Social Policy

Social Policy

SECOND EDITION

Edited by

John Baldock, Nick Manning,
and Sarah Vickerstaff

OXFORD
UNIVERSITY PRESS

Great Clarendon Street, Oxford OX2 6DP

Oxford University Press is a department of the University of Oxford. It furthers the University's objective of excellence in research, scholarship, and education by publishing worldwide in

Oxford New York

Auckland Bangkok Buenos Aires Calcutta Cape Town Chennai Dar es Salaam Delhi Hong Kong Istanbul Karachi Kolkata Kuala Lumpur Madrid Melbourne Mexico City Mumbai Nairobi São Paulo Shanghai Taipei Tokyo Toronto

Oxford is a registered trade mark of Oxford University Press in the UK and in certain other countries

Published in the United States by Oxford University Press Inc., New York

First published 1999

British Library Cataloguing in Publication Data

Data available

ISBN-01992 58945

10 9 8 7 6 5 4 3 2

Typeset by Newgen Imaging Systems (P) Ltd, Chennai, India
Printed by Ashford Colour Press Limited, Gosport, Hampshire

Contents

Detailed Contents

Guide to the Book

Welcome to Social Policy

That you are reading these words suggests something about you, your interests, and even your values. You may have done no more than pick up this volume in a bookshop or library. Alternatively, perhaps you are already a student on a social policy course, have bought or borrowed this book, and are expecting it to provide some quite specific information. Whatever the reason, there is a good chance that the term 'social policy' resonates with definite positive or negative views you have. This is because 'Social Policy', the academic subject, is not one that is easily neutral in its content or implications. Rather, it tends to involve aspects of life where values and commitments are important.

Why is this? A social policy is always a proactive attempt to change a given social order—to make things different from how they would otherwise have been. In the post-communist era of the new millennium, this inevitably means intervening to modify market forces and to redistribute resources amongst a population. The reasons for these interventions are varied, and they change as the economic, social, and political character of society changes. Social policies have most commonly been associated with the meeting of recognized needs, such as the provision of incomes to the old, sick, and unemployed, or of services such as education and healthcare. More recently the consequences of globalization and environmental change have required new social policies to minimize or protect against a growing variety of risks and forms of social exclusion and disadvantage. Social Policy is increasingly concerned with the study of risk and its management by the state and by international organizations.

What is social policy?

The term 'social policy' is used to refer both to the academic discipline Social Policy and to what it studies, social policies themselves. Part I of this book explores both concepts and shows how they relate to the nature, evolution, and politics of welfare systems. Two fairly conventional definitions provide a starting point:

- A 'social policy' is defined as a deliberate intervention by the state to redistribute resources amongst its citizens so as to achieve a welfare objective.
- A 'welfare system' is defined as the range of institutions that together determine the welfare of citizens. Amongst these are the family and the community networks in which the family exists, the market, the charitable and voluntary sectors, the social services and benefits provided by the state, and, increasingly, international organizations and agreements.

Clearly these two definitions raise further questions, in particular what is meant by 'welfare'. Seeking answers to that question is very much what studying the academic discipline of social policy is about.

The classic justification for a social policy is that it will lead to greater social justice, though that is by no means the classic outcome. And the classic statement of that justification is the Beveridge Report's call for an 'attack upon five giant evils': want, disease, ignorance, squalor, and idleness (Beveridge 1942: 170; the full quotation appears in Chapter 1). This conception of what social justice required formed the basis for the post-war British welfare state. But it does not apply so readily in other times or places. Different societies and different groups within those societies have varied and conflicting views about what is socially just. This means that social policy has become the central task of modern politics: deciding which risks should be tackled through state intervention, and what redistributions should be enforced with the authority of the state.

Beveridge's Report was produced in wartime, and he saw social policy largely in terms of redistribution between whole categories of people: from the employed to the unemployed, from those of working age to those in retirement, and from the healthy to the sick. However, today welfare is often seen in more individualistic terms. State social policies help provide the context in which individuals choose and organize their own lives. This perspective sees individual lives as subject to a whole range of risks, particularly risks of dependency and exclusion. Richard Titmuss, who in 1950 was appointed to what was effectively the first professorship of social policy in Britain, distinguished between 'natural dependencies, as in childhood, extreme old age and child-bearing', and 'manmade dependencies' such as the risks of industrial injuries and of unemployment and underemployment (Titmuss 1976: 42–4). He suggested that as economies and societies became more complex and industrialized so the numbers of these manmade risks increased, turning life into something of a lottery unless social insurance and welfare services were developed to meet the new dependencies.

Today many of us are able to live our lives taking for granted the guarantees provided by the welfare state and social policy. It is this context which allows what a more recent commentator, Ulrich Beck, has called 'institutionalized individualism', a self-centred consumerism which nonetheless depends on a welfare system constructed when people subscribed to more communal values (Beck 1998). Social policies are fundamental to the organization of our societies and implicit in the choices we make every day of our lives.

So it is unlikely that you will be neutral, disinterested, or uninterested in the issues of social justice and redistribution described in this book. They are part of what makes social policy an exciting subject; it is relevant to both our values and our lives.

The scale and volume of social policy

The moral and political importance of social policy is also reflected in the sheer scale and number of activities it represents. To study the operation of welfare systems is not to study some marginal aspect of the economy. The fifteen nations of the European Union spend very close to an average of 30 per cent of their gross national products on 'social protection' (Eurostat 2002: ch. 3). This amounted in 1998, to between € 9,395 per person in Luxembourg and € 2,239 in Greece with the figure for the UK being close to the average at € 5,715 (ch. 3: 12). (Throughout this book technical or specialist terms like **gross national product** and **social protection** are printed in bold when they are first used and a definition is supplied in a glossary at the end of the chapter.) These levels of expenditure effectively make welfare provision what might be called the largest industry in developed economies. Certainly, organizations such as the National Health Service or the state education system in the UK are substantially larger, in terms of amounts of money they spend each year and the numbers of people they employ, than most major corporations in the private sector. For example, in 2001 the National Health Service spent just over £60,000 million and employed just under one million people (Treasury 2003). In contrast, the private company with the largest turnover in 2001 was Shell Transport and Trading, which reported a turnover of £49,249 million and employed 90,000 people (Shell Transport and Trading Annual Report 2001: 15). If the number of employees is preferred as the key measure of size, then Unilever, with 295,000 employees in 2000 (Corporatewatch 2003), came closest to the NHS. The production of social welfare is arguably the largest industrial sector found in the richest economies of the world.

What does studying social policy involve?

While the making of social policy may be driven by values and politics, the study of social policy should be informed by evidence. Social research, collecting data about how people live, is central to the traditions of 'social policy' as an academic subject, and it has a long history rooted in the work of the early social scientists such as Edwin Chadwick (1800–1890), Friedrich Engels (1820–95), Charles Booth, (1840–1916), and Seebohm Rowntree (1871–1954).

Consequently you will find a great deal of empirical data in this book—particularly evidence about how resources are allocated. Studying social policy is an excellent way of getting to know about the material world and how people live in it. In this book much of the material is about the United Kingdom. Social policies are still largely the product of the nation-state, and therefore even a more international approach has to take the form of comparing the detail within one nation with that in another. But, as market forces are increasingly global in their operation, so social polices will have to follow if they are to have any redistributive impact. We have recognized the developing internationalism of social policies in this book by giving some account of what is happening in other countries.

The objectives of the book

- to provide a comprehensive introduction to the subject matter of Social Policy as it is currently studied in schools, colleges, and universities. It does this by reviewing the key debates and issues, and by setting out some of the basic evidence that is relevant

- to provide students with a substantial proportion of the information they will need to prepare for seminars, classes, and presentations and to write essays.
- to provide gateways to the further study of social policy issues. This is done by defining and structuring the core topics, by explaining the meaning of key terms (particularly in the glossaries at the end of each chapter), and by listing a large and accessible literature (in the references and guides to further reading at the end of each chapter).

The structure and organization of the book

The chapters are the basic building blocks of the book. It will often be necessary to read a whole chapter to understand an area of welfare needs and the social policy interventions designed to deal with them. Each chapter is an essay within its area. This is because Social Policy, the academic subject, takes the form of sets of interconnected arguments and evidence. There are limits to which particular topics can be taken out of their contexts.

The core chapters are those in Part IV, 'Delivering Welfare'. Here the main ways in which governments intervene to redistribute resources and to provide services are described. All the main organized service areas are found here: social security, education, healthcare, social care (including childcare), housing, and criminal justice. To these we have added two areas which are increasingly seen as important for our understanding of the core social policy responsibilities of government: the natural environment and the comparative organization of social policy in other countries, especially in Europe.

The chapters found in the other four parts of the book are designed to set the core activities of welfare systems in a broader context These sections are designed to add background and depth to the accounts in Part IV. Thus readers of the core chapters will often find they are referred to chapters in the other sections for further explanation of the context or related issues.

Part I, 'The Origins, Character, and Politics of Modern Social Welfare Systems'. is designed to introduce the subject of social policy, and to examine the different meanings of terms such as welfare, risk, and social exclusion. Since the Industrial Revolution, the state's responsibility for managing the welfare of its citizens has grown, especially through most of the twentieth century. In the twenty-first century there has been a widespread re-examination of the nature and performance of welfare states, with a halt to rising expenditure. This process has pushed social policy increasingly towards the centre of politics. The social policies of the present are rooted in their historical origins, and in the political conflicts and ideological differences that determine what the state does.

Part II, 'The Social and Economic Context', is designed to give substance to a fundamental truth that is often ignored by students of social policy: that the vast bulk of human needs are not met by the public welfare system but by the market economy and by the family. It is these last two institutions that define the context and the starting point of social policies, and readers of Part IV will often be referred back to these chapters. In Chapters 5, 6, and 7 we have sought to provide much of the fundamental evidence about how the family and the market both meet many needs and produce others. It is also in these chapters, particularly Chapters 5 and 7, that important data about population and demographic change are presented. Social Policy is rightly called a multi-disciplinary subject, and Chapter 3 seeks to provide students with some of the social theory that they need to weigh arguments, while Chapter 4 shows how this knowledge of social issues is shaped through the mass media and embedded in culturally relative understandings. Chapter 8 complements this discussion by showing that social needs are differentiated with respect to the different ethnic and gendered elements of people's lives, and according to their ages and abilities. These chapters are designed for the non-specialist reader, and any student planning to do a substantial or extended piece of work on a social policy issue should read them.

Part III, 'Planning, Financing, and Implementing Welfare Policies', is intended to explain and document how social policies are managed and how they are paid for. The state largely intervenes by using public servants to inspect and provide welfare services, and by making decisions about taxation and expenditure which allow it to pay for what is provided. Chapters 9 and 10 contain the subject matter of what are often called Public Policy Studies, and they form a fundamental foundation to any discussion of social policies and social services. In addition, Chapter 11 discusses the ways in which welfare services are increasingly delivered through the voluntary and non-governmental sector.

Part V, 'Consequences and Outcomes of Social Policy', consists of two essays; one on the achievements of social policy in the United Kingdom, the second on trends and debates about the future role of social policy and the welfare state. Broadly, they seek to outline how far social policy has come and where it might be going. Both the chapters are inevitably speculative and involve judgements about what the evidence means. Some readers might wish to start their investigation of social policy with these two chapters. Earlier, we described state welfare systems as the largest 'industries' to be found in developed economies. Social Policy, the academic subject, might well be expected to offer an account of whether the resources these industries consume are well spent, of whether they have produced welfare gains, and of how they may develop in the future.

How to use the book

The book is designed to be used by a student seeking to prepare for a class or seminar discussion, for a presentation or an essay on a social policy topic. The following route is suggested:

- Chapter headings. If there is a chapter title which broadly covers the topic you are researching, then read all or most of that chapter.
- Subheadings. At the beginning of each chapter is a list of the subheadings used and these may refer to the particular topic or area you are interested in. If not, consult:
- The index. This is at the back of the book and lists the pages on which a topic is discussed. Where a word is **emboldened** in the index then a glossary definition of the term appears on the page also indicated in bold. This will be at the end of one or a number of chapters. The references to the term within the chapter (the first use is also emboldened) and the context in which they appear will also be worth exploring.

- The glossaries. A particular term may occasionally appear in more than one glossary and be slightly differently defined in each. This is because Social Policy is a multidisciplinary subject and one where argument and differences in emphasis are normal. These differences are usually worth exploring.

We are keen to hear your ideas about the book. Visit our website on www.oup.co.uk/best.textbooks/socialpolicy or email us at highereducation.europe@oup.com and let us know what you think of it.

References

Beck, U. (1998), 'The cosmopolitan manifesto', *New Statesman*, 20 Mar.

Beveridge, W. (1942), *Social Insurance and Allied Services: A Report by Sir William Beveridge*. Cmd. 6404. London: HMSO.

Corporatewatch (2003) www.corporatewatch.org

Eurostat (2002), *Eurostat Yearbook 2002*. Office of Official Publications of the European Communities, Luxembourg. europa.eu.int/comm/eurostat/

Shell Transport and Trading Annual Report (2001), www.shell.com/home/Framework

Titmuss, R. M. (1976), *Essays on the Welfare State*, 3rd edn. London: Allen & Unwin.

Treasury (2003), www.hm-treasury.gov.uk/

Glossary

gross national product All of a country's output of goods and services (usually in a calendar year) plus income from assets abroad but with no deduction (i.e. gross, not net) for depreciation in the value of the country's assets. Gross domestic product is this but not including income from assets abroad.

social protection benefits Direct transfers in cash or kind to households and individuals which are organized by the state to meet risks and needs associated with old age, sickness, child-bearing, family expenses, disability, and unemployment. Within the European Union the constituents of social protection statistics have been harmonized according to ESSPROS, the European System of Integrated Social Protection Statistics. These include the bulk of public health and social services and social assistance benefits but do not include state education expenditure.

Acknowledgements

Grateful acknowledgement is made to all the publishers of copyright material in this book. Crown copyright material is reproduced with the permission of the controller of HMSO. Every effort has been made to seek permission for copyright sources. Should any source have been overlooked the publishers will be pleased to rectify omissions at the earliest opportunity.

About the Contributors

John Baldock is Professor of Social Policy at the University of Kent at Canterbury. His main research and teaching interests concern the ageing of the populations in industrial societies and the provision of care services for older people. He has recently co-written *The Young, The Old and The State: Social Care Systems in Five Industrial Nations* (with Anneli Anttonen and Jorma Sipilä and published by Edward Elgar, 2003). He is editor of the journal *Social Policy and Administration*. His current research involves the maintenance of identity in old age (as part of the ESRC's Growing Older Programme directed by Alan Walker) and a study of how families in Europe combine employment with social care responsibilities (as part of the SOCCARE project funded by the European Commission).

Michael Cahill is Reader in Social Policy at the University of Brighton. He is the author of *The New Social Policy* (1994) and *The Environment and Social Policy* (2002). Other recent publications include: *Environmental Values and Social Welfare* (2002) and *Environment and Welfare: Towards a Green Social Policy* (2002) (both edited with Tony Fitzpatrick). He currently teaches courses on Transport, Environment, and Society, and Social Policy and the Environment

Jochen Clasen is Professor of Comparative Social Research and Director of the Centre for Comparative Research in Social Welfare (CCRSW), University of Stirling. His research interests include comparative social policy, social security policy, and unemployment and employment policy in cross-national contexts. Recent publications include: *Comparative Social Policy: Concepts, Theories and Methods* (ed.) (Blackwell, 1999); 'Motives, means and opportunities: reforming unemployment compensation in the 1990s', *West European Politics*, 23(2) (2000); 'Social insurance and the contributory principle: a paradox in contemporary British social policy', *Social Policy and Administration*, 35(6) (2001); 'Changing principles in European social security' (with W. van Oorschot), *European Journal of Social Security* 4(2) (2002); and 'Unemployment protection and labour market reform in France and Great Britain in the 1990s: solidarity versus activation?' (with D. Clegg), *Journal of Social Policy* 32(3) (2003).

Hartley Dean is a Lecturer in the Department of Social Policy at the London School of Economics. He previously worked for twelve years as a welfare rights worker in Brixton, south London. Over the past eighteen years he has undertaken research and teaching at the universities of Kent, Luton, and Nottingham in areas relating to poverty, exclusion, welfare rights, and citizenship. His publications include: *Social Security and Social Control* (Routledge, 1991); *Dependency Culture: The Explosion of a Myth*, with Peter Taylor-Gooby (Harvester Wheatsheaf, 1992); *Parents' Duties, Children's Debts: The Limits of Policy Intervention* (ed.) (Arena, 1995); *Welfare, Law and Citizenship* (Prentice-Hall, 1996); *Poverty, Riches and Social Citizenship*, with Margaret Melrose (Macmillan, 1999); *Begging Questions: Street-Level Economic Activity and Social Policy Failure* (ed.) (Policy Press, 1999); *Welfare Rights and Social Policy* (Prentice-Hall, 2002).

Tina Eadie is a Lecturer in Community Justice in the School of Sociology and Social Policy at the University of Nottingham. Having worked in the criminal justice system as both a probation officer and manager, she currently teaches trainee probation officers in the Midlands region. Her research interests are predominantly in the areas of probation policy and practice, both in relation to enforcement and enabling probation officers to understand the organizational context of their work. She is particularly interested in the professional development of newly qualified probation officers and the extent to which they are achieving job satisfaction in their chosen career. She is also involved with a three-year research project funded by the Diana Fund exploring best practice with adolescents with learning disabilities whose behaviour ranges from sexually inappropriate to abusive.

Tony Fitzpatrick is a Senior Lecturer in the School of Sociology and Social Policy at Nottingham University. He is the author of *Freedom and Security* (Macmillan, 1999), *Welfare Theory: An Introduction* (Palgrave, 2001), and *After the New Social Democracy* (Manchester University Press, 2003). He has also co-edited *Environmental Issues and Social Welfare* (Blackwell, 2002), and *Environment and Welfare* (Palgrave, 2002), and is chief editor of the forthcoming *International Encyclopedia of Social Policy* (3 vols., Routledge). In addition, he has published widely in journals such as the *Journal of Social Policy, Environmental Politics* and the *International Journal of Social Welfare*. He became Treasurer of the UK's Social Policy Association in 2003.

Andrew Gray is Emeritus Professor of Public Management (University of Durham), Vice-Chairman of the Durham and Chester-le-Street Primary Care Trust, and a freelance academic working for a variety of universities. His recent publications include *Collaboration in Public Services: The Challenge for Evaluation* (ed. with W. I. Jenkins, J. Mayne, and F. F. Leeuw) (Transaction Publishers, 2003); 'Government and administration: paradoxes of policy performance' (with W. I. Jenkins), *Parliamentary Affairs* (2003); 'Democratic renewal: continuity and change' (with W. I. Jenkins), *Local Government Studies* (1999); and *Business-Like but Not Like a Business: The Challenge for Public Management* (Public Finance Foundation, 1998). He is Editor of *Public Money and Management*, has served on the Business and Management Studies Panel of the UK Higher Education Funding Councils' Research Assessment Exercise (2001), and from 1999–2002 was Chairman of the UK Public Administration Committee, the Learned Society for public policy and administration.

Bill Jenkins is Professor of Public Policy and Management at the University of Kent at Canterbury. His main research interests are public-sector management, public administration, modern British politics, and public policy evaluation. Together with Andrew Gray he has published a range of books and articles in these areas, most recently *Collaboration in Public Services: The Challenge for Evaluation* (ed. with Andrew Gray, Frans Leeuw, and John Mayne) (Transaction Publishers, 2003). He is collaborating with Professor Edward Page of the London School of Economics on an edited set of volumes, *The Foundations of Bureaucracy in Social and Economic Thought*, for Edward Elgar. He is currently Deputy Editor of the journal Public Administration.

Derek Kirton is Lecturer in Social Policy at the University of Kent at Canterbury. His main research interests are childcare policy and practice, and particularly the areas of adoption and foster care. He has published widely on the question of transracial adoption, including *'Race', Ethnicity and Adoption* (Open University Press, 2000). He is currently leading a Department of Health-funded research project on payment issues in foster care, and he is also interested in the adult experiences of people who have been adopted or grown up in care. He teaches modules related to child social care, children's rights, the sociology of childhood, social security, and research methods.

Mark Liddiard is a Senior Lecturer in Social Policy at the University of Kent at Canterbury. He has worked on a variety of research projects and has a particular interest in qualitative methods. He is co-author, with Susan Hutson, of *Youth Homelessness: The Construction of a Social Issue* (Macmillan, 1994). More recently, he has focused specifically upon cultural policy issues and published on museums, art subsidies, and the impact of the mass media on public attitudes and on policy-makers. He has recently published *Making Histories of Sexuality and Gender* (Cassell, 2003), an account of historical exclusion in museums.

Nick Manning is Professor of Social Policy and Sociology in the School of Sociology and Social Policy, University of Nottingham. He is seconded to the Nottinghamshire Healthcare NHS Trust, as Head of Research and University Liaison, 2003–6. Recent books and editions include: *New Risks, New Welfare: Signposts for Social Policy* (ed. with Ian Shaw) (Blackwell, 2000); *Work and Welfare in the New Russia* (with Ovsey Shkaratan and Nataliya Tikhonova) (Ashgate, 2000); *After the Fall: Central and Eastern Europe since the Collapse of Communism* (ed. with Roy Bradshaw and Stuart Thompstone) (Olearius Press, 2003); *Global Social Policy*, special issue on Globalization and Europeanization (ed. with Bruno Palier), (Sage, 2003); *A Culture of Enquiry: Research Evidence and the Therapeutic Community* (ed. with Jan Lees, Diana Menzies, and Nicola Morant) (Jessica Kingsley, 2003); *Poverty and Social Exclusion in the New Russia* (with Nataliya Tikhonova), (Ashgate, 2003).

Rebecca Morley is a Lecturer in the School of Sociology and Social Policy at the University of Nottingham. She has taught and researched for many years in the area of men's violence to women. She edited, with Audrey Mullender, the first book in Britain dealing with children and domestic violence, *Children Living with Domestic Violence: Putting Men's Abuse of Women on the Child Care Agenda* (Whiting & Birch, 1994). She has recently completed a study funded by the Economic and Social Research Council's Violence Research Programme on the impact of housing policy on women escaping domestic violence, and is currently part of a team contracted by the Home Office to evaluate the multi-service project package in the Crime Reduction Programme's Violence Against Women initiative.

Jan Pahl is Professor Emeritus of Social Policy at the University of Kent. Her research interests include the control and allocation of money within the family, financial services and financial exclusion, domestic violence, and health and social care. Her publications include *Private Violence and Public Policy* (Routledge, 1985), *Money and Marriage* (Macmillan, 1989), and *Invisible Money: Family Finances in the Electronic Economy* (Policy Press, 1999). She is currently working with the Department of Health on the implementation of the Research Governance Framework in the field of social care.

Gillian Pascall is Reader in Social Policy in the School of Sociology and Social Policy at the University of Nottingham. She teaches health and health policy, gender and social policy, and international and comparative policy to undergraduate, MA, and PhD students. Relationships between welfare states and gender have been at the centre of her research and publication since *Social Policy: A Feminist Analysis* was published in 1986. A consultancy with UNICEF in 1998 on *Women in Transition* led to work on gender and welfare regimes in the former soviet region, and on the social policy implications of EU expansion to the East. She has ongoing research with Professor Anna Kwak at the University of Warsaw on *The Gender Relations of Care: Parents and Social Policy in Poland*. This uses qualitative methods to study parenting in the changing social policy environment of the post-communist era. *Disability and Transition to Adulthood* (Pavilion

2001) was funded by the Joseph Rowntree Foundation and written with Nicola Hendey. This again is based on qualitative research. Interviews with young adults who have grown up with disability focus on their achievement of employment and independent households.

Chris Pickvance is Professor of Urban Studies at the University of Kent at Canterbury. A sociologist by background, his research interests include housing, local government, and urban protest. He is co-editor of *Place, Policy and Politics: Do Localities Matter?* (Unwin Hyman, 1990); *State Restructuring and Local Power: A Comparative Perspective* (Pinter, 1991); and *Environmental and Housing Movements: Grassroots Experience in Hungary, Russia and Estonia* (Avebury, 1997). *Local Environmental Regulation in Post-Socialism: A Hungarian Case Study* will be published by Avebury in 2003. His articles have appeared in the journals *Sociology*, the *Sociological Review*, and the *International Journal of Urban and Regional Research.*

Duncan Scott is a Research Fellow in the Centre for Applied Social Research, Department of Sociology, University of Manchester. He was formerly Senior Lecturer in Social Policy, Department of Applied Social Science, University of Manchester. He has been a local voluntary sector activist, consultant, teacher, and researcher in relation to the third sector for over 30 years. He is currently co-directing a Charities Aid Foundation study on Social Enterprise in the UK voluntary and community sectors. With others he authored *Moving Pictures: Realities of Voluntary Action* (Policy Press, 2000).

Julia Twigg is Professor of Social Policy and Sociology at the University of Kent at Canterbury. She has written extensively on the subject of informal carers, in particular the role of services in support of them. She is currently working on a study of the body in social and public policy which extends her earlier work on the management of the body in community care: *Bathing, the Body and Community Care* (Routledge, 2000). At present she teaches on issues in social care and on the social politics of food.

Sarah Vickerstaff is a Reader in Employment Policy and Practice at the University of Kent at Canterbury. She has a long-standing research interest in training and vocational education, with a current focus on apprenticeship, traditional and modern. A recent publication in this area is 'Apprenticeship in the "golden age": were youth transitions really smooth and unproblematic back then?', *Work Employment and Society* 7(2), (2003). She is currently completing a Joseph Rowntree Foundation-funded research project into the 'Organisational Context for Retirement: the impact of employers' age management policies and practice on the process of retirement'.

PART ONE

THE ORIGINS, CHARACTER, AND POLITICS OF MODERN SOCIAL WELFARE SYSTEMS

1

Social Policy, Social Welfare, and the Welfare State

John Baldock, Nick Manning, and Sarah Vickerstaff

CONTENTS

INTRODUCTION: A SOCIAL POLICY TEXTBOOK

This is a book about something called **social policy**. You may be using it as a student on a Social Policy programme at university or college; or you may be taking a Social Policy module as part of a professional training in, say, social work or nursing; or because you have chosen a Social Policy option as part of a course in sociology, economics, politics, or history. There are many, particularly social science, disciplines in which questions to do with social policy and the welfare systems of Britain or other countries are likely to be relevant. This is essentially because social expenditures by governments are so large a part of the economies of industrial societies.

Three terms are central to the subject matter of this book: 'social policy', 'social welfare', and 'the welfare state'. This chapter provides an introduction to the meanings that are attached to these and the debates that surround them.

SOCIAL POLICY

The phrase 'social policy' generally has two possible meanings. It is used to refer to the academic subject called Social Policy or, more importantly, it means social policies themselves, that is to say the intentions and activities of governments (and sometimes other organizations such as the European Union) which are broadly social in their nature. It is not very useful to spend a great deal of time trying to pin down the best definition of social policy. There is no right answer. It is much more helpful simply to look at examples of what are generally called social policies. This book contains a great many such examples, and in that sense our definition of social policy is simply demonstrated in the things that are described in this book. A similar approach was taken by a working party that produced a 'Benchmarking Document' to guide the curriculum for social policy in British universities. Rather than define what social policies are, the working party chose to list the main topics that were commonly studied under that heading, though it admitted that the list would have to change over time (see Box 1.1).

The classic examples of social policies are the activities of governments in providing money and services to their citizens in five main areas: social security benefits, health care, education, housing, and personal social services. These five areas form the core of this book, contained in Chapters 12–17. They can in part be traced back to a much-quoted paragraph in the Beveridge Report of 1942 that outlined five main areas where the state should construct social policy after the war. Beveridge's five did not include personal care services. Rather, he laid great emphasis on policies to maintain full employment, which he believed would make personal intervention in people's lives less necessary (see Box 1.2). Since Beveridge, as the titles of other chapters in this book show, social policy has come to be defined even more broadly, to include areas of government activity such as arts and culture, the criminal justice system, and environmental policies.

Box 1.1 Optional units currently found within UK Social Policy degree courses

'Social policy knowledge is typically taught and learnt through a focus upon particular themes, topics, and issues within degree courses. [Below is] a list of the optional units commonly found within UK Social Policy degree courses. However, it is not intended to be exhaustive or prescriptive, and different Social Policy courses are likely to include within them various combinations of a number of these, or other, units.

- Ageing and social policy
- Child care and child protection
- Community care
- Comparative social policy
- Crime and criminal justice policy
- Disability and social policy
- Economics, economic issues, and social policy
- Education and social policy
- Environmental issues and social policy
- Equal opportunity policies and their impacts
- European social policy
- Family policy
- Gender and social policy
- Health and health care policies
- Housing and urban policies
- Income maintenance and social security policy
- Local governance, local welfare institutions, and their policies
- Organization, administration, and management in welfare institutions
- Philosophy of welfare
- Political and social theory, ideology, and social policy
- Poverty, social exclusion, and social policy
- Race, ethnicity, and social policy
- Sexuality and social policy
- Social policy and the mass media
- Transport and transport policy
- Voluntary sector welfare services
- Welfare rights and social policy
- Work, employment, and labour market policies
- Youth, youth work, and associated policies

(Quality Assurance Agency for Higher Education 2000: Section 3.3)

Box 1.2 William Beveridge's 'five giants'

'The Plan for Social Security is put forward as part of a general programme of *social policy*. It is one part only of an attack upon five giant evils: upon the physical *Want* with which it is directly concerned, upon *Disease* which often causes that Want and brings many other troubles in its train, upon *Ignorance* which no democracy can afford among its citizens, upon the *Squalor* which arises mainly through haphazard distribution of industry and population, and upon the *Idleness* which destroys wealth and corrupts men, whether they are well fed or not, when they are idle.

(Beveridge 1942: 170; emphasis added)

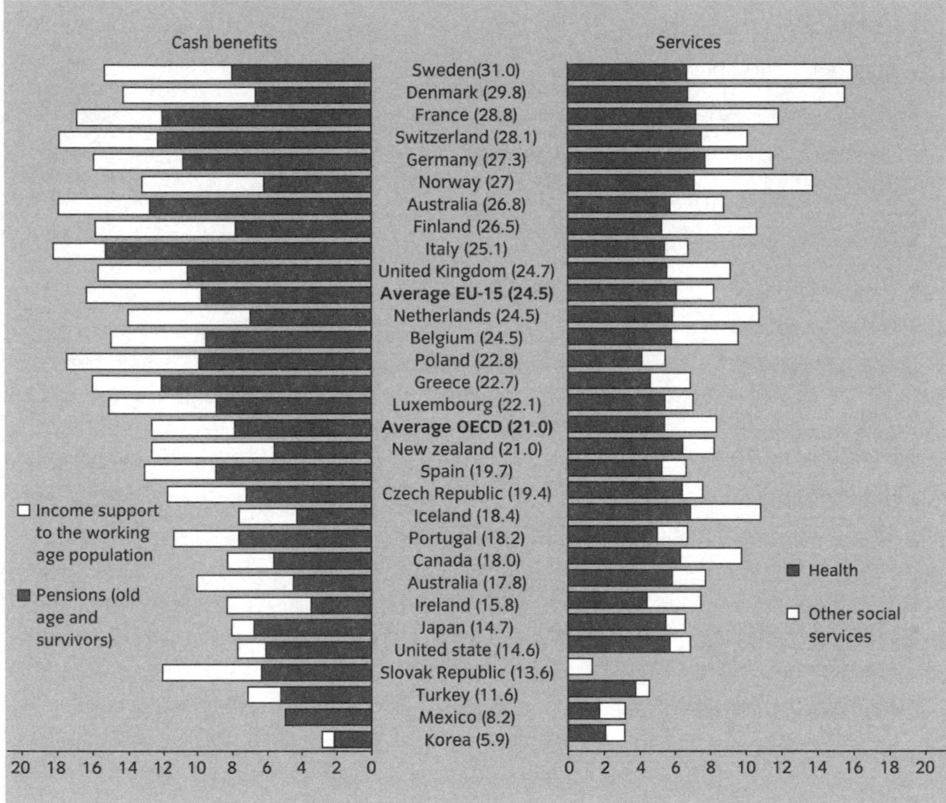

Figure 1.1 Public social expenditure by broad social policy area, 1998 (% of GDP)

Source: OECD 2001.

A key aspect of the importance of social policies is that they consume a large proportion of the economic output of most industrialized countries. Put more bluntly, social policies can cost a lot of money. Fig. 1.1 shows the share of the **gross national product** (GNP) of various countries taken up by what the OECD (Organization for Economic Cooperation and Development) defines as 'social expenditure by broad social policy area'. As the chart demonstrates, in 1998 this expenditure varied amongst the more industrial nations of the world from about 6 per cent of South Korea's economy to 31 per cent of the Swedish economy. The definitions that the OECD researchers use to construct this data are an interesting example of the practical choices that have to be made when one needs a definition of social policy. They use what they call 'the international consensus as to the scope of social protection'.

> Social protection usually covers income support or special assistance for elderly people, temporary or permanent departure from the labour market, illness or invalidity, difficult family circumstances, poor housing, or other poverty or insecurity related cases. These areas may be targeted by government policies via either agencies or regulations . . . To conclude, social protection is the share of individual protection that society decides to shoulder collectively, through rules and institutions established for that purpose.
>
> Social expenditure is the provision by public (and private) institutions of benefits to households and individuals in order to provide support during circumstances which adversely affect their welfare. Such benefits can be cash transfers, or can be the direct (in kind) provision of goods and services. (OECD 2001: 9)

An interesting practical point is that the OECD researchers who compile these widely used statistics choose not to include spending on education, because they argue that governments do not provide education in order to provide support 'during circumstances which adversely affect people's welfare' but rather as a form of investment. Others prefer to regard investment as a central part of welfare. One of the most influential commentators on social policy, Gøsta Esping-Anderson, has argued that we need a new form of welfare state that is more a 'social investment state' (Esping-Andersen 2002: 26–67) which focuses on children and families because they will provide the welfare of the future. If public expenditure on education is added to the figures in Fig. 1.1, then Sweden's social expenditure rises by 13 per cent to 44 per cent, and Korea's figure by 17 per cent to 23 per cent.

ANALYSING SOCIAL POLICY

We have argued so far that there is no general agreement as to the definition of a social policy, and that it is probably best that this is so. Students of social policy are no more likely to wish for tight boundaries defining their subject than historians would set strict limits on what counts as history, or physicists on what should be included in physics. However, there have developed a number of standard ways in which writers on social policy have chosen to analyse the phenomena they wish to present as social policy. Social policies can be examined in terms of:

1. the intentions and objectives that lie behind individual policies or whole groups of them;
2. the administrative and financial arrangements that are used to deliver policies;
3. the outcomes of policies, particularly in terms of who gains and who loses.

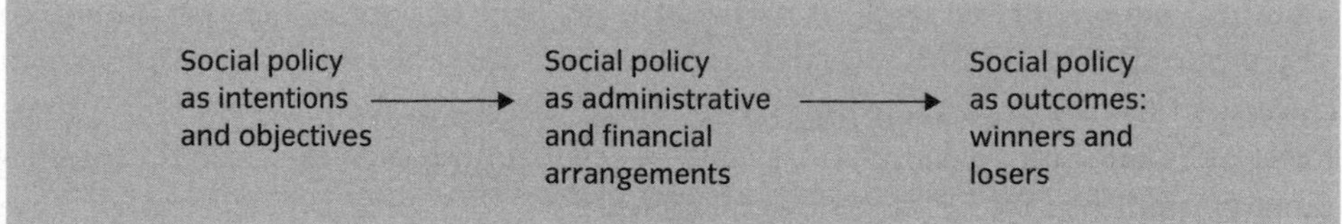

Figure 1.2 Social policy: an analytical framework

This framework is summarized in Fig. 1.2. Over the next few pages we elaborate each of its three parts.

Social policy as intentions and objectives

Sometimes the intentions that inform a social policy or even a whole policy area are fairly clear. For example, in 2001 the British government introduced a new policy to provide an enhanced form of community care called 'Intermediate Care' for older people newly out of hospital or at risk of returning to hospital (see Chapter 15). The policy requires the health service and local government to cooperate in precise ways and to particular deadlines set out in a policy document issued by the Department of Health (DoH 2001: 49–50). At the same time the necessary legislation allowing them to work together in these ways was contained in the Health Act 1999.

However, it is more often the case that there are substantial disagreements or uncertainties either within government or between central government and local authorities which lead to vagueness and ambiguity about policy intentions. For example, in 1990 Mrs Thatcher's government issued guidance on its plans to reform community care (DoH 1990) and passed legislation to enable the changes to take place: the NHS and Community Care Act 1990. However, the next decade showed that the intentions had not been clear enough, and local authorities which did not entirely share the government's ambitions were able to find room to do things differently (see Chapter 15). Another example of ambiguous policy goals was the 2003 White Paper *The Future of Higher Education*, which set out the Government's plans for radical reform and expansion in universities and further education colleges (DfES 2003). White Papers are a key way in which British governments set out their policy intentions; but because of disagreements in the cabinet about the right way to fund higher education and subsidize students, the policy was to a degree 'fudged', leading to uncertainty rather than a clear policy.

In many areas of social policy, especially where the particular benefits and services have been accumulating over a long period, it is particularly difficult to distinguish what the intentions are now or even what they originally were. These can vary, and involve contradictions. Some goals may be stated clearly, but others remain largely hidden and can only be untangled by looking at the political processes that first created and now sustain social policies and the broader ideologies that influence the key decision-makers. These issues are covered in detail in Chapters 2 and 3.

An essential part of the study of social policy is to go beyond the analysis of particular policies and search for common patterns both within one country and comparatively across a number of countries. A number of key common types of intention and objective are suggested by the social policy literature. They are grouped under three headings: redistribution; risk management; and reducing social exclusion.

Redistribution In the preface to this book we suggest that redistribution is a defining characteristic of social policy: 'A social policy is defined as a deliberate intervention by the state to redistribute resources amongst its citizens so as to achieve a welfare objective'. There is a sense in which this is always true. No government would intervene through policy if it believed that the existing allocation of resources was satisfactory. So social policy always involves changing what would have been the status quo. However, two kinds of redistribution are particularly important.

First, there is redistribution away from those who have more to those who have less in order to create greater equality along a particular dimension such as income, or access to a key service such as education or health care. This is what is sometimes called the 'Robin Hood' function of social policy. This kind of redistribution is essentially driven by ethical and moral considerations to do with fairness and justice. There are many people who believe inequalities of income and wealth beyond a certain point are simply unacceptable and should be corrected through **vertical redistribution** from the richer to the poorer. There is also growing evidence that the experience of living in materially unequal society is harmful to people and may lead to ill health and even early death (see Chapter 14). This argument is particularly associated with the work of Richard Wilkinson, who has argued that there are 'psychosocial pathways' between inequality and illness (Box 1.3).

Secondly, the state may use social policy to redistribute resources because the existing allocation is inefficient. This is a justification in terms of what economists call **market failure**. Classic examples are the provision of free schooling or of compulsory schemes making people save for old age. Without these interventions, people would not be prepared to pay for enough education to meet the needs of the economy, or, because individuals tend to discount their future needs, they would not save enough for old age.

Box 1.3 Inequality and ill health

'The results [emerging from recent studies] indicate that psychosocial pathways have a central role in linking health to socio-economic circumstances. It has often been found that the smaller the degree of socio-economic inequality, the healthier the society. In societies where there are small income differences between rich and poor, death rates tend to be lower and people live longer. It turns out that this is probably because more equal societies are less stressful: people are more likely to trust each other and are less hostile and violent towards each other.'

'Excuses for governments to drag their feet over the reduction of inequality are thin on the ground. If we are to improve health and social capital, if we are to free ourselves from antisocial prejudices and create a more inclusive society, the reduction of inequalities must surely be a key political objective.'

(Wilkinson 2000: 3, 67)

Much of this kind of redistribution may be **horizontal redistribution** and **lifetime redistribution**. Through these social policies the state forces people to spend more on education than they otherwise would, by taxing them and spending the money on their behalf. In this way what can happen is that the state redistributes people's incomes across their lifetimes, by taking from them when they are in work so that they may benefit in retirement, sickness, or unemployment. (Chapter 21 explores the degree to which social policies succeed in achieving these sorts of redistribution.)

The management of risk A powerful way of understanding social policies is to see them as ways in which societies collectively protect themselves from the risks of harm that individuals face in life. Risks are a natural part of the human condition, and they are also the products of our civilization and its technologies. Richard Titmuss distinguished between natural risks or dependencies, such as childhood, sickness, and old age, and manmade risks that are products of our civilization, such as unemployment and industrial injury (Titmuss 1976: 42–4). In the language of the time he defined those upon whom those risks had fallen as being 'in need'. He argued that the social policies of the postwar welfare states were designed to meet certain natural and manmade needs collectively through the mechanism of government. Thus social security systems to provide incomes to the unemployed, the sick, and the retired were set up, as were comprehensive education and health care services. In this sense social policy existed to meet **social need** (see Chapter 5).

More recent social theorists have extended this analysis to point out that, as societies become more complex and interconnected, so these manmade risks increase in number to include the effects of industrial pollution and the negative consequences of technology which may, for example, introduce dangerous particles or drugs into our environment or even accidentally contaminate huge areas, as happened when the explosion at the Chernobyl nuclear power station released radioactive clouds across Europe. The sociologist Ulrich Beck argues we now live in a '**risk society**' in which people are confronted with socially and economically created risks that even endanger the survival of the species. He points to 'organized irresponsibility' in which many leading social institutions, including private companies, large government bureaucracies, and the legal system, produce risks of harm or disadvantage against which individuals have little power to protect themselves (Beck 1992). This is an analysis that links the nature of postmodern industrial societies, which are dominated by private capital and market interests, to a need for the state to counteract their effects through social policies.

As the pace of change increases and as the risks become more global in nature, so the kinds of policies required changes. Only policy agreements on a world scale will now protect us from some environmental risks (see Chapter 19). There is also likely to be conflict between different groups seeking to use the state or international agreements to protect themselves. An example of these new, global, and unpredictable risks is the transmission of BSE (bovine spongiform encephalopathy) from cattle to human beings through the food chain. The inquiry into the British government's response showed how the existing divisions between government departments and the broad assumptions about their responsibilities held by civil servants and ministers made it difficult to come up with appropriate 'social policies' to protect the public (House of Commons 2000).

Social inclusion During the 1990s a growing number of social policies have been justified in terms of their capacity to reduce **'social exclusion'**. In 1997 the New Labour government of Tony Blair set up an interdepartmental Social Exclusion Unit to coordinate public policy (www.socialexclusionunit.gov.uk). The term social exclusion and its twin, **social inclusion**, are particularly associated with European Union social initiatives. The Lisbon summit in March 2000 committed member states to promotion of social inclusion through a range of social initiatives (see Box 1.4).

There is ambiguity about what social exclusion actually refers to. It is what is known as a 'contested term'. Some social policy analysts argue that it is just another word for poverty, but one that is preferred in a political context where governments are unwilling to be explicit about the existence of poor people. The European Union, as Box 1.4 shows, links poverty and social exclusion but sees a difference between them. It suggests that as economies develop, some people become excluded from skills and knowledge and thus become vulnerable to unemployment and poverty. Policies are therefore needed to re-include such people, largely by giving them the skills that will get them into paid work. However, these policies do not always reach the people who need them most. The concept of social exclusion, in the form 'les exclus' (the excluded), was first used in the context of French social policy debates in the 1970s, where it largely referred to people who slipped through the network of services and benefits designed to help the disadvantaged, particularly the less educated, the disabled, lone parents, and young adults. The exclusion in this sense was exclusion from the social policies of the state, and the danger was that such people would become less committed to central values of a society and thus threaten its stability and solidarity.

Box 1.4 Conclusions of the Lisbon European Council meeting 23–4 March 2000

'No 32. Promoting social inclusion

The number of people living below the poverty line and in social exclusion in the Union is unacceptable. Steps must be taken to make a decisive impact on the eradication of poverty by setting adequate targets to be agreed by the Council by the end of the year. The High Level Working Party on Social Protection will be involved in this work. The new knowledge-based society offers tremendous potential for reducing social exclusion, both by creating the economic conditions for greater prosperity through higher levels of growth and employment, and by opening up new ways of participating in society. At the same time, it brings a risk of an ever-widening gap between those who have access to the new knowledge, and those who are excluded. To avoid this risk and maximise this new potential, efforts must be made to improve skills, promote wider access to knowledge and opportunity and fight unemployment: the best safeguard against social exclusion is a job. Policies for combating social exclusion should be based on an open method of coordination combining national action plans and a Commission initiative for cooperation in this field to be presented by June 2000.'

The attractiveness of the terms 'social exclusion', as the definition of the problem, and 'social inclusion', as the policy goal that will combat it, is that they combine most of the intentions and objectives that we have already listed as informing social policies.

- Social exclusion is produced when incomes are excessively unequal. The pioneering researcher into poverty Peter Townsend (1979) showed how families with low incomes cannot participate in the lives of the communities in which they live. They become excluded in part because they cannot pay for the things that make one part of a society: going on holidays; entertaining others in one's home; kitting out their children suitably for sports or going out with their friends. Providing these people with the ability to re-include themselves in their communities requires vertical redistribution.
- Social exclusion is inefficient. It is an expression of market failure that wastes the potential of people who could work but lack the skills to do so, and it reflects inadequate redistribution to those who are unable to work through youth, illness, or age. It therefore requires horizontal redistribution.
- Social exclusion reflects a failure to tackle the risks that face people in complex societies and it creates new risks, particularly if the excluded become alienated from the wider society. Social policy is therefore required both to tackle the risks that lead to exclusion (for example, unemployment, low skills, illness, low wages, old age) and to prevent the development of new social problems.

Social policy as administrative and financial arrangements

Social policy as social administration In order to deliver the intentions that lie behind social policies in ordered and predictable ways, governments must set up procedures and sometimes organizations to carry them out. A large part of the Beveridge Report (1942) was not about the overall goals but about planning the detailed administrative arrangements that would be required to realize them. In most industrial countries the years 1945–70 witnessed the construction of large government bureaucracies, employing substantial proportions of the workforce and charged with providing the new social security, health, social care, education, and housing policies. In those years in the UK the academic subject now called Social Policy was more often known as Social Administration, and to some extent this reflected that what was of interest was less the social policy intentions themselves but rather the administrative arrangements that would best achieve them. There was broad agreement between political parties about the social policies that were needed. This is sometimes referred to as the '**post-war settlement**' or in 1950s Britain as 'Butskellism', a term coined by the *Economist* magazine to highlight the fact that the Tory Chancellor of the Exchequer, Rab Butler, was following very much the same social policy principles as his Labour predecessor, Hugh Gaitskell.

There is, indeed, often more difference between political parties over administrative arrangements than policy goals. Social policies generally use one of three main administrative forms to achieve their goals. The first and the cheapest is **regulation**. Governments pass laws that require individuals and organizations to do, or not to do, particular things: wearing seat belts, observing food hygiene regulations, not selling tobacco to minors.

There are likely to be many thousands of government regulations in an industrial society that are intended to achieve broadly social goals. The main advantage from the state's point of view is that regulation is relatively cheap. The cost of compliance falls on the individual or firm rather than on the state. The main cost to the state is some form of inspection and enforcement to ensure that people abide by the regulations. The second key administrative method of achieving social goals through social policy is by providing people directly with **services in kind**, such as health care, education, or housing. Governments can set up state organizations to do the job—large public bureaucracies like the National Health Service—or they can delegate the delivery of services to **private-for-profit** companies or to voluntary organizations (sometimes known as the **not-for-profit** sector). The third fundamental method of achieving social goals is to provide individuals and households with **cash benefits**. The cost of cash benefits is the largest area of social policy expenditure in Britain, and has a whole chapter to itself in this book (Chapter 12).

Organizational arrangements can make a great deal of difference to the success of a social policy. For example, in 1998 the British government set out its National Childcare Strategy designed to make available a nursery school place for every preschool child whose parents wanted one. Provision is by a mixture of local government, voluntary, and for-profit nurseries and approved childminders. Funding is a mixture of central government, through Child Care Tax Credits, local government education and welfare budgets, and direct charges to parents. Current debate about this policy revolves less around its main goals and more around whether the administrative and financial system is the appropriate one to deliver it (Lewis 2003).

Administrative arrangements go wrong in two main ways. First, the detailed rules and procedures that are used to deliver a policy may develop in ways that actually undermine its original intentions. In the case of the National Childcare Strategy, Jane Lewis (2003: 235) concludes that 'the choices parents currently face are determined more by the complex nature of the system that has been created than by the needs of the child. In this crucial sense, the development of childcare in the UK has not been "child-centred"'. Secondly, the organizations involved can develop goals of their own, sometimes as a result of their sheer size, sometimes because particular groups, such as professionals, use them to advance their own interests rather than policies themselves. These problems, and finding solutions to them, are fundamental to understanding social policy, and are discussed in much greater detail in discussion of professions and bureaucracy in Chapter 9. They have also tended to preoccupy governments. In Britain in the 1980s and 1990s the governments of Margaret Thatcher, John Major, and Tony Blair devoted a great deal of effort to reorganizing welfare bureaucracies and changing the way they are managed. Getting welfare bureaucracies to do what these governments believed they were intended to do involved **privatization** and **contracting out** and the setting of precise targets and rewarding their achievement, often referred to as the **new managerialism**. Privatization dominated the social policy of British governments in the 1980s and new managerialism the 1990s.

Social policy as public finance As Fig. 1.1 shows, the social policy activities of governments constitute substantial proportions of the economic output of industrial nations. Both obtaining the money and managing how it is spent are key aspects of social policy.

The two main ways which social policies are financed are by taxation (the **direct taxation** of incomes and profits and the **indirect taxation** of other economic activities) and by **social insurance contributions**. Paying these taxes and contributions has effects on people's wellbeing. In this sense taxation policies are also social policies. Governments can recognize this by adjusting taxes and contributions to incomes, for example, through **progressive taxes**, or by allowing individuals and households exemptions from the payment of tax. In Britain, exemptions are allowed, for example, if one is contributing to a pension scheme, aged over 65, suffering from blindness, or part of a married couple. Up until 1988 allowances were available for those supporting a dependent relative and until 2000 for owner occupiers paying a mortgage. These, like many other allowances that have existed in the past, have come and gone as governments have sought to adjust revenue and the social policy effects. Increasingly governments are introducing **tax credits** in order to achieve social policy goals. From April 2003 most parents in Britain have been able to claim a Child Tax Credit which adds to their income rather than takes away from it. Those in work are eligible for the Working Tax Credit which provides extra income for workers in low-income households, including those who have a disability.

The management of the public finances is a fundamental part of social policy. Two aspects of this management are critical; planning and controlling public expenditure. Delivering services such as health care or education require long-term investment in people and buildings, and advance knowledge of how much is likely to be spent in a particular year. For these reasons planning social policy and planning public expenditure often amount to the same thing. Governments must be able to describe their intended social policies in terms of how much they will cost. Chapter 10 describes how the political and technical aspects of these planning processes have evolved in recent years.

Controlling the amount and pattern of expenditures is similarly central to social policy. In industrial societies the sums involved are so large that preventing waste, inefficiencies, overspending, and underspending require sophisticated financial management systems. When these fail the consequences can be profound. As Chapter 10 describes, in 1975 the unexpected rise in inflation meant that public spending outran both planned expenditure and tax receipts to such an extent that a major financial crisis arose. The British Chancellor of the Exchequer at the time, Denis Healey, had to go cap in hand to the International Monetary Fund in order to prevent a collapse in the international value of the pound. The consequences for social policy over the next twenty years were profound as governments gave greater priority of controlling expenditure on social policies, often leading to cuts in previously planned expenditure.

Social policy as outcomes

The proof of the pudding is in the eating. Many analysts of social policy have suggested that the intentions that lie behind policies are less important than what they actually achieve. Richard Titmuss, when seeking to define the academic discipline called 'social policy', headed his list with 'the analysis and description of policy formation and its consequences, intended and unintended' (Titmuss 1968: 22). In much of his research he focused on the evidence of the results of policy interventions, and showed how many policies did not have the outcomes claimed for them, that some achieved almost the opposite of what was intended, and that there were other interventions by governments that had social consequences but were not recognized as social policies.

Clearly it is important, given the substantial proportion of countries' resources redistributed through social policies, that results be carefully monitored. Much of the content of the chapters in this book reports research designed to discover the outcomes of social policies. Chapter 21 is entirely devoted to the question. There is not the space here even to summarize all the issues involved in assessing the consequences of social policy. We shall merely draw attention to one of the more fundamental aspects of the question: the degree to which social policies have been successful in defeating the 'five giant evils' highlighted in William Beveridge's report (see Box 1.2).

As the chapters in this book explain, in the Britain of the first decade of the twenty-first century these 'evils' have been altered and, by most measures, greatly reduced. 'Want', in the sense of grinding poverty, has been almost eliminated by the cash benefits that Beveridge recommended. Poverty is now a matter of relative deprivation (see p. 118). The consequences of 'disease' have at least been delayed as average life expectancy has been extended. 'Ignorance' has been reduced insofar as people spend longer in full-time education and many more obtain formal qualifications. 'Squalor' in the form of poor-quality homes and large urban slums has been replaced, and 'idleness' has been reduced by a much higher level of participation in paid work. However, the difficulty is demonstrating how far these changes have been the outcomes of social policies. It is arguable that they are largely the results of economic growth and improvements in people's material living standards. Figure 1.3 shows how average household income, along with the economy

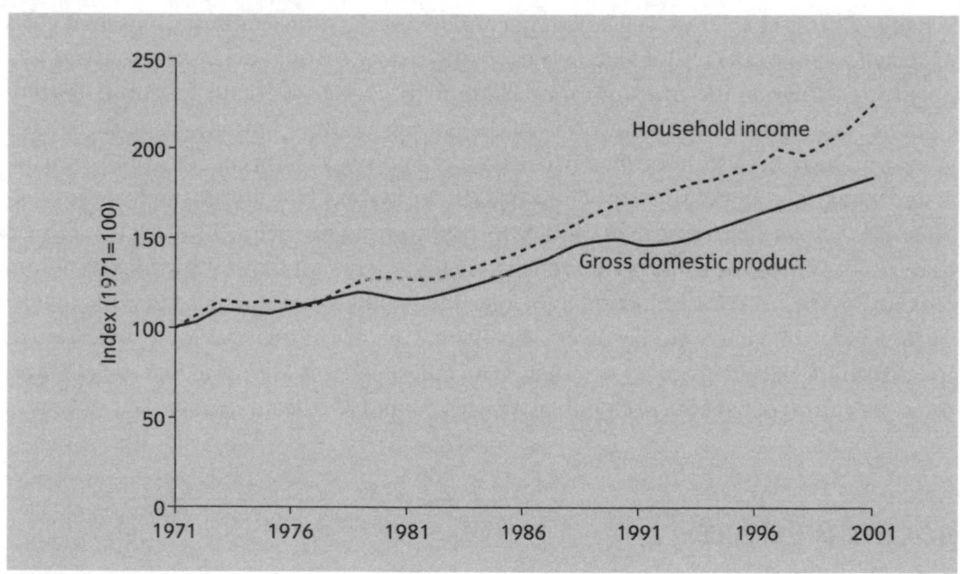

Figure 1.3 Real household disposable income per head and gross domestic product per head, UK

Source: ONS (2003: chart 5.1).

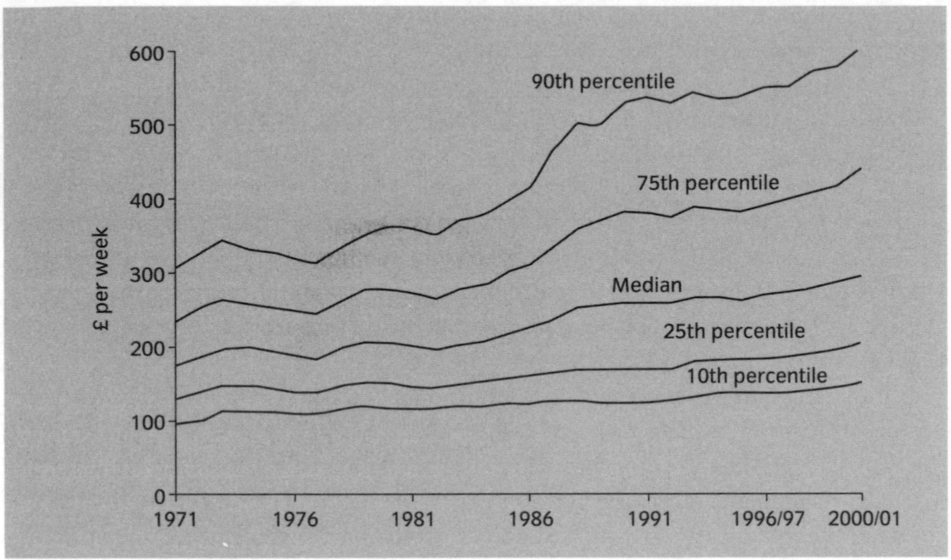

Figure 1.4 Distribution of real household disposable income, UK

Source: ONS (2003: chart 5.14).

as a whole (measured by **gross domestic product**, GDP) has more than doubled over the last thirty years. Many commentators suggest that it is this economic growth that has been the main engine behind improvements in people's standards of living and which provides the resources that have reduced the severity of Beveridge's 'five giants'.

Earlier in this chapter we suggested that another of the more commonly asserted goals of social policy was to redistribute resources and reduce inequalities, partly so that more people can share in the fruits of economic growth. However, Figure 1.4 shows that inequality, and particularly the incomes of the poorest tenth of households in the United Kingdom, have been stubbornly resistant to social policy. In terms of 2001 prices and adjusted to take account of the size of households, the average after-tax incomes of the poorest tenth of households rose over the last thirty years from just below £100 per week to less than £150. During the same period the incomes of the richest tenth nearly doubled from £300 to £600 a week. If a reduction in income inequality is a measure of a key outcome of social policy, then it has not been very successful. Chapter 21 includes more discussion of the distributional effects of social policies, including what is known as the **social wage**, the distribution of benefits from public services in kind like health care and education.

SOCIAL WELFARE

By focusing on the meaning of the term 'social policy' so far, we have concentrated on the activities of governments and their success or otherwise in achieving social objectives. However, many students of social policy are more interested in what can broadly be called **social welfare** and which is only partly the product of what governments and policy-makers do. Social welfare is again a term that gains little from being defined very tightly. Writers use it in slightly different ways depending on the issues they wish to cover. Sometimes it refers to very material aspects of wellbeing such as access to economic resources. At other times it is used to mean less tangible conditions such as contentment, happiness, an absence of threat and confidence in the future. A whole area of research called 'quality of life studies' that seeks to understand and measure what people believe to be the main ingredients of their welfare (see e.g. Baldwin et al. 1990). Social welfare can be thought of in terms of individuals, the concept of individual welfare, but as its name suggests it is also used on occasion to refer to more collective forms of wellbeing (collective welfare), such as those of a whole community or nation.

Researchers in social policy are often concerned with how social welfare is produced and sustained, and this work tends to draw attention to the great variety of sources that are involved. A useful and influential way of understanding this complexity is the 'welfare triangle' (Fig. 1.5).

The purpose of Fig. 1.5 is to illustrate the main sources from which people obtain their welfare or wellbeing. All of us depend for the quality of our lives, to different degrees, on our links to the market, to the state, and to the families and communities in which we live. Consider for a moment two particularly important measures of social welfare in a society: how it looks after its children and how it looks after its older people. In all societies parents and families are the primary providers of care for children. As the children grow older so the state, for example in the provision of education, becomes more important. But in some cases where parents cannot or are not there to provide care, the state or the wider community may have to step in. The care of dependent older people can similarly be the product of all three sources. In poor societies, frail older people are usually entirely dependent on the family for income and care. There also is much

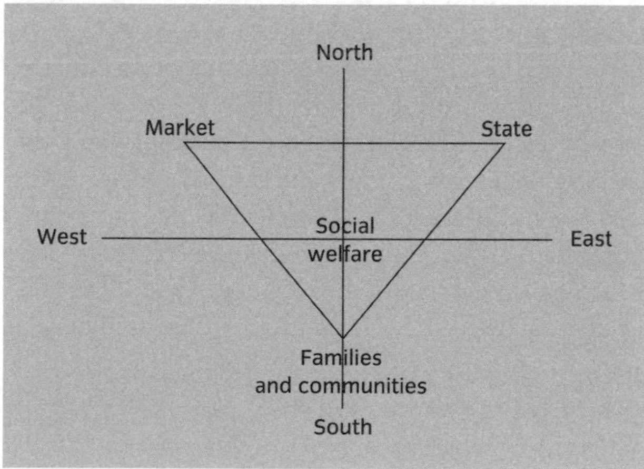

Figure 1.5 The production of social welfare

Source: adapted from Evers (1988: 27).

evidence to show that even in rich societies most personal care for older people is provided by their families. However, assistance is available from the state, in the form of social services. The market too may play a large role, in terms of paid care and the pensions that help finance it. The key point here is that welfare is generally a product of all three sources, or what is called the **mixed economy of welfare**. It is a matter of history and politics how the actual balance of sources has developed in a particular country.

Imposed on Fig. 1.5 are the four points of the compass. This again is merely an illustrative device. But it reminds us that in poor, southern societies the family and community are most important in the production of social welfare. Western countries, particularly the United States, have been associated with a greater use of the market to provide welfare, while eastern European nations, particularly before the collapse of communism, made greater use of the state. In choosing to develop social policy in a particular area, politicians and administrators always face decisions as to the respective roles of the market, the state, and the family in achieving their goals. For example, this is exactly the basis of the debate about the appropriate funding and provision of university education in Britain.

THE WELFARE STATE

Defining the welfare state

Societies in which a substantial part of the production of welfare is paid for and provided by the government have been called 'welfare states'. Within the academic subject of social policy there are continuing debates about what is necessary to qualify as a welfare state. Does, for example, the United States provide, through its federal, state, and local welfare provisions, sufficient help to its citizens to be labelled a welfare state? Or should the term be reserved for the Scandinavian countries such as Sweden or Denmark, in which state welfare services constitute a much larger proportion of the economy? Some regard this debate about what actually constitutes a welfare state as a sterile one, and suggest we should abandon the term and use instead that of a **welfare system** (Wincott 2003 provides a useful summary of this debate). However, even if a strict definition of 'welfare state' is not necessary from an analytical point of view, the term remains important because of the frequency with which it is used, by politicians, in the media, and by ordinary people, and because, historically, the welfare state was at one time understood as the twentieth century's most complete answer to social need.

In a speech to the annual conference of the Labour Party in 1950, Sam Watson, leader of the Durham coalminers, listed the achievements of the welfare state: 'Poverty has been abolished. Hunger is unknown. The sick are tended. The old folks are cherished, our children are growing up in a land of opportunity' (Hennessy 1992: 423). This turned out to be a rather rosy view, but it captures the confidence of the time in the role of state welfare. It was a conception of its function as setting minimum standards in income, health, housing, and education below which citizens would not be allowed to fall: the idea of the welfare state as a social safety net.

Comparing types of welfare state

Alongside discussion about what counts as a welfare state has been a parallel debate about how welfare states or welfare systems differ from one another. Investigating these differences is fundamental to the comparative study of social policy. Researchers have classified countries in terms of ideologies that inform their welfare policies, the levels and comprehensiveness of benefits they offer their citizens, and the organizational arrangements used to fund and deliver those benefits. This has been called by one commentator 'the welfare modelling business' (Abrahamson 2000). The main object is to understand whether welfare states are becoming more alike or more different, and to analyse whether some types of welfare state are more likely to survive in the context of global economic change. The best-known typology of welfare states is that suggested by Gøsta Esping-Andersen in his important book, *The Three Worlds of Welfare Capitalism* (1990). This divides welfare states into three main types; the neo-liberal (for example the United States), the social democratic (Sweden), and the corporatist (Germany). Esping-Andersen's analysis is described in more detail in Chapter 2, pp. 47–48.

THE DEVELOPMENT OF THE WELFARE STATE

Sir Robert Walpole, when he was old and poor-sighted, asked his son to read to him, but is reputed to have said, 'Anything but history, for history must be false.' Walpole may have been expressing a view more famously stated by Henry Ford many years later ('History is more or less bunk. It's tradition. We don't want tradition'), but he was more probably thinking of two problems that all history has to face. First, it inevitably involves selection and simplification. Secondly, the selection process may be biased or inaccurate. For these reasons it is not appropriate in the context of a textbook such as this to attempt a brief summary of the history of welfare states or even of the British welfare state. This would just exaggerate the problems of selection and misrepresentation. There are available some excellent general histories of the welfare state, and some of these are recommended in the guide to further reading at the end of the chapter. Here we limit discussion to highlighting two key themes that may be borne in mind when reading the history of welfare states. Then we provide an outline of the developments that have followed the election of 'New Labour' to government in 1997 and 2001.

A consequence of industrialization or of political competition?

Two accounts of the evolution of welfare states dominate the literature. Some argue that industrialization and the social needs it generates, particularly unemployment and poverty, make the provision of state welfare more or less inevitable. Classic accounts are found in Rimlinger (1971) and Wilensky (1975). Others argue that state welfare is won through political competition and follows the coming to political power of representatives of the interests of industrial workers or, more recently, other key groups such women, ethnic minorities, and disabled people. As a result, the scale and comprehensiveness of the

Box 1.5 Less eligibility: from the Report of the Poor Law Commissioners, 1834 (The principle of less eligibility that informed the 'New Poor Law' in England from 1834)

'The first and most essential of all conditions, a principle which we find universally admitted, even by those whose practice is at variance with it, is, that his situation [that is, the situation of the 'pauper', the recipient of Poor Law relief] on the whole shall not be made really or apparently so eligible as the situation of the independent labourer of the lowest class. Throughout the evidence it is shown, that in proportion as the condition of any pauper class is elevated above the condition of independent labourers, the condition of the independent class is depressed; their industry is impaired, their employment becomes unsteady, and its remuneration in wages is diminished. Such persons, therefore, are under the strongest inducements to quit the less eligible class of labourers and enter the more eligible class of paupers. The converse is the effect when the pauper class is placed in its proper position, below the condition of the independent labourer. Every penny bestowed, that tends to render the condition of the pauper more eligible than that of the independent labourer, is a bounty on indolence and vice. . . .

A well-regulated workhouse meets all cases, and appears to be the only means by which the intention of the statute of Elizabeth [of 1601], that all the able-bodied shall be set to work, can be carried into execution.'

(Report of the Poor Law Commissioners, 1834)

welfare state varies between countries depending on their political histories and which groups of citizens win the power to make the state attend to their interests. This historical analysis is represented in various ways by Miliband (1961), Addison (1975), and Gough (1979), and is discussed in Chapter 2.

Most histories of the welfare state give considerable weight to the processes of industrialization. Britain, particularly England, became an industrial and predominantly urban society significantly before most other countries, and many forms of state intervention in the welfare of citizens appeared there at an early stage too (Mathias 2001). There are also substantial similarities in the histories of public welfare across industrial societies, though the pace of development has varied. All developed a version of the Victorian Poor Law in the nineteenth century (Box 1.5), and all exhibited the basic infrastructures of the modern welfare state by around the middle of the twentieth century (Esping-Andersen and Korpi 1987). These issues are also explored in Chapter 3.

A 'golden age' of the welfare state?

It is not yet clear whether the post-Second World War welfare state will turn out to represent a relatively brief stage in the histories of a few countries or whether it will be a permanent and coherent feature of most developed economies. Some dispute there ever was a golden age (Glennerster 2000), but most broadly accept that from the 1940s to the mid-1970s funding for welfare benefits and services in Britain and other European countries grew year by year as a proportion of national income, and the major political parties shared a consensus that the core institutions of the welfare state were a good thing

(Lowe 1993). There is even more agreement that since the 1970s the welfare state has been under threat. To some extent this is explained by the coming to power of governments of the 'new right' (see Chapter 3), such as those of Mrs Thatcher, which did not share the welfare values of the postwar period. However, a more fundamental argument is that the growth of a global economy requires the driving down of costs in order to compete in economic markets, and this has made it very difficult for governments to expand welfare expenditures and sometimes made it necessary to cut them. Globalization (see Chapter 22) may have brought to an end the golden age of the welfare state. Furthermore, the competitive pressures have been compounded by demographic changes that reduce the number of workers in societies in relation to the non-working young and old, and by the appearance of new risks which are difficult for the established welfare state to deal with.

> For two reasons the continuing viability of the existing welfare state edifice is being questioned across all of Europe. The first is simply that the status quo will be difficult to sustain given adverse demographic and financial conditions. The second is that the same status quo seems increasingly out-of-date and ill suited to meet the great challenges ahead. Our existing systems of social protection may hinder rather than promote employment growth and competitive knowledge-intensive economies. They may also be inadequate in the face of evolving and possibly far more intense social risks and needs. It is against this backdrop that new political entrepreneurs and welfare architects are coming to the fore with calls for major [welfare] regime change. (Esping-Andersen 2002: 4)

A significant example of a new approach to welfare—and a potential way out of the problems Esping-Andersen is summarizing—has been what is called 'the Third Way'. This is particularly associated with social theorist Tony Giddens (1998; 2000; 2001) and politicians such as Bill Clinton and Tony Blair.

New Labour and the 'Third Way'

In opposition in the 1980s and 1990s, the Labour Party began to articulate a distinctive approach to the welfare state, social policy, and citizenship. The Report of the Commission on Social Justice, published in 1994, brought together a broad range of ideas and proposals, which have come to be identified as a 'third way' approach. This is neither a simple continuation of the Conservative Party's neo-liberal, privatizing, and individualizing stance towards the welfare state nor a return to the 'Old Labour' support for a comprehensive, centralized, redistributive welfare state (for a broader discussion of the Third Way see Powell 2000). The report emphasized the need for developments which have since become the bedrock of New Labour government policies:

> We must transform the welfare state from a safety net in times of trouble to a springboard for economic opportunity. . . . The welfare state must enable people to achieve self-improvement and self-support. It must offer a hand-up, not just a hand-out. (Commission on Social Justice 1994: 8)

In the 1997 general election the Labour Party stressed that its approach to welfare issues would be very different from that of the Tories: that a new emphasis would be on modernizing public services and more spending on education and the National Health

Service. New Labour's policies are discussed throughout this volume in the chapters dealing with specific service areas. Here we provide a broad overview of the philosophy and practice that has been adopted and of some of the debates that accompany them.

The 'New Deal' A key theme of New Labour's approach to the welfare state is that citizenship involves both rights and obligations. The welfare state is there to help those who are willing to help themselves. As Lister has put it: 'The shift in new Labour's welfare philosophy can be understood as a paradigm shift from concern with equality to a focus on social inclusion and opportunity, with which comes responsibility' (2001: 431). Thus work and employment are central to the social policies of New Labour. 'Off welfare and into work' is the cornerstone of the New Deal and its Welfare to Work policies (see Chapter 6). Policy has been directed as much to getting people into paid employment as to protecting them from both poverty and social exclusion. Young unemployed people, single parents, the disabled, and older workers have been targeted. A raft of policies and initiatives, including one-to-one job guidance and help, support for further education and training to help make people employable, a national child care strategy to help parents of young children back to work, and modifications to the tax and benefit system to 'make work pay', have been introduced to encourage people back into paid employment. The obligation on individuals to make the best of these opportunities is stated explicitly. As Gordon Brown, Chancellor of the Exchequer, said of the New Deal for Young People, there is not the option 'to stay at home in bed watching television' (quoted in the *Financial Times*, 26 June 1997). If a young unemployed person does not take up the available training and employment under the New Deal, their entitlement to benefit is withdrawn.

For New Labour, employment is:

- the first responsibility of citizenship;
- a route out of dependency into independence and economic self-sufficiency;
- a solution to poverty;
- a point of connection that individuals have to a wider society;
- a role model to offer children (both by mothers and by fathers);
- a glue that binds society together and so reduces social exclusion. (Williams 2001: 474)

The modernization agenda Another important theme in New Labour policy has been modernizing government and changing governance:

> Networks and partnerships, public participation and democratic renewal, are all symbols of what has been termed a new form of governance in the UK. (Newman 2002:7)

The modernization programme has many different elements. In part it is a continuation of earlier Conservative policies in areas like the **Private Finance Initiative (PFI)**, which uses private money to fund public services, for example where private companies construct public buildings like hospitals or colleges which are then rented by the public service. The modernization programme also seeks to coordinate the work of many 'stakeholders' in a policy area rather than government taking all the responsibility. The Teenage Pregnancy Strategy provides an example of some of these newer ideas.

The Government's Social Exclusion Unit reported on teenage pregnancy in 1999 and this was followed by the establishment of a Teenage Pregnancy Unit in the Department of Health which was also funded by four other government departments, including the Department for Work and Pensions. The Unit's members include civil servants and external experts from areas such as teaching, health, and youth work. In 2000 an independent advisory group was set up to provide advice on the issue and to monitor the success of the strategy. This blend of interdepartmental action and external stakeholders is replicated at local levels by Local Teenage Pregnancy Coordinators (see the Teenage Pregnancy Unit website accessible from the department of health website: www.info.doh.gov.uk).

Conclusion: the end of the universalist welfare state? There is inevitably debate about New Labour's philosophy and the effects of its policies on the nature of the welfare state. It is possible to point to a considerable redistribution of resources and a genuine focus on issues such as child poverty. Others are more concerned about the moralizing and punitive aspects of policies such as the New Deal. Two aspects of the approach are more generally agreed upon: the individualizing tendency of new social policies and their acceptance of inequality of outcome in most areas of life.

> Welfare policy is moving in new directions which emphasize individual responsibility and bias the role of the state increasingly to the promotion of equality of opportunity and the provision of services targeted on specific lower income or disadvantaged groups. This approach rests ultimately on an intellectual underpinning which sees the problems state welfare is designed to meet as individual disasters of a risk society rather than the product of a consistent collective disadvantage. (Taylor-Gooby 2000: 346)

REFERENCES

Abrahmson, P. (2000), 'The welfare modelling business'. In N. Manning and I. Shaw (eds.), *New Risks, New Welfare: Signposts for Social Policy*. Oxford: Blackwell, 57–78.

Addison, P. (1975), *The Road to 1945: British Politics and the Second World War*. London: Cape.

Baldwin, S., Godfrey, C., and Propper, G. (1990), *Quality of Life: Perspectives and Policies*. London: Routledge.

Beck, U. (1992), *Risk Society: Towards a New Modernity*, trans. M. Ritter. London: Sage.

Beveridge, W. (1942), *Social Insurance and Allied Services: A Report by Sir William Beveridge*. Cmd. 6404, London: HMSO.

Cahill, M. (1994), *The New Social Policy*. Oxford: Blackwell.

Commission on Social Justice (1994), *Social Justice: Strategies for National Renewal*. London: Vintage.

DfES (Department for Education and Skills) (2003), *The Future of Higher Education*. London: Stationery Office.

DoH (Department of Health) (1990), *Community Care in the Next Decade and Beyond: Policy Guidance*. London: HMSO.

DoH (Department of Health) (2001), *A National Service Framework for Older People*. London: DoH.

Donnison, D. V. (1975) *An Approach to Social Policy*. Dublin: National Economic and Social Council and Republic of Ireland Stationery Office.

Esping-Andersen, G. (1990), *The Three Worlds of Welfare Capitalism*. Cambridge: Polity Press.

—— (2002), 'A child-centred social investment strategy'. In G. Esping-Andersen (ed.), *Why We Need a New Welfare State*. Oxford: Oxford University Press, 26–67.

—— and Korpi, W. (1987), 'From poor relief to institutional welfare states: the development of Scandinavian social policy'. In R. Erikson, E. J. Hansen, S. Ringen, and H. Uusitalo (eds.), *The Scandinavian Model*. Armonk, NY: Sharpe.

Evers, A. (1988), 'Shifts in the welfare mix: introducing a new approach for the study of transformations in welfare and social policy'. In A. Evers and H. Wintersberger (eds.), *Shifts in the Welfare Mix: Their Impact on Work, Social Services and Welfare Policies*. Vienna: European Centre for Social Welfare.

Giddens A. (1998), *The Third Way: The Renewal of Social Democracy*. Cambridge: Polity Press.

—— (ed.) (2000), *The Third Way and its Critics*. Cambridge: Polity Press.

—— (ed.) (2001), *The Global Third Way Debate*. Cambridge: Polity Press.

Glennerster, H. (2000), *British Social Policy since 1945*, 2nd edn. Oxford: Blackwell.

Gough, I. (1979), *The Political Economy of the Welfare State*. London: Macmillan.

Hennessy, P. (1992), *Never Again: Britain 1945–51*. London: Cape.

House of Commons (2000), *The BSE Inquiry: report, evidence and supporting papers of the inquiry into the emergence and identification of bovine spongiform encephalopathy (BSE) and variant Creutzfeldt-Jakob disease (vCJD) and the action taken in response to it up to 20 March 1996*. London: Stationery Office; also available at www.bseinquiry.gov.uk

Lewis, J. (2003), 'Developing early years childcare in England, 1997–2002: the choices for (working) mothers', *Social Policy and Administration* 37(3): 219–38.

Lister, R. (2001), 'New Labour: a study in ambiguity from a position of ambivalence', *Critical Social Policy* 21(4): 425–47.

Lowe, R. (1993), *The Welfare State in Britain since 1945*. London: Macmillan.

Mathias, P. (2001), *The First Industrial Nation: The Economic History of Britain 1700–1914*. London: Routledge, Taylor & Francis.

Miliband, R. (1961), *Parliamentary Socialism*. London: Allen & Unwin.

Newman, J. (2002) 'Changing governance, changing equality? New Labour, modernization and public services' *Public Money and Management* (Jan.–Mar.): 7–13.

OECD (Organization for Economic Cooperation and Development) (2001), *20 Years of Social Expenditure: 1980–1998*. Paris: OECD.

ONS (Office for National Statistics) (2003), *Social Trends No. 33*. London: Stationery Office.

Powell, M. (2000) 'New Labour and the Third Way in the British welfare state: a new and distinctive approach?', *Critical Social Policy* 20(1): 39–60.

Pierson C. (1991), *Beyond the Welfare State? The New Political Economy of Welfare*. Cambridge: Polity Press.

Quality Assurance Agency for Higher Education (2000), *Social Policy and Social Work*. Gloucester: QAAHE. www.qaa.ac.uk/crntwork/benchmark/socialwork.pdf

Rimlinger, G. V. (1971), *Welfare Policy and Industrialization*. New York: Wiley.

Taylor-Gooby, P. (2000) 'Blair's scars', *Critical Social Policy* 20(3): 331–48.

Titmuss, R. M. (1968), *Commitment to Welfare*. London: Unwin University Books.

—— (1974), *Social Policy: An Introduction*. London: Allen & Unwin.

—— (1976), *Essays on the Welfare State*, 3rd edn. London: Allen & Unwin.

Townsend, P. (1979), *Poverty in the United Kingdom*. Harmondsworth: Penguin.

Wilensky, H. L. (1975), *The Welfare State and Equality: Structural and Ideological Roots of Public Expenditures*. Berkeley: University of California Press.

Wilkinson, R. G. (2000), *Mind the Gap: Hierarchies, Health and Human Evolution*. London: Weidenfeld & Nicolson.

Williams, F. (2001), 'In and beyond New Labour: towards a new political ethics of care', *Critical Social Policy* 21(4): 467–93.

Wincott, D. (2003), 'Slippery concepts, shifting context: (national) states and welfare in the Veit-Wilson/Atherton Debate', *Social Policy and Administration* 37(3): 305–15.

FURTHER READING

A complete and accessible history of the British welfare state is provided by Derek Fraser's *The Evolution of the British Welfare State* in a new edition which takes the story up to 1997 (London: Palgrave Macmillan, 2002). Excellent more recent histories are Howard Glennerster's *British Social Policy Since 1945*, 2nd edn. (Oxford Blackwell, 2000), Nick Timmins's *The Five Giants: A Biography of the Welfare State*, 2nd edn. (London: HarperCollins, 2001), and Rodney Lowe's *The Welfare State in Britain since 1945*, 2nd edn. (London: Macmillan, 1999). Pete Alcock's *Social Policy in Britain: Themes and Issues* (London: Macmillan, 1996) is a clear introduction to the character of the British welfare state and the ideas that it represents. Howard Glennerster's *Understanding the Finance of Welfare: What Welfare Costs and How to Pay for it* (Bristol: Policy Press, 2003) is an excellent social policy textbook that focuses more on resourcing issues. Michael Cahill, *The New Social Policy* (Oxford: Blackwell, 1994) is still an innovative exploration of social policy in communications, arts, transport, and other often neglected areas. Gøsta Esping-Andersen is one of the key thinkers about where the welfare state is going, and his and other authors' latest ideas can be explored in *Why We Need a New Welfare State* (Oxford: Oxford University Press, 2002). John Hills and others provide a review of what social inclusion policies in areas like low pay, child poverty, and education have achieved in *Understanding Social Exclusion* (Oxford: Oxford University Press, 2001). A good review of New Labour's social policy record is Martin Powell's edited book *Evaluating New Labour's Welfare Reforms* (Bristol: Policy Press, 2002). *Comparative Social Policy: Theories and Methods*, ed. Jochen Clasen (Oxford: Blackwell, 1998), is a good introduction to a complex area. *The Young, the Old and the State: Social Care Systems in Five Industrial Countries*, ed. A. Anttonen, J. Baldock, and J. Sipilä (Cheltenham: Elgar, 2003) compares how industrial nations look after children and older people. Vic George and Paul Wilding, *Globalization and Human Welfare* (Basingstoke: Palgrave, 2002) is an excellent analysis of the concept of globalization itself as well as of the welfare implications for both rich and poor nations.

USEFUL WEBSITES

The OECD (Organization for Economic Cooperation and Development) publishes very useful documents many dealing with comparative social policy issues at: www.oecd.org

British Government publications can be explored and accessed from: www.official-documents.co.uk;

www.letsallgeton.gov.uk. A great many of the publication of the Stationary Office are available at: www.tso.co.uk

Particularly useful government sites for getting up to date information about social policy issues are the Department of Health website, www.doh.gov.uk, particularly the links to social care issues, and the Treasury website, www.hm-treasury.gov.uk.

GLOSSARY

cash benefits where the state provides welfare in the form of money (rather than services in kind) such as unemployment benefits (called Job Seeker's Allowance in the UK), pensions, disability benefits, and a minimum income (Income Support in the UK).

contracting out when the public sector contracts the provision of social services to an independent for-profit or a not-for-profit organization.

direct taxation when government levies taxes on people's incomes and not on goods that they purchase (indirect taxation). Income tax is the main form and is usually progressive, taking proportionately more the more people earn.

gross national product (GNP) all of a country's output or goods and services (usually measured in a calendar year) plus income from assets abroad, but with no deduction (that is gross not net) for depreciation in the country's assets.

gross domestic product (GDP) is gross national product, but excludes income from assets abroad.

indirect taxation when government raises money by adding taxes to other things that people do (drive cars) or to goods and services that they buy (value added taxes, duties on fuel, liquor, and cigarettes). Indirect taxes tend to be regressive and to hit the poor harder as a proportion of their incomes.

individual welfare the good of the individual citizen.

horizontal redistribution contrasts particularly with vertical redistribution and is where resources are taken from some (usually in the form of tax) and given to others no worse off but who have particular characteristics or needs (such as children in state schools or who are ill or disabled).

lifetime redistribution an understanding of state provision of benefits and services which interprets it in terms of taking resources from people at points in their lives when they are well off (usually through taxes and social insurance contributions paid by the employed) and returning them when they are less well off or in need (when they are unemployed, ill, or retired, for example).

market failure when the market fails to produce what is most wanted at the lowest possible price; usually reflected in unemployed resources, unconsumed output or unmet demand.

mixed economy of welfare a term used to indicate that social welfare is produced not just by the state but also by families, communities, for-profit, and not-for-profit (charitable) sources.

not-for-profit organizations those that seek only to cover the costs of providing services, as do most charitable welfare organizations, and not to make a profit.

postwar settlement the political consensus, accepted by most major political parties in Britain and elsewhere, that the welfare state institutions established after the Second World War should be maintained.

private finance initiative (PFI) an arrangement where the state uses a for-profit company to find and invest the capital required to provide a government service. Thus a private company might finance and build a hospital or a school that the state then guarantees to rent for a specific length of time. This method reduces public borrowing, may lead to more efficient management of the capital investment, but commits the state to current expenditure in the future.

private-for-profit organizations are those which, in the context of social policy, provide welfare services, such as social care or nursing home care, but seek not only to cover their costs but also to make a profit for their owners.

privatization when publicly owned service providers are transferred into the for-profit sector and run by private owners.

progressive taxes taxes that take a growing proportion of people's incomes as their incomes go up. Income tax is usually progressive, the percentage rate of tax going up as particular income thresholds are passed. Taxes that do not rise in this way are said to be regressive.

regulation achieving social policy objectives by requiring people or organizations to do things such as wear seat belts, send their children to school, or abide by health and safety standards and practices.

risk society a term coined by Ulrich Beck to refer to the way in which complex industrial societies present individuals, and even whole populations, with a range of risks created by technology, the economic market, and powerful organizations and institutions.

selective benefits commonly used to describe 'means-tested' benefits; those only provided to those whose incomes and resources fall below a prescribed level.

services in kind social services which are provided to users directly, such as education, health care, or housing, rather than money (cash benefits) for them to purchase the benefits themselves.

social exclusion the processes by which people become disconnected from the wider society and the communities they live in because of characteristics they have (low incomes, age, poor education) or because of the ways in which they are discriminated against by other people or institutions.

social inclusion policies those that seek to combat the processes of social exclusion (see below).

social need a judgement that someone is lacking something (income, education, housing, or social care for example) that they ought to have, or has fallen below some minimum level in some area. The term can be given more precision by unpacking it into felt need, expressed need, normative need, comparative need, and technical need (see Chapter 5).

social policy the principles and practice of state activity—including state policy for private or voluntary action—relating to redistribution in pursuit of, or leading to, welfare outcomes.

social welfare the wellbeing of individuals or of families, households, and whole communities, in both material but also non-material terms such education and health, which is produced through the provision of goods and services by families, the community, the voluntary sector, the market, and the state.

tax credits instead of taking from incomes as they rise, the tax authorities add to people's incomes as they fall below a defined amount. Tax credits are an alternative to a separate system of means-tested cash benefits.

universal benefits conventionally, welfare benefits provided to all who fall into certain contingencies (such as having children, in the case of Child Benefit; being of school age; being over the age of retirement; having become unemployed) regardless of their income or wealth.

vertical redistribution the taking away of resources (usually in the from of taxation) from those who have more and the distribution of them to others who have less (usually in the form of cash benefits or services in kind).

welfare state the institutional arrangements through which the state provides money, goods, and services to its citizens. This concept is usually used to refer to main institutions of the postwar welfare settlement: the National Health Service, the social security system, the state-funded education system, the state role in the provision and funding of housing, and state personal and social work services. Some observers insist that a welfare state, as distinct from some welfare services, can only be said to exist where the state guarantees that citizens will not fall below defined minima in terms of income and possibly health and education.

welfare system the organizations and mechanisms primarily concerned with providing or guaranteeing the social welfare of citizens. These may include non-state organizations such as those in the voluntary sector and those in the private (for-profit) sector. This is a wider definition than the more traditional one of 'the welfare state'.

2

The Politics Of Welfare

Nick Manning

CONTENTS

INTRODUCTION: POLITICS AND WELFARE

Social policy is inextricably bound up with governments and politics. Political party manifestos routinely include substantial proposals for changes in social policies. Social policy itself involves attempts to change current social arrangements in one way or another, and hence involves the exercise of power. There are strongly held views about what these changes should amount to. Individuals, pressure groups, professionals, community groups, industrial and trade union groups, and others try to influence the direction of social policy.

In this chapter we will present some of the institutions, structures, and people who are involved in the politics of social policy, and who try to alter its course.

Case Study 2.1 Healthcare reform in the UK and the USA

A major commitment made by Bill Clinton when he was elected President in 1992 was to reform the delivery of healthcare to US citizens. The USA is unique amongst industrial nations for its inability to deliver healthcare insurance to 40 million people—about 15 per cent of the population, many of them black. There has been a long history of attempts to reform healthcare services in the USA. The vested interests of the American Medical Association and the private insurance industry combined forces to exclude health insurance from the 1935 Social Security Act. Only with the successful Democrat years of the 1960s was it possible to get limited support for the healthcare costs of poor people and older people in the 1965 'medicaid' and 'medicare' amendments to the 1935 legislation. In 1992 Clinton faced the same coalition of interests, now bigger and stronger with the growth of the healthcare industry since the 1960s, but with a weaker command of political resources. Perhaps it is not surprising that he failed to get his reforms through.

A major reform of the NHS was similarly initiated by Margaret Thatcher in 1994. In contrast to the US, British healthcare has been delivered since 1948 to all citizens free at the point of consumption, and independent of their employment status. Healthcare indicators are relatively good, and the cost is about half of the US system, at 7 per cent of GNP. However, market mechanisms were introduced into the system, so that both private and public providers could compete, and a large number of new bureaucrats were employed to undertake the detailed paperwork caused by the complex commissioning and contracting system set up to ensure that the marketplace worked.

The outcomes of Clinton's and Thatcher's attempts at healthcare reform were determined by politics, rather than rational planning. 'Politics' in this case means both the rules under which each leader has to operate and the resources they can bring to the debates and the decision-making arena. These are shaped by the context in which each leader has to work.

One of the reasons for the British state's relative success in 1948 was that under British political rules the ruling party has greater freedom of action than the US equivalent. The US Constitution is designed to restrain any particular part of the state, including the President, from any great freedom of action. Since the foundation of the NHS, the British state has managed to exercise much greater control over healthcare than its US counterpart, keeping costs very much lower, but with a comprehensive service. In a series of reforms in the 1970s and 1980s, state direction of the NHS steadily increased, and the independent power of the medical profession has slowly weakened.

CONCEPTS

Politics: institutions and structures

Modern **welfare states** are so called because they are part of the modern nation-state. States as such are a relatively recent invention. Although we think of England as having a very long history, some nation-states, such as Germany and Italy, only emerged in the nineteenth century. States in general have a familiar set of structures and institutions for administering those concerns of their citizens that are considered as legitimately within the public domain. In the welfare area, for example, these might typically include a **government department** or **ministry** for dealing with different aspects of healthcare. In the UK this is called the Department of Health, in France and in Russia it is called the Ministry of Health.

The staff of these government departments would typically be full-time career **civil servants**—an essential component of the modern welfare state. It is the role of these bureaucrats to carry out and implement whatever **policies** are laid down by the government of the day. For example, where a new government, such as New Labour in the UK, plans a new scheme, such as the movement of more young people from unemployment into employment (from 'welfare to work'), then civil servants are duty bound to implement this policy. More details on the complexities of this process are discussed in Chapter 9.

The right of governments to develop and implement such policies within the state is conferred mainly, although not exclusively, through the process of **liberal democracy**. This is a mechanism, now very widely diffused throughout the world, for registering the **consent** of citizens to government action of various sorts, and for making the legal, financial, and military **resources** available to the government to act. In the field of social policy, financial resources or lack of them are a pre-eminent constraint on government action, but legal arrangements are also of great significance. For example, modern medicine seems to cost more and more each year, partly as the result of the progress of medical science in developing new technology, but also partly as a result of the ageing of the population and the survival of people with significant healthcare needs. Both the medical profession and the public often turn to governments to find the money for this steady expansion of healthcare.

In addition to these resource problems, the **rules** under which such services operate, many of them inscribed in law, are both a mechanism for government control—through new legislation, for example—and a site for argument and dispute. For example, where a child has become very disruptive in her classroom, there might be a clash between the child's right to education, the parent's obligation to secure that education, the teacher's right to particular conditions of employment, and so on.

One source of such rules in modern states is the existence of a **constitution** which lays down the structure of government, and the various rules through which it should be set up and should operate. This can be very important indeed for social policy changes and provision. A good example is provided by the USA. After the Declaration of

Box 2.1 US constitutional amendments

13th	'Neither slavery nor involuntary servitude . . . shall exist within the US'
14th	'All persons born or naturalised in the US . . . are citizens of the US'
15th	'The right of citizens of the US to vote shall not be denied . . . on account of race, colour, or previous condition of servitude'

Independence in 1789 at which Jefferson famously declared that 'all men are created equal', the Constitution and the first ten amendments (such as freedom of religious expression) were adopted. There have been more than twenty subsequent amendments to the Constitution, many of which have had profound consequences for social policy. For example, the abolition of slavery, and the right of black Americans to equal access to services such as education, was guaranteed in a series of three amendments (the 13th, 14th and 15th—see Box 2.1) passed soon after the northern States won the American civil war in 1865.

Britain never rejected or completely neutralized the monarchy, as did the French, the Russians, and the Americans in their revolutions. Without this break, it has been difficult to establish a case for a written constitution in the UK, which makes it difficult to lodge an appeal to the basic rules which govern British society in a case where some feel that there is a fundamental injustice to be corrected. The members of Charter 88, for example, have argued that a written constitution would provide safeguards for citizens against welfare injustices perpetrated by mistake or intent.

However, in the case of the US, the varied interpretation of constitutional amendments by the Supreme Court has in any case often undermined their original intentions. This was most explicitly the case for the access of black Americans to education from the late nineteenth century through to the civil rights movement of the 1960s. There were two Supreme Court interpretations of the Constitution that clearly show how a written constitution can be undermined. In the first, the court ruled that discrimination on the grounds of race did not take place where service provision was 'separate but equal' (in the case of *Plessy* v. *Ferguson*, Louisiana, 1896). This justified the rapid development in the late nineteenth century of effective apartheid in the southern US states. In most areas of welfare and public service provision, including education, and in private provision such as bus transport and restaurants, blacks were excluded, by force if necessary, from white services up until the 1960s.

In the second example, the Supreme Court reversed the 'separate but equal' ruling in 1954 in relation to the access of black children to white schools (*Brown* v. *Board of Education, Topeka*, Kansas). However, it ordered that the new ruling should be implemented 'with all deliberate speed', which was taken to mean as slowly as possible. Almost no school desegregation took place over the next ten years, which was a major stimulus to the development of the 1960s civil rights movement. The rules of government enshrined in constitutions are not therefore independent of interpretation, and cannot in themselves guarantee particular outcomes.

The rules and resources which shape political institutions and structures typically give rise to a pattern of government action in the arena of social policy which has been classified by Julian Le Grand (1993) into three mechanisms: direct provision, financial support, and regulation.

Direct provision is where the state provides both the resources and the rules by which they are to be used. For example, in the UK health 'insurance' was provided from 1948 to 1994 through the National Health Service directly supplied by the government to citizens who needed healthcare. This approach was felt by British Labour governments for most of the twentieth century to be the most efficient and fairest mechanism for social welfare provision. This entailed either nationalizing existing services, such as the hospitals in 1948, or providing services from scratch, such as local authority housing from the early 1920s, or local authority social work since 1968. Taking these services into public ownership was part of a wider strategy of enlarging direct state provision where capitalism was seen to be inefficient or unfair, and included rail and air transport, steel production, and, for a time, car manufacture.

This policy was tolerated reluctantly by British Conservative governments as an unpleasant but practical necessity. It had been necessary for the development and coordination of the many activities essential to the prosecution of the Second World War, including the Emergency Medical Services. This had amounted in effect to the nationalization of many aspects of the country's production and service provision, and demonstrated that widespread direct state provision could work. Much of the British welfare state set up in the immediate postwar years was typified by this means of direct service provision.

For other services, however, **financial support**, but not direct provision, typifies state action. Here the state provides the financial resources, but not always the rules for their disbursement. This form of state intervention has often developed in areas where existing private provision is defended through well-organized interests. For example, British governments give people financial help to get privately provided legal services, because lawyers do not wish their service to be nationalized. Housing is also mostly provided by the private sector, but the British and US governments have spent large sums in helping purchasers to acquire cheaper finance for their houses, for example by defraying income tax where income is spent on repaying mortgages. Indeed, this idea of government relief from paying income tax on money spent on services amounts in effect to extensive government spending in terms of 'tax expenditure', discussed in more detail in Chapter 10.

In many countries, healthcare provision operates in the same way, through the government subsidizing private provision, since doctors have been powerful enough to resist nationalization. The American Medical Association has been notoriously successful in this respect, but private insurance companies have also lobbied hard to defend their interests. However they have also lobbied hard to attract government financial support, and on occasions they have been tempted to corruption, when for example they have submitted claims for the funding of fictitious treatments.

For this reason government financial support often requires the monitoring of service providers to check that the money is being used in a proper manner. This leads us to consider the third area of state action, **regulation**. Here the state is concerned more with the rules than the resources necessary for any particular action. In France, for example, the government merely legislates that all citizens should be insured through non-profit independent 'insurance societies' who pay for healthcare, and in the USA most citizens have private health insurance paid for by their employers, or, for about 15 per cent of the population, no cover at all. Regulation is a non-market method of state intervention to ensure the delivery of services to, or requisite behaviour from, defined groups or individuals in a manner defined in law or subject to bureaucratic surveillance. Parents are required to ensure children's education takes place, normally of course at a recognized school. Those children are known to the state, since all births must be registered with the state. The provision of medicines is closely regulated, as they may be dangerous; those of working age seeking income support are required to seek work; all car drivers must take out insurance against the costs of accidents; and so on. What the law requires, and the efficiency or fairness of bureaucratic surveillance, is the subject of sharp dispute from time to time, often organized by **pressure groups** concerned to secure the wellbeing of particular groups such as poor, older, or disabled people. We will look at the political practices of such groups below.

State action also takes place in most countries through lower levels of government. These also have considerable consequences for social policy. In very large countries such as Russia or the USA the next layer of government structures below the national level are what amount to 'mini-states' within the state. These will have considerable powers of their own, including the ability to raise finance independently from the central state, upon which they will nevertheless usually be partly dependent. In smaller countries—in Europe, for example—these lower tiers of government are likely to have rather less autonomy, and may range from rather loose regional groups to specific counties, as in the UK.

Social provision such as education is often undertaken at these lower levels of government. However, this raises a problem of the relative affluence of different areas, and hence the possibility of social provision varying between citizens of the same country as a result of geographical location. This variation may well be cumulative, so that relative differences are compounded for education, housing, healthcare, employment, and so on. Such regional disadvantages have been termed '**territorial injustice**' by Bleddyn Davies (1978).

Local governments also have rules, resources, and different modes of intervention, as we have seen for central government. For example, in the UK local governments can significantly vary the types of schools provided, typically between comprehensives and grammar schools. They can also vary the level of funding they choose to give to schools, and hence the size of classes, as well as provision of books and equipment and kind of food. As for central government, these local variations in rules and resources lead to different types of intervention. Some local authorities provide most schooling directly themselves, as in Nottinghamshire, whereas in others almost all schools are independently organized, as in Kent.

Power and authority

It is important to remember at this point that governments are not the only providers of welfare services, although they remain extremely important, especially when we are considering political aspects as in this chapter. Elsewhere in this book we suggest also that the private market, the voluntary and social movement sector, and informal, neighbourly, and family networks are significant shapers and providers of welfare. Politics, and especially power, suffuse these areas, too.

The rules and resources deployed by governments and other groups involved in the field of welfare are an exercise in power—the ability to implement plans of action and persuade or coerce others to follow suit. **Power**, in Stephen Lukes's view (1974), is not merely about the ability to pursue those options that are 'on the table', but also crucially the ability to control what the options are in the first place—either including the unthinkable, as Margaret Thatcher so often did, or more often excluding what some might think should be considered, but which governments or other powerful groups do not favour. Politics in the field of welfare can often be a struggle over the agenda for policy debate as much as the policies themselves, as we shall see when we look closer below at the key political players and processes of change.

Power, in a government which is legitimate, is normally defined as **authority**. The classic work on authority was by Max Weber (1947), who suggested that modern governments exercised authority on a rational-legal basis (Box 2.2). This meant that there were clear and explicit rules understood by all citizens as to the basis for a government's claim to have power. For example, where a new need comes to be widely recognized, such as those at risk of HIV/AIDS infection, or those unable to find work, government is the accepted source of authority for action: 'someone should do something about it,' we say.

The frequent response is either to provide a new service or finance some new activity such as healthcare or to produce new regulations to guide behaviour—even intimate sexual behaviour. These are accepted as legitimate because we understand these state actions as rational and legal.

Legitimate authority can also be seen in the operations of the market, where the price mechanism regulates the legitimate exchange of money for goods and services. Similarly, charities such as those concerned with the welfare of children have a powerful and legitimate voice, raised from time to time in the interests of children's needs. Even in family life much—but by no means all—parental authority stems from the rational basis for action in the superior knowledge of parents about the best interests of the child.

However, from time to time the rational basis for authority in all these areas, including that of the state, is contested. A major independent source of authority which is

Box 2.2 Max Weber on the basis of authority: rational-legal, traditional, charismatic

Rational-legal authority: the ability to command support for policies because they are in accord with widely accepted rules.

Traditional authority: the ability to command support for policies because they appear natural or sensible as a result of long use.

Charismatic authority: the ability to command support for policies through personal magnetism.

frequently brought to bear on questions of welfare, whether within the state or the family, is based on the **professions**, such as medicine, teaching, or social work. Here, although authority is ultimately state-sanctioned, for example by the state registration of practitioners, specialized knowledge is deployed to criticize and develop welfare policies in many ways. Another claim to legitimate authority is made by pressure groups operating in the particular interests of sections of the community, whose needs may be felt to have been overlooked, or for whom the very definition of appropriate needs has been challenged. A very significant example of this challenge to existing legitimate authority, and the posing of alternatives, has been the achievements of the women's movement over the last thirty years. For example, this movement has successfully challenged the rational-legal basis of the notion of the dependence of mothers on the 'family wage' of their husbands, enshrined in state employment policy and social security for much of the postwar era. Similar challenges have been made to medical treatments, for example of women's mental illness, or to the expression of husbands' authority over sexual or physical matters in the home.

However, a number of widely accepted activities by government and other welfare groups have been around for such a long time that the original reasons for them may have become obscured over time. An example is the close association between the aristocracy or senior church figures and voluntary charities, which gives charities their good status, and provides for some an important asset for raising money. Here Weber talks of authority as having a traditional basis, sanctioned more by its longevity than by its intrinsic merits. The American and French revolutions were a general replacement of traditional by rational-legal authority. But in England this did not occur, and there is consequently a long tradition of historical analysis of social policy which stresses the tradition of *noblesse oblige* on the part of the aristocracy to help those less fortunate than others.

Tradition is not a monopoly of the aristocracy. Traditional authority can also be found in the deference of many of us to 'the doctor' or to 'the teacher', or to senior members of our families. Here we can see power exercised in terms of obligations, such as to take the medicine, to undertake the duties of caring, or to be grateful for charitable help. However, traditional authority at the level of our daily lives is not as easy to overthrow as the *ancien régimes* of old, and may perpetuate the following of rules or the use of resources that, on reflection, we would not consider rational. For example, where medical treatments have grown out of accepted practice, rather than scientific assessment, patients have been asked to accept them on the basis of traditional medical authority. There is now a growing movement in favour of 'evidence-based medicine', which raises by its very nature doubts about accepted practice such as hospital treatment for heart attacks, or for giving birth. These are discussed in Chapter 14.

Turning to change rather than stability, it is clear that some new ideas in government or other areas of welfare can develop through the exercise of exceptional personal qualities that can persuade citizens that the merits of the person themselves are a satisfactory form of authority, and on that basis the ideas can be accepted. This personal form of authority was described by Weber as 'charismatic'. It can open up room for changes normally regarded as 'unthinkable': for example, for many people Margaret Thatcher possessed this personal quality, through which she was able to exercise power for a considerable period of time and to make a number of radical changes to the British welfare state.

Charismatic authority can be a force for good or ill. It may be the vehicle for challenging and overcoming policies that have become ossified by tradition, even if rational at one time. Margaret Thatcher felt that this was true of many areas of public life, including central and local government, and some of the professions. Echoing Joseph Schumpeter's characterization of capitalism as causing waves of 'creative destruction', she felt that many traditional ways of delivering welfare services, in the National Health Service, in housing, or in education, should be subject to market forces to weed out cosy but irrational practices that had accumulated unjustifiably over time. The eventual acceptance of some of her ideas by many of her critics, both in other countries and by New Labour, indicates how new her ideas were, from the use of contracting in health and social services to greater independence for schools or increased owner-occupation. Other ideas were dropped, the poll tax being the best known of these.

But charismatic authority is also common elsewhere in the welfare field, particularly in the voluntary sector. Many well-known voluntary agencies were built up by a charismatic innovator who managed to carry the authority to develop new ideas and services by sheer personal drive. Leonard Cheshire, Cecily Saunders, Elly Jansen, Maxwell Jones, and Paolo Freire are contemporary innovators of this type, just as Florence Nightingale, Octavia Hill, the Webbs, Lord Shaftesbury, and Elizabeth Fry were for an earlier generation.

Box 2.3 Charisma and welfare innovators

Leonard Cheshire: founder of the Cheshire homes for permanently disabled people

Cecily Saunders: founder of the hospice movement for people who are dying

Elly Jansen: founder of Richmond Fellowship houses for people with mental illness

Maxwell Jones: founder of therapeutic community movement for radical democracy in mental healthcare

Paolo Freire: founder of a radical movement for education for the 'real world'

Florence Nightingale: originator of the nursing profession

Octavia Hill: founder of the Charity Organization Society for the improvement of the lives of poor people

Sydney and Beatrice Webb: social reform campaigners in a variety of areas, and founders of the Fabian Society and the London School of Economics

Lord Shaftesbury: social reform campaigner, for example to protect working children

Elizabeth Fry: prison reformer

Once again, while much of the work of these welfare innovators was good, charisma does not always coexist with critical reflection, and can result in such leaders overreaching themselves, and rejecting criticism.

Thus while rational-legal and traditional bases for authority are relatively stable, charismatic authority is doomed to decay because it is dependent on a particular person's powers, and by definition these cannot be exceptional for ever—they will become normal, routinized, or mundane after a while, and disenchantment with their ideas may develop. Generally, as in the Catholic Church, a division of labour develops between the exercise of charisma and the maintenance of normal government. In the case of Thatcherism this can be seen in the way new leaders, such as William Hague, have sought the official blessing of Thatcher. In general, however, charismatic decay leads to changes in government or voluntary organization in time, and a new round of normal authority ensues.

Citizens may or may not comply with the exercise of government or other authority. Where this is seen as a problem for the community at large, it might typically be classified as illegal. However, the problem may be of little concern to the community, but of some consequence to the individual or her family. In social policy, for example, the non-take-up of benefit entitlement may increase poverty in a family, or for children, in a way which can undermine the assumptions that a government might make about the extent of its support for family needs. In other cases the individual's and the community's interests might both be threatened where, for example, a potentially violent schizophrenic fails to take the medication which makes continued community living possible.

Etzioni (1975) has classified examples of compliance into a number of different types, depending on the nature of the individual's compliance and the means at an organization's disposal to enforce compliance, which we can usefully adapt here. The government can achieve compliance because it can coerce people, reward them, or persuade them. These latter mechanisms show a close resemblance to Weber's types of authority—and perhaps students could take the time to compare and contrast the ideas of these two authors.

The individual can comply with government rules for different reasons. Those, such as Max Weber, who have defined government as the legitimate monopoly of the means of violence in a society, may observe that ultimately citizens comply because they have to. This begins with the obligation to have one's birth registered. Thereafter, as Michel Foucault (1973) has observed, a citizen is subject to continued, if mostly discreet, surveillance by the state in one form or another. A periodic mandatory population census

Box 2.4 Etzioni's types of compliance

Coercive compliance: where a person has little power to resist a policy.

Calculative compliance: where a person perceives it to be in her interest to comply with a policy.

Moral compliance: where a person strongly believes in the basis for a policy.

supplements this, as do childhood vaccination requests and school attendance checks. There are technical limits to this surveillance, although, as was the case in Eastern Europe, with enough effort it can become almost all-encompassing in its reach—and highly resented.

Some have argued that the use of surveillance to compel compliance is particularly marked in the social security services, where concerns that citizens should seek and accept legitimate, even if low-wage, work, have overridden the original spirit of this most expensive part of the welfare state—to provide income for the destitute. New Labour's 'welfare to work' programme, discussed in Chapter 6, continues this element of compulsion.

However, there are two more common reasons for compliance. Most people comply because they can see some advantage to themselves in doing so. This is akin to Weber's rational-legal basis for authority. For example, in Talcott Parsons's famous model of the 'sick role' (1951) he characterized the role of the patient as being excused the normal obligations of work and family life, but only in return for a commitment to follow the doctor's orders. Similarly, students may work hard in the expectation that exam passes will bring future rewards. Etzioni suggests that such instrumental calculations are widespread in modern societies. However, there are limits to the calculations that individuals are capable of making. For example, left to their own devices people heavily discount contemporary or future risks that we know statistically they face, such as health misfortunes or the problems of old age, and fail to undertake sufficient insurance.

But others are not as calculating as this, and are actively committed to complying because, Etzioni observes, they see this as a moral commitment to a belief in what the government or another group is aiming to achieve. This third type of compliance includes the acceptance of duties. Duties can be borne positively and happily: for example, traditional analyses of the welfare state stressed the positive altruism exercised by British citizens for the unknown stranger, typified by the 'wartime spirit' of the 1940s in Britain. The generalization of this type of compliance to an explanation of social policy in general has been a naive and idealized view held by parts of the political centre in Britain which has mourned the supposed loss of such spirit. Richard Titmuss's 1970 analysis of the British blood donor service (the only one in the world to be entirely voluntary) was a classic statement of this concern. But duties can also be owed to the community which may in themselves feel burdensome, such as the obligation to help one's family, pay taxes, or do voluntary work. The fostering of commitment to obligations has been a prominent feature of right-wing welfare analysis, such as Mead's *Beyond Entitlement* (1987), and found its way into New Labour policy through Frank Field's 1998 Green Paper on Welfare Reform (see Chapter 12). The argument is that, in reality, the acquisition of full citizenship rights depends on being able to discharge one's obligations as a citizen.

WELFARE POLITICS: THE PLAYERS

Who raises the issues that are to be dealt with through the political processes which permeate the welfare field? The main players include welfare clients, social movements, professionals, bureaucrats and policy networks, and politicians and political parties.

Box 2.5 Hirschman's 'exit, voice or loyalty'

Where a person disagrees strongly with a policy, there are only three options:

exit: leave the situation;
voice: express dissent and try to change the situation;
loyalty: change position and learn to accept the situation.

A simple model of the dynamic interplay of these social actors might be to consider the way in which social problems arise in society. When there appears to be a problem, for example the appearance of a new disease such as AIDS or a sharp rise in unemployment, this would normally be brought to the attention of government agencies by professionals such as doctors, **social movements**, or pressure groups. The latter two groups overlap considerably, and can be thought of as organized associations with the primary aim of changing the direction of state intervention in a particular area, generally through raising an issue on the agenda of public debate. Politicians and government bureaucrats might then be expected to respond to these collectively expressed requests.

Welfare clients such as patients, unemployed workers, and students may also be active in these attempts to change social policies. In this way they are making their voices heard rather than passively accepting existing arrangements. Hirschman (1970) has described the alternatives here in terms of 'exit, voice or loyalty' (Box 2.5). Attempts to change policies are an example of 'voice', when collective or individual disquiet or innovation is expressed in the political arena. Loyalty is the option to support existing policies and welfare arrangements—perhaps the most typical. The final option is to try to escape the situation through individual solutions: for example by setting up a new business rather than expecting government to solve unemployment; or choosing private medicine instead of trying to persuade the government that health policy is wrong.

However, this model of attempts to solve social problems through professional concern, collective action, or individual solutions is too simple to adequately understand political actions in the welfare field. This is for three reasons. First, much social policy is directed not at new social problems, but at ongoing issues of long standing. Second, much debate about policy arises from within government agencies rather than outside them. Third, much state intervention has unanticipated consequences—indeed, not infrequently having little effect or even making matters worse.

Routine issues: political party debates

New social problems are only infrequently the reason for changes in social policy. For example, expenditure on social security is dominated by the costs of pensions, and of unemployment. These problems have been around ever since the origins of income insecurity arose as a consequence of the rise in wage labour in the eighteenth century. For these areas of relatively routine party politics it has been suggested that a consensus of 'normal' policies can develop, where political disagreement between political parties can recede in favour of a consensus. A striking example of this was the general social policy agreement that existed between the postwar Labour Party and subsequent Conservative administrations for the first thirty years of the British welfare state. This was known as the 'Butskill' consensus, after the two ministers Butler and Gaitskill, from the two parties, who were in broad agreement over public expenditure.

However, of course, on many matters there is serious disagreement between the parties over social policy—especially clear during the years when Margaret Thatcher was Prime Minister. As described in Case Study 2.1, the British governmental system does enable a determined political party to pursue its policies relatively unchecked. During the 1980s this resulted in the introduction of market principles into many areas of social policy, the weakening of local government control, and the development of more independent **QUANGOS** (quasi non-governmental organizations) and agencies to undertake government work. Many of these agencies were staffed by conservative sympathizers, for example school governing bodies or health service trusts, who became in effect an extension of the party into government work that bypassed the traditional civil service (see Chapter 9 for more details on this).

The ideas that sustain political parties are frequently developed through pressure groups and **think tanks** who take on the task of thinking the unthinkable as far as future policy options are concerned. For the last Conservative government, the Institute of Economic Affairs (IEA) and the Adam Smith Institute were important influences. The current Labour government draws on ideas from the Fabian Society, the Child Poverty Action Group (CPAG), Demos, and others. In addition, **professional associations** such as the British Medical Association (BMA), the medical Royal Colleges, and **trade union** and **business groups** offer advice or warnings to the government, and may be actively consulted from time to time.

Debates internal to professional and government bureaucracies

Debates about policy changes, however, often arise within those groups of professionals and bureaucrats with responsibility for the area in question, rather than from political parties or pressure groups. The key players here are seen to be a constant set of state functionaries, regardless of which party is in power. Rhodes (1988; 1992) has proposed that government within the UK can be usefully conceptualized in terms of five types of **policy network**, ranged between two polar types of network: the policy community, and the issue network (see Box 2.6). The continuum between them concerns their relative integration, stability, and exclusiveness. Policy communities, for example legal services, are characterized by relatively tight-knit and stable relationships, continuity of a restricted membership, vertical interdependence based on service delivery, and insulation from other networks, the public, and Parliament. Issue networks, on the other hand, for example local campaigners, typically have a large number of participants, limited interdependence, less stability and continuity, and a more atomistic structure. In between these polar types, varying both in stability and in interests, are professional and producer networks, serving professional (for example, doctors) and economic (for example, manufacturers) concerns respectively; and finally there are intergovernmental

Box 2.6 Policy networks

There is a range of networks, depending on how tightly they are integrated:

Policy community: tight-knit and stable relationships, continuity of a restricted membership, vertical interdependence based on service delivery, and insulation from other networks, the public, and Parliament.

Professional/producer/intergovernmental network: These networks are intermediate in terms of how tightly they are organized, and in addition they are focused on different substantive areas, respectively a profession (such as medicine), producers who deliver goods and services (such as the pharmaceutical industry), government units (such as regional or local government).

Issue network: large number of participants, limited interdependence, less stability and continuity, and a more atomistic structure.

networks oriented horizontally towards common positions within the structures of government, such as local councillors.

A network is defined primarily in terms of 'resource dependencies', with network interactions chiefly oriented towards resource maximization. However, Rhodes has also included a wider range of factors when considering the way in which policy networks change. Not only are economic considerations relevant, but ideological, knowledge-based, and institutional issues are also identified by him as significant. Thus, although he stresses the effects of changes in party ideology (for example, the rise and fall of Thatcherism), clearly this could be extended to include a more general consideration of the world-views of those individuals who make up the network—their social values, normative assumptions, and so on. A popular image of this is captured in the television portrayal of the civil service control of ministers in *Yes, Minister*.

As far as knowledge-based change is concerned, Rhodes cites examples from professional networks, such as the health service. While this may seem a straightforward case of a particular variety of resource dependency, work in the sociology of science alerts us to the possibility that scientific and technical knowledge is socially constructed and constrained by pre-existing structures of power (Manning 1985: ch. 7). For example, medical knowledge about mental and physical health, insofar as it underpins closing hospitals in favour of community care, may in fact be a contestable justification for policies favoured more for their economic than for their health implications.

When policies go wrong: public inquiries and citizens' movements

Key political players in the field of social policy may, however, only be revealed at times of change. For example, when policies go badly wrong, there may be an **official inquiry** to ascertain the exact role that different groups and individuals played. An illustration of this process is given by the long series of public inquiries into cases in which vulnerable children have died in family circumstances where social workers and other professional groups have been unable to help, such as those of Maria Colwell and Victoria Climbié. A similar series of inquiries have examined failures of institutional care in mental hospitals, children's homes, and schools.

In other circumstances we can see policies being undermined by the resistance of ordinary citizens who either cannot or will not accept the policies. The single largest example was the sudden collapse of the East European welfare states in 1989–91, when citizens gained the confidence to engage in mass defiance of government policies. But specific cases can also be found. For example, when the US federal government decided in the 1960s to force local governments to develop racially integrated schools in the southern states and many northern cities, this led to the active physical resistance by parents of children being 'bussed' between school districts, and to the effective undermining of the policies through 'white flight', where white parents moved house, or moved their children to private schools, in order to avoid the effects of the policies.

MODELS OF WELFARE POLITICS

So far we have described some of the main institutions of government and the key players involved. There are major questions we have not yet asked, such as that of how much room for manoeuvre there is in the system, and whose voice is the strongest in this complex process. What is the range of options, and do all the players have an equal voice? There are a number of well-known approaches to answering these questions.

Pluralist

The classic liberal view from within American political science is that the political system is pluralist: it is open to external influence in a myriad of ways, and that concerned citizens, individually or in organized groups, have many opportunities to influence the shaping and implementation of social policy. For example, the fact that politicians have to be elected means that they will be keenly aware of their constituents' interests. They will invite representations from citizens through regular clinics, and attempt to take up cases of concern. In addition, many interests are represented through the many pressure groups, voluntary associations, churches, trade unions, and business organizations that lobby politicians about matters of concern. Within this general process, it is argued that social policy interests are well represented.

Elites

Criticisms of this model have been raised on the grounds that in reality it is very difficult for ordinary citizens to have an impact on social policies in this way. The idea of policy networks introduced earlier illustrates the relatively closed world of policy-making that actually characterizes particular social policy areas. This is a world of elites, where influential individuals and groups from particular backgrounds, and with common world views, actually dominate the agenda. For example, top French civil servants are almost exclusively recruited from graduates of the École Nationale d'Administration.

In the UK, pupils from public school and Oxbridge backgrounds are commonly to be found amongst higher civil servants and politicians of all parties. These key players tend to have common ideas about appropriate and sensible social policies, and to share assumptions or—at worst—prejudices about what policy options there might be for particular issues. For example, many of the groups cited in the pluralist model of open government are in reality run by elite members. These people have careers that may have encompassed the professional administration of different, and possibly opposing, organizations. The argument here is that their elite status in effect narrows the policy options, and can exclude the views of ordinary citizens from serious consideration.

Corporatist

In another view, the groups that shape social policy derive less from a culturally integrated elite than from several elites generated by the corporatist structure of power in modern industrial societies. The three key corporate groups are proposed as the trade unions, representing the power and interests of working people, the business community, and the state itself. These three, often called 'social partners' in EU policy debates, are held to be in effect the key organized blocks of power that between them determine the shape and structure of social policy. They bargain between themselves in a corporate round of regular discussions to determine general wage rates, public expenditure on social and other services, rates of tax which are needed to pay for these, and the type of state intervention (provision, regulation, and so on). This is typical of many European countries, especially Sweden, Germany, and France. One consequence of this bargaining process is that the needs of weak or vulnerable groups can be ignored, for example disabled people.

Marxist

A final model of the politics of welfare argues that the group with most power in the system to shape the way in which social policy develops is the business community. This combines elements of the previous two models to suggest that indeed there really is only one main elite, but that its essential nature derives less from a common cultural world view than its possession of economic power. This is a Marxist analysis, which proposes that the whole level, shape, and structure of social policy is bent to accommodate the interests of economically powerful groups. Where there might be conflicts arising between the economically powerful and other groups, such as the trade unions, the professions, or local and central government departments, that have vested interests in particular policies, then this model argues that economic interests will tend to prevail. For example, Bowles and Gintis (1976) have demonstrated how educational policy has evolved to match students to the needs of industry for particular types of labour.

MODELS OF WELFARE POLICY CHANGE AND DEVELOPMENT

In the previous section, four different models were presented of the way in which the politics of welfare operate in the contemporary world. However, the historical development of political conflicts over welfare are also important for two reasons. The first is that many current issues are shaped by structures and processes that are rooted in the past—particularly the nineteenth century, when the current system of wage labour and its associated insecurities matured—some of them even as far back as the Elizabethan Poor Law of 1601. The second reason is that many of the ideas used in welfare debates originated in the past. In this section we shall explore three influential ideas about the way in which welfare policies have developed.

Wage labour and labour markets

The first approach is to locate the origins of the welfare state in the emergence of wage labour and labour markets in the late eighteenth century in Britain. The insecurities of wage labour underlay the origins of much demand for and rationalization of the growth of welfare policy, in both the voluntary and state arenas. Since that time, labour market changes have repeatedly been critical to social policy development.

The defining moments of twentieth-century welfare innovation—such as the 1930s US New Deal, the 1940s UK Welfare State, and more recently the 1990s renovation of those systems in Clinton's 1996 US welfare reforms, and the British Labour party's 1997 'welfare to work/ minimum wage' package—have gone hand in hand with assumptions about the labour market.

This was most explicit in the American case through the simultaneous enactment in 1935 of the Wagner Act alongside the Social Security Act. These Acts were the culmination of actions by the federal government to deal with the consequences of the 1929 Wall Street crash, and the subsequent depression that spread round the world. The Wagner Act attempted to regulate American industrial relations by granting greater trade union rights and placing obligations on employers. This, it was hoped, would stabilize the economy and hence provide the means for funding pensions and unemployment benefits which were introduced by the Social Security Act. In turn these arrangements, it was hoped, would reduce the need for poverty relief.

At the founding of the British Welfare State a decade later, the 1942 report on social security prepared by Beveridge also made it clear that the design adopted depended on a crucial assumption: that full employment would ensure the funds to pay for pensions, and minimize expenditure on unemployment benefit and poverty relief.

However, full employment in the West has proved unattainable. Unemployment has been a plague for European governments for the last twenty-five years, both because it drives up the costs of social security and also because it generates political instability and a host of related social and health problems. Governments in eastern Europe are faced with the same problems. The creation of social needs and the social policies designed to meet them are crucially related to the operation of the labour market. Work not only provides the means to exist through meeting income needs (in Beveridge's time at the level of the 'family wage'), but on the whole is good for our psychological and physical health.

In general, work has become an essential passport to other benefits—either through entitlement to social security benefits (typically pensions or unemployment benefit) or through work-related provision such as occupational pensions, subsidized housing, and healthcare. In both the US and Russia, for example, this so-called 'occupational welfare' has been very extensive. In the European Union the very definition of social policy is closely related to employment issues. Thus, in the EU, the right to the free movement of labour and other employment rights (such as equal opportunities), the relatively high levels of expenditure on education, and on employment initiatives, and the relatively low levels of expenditure on health, housing, or social security highlight the close relationship of social and employment concerns. This was symbolized in the replacement in the final draft of the 1989 Social Protocol of the term 'citizens' by the term 'workers'.

Citizenship

A second approach to understanding the development of state intervention in welfare has used the concept of citizenship.

> Novel, important and true ideas are rare. Such ideas which are then developed into a coherent theory are even scarcer. T. H. Marshall is one of the very few to have had at least one such idea, and to develop it. That is why it is important to understand and to improve upon his theory of citizenship (Mann 1987: 339)

The classic formulation of citizenship rights in industrial society by Marshall contained three elements (see Box 2.7). First was the legal constitution of citizens as of equal standing in relation to the law; second was the access of all citizens to democratic apparatus for the exercise of political power over the state; and third was the provision of sufficient means for all people to engage in full social participation. The coexistence of these civil, political, and social rights, which he argued amounted to the conditions necessary for full citizenship, seemed to Marshall to be both a historical description of the development of industrial societies and the necessary precondition for their continued existence.

However, Marshall was at pains to point out that these rights did not exist without tension. Ironically, the development of citizenship rights had occurred alongside capitalism and its associated inequalities. In particular, the limitation of political rights to the formal exercise of voting rights resulted in the juxtaposition of multiple inequalities in the economy and in family life, with political interventions that attempted to mitigate these inequalities through social and other policies. Moreover, he argued that the best condition for the successful development of industrial societies was to maintain a balance between the economy and social rights. Too much economic freedom would undermine the long-term stability of the economy through the loss of political

Box 2.7 Marshall's model of citizenship

eighteenth century: civil rights

nineteenth century: political rights

twentieth century: social rights

In combination these have resulted in the 'hyphenated society' of democratic-welfare-capitalism.

legitimacy and the breakdown of social reproduction. Too much political and social intervention, on the other hand, would stifle the dynamic growth of the economy, upon which everything else depended. In sum, Marshall argued that a balance between economic growth via capitalism, political empowerment through democracy, and social integration/participation sustained through social policy was both historically and theoretically necessary for the sustained achievement of any one of these goals.

In recent years, the globalization of economic and political relations, and political challenges mounted to the traditional provision of social rights via the welfare state, have thrown some doubt on aspects of this model, and have stimulated new debates about citizenship. There are several problems. First, Marshall only ever referred to England in his discussion of citizenship, but other regimes have also achieved citizenship integration: for example fascist or state socialist regimes.

A second problem relates to the decline in the strength of organized labour, and the growth of single-issue politics. Citizens are also concerned about the environment, about gender, about race, about religion, and so on. Marshall's model is thus in need of extension, not only geographically, but in terms of the history of the substantive issues that are in contention. Turner (1990), for example, argues that Marshall neglects the realm of the 'private', including the experience of religious tradition and beliefs, and ethnic and racial identity, and suggests that more emphasis could be given to citizenship struggles from below (such as social movements), in contrast to a view of citizenship as a privilege handed down by ruling groups.

A final problem with Marshall's model is its normative emphasis. He describes the sequential unfolding of rights of different kinds to the point at which full citizenship has been achieved. But this ignores the great variation with which such rights are actually exercised in civil society. This is particularly the case for eastern Europe, where the lived experience of citizens until 1989 was increasingly at odds with the official state view of a citizen's rights.

Welfare 'regimes'

A third model for understanding the way in which the state has intervened in the field of welfare contrasts sharply with Marshall in that it is explicitly comparative across different countries, eschews normative commitments to any 'best' welfare arrangement, and explicitly incorporates political forces in its analysis. It draws on a tradition of analysing different types of welfare state, often contrasting less generous with more generous welfare provision. This work culminated in Esping-Andersen's (1990) highly influential book, in which he described three types, or 'regimes' as he called them, of 'welfare capitalism'. These were generated by considering the welfare situation of male wage workers only; and while there has been substantial criticism of them for ignoring gender issues, they nevertheless have dominated social policy debates in the last ten years. His argument was that in different countries social policies were organized around certain internally integrated features so that social policies of different types shared certain consistent assumptions and effects: in terms, for example, of the nature of state intervention, the stratification of social groups, and—most crucially—the extent to

Box 2.8 Esping-Andersen's three worlds of welfare capitalism

Neo-liberal (American)

de-commodification	low
stratification	high
state intervention	regulation of markets

Social democratic (Scandinavian)

de-commodification	high
stratification	low
state intervention	direct provision or finance

Corporatist (Franco-German)

de-commodification	high
stratification	high
state intervention	regulation of markets or finance

which markets were replaced by bureaucratic distribution in a process of 'decommodification' (see Box 2.8), in favour of the distribution of goods and services according to needs.

Esping-Andersen suggested that there were three such types: neo-liberal (American), social democratic (Scandinavian), and corporatist (Franco-German). The neo-liberal type had a relatively low (and falling) level of de-commodification, a relatively high level of stratification in terms of income inequality, and state intervention typified by regulation of markets rather than the provision or finance of social welfare. By contrast, the social democratic type had a high level of de-commodification, low level of stratification, and direct state provision or finance, as well as regulation. Corporatist types had a mixture of these features: heavily stratified by both income (especially in France) and social status, yet with considerable de-commodification, if only through the heavy regulation of non-profit providers rather than direct state provision.

The origins of these different regimes is linked to the political strength of labour movements in different countries, against a context of relatively similar levels of economic growth. Esping-Andersen here follows a well-worn path of attempts to explain the origins of different levels of 'welfare effort' in different countries. The crucial question is why welfare state effort—for example, the percentage of GNP spent on social security—has grown to a relatively higher level in some societies than others. Explanations typically include either the direct effect of economic growth or the indirect effect of economic growth through the development of left-wing political power, centred on trade union strength and its political representation in government.

From this perspective the origins, size, and generosity of welfare states are contingent on political forces, and especially the alliances that can form between different social classes. Where the middle classes are persuaded that it is in their interests to side with working-class demands for an expanded welfare state, as in Scandinavia, then private-sector service provision is crowded out and middle-class concerns for quality permeate the state sector. Where, however, working-class interests are poorly organized (as in the USA, for example), or where middle-class interests have turned away from state provision towards the private market (as in the UK), then welfare effort and quality will suffer.

BEYOND THE NATION-STATE

Much of our discussion has been about the politics of welfare at or below the level of the nation state. As we observed earlier, however, the nation-state has only existed for about 500 years, and much less in many instances. Some observers have wondered whether the nation-state is in decline, and suggested that we should also look at higher levels of organization in order to capture the full range of contemporary and future politics. For example, the European Union has grown in importance for social policy over the last twenty-five years, particularly in relation to issues of social security and employment (see Chapter 20). A growing volume of legislation and legal precedence is accumulating at the European level. Many local authorities now have direct administrative and financial connections to Brussels, and some maintain permanent offices in Brussels to keep abreast of new developments. A parallel development has occurred in voluntary sector organizations which are particularly relevant to social policy. With the commitment of the UK government to the social chapter, and the development of the European Monetary Union, this growing integration is set to continue. Moreover, with the number of countries in the European Union also set to grow, perhaps the nation-state is in decline?

A further erosion of nation-states can be traced through the development of global institutions which are increasingly moving into the area of social policy. While the World Health Organization may have always been concerned with social policy, the World Bank and the International Monetary Fund have only recently developed clear views on social policy, particularly in the field of social security in countries which are deemed to require 'structural adjustments' in their public expenditure profile, for example in eastern Europe, South America, and Africa. Very often an individual country which needs credit from the IMF will have to commit itself to a detailed social security policy which in the past was traditionally under the control of the nation-state and its political elite.

For some commentators this represents the 'end of history' as it has traditionally developed, such that in future a global society will develop with an increasing convergence towards one type of (limited) welfare policy. Others disagree, and suggest that with economic growth comes choice over social expenditure, and that there is a parallel regionalization of social politics through which a variety of social policies will continue to evolve. For example, the development of Irish, Welsh, and Scottish assemblies in the UK may lead to greater social policy divergence. The evidence from 200 years of US federal efforts to integrate American social policies suggests that local autonomy can indeed survive and flourish for long periods of time; and it may therefore be premature to anticipate a decline in the politics of welfare.

REFERENCES

Bowles, S., and Gintis, H. (1976), *Schooling in Capitalist America*. London: Routledge & Kegan Paul.

Davies, B. P. (1978), *Universality, Selectivity and Effectiveness in Social Services*. London: Heinemann.

Esping-Andersen, G. (1990), *The Three Worlds of Welfare Capitalism*. Cambridge: Polity Press.

Etzioni, A. (1975), *A Comparative Analysis of Complex Organisations*, 2nd edn. London: Macmillan.

Foucault, M. (1973), *The Birth of the Clinic*. London: Tavistock.

Hirschman, A. O. (1970), *Exit, Voice, and Loyalty: Responses to Decline in Firms, Organisations, and States*. Cambridge, Mass.: Harvard University Press.

Le Grand, J. (1993), 'Paying for or providing welfare'. In N. Deakin and R. Page (eds.), *The Costs of Welfare*. London: Avebury.

Lukes, S. (1974), *Power: A Radical View*. London: Macmillan.

Mann, M. (1987), 'Ruling-class strategies and citizenship', *Sociology* 21: 339–54.

Manning, N. (1985), *Social Problems and Welfare Ideology*. Aldershot: Gower.

Mead, L. M. (1987), *Beyond Entitlement: The Social Obligations of Citizenship*. London: Free Press.

Parsons, T. (1951), *The Social System*. London: Free Press.

Rhodes, R. A. W. (1988), *Beyond Westminster and Whitehall*. London: Unwin Hyman.

—— and Marsh, D. (1992), 'New directions in the study of policy networks', *European Journal of Political Research* 21: 181–205.

Titmuss, R. M. (1970), *The Gift Relationship: From Human Blood to Social Policy*. London: Allen & Unwin.

Turner, B. S. (1990), 'Outline of a theory of citizenship', *Sociology* 24: 189–217.

Weber, M. (1947), *The Theory of Social and Economic Organization*. Oxford: Oxford University Press.

FURTHER READING

Martin Powell and Martin Hewitt, *Welfare State and Welfare Change* (Milton Keynes: Open University Press, 2002) explains very clearly why and how the modern welfare state has developed.

Robert Geyer, *Exploring European Social Policy: Introduction and Exploration* (Bristol: Policy Press, 2000) provides a clear history of the evolution of the European Union's role in social policy and its effects on the nation states.

Kathleen Jones, *The Making of Social Policy in Britain: From the Poor Law to New Labour* (London: Athlone Press, 2000) is a classic history of the making of social policy brought up to date.

Will Hutton, *The World We're In* (London: Abacus, 2003) sets the broader global political and economic context in which he argues Europe needs to maintain a more welfare-based alternative and counterbalance to the United States.

The annual *Social Policy Review* published by the Policy Press, Bristol, on behalf of the British Social Policy Association includes accessible accounts of recent debates and policy initiatives.

GLOSSARY

authority legitimate power.

business groups representative organizations for employers whose major allegiance is to further the interests of their members' economic interests.

civil servants permanent salaried administrators available to a government whose duty it is to undertake to develop and implement policies determined by government ministers, and who take a neutral stance to the ideological position of the government.

consent uncoerced agreement to a course of action.

constitution basic rules formulating the structure of and procedures for government, either written or customary.

direct provision where a social service is organized, financed, and provided by permanent government employees.

financial support where a social service is financed by government but organized and provided by non-government organizations.

government department a major branch of central government responsible for a significant section of state activity, such as healthcare or social security.

liberal democracy the system of government based on the universal right to vote for candidates chosen from a range of alternatives to represent the interests of sections of the community, combined with the freedom to organize and propose policies on issues of the day.

ministry see **government department**.

official inquiry government-sponsored review of the operations of a particular area of policy.

policies plans of action formulated in general terms by political parties, and their representatives in government, especially ministers, and often developed in detail by civil servants.

policy networks informal affiliations of actors with a conscious interest in shaping policies and their outcomes.

power the ability to bring about preferred policy outcomes, or to prevent unwanted outcomes, or to shape the way in which policy options are considered.

pressure groups organized groups aiming to develop or influence government policies.

professional associations representative organizations for different professions, sometimes with a legal monopoly over the interests of a particular profession.

professions occupational groups based on a presumed monopoly of specialist knowledge attained through a lengthy training.

QUANGOS QUAsi Non-Governmental OrganizationS; that is, only partly independent of government influence, often appointed by government, but supposedly free to pursue policies independently.

regulation where social service provision, whether by government or by other organization, is monitored carefully in accordance with legally enforceable rules and standards.

resources capacities for action, often financial, but also personal, cultural, scientific, or political.

rules agreed course of action, established in law or by custom and practice.

social movements collective non-parliamentary attempts to change substantial areas of social life, major social institutions, prevailing ideologies and identities, or government policies. Often split between 'old' social movements, such as the labour movement, and 'new' social movements, such as environmentalism, feminism, or anti-racism.

territorial injustice where social service provision in relation to need is unequal between different geographical areas.

think tanks groups relatively autonomous from government which specialize in policy innovation and advice.

trade unions representative organizations for working people whose major allegiance is to further the interests of their members' working conditions and wages.

welfare states those that have a self-conscious commitment to the provision of adequate minimal access to income, healthcare, education, and housing for all citizens.

PART TWO

THE SOCIAL AND ECONOMIC CONTEXT

3

Welfare, Ideology, and Social Theory

Nick Manning

CONTENTS

INTRODUCTION

For the major part of this chapter we will examine the characterization of social policy along various ideological dimensions, and the ideals that have been at the heart of social policy debates for the last 100 years. Social policy has been more urgently discussed by politicians since conservative-oriented governments came to power in the 1980s in the United States of America and the United Kingdom. Yet the implementation of supposed right-wing policies of the 1980s and more left-wing policies of the 1990s has not been straightforward (Case Study 3.1). There is sharp ideological dispute over social issues, but also confusion about what traditional political ideologies dictate in specific policy terms.

What does this mean? We seem to have in both the UK and the USA a long period of relative cross-party agreement, followed by a sharp swing towards the right in public debate combined with a relatively weak implementation of the new political hopes. Yet with the exhaustion of these views in the 1990s and the election of ostensibly centre-left parties we find some of the most draconian welfare reforms being implemented, highlighted in the cartoon. In the remainder of this chapter we will discuss the significance of ideologies for social policy.

Case Study 3.1 Swings in welfare ideology in the United States and the United Kingdom

In the USA, the main lines of modern social policy were laid-down in Roosevelt's New Deal in 1932. This was a pragmatic response to the economic depression which had engulfed America shortly after the famous Wall Street stock market crash in 1929. There was cross-party agreement on the New Deal until 1980, when President Ronald Reagan was elected on a distinctly right-wing programme that appeared to spell the end of the New Deal consensus. In the event, Congressmen lost their political nerve and failed to follow through the dramatic reversals to welfare programmes that were expected. In the UK we can trace a remarkably similar pattern. The British welfare state was laid down in the pragmatic 1942 Beveridge report, *Social Insurance and Allied Services*. This had long-standing cross-party support too until 1979, when Margaret Thatcher was also elected on a right-wing programme. During the 1980s, however, the welfare state was not dismantled in the manner expected, and public expenditure actually rose for some central areas such as healthcare and social security.

Ironically, during the 1990s in both countries more ideologically moderate leaders, Clinton and Blair, undertook strong welfare reform policies, attacking groups such as lone parents in an attempt to get them 'off welfare' and into work. This shows how welfare ideology and welfare policy can oscillate dramatically, but not always in the same direction.

Cartoon 3.1 Blair's election pledges

Source: Steve Bell, 1997.

CONCEPTS: THEORIES OF IDEOLOGY

The concept of ideology, while an essential part of debates about social policy, as we shall see later in this chapter, has been much debated within social theory. Two theorists have dominated discussion about ideology: Karl Marx and Karl Mannheim. Marx's theory was embedded in a much wider project to analyse the nature of capitalism. Mannheim was more interested in a theory of knowledge, of how we think and know about the world we live in.

Marx

Marx initially suggested that ideology, like religion, reflects the frustrations of the physical and secular world. Indeed, religion itself, he claimed, was an ideology. He suggested that ideological thought was misleading as to the real relations involved in any particular issue, including social policy: 'it is not consciousness that determines life, but life that determines consciousness' (Marx and Engels 1976). Writing in the nineteenth century, he felt that the production of commodities lay at the heart of the new industrial society dominated by market mechanisms. He wondered why the real work involved in making a product is not actually reflected directly in its real nature for us, but in its market price. In the market it loses its real character, for example that of a painting, sculpture, football team, that of mass-produced clothing and so on, and turns into something quite different—a commodity or an investment. This, he implies, distorts our relationship to and understanding of the real world, usually for the worst: either we don't appreciate the real circumstances under which products are made, or on occasion (as with bad art) we value things for the 'wrong' reasons. Even people can become commodities in the market, and lose their character as people *per se*. Naomi Klein's polemical book about clothing brands, *No Logo* (2000), argues much the same point. For this reason Marx would have been alarmed at the development of an internal market in the NHS.

This distortion in the 'life process' under market society, Marx suggested, can be generalized to suggest that other relations can also be distorted: social security may not really provide security, healthcare may not make us well, education may not make us better-informed, professionals may not really serve their clients' best interests, and so on. The official ideas about how these major institutions in our societies are supposed to work may be ideologies.

Mannheim

Mannheim (1968) developed Marx's ideas as a special case of a more general issue. To what extent is the common intellectual currency of an historical period ideological? Are the totality of perceptions and ideas shared by members of a society about their world, including social policy, ideological? These ideas cover such fundamental areas as human nature and the society on which we all depend in one form or another. Mannheim suggested two different types of ideology: the particular and the total.

By the **particular conception of ideology** he refers to doubts we might have about the validity of someone's ideas. We suspect that he or she might be more or less consciously disguising the real nature of a situation which, if it were revealed, might be disadvantageous to them. We often hear politicians extolling the virtues of a social policy, such as 'welfare to work' or 'evidence-based medicine'. Such ideas might be discredited by showing that they spring from undisclosed personal, group, or class interests. For example, commercial companies that sponsor academic research in medicine or economics may ask for answers to questions that directly or indirectly generate knowledge that is in their interests: to sell pharmaceutical products, or financial services.

Mannheim's second type, the **total conception of ideology**, is a more sophisticated concept than the first. He argues not just that a particular deception is in someone's interests, but that there is a correspondence between their social situation and the total perception of the world that they and their associates profess. For example, the government's definition of a social issue will be bound up with its job of maintaining an ordered equilibrium in society—of maintaining law and order, employment, and so on. The poor must be educated and motivated to 'join in'. This might suggest that, while ideological differences are stressed by political parties in opposition, in power the constraints of government begin to change the ways in which governments and ministers think. Similarly, feminists and ethnic minorities have frequently noted how men and white people may see and act in the world from a male or white viewpoint, which has clearly shaped social policies over the years, from Beveridge's assumption that wives were dependent on their husband's 'family wage' to the idea that ethnic groups should be culturally assimilated to white society.

The end of ideology?

In more recent years there have been two challenges to the arguments of Marx and Mannheim. They suggest that mature industrialism has resulted in the exhaustion of ideological differences—the 'end of ideology'. The first argument is associated with Daniel Bell's book *The End of Ideology* (1960). Writing in the late 1950s, Bell argued that the big ideologies of communism and fascism had become exhausted. Fascism had been eliminated with the Second World War, and communism, once the excesses of Stalin's terror of the 1930s came to light, and with Khrushchev's criticism of him after his death in 1953, no longer held an alternative beacon to the world.

A more recent reworking of this theme emerged with the fall of the Iron Curtain, and the collapse of the USSR. Here a similar idea was taken up by Francis Fukuyama (1992) and described as the 'end of history'. His starting point was to claim that there was no longer any practical alternative to liberal democratic capitalism. This is explained through the effects of scientific and technological change, which is irreversible and cumulative, and which gradually constrains all societies onto a common developmental path. In addition there is a deep-seated aspiration in all people for 'recognition'. This, he argues, is a basic aspect of individual identity, and results inevitably in a steady struggle towards democratic political systems since they are the best—indeed only—way in which individuals can gain such recognition. Technology and democracy will also drive welfare states towards common solutions to common social problems.

The second type of criticism is that there has never really been a pre-eminent ideology. Mann (1970) and Abercrombie et al. (1980) argued that the **dominant ideology** in any society was merely the shared values of the ruling elite. Most people neither need nor want such an overarching ideology, but get by in daily life through a pragmatic adjustment to the constraints of work and family obligations. Survey evidence from the West suggests that a variety of values are held by ordinary people, and a range of accounts from eastern Europe confirms that many, probably the majority, did not really believe in the ideological prescriptions of state socialism.

This scepticism about the adherence of ordinary people to big ideologies has now widened into a new descriptive term for the current era: **post-modernism**. This term started in architecture as a means of denoting dissatisfaction with modern architecture, particularly the production of high-rise, pre-fabricated mass housing which was disliked by those who lived in it. It represented the rejection of the expression of the big idea or **grand narrative** in architecture, associated more than anything with Le Corbusier's designs for high-rise housing. Social policy took about ten years to catch up with this change in architecture, and in the mid-1980s developed the idea that industrial society in general had entered a new era, the post-modern (Harvey 1990). Drawing heavily on the work of Foucault, the argument was that different ideas or viewpoints, or 'knowledges', as Harvey termed them, coexisted, and that none was to be seen in any essential sense as dominant or superior. This helps us to understand the ideological and policy confusions that seem to characterize UK and US social policy in the 1990s.

IDEAS AND IDEOLOGIES: WHAT 'OUGHT' TO BE AND WHAT IS

Ideas about how welfare states should be constructed have been hotly contested in recent years. Frequently these ideas have been expressed in terms of left- and right-wing ideologies. Following the discussion of Marx and Mannheim, we can define an ideology as having three components. First is a particular view which emphasizes or weights an argument, explanation, or judgement to the exclusion of other points of view. For example, in developing an approach to unemployment we might choose to emphasize the individual characteristics of a worker and her particular capacities or attitudes. These might be seen as causing unemployment, and hence remedies might be sought in terms of skill training or the development of better work habits for that individual. The argument might even extend to blaming the individual for their unemployment. This approach, however, tends to hide alternative explanations, for example in terms of industrial restructuring or global competition (see Chapter 6).

A particular, possibly one-sided emphasis in an argument could be a mistake, or oversight. However, the term 'ideology' is used to denote in addition a second aspect—the interests of individuals or groups in the outcome of the argument or characterization. This means that they have something to gain from the argument being put in a particular way. For example, to continue the discussion of unemployment, whether an individual or a whole industry is the most appropriate level for explaining and dealing with unemployment is likely to vary with the interests of the individual or group concerned. Industrialists have tended to consider unemployment in terms of the inability of individuals to adapt to changing employment opportunities, or, in a famous phrase, to resist 'getting on their bikes' to search for work. This, it could be supposed, is because industrialists require a flexible workforce.

A third aspect of an ideology is the way it spills across more than one particular issue, referring to a wider set of relatively coherent ideas which might include not merely a specific item of social policy but also ideas about family life, the nature of individuals, the rights and duties of citizenship, the authority of the state, and so on. Thus, to continue our example, industrialists might also consider that it is the responsibility of all adults to seek work in order to support their families, that people will find work if the alternatives are unpalatable enough, and that the state should ensure that such incentives are clearly structured and known to citizens.

To sum up, ideologies are particular, sometimes biased, sets of ideas which are held because they are in the interests of the groups of people articulating them, and which integrate views about a range of issues and social institutions.

NORMATIVE IDEALS

While ideologies include ideas about the way welfare states or specific social policies have developed and work, they particularly include ideas about how things ought to be. These are statements about **normative ideals**. These can be end states but also the means of attaining those states.

End states

The desirability of health, happiness, or economic growth can be endlessly debated, and frequently they are. In the field of social policy, one of the most commonly desired end states is the meeting of a 'social need' (discussed in Chapter 5). It has been argued by Doyal and Gough (1991), for example, that there are two basic human needs: for health and for the capacity to survive and reproduce (which they interpret as the need for education in an industrial society). We might all be able to agree on such basic needs, but one of the problems is that some end states are incompatible with others. For example, economic growth can lead to pollution and ill health; more widespread education can lead to the devaluation of educational qualifications. This potential for end states to interact and even conflict means that arguments about the choice between them will revolve less around evidence and more around ideological divisions between individuals, groups, and political parties over the right goals to pursue.

Means

Not only are end states disputed, but also the means of attaining those states. In the early years of industrialization, when rapid urbanization had changed traditional family and community life, mutual aid and cooperative arrangements within working class communities sprang up to deal with new risks: illness, for example, or lack of shelter. Voluntary charitable societies were founded by energetic reformers to help find, or to impose, solutions to the new social problems accompanying industrialization. New professional groups emerged to deal with issues of healthcare, planning, and social statistics. These in turn emphasized different means of working towards the desirable ends concerned, using the authority of knowledge and professionalism. And behind much of this change lay the growth of state intervention, sometimes as provider, sometimes as funder, and sometimes merely as regulator, but always raising issues about who should determine goals and the means of attaining them.

As with end states, there are incompatibilities between different means. Do professionals know best? Is the knowledge base on any particular issue partial or complete? Should local communities be consulted on new developments in their area? Can the state be trusted to represent the interests of minorities? Participation on the basis of ignorance might not be helpful to communities; democracy might lead to the comfortable majority ignoring or even oppressing minorities. Professions may misuse their power to protect themselves at the expense of their clients. Again, the room for disagreement and incompatibility between these means of social change opens up plenty of space for ideological debate.

EXPLANATORY IDEALS

Although ideologies are typically concerned with statements about what ought to be, they also express coherent views about why and how social policies have got into the position they are in. These are ideas about explaining social policies, rather than trying to change them. Of course, explanation and prescription are often inextricably linked, but we can separate them for the purpose of exposition here. Moreover, just as we can separate ends and means when considering social ideals, we can separate social policy explanation into questions of why and how: why policies have developed in different times, places, and issues; and how they work in practice.

Why did welfare states appear?

There is widespread agreement that this was in reaction to the dislocating effects of the dependence of individuals and families on waged work which had spread throughout the United States and Europe during the nineteenth century. However, there are two ways of looking at the origins of welfare states. The first is to consider them the rational response to economic insecurity created by industrialization. From this point of view technocratic elites realize that it is neither in their own interests nor in the interests of those affected for severe poverty or inadequate access to health, education, and housing to develop. They organize a collective sharing of the risks of these misfortunes, often provided or regulated by the state, and justify this sometimes through the idea of social needs that ought to be met, and sometimes through the idea of investment in creating a healthy and happy (and therefore more productive) workforce.

From this point of view the growth of welfare states can be thought of as a functional or technical issue, and has often been written about as an inevitable by-product of industrialization. The traditional study of **social administration** as the progressive uncovering and meeting of social needs (discussed in Chapter 1) is typical of this **functionalist explanation**. Broader explanations, as in Kerr et al. (1960), recognized that industrial elites could organize this process in more than one way, but argued that in the end all industrial societies are moving in the same direction, whether the UK, USA, Russia, Japan, or south-east Asia.

A second way of understanding the origins of welfare states is to regard their development as a highly political process of social conflict. From this point of view there was a series of intense struggles between different groups, working people represented by labour parties, the liberal middle classes represented by democratic parties, and elites represented by conservative parties. All these groups saw that industrialization had created economic insecurity and exclusion, but they had very different ideas about what the appropriate mechanisms should be for dealing with this, and especially disagreed about the ideal social policies that they would like to see in place.

Celebrated examples of these more political analyses of welfare states include Marshall's (1963) account of welfare states as part of a wider political struggle for the establishment of **citizenship** rights (see Chapter 2). From this point of view social citizenship (that is, access to welfare) has only developed as a result of political struggle

Box 3.1 Evidence for political explanations of welfare

Evidence for political explanations of the development of welfare state expenditure was first explicitly presented by Castles and McKinlay (1979). This statistical study of Western industrial democratic states measured public welfare in terms of social security transfer payments, educational expenditure, and infant mortality. It found that political factors, such as left-wing mobilization, and the absence of right-wing government have the strongest statistical association public welfare.

Several further studies in the 1980s confirmed this finding, even when the measures used for welfare changed, and when the period of time covered was extended. For example, Hicks and Swank (1984) measured the impact of political 'capitalist and working class-linked actors' on changes in direct cash transfer payments for income maintenance between 1960 and 1971 in 18 'advanced capitalist democracies'. Political actions by both right-of-centre parties and trade unions were the main determinants of transfer spending. In a supplementary study, Hicks et al. (1989) confirmed this finding over the period 1957 to 1982. An extensive discussion of 'state activism' is presented in Hage et al. (1989).

and political mobilization, rather than technical or elite intervention. For some writers such as Stephens (1979), this struggle has been characterized as the success of left-wing parties in taming capitalism; others have argued more cautiously that where there has been generous welfare state development this is almost always due to the relative strength of the Left in government. This approach now has an extensive body of empirical support for its approach (see Box 3.1).

Political analysts, moreover, argue that the technical or functionalist approaches to explaining welfare states only developed in the context of an unusually quiet period of political consensus about the means and ends of welfare states in the middle fifty years of the twentieth century. This, they argue, misled some writers to consider this as typical, whereas in fact struggle, debate, and dissent are more typical of public debates over social policies. There are two points being made here: first, that social policy is a politically disputed arena, and second, that left-wing political ideas are supportive of more extensive social policies. In short, social policy is about ideals rather than technique, and therefore requires an analysis that examines the ideological context of policy debate and development.

How social policies work

In addition to this debate about the reasons why welfare states developed, there are passionate discussions about how ideals are turned into practice. In part these discussions overlap with normative issues about the ends and means of social policies, and many writers cover both simultaneously. Nevertheless, the way in which social policies work is not as simple as we might suppose. Social policy refers to some kind of intervention into social structures and processes (and occasionally a deliberate non-intervention). We have seen in Chapter 1 that there are basically four types of social provision: state, voluntary, market, and informal. Government intervention is particularly powerful, since the state can both regulate (through laws) and provide resources (through taxation) for social policies. But the state is itself controlled through the ballot box, and therefore the commitments organized around political party ideologies are of central importance. The voluntary sector, typified by charity organizations, is also driven by social ideals, often associated with the beliefs of a key founding individual (for example the Rowntree Trust and the ideas of **Seebohm Rowntree**).

Beyond this, the market and the informal sector appear less overtly ideological. The market simply enables the production and distribution of those social services which people purchase directly, or indirectly through private insurance. Informal care, typically unwaged work by women, arises most often through family obligations. It can nevertheless be argued that the market and the informal sector contain fairly explicit though hidden ideologies. Markets inevitably imply that the possession of money, or more often credit, is the measure of a citizen's rights. Access to money, typically through wage labour, is from this point of view the morally preferable route to social welfare. This is why New Labour argues that paid employment is an ideal solution to a variety of social problems. Finally, feminists have argued that informal, unwaged work both sustains and is justified by an ideology of family privacy in which men as a class exercise unwarranted power over women.

Other key actors in social policy implementation include the professions and the bureaucracies that occur throughout the state, voluntary, and market welfare sectors. In many respects they reflect and reproduce ideologies appropriate to their sector. Professions also have a long tradition of independent values, of which the doctors' **Hippocratic oath** is perhaps an archetypal expression. Commitment to public service, discretion, honesty, and knowledge-based practice have been proffered by professional associations as a set of beliefs and practices which are detached from the interests and commitments of politics or markets. Their ideology is perhaps a claim to rise above ideology itself.

IDEOLOGIES OF WELFARE

Social policy, it has been argued so far, is not a neutral or technical matter. Typically, given the dominance of the state in social policy, social policy ideologies have been analysed through the familiar left-to-right framework used as a shorthand for identifying different political ideologies. There are a number of examples of this in the literature (see Box 3.2).

Clearly it is not easy to separate different ideologies cleanly: they tend to shade into each other. A major reason for this is that writers have tended to blur the normative ('ought') parts of an ideology with the explanatory ('why and how') parts. Thus two ideological positions might share the same ideals, or end states, but differ over their analysis of the 'why and how' of social policies, and hence the means advocated of attaining common ideals. For example, Marxists and socialists mainly differ over their analysis of how to attain a fairly similar ideal. Even Marx's description of life under communism is expressed in the kind of individualist imagery of personal choice that supporters of the new right would not disagree with: 'Communist society . . . makes it possible for me to do one thing today and another tomorrow, to hunt in the morning, fish in the afternoon,

Box 3.2 Ideologies of welfare

Wedderburn (1965)
anti-collectivism; citizenship; integrationism; functionalism

Titmuss (1974)
residualism; industrialism; institutionalism

Taylor-Gooby and Dale (1981)
individualism; reformism; structuralism; Marxism

George and Wilding (1994)
New Right; Middle Way; democratic; Marxism; feminism; Greenism; socialism

(Adapted from George and Wilding 1994: 9)

rear cattle in the evening, criticise after dinner, just as I have a mind' (Marx and Engels 1976). Perhaps this explains how from time to time social policy analysts have crossed over and changed their ideological position as a result not of changed ideals but of their analysis of how to get to them.

Fine distinctions between ideologies are therefore difficult to work with, and here we will present a relatively simple three-dimensional view. On the one hand, the Left and the Right can be separated from a middle position. Second, there are a number of new social movements (NSMs) that cut across this traditional political spectrum, such as feminism and environmentalism. Finally, there is a group of beliefs ignored in the studies illustrated in Box 3.2, but possibly more significant than any other for social policy around the world—religious beliefs.

The Left

The Left draws its inspiration either from Marx or from the variety of democratic socialist ideas embedded in the European labour movements of the late nineteenth and early twentieth centuries. In many respects their ideals are quite similar. They are both concerned to harness industrialization (which they do not especially criticize) for the good of all members of society. An egalitarian distribution of goods and services is thus a central concern. The main disagreements between Marxists and other socialists is over means rather than ends. Marxists have been perfectly happy to advocate quite authoritarian means, including a powerful state, to achieve these ends: the USSR was a particularly clear example of this. Other socialists, on the whole, have been concerned to empower ordinary people through democratic parliamentary mechanisms in order to secure their active consent to social policies. Getting the majority of citizens to support policies is critical not merely to retain parliamentary power but to crowd out alternative services, such as private market-based ones. A particularly good example of this approach has been realized in Sweden for much of the postwar period.

The middle

In the middle is a wide range of views united not so much by ends, as was the Left, but by the means for developing social policy, with a much less clear idea of what the ends might be. The means they are concerned about are on the whole defined negatively in terms of avoiding the dangers of either too much unregulated capitalism or too much collectivism. This was classically defined by Marshall (1963) in his idea of **hyphenated society**, by which he meant democratic-welfare-capitalism. He argued that in the twentieth century the development of social policy was an essential element in the functioning of modern industrialism, just as the development civil rights and political rights had been in previous centuries. This is a functionalist model in which the modern welfare state is seen as a pragmatic way of adjusting society to the inevitable market failures that are thrown up by capitalism from time to time. Much policy-making, from this perspective, is concerned with anxiously avoiding pitfalls that might arise from the unintended consequences of policy intervention, such as undermining work incentives, erecting poverty traps, condoning professional arrogance, missing unrecognized need, or encouraging fraud.

This pragmatic response to social ills as they appear and are recognized has little time for passionate debate about the ideals of social policy. Notions of fairness and balance in social affairs, combined with the support of social institutions such as the family, are the goals of the middle way, anodyne enough for George and Wilding (1994: 73) to observe that 'few would quarrel with Middle Way goals'.

The Right

The Right is exceptional in the energy with which it has stated both its ideals and its favoured policy mechanisms in the last two decades. It has made the running in terms of policy debate around the globe, both within nation-states and within the numerous multinational agencies that advise and cajole those states over social policy, such as the World Bank, International Monetary Fund, and the Organization for Economic Cooperation and Development. While the Right can trace its ideals at least as far back as Adam Smith in the eighteenth century, its basis can be located in **Social Darwinism**, which was proposed by Spencer and Sumner in the nineteenth century. Unlike the European roots of socialist ideas, the right has thus been typically an Anglo-American development; modern exponents such as Murray, Friedson, and Hayek have been based in the USA and the UK.

Social Darwinism drew on Darwin's ideas to suggest that, as in the animal world, social and economic success depended on the fitness of individuals and groups to survive in the brave new world of competitive industrial society. Indeed, it was seen as a useful mechanism for weeding out weakness naturally, and against which there was little point in intervening—intervention, it was thought, might well have highly adverse consequences. This view has reappeared in modified form in recent writings from the so-called New Right. Their central argument is that society is not perfectible in any particular form. They claim that they do not, therefore, have an ideal society in mind, but argue instead that we should devote our attention to the appropriate means or mechanisms which will allow the maximum chance for any particular pattern of life favoured by an individual or group. Thus freedom from constraint, and the recognition of individuals as paramount judges of their own welfare, are central ideas to the

New Right. The key mechanism for ensuring these possibilities is the market; the state should have a substantially reduced role.

New social movements

The previous familiar political spectrum has been extremely important in debates about social policy over the last 100 years. However, since the 1960s a number of new ideologies have to come to prominence in social policy discussions and analysis which cannot be located on that single left-right dimension. They are frequently referred to collectively as the **new social movements**. They share a criticism of the standard Left/Right model that the dimensions are either incomplete or wrong.

There are three sets of values highly pertinent to social policy issues which the traditional ideological division cannot accommodate: feminism, anti-racism, and environmentalism. The first two are discussed by Williams (1989). She argues that while the move away from traditional social administration in the 1970s was made possible by the critical appreciation of the impact on social policy of the social and economic organization of work and production, which informs much left-oriented analysis, such an analysis in relation to work leaves two further themes, of family and nation, unexamined:

> These themes, Work, Family, Nation, which shape welfare policies, reflect the divisions of class, gender, and 'race' respectively. In this picture the welfare state has to be understood as developing within the social relations of imperialism and the social relations of patriarchy, which themselves have changed over time. (Williams 1989: xiv)

For feminist social policy writers, such as Wilson (1977), Dale and Foster (1986), and Pascall (1997), the central questions include those about why women play such a major role in social reproduction, both in the family and as state welfare workers, and how the division of labour in both waged and unwaged work affects their interests. Since social policy is concerned with **social reproduction**, that is the physical, emotional, ideological, and material processes involved in caring for and sustaining others (both children and adults), feminist writers argue that it is incomprehensible why feminist work should not be at the heart of social policy analysis. As feminist questions and analysis have expanded they have become entwined with some of the traditional Left/Right debates, such as those about commitment to equality, or the appropriateness of the state or the market for engineering change. Within feminist writing, therefore, we can locate relatively left, middle, or right-wing positions.

Anti-racism reflects the omission of issues of nation from social policy concerns. Within the welfare state, welfare services are labour-intensive, and black and immigrant workers have played an important role as a reserve army of cheap labour: doctors, nurses, cleaners, caterers. Moreover, welfare services contribute to the reproduction of inequalities in British society. Black children do less well at school and in the youth training and labour markets than their white counterparts. Access to appropriate healthcare and housing have been repeatedly documented as discriminatory against black people (see Chapter 8). Finally, it can be argued that the welfare state has historically been as much about the maintenance of political stability as about the meeting of social needs, and the presence of black people has been used to justify the frequent revamping of technologies of social control to contain and incorporate a perceived cultural threat. Mechanisms for this have ranged from the pathologizing of black diets, family life, and psychologies to direct policing.

Environmentalism is not central to Williams's 1989 analysis, but is included (along with feminism but not anti-racism) in the 1994 edition of George and Wilding's influential book on welfare ideologies. Green ideology is of two varieties—light green and deep green (Ferris 1991). The first is compatible with the current aspirations for most industrial societies, especially the attempt to solve social problems through economic growth. Concern here is that economic and social policies should be sensitive to their effects on animals and the environment. So, within housing there is concern about energy conservation, or within healthcare there is concern about testing drugs on animals, or the development of genetic manipulation without proper ethical and legal controls. Whether these ends are best pursued via market pricing or state intervention is now discussed more extensively by light greens, as their agenda has seeped into the mainstream of Left/Right debate. Deep greens, on the other hand, see the welfare state as little more than an extension of the over-industrialization and overpopulation that is ruining the planet. There is little debate about social policies *per se* in deep green ideology.

Other smaller social movements, ranging from more traditional political interest groups to protest groups, have developed, or in some cases renewed and reinvented themselves, within the welfare arena in recent years. For example, action to highlight the needs and rights of disabled people, older people, children, and sufferers from various medical conditions appear from time to time. Some of these groups have developed more extensive ideologies than others, such as Disability Alliance (Oliver 1990).

Religions

Missed almost universally from these debates over ideologies around welfare issues are the ideas embedded in the major religions of the world. These are important for several reasons. In terms of ideals, religious beliefs affect the functioning of family life, community organization, and the vigour and focus of the voluntary sector. Understanding south-east Asian welfare states, for example, is impossible without appreciating the values embedded in Confucian beliefs, especially about family life. With migration, religious beliefs of all kinds have been transplanted across industrial societies, and understanding and respect for religious belief are important components of discussions about anti-racism and social policy. Second, with the apparent end of ideology discussed earlier, religious ideas have become increasingly central to issues of national and regional identity both in the UK and in other countries. The biggest example would be the resurgence in the Orthodox Church in Russia, and Islam in the central Asian republics; but also within western Europe, in the Netherlands, for example, we find that religion can be the main organizing principle and structural division in the national society. Without taking into account its religious component a clear understanding of the Dutch welfare state is impossible.

In addition to ideals, religion affects the structure and functioning of welfare states. There is comparative evidence from the statistical analysis of western industrial societies that central government welfare state development is affected by the extent to which Catholicism is predominant in a society (Wilensky 1981). Moreover, insofar as the charitable and voluntary sector is an important component of welfare activity both within a society and in the international aid and relief business, religious inspiration has been an important element in the motivation for and justification of welfare work.

NORMATIVE CONCEPTS IN SOCIAL POLICY

Whatever the source of ideals about welfare ends and means, there have emerged a number of middle-range **normative concepts** in debate and analysis of welfare states that merit discussion and clarification. These will appear in all or most welfare ideologies, and form the building blocks of many debates between proponents of different positions. We will present four pairs of concepts that are central to many debates. It is interesting to notice how new social movements take the traditional left-wing position for some items, but very much the right-wing position for others. This confirms that they are in many respects different from the traditional Left/Right dimension, and deserve separate consideration on many issues.

It is difficult to encompass all these ideas in a neat classification. A particularly fundamental issue that runs through most of the following concepts is that of inequality. Equality and inequality have been at the heart of most social policy debates throughout the twentieth century. A major issue has been that the welfare state has been seen as a vehicle for egalitarian redistribution, welcomed by the Left and disliked by the Right. In fact, however, the evidence is complex and not wholly supportive of this assumption. In recent decades, income and health inequalities have grown, while educational and housing inequalities have probably not. However, it is difficult to come to a clear judgement when the units of measurement, such as health or educational needs, and the period of time over which they should be measured, can vary widely. It is also clear that interventions powerful enough to have a significant impact on inequality can have undesirable side effects. Against this view is the observation that too much inequality can also have undesirable side effects, on health needs, educational achievement, crime, and economic productivity. Nevertheless, for mainstream social policy writers the question of the extent of inequality, and what to do to reduce it, continues to be dominant. The intersection of this fundamental issue with other normative concepts will be presented in the following sections.

Needs and choice

The first concept is regarded as central to much classic social policy analysis, and discussed in more detail in Chapter 5. **Needs** are regarded as the main underlying reason for developing social policies by traditional proponents who have occupied the middle ground between the Left and the Right. The needs that should be met have generally been identified as those that alternative institutions such as the market and the family have failed to meet. Thus, where the labour market provides insufficient wages, or none at all, the need for income in order to buy food, clothing, shelter, and so on is identified as a moral imperative that should be met. The difference between Left and Right here centres on the means for meeting this need, and at what level it should be met. The Left has traditionally favoured state provision at levels not too far removed from basic adequacy. The Right has favoured compulsory insurance, or a very meagre state safety net at such low levels that if at all possible people would avoid it (for example the nineteenth-century workhouse).

The identification of needs remains at the heart of ideological differences over welfare. The newer ideologies use the same general argument, but in relation to specific groups such as women, ethnic minorities, disabled people, and older people. Evidence and arguments are assembled to demonstrate that these groups have been left out of provisions for the population in general. In the case of environmentalists, the needs of future generations are a central focus in the concept of sustainability, where current needs should only be met where they do not render the meeting of future needs impossible.

Meeting needs is a complex problem, since needs are difficult to measure unambiguously, and the means of meeting them can have unintended side effects some of which can render the original effort ineffective. For example, other than very basic needs for water, food, and protection from the weather, many needs are culturally relative. Thus the legitimate types of food, drink, clothing, shelter, we need vary markedly over time, between regions, between genders, ethnic groups, and so on. This suggests that a closely related concept of **choice** should be considered in parallel to need. Here the various ideologies differ more sharply than over need. The Right champions the idea that individuals are best helped by being able to exercise choice as a major starting point in arrangements for people's welfare. Since markets are the best way of providing choice, where people have the money to pay the Right is very supportive of the use of markets and the minimum use of bureaucratic state provision. However, feminists argue that women very often do not have access to the money or the freedom to spend it as they wish, even in more affluent households, and environmentalists argue that too many of us exercise choices that will damage our own futures, let alone those of our children, through pollution, resource depletion, and genetic manipulation. In other words, choice only works where the consumer has the knowledge and capacity (which usually means money) to make choices.

The **empowerment** of welfare clients that has been proposed by social policy ideologies concerned with ethnic minorities, disabled people, or elderly people may or may not be accomplished through markets. The Right tends to conflate choice and the market mechanism. In fact markets are difficult to control, and appear to have side effects that can simultaneously restrict choice. For example, the establishment of **quasi-markets** for schools may increase choice for some parents initially; but if some schools select the more able pupils, and others slowly run out of pupils and funding and eventually close, parents with children in those schools, or who live near them, may well find their choices severely restricted. Quasi-markets in health may have the same effect; in addition, the costs of preparing complex contracts in health tend to drive up costs, and to lead quickly to **producer capture**, whereby purchasing is routinized and insulated from real consumer choice.

Rights and obligations

If people have needs that are not being met, the welfare state in principle grants them the right to expect them to be met either directly, by the state, or under its jurisdiction financially or legally. **Rights**, then, are an intimate part of social policy. However, the meaning of 'rights' varies with the legal context of the welfare state, and de facto with the way in which welfare professionals and bureaucracies work in practice. For example, in Germany welfare rights are legally enshrined, whereas in the UK they are usually not (Box 3.3).

In the USA the Constitution guarantees US citizens equal rights, whether they are black or white, yet even here interpretation has varied. A famous example is the 1954 Supreme Court ruling in the *Brown* case that all black US children had the right to educational provision equal to that for white children. This was very nearly 100 years after the civil war had been fought on the issue of slavery, and resulted in several constitutional amendments (numbers 13, 14, 15) that tried to guarantee equal citizenship for black people in the US. Even after the 1954 ruling, however, education changed very slowly, until the civil rights movement changed the political climate in the southern states ten years later.

An important discussion of the relationship between rights and social policy was set out in Marshall's seminal analysis of the growth of citizenship in the UK (see Chapter 2, Box 2.7). He suggested that the development of rights under the British state had taken place in three stages: in the first, civil rights were recognized in the eighteenth century; in the second, political rights were recognized in the nineteenth century; and in the third, social rights were recognized with the foundation of a mature welfare state in the UK in the twentieth century. As noted earlier, this was part of a wider characterization of

Box 3.3 Social security rights for unemployment in the Great Britain and Germany

Jochen Clasen's (1992) study of the comparative erosion of unemployment benefits in Great Britain and in Germany in the 1980s shows how much easier it was for a government to achieve this in Great Britain. Here, with a central ministry responsible for both insurance and means-tested benefits, and no particular legal entitlement for citizens to receive from the insurance system the equivalent of the amounts deposited, the British government was free to reduce unemployment benefits in favour of means-tested assistance.

By contrast, while the German government started to try to make the same kind of fiscal savings by reducing German workers' entitlements, this strategy failed because of three factors. First, unemployment benefits are legally insulated from other pressures on the social security system in a separate agency; second, they are funded by legally separate earmarked contributions; third, there is by law an automatic consolidation of the accumulated fund, which can then be used to retain or finance improvements in benefits for the unemployed.

the UK within a Middle Way ideology as a compromise mixture of democratic-welfare-capitalism.

Rights, then, are contested and struggled for. They are not permanent. For the ideology of the Right, rights are negative rights about freedom from constraint, particularly interference by the central or local state, and minimal guarantees that social rules, such as those of the market, operate fairly. Although these cost money to police they are felt to be relatively cheap. By contrast, the rights favoured by the Left, such as positive rights to certain levels of welfare services, are much more expensive to provide. For ideologies associated with the new social movements, rights are about making sure that excluded groups get equal treatment. In this sense they share common ground with the Left. Women, ethnic minorities, future generations, disabled people, and so on have, or should have, the right to a level of service commensurate with their needs. This may mean that in some circumstances they get a level of provision considerably in excess of that typically provided to other citizens.

In recent years **obligations** have come to be seen as an intimate corollary of welfare rights. Citizens, it has been argued, should be active not merely in their pursuit of rights for themselves but also in their contribution to the social context on which we all, from the richest to the poorest, depend in one form or another. For example, we should not only expect the state to help us if we are poor, but we should expect to take paid work if we can. If we have children, we will be helped through social policy, but we should also strive to be good parents; in state-provided education we should try to achieve our potential. In the health service, we should cooperate with medical staff, and try to get better.

Such expectations are part of a fundamental aspect of social life: the process of reciprocity. This was a major theme of nineteenth-century social analysis. The spread of industrialization across Europe and America led to the contrast being drawn between the dense network of social relations in traditional communities and the open exchanges typical of industrial market societies. Toennies termed this the move from 'community' to 'society'; Durkheim, from 'organic to mechanical solidarity'; Main, from 'status to contract'. All these writers found the changes wrought by industrialization heightened their consciousness that, as Mauss (1967) described it, when a gift is offered between two parties, this sets up a reciprocal obligation to repay it in some sense, whether in markets, families, or governments. The move from reciprocal obligations central to the closely woven textures of pre-industrial communities, to contract obligations typical of industrial society, however, had not eliminated Mauss's central observation that with a gift was given an obligation to repay it. Inability to repay left the recipient with reduced social power and lower status. This is the anthropological source of the stigma so often experienced by welfare recipients, and it alerts us to the complexities that underlie the apparent selflessness of altruism that some have naively argued as the basis of a good welfare state.

Such obligations, epitomized in the title of a book by Laurence Mead, *Beyond Entitlement* (1986), have increasingly been stressed within right-wing ideology. Active citizenship is not new however; President Kennedy, in his inaugural speech in 1960 admonished us, 'Do not ask what your country can do for you, but what you can do for

Box 3.4 New Labour's Green Paper on welfare reform

'At the heart of the modern welfare state will be a new contract between the Citizen and Government, based on responsibilities and rights.

Towards a new welfare contract

Duty of government	*Duty of individual*
Provide people with the assistance they need to find work.	Seek training or work where able to do so.
Make work pay	
Support those unable to work so that they can lead a life of dignity and security.	Take up the opportunity to be independent if able to do so.
Assist parents with the cost of raising their children.	Give support, financial or otherwise, to their children and other family members.
Regulate effectively so that people can be confident that private pensions and insurance products are secure.	Save for retirement where possible.
Relieve poverty in old age where savings are inadequate.	Not to defraud the taxpayer.
Devise a system that is transparent and open and gets money to those in need.	

Duty of us all

To help individuals and families to realise their full potential and live a dignified life, by promoting economic independence through work, by relieving poverty where it cannot be prevented and by building a strong and cohesive society where rights are matched by responsibilities.'

(DSS 1998: 80)

your country.' More recently, New Labour in the UK have also taken up the idea that welfare recipients should feel obliged to return such largesse in some way (see Box 3.4).

Thus the 'welfare to work' scheme obliges benefit claimants to undertake some activity in return for benefit, such as training, or community service. The new social movement ideologies also stress such obligations. For example, feminists are concerned that men undertake the obligations of fatherhood, but they are also concerned that typical family obligations have meant obligations for women rather than men, particularly to undertake unpaid social care. Such obligations seem in fact to arise not out of reciprocal social exchanges, but from expectations about the family duties of women. Other groups stress the obligations of polluters to pay, or the obligations of able-bodied people to others.

Justice and merit

Meeting needs and fulfilling rights where resources are scarce raise questions of distribution, and rationing. What is **justice** in social distribution? In principle a just provision of welfare implies the equal meeting of equal needs. However, as we have seen, it can be difficult to determine what needs are when cultural relativities influence judgements. Geographical peculiarities may also lead to territorial injustice. When we have to compare needs for very different services, such as medical intervention and educational provision, the possibilities for relative injustice are compounded. What is the relative welfare effort that should be devoted to education or healthcare?

One answer proposed by John Rawls (1972) is that, in principle, we could plan a society as if we were screened behind a veil of ignorance. What would we choose for ourselves if we did not know what lay in store in our own lives? He argues that we would choose a relatively equal society, without large disparities of wealth and income. The rationalization for this is that it would be the safest way of ensuring that we were unlikely to suffer too much. However, there are other ways of answering this question. We might choose to risk poverty for the opportunity of greater wealth available to only a few. It can also be argued that a relatively egalitarian society is not, in fact, practicable. Inequality may be inevitable and necessary to motivate or reward the talented, or would otherwise only be possible through a suffocating blanket of state control. The fate of eastern Europe in the forty years after Second World War lends support to such a conclusion.

Another idea, developed by health economists, is that we should provide services in relation to the **quality of life** they can subsequently sustain (see Chapter 14). In healthcare, for example, a medical intervention might be considered as just where it can provide a greater increase in the quality of life for a patient than an equivalent intervention for an alternative patient. This can be refined to take into account the number of years over which the improvement in the quality of life is likely to last. Thus many years of modestly greater quality for a child might be preferable to a few years of a considerable increase in quality for an older person. This idea could be extended, in principle, to the calculation of the relative benefit and costs of different social policies, and hence the ideal just distribution of welfare effort. However, it would be difficult to do these calculations and plan social policy in sufficient detail.

Rawls's conception of justice as equality is really a popular or democratic approach to the rationing of scarce resources, whereas health economists are trying to develop a technical solution. Either way, social justice has been associated most strongly with ideologies of the Left and the new social movements, and arguments in favour of equality achieved through positive policy interventions. Equality is a simpler goal than the technical targeting of interventions very precisely where their benefit will be greatest. For the Right, justice is more concerned with civil equality under the law, with an otherwise laissez-faire approach to social planning, in which inequalities could be allowed to arise spontaneously.

Inequality is not necessarily incompatible with both justice and **merit**. If inequality motivated the talents of some for the good of all, would we choose to tolerate inequality from behind the Rawlsian veil? In the absence of detailed social welfare calculations, can we trust professionals such as doctors, planners, social workers, or teachers to provide services to those who need them most? What about functional effects for the whole community? These questions raise a classic issue in social policy: the extent to which policies should strive for equality of outcome or equality of opportunity.

Equality of outcome means that after social policy interventions, differences between people in terms of their welfare are less. Their incomes, housing space, educational qualifications might all be more similar than before. This might be possible to achieve through the expansion of some kinds of welfare available to all, for example total income, total healthcare, or total housing. In such cases everyone gains, although at different rates, and this is less likely to cause political controversy. However, other welfare is not expandable in the same way. Education is the classic case. While education is designed to give everyone the skills they need for adult life, it also has a major function of identifying and stratifying people by ability. In this respect it is a **positional good** (Box 3.5) in that there are only so many top positions, for example in business, medical, legal, or academic life, that can be occupied, just as there are only so many geographical points that can provide a panoramic view. If educational qualifications are expanded, they tend to lose their exclusivity at the same rate—the result of educational inflation.

In reality many kinds of welfare cannot be expanded indefinitely either, and the question arises of who merits access in preference to others. The alternative to equality of outcome is **equality of opportunity**, whereby we are all given equal support and help, but thereafter inequalities are allowed to multiply as individuals make what they can of their

Box 3.5 Positional goods

In his book *The Social Limits to Growth* (1977), Fred Hirsch observed that we desire some goods and services that are valuable to us in part because they are not available to everyone. For example, not everyone can enjoy a beautiful countryside view from a commanding height above the potential viewing-points of others. While there is a limited technical solution to the problem of mass viewing (as in football stadia and theatres), in the end there will have to be an unequal distribution of the view. He described these goods and services as 'positional goods'.

In social policy, educational achievement is such a good, since part of the function of education is to stratify people, regardless of their objective achievement: only some will get the highest grades, get to the best universities, and develop high-status careers. For some people the attractions of privatized social services (experienced as exclusive and only available to the few) are also in part because they are positional goods. There are many other such goods: traffic-free roads, empty beaches, unpolluted atmosphere, personal autonomy. Hirsch argued that there is a compelling myth that we can all have access to such goods if only economic growth can be sustained at a fast enough pace. This, sadly, is an illusion.

opportunities, and education, employment, income, housing, and so on are distributed according to merit rather than justice. The Left has had a very ambivalent attitude to the question of equality. In principle it has supported equality of outcome, but in practice it has adopted equality of opportunity in its policies. For example, in the 1960s the Labour government removed the strongly symbolic secondary/grammar school divide and developed comprehensive secondary education in the state sector as a radical push towards equality in education, yet at the same time left the private ('public') schools in place and rapidly expanded university education for middle-class children.

The Right has also been inconsistent on issues of equality and merit. In principle the Conservative government in the 1980s strongly supported equality of opportunities, but not equality of outcome. Yet in housing it has enabled many millions of tenants of state-owned housing to become highly satisfied property-owners, and in higher education it engineered such a major expansion of university provision that BA degrees have become widely in reach of working-class children in a more radical manner than ever before (see Chapters 13 and 17). For other ideologies, the relative emphasis on equality of outcome or equality of opportunity has tended to produce disagreements within the movement. Light greens, liberal feminists, and the Asian minorities favour equality of opportunities; dark greens, socialist feminists, and the African-Caribbean minorities favour equality of outcomes.

Citizenship and status

In recent social policy analysis, the concepts we have discussed—need, choice, rights, obligations, justice, merit—have been brought together under the term **citizenship**. Marshall argued that civil, political, and social rights define the conditions for citizenship to exist. His key observation was that there had been a steady expansion of areas in which citizens had defined rights. Citizens were, Goodin (1988) has argued, gaining membership of a community, and as a result gaining entitlements available to all members of that community. Community membership ensured that needs would be met if possible, but that there would be obligations too. Being a community member was thus the key to welfare citizenship. It implied access to universal services, and a sense of social inclusion.

However, the term 'community', while it might imply relative homogeneity when applied to small groups or pre-industrial societies, is misleading with respect to modern industrial societies. Class stratification, and gender and ethnic differences can multiply within a community, and hence between formally equal citizens. Citizenship equality is affected by people's positions in the social and economic structure; hence the term tends to carry quite different meanings for the ideological positions we have considered in this chapter. For the Left, citizenship is about the solidarity expressed through a relatively altruistic welfare state built on the common experience of the Second World War. Participation in the normal life of the community is the mark of the citizen, and indeed has been used by Townsend (1979) as a sociological method of defining poverty as that condition which prevents full social participation. But, for the Right, citizenship is confined to formal equality in law and politics, without any prescribed level of social support. The new social movements have also been critical of defining citizenship as community membership. Lister (1990) points out that membership can mean very different things for men and women, black and white people, able-bodied and non-able-bodied people. Greens have worried that animals have been denied rights to their own welfare, and are thus clearly not regarded as full members of the community.

This critique of citizenship as community membership has highlighted the question of the **status** of people, and especially whether they are excluded or included in the life of the community. Weber famously argued that modern societies are stratified not only by social class and by political power, but also by social status, meaning by this the esteem in which people are held. Status can be quite varied within any community, and may systematically exclude certain groups. Where community values celebrate ideals of masculinity, white culture, work, or mobility, those who are unable to embody such values tend to have a lower status or social esteem, and may find themselves excluded from the goods and services commonly available in that community. With the growth of income inequality over the 1980s and 1990s there has been increased concern amongst social policy analysts that large sections of the UK community may have become excluded from the mainstream. While the Left has expressed concern about this process, it has been the new social movements that have been particularly active in challenging the exclusion that results from low status. Feminists have challenged the male domination of public and private values which undervalues women; greens have challenged the celebration of continued economic growth and the dominance of paid work; anti-racists have celebrated ethnic diversity and dignity; and disabled people have affirmed the disabling effects for them of conventional architectural and technological arrangements.

IDEOLOGY, IDEOLOGIES, AND THE 'GOOD SOCIETY'

In this chapter we have observed that the major positions used in social policy debate are contested. Where there are attempts to persuade us of the inevitability or common sense of any particular policy, we should beware and consider the interests of those who support the policy. These interests are often organized into ideological positions which spill over into a range of issues. In recent years the previously simple choice between Left and Right has been complicated by new social movements and religious ideas which cut across the traditional political spectrum. The search for the 'good society' has become more uncertain.

Debate about social policy will always be inherently ideological. Nevertheless we can identify many of the middle-range, normative concepts that form the building blocks of any particular ideological position. All ideologies use ideas such as needs, choices, obligations, merit, and status. Indeed, much policy debate consists of teasing out where a particular policy stands on these issues. This is because the policy goals and means that different sections of society would prefer to see, and think of as right and just, are determined both by their interests and by their ideals. This chapter shows how interests and ideals combine particular normative principles into coherent sets of ideas constituting the competing ideologies that ultimately define the politics of welfare.

REFERENCES

Abercrombie, N., Hill, S., and Turner, B. S. (1980), *The Dominant Ideology Thesis*. London: Allen & Unwin.

Bell, D. (1960/1965), *The End of Ideology*. New York: Free Press.

Beveridge, Sir W. (1942), *Social Insurance and Allied Services*. Cmd. 6404, London: HMSO.

Castles, F. G., and McKinlay, R. (1979), 'Public welfare provision, Scandinavia, and the sheer futility of the sociological approach to politics', *British Journal of Political Science* 9: 157–71.

Clasen, J. (1992), 'Unemployment insurance in two countries: a comparative analysis of Great Britain and West Germany in the 1980s', *Journal of European Social Policy* 2(4): 279–300.

Dale, J., and Foster, P. (1986), *Feminists and State Welfare*. London: Routledge & Kegan Paul.

Doyal, L., and Gough, I. (1991), *A Theory of Human Rights*. Basingstoke: Macmillan.

DSS (Department of Social Security) (1998), *New Ambitions for Our Country: A New Contract for Welfare*. Welfare Reform Green Paper (Cm. 3805). London: Stationery Office.

Ferris, J. (1991), 'Green politics and the future of welfare'. In N. Manning (ed.), *Social Policy Review 1990–91*. Harlow: Longman.

Fukuyama, F. (1992), *The End of History and the Last Man*. London: Hamish Hamilton.

George, V., and Wilding, P. (1994), *Welfare and Ideology*. Hemel Hempstead: Harvester Wheatsheaf.

Goodin, R. E. (1988), *Reasons for Welfare: The Political Theory of the Welfare State*. Princeton: Princeton, NJ University Press.

Hage, J., et al. (1989), *State Responsiveness and State Activism*. London: Unwin Hyman.

Harvey, D. (1990), *The Condition of Postmodernity: An Enquiry into the Origins of Cultural Change*. Oxford : Blackwell.

Hicks, A., and Swank, D. (1984), 'Welfare expansion: a comparative analysis of 18 advanced capitalist democracies, 1960–71', *Comparative Political Studies* 17(1): 81–119.

—— —— and Ambuhl, M. (1989), 'Welfare expansion revisited: 1957–1982', *European Journal of Political Research* 17: 401–30.

Hirsch, F. (1977), *Social Limits to Growth*. London: Routledge & Kegan Paul.

Kerr, C., Dunlop, J. T., Harbison, F., and Myers, C. A. (1973), *Industrialism and Industrial Man*. Harmondsworth: Penguin.

Klein, N. (2000), *No Logo*. London: Flamingo.

Lister, R. (1990), 'Women, economic dependency and citizenship', *Journal of Social Policy* 19(4): 445–68.

Mann, M. (1970), 'The social cohesion of liberal democracy', *American Sociological Review* 35: 423–39.

Mannheim, K. (1936/1968), *Ideology and Utopia: An Introduction to the Sociology of Knowledge*. London: Routledge & Kegan Paul.

Marshall, T. H. (1963), *Sociology at the Crossroads*. London: Heinemann.

Marx, K., and Engels, F. (1976), *The German Ideology*. Moscow: Progress.

Mauss, M. (1967), *The Gift: Forms and Functions of Exchange in Archaic Societies*. New York: Norton.

Mead, L. (1986), *Beyond Entitlement: The Social Obligations of Citizenship*. New York: Free Press.

Oliver, M. (1990), *The Politics of Disablement*. Basingstoke: Macmillan Education.

Pascall, G. (1997), *Social Policy: A New Feminist Analysis*. London: Routledge.

Rawls, J. (1972), *A Theory of Justice*. Oxford: Clarendon Press.

Stephens, J. D. (1979), *The Transition from Capitalism to Socialism*. London: Macmillan.

Taylor-Gooby, P., and Dale, J. (1981), *Social Theory and Social Welfare*. London: Arnold.

Titmuss, R. (1974), *Social Policy: An Introduction*. London: Allen & Unwin.

Townsend, P. (1979), *Poverty in the United Kingdom: A Survey of Household Resources and Standards of Living*. Harmondsworth: Penguin.

Wedderburn, D. (1965), 'Facts and theories of the welfare state'. In R. Miliband and J. Saville (eds.), *The Socialist Register*. London: Merlin Press.

Wilensky, H. L. (1981), 'Leftism, Catholicism, and democratic corporatism: the role of political parties in recent welfare state development'. In P. Flora and A. J. Heidenheimer (eds.), *The Development of Welfare States in Europe and America*. London: Transaction.

Williams, F. (1989), *Social Policy: A Critical Introduction: Issues of Race, Gender and Class*. Cambridge: Polity Press.

Wilson, E. (1977), *Women and the Welfare State*. London: Tavistock.

FURTHER READING

V. George and P. Wilding, *Welfare and Ideology* (Hemel Hempstead: Harvester Wheatsheaf, 1994). This is the third edition of a classic book on ideology and social policy, which tackles many of the issues very succinctly. It may be difficult to obtain other than from libraries.

N. Malin, S. Wilmot, and J. Manthorpe, *Key Concepts and Debates in Health and Social Policy* (Milton Keynes: Open University Press, 2002) adopts a similar 'ideologies of welfare' approach to George and Wilding and includes discussion of the Third Way and New Labour policies.

Section 1 of C. Pierson and F. Castles (eds.), *The Welfare State Reader* (Cambridge: Polity Press, 2000) provides some key statements of welfare state ideology from the Left, the Right, and feminists.

B. Jessop, *The Future of the Capitalist State* (Cambridge: Polity Press, 2002) provides a polemical but very illuminating interpretation of welfare regimes and their futures.

N. Deakin, *In Search of Civil Society* (London: Palgrave, 2001) is a complex and thoughtful book which goes beyond the more usual territory and deals with voluntary welfare activities at local, national, and global levels.

GLOSSARY

choice Choice over goods and services can be established in markets through the act of buying. However, where these are distributed through administrative and professional means, the question of clients exercising choice can challenge received wisdoms about accepted welfare arrangements. It is difficult to increase choice for everyone, since the choices of some may restrict the choices of others.

citizenship This is the formal status conferred on a member of a national community. With it normally come a set of rights to equal treatment under the law, to vote and to social support. It has famously been used by Marshall to analyse the twentieth-century welfare state (see Chapter 2, Box 2.7).

dominant ideology A term which comes out of a tradition of Marxist writing which argues that the economic relationships in a society allow an elite to determine the main social, political, and intellectual views of the day.

empowerment Recent developments in welfare debate have acknowledged that under the original 1948 arrangements, many clients of the welfare state were expected to be passive and grateful recipients of state handouts. There has now been a common criticism of this assumption on all sides, in favour of clients having more power, dignity, respect, and autonomy through a process of empowerment.

equality of opportunity This means that citizens will be given an equal start in life, but thereafter will be allowed to make what they can of their talents and opportunities.

equality of outcome This means that those with equal needs receive equal treatment. This may mean that some disadvantaged people might receive more support than others.

explanatory ideals Social policy debate about the ideal goals of policies and the means of achieving them frequently includes discussions of the circumstances under which welfare states developed, and especially the way in which policies operate in the real world. Writers advocating particular policies may also have strong views about why welfare states exist and how they work. For example, 'defending' the welfare state makes assumptions about the circumstances under which welfare states exist or can be changed; or advocating a specific policy, such as to introduce market mechanisms or encourage professional change, will involve assumptions about how the policy will work in practice.

functionalist explanation A kind of explanation which views the social system as a whole, and tends to argue that social arrangements exist because they work well to fulfil the functional requirements of the system. If those functions are not yet manifestly identified, they are assumed to exist latently. This analysis thus tends to be circular, in that it both assumes functions and then uses functions as an explanation. It is also teleological, in that it assumes that social development is evolving towards some kind of preferable end state.

grand narrative A term in post-modernist writing applied to wide-ranging and comprehensive schemes such as communism or fascism, designed to perfect human society.

Hippocratic oath The commitment, recorded from ancient Greece by Hippocrates, still traditionally given by medical doctors to work for the good of the patient, and to 'do the sick no harm'.

hyphenated society Marshall (1963) argued that industrial society in the UK had by the middle of the twentieth century developed to a balanced point that included a strong but not uncontrolled capitalist economy, and a comprehensive but not too intrusive welfare state brought about by democratic means. This balance, which he felt was a good one, was a mixture, or hybrid, whereby the various parts kept each other in a check in a hyphenated society of democratic-welfare-capitalism.

justice A fair action in accordance with the rules. In social policy it has either come to mean the allocation of social services according to need or, in the absence of our ability actually to measure all the many individual needs there are, it has been used to define an egalitarian society in which needs are most likely to be met equally. In complex societies it may be that an unequal distribution of services can increase the capacity of the whole system to meet needs, and simple egalitarian justice is thus difficult to operationalize.

merit Merit means that under the rules an individual receives what they deserve. For some writers this is an essential incentive for individuals to produce effectively for the whole system, and to deter others from non-production. For other writers, the rules are seen to be devices for exclusion, such that the term 'merit' camouflages the systematic reproduction of inequalities.

needs The most central concept to social policy debate. Where goods and services are distributed outside the market, in which we can express our preferences through the act of buying, it is difficult to identify who should have what. What people need is established in relation to administratively or professionally defined norms, but these are inherently open to debate and challenge. In particular, beyond very basic needs for food and shelter, there is considerable cultural variation in socially defined needs (see Chapter 5 for an extended discussion).

new social movements Social movements are collective attempts to change social arrangements through public campaigns. Traditional movements included the labour movement and the suffragette movement. Since the 1960s a number of new social movements have developed or renewed themselves as part of the general liberalization of social values at that time. These include movements focused on environmentalism, women, and anti-racism.

normative concepts Much debate in social policy between different major ideological positions, such as left and right, takes place at a middle range, or intermediate level, over particular concepts that are prescriptive—that is, they say what ought to be or should be the case. The case for more or less state intervention, or equality, for example, is often made through appeal to these middle-range normative concepts, such as needs, choices, justice, merit, rights, and obligations.

normative ideals Social policy debate is not just about the scientific evidence for engineering social change, but also about the way society ought to be. This involves normative ideals, including both the desired end states we would like to push towards and also the means by which we would like to get there. Many writers mix up ends and means in their writing, which we have to reflect on carefully in order to appreciate their views.

obligations In recent years most shades of ideological opinion have come to place increasing emphasis on the obligations that go along with the rights that individuals can acquire. This is in part a recognition of the anthropological observation of the central place of reciprocity in social life: exchanges are usually balanced, and in the case of a right the balance is an obligation. Thus an individual is expected to work hard, get better, or take employment in exchange for education, healthcare, and income support.

particular conception of ideology A concept used by Mannheim to indicate those ideas that an individual or group might express about particular circumstances, which are erroneous, and which may or may not be deliberately false, but which the proponent of the view has an interest in sustaining.

positional goods Some goods and services are valuable to us in part because they are not available to everyone. For example, not everyone can enjoy a beautiful countryside view from a commanding height above the potential viewing points of others. Some social services, such as higher education, can be thought of in this way. While there is a limited technical solution to the problem of mass viewing (as in football stadia and theatres), in the end there will have to be an unequal distribution of the view. We can describe these goods and services as 'positional goods'.

post-modernism This is a new historical era, after the modern era, identified initially in architecture in the mid-1970s as a reaction to the functional designs of housing estates in the middle of the twentieth century all over the world. The term has since spread into social analysis through French intellectual work in the 1980s. An important part of this work has been to argue that there are no longer any grand ideas or schemes (see **grand narrative**) such as communism or fascism, that human society can follow to improve itself.

producer capture This occurs where the producer of a service is able to 'capture' and dictate the preferences of consumers and terms of service delivery. Professional groups such as doctors are accused of this control from time to time. Where consumer representatives or advocates have been set up, there is concern that in a more narrow sense they may also be captured and come to espouse the interests of the producers rather than the consumers.

quality of life The basis for one attempt at measuring medical need, and hence distinguishing between different medical cases where resources are limited and have to be rationed. The argument is that medical care should be used to maximize the number of years and the quality of life of the patient. In principle this allows a rational choice to be made, for example between a case where the quality of life will only be increased modestly, but over many years, and a case where quality may be increased substantially but for a short period only. This might favour the treatment of children over the treatment of older people, for example.

quasi-markets Markets in social services, such as schools and healthcare, set up administratively to encourage different providers to compete with each other in the hope that this will motivate them to increase quality, or at least cut costs, and that consumers will get greater choice as a result. They are not full markets, since there are many areas where natural monopolies operate, where real prices are difficult to set for complex services, or where it is not politically acceptable for services to be driven out of business. Experience to date suggests that the costs of inter-unit contractual development have been high, and that choice has not been greatly increased.

rights Constitutionally or legally defined capacities, such as the capacity to vote, usually conferred on members of the relevant community or society, often through the acquisition of citizenship. Where these involve freedom from constraint, such as the capacity to engage in religious worship, they are relatively simple to define and cheap to guarantee. Where they involve capacities that depend on the provision of services such as education or healthcare or income maintenance, they are difficult to define and expensive to guarantee. The Right has tended to argue for rights to freedom from constraint; the Left has tended to argue for rights to services.

Seebohm Rowntree The Rowntree family owned the York-based chocolate business. Seebohm undertook several famous surveys of working families in York between 1898 and 1951. He showed in his early surveys that severe poverty was widespread, but that the postwar welfare state had all but eliminated it by 1951. There is a continuity of definition of the poverty line between his work, the Beveridge report, and current social security income support benefit levels. The Rowntree Foundation, which commemorates his work, now funds a wide range of social policy research into the circumstances of poor and disadvantaged people.

social administration The management of the production and distribution of social services in general. It was used to define the academic discipline of social administration from the late 1940s, when the first chair in the subject was established at the University of Nottingham, and the national association which dealt with the subject, the Social Administration Association. In 1988 the title was changed to the Social Policy Association to reflect a wider academic interest in the sociological and political science analysis of the welfare state. 'Social administration' now connotes a rather limited and uncritical approach to the subject, dominant between the 1940s and the 1970s.

Social Darwinism In the nineteenth century the revolutionary biological ideas of Charles Darwin were applied to society and social relations by writers such as Spencer in the UK and Sumner in the USA. The main point taken from Darwin was the idea of the survival of the fittest, suggesting that state intervention to protect or support the weak was not only self-defeating but might be positively harmful if it allowed the weak to flourish at the expense of the strong.

social reproduction The idea that in addition to the biological reproduction of human beings, there is an equally important activity of reproducing the fundamental social relationships necessary to the continuity of human society. These include the capacity for relating to a group and responding appropriately to emotions, mostly learnt in families, and the capacity to learn and to work cooperatively, mostly learnt in schools.

status The esteem in which we are held in a community in relation to some of the central values cherished in that community. Max Weber argued that it was the third basic dimension that stratified societies alongside class and power. The new social movements have increasingly drawn attention to the way in which social values can divide people by esteem. Where maleness, whiteness, and physical and mental dexterity are esteemed, this can lower the status of women and of black and disabled people.

total conception of ideology In this term Mannheim refers to the 'world-view' of an individual or group, i.e. their total way of looking at the world. It ranges across a number of social issues, and may include erroneous ideas. It is bound up with their way of life and identity in such a way as to make it difficult for them to see issues from any other point of view. It has some similarity to the term **dominant ideology**, although Mannheim did not hold to the Marxist view that this was determined by prevailing economic relations in a society.

4

Welfare, Media, and Culture

Mark Liddiard

CONTENTS

INTRODUCTION

In contemporary British society at the start of the twenty-first century, we are surrounded by a dazzling array of mass media. Television, radio, newspapers, and increasingly the Internet are all important and influential sources of information, and have enormous potential for framing the ways in which we understand and interpret current affairs and social issues. As a starting point, it is clear that many of the social policy issues covered elsewhere in this book have largely entered the public arena by virtue of the mass media. The fact that we live in an increasingly media-conscious political and social environment means that the mass media are simply too important for social policy to ignore.

It is certainly clear that the media have become a crucial component in how we understand the world. What is considerably less clear, however, is the precise way in which audiences interpret and receive the myriad of messages and images that they receive. There are important questions here about the role of the mass media in terms of influencing public opinion in relation to welfare issues and even the welfare state itself—questions which, with just a few notable exceptions (eg. Golding and Middleton 1982; Franklin 1999), are largely neglected by social policy. Yet given the very real importance that some interest groups and agencies attach to securing favourable media coverage and exposure in their efforts to secure policy changes, just what influence do the mass media have upon policy-makers? Given their potential power in influencing and even manipulating policy debates, what should be the appropriate role of the state in terms of the control and regulation of the mass media?

There has been a long history of interest in media coverage of social issues and the corresponding influence that this may have upon both public perception and policy outcomes. Stanley Cohen's study of the Mods and Rockers phenomenon in the 1960s, and the role of the media in creating and amplifying 'folk devils' and 'moral panics', was one of the earliest studies to focus on the treatment of crime and delinquency in the media (see Cohen 1972). Similarly, the ground-breaking work of Stuart Hall and the Centre for Contemporary Cultural Studies in the 1970s examined the role of the media in creating a moral panic surrounding mugging, which then fed directly into the criminal justice system (see Hall et al. 1979).

More recently, media coverage of a number of social issues has attracted considerable debate and controversy. In 1999, for instance, an independent inquiry by the charity MIND found that people with mental health problems were seriously socially excluded in British society. In particular, a key finding was that misleading media coverage had led to growing intolerance of the mentally ill. The fact that some two thirds of news and current affairs coverage made a link between mental illness and violence was felt to have very real and damaging implications for public attitudes towards those with mental health problems.

Similarly, misrepresentation of asylum-seekers with inaccurate and often inflammatory coverage—particularly in the tabloid press—has provoked very real anger amongst those working with refugees and asylum-seekers. The numerous stories of asylum-seekers enjoying generous benefit payments and services fit incongruously with the reality of destitution faced by many asylum-seekers and refugees.

The suggestion that hostile media coverage has had a negative impact upon race relations and policy debates about asylum and immigration also came to a head in the summer of 2001, when race riots and violence erupted in a number of northern towns such as Oldham, Bradford, and Burnley. In Oldham in particular, local and national media coverage was widely criticized as partial and misleading. Indeed, the suggestion was that the media themselves played a crucial role in influencing subsequent events.

Box 4.1 'Ode of an Asylum Seeker'

'I come for a visit, get treated regal,
So I stay, who care illegal?
I cross border, poor and broke,
Take bus, see employment folk,
Nice man treat me good in there,
Say I need to see welfare.
Welfare say "You come no more.
We send plenty cash right to your door."
Welfare cheques they make you wealthy,
NHS, it keeps you healthy!
Bye and bye, I got plenty of money,
Thanks to you, British dummy.'

(*Daily Mail*, 31 January 2003)

The above extract is from a poem published in the *Daily Mail* in the context of a story about a civil servant facing disciplinary action for circulating it via e-mail. The editorial went on to say: 'Yet doesn't the ode present a more honest picture of the asylum crisis than any number of soothing official circumlocutions? Instead of threatening an inquiry, the Government should be fast tracking him to the top of the diplomatic service, with a knighthood to boot.'

Questions

- Do you consider this poem to be misleading or inflammatory in any way?
- Should this poem have been published in a national newspaper?
- In your view, what might be the implications of publishing this poem?

The impact of the mass media upon race relations is not a new concern. Debates about immigration have long featured in press coverage in different ways, as the following cartoon illustrates.

Of course, it is easy to dismiss the impact of poems and cartoons as being little more than harmless sources of humour and ridicule. Indeed, similar points were made about the treatment of race in 1970s comedy programmes, such as the controversial *Love Thy Neighbour*. In retrospect, it seems clear that even if such programmes reflected some prevailing attitudes of the time, they also served to negatively reinforce and perpetuate popular stereotypes.

Questions about the impact of media coverage have certainly pervaded a host of social issues. The influence of 'waif' fashion models in advertising has also been a source of some controversy, particularly because of a concern about the impact on body image amongst young women, and has been linked by some to the incidence of serious health issues such as anorexia and bulimia. In short, there have been long-standing concerns

Cartoon 4.1 What impact does mass media content have upon public opinion and policy-makers?

(*The Sun*, 16 October 1986).

about the impact of the mass media upon a range of social issues and welfare debates. The degree to which media coverage does actually influence popular perception and attitudes, however, is far from clear.

THE IMPACT OF THE MASS MEDIA UPON PUBLIC ATTITUDES

It is interesting—and perhaps not surprising, given the increasingly media-conscious environment in which we live—that considerable importance is often attached to achieving favourable media coverage of social and welfare issues. There is often something of an implicit assumption on the part of involved agencies and commentators that media coverage is important for changing public perceptions and helping to change and modify policy. But is this really the case? What kind of impact do the mass media really have upon public attitudes towards different social problems?

The first point is to recognize that the media are far from homogeneous. The content and style of presentation, for example, may vary widely and dramatically between the press and television. Moreover, even if one is only considering the press, they too are far from uniform. On the simplest level, there is an obvious distinction between the tabloids and the broadsheets. The heterogeneity of the mass media, however, may be important because their impact upon public attitudes may differ widely. A recent survey, for instance, showed that in the UK the public view the credibility of news coverage very differently depending upon the medium concerned. Whilst some 85 per cent of respondents believed that television news reporting was exactly in line or approximately in line with what really happened, the corresponding figure for newspaper coverage was just 48 per cent (Smith 1998).

The styles of media presentation can also be important because of the influence that they may have upon the public. Often, serious social issues may be treated as if they were a form of public entertainment. Whilst this may be useful for encouraging public interest in a topic such as homelessness, it can nonetheless leave misconceptions and stereotypes, trivialize serious social issues, and may ultimately do little to rectify misapprehensions or modify attitudes (Hutson and Liddiard 1994).

It is important too to recognize that the media operate with their own agendas, which can take many different forms. The implication is an important one because of the way in which only the issues, notions, and concepts which are consistent with pre-existing media agendas will be accepted and promoted. In this sense, whilst agencies may rightly or wrongly view the media as being in a position of enviable power to influence public opinion and policy-making, in order actually to attract media interest, agencies must first subscribe to media agendas and modify their messages and concerns. For instance, in the context of homelessness, journalists and politicians regularly employ crude and stereotypical images of the homeless—focusing on prostitution and drug abuse, for instance—because they make good copy (Kemp 1997). Importantly, homeless agencies may often collude with such images in their enthusiasm to attain coverage (Beresford 1979; Liddiard and Hutson 1998).

There is no doubt that the media can provide a very important and powerful source of communication, enabling issues to be conveyed to millions of people who may not otherwise have been involved or particularly interested. The ability to sensitize so many people to social policy concerns is not to be minimized. Yet the assumption that media coverage of a social issue will have a direct impact upon both public opinion and policy-makers is questionable.

Public attitudes towards many different areas of social welfare are notoriously difficult to delimit. Public opinion is profoundly heterogeneous, and levels of knowledge and interest in social issues vary widely. As studies such as the British Social Attitudes Survey have shown, eliciting accurate information about public attitudes towards different areas of welfare is difficult and laden with methodological problems. Nonetheless, a number of points can be made about the role of the media in terms of public attitudes.

The question of how the media impact upon public attitudes has long concerned academics, and there have been a number of important shifts in how they have approached the issue. One traditional view, and one which still pervades some of the debates here, is known as the 'hypodermic syringe' model. This approach perceives the media as somehow having a direct and inherently straightforward impact upon the viewing audience. However, this approach has now been largely discredited because of the way in which it implies a passive audience—unquestioningly absorbing whatever they are presented with by the media. The impact of the media upon the public is more complex, not least because there is now much agreement about the fact that the public select and interpret media messages according to their existing viewpoints. In other words, far from being passive recipients of media messages, the public are actually highly active in their interpretation of the images and messages with which they are presented. Only those media messages which generally reinforce what individuals already believe tend to be selected by the audience. In other words, media messages may simply resonate with the public. In this way, the same media item can be interpreted differently by different categories of people.

Arguably, the result is a mass public largely ill-informed of key social issues, whose knowledge is only modified or mediated on the basis of their own pre-existing agendas and misapprehensions. In short, the role of media coverage upon public attitudes towards social issues is far from clear. Yet just what impact does the media coverage have upon policy-making?

THE IMPACT OF THE MEDIA ON POLICY-MAKING

Does media coverage of homelessness and other social problems have a significant influence upon policy-makers, promoting the importance of some issues over others? This is a difficult issue to address, because we know surprisingly little about the impact of the mass media upon the decision-making process. Nonetheless, a number of points can be made. In the initial stages of policy germination, for instance, pressure groups will seek to place certain issues on the political agenda. The media certainly perform an important role at this early stage of the policy and decision-making process, with pressure groups depending heavily upon their ability to excite media interest. Without such assistance, many campaigns would never get off of the ground.

However, it remains very difficult actually to identify concrete effects that media coverage—and in turn public concern—may have had upon subsequent policy, although it does seem that the influence of media coverage depends in part upon the wider social context in which this coverage is taking place. If media coverage is compatible with the surrounding socio-economic and political environment, then it is likely to have more impact. The implication is that policy responses to social problems such as homelessness may have much less to do with media coverage and public opinion and much more to do with dominant political ideologies and agendas (Liddiard 1998).

It is important, too, to remember that the link between the media and policy-making operates in both directions, with policy-makers and politicians often playing a crucial role in terms of informing, even manipulating, the media. The work of the Glasgow University Media Group and others have shown how government accounts and interpretations can permeate into mass media accounts, often through subtle manipulation of journalistic processes and information collection (see Broadbent 1993; Miller 1994).

The New Labour government has consistently been accused of misusing 'spin' in its attempts to secure favourable media coverage for its policy initiatives.

For these reasons, it is probably fair to suggest that the media may have only a limited impact upon policy-making. After all, policies are made in response to a variety of diverse pressures, of which agenda-setting by the media is only one. Nonetheless, it does seem that the media may have a role to play in terms of actually setting the parameters for policy debates, and may play at least a small part in framing policy discussions. Golding and Middleton, for instance, claim that the mass media are important for shaping the political climate:

> so that ultimately legislation and the overall allocation of resources are influenced by mass mediated versions of priorities and necessities (and) they influence the cultural context . . . by setting the tone for public discussion and providing the imagery and rhetoric . . . [for] administrators. (1979: 19)

In light of the potential of the mass media for influencing social policy debates on the part of both the public and policy-makers, some concern has been raised about their role and content in the UK and elsewhere. How can we ensure that the mass media are free to deal with whatever issues they wish, while at the same time ensuring that they behave responsibly? These issues have come to the fore in recent debates concerning the freedom and regulation of the mass media, particularly in the context of the press.

REGULATION OF THE PRESS?

The freedom of the press is often presented as a central feature of democracy. Indeed, it is often argued that censorship and other restrictions on the press are the hallmark of totalitarian and suppressive regimes. In fact, this is a somewhat simplistic notion and censorship can be both subtle and insidious. In the UK, for instance, government interference with the media has regularly taken a number of subtle forms, such as restricting access to information and the scene of events and making accurate reporting more difficult, as well as more explicit legal intervention to prevent publication.

The debate about media control and regulation, however, also rests heavily upon the media themselves. Those who gather, report, edit, and disseminate the news and views have a very large responsibility to report events and views in an accurate and objective manner. However, the growing competition and dramatic requirements of the modern mass media are often seen to be encouraging irresponsible practice—a debate which came most poignantly to the fore with the death of the Princess of Wales in 1997 and the question of privacy and press intrusion. This case and a variety of other examples of press excesses have led to repeated calls in the UK for greater state intervention in the press. There is certainly no doubt that the popular press in particular is often guilty of gross errors of taste, in terms both of the kind of news that it provides and of the methods used to obtain it. Soothill and Walby (1991), for example, show how sex crimes have been exploited as a form of titillation by the press, in their efforts to increase circulation. In an attempt to address some of the worst excesses of the tabloid press, the UK has a system of self-regulation for the press. The focus for self-regulation in the UK is the Press Complaints Commission, which deals with complaints about newspaper coverage and establishes a code of practice which UK newspapers are expected to meet (see Box 4.2)

While the success or otherwise of press self-regulation remains a contentious point, moves towards state regulation and control of the press have been fiercely opposed. Indeed, when giving evidence to a Commons committee investigating privacy and media intrusion in March 2003, both Piers Morgan (editor of the *Mirror*) and

Box 4.2 Press Complaints Commission Code of Practice

Newspaper editors and publishers are expected to ensure that the Code of Practice is observed, including the following clauses:

- Newspapers and periodicals must take care not to publish inaccurate, misleading or distorted material.
- Everyone is entitled to respect for his or her private and family life, home, health, and correspondence.
- The use of long-lens photography to take pictures of people in private places without their consent is unacceptable.
- Journalists and photographers must neither obtain nor seek to obtain information or pictures through intimidation, harassment, or persistent pursuit.
- Journalists must not obtain or publish material obtained by using clandestine listening devices or by intercepting private telephone conversations.
- Journalists must not generally obtain to seek to obtain information or pictures through misrepresentation or subterfuge.
- The press must avoid prejudicial or pejorative reference to a person's race, colour, religion, sex, or sexual orientation or to any physical or mental illness or disability.

There may be exceptions to some of these clauses, where they can be demonstrated to be in the 'public interest'. The 'public interest' includes:

- detecting or exposing crime or a serious misdemeanour;
- protecting public health and safety;
- preventing the public from being misled by some statement or action of an individual or organization.

For a full list of the Codes of Practice and more information on the work of the Press Complaints Commission, including a discussion of the virtues of self-regulation, go to their website: www.pcc.org.uk

Questions

- To what extent do you think the UK press have met the Code of Practice?
- How successful has self-regulation of the press been?

Rebekah Wade (editor of the *Sun*) argued forcefully that the PCC had dramatically improved standards in the press and that further regulation was not appropriate. Ultimately, of course, the law of the marketplace prevails. In other words, the public buy what the public want—and if they do not want to read or watch something, then they will not buy the newspapers or watch the television channels. There is certainly an element of truth to this claim, although it fails to acknowledge that the media may also be instrumental in determining public tastes. Nonetheless, there are some interesting examples of this—the mass boycott of the *Sun* newspaper in Liverpool, following its coverage of the 1989 Hillsborough disaster, is one such example. Similarly, advertisers can and do withhold their advertising for various reasons, hitting at the financial heart of the media.

Indeed, it can be argued that the true function of the mass media—the dissemination of information—has been distorted by the pressures of financial interests. The tabloid press in particular may often resort to sensationalist and superficial entertainment in a bid to boost their circulation figures. This relates to the important question of media ownership. There is no doubt that the presentation and interpretation of news may be subject to the personal predilections of the proprietors and the interests that they openly or otherwise represent, as the following cartoon graphically illustrates in the context of the 1987 general election.

Cartoon 4.2 Is there a case for more regulation and control of the press?

(*Sun*, *11 June 1987*).

The power and influence of Rupert Murdoch and his News International empire has long been the focus of scrutiny, given his ownership of a number of national newspapers in Britain including the *Sun* and the *Times* (see Williams 1996). Indeed, it is important not to underestimate the sheer size of the potential audience for this media. Even in the age of electronic and televisual news dissemination, the scale of newspaper circulation in the UK remains very high, as Table 4.1 illustrates.

In short, Britons purchase more than 10 million newspapers every day—more than any other Europeans. Yet the figures for the readership of these newspapers are even higher than their circulation. The *Sun*, for instance, is the nation's most popular weekday newspaper and has a daily readership of over 10 million people. With such a huge potential audience, the crude political bias of such newspapers and their proprietors certainly strengthens the case for greater regulation of press content and ownership.

Table 4.1 National newspaper circulation, February 2003

Dailies	
Sun	3,516,129
Mirror	2,042,092
Daily Record	515,173
Daily Star	842,960
Daily Mail	2,386,580
Daily Express	904,655
Daily Telegraph	912,252
Guardian	393,367
Times	635,196
Independent	185,719
Financial Times	427,722
Sundays	
News of the World	3,928,895
Sunday Mirror	1,691,863
People	1,142,294
Daily Star Sunday	464,333
Sunday Mail	630,733
Mail on Sunday	2,305,347
Sunday Express	883,962
Sunday Times	1,403,964
Sunday Telegraph	730,739
Observer	449,953
Independent on Sunday	186,681

Source: Audit Bureau of Circulations.

THE INTERNET

If newspapers are the traditional medium for publicly airing many social policy issues and debates, the Internet has provided a quite new and exciting arena. It is estimated that worldwide use of the Internet rose dramatically from approximately 3 million people in 1994 to 377 million by 2000, and it continues to rise at an astonishing rate (Gardner and Oswald 2001). The dramatic growth in websites, and the fact that more and more of us are online, offers a quite different forum for discussing social issues and for sharing information and experience.

Information, and our access to it, is experiencing a profound revolution which seems set to alter many aspects of our lives in fundamental ways. Yet these developments are also poised to present difficult conundrums for policy-makers and social policy. It is perhaps ironic that the contents of this chapter are destined for a printed book, when increasingly information and data, and in turn political and academic debate about social issues, is taking place not through the medium of the printed word but electronically, through the medium of the Internet and the World Wide Web.

The development of the Internet evidently has many implications. It is certainly an excellent illustration of globalization, and some of the dilemmas that this may imply. A global village of information already exists, and is growing in size and importance at

Box 4.3 Internet use in Great Britain

- By September 2002, the proportion of households in the UK who could access the Internet from home had risen to 46 per cent, representing 11.4 million households, compared to just 14 per cent at the start of 1999.
- By October 2002, 62 per cent of adults in Great Britain had accessed the Internet at same time in their lives, representing 28.6 million adults.
- Among those adults using the Internet for private use, 76 per cent used it for e-mail, 71 per cent used it to find information about goods or services, and 36 per cent used it for finding education-related information.
- Men use the Internet more than women. 68 per cent of men who accessed the Internet for private use did so more than once a week, compared with 50 per cent of women.
- There is considerable geographical variation in household access to the Internet. In 2002, London had the highest proportion of households with access to the Internet, at 49 per cent, compared to just 32 per cent in the north-east of England.
- There has been a substantial rise in ownership of a personal computer. By 2001, two-fifths of all households owned a PC, compared to just 13 per cent in 1985.
- There is a significant class disparity in ownership of a PC. In 2001, 70 per cent of households whose head belonged to the managerial class owned a PC, compared to just 39 per cent for partly skilled households.

(Office for National Statistics)

a staggering rate. The opportunities to transmit and access huge quantities of data globally could have many consequences, some of which are of real importance for social policy. The manner in which Internet content is able to transcend national barriers with ease has raised interesting questions of regulation and control. Restricting access to some Internet content raises not simply technological difficulties but also profound questions of censorship which go to the heart of democratic society. This area is further clouded by ambiguity surrounding the ownership of material available in cyberspace. Yet these conundrums are not going to go away for policy-makers and social policy. On the contrary, it seems certain that they will continue to grow in importance and significance.

Of particular interest, however, are the social implications of the Internet and Information Communication Technologies (ICTs) more generally. There is no doubt that some groups and campaigners have employed the Internet to develop powerful networks of support, which transcend geographical obstacles. Those working with refugees and asylum-seekers, for instance, have actively used the Internet as a tool for mobilization and organization, while a myriad of online support groups have now firmly established themselves, offering valuable advice. In this sense, the Internet has the potential to transform the delivery of social policy, and the New Labour government have been active in promoting the expansion of online services.

However, the rise of the Internet is not without potential problems. Some commentators have been very vocal in expressing concern about the impact of the Internet upon social skills and interaction. In 2000, for example, the Archbishop of York warned that the Internet was creating a 'society without a soul'. He went on to say: 'The danger is in having all this wizardry in individual homes which people never leave and where there is, as a result, no social interaction . . . There is in the Internet the potential for destroying ourselves.' It is interesting, however, that this view is not supported by evidence, such as the British Social Attitudes Survey:

> Contrary to what many believe, internet users are much more likely to take part in social activity and be good citizens . . . The image of the world-wide web user as an anti-social loner is simply wrong: internet use and 'social capital' seem to be complimentary. (Gardner and Oswald 2001: 168)

A more compelling social policy concern, however, has been the long-standing anxiety that the information revolution may serve simply to compound and exaggerate the inequalities that already pervade society and which are discussed elsewhere in this book. We have seen that there are significant socioeconomic differences in terms of access to computers and the Internet and the long-term educational implications of this remain to manifest themselves fully. But there is growing concern that access to information is likely to be highly inequitable, in turn reflecting and compounding existing inequity in educational performance, already marked as it is by stark divisions of class and income. This point has not been lost on the British government, which has made interesting comments about the 'digital divide' in the UK. In launching the 'Computers for All' initiative in March 1999, Chancellor Gordon Brown described mastering IT as one of the 'newest and most decisive economic challenges of the twenty-first century'. He went on to say: 'Inequality in computer learning today will mean inequality in earning power tomorrow.' At the same time David Blunkett, then Education Secretary, said that it was 'vital that we prevent a generation of children emerging as the information-poor'.

Despite the rhetoric, however, it remains to be seen how successfully the UK government will be able to navigate these problems and bridge the gap between the 'information-rich and the information-poor' and, in turn, avoid compounding existing patterns of social exclusion. Some commentators, such as Selwyn (2002), are far from optimistic.

The inequalities and inequities of Internet access are interesting, not least because they have clear parallels with the inequalities that have long pervaded cultural participation in British society and which in turn raise important questions about cultural need. It is to the arts and culture—and the vexed issues that they raise for social policy—that the next section turns.

SOCIAL POLICY AND THE ARTS

The **arts** and **culture** pervade almost every aspect of social life. Whatever our appreciation of the arts, all of us are enveloped by the ubiquitous culture—popular and otherwise—that surrounds us. In simple terms, the arts and culture are a fundamental and highly pervasive feature of society. Yet this is an area which has been woefully neglected by social policy, with just a few notable exceptions (e.g. Cahill 1994). This is all the more surprising when one considers that there are a number of ways in which issues surrounding the arts and culture closely reflect wider social policy debates and present policy-makers with a variety of conundrums. The very real inequity in people's participation and enjoyment of the arts and culture has many implications for society, and closely reflects some of the wider debates about inequality. Just as questions of inequality in other areas of social provision lead to questions of social need, so the clear inequity in participation in the arts and culture raises important questions about **cultural need**. How important are the arts and culture, and participation in them, for creating a balanced and healthy society? Might they conceivably be a part of citizenship? In which case, what should be the role of the state in providing for cultural enrichment? Should it subsidize the arts? Yet how does one decide how much the arts and culture should get in relation to other areas of social need? Moreover, what are the most appropriate ways to raise and distribute money and financial support for the arts? These are important policy questions which have long challenged policy-makers and have recently been closely examined in the UK as the **National Lottery** has been established. Let us begin by looking at participation in the arts and culture, and the vexed question of cultural need.

CULTURAL NEED

Participation in the arts and culture is often profoundly inequitable. Divisions of class, age, gender, and ethnicity can all have a dramatic impact upon participation in various cultural endeavours. Even a cursory examination of Table 4.2 reveals profound differences in the level of participation in selected leisure activities.

Table 4.2 Attendance at selected events, by socio-economic group, Great Britain, 2000–2001 (%)

	Managerial/ professional	Other non-manual	Skilled manual	Semi-skilled manual	Unskilled manual
Sporting events	24	20	18	15	7
Plays	29	17	8	6	5
Opera	9	3	2	1	1
Ballet	7	3	1	1	1
Contemporary dance	4	2	1	1	1
Classical music	17	8	4	2	2
Concerts	19	17	13	9	5
Art galleries/exhibitions	30	18	8	6	7

Source: Office for National Statistics.

It is evident from this table that there are considerable class disparities in the level of participation for a range of cultural and leisure pursuits. The question is why? Of course, these disparities may simply be a consequence of choice. However, in recent years, access to the arts and culture has increasingly been left to the vagaries of the market. Consequently, many in the arts world have argued that those in financial poverty have effectively been condemned to a cultural poverty—unable to afford even to enjoy their own heritage, for instance, excluded from museums by the gradual introduction of entry charges. The question arises, therefore, as to whether or not the arts and culture should be included in the wider debates about social need. In short, what should be the role of the state in the context of the arts, culture, and leisure? Should the state invest resources to ensure that no one is financially excluded from the benefits of cultural participation? These are complex debates, which raise a number of different issues. Let us consider some of these questions.

ARGUMENTS AGAINST STATE SUPPORT

The arts account for a tiny proportion of state expenditure. Yet state support for the arts is a highly contentious issue, which has attracted vociferous comment from a variety of sources. The launch of the National Lottery in 1994, and the expressed commitment to using the proceeds to subsidize and support areas, like the arts, otherwise receiving scant state assistance, has ensured that the issue of state support for the arts has remained firmly on the popular agenda. But this has been a recurring issue for some time. The widespread closure of many provincial theatres and cinemas, and restricted opening hours imposed on many libraries, have all precipitated a wide-ranging debate about whether or not local authorities have an obligation to provide cultural amenities, such as cinemas or libraries, or whether their provision must rest wholly in the hands of the free market.

In principle, and with largely unlimited funds, the arts may indeed have a strong claim upon government resources. However, government funds are limited, restrictively so in many areas of social policy, and so it may be difficult to justify government financial support for the arts when other areas of need present themselves. Nevertheless, the fact that more money should be spent by the state on concrete social need, such as education or housing, does not—or at least should not—consequently imply that less should be spent on the arts and on meeting cultural need.

Of course, one can argue that state support is simply not necessary for the artistic and cultural enrichment of society. Namely, good art and culture will prosper regardless of whether or not the state is offering support. This is a very interesting point, not least because it introduces some of the many difficulties relating to measuring and quantifying the impact and effectiveness of the money which is spent on the arts and cultural activities. In short, how does one quantify or measure the impact of public money spent on the arts? While he was Secretary of State for National Heritage, Peter Brooke declared that a good test of the state's financial involvement in the arts was the extent to which the arts 'flourish'. Yet just what does this mean? Does it refer to the attainment of critical acclaim? Does it mean commercial recognition and success? Does it concern an expansion in the number of artistic and cultural endeavours? Does it refer to a broadening of the types of artistic and cultural endeavour? In the context of museums, for example, the efficient use of funds is frequently assessed simply in terms of the number of visitors that a particular museum attracts. Yet such a measure can be highly unsatisfactory in terms of assessing the effectiveness of subsidies and the quality of the experience that they provide.

Some have actually gone so far as to suggest that state support may actually be to the detriment of the arts and culture. On the one hand, government funding may mean that cultural organizations and institutions become complacent, immune to market and commercial pressure, and may subsequently err towards financial irresponsibility. Whilst this has often been a dominant theme in government attitudes towards the arts, the fiscal prudence which has now come to permeate the arts world means that notions of financial complacency and irresponsibility are somewhat misguided.

A more potent suggestion is that art subsidies can be detrimental by effectively stifling innovation. The way in which financial support is often directed at well-established bodies and organizations is such that, conceivably, artistic projects may come to lack originality and become somewhat staid, because established projects are seen to be a 'safe bet' for support. The result is that the dynamism and innovation on which art so clearly rests can become somewhat stifled—a point which has often been raised concerning the **Arts Council of England** and similar bodies abroad. This is a difficult point. Namely, because the finance available for the arts is so restricted, decisions—very difficult and vexed decisions—have to be made about which art is worthy of support and which art is not, such that good art is financed and encouraged while poor art is not.

Yet these issues rest heavily upon questions of artistic quality and how one assesses it, which are notoriously subjective and to which there are no agreed answers. However, these concerns are not necessarily questioning the appropriateness of art subsidy, simply questioning the way in which the financial cake is divided and the criteria by which it is divided.

Perhaps the most vociferous attack on art subsidies of late—and one which has especially been highlighted by the advent of the National Lottery—is their inequity. Why should the many fund and subsidize the entertainment of the few? As Anthony Everitt said about the Royal Opera House's annual grant of some £20 million: 'Never in the history of British culture has so much been given by so many for so few' (1994). By the logic of supply and demand, if audience demand for the arts is insufficient to cover the costs of supplying opera or ballet through admission charges, why should society and taxpayers as a whole subsidize them? After all, art subsidies involve the application of resources which are supplied involuntarily by all the public in the form of taxes, and yet these resources are inevitably distributed inequitably.

Of course, this inequity may be more perceived than real—and the media have undoubtedly played an important role, particularly in the context of the National Lottery, in shaping public perception of injustice. Nonetheless, there is still good evidence to suggest that this concern with the inequity of state support for the arts has some foundation. The influential work of Julian Le Grand, for instance, focused on the inequitous workings of the welfare state and claimed that, in the UK, the top 20 per cent of households benefit from some 40 per cent of public expenditure on the arts, while in contrast the bottom 25 per cent benefit from just 4 per cent (1982: 157–8). These calculations are unsurprising—opera and ballet, for instance, are regular recipients of very considerable support from the Arts Council and yet, as we have already seen, the audiences for these activities are disproportionately distributed between different social classes.

These are potent arguments, although it is important to ensure that meeting cultural need is not viewed any differently from meeting other social need. After all, it is now widely acknowledged and accepted that the welfare state itself is permeated by inequity. Indeed, one can also argue that precisely because access to the arts and culture is so inequitable, this is even more justification for state intervention. Nonetheless, the perceived inequity in state support for the arts—whether real or not—is important because of the impact that it has upon public perception and attitudes to which, in theory at least, politicians and policy-makers are ultimately subservient.

It is very interesting that some survey evidence, such as the data in Table 4.3 from the British Social Attitudes Survey, appears to suggest that state support for the arts is generally not perceived as a legitimate use of public money by the public. In short, for every person who wants more money spent on the arts, more than four people want less spent. Additionally, there is a very interesting class influence upon this figure—amongst the **salariat**, one in seven want more public money spent on the arts and culture, which compares to just one in twenty amongst the working class. Clearly, there may be a variety of reasons for this pattern of support. One explanation rests with the pattern of participation in the arts and culture. In short, the higher social classes are generally more

Table 4.3 Attitudes to government spending

Item of spending	% wanting government to spend		
	More	Same as now	Less
Health	87	9	1
Education	79	16	1
Unemployment benefits	48	39	8
Culture and the arts	10	38	44

Source: Jowell et al. (1994).

likely to participate in the arts and high culture and are therefore more likely both to appreciate the virtue of investing more money in the arts and, of course, to benefit directly from any increase in spending. We have seen elsewhere that public attitudes to welfare closely reflect self-interest. Other factors may also play a role here, not least the fact that the media often present state support for the arts and culture as necessarily inequitable, when this may not necessarily be the case.

To reiterate, in recent years there has been a marked shift in policy towards the arts on the part of government in the UK—a move away from state subsidies and towards market provision. In other words, people are expected to pay the market price for their enjoyment of the arts. The arts have therefore become increasingly dependent upon a simplistic 'market test'—in a crude supply-and-demand scenario, if the public are not prepared to pay the market price to see or enjoy something, then the state cannot be expected to support it. This is a policy approach which has applied the free-market ideology of the New Right to the arts, an arena in which crude notions of financial supply and demand are simply inappropriate. In response, a number of pertinent arguments have been presented to justify state expenditure on culture.

ARGUMENTS FOR STATE SUPPORT

The widening of opportunity, allowing all to appreciate the arts and culture, irrespective of their financial power, lies at the heart of arguments in favour of state subsidy. Indeed, this is why the Victorians were such avid supporters of cultural endeavours like museums, and it is why the widespread introduction of museum charges was met with such disdain throughout the profession. One of the core functions of the Arts Council of England, for example, is to increase the accessibility of the arts to the public and yet it is difficult to see how this role can be compatible with a crude market test. It may be true that opera or ballet only have a limited audience, but with average ticket prices of £30 or more, this may be more indicative of the public's economic weakness than a lack of interest. Indeed, even if there is less apparent demand for opera or ballet amongst some of the public, this may simply reflect the fact that much of the population have never had the opportunity to appreciate opera or ballet. In this sense, subsidies are necessary in order to nurture the audiences of tomorrow. This relates to the next point.

The opportunity to enjoy and appreciate the arts and culture are crucial for the development of a healthy and balanced society, which is far from amenable to the notion of a crude market test. This is even more pronounced if one is considering the nebulous and ultimately very broad notion of 'cultural enrichment'. However, there is no doubt that Britain has considerable international prestige courtesy of its performing arts—indeed, this is a point that respective governments are often very fond of reiterating—and yet it is difficult to see how this can possibly be compatible with a crude market test.

There is a wide range of potent arguments to be made in favour of public arts subsidy, and there are also powerful arguments by precedent—the Victorians were avid funders of leisure and cultural facilities, believing as they did in the central notion of self-education and the role of cultural fulfilment in pulling together a highly polarized society. Similarly, it is important to recognize that cultural need is not necessarily unrelated to other forms of need which are often unquestionably the role of the state. The arts and culture have a real role to play in the provision of employment opportunities. Similarly, the advent of the National Curriculum has seen an enhanced acknowledgement of the important educative role of museums. In a variety of respects, therefore, state support for the arts closely impinges upon areas of social need which are more widely acknowledged as appropriate recipients of state intervention, such as employment and education.

It is true that there are a number of real problems and difficulties with the notion of cultural need, not least the fact that cultural need is such a nebulous notion that it can be difficult to assess or quantify the impact of state expenditure upon the arts. Nevertheless, the meeting of other areas of need are also beset with problems in terms of quantifying the impact of state intervention. Indeed, in the same way as other types of social need form an important component of citizenship, so one can argue that cultural need—which can take many different forms—should also be a component of citizenship. Certainly, T. H. Marshall, in his exposition of citizenship, implied that full citizenship should include the right to culture:

> By the social element I mean the whole range from the right to a modicum of economic welfare and security to the right to share to the full in the social heritage and to live the life of a civilised being according to the standards prevailing in society. (1963: 74)

The problem, however, is that since the 1970s access to the arts and culture, and indeed access to many areas of social life, has been generally determined not by citizenship but by consumerism and the workings of the market. The result has been a predictable one, as economically weak individuals have experienced varying degrees of exclusion from many areas of social life, especially the arts and culture, where access has been left largely to the vagaries of the market. The result has been effectively to compound the existing inequalities in participation in the arts. One can claim, therefore, that access to culture is an important, even fundamental, component of a citizen's rights. The exclusion and inequalities in access which result from this move towards the operation of the market, and the emphasis on individual consumption, arguably necessitate state support and intervention.

The New Labour government has certainly shown itself to be more willing to engage with enhanced state involvement in the arts and culture, in many ways. From its encouragement of the British film industry through favourable tax regimes, to ensuring free entry to national museums and galleries from December 2001, the arts world has broadly welcomed the arrival of a new government, albeit with some reservations. However, the area in which the Labour opposition most successfully courted public opinion in relation to the arts before the 1997 general election was in the context of the National Lottery.

THE NATIONAL LOTTERY

To some extent, the advent of the National Lottery was widely seen as the answer to some of these dilemmas concerning state funding of the arts and culture. Run by Camelot, the National Lottery was established in the UK in November 1994. Since then

Box 4.4 What happens to money spent on a National Lottery ticket?

Every pound spent on the National Lottery is shared out in the following way:

- prizewinners: 50 pence
- National Lottery Distribution Fund (for good causes): 28 pence
- the Treasury, through Lottery Duty: 12 pence
- retailers: 5 pence
- Camelot operating costs: 3 pence
- Camelot Corporation and Business Taxes: 1 penny
- Camelot profit: 1 penny

Income to the National Lottery Distribution Fund for good causes is divided in the following way:

- arts: 16.66 per cent
- sport: 16.66 per cent
- heritage: 16.66 per cent
- charities: 16.66 per cent
- health, education, and the environment: 33.33 per cent

Before August 2001, 20 per cent of funds went to projects to mark the millennium—including the Millennium Dome—and 13.33 per cent to education, health, and environment projects.

When one considers that UK lottery sales had reached almost £36 billion from inception to the start of 2002, one can appreciate just how much revenue has been raised by the National Lottery.

it has become firmly established in the nation's psyche. Indeed, the initial scale of uptake was quite phenomenal.

In the first thirteen months of its operation until the end of 1995, for instance, Lottery sales totalled some £5.1 billion—approximately 3 per cent of all retail spending. Clearly, this is a very significant economic development, diverting discretionary consumer spending away from other retail sectors. In short, the National Lottery was, initially at least, a huge success, beyond the expectations of both its promoters and detractors. It has also generated huge revenue for the government in terms of lottery duty—approximately £3.83 billion over the seven year licence period—along with almost £10 billion for good causes. Indeed, by sales, the National Lottery in the UK is the second largest of 192 international lotteries.

In many respects, therefore, the Lottery has been a profound success. Many in the arts world were initially hopeful that Lottery funds would help to revitalize the arts and culture in this country, and begin to resolve the notable inequity in cultural participation. In reality, however, the National Lottery ran into a variety of difficulties, particularly early on.

PROBLEMS WITH THE NATIONAL LOTTERY

The number of grants made by bodies distributing cash to the 'good causes' was far lower than originally expected, although the average size of the grants given was considerably larger than anticipated. The original promise was that literally thousands of grants would be made, reaching every corner of the country. Yet this was simply not the case. The net result was that smaller organizations seeking Lottery money were largely excluded. In terms of grants given to the arts in England, projects requesting more than a million pounds received more than 80 per cent of the total cash distributed. Just 1 per cent went in grants of less than £30,000 (Fitzherbert et al. 1996).

There was also a very real concern about the geographical distribution of grants. At the inception of the Lottery, there were fears that arts and heritage grants would be heavily concentrated in London and the south-east. This concern appears to have been justified. London, for instance, certainly received a considerably higher share of arts, heritage, and sport money. Per head of population in the first year of operation, London got an average of £26.07 from these sources, compared to the East Midlands—which is already experiencing fewer resources—which received £3.21 (Fitzherbert et al. 1996).

From the inception of the National Lottery, concern was also voiced about its impact upon charitable giving, so important in many areas of social need. To some extent, these concerns were borne out by the initial evidence. The National Council of Voluntary Organizations, for instance, found that individual donations to charities dropped by £344 million in 1995. Whilst the National Lottery Charities Board made grants of £240 million, the net loss to charities was nonetheless some £104 million (Fitzherbert et al. 1996). However, the evidence on the precise impact of the Lottery upon charities remains unclear.

Table 4.4 Percentage of UK households participating in the National Lottery, by social class of head of household

	Saturday draw		Wednesday draw	
	1995	1997	1998	1998
Professional	63	54	43	23
Managerial and technical	70	62	58	36
Skilled non-manual	82	67	58	38
Skilled manual	89	80	75	50
Partly skilled	75	69	66	43
Unskilled	79	68	64	45
Retired and unoccupied	62	52	55	33
All households	72	62	61	38

Source: Office of National Statistics.

In short, the National Lottery was welcomed initially as a development which had the power and potential to redress the real inequity in people's enjoyment and participation in the arts, culture, and their own heritage. Yet this potential was not immediately realized. This inequity is even more difficult to accept when one considers that, in many respects, it is the lowest income groups who invest most in the Lottery and yet receive the fewest benefits. The Family Expenditure Survey has shown, for instance, that in the first three months of 1995, amongst purchasers of Lottery tickets, the families from the very poorest 10 per cent of the population spent just under £2 per week, although this represented some 30 per cent of their leisure spending. In contrast, whilst the families from the richest 10 per cent spent about £4 per week, this represented just 4 per cent of this group's leisure spending. Moreover, the lower socioeconomic groups, through volume of numbers, purchase more Lottery tickets and so in turn contribute most to the money available for good causes (see Table 4.4). Yet it is felt that the National Lottery money is being largely distributed to artistic endeavours more commonly frequented by higher social groups.

CREATION OF SOCIAL PROBLEMS

It is still very difficult to know whether or not the National Lottery has created or exacerbated social problems, such as gambling. Certainly, the experience of national lotteries elsewhere, such as the US and Canada, suggest that problem gambling can increase, although studies conducted for Camelot have suggested that fewer than 1 per cent of those who play the National Lottery were 'problem gamblers'. However, despite initial

Cartoon 4.3 How has the National Lottery contributed to social problems?

© Austin, *The Guardian*, 1996

government assurances to the contrary, the National Lottery has signalled a widespread dismantling of restrictions on other forms of gambling and has certainly helped to make gambling more socially acceptable. In October 2001, for instance, betting tax was abolished and in March 2002 UK gambling laws were relaxed. Indeed, as Table 4.5 illustrates, the proportion of the population who participate in gambling of one form or another is striking.

To summarize, the National Lottery has had a profound impact upon many areas of social and economic life. Yet whilst it was initially hailed as the shot in the arm that the arts needed, it has arguably failed to deliver on its potential. If anything, the workings of the Lottery appear to have made existing inequity in participation in the arts—both social and geographical—more pronounced, at least initially. More recently, the fact that Lottery sales fell by 5 per cent in 2002—despite a £72 million relaunch and renaming—has raised concerns about the future of income for the good causes. The perceived inequity in benefits from the Lottery has certainly attracted much debate, and has raised wider questions about the role of public finance in terms of cultural life. It is certainly interesting that in 1994, at the inception of the National Lottery, some 12 per cent of the populace thought that there should be more spending on culture and the arts.

Table 4.5 Percentage participation in gambling activities, UK, by age, 1999

	16–24	25–34	35–44	45–54	55–64	65–74	75 and over	All
National Lottery	52	71	72	72	69	61	45	65
Scratchcards	36	32	23	17	16	11	6	22
Fruit machines	32	22	15	8	6	3	1	14
Horse races	12	19	15	14	11	9	5	13
Private bets	21	18	11	10	6	5	3	11
Football pools	4	9	8	11	13	10	6	9
Another lottery	8	9	8	9	9	8	6	8
Bingo	7	7	7	6	7	9	10	7
Dog races	6	7	4	4	2	1	1	4
Other betting with a Bookmaker	5	5	3	2	2	1	–	3
Table games in a casino	4	5	3	2	1	–	–	3
Any gambling	66	78	77	78	74	66	52	72

Source: Office for National Statistics.

Yet within just two years, this figure had halved to only 6 per cent. In the sense that the Lottery has provoked debate about the role of public financial support for the arts and culture, it has been very important indeed.

CONCLUSION

This chapter has sought to achieve a number of things. Most importantly, it has attempted to illustrate the importance of the mass media, arts, and culture for social policy. It is a field which lies at the very heart of society, its cohesiveness, and its problems. Some of the themes raised in this field mirror fundamental debates in social policy. The whole question of cultural need and the inequity in cultural participation raises similar dilemmas to those surrounding social need. The long-standing debate about the importance of cultural need and the appropriateness of state intervention for meeting such need—a debate which has come to some prominence with the National Lottery—is finally being acknowledged by the Labour government. Yet social policy continues to see the arts and culture as largely irrelevant. This is even more surprising when one considers that many social policy debates, and their political manifestations, take place in an increasingly media-conscious and media-dominated environment. The impact of the media upon social policy debates should be viewed with much more urgency and importance by the social policy community than it currently is. Many of these issues, and their social implications, are set to become increasingly important. It is time for social policy to broaden its traditional focus, and to view these concerns with the seriousness that they deserve.

REFERENCES

Beresford, P. (1979), 'The public presentation of vagrancy'. In T. Cook (ed.), *Vagrancy: Some New Perspectives*. London: Academic Press.

Broadbent, L. (1993), 'Backyard on the front page: the case of Nicaragua'. In J. Eldridge (ed.), *Getting the Message: News, Truth and Power*. London: Routledge.

Cahill, M. (1994), *The New Social Policy*. Oxford: Blackwell.

Cohen, S. (1972), *Folk Devils and Moral Panics: The Creation of the Mods and Rockers*. London: MacGibbon & Kee.

Curran, J., and Seaton, J. (1991), *Power without Responsibility: The Press and Broadcasting in Britain*, 4th edn. London: Routledge.

Everitt, A. (1994), 'Lose the life support?', *Guardian*, 23 May.

Fitzherbert, L., Giussani, C., and Hunt, H. (eds.) (1996), *The National Lottery Yearbook*. London: Directory of Social Change.

Franklin, B. (ed.) (1999), *Social Policy, the Media and Misrepresentation*. London: Routledge.

Gardner, J., and Oswald, A. (2001), 'Internet use: the digital divide'. In A. Park et al. (eds.), *British Social Attitudes: The 18th Report*. London: Sage.

Golding, P., and Middleton, S. (1979), 'Making claims: news media and the welfare state', *Media, Culture and Society* 1: 5–21.

—— —— (1982), *Images of Welfare: Press and Public Attitudes to Poverty*. Oxford: Robertson.

Hall, S., Critcher, C., Jefferson, T., Clarke, J., and Roberts, B. (1979), *Policing the Crisis*. London: Macmillan.

Hutson, S., and Liddiard, M. (1994), *Youth Homelessness: The Construction of a Social Issue*. London: Macmillan.

Jowell, R., Curtice, J., Brook, L., and Ahrendt, D. (eds.) (1994), *British Social Attitudes: The 11th Report*. Aldershot: Dartmouth.

Kemp, P. (1997), 'The characteristics of single homeless people in England'. In R. Burrows, N. Pleace, and D. Quilgars (eds.), *Homelessness and Social Policy*. London: Routledge.

Le Grand, J. (1982), *The Strategy of Equality: Redistribution and the Social Services*. London: Allen & Unwin.

Liddiard, M. (1998), 'Homelessness: the media, public attitudes and policy-making'. In S. Hutson and D. Clapham (eds.), *Homelessness: Public Policies and Private Troubles*. London: Cassell.

—— and Hutson, S. (1998), 'Youth homelessness, the press and public attitudes', *Youth and Policy* 59: 57–69.

Marshall, T. H. (1963), 'Citizenship and social class'. In *Sociology at the Crossroads*. London: Heinemann.

Miller, D. (1994), *Don't Mention the War: Northern Ireland, Propaganda and the Media*. London: Pluto Press.

Negrine, R. (1994), *Politics and the Mass Media in Britain*, 2nd edn. London: Routledge.

ONS (Office for National Statistics) (2003), *Social Trends No. 33*. London: Stationery office.

Sawers, D. (1993), *Should the Taxpayer Support the Arts?* London: Institute of Economic Affairs.

Selwyn, N. (2002), ' "E-stablishing" an inclusive society? Technology, social exclusion and UK government policy making', *Journal of Social Policy* 31(1): 1–20.

Smith, A. (1998), 'Britons buy more papers than other Europeans but doubt contents', *Guardian*, 29 Jan.

Soothill, K., and Walby, S. (1991), *Sex Crime in the News*. London: Routledge.

Williams, G. (1996), *Britain's Media: How They are Related—Media Ownership and Democracy*, 2nd edn. London: Campaign for Press and Broadcasting Freedom.

FURTHER READING

M. Cahill, *The New Social Policy* (Oxford: Blackwell, 1994). A very influential book and one of the few attempts to broaden the traditional focus of social policy towards new areas such as communicating, viewing, travelling, shopping, and recreation. Cahill argues that the development of an increasingly consumerist society has led to the emergence of profound inequalities in these areas, which warrant much more attention from the social policy community than they generally receive.

J. Curran and J. Seaton, *Power without Responsibility: The Press and Broadcasting in Britain*, 4th edn. (London: Routledge, 1991). An excellent overview of the debates surrounding media freedom and regulation in the UK. For those interested in the freedom of the press, media ownership, or the development of satellite television, this is a good starting point.

J. Eldridge (ed.), *Getting the Message: News, Truth and Power* (London: Routledge, 1993). A collection of some of the more recent research by the Glasgow University Media Group. A variety of rich empirical articles on a diverse array of topics illustrate the complexities of the transmission and reception of ideological messages through the mass media.

B. Franklin (ed.), *Social Policy, the Media and Misrepresentation* (London: Routledge, 1999). An overdue and timely book which draws together a range of articles exploring the media treatment of social policy issues and some of the implications of this. It is an excellent source of examples and illustrations of social policy media coverage, as well as offering some very thought-provoking commentary.

P. Golding and S. Middleton, *Images of Welfare: Press and Public Attitudes to Poverty* (Oxford: Robertson, 1982). One of the few attempts in social policy to unpack the influence of media accounts upon welfare debates and public perception of social problems, like poverty. Somewhat dated in places, but the authors still make some astute points of considerable contemporary relevance.

R. Negrine, *Politics and the Mass Media in Britain*, 2nd edn. (London: Routledge, 1994). A comprehensive overview of the many arguments and debates surrounding the mass media in Britain. Negrine's examination of the relationship between media coverage, public opinion and policy-making is an excellent introduction to the topic, presenting a wealth of ideas and evidence.

Office for National Statistics, *Social Trends: The 33rd Report* (London: HMSO, 2003). An invaluable sourcebook of statistical data for social policy students and academics alike. It draws together a wealth of information on the arts, culture, and leisure from a number of sources, such as the Family Expenditure Survey, the General Household Survey, and the British Social Attitudes Survey, which it then presents in a highly accessible manner.

USEFUL WEBSITES

There are a wide range of relevant websites on these issues, although some of the most useful include:

www.ukonline.gov.uk The site that allows you to search for and read a wide variety of government reports and publications on a diverse array of issues and topics, such as government strategies on the Internet, the National Lottery, and the arts.

www.statistics.gov.uk Site of the Office for National Statistics. A rich source of official statistics and data, including online access to the latest social trends.

www.pcc.org.uk Site of the Press Complaints Commission, offering details about their work and their full Code of Practice. It also offers some commentary about the virtues of self-regulation of the press.

www.natlotcomm.gov.uk Site of the National Lottery Commission, offering a variety of information and news about the National Lottery.

www.diversity-online.org Site run by the International Media Working Group Against Racism and Xenophobia. It offers a rich source of media stories and articles on issues such as immigrants, asylum-seekers, and refugees. A good source of examples of questionable media and press coverage.

GLOSSARY

arts The diverse body of creative endeavours concerned not simply with the visual arts, but also with music, theatre, cinema, and literature.

Arts Council of England The major state-funded arts organization in England, supporting music, drama, and the visual arts with government funds, and which is responsible to the Secretary of State for Culture, Media, and Sport. In 1994 the Scottish and Welsh Arts Councils became autonomous, directly accountable to their respective Secretaries of State.

censorship The suppression by authority of material deemed to be immoral, heretical, subversive, libellous, damaging to state security, or otherwise offensive. Censorship is not always the prerogative of government—the media can and do exercise a degree of self-censorship, in the film industry, for instance.

cultural need Need defined as being unable to participate fully in the cultural life of society. The growing commercialization of culture and leisure has exacerbated the exclusion of economically weak individuals from even the most basic cultural and leisure opportunities.

culture A very broad term, which literally means the way of life of a particular society or group of people. The term is often used more specifically to refer to art, music, and literature.

Internet A global system of electronic networks or a World Wide Web, through which global sites and addresses—and in turn the information they contain—can be easily accessed via a computer and a modem. The Internet is not owned or controlled by anyone.

mass media The techniques and institutions through which information and communication is broadcast to a large, heterogeneous and geographically dispersed audience. In the twentieth century, the mass media include books, newspapers, radio, cinema, television, and the Internet.

National Lottery A national game of chance in which tickets sold may win a substantial prize. Established in 1994, the main National Lottery game in the UK involves trying to guess correctly the numbers of six balls randomly drawn from a choice of forty-nine—at odds of 14 million to one!

philanthropy Practical benevolence, often in the form of funding.

salariat The salaried class.

5

Social Need and Patterns of Inequality and Difference

Mark Liddiard

CONTENTS

INTRODUCTION: A CONTESTABLE CONCEPT AT THE HEART OF SOCIAL POLICY

The concept of 'social need' lies at the heart of social policy. Arguably, the recognition and satisfaction of need distinguishes the welfare function of the state from its other roles and activities. Inseparably linked to the debates about the nature, effectiveness, and cost of the welfare state has been the issue of how far it meets which needs. Yet the concept of 'need' poses difficult conceptual and normative questions. How do we decide which are valid needs and which are not? If some needs are more or less legitimate than others, how do we decide which needs are a priority, and which are not? Are there any needs which are so basic and fundamental that ensuring they are met may be part of an individual's rights and an obligation of the state? Even if one can establish a measure of basic needs, as some authors claim, should the meeting of these be the responsibility of the government, or rather the responsibility of others, such as the family and charity?

These questions are fundamental to social policy, and the subject has long acknowledged the significance of need as a rationing device, whereby resources of different kinds are distributed according to various criteria of entitlement. Different groups and individuals have radically different ideas about what should be defined as 'need' and what should not. Often, the concept of need has seemed to be highly subjective and beyond objective agreement. These dilemmas have come to the fore in a number of areas, most publicly in the context of health care, where medical professionals have been in the unenviable position of having to decide upon the validity of some people's health needs over others.

The definition of social need is thus crucial to social policy, and the lack of consensus about which needs should take priority lies at the conceptual heart of welfare. Whilst it may be possible to justify state involvement in the provision of welfare in terms of meeting social need, if the needs which state welfare and ultimately state resources are supposed to be meeting are vague and ill defined, so the arguments in favour of state welfare are weakened. Yet clarifying the nature of social need is more than simply a theoretical debate—it has real practical significance. Access to resources and the distribution of these resources are often heavily dependent upon notions of need.

DEFINING NEED

A key characteristic of 'need' is the fact that it can be defined and measured from a variety of perspectives. Jonathan Bradshaw (1972) made this diversity the basis of his taxonomy of social need, in which he outlines four types of need:

- Normative need: how an expert or professional may define need in the context of a set of professional or expert standards.

  Welfare professionals reach judgements about what may or may not be legitimate need. They are active in the processes which decide whether or not a need exists and, if it does, how this need may best be met within the confines of existing resources. The judgements of welfare professionals, and the bodies of knowledge and standards that they use, are clearly an important feature in defining need.

- Felt need: what a person or a group believe they 'need'.

  This conception relies upon the individual's own perception of need, and any discrepancy between their situation and what they believe it ought to be. However, this self-perception is likely to be subjective and may be better described as a 'want'. Felt need is necessarily affected by the knowledge and expectations of the individual, which may be unrealistic. Alternatively, researchers have shown that the poorest sections of society may be only marginally aware of their poverty and the extent of their need.

- Expressed need: a felt need that has become a demand.

  Academics have argued that social need can be closely associated with either an effective economic or an effective political demand. Yet it is important to acknowledge that just because people have the power to demand something, this does not necessarily imply that they need it. In this sense, it is important to distinguish between need and demand.

- Comparative need: need defined by comparing the differences in people's access to resources.

  This approach recognizes that need is a relative concept, and so any debate about need must take place in the context of a comparison between people. Need may be defined in terms of the average standards found within a community or society, or by comparing the resources available to some in contrast to others who are defined as similarly entitled. A comparative approach has, of course, been most widely employed in the context of debates about poverty.

Bradshaw's taxonomy is very helpful in setting out the range of ways in which need can be approached and understood. A number of authors have developed further these ideas in a number of ways, one of whom was Forder (1974), with his concept of **technical need**.

- Technical need: in simple terms, technical need arises when a new form of provision is invented, or existing provision is made much more effective. This in turn creates a need for a solution that previously did not exist. Once a new invention has occurred, it can then lead to forms of felt, expressed, normative, and comparative need. Advances in medical technology are the most common example of this, and one of the most pertinent illustrations is the development of Viagra, the male anti-impotence pill (Box 5.1).

The question remains, however, as to the degree to which it is possible to reach any consensus about need, and whether or not there are any features of need which can be identified as essentially incontestable. Many social theorists have sought to establish basic needs with which all would be likely to agree. The importance of trying to establish a list of basic needs should not be underestimated. If one can establish a concrete and agreed set of basic needs, which really should be met in a society, it may be much easier to add legitimacy to the very existence of welfare states, whose ultimate objective is to meet need.

Attempts to produce a list of human needs have taken a variety of different forms, and one of the first to construct such a list was Maslow (1954), who set out a hierarchy of five

Box 5.1 Viagra and the NHS

The successful development of Viagra for the treatment of male impotency, and the ensuing debate about its availability on the NHS, is an excellent illustration of **technical need** and the issues it raises for considering need more generally. The publicity surrounding Viagra has certainly generated a **felt need**. Interestingly, however, it has also led to much more **expressed need** by legitimizing a request that had previously been highly stigmatized. There has also been a strong element of **comparative need** in this debate—people may have access to it in some countries or areas and not in others. The government are certainly keen to avoid 'prescription by postcode', but whilst Viagra is currently not available on the NHS, it is nonetheless freely available to those able and willing to pay for a private consultancy. The debate here is also very much about **normative need**, and about who should be the arbiter of need: government, medical professionals or consumers?

Questions:

- Should Viagra be freely available on the NHS?
- Who should decide whether Viagra is available or not?

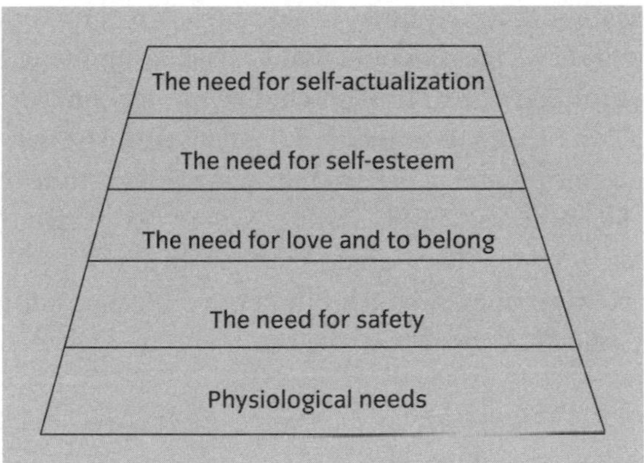

Figure 5.1 Maslow's (1954) hierarchy of basic needs

basic needs (see Fig. 5.1), and argued that once the most basic need for survival (physiological need) was met, so, in succession, further ones demand attention.

Whilst Maslow's basic human needs are of some theoretical interest, it is immediately apparent that they present real practical difficulties. Not only are they difficult to measure, but they will also vary from individual to individual. Given the fluidity of such needs, it would evidently be impossible to expect state action to ensure that every citizen had them met.

David Harvey (1973) sought to move this debate on by identifying nine categories, goods, and services that people require in order to meet the human needs Maslow had set out:

- food
- housing
- medical care
- education
- social and environmental services
- consumer goods
- recreational opportunities
- neighbourhood opportunities
- transport facilities

The real difficulty with such lists of need, however, comes when considering the relative importance of each of these categories. Clearly, not all forms of need carry equal significance and importance. According to Maslow, only the basic physiological needs are essential for sustaining life, and these must necessarily be met before higher needs. Yet how do we rank the remaining needs? The real problem here is that what we perceive and define as valid and legitimate needs may be little more than subjective judgements, relative to the society and time period in which they are being made. The implication is that, whilst real and important steps may be taken in addressing various agreed needs in society, as social values and ideas about what is essential to living as a full member of society shift, so in turn may the notion of what people legitimately need. In short, the debate about 'need' can be seen to be inherently relative, and heavily influenced by time and social context. Some observers believe that the relative nature of social need means that attempts to measure and order forms of need are essentially misguided and ultimately doomed to failure. They argue that debate about need may ultimately be little more than a political one, in which different political positions succeed or fail in insisting on their particular conception of need.

CAN WE ESTABLISH A LEVEL OF BASIC NEEDS?

Is it possible to say that there are any basic needs which, once they have been identified, really ought to be met? This is an important question: if one can establish that there are certain basic needs, the meeting of which are essential to being a civilized human being, then this may begin to establish an argument in favour of the welfare state.

A starting point for establishing basic needs is the notion that needs are related to ends—in order to achieve certain ends in life, such as a high level of education, one may have first to fulfil a variety of needs—the need for financial support; the need for child care; the need for adequate transport; and so on. Indeed, the distinction here is between **ultimate needs** and **intermediate needs**. Ultimate needs are the ends to which other activities are directed. In contrast, intermediate needs are not ends in themselves but are rather a means to an end. For instance, we may need something, such as a basic education, in order to fulfil other needs, such as finding a job.

Yet we all have many different ends in sight, and we believe we need different things in order to achieve our ends. We could never say that everyone should have whatever they require in order to fulfil their ends in life—the list of potential needs is infinite. Nonetheless, some writers, particularly Raymond Plant, have made some important progress here by attempting to identify what people need in order to achieve any ends in life at all.

> These needs might be regarded generally as physical well-being and autonomy: an individual would have to be able to function efficiently as a physical entity and have freedom to deliberate and choose between alternatives if he is to pursue any conception of the good. (Plant 1985: 18)

Simplified, Plant suggests that it is possible to identify two basic needs in any society. First, there is a need for physical survival. We obviously cannot hope to achieve anything without physical survival. Secondly, he argues that there is a basic need for autonomy, or freedom. In order to make genuine choices about our paths in life, we need to have autonomy and the freedom to make informed choices. These two basic needs are crucial, argues Plant, because unless they are met, we cannot hope to achieve any ends at all in life.

These arguments seek to derive needs from basic human goals upon which we might all agree. Nonetheless, there do seem to be a number of problems here, not least of which is the question of what rights to survival and autonomy actually justify in practice. Plant, for instance, interprets survival as effectively referring to health. In this sense, one can argue that this justifies the provision of healthcare. However, the level and extent of healthcare being argued for remains very unclear. Does the argument that people need healthcare to ensure survival really extend to saying that they should have as much healthcare as technically possible? If this were the case, it would place unacceptable and unachievable demands upon a health service. In which case, where does one draw the line between what is a justifiable need for healthcare which should be met and what is not? Similarly, in order to guarantee physical survival, one could argue that it is necessary to guarantee an income to ensure subsistence—thus again raising problems concerning what minimum of income is sufficient.

A further and very real problem with Plant's approach concerns the role of the state. Even if one can establish that there are indeed a number of basic needs which can and should be met, it does not simply follow that the state should be the vehicle for meeting these. Presenting a strong and coherent argument for the meeting of certain basic needs may be one thing, but deducing a state obligation—as opposed to those of individuals, families, or charity, for instance—may be a quite different matter.

NEED IN TERMS OF BASIC MINIMA

Much social policy debate about need takes place in terms of minima, or basic levels below which some individuals may be defined as being in real need. The difficulty is just how to decide upon the nature of any minimum. For example, some have argued that there is a minimum living standard which applies to all societies, below which one is evidently in need of assistance. Usually based upon various ideas of subsistence, and the very minimum required for survival, this is the notion of **absolute poverty**. The measurement of absolute poverty generally limits poverty to **material deprivation**, and seeks to establish a price for the basic necessities in life. Those who are then unable to afford these necessities are deemed to be in absolute poverty, unable to afford to maintain even basic subsistence levels.

The work of Seebohm Rowntree (1871–1954) was one of the first to attempt to define and measure need in this way, and establish a basic minimum income, below which subsistence was not possible. Applying his measure in 1899, Rowntree discovered that a third of the working-class households in York were in absolute poverty—and lacked the minimum income necessary for subsistence. In his third survey of York in 1950, this proportion had dropped to just 1.5 per cent of his total sample, leading some to argue that poverty in the UK had effectively been eradicated.

The concept of 'absolute poverty', however, is not a concrete and objective measure of need. On the contrary, it is very much open to debate and interpretation, and there have been a variety of differing attempts to operationalize this concept, or put it into a form which can be empirically measured. The problem comes in terms of what are defined as the minimum needs necessary for subsistence—do these only refer to physical needs, and the basic need for food; shelter and good health? Or could we—indeed, should we—include in this approach other needs which may be equally important for becoming a full and involved member of society—access to leisure such as holidays or to sources of cultural enrichment such as museums or art galleries?

Even when focusing exclusively upon nutritional requirements, it is unclear what basic nutritional requirements should be. Different individuals in different occupations, for instance, may have very different nutritional needs. This variety is even more pronounced in the case of other dimensions of need such as housing, clothing, or education.

Official poverty

Despite these difficulties, the idea of need defined in terms of basic minima has proved to be pervasive. Many official definitions of poverty tend to be related in some way to an absolute or subsistence poverty line. In the UK, for instance, 'official' poverty has conventionally been measured in terms of benefit levels. Benefits such as Income Support are paid to those who can demonstrate a low income, and are intended to provide a basic minimum income for those experiencing material hardship. Those individuals whose incomes are at or below this level are deemed to be in poverty. In Britain until the 1980s, the government based its estimate of the extent of poverty and need in society on the numbers living at or below benefit levels. Those receiving an income of between 100 and 139 per cent of benefit levels were often defined as on the margins of poverty.

This approach, however, attracted considerable criticism, not least because it implied that every time benefit levels were increased, this paradoxically increased the number of those defined as being in poverty. From 1985 the government chose instead to publish figures on the numbers living below incomes which were 50 per cent of the average adjusted for household type. The number of people living in households with less than

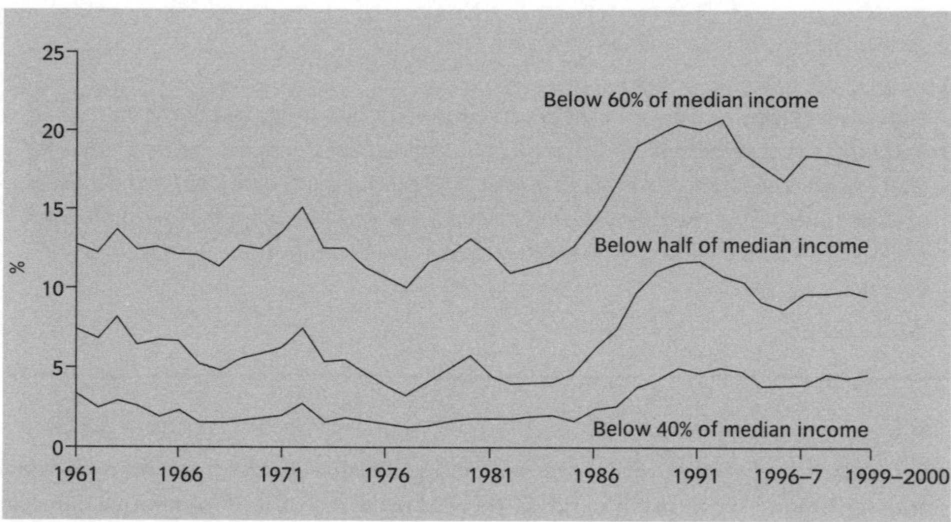

Figure 5.2 Percentage of people whose income is below various fractions of median income, UK. (Housing costs excluded. Data from 1993–4 onwards are for financial years; data for 1994–5 onwards exclude Northern Ireland.)

Source: ONS 2003.

60 per cent of median income is now one of the preferred indicators of poverty for both the UK government and the European Union. In 1999/2000, it was estimated that some 13.3 million people were living in households with below 60 per cent of median income (Rahman et al. 2001).

This has been described as the **relative income standard of poverty**. Interestingly, the government also modified the way in which it calculated its figures. Originally, it sought to calculate the income for each household member separately. However, this was changed, and all members of a household were assumed to have an equal share of the total household income, which is evidently questionable. The result, however, was that this change actually reduced the numbers on low incomes by more than a million people. The problem with such a measure of need, however, is the arbitrary point at which one draws a poverty line.

Relative poverty

Peter Townsend was a vocal proponent of the idea that poverty must be related to the society in which it may be present. However, he argued that the relative income standard of poverty is arbitrary: it is unclear why the poverty line should be drawn at 50 per cent of average income—70 per cent could have just as much validity. Townsend was therefore keen to establish a more objective and less arbitrary measure of poverty and need, but one which was necessarily relative to wider standards in society. After all, given economic and social change, so standards and expectations may shift, and luxuries may become comforts and comforts in turn may become necessities. Townsend argued, therefore, that poverty had to be related to and defined by the standards of

Box 5.2 Townsend's definition of poverty

Individuals, families, and groups in the population can be said to be in poverty when they lack the resources to obtain the types of diet, participate in the activities, and have the living conditions and amenities which are customary, or at least widely encouraged or approved, in the societies to which they belong. Their resources are so seriously below those commanded by the average individual or family that they are, in effect, excluded from the ordinary living patterns, customs and activities.

(Townsend 1979)

a particular society at a particular time and, moreover, reflect more than simply material impoverishment. With this in mind, he focused upon the concept of **relative deprivation**. He suggested that any definition of poverty should include some measure of an individual's ability to participate in social activities which are generally customary in society (see Box 5.2).

With this in mind, Townsend constructed what he described as a **deprivation index**. This covered some sixty types of household activity relating to diet, clothing, health, recreation, travel, and so on, from which he chose twelve items that he saw as relevant and necessary to the whole of society. He then calculated the proportion of the population deprived of these. Each household was given a score on a deprivation index, and the more respects in which a household was found to experience deprivation, the higher its score. Townsend then related deprivation to income levels. In particular, he related the average score of households to different levels of income, expressed as a percentage of basic benefit levels. From this, he claimed to have identified a poverty threshold, in terms of a level of income below which the amount of deprivation suddenly increased dramatically—at approximately 150 per cent of benefit levels. Townsend therefore argued that all households without this level of resources were suffering from poverty and in need. Importantly, he also felt that his figures and his definition of poverty, were not arbitrary, but were ostensibly objective.

Problems with this approach

Townsend's approach to poverty, and hence to need, was path-breaking. He developed a social measure in terms of household integration into the surrounding community, and so moved measurement on from arbitrarily chosen minimum standards. But his work also attracted criticism, not least from David Piachaud (1981), who makes a number of pertinent points.

Townsend claimed to have found an 'objective' point at which to draw a poverty line, below which deprivation increases very rapidly. In fact, Piachaud argues that a poverty line based on 150 per cent of benefit levels is as arbitrary as any other. Indeed, after examining Townsend's data, Piachaud disputes the suggestion that deprivation starts to rapidly increase below this level of 150 per cent of benefit levels.

It is also not clear why the items employed in Townsend's index have been selected. For instance, it is unclear why not eating cooked meals should necessarily be equated with deprivation, as Townsend claims. After all, some people may prefer to eat sandwiches and salads! This is a crucial point—namely, Townsend does not seek to establish whether scoring high points on his 'deprivation index' is actually a consequence of shortage of money, or a consequence of choice!

Mack and Lansley: breadline Britain

Mack and Lansley (1985; 1991) follow Townsend's social approach to the measurement of need and poverty, defining poverty in relative terms, but attempting to improve the approach in two important ways.

First, they sought to clarify whether or not people lacked something by choice, or whether it was a consequence of financial pressure.

Secondly, they were concerned about the accusation that any items included in their deprivation index would be necessarily arbitrary. They therefore adopted a **consensual approach to poverty**, and asked their respondents what they considered to be necessities in contemporary Britain. An item became a necessity if a majority (or more than 50 per cent of the population) classified it as one. On the basis of this deprivation index, they then went on to measure the extent of poverty, which they defined as 'an enforced lack of socially perceived necessities'. Later surveys have used the same method.

The last survey using this 'consensual approach' to measure poverty in Britain (Gordon et al. 2000) came up with some startling and disturbing results:

- In 1983, 14 per cent of households (approximately 7.5 million people) were living in poverty; this had increased to 24 per cent (approximately 14 million people) by 1999.
- Around 9.5 million people in Britain today cannot afford adequate housing, free from damp and adequately heated.
- Some 6.5 million adults go without essential clothing, such as a warm waterproof coat, because of a lack of money.
- About 8 million people cannot afford one or more essential household goods, like a fridge, a telephone, or carpets for living areas.

It is evident that attempting to establish any measure of need in terms of a basic minima is fraught with problems. Absolute or subsistence definitions of need and poverty are to a degree arbitrary, or a matter of subjective judgement. In any event, many commentators argue that any attempt to measure deprivation and need must be relative to the standards and expectations of wider society. In other words, the nature of poverty necessarily varies over time, and reflects the contemporary social circumstances in which it is experienced. In this sense, poverty and deprivation are related to social inequality: the poor are those whose incomes or resources are so far short of society's average that they simply do not have an acceptable standard of living. If poverty is measured and gauged in terms of average expectations and average incomes, then reducing poverty and meeting need may actually be impossible without attacking inequality. In the UK, inequality pervades many features of society, most notably in terms of income.

NEED AND INEQUALITY

One of the most significant forms of inequality in the UK is in terms of income distribution. Data on income distribution have been used to chart changing patterns of poverty and need over time. Indeed, according to this measure there has been a considerable increase in the scale of poverty in the UK over the past twenty years or so. In 1979, for instance, 5 million people (or 9 per cent of the population) were living on below half average incomes after housing costs. By 1999/2000 this figure had risen to approximately 14 million people, or a quarter of the population, the worst poverty record in the EU, with the exception of Greece (Howard et al. 2001)

Whilst many industrialized countries experienced moves towards greater income inequality, this grew more rapidly in the UK than in almost any other. Between 1979 and 1995, for instance, incomes for the richest tenth of the population rose by more than 60 per cent, while the real incomes of the poorest tenth showed a fall of 8 per cent, when housing costs were taken into account (Hills 1995).The reasons for these increases in inequality are complex. In particular, they reflect the fact that, during the 1980s, more people became dependent upon state benefits, not least because of increases in unemployment. Yet, simultaneously, the gap widened between the income of those dependent on benefits and the income of that part of the population with earnings. This was a consequence of the fact that, since the early 1980s, benefit levels have generally been linked to prices rather than to income levels. These changes in inequality have affected some social groups more than others.

There are, for instance, important differences between ethnic groups. The incomes of some ethnic minority groups are well below the national average, and a significant percentage of their populations live in areas high in indicators of deprivation. Households where the head of household is from an ethnic minority group are much more likely to appear in the bottom 20 per cent (or quintile) of the income distribution than their white contemporaries. For example, over 60 per cent of individuals of Pakistani or Bangladeshi origin are in the bottom fifth of income distribution—three times more than white people and almost twice as many as black people (Howard et al. 2001). This is, of course, partly related to unemployment and its high incidence amongst some ethnic minority groups. In 2000, for example, unemployment rates for black and Pakistani/Bangladeshi people were three times higher than that for white people. Children from ethnic minorities are more likely to be living in poverty than white children.While around a third of children in Britain are living in poverty, for Bangladeshi and Pakistani children, the figure is 73 per cent (Platt 2002).

There are also important differences between men and women here. Whilst men are much more likely to be in the professional and skilled manual groups, women are more likely to be in the skilled and unskilled non-manual groups, reflecting the dominance of women in some occupations such as clerical and secretarial work and their importance in some professions such as teaching and medicine. Women have been heavily concentrated in low paid and low-status employment in the UK, and in 2000 women's full time average earnings were just 82 per cent those of men.

Box 5.3 Child poverty

The Blair government made poverty reduction—particularly child poverty—a key element of its policies. This was one of the objectives behind the introduction of schemes such as the Working Families Tax Credit and the Child Tax Credit. In particular, in 1998 it established a target to reduce the number of children in low-income households by at least a quarter by 2004 and by half by 2010. Yet the challenge is a formidable one. In 1968, just 10 per cent of children lived in households with below half the average income. By 1996 this had risen to a third of all children (over 4.3 million). Nonetheless, the government has made some progress here, and by 2002 the number of children living in poverty had dropped by approximately 500,000 to 3.9 million. Much of this reduction—approximately 300,000 children—appears to have been a consequence of rising employment and more parents obtaining paid work (Piachaud and Sutherland 2002). Despite such progress, many commentators remain doubtful as to whether the government can meet its targets to reduce child poverty, at least not without a substantial increase in resources.

An important question for social policy concerns the extent to which the welfare state should seek to reduce inequalities. Which inequalities are the most damaging in the sense of reducing people's opportunities or in contributing to other needs such as poor health? There is also the risk that welfare allocations, or the taxes necessary to pay for them, may actually have been contributing to forms of inequality.

THE WELFARE STATE AND INEQUALITY

It is clear that some households will pay considerably more in taxes than they receive in benefits, while others will benefit more than they are taxed. Overall, one can say that there is some redistribution of income from households on higher incomes to those on lower incomes. In 2000–1, for example, UK households in the bottom quintile group had an average original income (or income derived from various non-governmental sources, such as employment or occupational pensions) of £3,090. Once redistribution through taxes and benefits had occurred, such households were left with a final income of £9,670. In other words, on average, these households had gained some £6,580 through redistribution. In contrast, households in the highest quintile group (or the top 20 per cent) had an average original income of £55,740 and a final income of £39,080. In other words, on average, these households had made a net loss of some £16,660 through redistribution (ONS 2003).

However, the welfare state also has an important redistributional role in terms of welfare services which are provided in kind, rather than as cash benefits; such as the National Health Service, state education, personal social services, and subsidized and social housing. It has been argued that the provision of such services should be considered as a non-monetary form of income, or a **social wage**, which forms an important addition to cash incomes. However, there has been intense debate about who actually benefits most from the provision of such services. Julian Le Grand, for instance, famously argued that state welfare provision does not in fact enhance redistribution and reduce inequality. Rather, he showed that state welfare services accentuate the divisions between those facing need and those who are comfortably provided for. In the use of transport, education, and possibly healthcare the better-off consume disproportionately relative to their needs (Le Grand 1982). It has been claimed by some commentators that the welfare state has increasingly been 'captured' by the middle classes.

In contrast, recent research by Tom Sefton (1997; 2002) has shown that the welfare state did go some way towards tempering the growing income inequalities witnessed in the 1980s. Whilst much attention was devoted to the widening income gap between rich and poor, most calculations failed to take into account the value of welfare services to different groups. In 2000–1 the social wage, or the value in kind of the main state services, such as healthcare and education, was worth an average of £1,700 per person or nearly £4,000 per household. On average, individuals in the bottom two-fifths of income distribution receive around twice the value of benefits in kind as those in the top fifth (Sefton 2002). However, there is considerable variety here between services—higher education, for instance, is certainly worth more to the better-off in society, while subsidized social housing and the personal social services strongly benefit the poor.

That income inequality has increased remains the basic fact. Between 1979 and 1999, for example, real incomes after housing costs rose by an average of 80 per cent. Yet the poorest 10 per cent saw a rise of just 6 per cent (Howard et al. 2001). The social wage has helped to offset this growing inequality of cash incomes, although it has still not prevented inequality from rising. Whilst one would anticipate that welfare services would mainly benefit lower income groups, the surprising reality is that the poorest half of the population receive just 60 per cent of the value of these services. Indeed, only in the context of social housing has there been a clear shift in the distribution of welfare spending towards the poorest individuals and families (Sefton 1997).

DEMOGRAPHIC CHANGE IN THE UK

Demographic trends are of fundamental importance for social policy and any debate about social need. Ultimately, demographic changes have a direct impact upon welfare provision, because they alter the size and composition of the population who contribute to and use the services provided by welfare states. One role of social policy is to chart and follow demographic trends—both in the short and in the much longer term—and anticipate the needs that different patterns of population change are likely to imply for welfare provision. Demography lies at the heart of social policy because of its close relationship to need and, in turn, demand upon the welfare state.

Knowledge about the size and structure of the population is essential for understanding and anticipating demand for all kinds of welfare service, such as education, healthcare, social security benefits, and pensions. Demographic change provides the best basis available for estimating future needs. Demographic change can also be interpreted as an indication of wider social shifts in values and forms of behaviour which may have implications for the needs faced by future governments and taxpayers.

Population structure

Since 1900 the world population has more than trebled—from around 1.6 billion to more than 6.1 billion by 2001. It is estimated that by 2050 world population will be

Box 5.4 Census 2001

Since 1801, the UK government has conducted a census every ten years of every household in the country, to collect a variety of important demographic information, which is then used for planning and targeting welfare services and provision. The last census took place on 29 April 2001 and cost £200 million to administer. The key findings included:

- The UK population on the day of the census was 58,789,194—about one million lower than estimates made in 2000.
- For the first time, the number of people over 60 exceeded the number of children aged under 16.
- Those aged 85 and over now make up nearly 2 per cent of the entire population, compared to 0.4 per cent 50 years ago.
- Boys outnumber girls up until the age of 21, but there are fewer men than women in all ages over 21.
- There has been significant regional variation in population change over the past twenty years, with a decline in the population of the north and an increase in the population of the south.

Question

- What are the implications of these findings for the design and delivery of welfare services?

Table 5.1 World population

	1800	1900	1950	2001
Asia	635	947	1,402	3,721
Africa	107	133	224	813
Europe	203	408	547	726
Latin America and Caribbean	24	74	166	527
North America	7	82	172	317
Oceania	2	6	13	31
	978	1,650	2,524	6,134

Source: ONS (2003).

between 7.9 and 10.9 billion. Yet within this pattern, there are important differences. Less developed areas, for instance, have much lower life expectancies than do more developed regions. Whilst life expectancy at birth is comparatively long in the UK—75 for males, and 80 for females—in some countries life expectancy is less than half this. In Sierra Leone, for example, life expectancy at birth is just 36 for males and 39 for females.

Europe has also had a considerably slower population growth rate than the world as a whole. Between 1950 and 2001, for instance, the population of Europe rose by less than 33 per cent, compared to an increase of 143 per cent for the population of the world as a whole over the same period. The UK population has similarly experienced a relatively subdued rate of population growth. In 1961, the UK population was approximately 53 million and by the 2001 census was under 59 million. Change in population is dependent on a number of variables—specifically, the number of births, the number of deaths, and migration in and out of the country.

Births and the family

One of the most important factors affecting population structure is the number of live births. The UK has seen a number of changes to fertility patterns. More women are now delaying having their first child, and the average age of mothers for all live births rose from 26.2 in 1971 to 29.1 in 2000. Women are also choosing to have fewer children. There has also been a dramatic increase in the number of births outside marriage. Of live births in Great Britain in 2001, around 40 per cent occured outside marriage—more than four times the proportion in 1975. However, it is important to remember that more than three-quarters of births outside marriage are jointly registered by both parents (ONS 2003).

The family is a central object of social policy intervention. However, the contemporary family is experiencing a variety of important changes, which in turn attract the attention of social researchers, politicians, and policy-makers. Many of these changes are linked and related in different ways, and have consequences for both the goals and the design of social policies.

Marriage, divorce, and cohabitation

One of the most striking areas of debate has been focused upon the question of marriage, and its centrality to modern British society. Whilst politicians regularly proclaim the virtues of marriage, and the benefits of dual parenthood, the contemporary family is now considerably more diverse in its characteristics. Some researchers and politicians have not been slow to attach many of the ills of our modern society to changing family forms. Whilst the main changes involved may be reasonably clear in their nature, what is far from clear are the implications of these for social welfare. A number of developments are notable, one of which has been the declining marriage rate and the corresponding increase in cohabitation.

Marriage may be an institution, but it is one to which growing proportions of the population are hesitant to subscribe. In 2000, for example, there were 180,000 first marriages, less than half the peak of 390,000 in 1970. Not only are fewer people actually marrying, but the average age of people getting married for the first time is increasing.

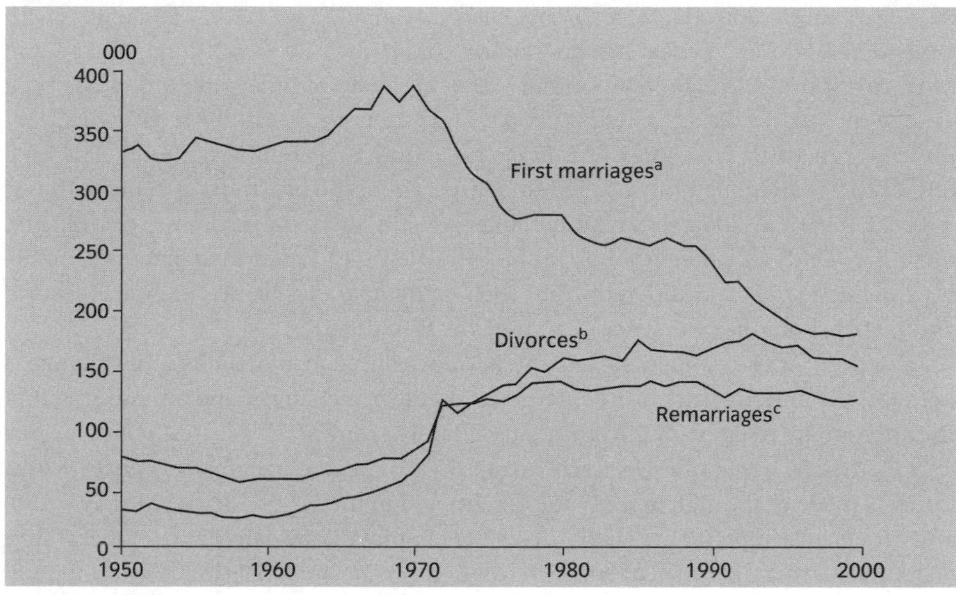

Figure 5.3 Marriages and divorces in the UK

[a] For both partners.

[b] Includes annulments. Data for 1950–70 for Great Britain only.

[c] For one or both partners.

Source: ONS 2003.

In 2000, for example, the average age for first marriage was 30.5 for men and 28.2 for women, compared to 25.6 for men and 23.1 for women in 1961. At the same time, there has been a sharp increase in the number of people cohabiting, together with a shift towards cohabiting for longer periods. For instance, the proportion of all non-married women aged 18 to 49 who were cohabiting in Great Britain almost tripled between 1979 and 2001, from 11 per cent to 30 per cent.

At the same time as a rise in cohabitation, there has been a dramatic increase in divorce. Since 1971, divorce has more than doubled. In 2001 there were 157,000 divorces in the United Kingdom. It is perhaps unsurprising that so many politicians and clergy claim that the concept of marriage in the UK is under threat. The rise in divorce has important and significant implications for social policy, in a number of ways. The complexity of reconstituted families may have important consequences for the meeting of social need in the future. The provision of old age care, for instance, has been the focus of concern. Traditionally a main source of informal care for the elderly has been by younger family members. Yet with the increase in divorce and, in turn, remarriage, it is less clear just how these family responsibilities may or may not be shared out.

Lone parents

A further shift in family form which has provoked concern amongst policy-makers and politicians has been the increase in the number and proportion of lone-parent families over the past thirty years. The UK has one of the highest rates of lone parenthood in the

European Union. In 2002, lone parents headed around 22 per cent of all families with dependent children in Great Britain—almost three times the proportion in 1971—and nine out of every ten are lone mothers. This high rate of lone parenthood has been viewed by many as being inherently risky, and a number of authors have argued that there is something necessarily advantageous about two-parent households. The high rate of lone parenthood has also led to debates about the provision of benefits to this group. Do their greater needs require higher benefits and more assistance, or will these merely 'reward' lone parenthood? Indeed, the identification of lone parents as somehow being distinct and different from their contemporaries lies at the heart of many arguments about the emergence of an underclass in the UK.

As with all social policy debates, the acknowledgement of demographic change is perhaps less important than the interpretation of such changes, and an assessment of the appropriate response by government. Certainly, many of the debates about lone parents in the UK have only selectively engaged with the demographic evidence. Whilst much is made of the high rate of lone parenthood in the UK by Charles Murray (1990) and others, it is important to clarify a number of points. Lone parenthood, for example, is not necessarily a permanent state. On the contrary, many lone parents go on to form new joint households fairly quickly. Moreover, contrary to the pervasive image of the teenage mother attempting to jump the housing queue, the majority of lone parents are actually divorcees in their 20s or 30s.

In short, the nuclear family is undergoing substantial change in the UK, arising from fewer marriages, more cohabitation, and more extra-marital births; increasing divorce and remarriage; declining fertility and smaller families; and a rise in the proportion of lone parents and reconstituted families. The nuclear family may still be dominant, but it is nonetheless only one possible family form.

Household change

The rise in divorce and the declining fashionability of marriage has led to other changes, all of which are important to social policy. The average size of households in Great Britain has almost halved since the beginning of the twentieth century to some 2.4 people per household in 2002 (ONS 2003). Of particular significance has been the rise in single-person households. More and more of us, it seems, are living on our own. In 1961, just 14 per cent of households were single-person households. By 2002, this proportion has increased to some 29 per cent, and seems set to climb further, as more of us live independently after leaving home and before marriage; as a consequence of divorce, or simply as a reflection of the growing proportion of the elderly, many of whom live in 'solo' households. The implications of this development may be profound, not least for housing policy. The growing number of single-person households—who in turn want somewhere to live—has figured strongly in recent debates about the need for 4.4 million new homes in the UK by 2016. Whilst the population of the UK may have remained reasonably static over the past few decades, it is important to remember that demand for housing can increase within a static population if new and smaller households are forming faster than old ones dissolve.

In short, demographic change has a very real and integral relationship with the issue of social need. However, it would be erroneous to assume that one can chart a clear and

Table 5.2 Households by size, UK (%)

	1961	1971	1981	1991	2002
One person	14	18	22	27	29
Two people	30	32	32	34	35
Three people	23	19	17	16	16
Four people	18	17	18	16	14
Five people	9	8	7	5	5
Six or more people	7	6	4	2	2
All households (= 100%) millions	16.3	18.6	20.2	22.4	24.1
Average household size (number of people)	3.1	2.9	2.7	2.5	2.4

Source: ONS (2003).

straightforward relationship between demographic change and the consequent needs faced by society. On the contrary, there may be common acknowledgment of a particular demographic pattern, but very different assessments of the implications for social policy. Nowhere is this more aptly illustrated than in the various debates about an ageing population, and the consequences of this for welfare provision.

Ageing of the population

The population age profile of industrialized societies is changing in important ways, not least of which has been the movement towards what is commonly described as an **ageing population**. The age structure of the population reflects variation in past births, increases in longevity, and the effects of migration. This is an important debate, reflecting concern about the welfare costs of an expanding **dependent population**—or the proportion of the population economically supported by those of working age. In other words, this is a crude measure of the number of people economically supported by those of working age—what is known as the **dependency ratio**. Those people aged under 16, and those over pensionable age, are often deemed to represent the dependent population, and, importantly, many countries are experiencing an increase in the proportion of the population above pensionable age. In 1961, for instance, just 12 per cent of the UK's population were aged 65 or over, and only 4 per cent were aged 75 and over. By 2001, this had increased to some 16 per cent and 7 per cent respectively.

The proportion of the population aged 65 or over is projected to rise further, as the post-Second World War 'baby boomers' reach retirement age. By 2025 it is projected that more than 20 per cent of the population will be aged over 65 (ONS 2003). Moreover, there will be a particular increase in the number of very elderly people. Whilst in 1961 there were nearly 350,000 people aged 85 and over, by 2001 this number had increased to 1.1 million. In 2000 there were more than three times as many people aged over 90 as

Table 5.3 Population by age, UK (%)

	All ages (= 100%) (millions)	Under 16	16–34	35–54	55–64	65–74	75 and over
Mid-year estimates							
1961	52.8	25	24	27	12	8	4
1971	55.9	25	26	24	12	9	5
1981	56.4	22	29	23	11	9	6
1991	57.8	20	29	25	10	9	7
2001	59.5	20	25	29	10	8	7
Mid-year projections							
2011	60.5	18	24	29	12	9	7
2021	61.1	18	23	26	14	11	8
2031	60.7	17	22	25	13	13	11

Source: ONS (2003).

there were in 1971. These developments clearly have profound implications in terms of future need for healthcare, social care, and pensions—and what this is likely to mean for national budgets, taxation, and welfare spending in the near future. Old people are higher users of health services than their younger peers. For example, patients aged 75 and over use approximately six times the average of NHS spending (Taylor-Gooby 1991). The stark implication is that a growing proportion of retired people will impose a burden of rising cost upon a shrinking population of working age. This has generated vigorous policy debate. Concern about the ability of the country to pay for growing pension costs in the future has led to a variety of reviews and changes to pension provisions in the UK, all of which claim to have at their heart a concern with this demographic trend.

Even here, however where the evidence about demographic change and its relationship to social need appears to be fairly uncontentious, all is not as clear as it initially seems. On the contrary, the impact of the ageing population upon welfare states into the next century may be more complicated than it appears at first. Rather than representing a demographic time-bomb, a number of competing points can be made.

Whilst it does seem likely that the ageing population will lead to greater costs in some areas, these are nonetheless likely to be matched by a reduction in other costs, such as childcare. Sefton (1997) shows that the effect of a smaller child population on education spending has already more than offset the effects of an ageing population on healthcare and personal social services spending. Indeed, those aged over 65 are not necessarily dependent. Far from being economically dependent, the elderly may make a number of important economic contributions to society—in terms of informal and unpaid childcare or care for other elderly people, for instance, and in terms of their important role as consumers of economic goods and services.

Certainly, those aged 85 and over are likely to increase as a proportion of the population, and to present a variety of needs in terms of health and social care. However, it is important to acknowledge that they still represent only a very small proportion of the entire population. The fact remains that economic growth could easily meet growing costs here. If current standards of provision are maintained, the cost of maintaining health and social services provision can be met by modest economic growth (Hills 1993). In other words, the issue here is not one of economic necessity, but one of political priority. Who should benefit from increases in economic productivity: existing workers or the retired? Moreover, the costs of an ageing population are not necessarily borne by the state—the movement towards private provision in terms of health and social care, and particularly in terms of pensions, are likely to alleviate some of the projected welfare costs.

Concerns about the demographic ageing of the population also ignore the fact that old age is to an extent a social construct, rather than simply a physical or biological fact. In other words, the current relationship between old age and physical dependency is changing. Old people in the future may be considerably healthier and more active than in the past, because of improvements in diet and lifestyle.

CONCLUSION: SOCIAL NEED, DEMOGRAPHIC 'FACTS', AND POLICY JUDGEMENTS

A logical mind might consider that social policy should be determined by 'social need' and that need should be measured in terms of empirical 'facts' such as changes in the size and structure of a population (demography) and evidence about deprivation (for example, measures of poverty). This chapter has sought to show that there can be no simple links made between facts about need and the necessary social policies. The very words we use to describe demographic change (e.g. 'the ageing population' or 'lone parenthood') involve elements of judgement. All attempts to measure poverty have been criticized for the normative assumptions they inevitably have to make about either minima or the forms of social inclusion and exclusion that count. Therefore, policy cannot follow directly from evidence of need. As Chapter 3 explains, a political process must intervene, determining which needs are recognized and the degree to which they are then to be alleviated by social policies.

REFERENCES

Abel-Smith, B., and Townsend, P. (1965), *The Poor and the Poorest*. Occasional Paper in Social Administration No 17. London: Bell.

Barry, N. (1990), *Welfare*. Milton Keynes: Open University Press.

Bradshaw, J. (1972), 'A taxonomy of social need', *New Society* No 496 (30 Mar.): 640–3.

Coleman, D., and Salt, J. (1992), *The British Population: Patterns, Trends and Processes*. Oxford: Oxford University Press.

Doyal, L., and Gough, I. (1984), 'A theory of human needs', *Critical Social Policy* No 10: 6–33.

—— (1991), *A Theory of Human Need*. Basingstoke: Macmillan.

Ermisch, J. (1990), *Fewer Babies, Longer Lives*. York: Joseph Rowntree Foundation.

Falkingham, J. (1989), 'Britain's ageing population: the engine behind increased dependency ratios', *Journal of Social Policy* 18 (2): 211–33.

Finch, J., and Mason, J. (1993), *Negotiating Family Responsibilities*. London: Routledge.

Forder, A. (1974), *Concepts in Social Administration: A Framework for Analysis*. London: Routledge & Kegan Paul.

Gordon, D., and Pantazis, C. (eds.) (1997), *Breadline Britain in the 1990s: The Full Report of a Major National Survey on Poverty*. Bristol: University of Bristol.

—— Adelman, L., Ashworth, K., Bradshaw, J., Levitas, R., Middleton, S., Pantazis, C., Patsios, D., Payne, S., Townsend, P., and Williams, J. (2000), *Poverty and Social Exclusion in Britain*. York: Joseph Rowntree Foundation.

Harvey, D. (1973), *Social Justice and the City*. London: Arnold.

Hills, J. (1993), *The Future of Welfare: A Guide to the Debate*. York: Joseph Rowntree Foundation.

—— (1995) *Inquiry into Income and Wealth*. York: Joseph Rowntree Foundation.

Howard, M., Garnham, A., Fimister, G., and Veit-Wilson, J. (2001), *Poverty: The Facts*. London: Child Poverty Action Group.

Jones, K., Brown, J., and Bradshaw, J. (1983), *Issues in Social Policy*, 2nd edn. London: Routledge & Kegan Paul.

Joseph Rowntree Foundation (1995), *Inquiry into Income and Wealth* (2 vols., York: Joseph Rowntree Foundation.

Joshi, H. (1989), *The Changing Population of Britain*. Oxford: Blackwell.

Kiernan, K., and Wicks, M. (1990), *Family Change and Future Policy*. York: Joseph Rowntree Foundation.

Le Grand, J. (1982), *The Strategy of Equality*. London: Allen & Unwin.

Mack, J., and Lansley, S. (1985), *Poor Britain*. London: Allen & Unwin.

—— —— (1991), *Breadline Britain*. London: Unwin Hyman.

Maslow, A. (1954), *Motivation and Personality*. New York: Harper.

Murray, C. (1990), *The Emerging British Underclass*. London: Institute of Economic Affairs.

ONS (Office for National Statistics) (2003), *Social Trends* No. 33. London: The Stationery Office.

Piachaud, D. (1981), 'Peter Townsend and the Holy Grail', *New Society* 57 (10 Sept.): 419–22.

—— and Sutherland, H. (2002), *Changing Poverty Post-1997*. London: London School of Economics.

Plant, R. (1985), 'The very idea of a welfare state'. In P. Bean, J. Ferris, and D. Whynes (eds.), *In Defence of Welfare*. London: Tavistock.

Platt, L. (2002), *Parallel Lives: Poverty among Ethnic Minority Groups in Britain*. London: Child Poverty Action Group.

Rahman, M., Palmer, G., and Kenway, P. (2002), *Monitoring Poverty and Social Exclusion*. York: Joseph Rowntree Foundation.

Sefton, T. (1997), *The Changing Distribution of the Social Wage*. STICERD Occasional Paper 21. London: London School of Economics.

—— (2002), *Recent Changes in the Distribution of the Social Wage*. London: London School of Economics.

Smith, G. (1988), *Social Needs: Policy Practice and Research*. London: Routledge.

Taylor-Gooby, P. (1991), *Social Change, Social Welfare and Social Science*. London: Harvester Wheatsheaf.

—— and Dale, J. (1981), *Social Theory and Social Welfare*. London: Arnold.

Townsend, P. (ed.) (1970), *The Concept of Poverty*. London: Heinemann.

—— (1979), *Poverty in the United Kingdom*. Harmondsworth: Penguin.

FURTHER READING

J. Bradshaw, 'A taxonomy of social need' (*New Society* No 496, 30 Mar. 1972: 640–43). An important and influential exposition of the different forms that social need might take.

D. Coleman and J. Salt, *The British Population: Patterns, Trends and Processes* (Oxford: Oxford University Press, 1992). A thorough and comprehensive guide to the many debates surrounding the British population, drawing together a wealth of evidence and argument.

L. Doyal and I. Gough, *A Theory of Human Need* (Basingstoke: Macmillan, 1991). A considered account of the key issues and dilemmas here, further developing the approach of Raymond Plant to the question of need.

D. Gordon, L. Adelman, K. Ashworth, J. Bradshaw, R. Levitas, S. Middleton, C. Pantazis, D. Patsios, S. Payne, P. Townsend, and J. Williams, *Poverty and Social Exclusion in Britain* (York: Joseph Rowntree Foundation, 2000). The latest report on the extent and nature of poverty in Britain using the 'consensual method' pioneered by Mack and Lansley.

J. Hills, *The Future of Welfare: A Guide to the Debate* (York: Joseph Rowntree Foundation, 1993). A comprehensive guide to the wealth of evidence and debate about the future sustainability of welfare spending, drawing upon some rich sources of data.

M. Howard, A. Garnham, G. Fimister, and J. Veit-Wilson, *Poverty: The Facts* (London: Child Poverty Action Group, 2001). The latest edition of a very useful publication, containing a wealth of figures and data on poverty in the UK.

Office for National Statistics, *Social Trends* No. 33 (London: Stationery Office, 2003). An invaluable source of government data on a range of topics, including the family, population change, and patterns of income and wealth.

D. Piachaud, 'Peter Townsend and the Holy Grail' (*New Society* 57, 10 Sept. 1981: 419–22). An influential challenge to Peter Townsend and the claim that need and poverty can be objectively measured.

L. Platt, *Parallel Lives: Poverty among Ethnic Minority Groups in Britain*. (London: Child Poverty Action Group, 2002). A comprehensive examination of poverty among ethnic minorities in Britain.

M. Rahman, G. Palmer, and P. Kenway, *Monitoring Poverty and Social Exclusion*. York: Joseph Rowntree Foundation, 2002. An annual report of indicators of poverty and social exclusion, providing some very useful data.

T. Sefton, *Recent Changes in the Distribution of the Social Wage*. (London: London School of Economics, 2002). An examination of the 'social wage' in the UK and the distributional impact of welfare spending.

P. Townsend, *Poverty in the United Kingdom* (Harmondsworth: Penguin, 1979). Essential reading for any consideration of poverty in the UK, in which Townsend spells out his 'poverty threshold'.

USEFUL WEBSITES

There are a wide range of relevant websites on these issues, although some of the most useful include:

www.ukonline.gov.uk The site that allows you to search for and read a wide variety of government reports and publications on a diverse array of issues and topics.

www.statistics.gov.uk A rich source of official statistics and data, including online access to the 2001 Census findings and the latest Social Trends.

www.jrf.org.uk Provides access to a variety of research findings and reports on poverty and other social issues produced by the Joseph Rowntree Foundation.

www.cpag.org.uk A very useful site for examining child poverty in the UK, with access to various figures and reports.

www.poverty.org.uk A site monitoring poverty and social exclusion in the UK and providing a wide range of figures and data.

GLOSSARY

absolute poverty Poverty defined and measured in terms of the minimum requirements necessary for basic subsistence and survival. Those deemed to be in absolute poverty are unable to afford even the basic necessities in life. They exist below even 'subsistence poverty', the level at which people can just continue to survive.

ageing population A change in the age structure of the population, whereby the proportion of older people increases relative to the numbers of younger people. The term is often used to describe a population in which the proportion over pensionable age is increasing, which in turn may imply more social spending on pensions and healthcare, and less revenue.

comparative need Need established by comparing the standards achieved by similar groups within one society—for example those living in different parts of the country—or in different societies—for example a comparison of the incomes of, or provision for, retired people in one nation compared with those in another. In other words, need is seen as an inherently relative concept, and any debate about need must be related to the wider context within which the debates are taking place.

consensual approach to poverty Attempting to establish a consensus about what the population consider to be necessities in that particular society, at that particular period in time, without which one could be defined as being in poverty.

dependency ratio Usually the ratio of those outside the labour force (for example 0–15 and 65 and over) to those defined as in the labour force or of working age.

dependent population The section of the population economically supported by those in employment.

deprivation index A list of items defined as essential to being a full member of society, without which one could be deemed to be experiencing deprivation.

expressed need Need that has become a demand. There is a close relationship between need and demand, but simply because someone demands or wants something does not necessarily mean that they need it.

felt need An individual's or group's belief that they need something. This relies heavily upon an individual's own perception of their need, and their perception of any discrepancy between what their situation may be and what their situation should be. This definition is very similar to a 'want'.

intermediate needs Needs which are not ends in themselves, but rather a means to an end. For example, we may need some things, such as a basic education, in order to fulfil other needs, such as finding employment, which in turn may answer the more ultimate need for income.

material deprivation Having insufficient physical resources—food, shelter, and clothing—necessary to sustain life either in an absolute sense or relative to some prescribed standard.

normative need How an expert, such as a doctor or welfare professional, may define need in a given situation or circumstance. Important because welfare professionals are closely involved in the identification of need, and the determining of how this may best be met within the confines of existing resources.

relative deprivation Deprivation measured by comparing one's situation to that of relevant others, or to standards accepted in a particular society at a particular time.

relative income standard of poverty A measure of poverty which relates it to average income levels within society. For instance, those found to be living at or below incomes which are 50 per cent of the average may be defined as being in poverty.

social wage The value of welfare services which are provided in kind, rather than as cash benefits, such as the NHS, state education, personal social services, and subsidized social housing.

technical need Need arising when some new provision is invented or existing provision is made much more effective, creating a need for a solution that was not previously available.

ultimate needs Needs which are seen as ends in themselves, and to which other activities and needs are directed: for example, survival, autonomy, and self-fulfilment may be defined as ultimate human needs.

6

Work and Welfare

Sarah Vickerstaff

CONTENTS

INTRODUCTION

I know the damage unemployment does. I remember my father telling me of working in this city in the 1930s in an era remembered for unemployed men standing on street corners when they wanted to work. I grew up in a mining area where once there were 66 pits which closure by closure were reduced to just one. For me since the time I went to school and grew up around a mining community and for a whole generation our political life has been dominated by unemployment—long term unemployment, youth unemployment, the fear of unemployment, the consequences of unemployment, the poverty caused by unemployment. (The Chancellor of the Exchequer, Gordon Brown, speaking to the Labour Party Spring Conference in Glasgow on 16 February 2000)

Employment is one of the best defences against poverty, unhappiness, and low self-esteem, which in turn are likely to affect adversely an individual's physical and mental health. In addition, paid work outside the home has traditionally been seen as a key mechanism of social integration: a person who 'works' is a full citizen, a useful and 'fully paid up', taxpaying member of society. People who are in paid employment have higher rates of involvement in other social, political, and sporting activities. This is partly a question of money—having the income to enjoy leisure activities—partly a matter of greater social inclusion or greater integration into public life. Thus, although we tend to conflate welfare with the welfare state and its policies, in fact work and employment are more fundamental producers of individual and societal welfare. In the first twenty-five years after the Second World War it was taken for granted in Europe and the USA that a key goal of government policy was the maintenance of **full employment**. The problem for many societies in Europe today is that there does not seem to be enough work to go round. Since the early 1970s, and especially in the 1980s, with the growth of persistent unemployment, this commitment to full employment, and the belief in its possibility, has been shaken throughout the advanced industrial (or increasingly **post-industrial**) world.

Unemployment tends to grab the newspaper headlines as *the* key employment issue but since the 1960s many other developments have been occurring in the world of work. The sorts of job available and the skills and attributes they require have been transformed; access to work is changing (who gets what kind of job); and for many people their experience of work, especially in relation to job security, has fundamentally altered. In order to consider the connection between work and welfare we must first look at all of these features of the **labour market**. We can then go on to review and evaluate some of the policy responses to these issues, and investigate contemporary debates on what to do about unemployment and access to work.

THE WORK AVAILABLE

In the period since the 1960s the UK economy has witnessed a progressive decline in manufacturing industry and hence the number of jobs available in this sector. At the same time there has been an increase in **service sector** and office or white-collar work. This shift from industry to services, and the related move from manual to non-manual work, have radically changed the pattern of demand in the labour market.

The transformation of the British economy from a strong manufacturing base to a 'post-industrial' service base has brought with it a collapse in the demand for the labour of unqualified youths. (Ashton 1992: 186–7)

In addition to this shift in the pattern of activity in the economy, technological changes and new standards of customer service have also meant that the skill and competence requirements for jobs have changed.

Twenty years ago, almost all the manual workers in my operation were men and a lot of the work consisted of humping sacks of potatoes around. Today, it's all fiddly work, putting sauce on the bits of chicken for Marks and Sparks, and the assembly line is 90 per cent women. Mostly men don't apply for it—it's part-time and they see it as women's work. (Food factory manager, quoted in Commission on Social Justice 1994: 187)

Even in the worst periods of unemployment since the late 1970s there have been simultaneous skill shortages and hard-to-fill vacancies. There is considerable debate about the overall trends in skill requirements for the jobs available in today's economy. Some argue that there is an upward trend in the skill levels required, pointing to the shift from manual to non-manual work and the impact of newer technologies, such as computer applications, whilst others indicate the growth of unskilled service sector jobs which require few skills or personal attributes. Far from the old disciplines of assembly-line work in factories becoming a thing of the past, these work techniques are increasingly being applied to all kinds of other work, for example fast-food restaurants and telephone call centre workers. (One version of this argument is the MacDonaldization thesis: see Box 6.1.)

A major piece of research into the trends in job skills in the UK found evidence for a polarization of skills (for a discussion of this research and the wider debate see Gallie 1991; 1996; Bradley et al. 2000). In other words, the middle ground of semi-skilled jobs is disappearing; instead skilled manual, managerial, and professional jobs are becoming

Box 6.1 The McDonaldization thesis

George Ritzer, in a book entitled *The McDonaldization of Society*, has argued that the process typified by the way fast food restaurants are run is extending into many areas of contemporary life:

First, a McDonaldized world is dominated by homogeneous products. The Big Mac, the Egg McMuffin, and Chicken Nuggets are identical from one time and place to another. Second, technologies like Burger King's conveyor system, as well as the french-fry and soft-drink machines throughout the fast-food industry, are as rigid as many of the technologies in Henry Ford's assembly-line system. Further, work routines in the fast-food restaurant are highly standardized. Even what the workers say to customers is routinized. In addition, the jobs in a fast-food restaurant are deskilled; they take little or no ability. The workers, furthermore, are homogeneous, and the actions of the customers are homogenized by the demands of the fast-food restaurant (for example, don't dare ask for a rare burger). The workers at fast-food restaurants can be seen as a mass of interchangeable workers. Finally, what is consumed and how it is consumed is homogenized by McDonaldization.

(Ritzer 1993: 155)

more skilled whilst many of the remaining jobs are becoming more routine and unskilled. In Britain, at least, this polarization has not changed the fact that many employers still argue that the unemployed (and especially the young unemployed) do not have the abilities and skills that they are looking for, whether these be specific skills or the more intangible quality of 'employability'. This mismatch in labour supply and labour demand is seen as one cause of unemployment. It is also in this context that debate about the role of education and training policy has taken centre stage in many European countries (see Chapter14).

Another feature of the way in which work has been changing is the growth of part-time and other forms of **flexible or casual work**. This growth is driven largely by the expansion of the service sector but also by increasing economic competition, leading employers to seek ways to improve efficiency and reduce labour costs. The degree of growth of part-time and flexible work across Europe varies considerably (see Gregory and Reilly 1996), depending in large measure on the prevailing context of employment regulation. Where part-time workers enjoy substantially the same employment protection as full-time workers, some of the flexibility that employers may gain from being able to deploy part-time or casual workers as and when they want is lost. One thing unites the experience of part-time employment across Europe, however, and that is the fact that it is overwhelmingly women who work part-time. The growth of part-time work is seen as contributing to growing income disparity between the rich and poor in society (see Case Study 6.1 below), which is another feature of the employment landscape in recent years, especially in the USA and Britain.

Employment security and labour intensification

These changes in the work available and in access to it raise issues about the experience of work and the impact this has on people's welfare. The growth of flexible and casual work has affected not only the unskilled but also white-collar, managerial, and professional workers. Many people in employment will have seen workforce reductions in their own workplace or have experienced job loss secondhand through friends and relatives. Many men may have had to change their jobs, perhaps losing the **occupational identity** they believed they would keep for all their working lives. In this context even the employed are likely to feel more insecure about their job prospects. In this respect the changes in the labour market over recent years may have gone some way to making men's patterns of working across the lifecycle more like women's: periods of work interspersed with periods of economic inactivity. Such broken career patterns and part-time or casual work obviously have implications for levels of income, and for any pension entitlement based on years of working service.

Along with a sense of the insecurity of employment, many employees have experienced an intensification of their work. In the public sector, following waves of workforce reduction in the 1980s and 1990s, the 'survivors' (those who have kept their jobs) in areas such as local government or higher education, for example, feel that they are now expected to work harder. The amount of work has increased but the number of people doing it has decreased. In the private sector the introduction of **lean production** methods has had a similar effect. This sense that people are working harder is borne out by two different measures of work effort: the extent of work, that is the hours worked, and the intensity of work, how hard people have to work whilst at work (see Green 2001: 56). Average working hours reduced considerably across the twentieth century, but since the 1980s the dispersion of hours has changed: more people work longer hours and more people work for a short number of hours, a pattern obscured by average hours calculations (Green 2001: 58–60). This change in the pattern of work has been noted in publicity about the fact that British fathers have the longest average working hours in Europe. Measures of labour intensity are more difficult to come by, but a range of research reviewed and added to by Green (2001) suggests that many people believe that they have to work harder, if not always longer, than they did in the past. These two measures of work effort put together suggest a number of potentially detrimental effects on the relationship between work and welfare. **Labour intensification** may well be having an impact on people's levels of stress and overall health, and in some households a long-hours culture may have the effect of putting strain on relationships.

PARTICIPATION RATES AND THE DEPENDENCY RATIO

If people spend up to a third of their lives being educated and a third of their lives in retirement, that only leaves a third in work to support the rest. . . . Do the maths. It just doesn't add up. (Alistair Darling, then Secretary of State for Work and Pensions, speech reported in the *Financial Times*, 6 February 2002)

Along with the changes to work already discussed, there has been a trend for the standard patterns of work across the individual's lifecycle to change, notably as the quotation above suggests, people are in paid employment for less time. Young people are staying in education longer (see Chapter 14) and many people, especially men, are retiring earlier. Rather than being a cause for celebration, as working less perhaps could be expected to be, this shortening of working life is seen as a major problem in many European societies. The growing tendency to early retirement, particularly by men in their 50s, has been recognized as an important social trend in western Europe and America (see Table 6.1). What appears rational and beneficial from the points of view of the individual or the employing organization may be irrational and costly in terms of the collective wellbeing and health of the whole economy. From a national point of view, early withdrawal from the labour market is seen as a risk and a cost, worsening the **dependency ratio**, raising public and private pension costs, and threatening additional welfare expenditure over the longer term. There is a tension between individual choice and social benefit (Esping-Andersen 1999). The British, along with many other European governments, are increasingly trying to encourage older workers to stay in employment.

For some social theorists such as Ulrich Beck these changes mark a radical development in the world of work. He charactersizes it as a movement from a **Fordist regime**, in which work and the products made were standardized and when people's work

Table 6.1 Economic activity rates,[a] by gender: EU comparison, 1992 and 2000 (%)

	1992			2000		
	Males	Female	All	Males	Female	All
Denmark	–	–	–	84.0	75.9	80.0
Finland	–	–	–	79.4	74.1	76.8
Sweden	–	–	–	77.2	75.4	75.3
United Kingdom	86.3	66.8	76.6	83.0	67.8	75.5
Netherlands	79.4	55.3	67.4	83.9	65.7	74.9
Austria	–	–	–	83.9	65.7	74.9
Germany	80.9	61.1	71.1	78.8	63.0	71.0
Portugal	80.0	58.6	68.7	78.8	63.6	71.0
France	75.5	58.9	67.0	75.3	62.5	68.8
Irish Republic	76.4	43.4	60.0	79.1	55.7	67.5
Belgium	71.8	49.3	60.6	73.8	56.6	65.2
Luxembourg	77.6	47.5	62.8	76.4	51.7	64.2
Greece	76.2	41.7	58.3	77.1	49.7	63.0
Spain	76.0	41.8	58.7	77.1	50.7	63.7
Italy	74.0	42.0	57.8	73.8	46.2	59.9
EU Average	–	–	–	78.1	59.8	68.9

[a] People aged 15–64, except for UK, where data refer to those 16–65.

Source: ONS (2002:73).

and life courses were predictable, to a **risk regime**, in which the experience of work is individualized and there is no longer a standard or common biography (2000: 67–92).

Gender and access to work

Although we talk about the period of postwar full employment, this is not really an accurate picture of typical **participation rates** in the past, as Pamela Meadows reminds us:

> If we take the household as the unit, 50 years ago the head of the household, whether male or female, was likely to be economically active, with other household members other than lodgers and adult or adolescent children likely to be inactive. This model, which had persisted since the industrial revolution, was envisaged by Beveridge as unchanging and still forms the basis of our social security system. However, it does not match present social reality (1996: 4).

Full employment meant that any man who wanted to find a job had a reasonably good chance of success. As Beveridge had defined it in 1944: 'Full employment . . . means having always more vacant jobs than unemployed men' (quoted in Rubery 1997: 63).

The **male breadwinner model** of the family underlay definitions of full employment, and the way in which social security provisions were framed, and also informed employers' and employees' notions of suitable workers for particular jobs. In Britain forty years ago the 'typical worker' (found in many sociological studies of the time) was a man, working full-time in industry in skilled or semi-skilled work. Today the average worker is more likely to be a woman working part-time in a service sector job such as retail.

These facts have profound implications for how we understand 'work', and for the role of public and social policy in responding to labour market problems. As many writers have pointed out, the old view of 'work' as paid employment outside the home in the public sphere served to downgrade the unpaid work which went on, undertaken mainly by women, in the domestic sphere: childcare, cleaning, cooking, etc. This led some feminists in the 1970s to develop a campaign for wages for housework. Women's access to paid employment outside the home was restricted by domestic responsibilities, especially childcare and the prevalent social belief that women's real place was in the home. One of the most dramatic trends in the labour market since the 1970s has been the steady increase in the numbers of women in paid employment outside the home; in particular, the participation rates of married women have seen very significant rises in most European countries. Table 6.2 gives some indication of these developments. It also begins to reveal another feature of recent labour market changes noted above: as female employment has increased, so male unemployment has grown. This is sometimes referred to as the **feminization** of work; however the changes are not typically because

Table 6.2 UK employee jobs,[a] by gender and industry (%)

	Males			Females		
	1981	1991	2001	1981	1991	2001
Manufacturing	32	25	22	17	12	8
Distribution, hotels, catering and repairs	17	20	22	26	26	27
Financial and business services	11	15	19	12	17	18
Transport and communication	9	9	9	3	3	4
Construction	9	8	8	2	2	1
Agriculture	2	2	2	1	1	1
Energy and water supply	4	3	1	1	1	–
Other services	17	19	18	38	40	41
All employee jobs (=100%) (millions)	13.2	12.1	12.8	10.0	11.5	12.7

[a] At June each year.

Source: ONS (2002: 69).

Table 6.3 The gender pay gap, Great Britain, 1982–1999

	1983	1985	1987	1989	1991	1993	1995	1997	1999
Female full-timers	72.3	73.8	73.7	76.5	78.3	79.4	80.2	80.9	81.6
Female part-timers	57.0	57.4	56.2	57.2	58.3	58.8	60.0	59.2	60.4

Average gross hourly earnings (overtime included) of female full-time and part-time employees as % of total male full-time earnings.

Source: Grimshaw and Rubery (2001).

of direct substitution (that would be women doing jobs that men once did) but rather because the kinds of job available have changed.

Although many more women are working outside the home, the labour market is still gendered in the sense that typically men and women work in different kinds of jobs, in different sectors. This is also illustrated in Table 6.2. Women are concentrated in service sector jobs, often occupations such as nursing, teaching, catering, and cleaning which mirror traditional domestic skills and tasks, or in jobs in retail, personal services, and tourism, where women may be in part employed to attract the customers. The distinction between women and men's jobs are surprisingly enduring, both in practice and in terms of the career expectations of young women and men. Such a gendered **division of labour** has implications both for women and for men's employment opportunities, but also for their relative average wages. This is often referred to by the notions of horizontal and vertical segregation, in which women are concentrated in certain industries and sectors and, within those, at the bottom of career ladders; and by the notion of a **gender pay gap**, in which women's average earnings are well below those of men (see Table 6.3). The number of women working part-time further strengthens the impact of these factors.

Lower earnings for women reflect their concentration in lower-paid sectors of employment and at the bottom of career ladders, but also the ways in which skills are defined:

> In manual work, 'skill' is socially constructed, so that jobs that involve tasks associated with masculine expertise—such as driving—are seen as more skilled than jobs that involve feminine dexterity—such as sewing (Abbott and Wallace 1997: 195).

Women's relatively lower earning power obviously has implications for their welfare in terms of their current standard of living but also in respect of pensions and hence the threat of poverty in older age. As Ginn and Arber comment:

> Among elderly people, inequality in personal incomes is structured by class and gender, and occupational pensions are the main means by which a disadvantaged position in the labour market during working life is translated into a low income in later life. The concentration of poverty among women in later life is well established. (1993: 47)

Case Study 6.1 The pros and cons of part-time work

'Since part-time employment almost never pays enough to support a family (and perhaps not even a single person), part-time jobs can only be taken by those with another earner in the family—often in practice, women married to men in employment. For this group the tax and benefits system offers a substantial incentive to work part-time. . . . For women whose partners are unemployed or earning a low wage topped up by family credit, benefit withdrawal starts at a much lower point; creating effective disincentives for the woman to work.

Thus, it is argued, the rise in part time working is helping to create a gulf between "work-rich" families, with more than one job, and "work-poor" families with no job at all, while offering little or nothing to the unemployed who need a full time wage.' (Hewitt 1996: 44).

Questions:

- Are the reasons why men and women take part-time work the same or different?
- Is the availability of part-time work a good opportunity for women who want to work?
- Why is part-time working much less in some European countries than in others?

The net effects of these changes in the labour market has been to reduce the numbers of traditional 'men's jobs' whilst at the same time increasing the numbers of jobs seen as suitable for women. However, many of the jobs which women are now doing are part-time, poorly paid, and with few prospects of career advancement. Some commentators see these developments as irreversible: 'Men, both the young and the old, may be waiting for the return of an era, which has gone for good' (Balls 1993: 23).

UNEMPLOYMENT AND SOCIAL EXCLUSION

Relatively high rates of unemployment have come to characterize many European economies; however, patterns of unemployment vary considerably in terms of age, race, gender, and geography (see Box 6.2 for the problems of defining unemployment). Unemployment rates are higher for young people, ethnic minorities, and those with no (or poor) educational or training qualifications, and generally higher for men than for women (see Table 6.4 for gender and age variations). In addition, there are regions of exceptionally high unemployment.

Youth unemployment

Young people throughout Europe have been particularly affected by unemployment (see Table 6.5). This has led some to talk about the restructuring of the youth labour market and the prolonging of the transition from school to work (see Chapter 14). As a result, possible responses to youth unemployment have been a major focus for debate and policy reform (see below). The implications of a hard core of long-term unemployed

Box 6.2 The problems of defining unemployment

We need to be cautious when looking at unemployment statistics, especially when comparing across countries. Unemployment can be defined for data-gathering purposes in a number of different ways, which have implications for the headline figure of unemployment, and hence public perceptions of the problem. Before April 1998 in the UK the main indicator of unemployment was the government figures based on the claimant count (i.e. those unemployed and claiming benefits). This calculation was much criticized, as it did not include (for example) people on government training schemes. From 1998 the International Labour Office definition is used. This definition of unemployment is accepted as a more workable one for comparative purposes: someone is unemployed if they do not have a job but are available to start work within two weeks and have looked for work in the previous four weeks or have been waiting to start a job. However, even this measure is open to debate. Some people may regard themselves as unemployed even though they may not be officially defined as such, for example someone who was forced to take early retirement but did not wish to give up work, or a disabled person not in work but who would actually like to work if suitable employment were available.

Also, defining someone as unemployed may not be strictly accurate: they may be engaged in work in the informal economy, doing voluntary work, or unpaid caring in the home, thus actually 'working' if not part of the formal economy.

young people have also fuelled the debate about the development of an underclass. A recent definition of the underclass underscores the potential relationship between unemployment and social exclusion:

> a social group or class of people located at the bottom of the class structure who, over time, have become structurally separate and culturally distinct from the regularly employed working class and society in general through processes of social and economic change (particularly de-industrialisation) and/or through patterns of cultural behaviour, who are now persistently reliant on state benefits and almost permanently confined to living in poorer conditions and neighbourhoods. (Macdonald 1997: 3–4)

Many young people only experience unemployment for a short period before going into further education, training, or a job, and therefore we must not assume that unemployment alone causes social exclusion or the basis for an underclass. Nevertheless, in certain localities such as Liverpool in England or amongst certain ethnic communities such as blacks in American inner-city ghettos unemployment may be more persistent and intra-generational, leading to the kind of social marginalization implied in definitions of the underclass (Roberts 1997: 45–7).

Lone parents and unemployment

Another group which has attracted special attention in the debate about unemployment, especially in the United States and the UK, are lone parents. In comparison with

Table 6.4 UK unemployment rates,[a] by gender and age (%)

	1992	1993	1994	1995	1996	1997	1998	1999	2000
Males									
16–17	17.7	18.8	1838	19.2	21.3	19.4	18.1	21.5	20.1
18–24	19.0	21.1	19.3	17.7	17.2	14.8	13.1	12.6	11.8
25–44	10.5	10.9	10.2	8.9	8.7	6.9	5.7	5.6	4.8
45–54	8.4	9.4	8.6	7.5	6.4	6.1	4.7	4.9	4.8
55–59	11.2	12.3	11.6	10.3	9.8	8.0	6.7	6.4	5.4
60–64	10.2	14.2	11.6	9.9	8.9	7.6	6.9	6.4	5.8
65 and over	4.9	4.6	3.7	–	4.0	4.1	–	–	–
All aged 16 and over	11.5	12.4	11.4	10.1	9.6	8.1	6.8	6.7	6.1
Females									
16–17	14.0	15.1	16.9	15.5	15.3	16.0	15.3	14.0	16.9
18–24	11.0	12.9	11.8	11.6	10.2	9.8	9.4	9.3	8.5
25–44	7.3	7.3	7.0	6.7	6.3	5.4	5.1	4.8	4.5
45–54	5.0	5.0	5.0	4.5	4.1	3.7	3.1	3.2	2.9
55–59	4.5	6.0	6.5	4.7	4.3	4.8	3.5	3.5	3.1
60 and over	3.1	3.9	2.9	–	–	2.1	2.0	1.9	–
All aged 16 and over	7.3	7.6	7.3	6.8	6.3	5.7	5.3	5.1	4.8

[a] At spring each year. Unemployment based on the ILO definition as % of all economically active.

Source: ONS (2002: 70).

other European countries the UK has a high number of lone-parent households; they are less likely to be in paid employment, and are therefore more likely to be dependent on state benefits.

In America the 'problem' of lone mothers has been seen as a key side effect of earlier welfare systems: income support for lone mothers is thought to have reduced the incentive to marry and to work. Hence, conservative critics have pointed to the growth in the numbers of lone mothers as evidence that the welfare state has contributed to the breakdown of the family and the work ethic. The ability of lone parents to go out to work is obviously dependent upon a range of factors: for example, the accessibility of appropriate and affordable childcare; a supply of jobs that pay sufficient to sustain the household; and the skills and disposition of the individual.

Explanations of unemployment

There is no single explanation of unemployment and indeed we should not expect one, as unemployment itself is a varied condition, for example differences between

Table 6.5 Young people,[a] by employment status: EU comparison, 2000 (%)

	In employment	Unemployed	Economically inactive	All (= 100%) (millions)
Austria	52.5	3.5	43.9	0.9
Portugal	42.0	3.8	54.2	1.5
Irish Republic	47.7	3.3	48.9	0.7
United Kingdom	55.9	7.7	36.4	6.9
Germany	46.1	4.3	49.6	8.9
Sweden	36.9	3.8	59.2	1.0
Denmark	67.0	4.9	28.1	0.6
Luxembourg	30.6	2.0	65.3	0.0
Netherlands	68.4	3.8	27.8	1.9
Italy	26.1	12.0	61.9	6.7
Finland	45.4	17.9	36.7	0.6
Belgium	30.3	5.5	64.2	1.2
Spain	31.8	10.8	57.4	5.8
France	28.3	7.4	64.4	7.2
Greece	26.9	11.2	61.8	1.4
EU average	39.9	7.6	52.5	45.5

[a] Aged 15–24.

Source: ONS (2002: 71).

short-term temporary job loss, long-term unemployment, or 'voluntary' redundancy or early retirement. However, debates about the causes of unemployment are important because they underpin different policy responses. It is generally agreed that the core of recent unemployment is structural: namely that declining employment in some sectors such as manufacturing is not compensated for by employment expansion in other sectors. Unemployment may occur because more jobs are lost than are created or because of constraints on mobility (i.e. the new jobs are located somewhere different from the old jobs), or because people are not prepared or able for a variety of reasons to accept different kinds of work. Another cause of structural unemployment is technological development: advances in process and methods means that fewer people are required to produce the same level of output as in the past. Thus, both the number of people and the kinds of people in demand in the labour market change.

In relation to policy discussions, we can draw a broad distinction between individualist and structuralist explanations of unemployment and hence different approaches to its remedy. Neo-liberals see high unemployment as a consequence of the uncompetitiveness of Western economies in comparison to emerging economies in other parts of the world. This uncompetitiveness is seen, in part, as a result of the market distortions created by the welfare state: individuals for a variety of reasons have failed to adapt sufficiently to the new economic circumstances. This may be because they refuse to accept lower wages and change the kind of work they do; because they fail to acquire the new skills needed to get work; or because, in the context of welfare benefits which ameliorate the effects of unemployment, they have lost the incentive to get work. Structuralist explanations, on the other hand, see the unemployed as victims of global economic forces and changes, locked into cycles of social and economic disadvantage beyond their power as individuals to change. All societies in Europe have to wrestle with the issue of unemployment, although the severity of the problem varies from country to country.

WHAT CAN POLICY DO?

There are various ways in which public policy can have an impact on work and employment. First, through broad macroeconomic policy in terms of how the economy is managed and the role of monetary and fiscal policy in encouraging economic growth and development and hence the impact on the demand for labour (see Chapter 5). Second, through specific employment regulation such as collective labour laws regarding the conduct of industrial relations and the role of trade unions and individual labour laws regarding aspects such as discrimination and unfair dismissal. Third, via education and training policies which seek to improve the supply of labour and hence the employability of individuals (see Chapter 14). Fourth, through what is often referred to as active labour market policy, which includes job creation or job subsidy policies. Fifth, through welfare and benefit systems which try to ensure a safety net for the inactive, unemployed, or low-paid. Social policy analysts have traditionally been concerned with the benefit systems, but in practice it is difficult to separate out policy in these different areas, as they inevitably affect each other.

Lying behind policy choices are political views about what government should do and can do. We will consider three different broad approaches to the question of what policy can and should do: the deregulationist or neo-liberal approach; the regulation or social democratic approach, which can take a number of different forms; and the radical alternatives, sometimes thought of as 'green' ideas (see e.g. Esping-Andersen 1996a: 10–21). In practice, as we shall see, real-life policies are sometimes a mixture of these different perspectives.

Deregulation or the neo-liberal approach

A liberal market approach of deregulation and minimal welfare is the approach that broadly characterized the US and UK in the 1980s and early 1990s.

> The case for a deregulated labour market rests on the belief that regulation—in very broad terms employment protection and minimum wage legislation, plus adequate legal backing for trade unions—renders markets less flexible and less adaptable, thus driving up unemployment. (Philpott 1997a: 12)

Simply put, the belief is that highly paid workers in the first world economies have priced themselves out of jobs in the face of competition from low-wage economies in other parts of the world. The solution, in part, is to reassert market forces with the aim of depressing wages. The answer to unemployment is to concentrate on restimulating the economy, and free up the labour market so that labour can find its true price. Often combined with this kind of analysis is the argument that the welfare state and its benefit safety net has created a dependency culture in which even when there is work people lack the incentives to go out and get it. One approach, advocated for example by Charles Murray in the United States, is therefore to withdraw benefits and force people back to work.

These arguments have found their strongest supporters in the United States, where policy has been directed towards the twin aims of creating a lower wage economy at the bottom end of the labour market and making participation in employment or training a condition of benefit entitlement. The latter approach to unemployment benefits is usually called **workfare**, and typically carries with it a strong moral undertone:

> Dispute over what can be expected of poor people, not lack of opportunity, is the main reason chronic poverty persists in America. (Mead 1997: 1)

These ideas have travelled from America to the UK and were influential in the Conservative governments of the 1980s and early 1990s. They still inform current policy thinking, as will be seen below. Of course, underlying such policy ideas is the assumption that there are jobs into which people can be forced, and in the American example the expansion of low-paid service sector jobs has been considerable. In Europe it is not so clear that such a policy could work without some element of government-sponsored job creation.

Regulation or the social democratic approach

A regulation or social democratic approach to unemployment and related employment issues starts from the premise that the difficulties are structural rather than individual, and therefore state intervention of some sort to secure the welfare of disadvantaged groups is legitimate. Thus, policy is expected to combine employment protection measures, such as unfair dismissal legislation and directives on working hours, with social protection for those who are disadvantaged in the labour market. Esping-Andersen (1996) sees Sweden as the archetype of such an approach: comprehensive and universalistic benefit systems combined with active labour market policies designed to create jobs, especially in the public sector, and provide continuing education and training to enable people to take up job opportunities. The problem with such an approach, simply put, is that it is expensive and requires a degree of social consensus accepting high levels of taxation as the price for a developed welfare system.

In other countries in Europe a different variant of the social democratic approach has been tried, leading to what Esping-Andersen has characterized as the 'labour reduction route':

> While the Scandinavians have managed the surplus of 'deindustrialized', largely unskilled, masses with retraining and job creation, and the Americans with wage erosion, the continental European

> nations have opted to subsidise their exit, especially through early retirement. This has arguably produced an 'insider–outsider' divide, with a small, predominantly male, 'insider' workforce enjoying high wages, expensive social rights, and strong job security, combined with a swelling population of 'outsiders' depending either on the male breadwinner's pay or on welfare state transfers. (1996a: 18)

The growth in the numbers of inactive men, that is retired and those on invalidity benefits, has been considerable in countries such as Denmark, Germany, and France. Not unsurprisingly, those most likely either to be forced into early retirement through redundancy or to opt for an early end to work are those whose employment was unskilled and/or poorly paid (OECD 1994: 27–35). As a result, the labour reduction route is liable to increase the dependency of older groups on welfare benefits of one sort or another.

Due to the welfare costs associated with such approaches to the problem of unemployment, social democratic ideas have increasingly come under pressure from the arguments of the neo-liberals. However, in most continental European countries the social costs of a deregulation approach as developed in America are seen as too high: unemployment may be reduced, but at the expense of growing poverty and social inequality. Social democratic or regulation perspectives have therefore increasingly argued for what Esping-Andersen (1996a: 3) has characterized as a 'social investment strategy'. This emphasizes the desirability of moving from passive (income support) benefits to active labour market policies. Thus, in addition to the concern with social security through benefits systems a regulation approach now typically also puts a premium on so-called 'supply side' measures, that is, policies on education and training designed to make people more employable. In recent debates about the future of the welfare state in Europe, especially in Britain, there has been discussion of the possibilities of a 'middle way', that is a basis for policy that borrows from both neo-liberal and social democratic ideas (see below in discussion of recent policy).

Radical alternatives

Although debate about employment and unemployment policy is dominated by the dispute between deregulation and regulation perspectives, a third set of ideas has increasingly tried to inject radical alternatives into the argument. Such alternatives do not form a coherent whole, but rather come from a number of different perspectives. What unites them is often an anti-state, self-help approach, and for this reason they are sometimes characterized as green ideas.

These ideas revolve around a rejection of continued economic growth as an overarching aim for government policy, or simply see the possibility of a return to postwar 'full employment' as utopian (Mayo 1996). Thus, if it will be impossible to find paid employment for everyone, the focus must shift to finding alternatives to work or attempts to share work out more evenly (see also Marsh 1991). This might involve facing the question of why we should continue to see paid employment as a defining characteristic of citizenship or social inclusion. Instead, participation through other activities such as voluntary or community work should rank equally as a contribution to society (see Box 6.3).

Box 6.3 Reconceiving work

But whatever employment levels pertain in the medium term, there are good reasons to recast the utopia from one of full employment to one (sometimes dubbed 'full engagement') which provides access to income and to meaningful work, paid or unpaid as citizens.

First, for the immediate future, the lead export sectors for the UK—such as financial services, tourism, and manufacturing—will remain central to national employment levels and to generating secondary employment and income. However, the evidence of 'jobless' communities is on the rise . . . So, in the face of mass unemployment there is a pressing need for alternative approaches to work within deprived neighbourhoods that meet people's needs and promote self-reliance. At the same time, there is a pressing social and economic need to reverse the low status and conditions of unpaid work, given the increasing stress and personal cost to those doing it.

Second, employment should be seen not as an end in itself, but as a means to achieving a better quality of life. This means distinguishing between forms of work, with the aim of promoting patterns of work that are socially useful and contribute to greater personal autonomy and fulfillment.

(Mayo 1996: 16–17)

Another set of ideas suggests that in the face of continued high unemployment, policy should focus on guaranteed incomes schemes. This would involve a universal guaranteed income for anyone who fell below an agreed acceptable threshold, whether or not they were in employment (Pixley 1993: 91–4). Critics of such an idea point both to the cost and to the effect on incentives, arguing that no one would take certain low-paid jobs if they were guaranteed an income regardless of whether they worked or not.

RECENT POLICY INITIATIVES IN THE UK

Up until the middle of the 1970s full employment was an avowed aim of governments in the UK, and there was a broad political consensus on the role of the welfare state in supporting the unemployed. Since that time, and especially since the early 1980s and the period of Conservative government, the agreement on policy objectives has broken down and policy has moved progressively away from the full employment ideal.

In the 1980s, Conservative governments followed in the footsteps of Republican politicians in the United States in arguing that the welfare state had resulted in perverse incentives, discouraging the unemployed from seeking work and leading to welfare dependency. As a result, policy shifted in a neo-liberal direction, reducing employment protection and the bargaining power of trade unions whilst simultaneously cutting levels of welfare benefits and increasingly moving to a more conditional system of entitlement to benefit.

Changes to social security benefits were focused around two main perceived problems. First, the need to reduce public expenditure and secondly to restructure work incentives. Thus, the targets for policy were to reduce the levels of benefit and require the unemployed to demonstrate their availability or willingness to work (see Chapter 11). As Evans summarizes:

> Social security changed from concerns about coverage in the 1970s to concerns about fiscal constraint and labour market incentives. Targeting, economic incentives, and efficiency became the central concerns of policy in the 1980s. (1998: 263)

The Jobseeker's Allowance introduced in 1996 marked the final point of these developments under the Conservative governments of the 1980s and 1990s. This marked the end of insurance-based unemployment benefit, replacing it finally with an allowance that required claimants to demonstrate that they were actively looking for work as a condition of receiving benefit. Critics of these developments viewed them as simply punitive:

> With declining employment prospects for the unskilled, for black people and for working-class youth, who figure disproportionately among the unemployed, the measures introduced by the Jobseeker's Allowance serve only as a form of punishment. (Novak 1997: 106)

The new Labour government of 1997 came to power committed to the reform of the welfare state. However, this was not heralded as a return to the ideas and policies of the 1960s and 1970s. Instead, the new government was keen to develop a new middle way, which took up some of the ideas of the neo-liberals whilst maintaining the social democratic commitment to social justice. This has been developed into the notion of an active welfare system (see Box 6.4). In relation to employment policies and issues this approach has taken three main forms: measures to encourage and subsidize people into

Box 6.4 An active welfare system

'The provision of benefits for workless people helps to achieve our social goals by increasing incomes and providing security for some of the most disadvantaged people in the country. But it may also reduce the incentive for some people to go out and look for work. The benefits system in the past has been passive in its administration of benefits. It has been content to hand out money without offering people opportunities to get ahead under their own steam. But people in work stand a much better chance of sharing in rising prosperity than those dependent on benefit. We want a welfare system that provides that all-important safety net for those who cannot work. But we want to ensure that in doing so it also provides people with the opportunities they need to fulfil their potential. This is consistent with the generally held view that it is the responsibility of those who are receiving unemployment benefit to be actively seeking work.'

(Department for Work and Pensions 2002: 24)

or back into work; measures to make work pay; and a range of training policy measures such as Modern Apprenticeships designed to improve the skills of the workforce (see Chapter 14 for the latter). We will consider the first two of these in turn.

New Deals

The centrepiece of the New Labour governments' approach is the New Deal, a raft of **welfare to work** policies announced in the first budget of the new Labour government in 1997. The avowed aim of the policy is to get the long-term unemployed back into work, on the basis that work is the best guarantor of welfare. The original, and still the primary, focus of the policy is the young unemployed: 18–24 year olds who have been claiming Jobseeker's allowance for 6 months or more will enter a 'gateway' to work, which involves job search and career advice and training before taking up one of four options (see Box 6.5). As Williams (2002: 54) comments:

> The New Deal for Young People contains two new elements which distinguish it from previous programmes of a similar kind (such as Youth Training). The first is that it is client-centred. Rather than places being available on certain schemes and young people being 'slotted into' what is there, the young person's wishes are intended to be the driving force. Each young person has a Personal Adviser (PA) who sees him/her regularly and works intensively to find an option that is right for him/her.

Any young people who refuse to take up one of these options will have their benefit cut. Gordon Brown (Chancellor of the Exchequer at the time of announcing the policy) said that there would be no fifth option 'to stay at home in bed watching television' (quoted in the *Financial Times*, 26 June 1997).

The scheme developed from its beginnings to cover a range of groups (see Box 6.6). To facilitate the re-entry of women with children into the labour market there is also a new national strategy on childcare. The policy is couched in terms of a new partnership between government and the private sector:

> New Deal will close the gap between what young people have to offer, and the needs of employers, with an intensive programme of training, further education and work experience.

Box 6.5 New Deal options

Young people enter a 'gateway' to the four options; this involves a period of one-to-one advice and guidance which may last up to four months, they then move onto one of the following options:

1. A job in the private sector: a job subsidy of £60 a week for six months will be paid to employers who employ an unemployed young person.
2. A job in the voluntary sector: on the same basis as (1) above.
3. A place on an environment taskforce: the young person will receive normal benefit plus £20 a week.
4. Full-time education and training.

Box 6.6 New Deals

New Deal for Young People: compulsory for 18–24 years who have been unemployed and on jobseeker's allowance for six months.

New Deal 25 Plus: compulsory for adults 25–49 who have been on jobseeker's allowance for eighteen of the last twenty-one months.

New Deal 50 Plus: voluntary for anyone 50 or over who has been on benefits for six months.

New Deal for Lone Parents: compulsory, though still being developed (2002). Lone parents on income support have a meeting with a personal advisor to assess employment opportunities.

New Deal for Disabled People: voluntary.

New Deal for Partners: voluntary scheme for partners of people in workless households.

> Employers have an important role to play in making New Deal a success, offering employment under the subsidised jobs option and providing training during that time. . . . In turn, the scheme benefits employers in a number of ways. It helps meet their manpower needs and it gives them a new source of potential recruits (Labour Party n.d.).

The various New Deals have been claimed by the government as a major success. By August 2002 nearly 400,000 young people had passed through New Deal into a job, and with a relatively buoyant economy some commentators see the job of New Deal for Young People as almost completed (*Financial Times*, September 2002). In August 2002 Gordon Brown, Chancellor of the Exchequer, when announcing new tax credits for children and workers also hinted at tightening up the New Deal. The 'Step Up' pilot programme gives long-term unemployed, who have not found a job after New Deal, a guaranteed job with an employer for fifty weeks. However, failure to accept this job would result in loss of benefit.

The New Deal scheme is inevitably controversial: neo-liberals point to the cost of the programme and argue that it produces no new jobs. Critics from the Left argue that it retains too much of the compulsion that characterized the neo-liberal policies which preceded it (see Case Study 6.2). Whatever one's view, the policy represents a new attempt at a social investment strategy with active labour market intervention in the attempt to reduce unemployment.

Making work pay

The second strand of employment policy involves measures designed to make sure that people entering low-paid jobs can afford to work and are no worse off than if they had stayed on benefits. The major measure was the introduction in April 1999 of the

Case Study 6.2 The right to work or the duty to work?

'The underpinning values implied in the New Deal are essentially *moral*. New opportunities are to be provided, the scheme will be client-centred, young people will be offered experience and training that is relevant and meaningful for them, but there will be . . . no fifth option. Those who "don't want to work" will be made to work by the imposition of financial sanctions.

People have got lots of mega problems in their lives, and they aren't terribly bright, and they need to sort themselves out. I feel that the government have not really grasped that. They've not really recognized that you can frighten people into taking jobs but if you've not solved the problems they've got it will emerge again at another point. (College Principal)

No one should have to work. I don't want to. If someone wants to live on the dole, why shouldn't they? Most people [who work] do awful jobs they don't like. . . . New Deal? Raw deal. They just want to make me do some s . . . job. (Davey)'

(Williams 2002: 57, 68, 70)

Questions

- Is it right to make schemes such as New Deal effectively compulsory for certain groups?
- What kinds of unintended effects might arise from making such schemes compulsory?
- Can society impose a duty to work on its citizens?

National Minimum Wage. From October 2001 the minimum wage was £4.10 per hour for workers aged over 22 and £3.50 per hour for those aged 18–21. The measure is thought to have raised the wages of some 1.5 million workers since its introduction (Department for Work and Pensions 2002: 46). In addition to this policy innovation the new Labour governments have introduced a number of tax credits to try to ameliorate the effects of in-work poverty. The Working Families Tax Credit and the Disabled Persons Tax Credit were introduced in October 1999. At the time of writing there are plans for an extension of this approach with the introduction of a new Working Tax Credit for low earners from April 2003 (Department for Work and Pensions 2002: 47).

The employment and training policies of the New Labour governments combine a mixture of philosophies and policies. The commitment to a minimum wage and a degree of trade union recognition puts the policies firmly in the social democratic camp, as does the emphasis on supply-side measures such as improved access to further education and training. However, there is no option for young people to stay out of the New Deal and still receive benefit. The policy introduced by earlier Conservative governments of making entitlement to welfare conditional on participation in work or training is maintained and owes much to the American examples of workfare schemes. This aspect of the policy is more in the tradition of neo-liberal thought.

Cartoon 6.1 Is any job better than no job?

CONCLUSIONS

Despite a number of decades of persistent unemployment and widespread popular fears about an emerging 'workshy', delinquent, and socially marginal underclass, work, or rather employment, seems to be as popular as ever. Most young people want to find a good job, many lone parents would like the opportunity to work, many disabled people feel unfairly excluded from the world of paid employment, and substantial numbers of those forced to take early retirement in the 1990s found other jobs or would have liked to. Employment is still seen by the majority as the ticket to full participation in society. The problem for the UK and other European societies is whether it is possible to produce both high levels of employment and social justice or equality. The American example of a low-wage, low-skills, high-employment economy is impressive in the number of jobs it provides but worrying with respect to the growing ranks of the working poor. This raises the question of whether any job is better for the individual's welfare than no job (see cartoon 6.1). The Swedish or German examples of high-wage, high-skills, high-employment economies have looked increasingly unsustainable as competition in the global economy heats up. The search for a 'middle way' between these two alternatives is bound to continue. Whether the UK is in the vanguard of such a new approach or merely the test-bed in which these ideas will prove unworkable remains to be seen.

REFERENCES

Abbott, P., and Wallace, C. (1997), *An Introduction to Sociology: Feminist Perspectives*. London: Routledge.

Ashton, D. (1992), 'The restructuring of the labour market and youth training'. In Brown and Lauder (1992: 180–202).

Balls, E. (1993), 'Danger: men not at work: unemployment and non-employment in the UK and beyond'. In Balls and Gregg (1993: 1–30).

—— and Gregg, P. (1993), *Work and Welfare: Tackling the Jobs Deficit*. London: Institute for Public Policy Research.

Beck, U. (2000), *The Brave New World of Work*. Cambridge: Polity Press.

Bradley, H., Erikson, M., Stephenson, C., and Williams, S. (2000), *Myths at Work*. Cambridge: Polity Press.

Brown, P., and Lauder, H. (eds.), *Education For Economic Survival*. London: Routledge.

Commission on Social Justice (1994), *Social Justice: Strategies for National Renewal*. London: Vintage.

Crompton, R., Gallie, D., and Purcell, K. (eds.) (1996), *Changing Forms of Employment: Organisations, Skills and Gender*. London: Routledge.

Department for Work and Pensions (2002), *Opportunity for All Fourth Annual Report 2002*, Cm. 5598. London: HMSO.

Equal Opportunities Commission (1996), *Briefings on Women and Men in Britain: Pay*. Manchester: EOC.

Esping-Andersen, G. (1996*a*), 'After the golden age? Welfare state dilemmas in a global economy'. In Esping-Andersen (1996*b*: 1–31).

—— (ed.) (1996b), *Welfare States in Transition: National Adaptations in Global Economies*. London: Sage.

—— (1999), *Social Foundations of Post-Industrial Economies*. Oxford: Oxford University Press.

Evans, M. (1998), 'Social security: dismantling the Pyramids?' In Glennerster and Hills (1998: 257–307).

Gallie, D. (1991), 'Patterns of skill change: upskilling, deskilling or the polarisation of skills?', *Work, Employment and Society* 5(3): 319–51.

—— (1996), 'Skill, gender and the quality of employment'. In Crompton et al. (1996: 133–59).

Giddens, A. (1993), *Sociology*. Oxford: Oxford University Press.

Ginn, J., and Arber, S. (1993), 'Pension penalties: the gendered division of occupational welfare', *Work, Employment and Society*, 7(1): 47–70.

Glennerster, H., and Hills, J. (eds.) (1998), *The State of Welfare: The Economics of Social Spending*. Oxford: Oxford University Press.

Gregory, A., and O'Reilly, J. (1996), 'Checking out and cashing up: the prospects and paradoxes of regulating part-time work in Europe'. In Crompton et al. (1996: 207–34).

Green, F. (2001), 'It's been a hard day's night: the concentration and intensification of work in late twentieth-century Britain', *British Journal of Industrial Relations* 39(1): 53–80.

Grimshaw, D., and Rubery, J. (2001), *The Gender Pay Gap: A Research Review*. Manchester: Equal Opportunities Commission.

Hewitt, P. (1996), 'The place of part-time employment'. In Meadows (1996: 39–58).

Labour Party (n.d.), *A New Deal for a New Britain*. London: Labour Party.

Macdonald, R. (ed.) (1997), *Youth, the 'Underclass' and Social Exclusion*. London: Routledge.

Manning, N. (ed.) (1991), *Social Policy Review 1990–91*. Harlow: Longman.

Marsh, C. (1991), 'The right to work: justice in the distribution of employment'. In Manning (1991: 223–42).

Mayo, E. (1996), 'Dreaming of work'. In Meadows (1996: 143–64).

Mead, L. M. (1997), *From Welfare to Work: Lessons from America*. London: Institute for Economic Affairs.

Meadows, P. (ed.) (1996), *Work Out—or Work In?* Layerthorpe: Joseph Rowntree Foundation.

Novak, T. (1997), 'Hounding delinquents: the introduction of the Jobseeker's Allowance', *Critical Social Policy* 17(1): 99–110.

ONS (Office for National Statistics) (2002), *Social Trends 32*. London: HMSO.

OECD (Organization for Economic Cooperation and Development) (1994), *New Orientations for Social Policy*. Brussels: OECD.

Pass, C., Lowes, B., Pendleton, A., and Chadwick, L. (eds.) (1991), *Collins Dictionary of Business*. Glasgow: Collins.

Philpott, J. (1997*a*), 'Looking forward to full employment: an overview'. In Philpott (1997*b*: 1–29).

—— (ed.) (1997*b*), *Working for Full Employment*. London: Routledge.

Pixley, J. (1993), *Citizenship and Employment*. Cambridge: Cambridge University Press.

Ritzer, G. (1993), *The MacDonaldization of Society*. Newbury Park, Calif.: Pine Forge Press.

Roberts, K. (1997), 'Is there an emerging British "underclass"? The evidence from youth research'. In Macdonald (1997: 39–54).

Rubery, J. (1997), 'What do women want from full employment?'. In Philpott (1997*b*: 63–80).

Trades Union Congress (n.d.), *Jobs, Unemployment and Exclusion*. London: TUC.

Williams, S. (2002), 'Individual agency and the experience of new deal', *Journal of Education and Work* 15(1): 53–74.

FURTHER READING

U. Beck, *The Brave New World of Work* (Cambridge: Polity Press, 2000). A leading social theorist of the last decade argues for a radical rethink of how we conceptualize society. In this book he addresses the implications of the emergence of a risk society for the world of work.

H. Bradley, M. Erikson, C. Stephenson, and S. Williams, *Myths at Work* (Cambridge: Polity Press, 2000). An excellent volume which systematically examines from a critical perspective prevailing popular assumptions about the world of work, for example the increase in non-standard and casual work, the feminization of work, and need for increased skills amongst today's employees.

G. Esping-Andersen, 'After the golden age? Welfare state dilemmas in a global economy', in Esping-Andersen (ed.), *Welfare States in Transition: National Adaptations in Global Economies* (London: Sage, 1996). This chapter provides a good review of the problems facing welfare states in the post-full employment period.

R. Macdonald (ed.), *Youth, the 'Underclass' and Social Exclusion* (London: Routledge, 1997). This is a recent collection of articles reviewing the debate about whether an underclass is developing in the UK with particular reference to the position of young people.

L.M. Mead, *From Welfare to Work: Lessons from America* (London: Institute of Economic Affairs, 1997). This book provides an introduction to Mead's work, a leading American thinker on welfare reform along with commentaries from a number of British social policy writers and thinkers, including Frank Field, who was Minister for Welfare Reform for the first fifteen months of the new Labour government in 1997/8.

J. Philpott (ed.), *Working for Full Employment*. (London: Routledge, 1997). Contributions to this collection examine the nature and consequences of contemporary unemployment and examine different policy responses. A number of contributions compare an Anglo-American deregulation approach with the more European regulation approach.

J. Pixley, *Citizenship and Employment* (Cambridge: Cambridge University Press, 1993). Reviews theoretical arguments about the centrality of work in our societies, and in particular the extent to which full employment is still a viable policy goal. Pixley also undertakes a critical analysis of alternatives to paid work such as guaranteed income schemes and communes.

GLOSSARY

dependency ratio Usually the ratio of those outside the labour force (for example 0–15 and 65 and over) to those defined as in the labour force and of working age.

division of labour 'One of the most distinctive characteristics of the economic system of modern societies is the development of a highly complex and diverse division of labour. In other words, work is divided into an enormous number of different occupations, in which people specialize' (Giddens 1993: 491).

feminization The idea that in education, jobs, and economic life more generally men are progressively losing out to women.

flexible or casual work This refers to jobs which are not full-time and permanent but rather temporary, on short-term contract, variable hours, or one-off contracts for a particular piece of work. Labour flexibility is the ability of a firm to modify the employment and utilization of its labour force in the face of changing labour and product market conditions (Pass et al. 1991: 328).

Fordist regime Referring back to Henry Ford's car factory as the archetype of factory production, the notion of a Fordist regime is that for much of the last century the economic growth and development of Western societies was based on mass production, mass labour and mass consumption. People's work and life experiences, like the products they bought, were standardized.

full employment Usually defined either as more jobs available than people seeking employment or as a job available for anyone seeking one.

gender pay gap 'The Equal Opportunities Commission (1996: 2) offers a definition: 'The gender pay gap is defined as women's earnings as a percentage of men's earnings. The pay gap is said to be narrow as this figure approaches 100 per cent.'

labour intensification Increasing the intensity of work means that people have to work harder and expend more mental or manual effort in a given period of work.

labour market The labour market refers to the process whereby firms look for employees (the demand side of the market) and people offer their labour power in return for a wage/salary (the supply side of the market). In practice, there can be said to be many different labour markets, for example local labour markets: the supply and demand for labour in a local area; or skilled and specialist labour markets.

lean production The original idea of lean production is usually associated with the 1990 book by J. Womack and colleagues *The Machine that Changed the World* (New York, Maxwell Macmillan), in which they advocated the need for organizations to restructure to reduce staffing and waste in order to survive in harsher competitive conditions.

male breadwinner model This model assumes a traditional nuclear family structure in which the man goes out to work and earns a family wage (enough for himself and his dependants) and the woman stays at home and works in the domestic sphere.

occupational identity In the past a lot of men, especially skilled workers, could expect to stay in their industry or craft throughout their working lives, and as a result there were often strong occupational identities, for example in shipbuilding, mining, and the steel industry.

participation rates This refers to the percentage of a particular group, for example women, who are in or seeking paid employment.

post-industrial As the share of employment in industry has declined and advanced capitalist economies such as Britain are dominated by non-industrial employment, the term 'post-industrial' has been used to denote a new phase for these economies.

risk regime The risk regime or risk society is usually counterposed to the earlier **Fordist regime** as being a society, economy, and polity in which insecurity, uncertainty, and loss of boundaries prevail. The life course is individualized and people can no longer rely on standard experiences and assumptions; they must chart their own paths.

service sector It is typical to characterize the economy as divided into three main sectors: the primary sector, which includes activities such as agriculture, mining, and fishing; the industrial sector, which includes manufacture and construction; and the service sector, which includes retail, banking, teaching, and health and personal services.

underclass 'a social group or class of people located at the bottom of the class structure who, over time, have become structurally separate and culturally distinct from the regularly employed working class and society in general through processes of social and economic change (particularly de-industrialization) and/or through patterns of cultural behaviour, who are now persistently reliant on state benefits and almost permanently confined to living in poorer conditions and neighbourhoods' (Macdonald 1997: 3–4).

welfare to work An umbrella term for policies focused on getting people off benefits and back into paid employment.

workfare This can be defined as any social policy in which participation in job search, training, or work is a condition of receiving benefits.

7

The Family and Welfare

Jan Pahl

CONTENTS

INTRODUCTION: A CHANGING SOURCE OF WELFARE

'The family' is a controversial topic. Some commentators deplore the changes which are taking place in family life, while others applaud the end of what they see as damaging patterns of family relationships. Some argue that 'family policy' has gone too far and has created a culture of dependency that loads intolerable burdens on the welfare state, while others insist that 'family policy' in Britain has not gone far enough in supporting families and their members. Behind these debates lie deep ideological divides and a fundamental division between the private sphere of the family and the public sphere where social policy is made and implemented.

In this chapter we shall be looking at the facts behind the rhetoric. What changes are taking place in the lives of families and their members? What part do families play in the production of welfare? What principles underlie family policy, and what has been the impact of recent policy changes? And what does 'the family' mean in a world of cultural diversity and rapid social change?

FAMILIES AND HOUSEHOLDS

Definitions

'Family' and 'household' are important terms for this topic, so we begin with some definitions. The **household** is a key unit in social policy, since it is the focus of many policy interventions. For example, means-tested social security payments are calculated on the basis of household income; the council tax is levied on households, not individuals; and many statistics are based on the unit of the household.

One definition of the household is given in *Social Trends*, the annual publication of the Office for National Statistics:

> A household is a person living alone or a group of people who have the address as their only or main residence and who either share one meal a day or share the living accommodation. (ONS 2002: 232)

So households are based on a common place of residence and some sharing of either food or accommodation. Of course, in many cases the 'household' contains a single 'family', but the concept of family is intrinsically much more complicated than the concept of household.

Many definitions have been suggested for the term **family**. In Britain it seems to be agreed that a married couple and their dependent children constitute a family, but when other social groupings and other cultures are concerned, definitions become less secure. The definitional possibilities can be explored by asking a range of different people whether, in their opinion, the following constitute 'a family':

- one parent and his or her children?
- a cohabiting couple and their children?

- an elderly person and an adult child?
- a lesbian couple and the children of one of them?
- a father living apart from his wife and children but supporting them financially
- a three-generation household with parents, their adult children, and their grandchildren

The answers are likely to suggest that the idea of the family is essentially subjective, reflecting each person's ideas about family life. The Family Policy Studies Centre concluded, 'There is no definition of a family. The UK Association of the International Year of the Family does not define a family, but aims to support families in all their possible forms' (Family Policy Studies Centre 1997: 1).

However, there do seem to be some characteristics which define a 'family' for most people. These include:

- marriage or a marriage-like relationships between adults;
- the presence of children who are or have been dependent on the adults;
- sharing of resources such as living space, money and property;
- continuity over time;
- links with other kin.

The official definition of the family, used in all government censuses and surveys, is that a family is:

> a married or cohabiting couple, either with or without their never-married children (of any age), including couples with no children or a lone parent together with his or her never-married child or children (ONS 2002: 232)

However, even this definition might be controversial, since it excludes households which some people would regard as families, such as lesbian or gay couples with children, and includes some households which might not be seen as families, such as cohabiting couples without children.

A useful distinction has been made between the nuclear family and the extended family. The **nuclear family** typically consists of one or two adults living together in a household with their dependent children. However, many nuclear families are embedded in larger kin networks, with whom they may from time to time share living space, money, and property, and which may include grandparents, aunts and uncles, cousins and so on. This larger kin network is described as an **extended family**, and though it is often described as being characteristic of more traditional societies, it remains an important source of support in Britain.

Another useful distinction is between those who focus on 'the family', a term which implies that there is one, ideal-type family, and those who focus on 'families', a term which allows for the increasing diversity of family forms. The idea of 'the family' rests on the assumption that the most natural and desirable family is composed of two married parents and their children, with the father as the main breadwinner and the mother as the homemaker, who fits any paid work around her responsibilities for the home and children. The idea of 'families' underlines the point that family life and relationships can take many different forms, as we shall see, and that no one type of family should be privileged over the others.

Debates about 'family values'

All the changes taking place in family life throughout Europe and North America have produced fierce debates. On the one hand, some people have argued that the 'breakdown of the traditional family' is to blame for a range of social problems, from unemployment and crime to violence and lone-parent families. On the other hand, other people have argued that the 'traditional family' is itself the problem. From this point of view, family violence and lone-parent families are symptoms of inequalities, and even exploitation, within the family, and the changes taking place in family life are to be welcomed rather than deplored.

The following quotations express these two different approaches to the changing shape of family life, both taken from Muncie et al. (1995: 59):

> Despite attempts to subvert it, our laws and systems must acknowledge the family as the basic building block of the nation. Instead of simply calling for more money as the solution to every problem, or even trying to accommodate unconventional lifestyles, the nation's spiritual leaders should unashamedly extol the virtues of normal family life. (Gerald Howarth, Conservative MP, 1991)
>
> Family policy needs to recognize that families come in all shapes and sizes . . . to claim that one kind of family is right and others wrong can do considerable harm by stigmatizing those who live in non-traditional family settings. (Harriet Harman, Labour MP, 1991)

These debates reflect profoundly different ideological approaches to families and family life. Since **ideology** will be a key concept for this chapter, it may be useful to begin with a definition.

> Ideologies are sets of ideas, assumptions and images, by which people make sense of society, which give a clear social identity, and which serve in some way to legitimise power relations in society. (McLennan 1991: 114)

This definition underlines the fact that ideologies not only influence the ways in which individuals think about themselves and their place in the world but also shape the development of social policy and social action in the broader political arena. One way of making sense of different ideologies concerning the family is to consider the theoretical perspectives which underlie them.

THEORETICAL AND POLICY PERSPECTIVES ON THE FAMILY

Many theoretical explanations of the social world have been developed within the discipline of sociology. In thinking about families, three theoretical perspectives are particularly relevant.

Three theoretical perspectives

The functionalist analysis of the family was developed by the American sociologists Parsons and Bales (1956). They suggested that the nuclear family, consisting of a breadwinner/husband and a homemaker/wife, is the type of family which fits most easily with the requirements of industrial society. Lacking close ties to a wider kin network, the nuclear family is able to move from place to place following the demands of the labour market, and generally to perform the functions necessary to the stable continuation of an industrial society.

From this theoretical perspective the modern nuclear family has two main functions: the socialization of children and 'personality stabilization' or 'tension management' for the adults. Parsons and Bales made a clear distinction between the roles of the husband/father and the wife/mother. They saw the father's role as being instrumental, with his employment providing for the economic wellbeing of the family, while the mother's role was affective, being concerned primarily with the emotional wellbeing of the family. In their analysis the tasks assigned to each sex arose out of biological differences, and in particular out of the mother's responsibility for childbearing and rearing.

Functionalist theories were linked with ideas about modernity, which assume that societies progress towards greater uniformity, leaving behind dysfunctional, or even simply diverse forms of family life. There was an underlying assumption that the middle-class American family of the 1950s and 1960s was by definition a superior form of the family and one to which other groups should aspire. It was often described as the 'normal' family.

Even though the functionalist perspective is now seen as old-fashioned and ethnocentric, there are ways in which the ideologies which underpinned this work are still powerful. For example, from time to time the British Social Attitudes Survey includes a question which asks respondents whether they agree or disagree with the following statement: 'A husband's job is to earn the money; a wife's job is to look after the home and family.' Every time that this question is asked there is a sizeable minority of people who agree: for example, in 1995, 24 per cent of respondents said that they 'agreed' or 'strongly agreed' with the statement, with men more likely to agree than women (Jowell et al. 1995). The functionalist conception of the family is still widespread. However, a powerful critique of functionalism has been developed by feminists.

The feminist perspective sees the 'normal' or traditional family as essentially unequal. It argues that the dependence of women and children on the male breadwinner creates a damaging power imbalance within the family which is the source of many problems, especially for women and children, and for those who do not fit into traditional family forms. As Charles put it:

> Feminism has developed a critique of 'the family', arguing that it ensures women's dependency on men and their ideological confinement to the domestic sphere and that it institutionalises heterosexuality and defines other forms of sexuality as deviant. (Charles 2000, 179)

Other feminists have seen the family as the site of a particular type of exploitation:

> [Families] are not just random sets of people united by bonds of affection and kinship who live together and share out the jobs that need doing so as to offer each other practical support in a joint

> endeavour to get along in the world. Rather they are . . . part of a system of labour relations in which men benefit from, and exploit, the work of women—and sometimes of their children and other male relatives too. (Delphy and Leonard 1992: 1)

To sum up, the feminist perspective on the family argues that:

- The traditional family is characterized by inequalities between women and men, and between children and parents, which continue despite the rhetoric of increasing equality.
- These inequalities are translated into inequalities in the allocation of resources, such as money, and in the work done within families, including childcare, domestic work, and caring for dependent members of families.
- These inequalities are maintained by the state, through social and economic policies which assume that families will contain a male breadwinner and a woman who is responsible for childcare and domestic work.

From the feminist perspective, the increases in cohabitation, in divorce, and in the numbers of lone-parent families are all symptoms of the dissatisfaction which women feel with the traditional form of the family.

However, from the New Right perspective the changes occurring in family life are evidence of a deterioration and decay which is damaging to all. The rise in births outside marriage, the increase in divorce initiated by women, and the failure of fathers to support their children are all symptoms of what is going wrong. The following quotation may be taken as an example of this perspective:

> We also see growing evidence of child homelessness, drug abuse among the young, the physical abuse and neglect of babies and children, high rates of teenage pregnancy and a continuing cycle of broken relationships. As the evidence continues to accumulate, there is one persistent factor which so often links all this unhappiness. It is the disintegration of the family. (Kirby 2002: iv)

The Institute of Economic Affairs has been active in setting out the agenda of the New Right in relation to the family, in publications such as those by Dennis and Erdos (1993) and Morgan (1995; 2000). Briefly, the New Right perspective can be summed up as follows:

- The 'normal', and most socially valuable form of the family consists of a married couple, with both parents committed to the care of their children, the father through his responsibility for the family's economic well-being and the mother through her responsibility for the home and family.
- This form of the family is currently under threat, because of demographic and ideological changes, which reflect the influence of feminism, individualism and a more general moral decay.
- The state has played a part in undermining the normal family, by providing support for other types of families, by failing to reward marriage and by tolerating high levels of unemployment among young males.

The state and family policy

There have been a number of attempts to produce a definition of **family policy**. Hantrais and Letablier concluded:

> For a social policy to be described as family policy . . . . the family would need to be the deliberate target of specific actions, and the measures should be designed so as to have an impact on family resources and, ultimately, on family structure. (1996: 139)

However, definitions of family policy tend to founder on the rocks of national and cultural differences. In particular, states vary greatly in the extent to which it is seen as appropriate for governments to intervene in family life. For example, within Europe, Britain has never had an explicit family policy. By contrast, in Finland, France, Germany, Greece, Ireland, Italy, Luxembourg, Portugal, and Spain, the constitution recognizes the family as a social institution and undertakes to afford it protection. Some countries, such as Germany and France, have a designated minister for the family (Hantrais and Letablier 1996).

However, in Britain there has always been a debate about the extent to which the state should be involved in family life. This debate emerged again during the 1997 election, and was apparent in the election manifestos put out by the main political parties. The relevant section in the Conservative Party election manifesto was entitled 'Choice and security for families'. It began by expressing concern about state interference:

> The family is the most important institution in our lives. It offers security and stability in a fast-changing world. But the family is undermined if governments take decisions which families ought to take for themselves. . . . Conservatives believe that a healthy society encourages people to accept responsibility for their own lives. A heavy-handed and intrusive state can do enormous damage. (Conservative Party 1997: 15, 17)

Despite the warning about state interference, the manifesto went on to promise new support for families where one parent was not in paid work because of caring for children or a dependent relative. The promised change took the form of allowing one partner's unused tax allowance to be transferred to an earning spouse, a change which would reward two-parent families with only one-parent in paid work, but which would be irrelevant to one-parent families or to families where both parents were unemployed. As the manifesto explained, 'We believe our tax system should recognize and support the crucial role of families in their caring responsibilities' (p.15).

The relevant section in the 1997 Labour Party election manifesto was headed 'Help parents balance work and family'; and the text explicitly supported women's right to take paid work, and endorsed the value of state involvement in family life:

> Labour does not see families and the state as rival providers for the needs of our citizens. Families should provide the day-to-day support for children to be brought up in a stable and loving environment. But families cannot flourish unless government plays its distinctive role: in education, where necessary, in caring for the young; in making provision for illness and old age; in supporting good parenting; and in protecting families from lawlessness and abuse of power. Society, through

government, must assist families to achieve collectively what no family can achieve alone. (Labour Party 1997: 24)

In November 1998 the Home Secretary, Jack Straw, took a first step in realizing the government's broad manifesto commitments by issuing a Green Paper, *Supporting Families: A Consultation Document* (Home Office 1998). This suggested a number of specific ways in which government could help families, particularly in their role in bringing up children:

- reducing child poverty;
- advice and support for families, including a new national parent helpline and an expanded role for health visitors;
- balancing work and home priorities through family-friendly policies;
- reducing the risks of family breakdown by providing a 'pre-marriage information package' to couples and encouraging pre-nuptial agreements;
- tackling serious problems like domestic violence, truancy, and school-age pregnancy, with a major publicity campaign to raise. awareness of domestic violence issues.

The consultation document was met with immediate criticism from many sides of the political spectrum, illustrating the political risks inherent in government statements about family policy. The Conservative Party warned of state intrusion into private lives, as did, for different reasons, representatives of lone parents and of gay and lesbian people. Later in this chapter we shall consider whether the aims of *Supporting Families* have been met.

Whether or not Britain has an explicit family policy, there is still an enormous amount of policy-making which is relevant to family life. This may take the form of tax and social security policy, legislation related to marriage and divorce, provision for children and dependent adults, and policies relating to health, housing, and employment. Later in this chapter we shall consider some of these in more detail.

DEMOGRAPHIC TRENDS IN FAMILY LIFE

Information about the changing patterns of family life comes from a variety of different sources, including the ten-yearly national Census of Population, the General Register Office, which collates certificates for births, marriages, and deaths, and a variety of quantitative and qualitative surveys. The annual review, *Social Trends*, presents a great deal of quantitative data in a very accessible form, and is an essential source of information about all areas of social policy in Britain (ONS 2002). In this chapter it is only possible to summarize a few of the most important trends in family life. Table 7.1 outlines some of the large-scale, quantitative surveys which have produced the data on which this chapter is based.

Table 7.1 Major social surveys in the United Kingdom

Survey	Frequency	Sampling frame	Type of respondent	Location	Sample size to nearest 1000	Response rate (%)	Reference
British Household Panel Survey	Yearly from 1991	Postcode address file (PAF)	All adults in household plus teenagers in 1994	GB	10,000 (first wave)	74 (1991)	Buck et al. (1994)
British Social Attitudes Survey	Annual	Electoral register PAF	One adult in household	GB	5,000	67	Jowell et al. (1994)
Census of Population	Every 10 years	Local address lists	Household 'head'	UK	58,000,000	98	Office for National Statistics (1997)
General Household Survey	Continuous	PAF	All adults in household	GB	12,000	82	Office for National Statistics (1997)
Labour Force Survey	Continuous	PAF	All adults in household	GB	60,000	83	Office for National Statistics (1997)
National Child Development Study	Five sweeps since 1958	All children born in one week in 1958	Children, parents, adult 'children'	GB	11,000	73 (1991)	Ferri and Smith (1998)
New Earnings Survey	Annual	Inland Revenue PAYE records	Employers supply data on employees	GB	210,000 (employers)	94	Office for National Statistics (1997)
Social Change and Economic Life Initiative	Interviews in 1985 and 1987	Electoral register	All adults in household	Six areas of GB	6,000	75	Anderson et al. (1994)

Changes in birth rates and in fertility

First results from the 2001 Census revealed that the population of the United Kingdom numbered 58,789,194, fewer than was expected (National Statistics Online 2002). Around one person in every fourteen described themselves as being a member of a minority ethnic group. The **age structure** of the population is a consequence of variations in the annual number of births and deaths. The population pyramid shown in Fig. 7.1 shows that these variations can be quite substantial. The bulge in the pyramid in those in their fifties represents the 'baby boom' which followed the Second World War, while the even bigger bulge among people now in their 30s is a result of the fashion for large families in the 1960s (ONS 2002: 28).

Figure 7.1 shows how individual experience can be strongly affected by the age cohort into which a person is born. Those born in the late 1940s, or during the 1960s, will be competing throughout their lives with a larger number of peers for school places, jobs, housing, healthcare, and so on. By contrast, the relatively small cohorts born during the 1930s and the 1970s will face less competition in all these areas. However, when the 'bulge' generations reach old age there will be a relatively small population of working age to support them financially or to care for them. There has been some concern about the effects of these changes in the **dependency ratio**, that is in the ratio of those who are dependent to those who are economically active.

The **total period fertility rate** (TPFR) measures the average number of children born to each woman if birth rates in the specific period persisted throughout her childbearing

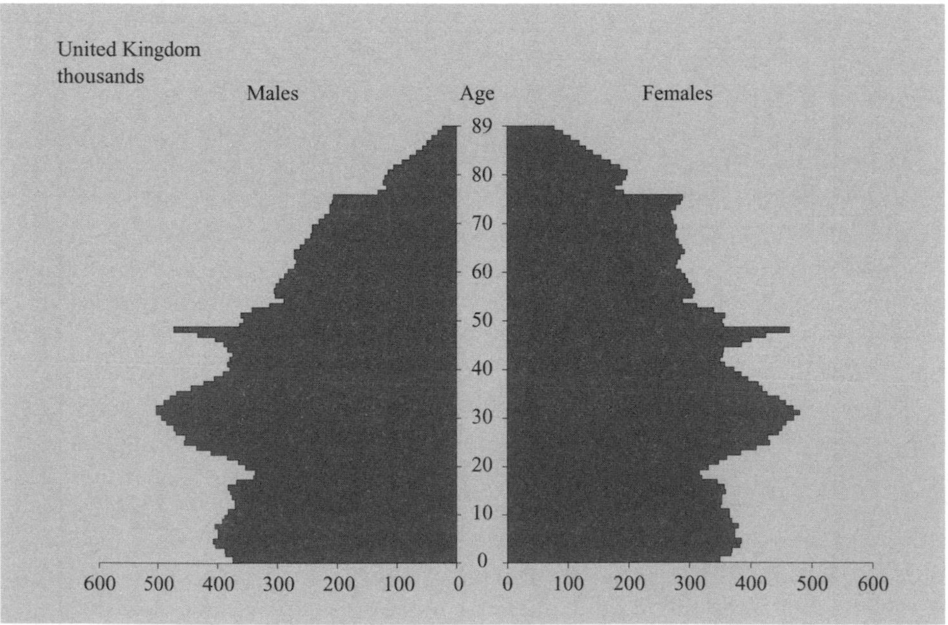

Figure 7.1 Population pyramid by gender and age, 1995

Source: ONS (1997).

life. In the UK the TPFR peaked at 2.95 in 1964 and then fell to a low point of 1.69 in 1977. The fall in the birth rate is partly a consequence of smaller family size, but it is also a result of the increase in the proportion of childless women. The percentage of women who were still childless at the age of 30 rose from just under a fifth among women born in 1947 to a third among women born in 1962. Changes in the TPFR are thought to have been influenced by more women receiving higher education, by an increase female participation in paid work, and by greater control over fertility because of the contraceptive pill (ONS 1997: 32).

Changes in households and families

Information about demographic changes is sometimes presented in terms of 'households' and sometimes in terms of 'families': when using this sort of data it is important to notice which term is being used.

The average size of household in Great Britain has almost halved since the beginning of the twentieth century, and in 2001 stood at 2.4 people per household. However, this figure conceals large variations in household type. There has been a decrease in the proportion of 'traditional' family households. In 1961 38 per cent of households consisted of married couples with their dependent children, while 26 per cent of all households consisted of couples with no children. However, by 2001 only 23 per cent of households consisted of the 'traditional' family, while couples without children made up 29 per cent of all households (ONS 2002: 40).

One-person households increased from 11 per cent of all households in 1961 to 29 per cent in 2001. This reflects a number of different factors, including the increasing numbers of young people who are financially able to leave the parental home but who delay marriage, the increases in divorce and separation among those who do marry, and the rise in the expectation of life, especially among older women. All these factors make it more likely, and more possible, for individuals to set up homes of their own. It is likely that the number of one-person households will continue to increase.

Turning from households to families, we can see that changes have also taken place in the demography of the family. In particular, there has been an increase in the proportion of **lone-parent families**, by comparison with other types of family. However, despite the alarms of the New Right, the two-parent family is still very much the norm. Lone-parent families made up 20 per cent of all families in 2001 compared with 7 per cent in 1972, but this still leaves the great majority of children living with both their parents. Most lone-parent families are headed by mothers, and lone fathers continue to be very much in the minority, making up 9 per cent of all lone parents, and in general caring for older children than lone mothers (ONS 2002: 48). In general, lone parents in Britain are less likely to be in employment than their counterparts in other European countries (Millar and Rowlingson 2001).

It is important not to regard being a lone parent as a permanent state. An analysis of the British Household Panel Survey found that in the early 1990s, on average, around 15 per cent of lone mothers per year ceased to be lone parents, usually as a result of forming new partnerships. If such a rate were maintained, half of all lone parents would only remain so for around four years (ONS 1997: 43; See Table 7.1 for details about the British Household Panel Survey).

Changes in marriage and divorce

There have been profound changes in the rate of marriage and in the age at which people marry. The marriage rate rose from 1931 to 1971 and then fell dramatically: between 1981 and 1992 the marriage rate per 1,000 of the population fell from 7.1 to 5.4. However, it has been argued that the period from 1950 to 1980 represented an anomaly, in that marriage rates were unusually high, and that rates in the 1990s represented a return to normal. The age at which individuals married rose by about two years between 1961 and 1994, to 28 years for men and 26 years for women, though this figure masks social class differences, in which those of higher social class tend to delay marriage longer. Similar patterns are found in other European countries, though the UK has one of the highest marriage rates in the European Union.

There has also been a change towards more cohabitation before marriage, to the extent that this has become the norm, compared with only 7 per cent of those marrying at the beginning of the 1970s (Kiernan and Wicks 1990: 8). Results from the British Household Panel Survey showed that nearly three-quarters of never-married, childless couples who were cohabiting planned to get married. Thus for the most part cohabitation is a part of the process of getting married and not a substitute for marriage. There has been a parallel rise in the percentage of children born to cohabiting couples; in the majority of cases these births are registered by both parents, who often go on to marry. However, cohabitations are more likely to break up than marriages. So 70 per cent of children born within marriage will live their entire childhood with both parents, but only 36 per cent of children born to a cohabiting couple will live with both parents throughout their childhood (Berthoud and Gershuny 2000: 40).

Attitudes towards cohabitation vary greatly. It has been seen as a threat to marriage, delaying it and creating an environment in which it is devalued (Morgan 2000). However, attitude surveys show that cohabitation is becoming accepted as normal and may even be preferred, particularly among younger people. In 2000 the British Social Attitudes Survey asked people whether they agreed with the statement, 'It's alright for a couple to live together without intending to get married.' The proportion agreeing varied from 84 per cent of those aged 18–24 to 35 per cent of those aged over 65 (Park et al. 2001). This same survey cast light on the assumption that cohabitation is concentrated among the less educated, less skilled, and unemployed, people sometimes conceptualized as being part of an 'underclass'. In reality the results showed that there was no significant relationship between cohabitation and social class, and that people on benefits were less likely than others to cohabit (Park et al. 2001: 43).

The other important trend is the increase in divorce. The UK has the highest divorce rate in the European Union, and it has been estimated that four out of ten new marriages will end in divorce. In 1994, over one half of all divorces involved couples with children under 16. Wives were much more likely to initiate divorce than husbands. Reasons for the divorce also varied, with women more likely to seek a divorce because of the unreasonable behaviour of their partners, and husbands more likely to cite adultery as the reason for the breakdown of the marriage (Haskey 1996).

The cumulative effect of these changes is that step-families are becoming more common. In 1991 8 per cent of all families with dependent children contained one or more stepchildren (Office of Population Censuses and Surveys 1991). The children in these families may have two parents and two step-parents, they may move between two different 'homes', and they may have up to eight grandparents. Some of the complexities involved in living in a step-family have been described by Robinson and Smith (1993), Ferri and Smith (1998), and Barnes et al. (1998). The evidence suggests that remarriages, and therefore step-families, are at greater risk of breakdown than first marriages (Burgoyne et al. 1987).

The main changes which have taken place in families and households are summarized in Box 7.1.

Changes in employment patterns

Changes in the labour market over the past few years have made a profound difference to the ways in which families are able to provide for the welfare of their members. There

Box 7.1 Recent changes in families and households

- lower fertility, older age at childbearing and increasing childlessness;
- smaller household and family sizes;
- growth in single-person households and in living alone;
- decline in adoption and a growth in lone parenthood;
- decline in first marriage rates;
- rise in cohabitation, often as a precursor to marriage;
- growth in the prevalence of divorce;
- increase in remarriages, reconstituted families, and step-families;
- growth in the ethnic minority population, resulting in greater diversity in family sizes, composition, and kinship patterns

(Haskey 1996: 8)

Box 7.2 Recent changes in patterns of paid work

- a decline in manufacturing industry and a growth in service sector jobs;
- a decline in the numbers of full-time, secure jobs and an increase in part-time and insecure jobs and in flexible working arrangements;
- an increase in women's employment, especially in part-time work and among younger women and women with children;
- a decrease in unemployment, from a peak in 1993, although people from minority ethnic groups are still more likely to be unemployed than others;
- introduction of the New Deal, targeting especially lone parents, ethnic minorities, younger and older people, and those with disabilities;
- a growing divide between 'work-rich' households, with two or more earners, and 'work-poor' households where no one has a paid job

is only space here to outline the main changes, which are discussed in more detail in Chapter 6 of this book. Important changes in patterns of paid work are highlighted in Box 6.2.

All these changes affect the extent to which families are able to provide for the welfare of their members and for the particular mix of strategies which they use in making that provision.

THE PRODUCTION OF WELFARE WITHIN FAMILIES

One theme of this book is that the welfare of individuals is produced, not only by the welfare state, but also by the market and by the family. This next section considers the ways in which families produce welfare for their members.

Types of welfare provided within families

Four general points have to be made at the outset. First, for many people the family is a first line of defence against the 'five giant evils' which Beveridge saw as the targets for the welfare state: want, disease, ignorance, squalor, and idleness (Beveridge Report 1942: para 8). When all goes well, families provide a means of redistributing income from those who earn to those who do not, in order to ensure that individual family members have enough food and clothing, and a roof over their heads. People with minor illnesses and long-term disabilities are usually cared for at home, and home is the place where children are nurtured and where their education begins. Of course, other types of welfare can also be provided within the family, from loving relationships to opportunities for leisure and pleasure of different sorts. However, for the purposes of this chapter the focus will be on the welfare associated with being fed and clothed and housed, and being cared for in childhood and times of physical dependence.

Second, it is important to remember that 'families' do not produce anything: it is the individuals within families who produce, and consume, any welfare which may created. So in this section we shall have to move the focus from the family itself to the individuals who make up the family. This change of focus reflects a move between disciplines. Traditionally economists have used the household/family as the key unit of analysis, while sociologists have been concerned about the different perspectives of individuals within households: the idea that there can be profound differences between 'the husband's marriage' and 'the wife's marriage' was first introduced by the American feminist sociologist Bernard (1982).

Third, creating welfare at home is work. This point was made vividly by John Masefield (1946: 61) in the following poem:

> To get the whole world out of bed
> And washed, and dressed, and warmed, and fed,
> To work, and back to bed again,
> Believe me, Saul, costs worlds of pain.

Work at home may be unpaid, but it is still work, according to the definition suggested in a sociology textbook:

Work is the carrying out of tasks, involving the expenditure of mental and physical effort, which have as their objective the production of goods and services catering for human needs. An occupation is work which is done for a regular wage. (Giddens 1997: 491)

One of the concomitants of the development of a welfare state is the move of many sorts of work out of the home: this has particularly affected women, as they have moved into paid work as nurses, social workers, teachers, nannies, and care assistants, doing the sorts of tasks which women have traditionally performed as part of their unpaid family duties.

Fourth, there is a trade off between different ways of producing welfare, which relates to the shifting boundaries between paid and unpaid work. A mother who does not have paid employment is able to look after her children herself, cook for the family, and clean the house, and she may produce goods such as soft furnishings and home-made clothes. If the same woman has a full-time job she is likely to have to pay for childcare and to buy more pre-prepared meals; she may employ another woman to clean the house and she will probably buy ready-made soft furnishing and clothes.

In the following pages we will consider three different types of work, each of which produces welfare for individuals within families. We begin with the work of childcare, and with the social policies which are most relevant to the support of children within families.

Childcare and child support

In 2000 there were 12.1 million children aged under 16 in the UK, with more boys than girls; 10 per cent of children belonged to a minority ethnic group. The majority of children were growing up living with both their parents, but just over 1 million lived in step-families (ONS 2002: 18).

Child poverty continues to be a serious issue. Defining poverty can be complicated but a commonly used measure is that it means living in a household with below half the mean income, after housing costs are taken into account. On this basis one-third of children were living in poverty in 1998/9 and the extent of poverty was three times as high as it had been in 1979. This meant that when the Labour government came into power in 1997, 3.4 million children were living in poverty and Britain had the highest proportion of children living in poverty of any European country except Italy (Piachaud and Sutherland 2002). As we have seen, an early aim of the Labour government, expressed in the Green Paper *Supporting Families*, was to reduce the numbers of children living in poverty.

Having children involves both expense and hard work. One study calculated that a child reaching his or her 17th birthday will have cost around £50,000 (Middleton et al. 1997). However, this calculation included only direct costs and did not take account of the lost income of the person who took the prime responsibility for child care, usually the mother. An estimate of the amount involved concluded that the total could be as high as £202,000 (at 1990 values), of which 40 per cent represented being out of employment during the child's early years, 36 per cent represented working shorter hours in order to fit in with childcare, while 25 per cent represented lower rates of pay because of loss of work experience (Joshi 1992: 121).

Mothers still carry the main responsibility for children, despite much rhetoric about the increased commitment of many fathers to their children. A study of the division of household tasks, carried out in 1991, showed that looking after a sick child would be the responsibility of the mother in 60 per cent of families and shared between both parents in 39 per cent of families; fathers took responsibility in just 1 per cent of families. The study showed that the situation had changed very little since 1983 (Central Statistical Office 1995: 32).

There are a number of different reasons why childcare has become an important issue in social policy. The first reason has been concern about the welfare of children, in a society in which many children live in poverty, in which some parents are divorced or separated, and in which a proportion of parents are failing in their parental responsibilities. For many years the law about caring for, bringing up, and protecting children from abuse had been inconsistent and fragmented. The Children Act 1989 aimed to bring about radical changes and improvements in the law and to provide a single and consistent statement of it.

The Children Act was a long and complex piece of legislation, which was generally welcomed when it came into force. It provided a single and consistent statement of the law that applies to the welfare of children. The introduction to the Act set out the underlying beliefs (Department of Health 1989: 1):

> The Act rests on the belief that children are generally best looked after within the family with both parents playing a full part and without resort to legal proceedings. That belief is reflected in the:
>
> - new concept of parental responsibility
> - ability of unmarried fathers to share that responsibility by agreement with the mother
> - local authorities' duty to give support to children and their families

A guide to the Act, and a discussion of the ideologies which are reflected in it, has been provided by Freeman (1992). He suggested that the Children Act expressed ideologies from both the Right and the Left. On the one hand, it presented the two-parent family as the ideal and warned of the dangers of too much state intervention. On the other hand, it gave new and stronger powers both to local authorities and to children.

The principles which underpinned the Children Act were the basis for its many and complex provisions. The first principle was that the welfare of the child should be paramount. This principle applied to any issue related to the upbringing of the child, the administration of a child's property, court proceedings, or disputes between parents.

The second principle was that there should be as little delay as possible, since delay was likely to prejudice the welfare of the child, because of the uncertainty which this creates, and also because of the damage which delay may do to relationships.

The third principle was incorporated into a checklist which courts should consider in any contested cases. The checklist included such issues as the child's physical, emotional, and educational needs, the likely effect of any change in circumstances, the capacities of the parents to care for the child, and the implications of the child's age, sex, and background. The child's 'background' included his or her religion, racial origin, culture, and language, and this principle reflected the increasingly multi-cultural nature of the British population.

The fourth principle was concerned with minimal intervention. The Act stated that a court should not make an order 'unless it considers that doing so would be better for the child than making no order at all' (section 1(5)). In this the Act reflected the then Conservative government's suspicion of state interference into family life.

Finally, the Act laid stress on the principle of **parental responsibility**, marking a shift of emphasis from parental rights to parental responsibilities. The aim was to stress that parents, rather than the state, have the prime responsibility for children. Mothers, and the fathers of legitimate children, automatically have parental responsibility, while fathers who are not married to the mother of the child can acquire parental responsibility in a number of different ways. In differentiating between married and unmarried parents in this way, the Act seemed to confirm the value attached to traditional family forms.

The second reason for childcare becoming a focus for social policy has been the rise in the numbers of lone-parent families. This has led to growing concern about the provision of financial support for dependent children. The key issue is whether children living in lone-parent families should be financially supported by the state, through the social security system, by the earnings of the caring parent, usually the mother, or by contributions from the absent parent, usually the father. Compared with other European countries, in Britain a relatively high proportion of lone parents depend on the social security system (Millar and Rowlingson 2001). Concern about the financial burdens which this laid on the state led to the passing of the Child Support Act 1993.

The aims of the Child Support Act were to:

- ensure that parents accept financial responsibility for their children whenever they can afford to do so;
- strike a fair and reasonable balance between 'first' and 'second' families;
- maintain parents' incentives to take paid work rather than depending on social security (Secretary of State for Social Security 1995: 10).

The Child Support Act led to the setting up of the Child Support Agency. This organization undertook to develop a system for ensuring that money would be transferred from the 'absent parent', usually the father, to the 'parent with care', usually the mother. A formula was developed for calculating the amount which should be paid, with an upper limit set at 30 per cent of the absent parent's net income.

When it was first set up the Child Support Agency was criticized from a variety of different positions. Some men's groups considered that the payments to parents with care were set too high and that the formula did not take adequate account of the cost of supporting second families. Some women's groups resented the pressure that was put on women to name the fathers of their children, and argued that the focus on lone mothers living on social security meant that the Treasury, rather than women and children, was the main beneficiary of the Act (Clarke et al. 1994; Bennett 1997).

From 1997 the Labour government introduced a number of policies to reduce child poverty and to provide more support for families with children. These included:

- Increasing Child Benefit between 1997 and 2001 by 26 per cent for the first child and 4 per cent for subsequent children. Child Benefit is a universal benefit paid to all mothers, regardless of their income, to help with the cost of bringing up children
- Introducing the Working Tax Credit in 2003. This is a means-tested benefit paid to people in low paid jobs. It replaced the Working Families' Tax Credit, the Disabled Person's Tax Credit, and the Employment Credit of the New Deal 50 plus. Its aim is to increase the incomes of those in low paid jobs and also to encourage paid work. It is administered by the Inland Revenue and couples can chose which one of them receives the benefit (Child Poverty Action Group 2003: 1260).
- Introducing the Child Tax Credit in 2003. This is a means-tested benefit paid to low income and middle income families who are responsible for a child under 16. It replaced payments for children which were previously paid with Income Support, Job Seeker's Allowance, Working Families' Tax Credit and the Children's Tax Credit. Payments go to the person who is the main carer of the child, that is typically the mother (Child Poverty Action Group 2003: 1249).
- Introducing the Childcare element to the Working Tax Credit. This can pay up to 70 per cent of the costs of childcare, with a limit of £135 a week for one child and £200 a week for two or more children (in 2003). Its aim is to make it easier for lone parents and couples on low incomes to take paid work, by giving them help with the costs of childcare. This benefit is paid to the person who is the main carer for the child (Child Poverty Action Group 2003: 1285).
- Introducing the National Childcare Strategy. This aims to increase the amount of good quality, affordable child care for children aged 0 to 14. It reflects a concern with the wellbeing of children, but also a commitment to helping parents to take paid work and to balance work and family life.

A number of other policies had similar aims, in terms of encouraging parents to combine paid work and childcare and to achieve a better balance between home and work priorities. These included the New Deal, the Parental Leave Directive, the Working Time Directive, the Part Time Work Directive, and the various maternity benefits. (For further information see Wasoff and Dey 2000; Hills et al. 2002; Child Poverty Action Group 2002; and the relevant websites among those listed at the end of this chapter).

How effective have all these initiatives been in reducing child poverty? At the time of writing the full effects have not yet been felt. However, it seems as if there have been real changes. It is estimated that the Labour government has adopted tax/benefit policies and active labour market measures that should by 2002 reduce the numbers of children in poverty by over one million (Piachaud and Sutherland 2002). However, that still leaves a substantial number of individuals spending their childhood in poverty. An alternative critique suggests that the focus on getting parents into paid work devalues the work of caring for children and the committed parenting which the Labour government wishes to promote (Driver and Martell 2002).

Domestic work

Under the heading of domestic work we shall consider such activities as cleaning, preparing meals, washing up, and shopping for food and household necessities. All these activities produce welfare for the members of the household, and carrying them out involves an enormous amount of time and effort. It has been calculated that the time spent in productive work in the home is equal to the time spent in paid work (Rose 1989: 124). Attempts to estimate the value of domestic work have indicated that including unpaid work in national income would add between a quarter and more than a half to measured income, depending on the methods used for the calculation (Hyman 1994: 63).

When the first path-breaking study of housework was carried out it was initially considered to be a frivolous topic and one not worthy of academic study (Oakley 1974). However, there is now an enormous literature documenting the changing patterns of domestic work. All the research suggests that women still carry the main burden, though there is some evidence of men increasing their involvement. There have been many attempts to calculate who does what types of domestic work. One approach has been to list all the different tasks for which family members may be responsible and to ask who was responsible for each one. The British Household Panel Survey asked both men and women what share they took of five activities: cleaning, cooking, shopping, laundry, and childcare. From this it was possible to calculate an index of the domestic division of labour. The results showed that:

- Women continued to do significantly more domestic work than men.
- There was a tendency for the division of labour to become more equal, especially when the wife moved into full-time paid work or the husband gave up paid work.
- Men and women differed in their reports of how much they did, with both partners tending to say they did more than the other. (Berthoud and Gershuny 2000)

Another approach has been to consider work within the household in terms of the time household members spend on different tasks. For example, the Social Change and Economic Life Initiative used time-budget diaries to investigate the relative amounts of time which men and women spent on 'childcare', 'shopping', 'odd jobs', and 'routine domestic work', such as cleaning, cooking, and washing up. The results showed that, despite increases in women's employment, they continued to spend more time than men on childcare, shopping and routine domestic work, while men were likely to spend more time than women on odd jobs around the house. However, between 1974 and 1987 there was a tendency for men to do more routine housework and shopping and for women, especially those in full-time employment, to do less (Anderson et al. 1994; see Table 7.1 for details about the Social Change and Economic Life Initiative).

Despite the importance of domestic work in terms of the welfare it creates, there is very little explicit social policy related to the topic. This probably reflects the fact that until recently domestic work was taken for granted, as something which women did, unpaid, as part of their roles as wives and mothers. Only since 1973 have judges been encouraged to take the unpaid work done at home into account in making the financial settlement when a marriage ends.

However, implicitly the welfare state still tends to assume that women will be responsible for domestic work and childcare. Welfare providers often take for granted that one parent will be free to take children to and from school, to accompany them to the doctor and the dentist, and to stay in for the health visitor and the social worker. Women who fail to carry out domestic work in the way expected of them risk being considered 'bad mothers' by those with responsibility for the welfare of children.

Caring for sick and disabled people

'Caring' is another type of work which was taken for granted until the late twentieth century: it was seen as something that wives and mothers did naturally, as part of their domestic responsibilities. So 'caring about' someone was assumed to involve 'caring for' them, to use the distinction first made by Graham (1983). The word 'carer' came into use during the 1980s, as feminists and pressure groups argued that caring for sick and disabled people was real work and that it reduced the costs of health and social services.

What sorts of people require, and give, care within the family? Besides those with ordinary short-term illnesses, care may be needed because of mental or physical disabilities, or long-term illness, either mental or physical. Most elderly people are fit and well, but there is a tendency for both physical and mental infirmities to increase with age. Care may be given by spouses to each other, by parents to their disabled children, by adult daughters and, less often, adult sons to their parents; increasingly it is also being recognized that some quite young children provide care for their disabled parents (Parker 1990; Twigg et al. 1990; Twigg 1992).

In 1985 the General Household Survey asked about caring, and produced the first national data about people who give and receive care. Respondents were asked whether they were 'looking after, or providing some regular service for, someone who was sick, elderly or handicapped'. When the results were applied to the whole population it was estimated that six million people were doing some sort of caring for others (Green 1988; see Table 7.1 for details about the General Household Survey).

However, the figure of six million has to be treated with some caution. Only about half of these people said that they were the sole or main carer, and only about a fifth spent more than twenty hours per week on caring activities. Nevertheless, this still amounted to a great deal of work done and welfare provided. The study showed that the different sorts of care included:

- personal help with dressing, bathing, toileting, and feeding;
- physical help with activities such as walking, getting in and out of bed, going up and down stairs;
- practical help, such as preparing meals, doing housework, or shopping or doing household repairs and gardening;
- other sorts of help, such as giving medication, changing dressings, taking the person out, or simply keeping him or her company.

The survey showed that needing personal and physical help tended to be associated with very long hours of work for the carer. Some carers, most of them women, were providing 100 or more hours of care per week, far more than any paid worker would undertake.

Caring is costly in a number of different ways. First, there are costs in terms of lost earnings. The rate of paid employment is lower for all adults providing care. However, the effect is greater for women than men and greatest in the case of a mother caring for a disabled child (Arber and Ginn 1995; Baldwin 1985). Secondly, there are the additional costs of disability. These may include additional heating, when someone is at home all day, adaptations to the house, special equipment, such as wheel chairs and other aids, extra clothes and bedding, and higher transport costs when a person is unable to use public transport. Thirdly, there are likely to be costs to the carer in terms of stress and strain (Glendinning and Millar 1992; Pahl and Quine 1987).

Social policy is now beginning to recognise the contribution which carers make to the welfare of individuals within families. The National Health Service and Community Care Act 1990 outlined a system of community care in which social services departments were responsible for providing care for disabled people and support for carers. The White Paper which preceded the Act said:

> The Government acknowledges than the great bulk of community care is provided by friends, family and neighbours. . . . But it must be recognised that carers need help and support if they are to continue to carry out their role . . . practical support for carers should be a high priority. (Secretaries of State for Health 1989: 4–556)

In 1985 the Carers (Recognition and Services) Act imposed an obligation on local authorities to assess the needs of carers as well as of those who are cared for. However, the support which carers can expect remains very limited: one study of people looking after a relative with Alzheimer's disease at home found that most carers had fewer than sixteen hours away from caring each week, out of a total of 168 hours in the week (Levin et al. 1994).

Financial support is provided by the social security system. The rules of eligibility change constantly, but the position at any one time can be checked in the handbooks produced by the Child Poverty Action Group (see e.g. Child Poverty Action Group 2002). At the time of writing the main benefits are:

- Disability Living Allowance for people under 65 who have a long term disability which prevents them taking paid employment;
- Attendance Allowance for people over 65 who need someone to help them with activities of daily living;
- Invalid Care Allowance for those who provide care for someone who is receiving the higher rate of the Disability Living Allowance. To qualify for this allowance the carer has to be caring for at least thirty-five hours per week. At the time of writing the rate was £42.45 per week, so the maximum that anyone could be 'paid' is just over £1.00 per hour: if caring at home is work, it is very badly paid work indeed.
- Disabled Person's Tax Credit, which is an allowance for low-paid workers with a disability. The effect is to top up the wages of those who work for more than 16 hours per week.

The question of the boundary between **public and private spheres** is central to any discussion about the production of welfare within the family. Are looking after children, doing housework, and caring for sick and disabled people essentially private matters, carried out because people love and care for each other? Is it appropriate for the state to become involved, through social policies focused on the work done within families? And if these issues become a matter of public as well as private concern, what forms should state intervention take, given that historically care and control have tended to advance together? These are likely to be central questions in any discussion of social policy as it relates to families.

DISADVANTAGE WITHIN FAMILIES

However, families can be sources of disadvantage or 'dis-welfare', as well as of welfare. Many people are ambivalent about their families, even when things are going well, but for some individuals the family becomes the place where they experience inequality, unhappiness, and even danger. In this section we consider three aspects of family life which can create problems for individual family members.

Financial inequalities

Throughout much of social policy the household is regarded as an economic unit. When a man and a woman live together, especially if they are married, it is assumed that they will share the income which enters the household. This assumption underlies the idea of the household means test. Being eligible for a means-tested benefit implies that the income of the household as a whole is below the minimum considered necessary: it is assumed that an individual cannot be poor if he or she lives within a household which has an adequate income.

However, it has become apparent that there can be considerable financial inequalities even within quite affluent families. In particular, women and children have been found living in poverty in households with adequate incomes (Pahl 1989; 2000). Most of the research on this topic has focused on married or as-married couples, with or without children, so in this context the word 'family' usually means a nuclear family living together in a household.

Over the past few years many typologies have been devised with the aim of making sense of the complexities of money management within families. One much-quoted typology was developed for the Social Change and Economic Life Initiative (Vogler and Pahl 1993; 1994; see Table 8.1 for details of the survey). Respondents were asked to identify which of several systems of money management came closest to the way in which they organized their finances. The researchers then went on to create a typology of allocative systems, which divided couples according to who managed and who controlled household finances. The allocative systems are summarized in Box 7.3.

The typology was used again in the British Household Panel Survey, which found very similar proportions of couples using each system in the years from 1991 to 1995, though with a slight reduction in couples using the housekeeping allowance system. The results showed that when women were in employment, especially if the employment was

Box 7.3 Systems of money management

- the 'female whole wage system', in which the husband hands over his whole wage packet to his wife, minus his personal spending money; the wife adds her own earnings, if any, and is then responsible for managing the financial affairs of the household (27 per cent of the couples in the sample);
- the 'female-managed pool', which involves the pooling of all or nearly all of the income, usually in a joint account: so both partners have access to the household income, but the woman has the main responsibility for managing and controlling finances (15 per cent of couples);
- the 'joint pool', which involves the pooling of all or nearly all the income, usually in a joint account, with both partners sharing the management and control of the pool (20 per cent of couples);
- the 'male-managed pool', which involves the pooling of all or nearly all of the income, usually in a joint account: so both partners have access to the household income, but the man has the main responsibility for managing and controlling finances (15 per cent of couples);
- the 'male whole wage system', in which the husband has sole responsibility for managing and controlling finances, a system which can leave non-employed wives with no personal spending money (10 per cent of couples);
- the 'housekeeping allowance system'. Typically the husband gives his wife a fixed sum of money for housekeeping expenses, to which she may add her own earnings, while the rest of the money remains in the husband's control and he pays for other items (13 per cent of couples in the sample).

(Vogler and Pahl 1993; 1994)

full-time, the couple were likely to be more equal in terms of how they managed their money and in terms of financial decision-making (Berthoud and Gershuny 2000).

Other studies have also identified an 'independent management system', with each partner keeping his or her income separate and each taking responsibility for particular bills. It has been suggested that this system is characteristic of couples who are cohabiting or who have remarried. One study found that among remarried couples a half were using independent management of money, compared with 2 per cent among couples in general (Burgoyne and Morison 1997). However, it may be that there is a more general trend towards individualizing finances, associated with increasing scepticism about marriage (Lewis 2001: 165).

There is now a considerable body of research showing that the system of money management adopted by a couple has significant implications for the lives of individuals within the household. These differences can be summarized as follows:

- When money is scarce women tend to get the job of making ends meet, since it is usually they who are responsible for finances in low-income households (see also Kempson et al. 1994; Kempson 1996; Goode, et al. 1998; Molloy and Snape 1999).
- Men tend to spend more than women on personal interests and leisure pursuits. Access to personal spending money reflects both total household income and the

management of money within the household. However, gender inequalities are greatest in households with male-controlled systems of money management and least in households with joint pooling of money (Pahl 1989; Vogler and Pahl 1993, 1994).

- Women are likely to bear the brunt of financial cutbacks. When money is short, women are more likely than men to cut back on such things as food, heating, social life, and entertainment. Again, these gender inequalities seem to be greatest in households with male-controlled systems of money management and least in households with joint pooling systems (Vogler and Pahl 1994; Goode et al. 1998).
- Women are more child- and family-focused in their spending. Money which is controlled by women is more likely to be spent on children, on food, and on collective expenditure for the household, while men tend to hold more back for their individual use. If the aim is to benefit children, women make more efficient use of household income (Pahl 1989; Kempson et al. 1994; Middleton et al. 1997).
- Individuals can be poor in households with adequate incomes. This finding has important implications for policy initiatives aimed at the relief of poverty (Pahl 1989; Kempson 1996).

Financial inequalities within families often seem to occur when one family member, typically a male breadwinner, uses money as a way of exercising power and of controlling other family members; another source of power and control is violence.

Violence against women within the family

Violence seems to be an enduring characteristic of family life, with women and children being the main victims. Throughout most of history this has been taken for granted, to the extent that in 1792 Judge Buller confirmed that husbands had the right to beat their wives, so long as the stick that was used was not thicker than a man's thumb. What is now described as 'wife abuse' or 'domestic violence' was then considered to be a private matter, lying outside the public domain and not amenable to legislation (Dobash and Dobash 1980).

Violence against women became a public issue in the 1970s, largely as a result of the growth of the women's movement and the work of feminists in documenting the nature and extent of the problem. The first refuge for abused women was set up in London in 1971, and refuges, or shelters, can now be found in most parts of the world. Male violence within the family has become recognized as a threat to the physical and mental health of women and children and as a major cause of morbidity and mortality (Kingston and Penhale 1995).

Domestic violence is also a crime. About half of all homicides of women are killings by a partner or ex-partner; one in five of all murder victims (male or female) is a woman killed by a partner or ex-partner; one-third of all reported crimes against women, and one-quarter of all reported assaults, are the result of domestic violence (Victim Support 1992: 4). A large-scale survey of the general population, carried out in London in 1993, showed that around 30 per cent of women had experienced domestic violence from their partners or ex-partners. Men could also be the victims of domestic violence, though to a lesser extent than women both in terms of frequency and severity. The study showed that most of the violence men experienced occurred in public places; by contrast, most violence against women occurred in private. Men were the main perpetrators of both public and private violence (Mooney 2000).

Despite the seriousness of much domestic violence, the appropriate agencies have often been reluctant to provide help for the victims. One problem is that so many different agencies are potentially involved. If a woman has injuries she may need medical and nursing care. She has been the victim of a crime, so the police can be involved, and she may have to go to court to get an injunction to prevent her husband from assaulting her again. Many husbands are not deterred by legal action, so she may decide to leave home to protect herself and her children. She may go to a refuge, or to the local authority housing department: if she has dependent children the 1985 Housing Act gives her the right to temporary accommodation. Lacking an income, she is likely to apply to the benefit office for income support. There is now ample evidence of the ways in which policy-makers and professionals have failed to meet the needs of abused women (Hague and Malos 1998; Mullender 1996; Pahl 1985).

The law relating to violence in the family was changed by the Family Law Act 1996. Previously the legal position was quite complicated, with different legislation applying in the case of married and unmarried couples. The 1996 Act consolidated existing legislation and set out the position with regard to the occupation of the family home and the right of individuals to protection against violence. More specifically, the Act:

- widened the scope for occupation and non-molestation orders, which now apply to 'associated persons', such as ex-partners, as well as to currently married and cohabiting people;
- increased the rights of courts to attach a power of arrest to court orders;
- simplified the position with regard to the different courts in which cases involving domestic violence can be heard.

Separation and divorce

Unhappy marriages are the root cause of much dis-welfare within families, while separation and divorce tend to create inequalities between the different members of families. When a couple separate, the result is typically a reduction in household incomes for women and children and a modest increase in the household incomes of men. The most effective route out of poverty for women in this situation is remarriage, a fact which reflects the greater earning power and job security of men, and the responsibility of women for childcare (Burgoyne et al. 1987).

Research on the impact of divorce on children has shown that the children of separated parents are more likely to have behaviour problems, perform less well at school, become sexually active at a younger age, and to turn to drugs, smoking, and heavy drinking. However, these outcomes may have been a product of the conflict leading up to the separation and of family poverty as well as of the parental separation (Rodgers and Pryor 1998; Kirby 2002).

The state has had an interest in marriage ever since the Marriage Act 1836. Throughout the nineteenth century divorce was only available to the very rich. This led to a situation in which many individuals were trapped in unhappy marriages, while those who had gone on to make new relationships were forced to do what was then called 'living in sin', being unable to divorce or to legalize the new relationship.

Attempts to remedy this situation produced the 1937 Divorce Law, which made divorce possible, but only when a 'matrimonial offence' had been committed: one partner had to prove that the other was guilty of adultery, cruelty, or desertion. Though this made divorce accessible to ordinary people for the first time, the idea that one partner must be to blame for the breakdown of the marriage made divorce procedures essentially adversarial.

Concern about the adversarial nature of the divorce process led to the Divorce Reform Act 1969. The main provisions of this Act were:

- The only ground for divorce was the 'irretrievable breakdown' of the marriage.
- Breakdown could be established by reference to one of five 'facts', which included adultery, desertion, unreasonable behaviour, two years' separation if both consented to the divorce, or five years' separation if one partner did not want the divorce.
- Unreasonable behaviour included financial irresponsibility, violence, alcoholism, constant criticism.

Those who did not want to wait two or five years for a divorce still had to rely on fault-based facts to prove that the marriage had broken down, so bitterness and blame continued to surround divorce proceedings.

At this time legal aid was made available to those who did not have enough money to obtain advice and take the case to court. Since the granting of legal aid was dependent on a means test on individuals, not couples, many wives qualified for legal aid and this made it possible for them to obtain a divorce. After the 1969 Act the divorce rate rose quite sharply, and continued to rise throughout the next twenty years, with about three quarters of all divorces being granted to women.

Concern over the fact that four in ten marriages were ending in divorce, and that couples were continuing to use fault-based facts to prove breakdown, led to a demand for a new law relating to divorce. This reached the statute book as the Family Law Act 1996. The aims of the Act were set out by the government as follows:

- to support the institution of marriage;
- to include practical steps to prevent the irretrievable breakdown of marriage;
- to ensure that spouses understand the practical consequences of divorce before taking any irreversible decision;
- to minimize the bitterness and hostility between the parties and reduce trauma for the children;
- to keep to the minimum the costs to the couple and to the taxpayer.

The Act attempted to send a message that ending a marriage is a serious business. Mediation was not compulsory, unless the courts ordered it because the couple could not agree. The voluntary organization National Family Mediation was charged with providing mediation services, but was nevertheless underfunded. In addition, the spouse who had applied for the divorce had to attend an information meeting at the court about financial and other consequences, and then there had to be a three-month 'period of reflection' after the meeting (Bird and Cretney 1997).

The Family Law Act 1996 ended the concept of fault: the single ground for divorce was that the marriage had broken down. The aim was to make couples think more carefully about getting divorced, but if they decided to go ahead then the aim was to minimize bitterness and harm to children. Some commentators have argued that the ending of the concept of fault devalued the marriage vows, while others suggested that the focus on mediation reflected an outmoded view of the nature of family relationships (Lewis and Maclean 1997).

SOCIAL POLICY AND FAMILIES IN THE FUTURE

Patterns of family life and the nature of family policy have changed greatly over the second half of the twentieth century. What do demographic trends tell us about the future shape of family life? As we saw earlier in this chapter, family policy reflects strongly held and often conflicting ideologies. What cultural and ideological forces will shape policy making in the future?

Future trends in family life

Predictions about the future must always be regarded with some scepticism. However, demographic trends provide a useful start. In general, these involve taking current patterns and projecting them into the future.

In some respects the future is already unrolling. For example, the population pyramid shown in Fig. 8.1 can be used to predict important aspects of the future. The relatively large cohort of babies born during the 1960s will mean a relatively large population of elderly people when these individuals retire from employment in the years around 2030. After that there will be a decline in the numbers of elderly people, and in the population as a whole, because of the low birth rate in the 1970s and 1980s. Changes such as this have implications for social policy, and may have lain behind the government decision to equalize the retirement age for men and women at the age of 65 by the year 2020.

The annual review *Social Trends* summarized some of the main demographic trends (ONS 1997). These included the following:

- More people will remain single, either because they have never married, or because they have yet to marry. This reflects three trends: the rise in the age of marriage, the increase in cohabitation, and increasing scepticism about marriage itself.
- More marriages will end in divorce. Among both men and women 7 per cent were divorced in 1992, but this is expected to rise to 11 per cent of men and 12 per cent of women by the year 2020: the larger percentage among women reflects the fact that women typically outlive men.

- More people will live alone. This is partly because of the increase in divorce and partly because of greater longevity; but it also reflects the fact that young people are financially able to leave their parents' homes without having to marry.
- More people will live in **reconstituted families**. Increases in divorce will mean that more children spend more time living with a step-parent, or being shared between two parents who live apart; some children may effectively find themselves with four parents and eight grandparents.
- Grandparenting will change. The rise in the employment rate of mothers with young children will make grandparents, and especially grandmothers, an important source of childcare. At the same time the increase in life expectancy will mean that grandparents will be fitter and more active than in the past, and indeed many will still be in employment themselves when their grandchildren are growing up (Dench et al. 1999; Wheelock and Jones 2002).

Another view on the future is provided by cultural theorists. Here the focus is on the development of post-modernity, and on the transformations which are said to be taking place in intimate relationships. It has been suggested that we may be seeing 'the end of marriage' (Lewis 2001). It has been argued that the focus is shifting 'from institution to relationship', that is from the institution of marriage, with its traditional structure, to the individually chosen relationship, which can be broken when it ceases to satisfy (Giddens 1992). A key concept has been the idea of **individualization**:

> Individualisation means that men and women are released from the gender roles prescribed by industrial society for life in the nuclear family. At the same time, and this aggravates the situation, they find themselves forced, under pain of material disadvantage, to build up a life of their own by way of the labour market, training and mobility, and if need be to pursue this at the cost of their commitments to family, relations and friends. (Beck and Beck-Gernsheim 1995: 6)

Whether or not the cultural theorists will prove to be right in their predictions for the future, it is likely that the concept of families will continue to be controversial. The struggle will continue between those who think that change has gone too far and those who think that it has not gone far enough.

European perspectives on family policy

Debates about family policy will increasingly take place in the context of the European Community. However, the different countries involved have very different approaches to family policy.

Nation-states differ greatly in the extent to which family policy is explicit or implicit. In many European countries the constitution explicitly recognizes the importance of the family, and the state undertakes to afford it special protection. In some countries, such as France, Germany, and Luxembourg, this commitment is translated into institutional structures for formulating and implementing policy. Other states, such as Greece, Italy, Portugal, and Spain, pledge themselves in their constitution to support the family, but do not have central institutions equipped to carry out family policy making.

Some countries, such as Denmark, Finland, the Netherlands, and Sweden, do not identify the family as an explicit area of policy; instead individuals, and particularly children, are the focus of policy. In others, such as Ireland and the UK, official government policy has not generally directly targeted the family as a policy area because of the concern of governments to avoid interfering in the private lives of individuals (Hantrais and Letablier 1996).

The tension between policies which support family life and those which encroach on family privacy is revealed in many of the documents which have shaped family policy in Europe. The European Convention on Human Rights (1950) stipulated that:

1 Everyone has the right to respect of his [*sic*] private and family life, his home and his correspondence.
2 There shall be no interference by a public authority with the exercise of this right except such as is in accordance with the law.

The main treaties of the European Union have not been explicitly concerned with family policy, despite growing pressure that the EU should be concerned with the welfare of families. However, many European initiatives have affected families, most notably in the areas of childcare, working hours and maternity, **paternity and parental leave**. Legislation in these fields has been presented in terms of equal opportunities or health and safety at work. The principle of **subsidiarity**, according to which actions should be taken at the lowest appropriate administrative level, has inhibited the making of substantive family policy at supra-national levels.

At national levels there are great variations, in terms of family formation and structure and in the nature and extent of family policy. These variations have been documented by the European Observatory on National Family Policies (Ditch et al. 1996: 5). Total Period Fertility Rates are declining throughout the continent and every country now has a fertility rate below replacement level: it is argued that this may have beneficial social, economic, and environmental consequences. Most European countries are experiencing increases in cohabitation and divorce and in the numbers of lone-parent families, with a consequent increase in step and other relationships. Policy responses to these changes in family life will reflect long-standing ideological, cultural, and political differences between individuals and between nations.

Despite a British tradition of non-interference in family life, the Labour government has been energetic in introducing new policies in this field. Many of these have reflected a dual concern with lifting children out of poverty and getting parents into paid work. Despite a statement in *Supporting Families* that 'marriage is still the surest foundation for raising children' (Home Office 1998: 8), most policies have focused not on marriage but on parents and children. At the time of writing, the effects of these policies are uncertain, but those who read this book will be better able to judge what their impact has been. What is sure is that in the future social policy will continue to be a sensitive indicator of the current state of opinion on the changing nature of family life. It will also continue to have a powerful effect on the living standards and welfare of individuals within families.

KEY LEGISLATION AND POLICY DOCUMENTS

Children Act 1989 see page 174.

Child Support Act 1993 see page 175.

Divorce Reform Act 1969 see page 184.

Family Law Act 1996 see page 183-4.

Housing Act 1985 see page 183.

National Health Service and Community Care Act 1990 see page 179.

REFERENCES

Anderson, M., Bechofer, F., and Gershuny, J. (1994), *The Social and Political Economy of the Household*. Oxford: Oxford University Press.

Arber, S., and Ginn, J. (1995), 'Gender differences in the relationship between paid employment and informal care', *Work, Employment and Society* 9(3): 445–71.

Baldwin, S. (1985), *The Costs of Caring: Families with Disabled Children*. London: Routledge.

Barnes, G., Thompson, P., Daniel, G., and Burchardt, N. (1998), *Growing up in Stepfamilies*. Oxford: Clarendon Press.

Beck, U. (1992), *Risk Society*. London: Sage.

—— and Beck-Gernsheim, E. (1995), *The Normal Chaos of Love*. Cambridge: Polity Press.

Bennett, F. (1997), *Child Support: Issues for the Future*. London: Child Poverty Action Group.

Bernard, J. (1982), *The Future of Marriage*. New Haven, Conn.: Yale University Press.

Berthoud, R., and Gershuny, J. (2000), *Seven Years in the Lives of British Families*. Colchester: University of Essex.

Beveridge Report (1942), *Social Insurance and Allied Services*, Cmd. 6404. London HMSO.

Bird, R., and Cretney, S. (1997), *Divorce: The New Law*. London: Bristol Family Law.

Burgoyne, C., and Morison, V. (1997), 'Money in re-marriage: keeping things simple—and separate', *Sociological Review* 45(3): 363–95.

—— Ormrod, R., and Richards, M. (1987), *Divorce Matters*. Harmondsworth: Penguin.

Central Statistical Office (1995), *Social Trends, No. 25*. London: HMSO.

Charles, N. (2000), *Feminism, the State and Social Policy*. Basingstoke: Macmillan.

Child Poverty Action Group (2002), *Welfare Benefits Handbook*. London: CPAG.

—— (2003), *Welfare Benefits and Tax Credits Handbook*. London: Child Poverty Action Group.

Clarke, K., Glendinning, C., and Craig, G. (1994), *Losing Support: Children and the Child Support Act*. London: Child Poverty Action Group.

Conservative Party (1997), *You Can Only be Sure with the Conservatives*. London: Conservative Party.

Delphy, C., and Leonard, D. (1992), *Familiar Exploitation: A New Analysis of Marriage in Contemporary Western Societies*. Cambridge: Polity Press.

Dench, G., Ogg, J., and Thomson, K. (1999), 'The role of grandparents'. In R. Jowell, J. Curtice, A. Park, and K. Thomson (eds.), *British Social Attitudes: The 16th Report*. Aldershot: Ashgate.

Dennis, N., and Erdos, G. (1993), *Families without Fatherhood*. London: Institute of Economic Affairs.

Department of Health (1989), *An Introduction to the Children Act 1989*. London: HMSO.

Ditch, J., Barnes, H., Bradshaw, J., Commaille, J., and Eardley, T. (1996), *A Synthesis of National Family Policies in 1994*. York: University of York.

Dobash, R., and Dobash, R. E. (1980), *Violence against Wives*. Shepton Mallet: Open Books.

Driver, S., and Martell, L. (2002), 'New Labour, work and the family', *Social Policy and Administration* 36(1): 46–61.

Family Policy Studies Centre (1997), *Putting Families on the Map*. London: Family Policy Studies Centre.

Ferri, E., and Smith, K. (1998), *Step-parenting in the 1990s*. London: Family Policy Studies Centre.

Freeman, M. (1992), *Children, their Families and the Law: Working with the Children Act*. Basingstoke: Macmillan.

Giddens, A. (1992), *The Transformation of Intimacy*. Cambridge: Polity.

—— (1997) *Sociology*. Cambridge: Polity Press.

Gittins, D. (1993), *The Family in Question*. Basingstoke: Macmillan.

Glendinning, C., and Millar, J. (1992), *Women and Poverty in Britain: The 1990s*. Hemel Hempstead: Wheatsheaf.

Goode, J., Callender, C., and Lister, R. (1998), *Purse or Wallet: Gender Inequalities and Income Distribution within Families*. London: Policy Studies Institute.

Graham, H. (1983), 'Caring: a labour of love,. In J. Finch, and D. Groves, (eds.), *A Labour of Love: Women, Work and Caring*. London: Routledge.

Green, H. (1988), *Informal Carers*. London: HMSO.

Hague, G., and Malos, E. (1998), *Domestic Violence: Action for Change*. Cheltenham: New Clarion Press.

Hantrais, L., and Letablier, M. (1996), *Families and Family Policy in Europe*. London: Longman.

Haskey, J. (1996), 'Population review: families and households in Great Britain', *Population Trends* 85(7): 13.

Hills, J., Le Grand, J., and Piachaud, D. (2002), *Understanding Social Exclusion*. Oxford: Oxford University Press.

Home Office (1998), *Supporting Families: A Consultation Document*. London: Stationery Office.

Hyman, P. (1994), *Women and Economics*. Wellington, New Zealand: Bridget Williams.

Joshi, H. (1992), 'The cost of caring'. In Glendinning and Millar (1992).

Jowell, R., Curtice, J., Park, A., Brook, L., and Ahrendt, D. (1995), *British Social Attitudes: The 12th Report*. Aldershot: Gower.

Kempson, E. (1996), *Life on a Low Income*. York: Joseph Rowntree Foundation.

—— Bryson, A., and Rowlingson, K. (1994), *Hard Times: How Poor Families Make Ends Meet*. York: Joseph Rowntree Foundation.

Kiernan, K., and Wicks, M. (1990), *Family Change and Future Policy*. London: Family Policy Studies Centre.

Kingston, P., and Penhale, B. (1995), *Family Violence and the Caring Professions*. Basingstoke: Macmillan.

Kirby, J. (2002), *Broken Hearts: Family Decline and the Consequences for Society*. London: Centre for Policy Studies.

Labour Party (1997), *New Labour: Because Britain Deserves Better*. London: Labour Party.

Levin, E., Moriarty, J., and Gorbach, P. (1994), *Better for the Break*. London: HMSO.

Lewis, J. (2001), *The End of Marriage*? Cheltenham: Elgar.

—— and Maclean, M. (1997), 'Recent developments in family policy in the UK'. In M. May, E. Brunsdon, and G. Craig (eds.), *Social Policy Review 9*. London: Social Policy Association.

McLennan, G. (1991), 'The power of ideology', in *Society and the Social Sciences*. Milton Keynes: Open University Press.

McRae, S. (1999), *Changing Britain: Families and Households in the 1990s*. Oxford: Oxford University Press.

Masefield, J. (1946), *Poems*. London: Heinemann.

Middleton, S., Ashworth, K., and Braithwaite, I. (1997), *Small Fortunes: Spending on Children, Childhood Poverty and Parental Sacrifice*. York: Joseph Rowntree Foundation.

Millar, J., and Rowlingson, K. (2001), *Lone Parents, Employment and Social Policy*. Bristol: Policy Press.

Molloy, D., and Snape, D. (1999), *Low Income Households: Financial Organisation and Financial Exclusion*. London: Department of Social Security.

Mooney, J. (2000), *Gender, Violence and the Social Order*. Basingstoke; Macmillan.

Morgan, P. (1995), *Farewell to the Family?* London: Institute of Economic Affairs.

Morgan, P. (2000), *Marriage-lite: The Rise of Cohabitation and its Consequences*. London: Institute for the Study of Civil Society.

Mullender, A. (1996), *Rethinking Domestic Violence: The Social Work and Probation Response*. London: Routledge.

Muncie, J., Wetherell, M., Dallos, R., and Cochrane A. (1995), *Understanding the Family*. London: Sage.

National Statistics Online (2002), www.statistics.gov.uk/Census2001/default.asp

Oakley, A. (1974), *The Sociology of Housework*. London: Martin Robertson.

Office of Population Censuses and Surveys (1991), *Social Trends 21*. London: HMSO.

—— (1996), *Living in Britain: Results from the 1994 General Household Survey*. London: HMSO.

ONS (Office for National Statistics) (1997), *Social Trends 27*. London: HMSO.

—— (1998), *Social Trends 28*. London: HMSO.

—— (2002), *Social Trends 32*. London: HMSO.

Pahl, J. (1985), *Private Violence and Public Policy*. London: Routledge.

—— (1989), *Money and Marriage*. Basingstoke: Macmillan.

—— (2000), 'Social polarisation in the electronic economy'. In: R. Crompton, F. Devine, M. Savage, and J. Scott (eds.), *Renewing Class Analysis*. Oxford: Blackwell.

—— and Quine, L. (1987), 'Families with mentally handicapped children'. In J. Orford (ed.), *Coping with Disorder in the Family*. London: Croom Helm.

Park, A., Curtice, J., Thomson, K., Jarvis, L., and Bromley, C. (2001), *British Social Attitudes: The 18th Report*. London: Sage.

Parker, G. (1990), *With Due Care and Attention: A Review of Research on Informal Care*. London: Family Policy Studies Centre.

Parsons, T., and Bales, R. (1956), *Family, Socialisation and Interaction Process*. London: Routledge.

Piachaud, D., and Sutherland, H. (2002), 'Child poverty', In Hills et al. (2002).

Robinson, M., and Smith, D. (1993), *Step by Step: Focus on Stepfamilies*. Hemel Hempstead: Wheatsheaf.

Rodgers, B., and Pryor, J. (1998), *Divorce and Separation: The Outcomes for Children*. York: Joseph Rowntree Foundation.

Rose, R. (1989), *Ordinary People in Social Policy: A Behavioural Analysis*. London: Sage.

Secretaries of State for Health (1989), *Caring for People: Community Care in the Next Decade and Beyond*. Cm. 849. London: HMSO.

Secretary of State for Social Security (1995), *Improving Child Support*. London: HMSO.

Twigg, J. (1992), *Carers: Research and Practice*. London: HMSO.

—— Atkin, K. and Perring, C. (1990), *Carers and Services: A Review of Research*. London: HMSO.

Victim Support (1992), *Domestic Violence*. London: HMSO.

Vogler, C. and Pahl, J. (1993), 'Social and economic change and the organisation of money in marriage', *Work, Employment and Society* 7(1): 71–95.

—— (1994), 'Money, power and inequality within marriage', *Sociological Review* 42(2): 263–88.

Wasoff, F., and Dey, I. (2000), *Family Policy*. Eastbourne: Gildredge Press.

Wheelock, J., and Jones, K. (2002), 'Grandparents are the next best thing: informal childcare for working parents in urban Britain', *Journal of Social Policy* 31(3): 441–63.

FURTHER READING

M. Anderson, F. Bechofer, and J. Gershuny. *The Social and Political Economy of the Household* (Oxford: Oxford University Press, 1994). Results from the Social Change and Economic Life Initiative illuminate the allocation of work, time, and money within households.

R. Bertoud and J. Gershuny, *Seven Years in the Lives of British Families* (Colchester: University of Essex, 2000). Results from the British Household Panel Survey document the changes which took place in family life in the 1990s.

L. Hantrais and M. Letablier, *Families and Family Policies in Europe* (London: Longman, 1996). A comparative study of family policy in the European Union.

D. Gittins, *The Family in Question* (Basingstoke: Macmillan, 1992). A reissue of a classic text on family life and family ideologies.

S. McRae, *Changing Britain: Families and Households in the 1990s* (Oxford: Oxford University Press, 1999). A series of case studies on trends in family life, kinship, older people, young motherhood, divorce, and new ways of living.

F. Wasoff and I. Dey, *Family Policy* (Eastbourne: Gildredge Press, 2000). A short and readable introduction to current debates in family policy.

USEFUL WEBSITES

For information about the National Childcare Strategy go to: www.dfes.gov.uk/childcare

The Child Poverty Action Group website gives information about family living standards and family policy at: www.cpag.org.uk

An account of the work of the Child Support Agency can be found at: www.childsupportagency.org.uk

The National Family and Parenting Institute, with its helpline for parents, can be found at: www.nfpi.org.uk

The government's New Deal initiative for lone parents is described at: www.newdeal.gov.uk

The National Council for One Parent Families has a useful fact file at: www.oneparentfamilies.org.uk

For facts about domestic violence go to: www.womensaid.org.uk/dv/dvfactsh3.htm

GLOSSARY

age structure This term is used to describe populations in terms of the relative numbers of people of different ages. The age structure of the population reflects variations in the past number of births, together with increased longevity and changes arising from migration (ONS 2002: 32).

child benefit This is a universal benefit, paid to the mother of a child under 16, or under 19 if the child is still in full-time education. At the time of writing there are higher rates of benefit for the first child and even higher rates for the first child of a lone parent (Child Poverty Action Group 2002: 187).

childcare This term is often used to refer to the support available outside the family to help parents to care for dependent children. It includes day nurseries and playgroups, as well as care by childminders and nannies. However, as much care is provided by grandmothers as is provided by all other sources of childcare put together (Wheelock and Jones 2002).

dependency ratio This term was coined by economists to describe the ratio between those who are 'economically active', in that they earn their own living in the labour market, and those who depend on other earners for their financial support. The definition does not, of course, recognize the fact that those who are economically active are often dependent on those who are 'economically inactive' for the provision of domestic services, **child care**, and other supports, and that 'economically inactive' people can be contributing valuable unpaid work to their family or community.

extended family This term was coined by sociologists to describe the wider kin group, in contrast to the 'nuclear family'. An extended family may link three or more generations, and will include people whose relationship is that of grandparent/grandchild, brothers and sisters, uncles and aunts, nephews and nieces and cousins.

family The official definition of the family, used in all government censuses and surveys, is that a family is a married or cohabiting couple, either with or without their never-married children (of any age), including couples without children or a lone parent together with his or her never-married child or children (ONS 2002: 232).

family policy 'For a social policy to be described as family policy . . . the family would need to be the deliberate target of specific actions, and the measures should be designed so as to have an impact on family resources and, ultimately, on family structure' (Hantrais and Letablier 1996: 139).

household A household is a person living alone or a group of people who have the address as their only or main residence and who either share one meal a day or share the living accommodation (ONS 2002: 232).

ideology 'Ideologies are sets of ideas, assumptions, and images by which people make sense of society, which give a clear social identity, and which serve in some way to legitimize power relations in society' (McLennan 1991: 114).

individualization This term refers to the process by which the individual, rather than the group, becomes the key unit in society. The idea implies the breaking down of the structures of class, occupation, locality, and gender. As one commentator said, 'The individual himself or herself becomes the reproduction unit for the social in the lifeworld' (Beck 1992: 130).

lone-parent family A lone-parent family consists of a lone parent living with his or her never-married dependent children, provided these children have no children of their own (ONS 1998: 235).

maternity allowance This is a benefit paid to women who are pregnant or who have recently given birth, who have paid sufficient contributions but who do not qualify for maternity pay, either because they have changed jobs during pregnancy or because they are self-employed (Child Poverty Action Group 2002: 84).

maternity leave The right for women to take paid leave from employment around the time of the birth of a baby (Ditch et al. 1995: 47).

maternity pay A contributory benefit paid to women who are pregnant or who have recently given birth. Entitlement to the benefit depends on women having been employed for at least twenty-six weeks and to have satisfied certain other conditions (Child Poverty Action Group 2002: 77).

nuclear family This term was coined by sociologists to describe the social group consisting of parents and their children; it is particularly contrasted with the 'extended family', which includes members of the wider kin group such as grandparents, uncles and aunts, cousins, nephews and nieces, and grandchildren.

parental responsibility The Children Act 1989 used this term to sum up the collection of duties, rights, and authority which a parent has in respect of a child. The aim was to stress that parents, rather than the state, have the prime responsibility for children. Mothers, and the fathers of legitimate children, automatically have parental responsibility, while fathers who are not married to the mother of the child can acquire parental responsibility in a number of different ways (Department of Health 1989: 1).

paternity and parental leave The first term refers to the right of a man to take paid leave from employment when he becomes a father. The second term refers to the right of parents to take leave when a child is ill. Currently neither is state policy in the United Kingdom, though some other European countries do give limited rights to such leave (Ditch et al. 1995: 47).

public and private spheres The separation of public and private has a long history in western European thought, deriving from the ancient Greek distinction between the *polis*, meaning the sphere of public life, and the *oikos*, meaning the private household. The involvement of the state in the private life of the family has been criticized as interference and control, or it has been welcomed as a support to the work done in this sphere and as a check on the tyranny which the strong can exercise over weaker members of families.

reconstituted families These are families in which one or both parents have been married before, so at least one parent–child relationship involves a step-parent and a stepchild.

subsidiarity This concept originated within the Roman Catholic Church and has been adopted as a central principle of the European Community. It expresses the idea that actions should be taken at the lowest appropriate administrative level. So actions should not be undertaken by nation-states if they can be carried out by regional bodies, and public agencies should not take on responsibilities which can be undertaken within the family (Hantrais and Letablier 1996: 45).

total period fertility rate (TFPR) The TPFR measures the average number of children born to each woman, if birth rates in the specific period persisted throughout her childbearing life (ONS 1997: 32).

8

Welfare, Identity, and the Life Course

Hartley Dean

CONTENTS

INTRODUCTION: DIFFERENCE AND DEPENDENCY

Human beings are not all the same. We are different. Our differences define our **identities** and affect what we may require for our welfare (or 'wellbeing'). Some of those differences are biological. We are born with different sexual characteristics, different skin colours, different physical propensities and abilities. In the course of our lives the differences between us multiply as we grow up and grow old, and as illness, injury, and other vicissitudes may or may not befall us. At the same time as being different from each other, as social beings we are also dependent on each other. The complex ways in which societies—as associations of interdependent human beings—organize and reproduce themselves result in a further range of differences that are socially determined and can lead to oppression. Our lives are shaped by differences of class, custom, and culture, and by the particular economic, political, and historical characteristics of the society we inhabit. This chapter is about how social policy is implicated in the way we understand difference and dependency.

The chapter will focus on four kinds of difference—gender, ethnicity, disability, and age. In the case of each we shall see how biological differences lay the foundations for differences that are socially constructed, how social difference can create social disadvantage, and the role that social policies play. In the conclusion we shall return to the question of identity and its significance for the future of social policy. First, however, we set the scene by discussing three rather different approaches towards difference and dependency.

The social welfare perspective

The classic justification for a welfare state is that it enables us to define and recognize what Richard Titmuss once called 'states of dependency' (1955: 64). Advanced industrial societies are characterized not only by their complex division of labour but by complex **divisions of welfare**. Different people may address the 'states of dependency' that will occur in the course of their lives and satisfy their welfare needs in different ways. Titmuss argued that state welfare provision should be universal: it should cater for the different needs of all the people and not just the specific needs of the poor. In practice, however, Titmuss identified class-based divisions of welfare: he noted that while the prosperous could benefit, for example, from generous fiscal and occupational benefits, the poor were dependent on stigmatizing state benefits. More recent commentators have similarly identified sexual, racial, and age divisions of welfare, and a case can be made 'for identifying . . . other specific divisions based on the failure of welfare to cater for the needs of the various and disparate groups which constitute the poor' (Mann 1992: 26).

From the social welfare perspective, one of the objectives of social policy is to achieve **social solidarity** and to mitigate the inequalities created by a market economy. Our frailty and interdependency as human beings necessitates collectively organized mechanisms of social protection. Provision for our welfare needs cannot be guaranteed if simply left to free market forces. However, precisely because human beings are so different, our needs are complex (see Chapter 5). Waltzer (1983), for example, has argued that the welfare state should not be like the Procrustean bed of Greek legend—upon which people were shrunk or stretched until they would fit. The challenge is to protect people from inequality, while accommodating their differences; to combat disadvantage not by mechanistic or proportional processes of redistribution or the provision of uniform entitlements, but by creative and affirmative intervention that recognizes difference and the particularity of people's needs. There is a risk, however, that in attempting this the welfare state can become paternalistic and impose its own definitions of people's various needs.

The politics of equal opportunity

A rather different approach to social diversity has been provided by liberalism. Liberalism values freedom of individual choice, and liberal thinkers—from Locke in the seventeenth century to Rawls in the twentieth—have recognized that individuals have different attributes and preferences. However, precisely because they see dependency as inimical to freedom, liberals have been less inclined to accept that the state should accommodate or provide for the diverse needs of different people. *Economic* liberalism favours free markets in which, subject only to the rule of law, individuals are equally free to exploit their attributes and satisfy their preferences, even though this may result in social inequalities. *Social* liberalism, on the other hand, recognizes that for individuals to compete in a market economy—whether as entrepreneurs or wage-earners—there must be a 'level playing field': there must, so far as possible, be **equality of opportunity** for all, regardless of class, gender, ethnicity, disability, or age.

The development of welfare state capitalism was informed as much by social liberal ideals as by the social welfare perspective: by the aspiration that 'equality of status is more important than equality of income' (Marshall 1950: 33). The priority is not necessarily to redress differences through a redistribution of resources, but to ensure that everybody is permitted an equal chance in life, regardless of individual difference. This means that everyone should have the opportunity to be educated, healthy, properly housed, and adequately provided for in the event of misfortune and during old age. Responding to such opportunities, however, is the responsibility of the individual. The state's primary responsibility is not necessarily to provide the things that are essential to human wellbeing, but to put procedural guarantees in place to ensure that people can access provision without discrimination. In this way, according to social liberals, we should establish a strictly meritocratic society in which differences of income and wealth are based on just rewards, rather than a class society in which such differences are based on accidents of birth and breeding. These arguments have been extended to contend that the state should guarantee equality of opportunity in ways that ensure that women, minority ethnic groups, and disabled people can achieve their full potential as individuals. This is the thinking that has informed the development of anti-discrimination legislation (see Box 8.1). A particular emphasis upon equality of opportunity over equality of income or outcome has been ascendant in the political rhetoric of both the New Right and, more recently New Labour (see Chapter 3). However, the implication of the liberal view is that its **formal** ideal of abstract human equality may sometimes obscure the **substantive** reality of everyday human difference.

Box 8.1 British anti-discrimination legislation[a]

Sex Discrimination Act 1975 (SDA)	The SDA *supplemented* the Equal Pay Act of 1970, which requires that employers should not provide less favourable pay and conditions on the grounds of an employee's sex (but which is often thwarted because labour market segregation makes it difficult to establish that work 'traditionally' performed by women is of 'equal value' to that performed by men). The SDA outlaws both direct and indirect discrimination on the grounds of sex in relation both to employment and to the provision of goods and services.[b] It created the Equal Opportunities Commission,[c] a quango with power to investigate complaints.
Race Relations Act 1976 (RRA)	The 1976 RRA *superseded* the weaker RRAs of 1965 and 1968, which had sought to outlaw incitement to racial hatred and direct racial discrimination in public places, in employment and housing, and to promote good 'community relations'. The 1976 Act outlaws both direct and indirect discrimination on the grounds of 'race', colour, national or ethnic origins in relation both to employment and to the provision of all goods and services.[b] It created the Commission for Racial Equality,[c] a quango with power to investigate complaints. It has been extended by the Race Relations (Amendment) Act 2000 to apply to the functioning of all public authorities.
Disability Discrimination Act 1995 (DDA)	The DDA outlaws both direct and indirect discrimination on the grounds of disability in relation both to employment and the provision of goods and services,[b] but is subject to exemptions where, for example, employers can establish a 'justifiable reason' for discriminating. (Additional exemptions that currently apply to small employers will be removed in 2004.) Amending legislation in 1999 created the Disability Rights Commission,[c] a quango with power to investigate complaints.
Age Discrimination Act (proposed 2006)	Following the European Community Employment Directive of 2000 the UK government is currently consulting with a view to legislating to combat age discrimination in the workplace. It is not clear how extensive the legislation will prove to be.

[a] In response to the European Community Employment Directive of 2000, the British government proposes in 2003 to introduce regulations under existing employment legislation to outlaw discrimination on the grounds of sexual orientation and religion. However, the protection proposed will not extend to discrimination in the provision of goods and services.

[b] Direct discrimination occurs when a person is treated less favourably than another. Indirect discrimination occurs when conditions are imposed that adversely affect members of a particular social group. Redress in respect of discrimination (including victimization) in employment may be sought before the Employment Tribunal, while redress in respect of discrimination in the provision of goods and services may be sought in the civil courts.

[c] The British government is considering possible models for unifying existing equality bodies and establishing a single Equality Commission, but it has no immediate plans to legislate and has declined the option of setting up a more broadly based Human Rights Commission.

The politics of identity and recognition

Theorists of post-modernity contend that the social democratic and liberal 'grand narratives' that originally informed the social welfare and equal opportunities perspectives have now been exhausted (see Chapter 3). Derrida (1978), for example, claims that the proliferation of difference has fragmented the very nature of human beings' identities. Certainly, we must acknowledge that global economic and social changes have been reflected in new forms of political and social scientific thinking. The nature of the class demarcations that once shaped domestic politics and the geopolitical tensions that characterized the international order have fundamentally changed. We have seen the emergence of **new social movements**—such as the women's movement, the anti-racist movement, and the disability rights movement—that have created a new kind of politics which actively celebrates social difference. At the heart of this new politics lie questions of culture and identity—as opposed to social structure and class. While writers like Giddens (1994) have hailed this as a form of politics that may somehow transcend the old divisions between Left and Right, it is also reflected in a more fundamental 'cultural turn' in the social sciences; in modes of analysis that accommodate the part played by human agency and discursive practices in the 'production of meaning' and the way we understand the world around us (Clarke 1999).

The task for the student of social policy, according to Fiona Williams, is to 'catch some understanding of the relationship between diversity and power, between the individual, their identity, their landscapes of choice and risk and the ways these are structured by societal relations of power and inequality' (1992: 214). Feminist thinkers have given this idea particular meaning. Fraser (1989; 1995), for example, has argued that while conventional social policy debates have been preoccupied with issues of redistribution, it is time that these were extended to encompass issues of recognition; that what is required is a politics of needs interpretation that focuses on recognizing the different identities through which human beings define their needs. This is more radical than either the social welfare or the equal opportunities approach, both of which envision a society that is informed by the work ethic; in which the primary social difference to be recognized is that between self-sufficient 'workers' and dependent 'others'. Recent feminist commentators have argued for an alternative politics, based on an **ethic of care** (see Sevenhuijsen 1998): a politics that acknowledges the frailty and interdependency of human beings, and the reality that our identities stem as much from the care that we may give and must necessarily ourselves receive in the course of our lives as from our place (if any) in the labour market.

GENDER

It is undoubtedly true that 'the traditional world of social policy (or administration) was peopled by ungendered subjects and objects of analysis; women and their concerns were marginalised' (Lister 2000: 22). More recently, while the makers of social policy still do not sufficiently address issues of gender, the study of social policy has been revolutionized by insights from contemporary analyses of gender and sexuality.

The social construction of gender

While sexual difference is biological, gender is socially or culturally constructed. That women have babies and men do not is a biological fact. The prevailing sexual division of labour—under which it is characteristically women who attend to the daily business of social reproduction while men are freed to engage in economic production and political governance—is a social artefact. With this in mind:

> [women's] pan-cultural second-class status could be accounted for, quite simply, by postulating that women are being identified or symbolically associated with nature, as opposed to men, who are identified with culture. Since it is always culture's project to subsume and transcend nature, if women were considered a part of nature, then culture would find it 'natural' to subordinate, not to say oppress, them. (Ortner 1972: 254)

There are strands of feminist thought that are implicitly founded in **biological determinism**: that assert that women are closer to nature, that they are 'naturally' more caring and less aggressive, and that they address the world 'in a different voice' (Gilligan 1982) than men. Other strands of feminism, however, reject such ideas, and assert that the gendered nature of society is a specific outcome of power relations and **patriarchy**. It is an effect of the dominance of men over women and can be resisted. Patriarchy, as a structural characteristic of human societies, rests upon a divide not between nature and culture, but between the socially constituted spheres of the private and the public. The sphere we regard as 'private' is the domain of hearth, home, and the ideologically constructed family (see Chapter 7). The sphere of the 'public', in contrast, is the domain of the market and the state. The power that accrues to roles assumed predominantly by men within the public sphere accounts for the perpetuation and subordination of the dependent roles assumed predominantly by women within the private sphere.

This presents a dilemma that Pateman (1989)—calling upon the writings of one of the earliest feminists—has characterized as 'Wollstonecraft's dilemma'. Mary Wollstonecraft (1792) contended that men and women are equal but different. In practice, however, women must choose between equality with men on men's terms, which requires the jettisoning of family responsibilities, or recognition of their different status as mothers and homemakers. The dilemma is reflected in an enduring tension between what Williams (1989) has characterized as welfare feminism and liberal feminism. Welfare feminists have argued for a greater degree of recognition and support—for example, through the benefits and tax system—for women's roles as mothers and carers, while liberal feminists have argued for equality of opportunity; for the chance to engage in the labour market and with the political process on equal terms with men. The risk for women of the former strategy is that of 'locking them out of the "public" sphere economically and politically'; that of the latter is that, so long as men do not share the roles of caring, it will 'simply increase the burdens on them' (Lister 1994: 42–3).

The architects of the welfare state were so inured to patriarchal assumptions about the respective roles of male breadwinners and female homemakers that the national insurance system, for example, was designed on the premise that married women would for the most part be financially dependent on their husbands. While many of the more overtly discriminatory elements of the British social security system have since been removed—primarily as a result of European Union Equal Treatment Directives—the legacy of the assumptions on which the system was founded remains. In common with other systems in the developed world, British social security provision incorporates a social insurance scheme, under which it is predominantly male heads of household who claim entitlements on behalf of predominantly female dependants, and a social assistance system, under which it is predominantly female-headed households—including large numbers of lone parents and single pensioners—who claim stigmatized means-tested benefits: the former have been characterized as 'masculine sub-systems', the latter as 'feminine sub-systems' (Fraser 1989: 111–12). Recent policy moves towards a system of tax credits, it has been argued, may portend a shift away from assumptions based on the 'male breadwinner household model' that informed the Beveridgian welfare state, and towards an 'adult worker model' (Lewis 2000) in which men and women alike are expected to sustain themselves through participation in the labour market. In practice, however, such policies take little account of women's preferences or the opportunities available to them, and would seem to be privileging paid employment at the expense of unpaid caring. Wollstonecraft's dilemma still applies.

There are, broadly speaking, two kinds of response. One, offered by radical feminists, may be characterized as the 'strategies of personal and political separatism' (Williams 1989: 54): put starkly, women should eschew men and provide for their own welfare. The other entails a range of strategies that have in various ways embraced the slogan 'the personal is political' (cf. Eisenstein 1984). What such strategies share is a desire to publicize (literally—to project into the public sphere) the issues of the private sphere, and to challenge the basis of gendered power relations though a politics of identity and recognition. Such approaches open up the possibility of addressing a wider range of issues, including:

- men's behaviour and the extent to which masculinity is as much a social construction as femininity;
- the specific experiences of different women, including women from minority ethnic groups for whom gender is but one component of their identity;
- issues closely associated with gender, such as sexuality and the particular experiences and needs of lesbians and gay men.

Experiences of disadvantage

The concept of poverty has already been discussed in Chapter 5. Some commentators have argued that we are now witnessing the '**feminization** of poverty' (Scott 1984). The term may be construed in different ways. It may refer to an increased risk of poverty for women, the increased visibility of women's poverty, or the reconstitution of poverty from a woman's perspective. Undeniably women do suffer more poverty than men, because their labour—both paid and unpaid—is undervalued. It is also true that changes in the labour market and demographic changes affecting household composition have brought the poverty of unemployed women, female lone parents, and older single women more sharply into focus. Arguably, women have always been poorer than men. Lewis and Piachaud (1992) have shown that the proportion of women amongst adults in receipt of poor relief or social assistance, at around 60 per cent, was much the same at the beginning as at the end of the twentieth century. Nonetheless, the Equal Opportunities Commission have observed that 'during the past 25 years there has been an increase in the poverty of mothers, and lone-mothers in particular' (EOC 2001: 3). This is in spite of the extent to which, in the post-Second World War period, the proportion of women participating in paid employment increased dramatically (see Chapter 6). In the 1990s, within the poorest 10 per cent of the population, around two-thirds of the adults were women, and these women had about half as much independent income as men (Webb 1993).

There are three principal reasons for the endurance of women's poverty. First, as is illustrated by the figures in Table 8.1, nearly a third of all women of working age still remain outside the labour market, almost twice the proportion for men; women do not have equal access to the 'core' of the labour market and are disproportionately represented within part-time and lower-paid jobs; and, on average, not only are women paid less than men, they obtain a smaller proportion of their income from employment and, in retirement, from occupational pensions (and a higher proportion from state benefits). Second, women undertake a disproportionate share of the tasks associated with social reproduction: that is, with unpaid care work and domestic labour (see Case Study 8.1).

Third, the distribution of income and resources within families does not necessarily work to the advantage of women. The evidence for this has already been discussed in Chapter 7.

Additionally, women are disadvantaged by other forms of discrimination within the public sphere. Gillian Pascall (1997) and others have argued that, although women now make up a high proportion of the public sector workforce—in healthcare, social work, and education—they remain under-represented at senior and managerial levels. As a result, it is largely men who control health and social services, including services that particularly affect women, such as reproductive healthcare and support for informal carers; and the education system, while no longer preparing girls for domesticity, is tending to equip them for relatively subservient occupations, especially in the public sector. Finally, although women in Britain have been permitted to vote and to participate in the democratic process on the same terms as men since 1928, in 2001 only 18 per cent of Westminster MPs and 28 per cent of local government councillors were women (EOC 2001).

Policies and their impact

Notwithstanding, it must be stressed that the welfare state has in many ways been good for women. It has had a major role in redistributing income and resources from men to women. In spite of the gendered assumptions that underpinned the original welfare state settlement, the parsimonious and begrudging nature of the benefits it sometimes offers to women, and men's continued dominance in the management of welfare, the National Health Service has improved health outcomes for women; the education system has expanded their opportunities in the labour market; some limited recognition

Table 8.1 Gender, labour market participation, and personal income in Great Britain

	Men	Women
Economic activity of 16–64 year olds, 2001 (%)		
In employment	80	67
as full-time employees	62	35
as part-time employees	5	27
as self-employed	12	4
Unemployed[a]	4	3
Outside labour market[b]	16	31
Occupations, 2001 (% of occupational group)		
Professional and managerial	66	34
Associate professional/technical	54	46
Administrative/secretarial/personal services/retail	22	78
Skilled trades/process, plant and machine operatives	88	12
Elementary	54	46
Earnings from employment, 2001		
Average hourly earnings (£ per hour)		
full-time	11.97	9.76
part-time	7.69	7.03
Average weekly earnings (£ per week)		
full-time	490	367
part-time	141	136
Income, 1999/2000 (% derived from)		
Employee earnings	68	62
Self-employment	11	5
Investments	4	4
Occupational pensions/annuities	8	5
Benefits (inc. state pension)	8	21
Other	1	3

[a] Unemployed by International Labour Organization definition, although the figures shown here do *not* reflect the official ILO unemployment rate but the proportions of those meeting that definition as a percentage of *all* men/women—i.e. including those outside the labour market.
[b] Sometimes also referred to as 'economically inactive'.

Source: based on Labour Force Survey data drawn from EOC (2002), with some calculations by the author.

has been accorded to the role of women as providers of informal social care; and housing and social security provision have provided at least some measure of independence to women, especially those needing to escape from violent or dysfunctional family relationships or choosing to live without dependency on a male breadwinner.

Case Study 8.1 Evaluating women's role in unpaid care work and domestic labour

Recent research has a great deal to tell us about the nature of women's experiences and about the work they do outside the formal labour market. For example, women, regardless of whether they also undertake paid employment, still undertake the bulk of unpaid domestic work (Kiernan 1992). When it comes to putting a value on the 'housework' and childcare performed by women, one commercial insurance company recently calculated that—at an average figure in 2001 of around £378 per week—this amounted to more than twice that contributed by men (reported in the *Guardian*, 24 March 2001). Looked at in terms of the personal cost to a woman, in earnings foregone, of a career break to have two children, this can typically amount to twenty times the value of her annual salary when she stopped work (Joshi 1992). There is also a considerable body of evidence to show that, over and above the contribution they make to childcare, women make a disproportionate contribution to the unpaid care that is provided at home for elderly or disabled parents, spouses, or other relatives, and this can have similar consequences in terms of the costs that are saved—by families and/or the state—and the income and opportunities that women themselves forgo (see Chapter 7 and Glendinning 1992).

In addition to the provision of mainstream social welfare, British governments in the 1970s introduced anti-discrimination legislation (see Box 8.1) that sought to outlaw all forms of sex discrimination. Insofar as such legislation is premised on the rights of individuals, it has had little effect upon the structural nature of gender segregation within labour markets, on the legacy of the gendered assumptions upon which the welfare state has been constructed, or on the nature of power relations within patriarchal families. Nonetheless, the legislation has brought advances for individual women, it has improved the practices of most employers, and it has contributed to public awareness of sex equality issues.

Classic accounts of modern welfare regimes (such as that by Esping-Andersen: see Chapter 1) have sought to understand their emergence as a process of 'de-commodification', by which state welfare provision ensures that (predominantly male) wage labourers may to an extent sustain themselves independently of the market. Equally, however, it may be argued that the development of the welfare state entailed a process of 'de-familialization', by which state welfare provision may lessen individuals' (including women's) reliance on families, an argument since conceded by Esping-Anderson (1999). The reality, however, is complex. On the one hand, as Janet Finch (1989) has shown, the changing nature of familial obligations is not necessarily influenced by state intervention but by negotiation within familial and kinship relationships. On the other, while it is sometimes supposed that functions 'traditionally' associated with families have passed to the state, post-structuralists such as Donzelot (1979) have observed that families seem now to have extended functions and are subject by the welfare state to far greater levels of surveillance and control. For example, women's performance as mothers and informal carers may be subject to supervision by healthcare and social service professionals (see Chapters 15 and 16).

> The family has not lost functions, but it has lost control. It is still the major arena for the care of dependants, but traditional female tasks are now defined and managed outside the family and by men. (Pascall 1997: 23)

The welfare state may also function directly to enforce women's dependency on men. Lone parents (90 per cent of whom are women) will have social assistance benefits withdrawn if they should cohabit, and they can be compelled to cooperate with the making of child support assessments against the father(s) of their child(ren). More recently, so far as lone parents are concerned, the emphasis of the New Labour government has been to provide incentives and encouragement for them to engage with the labour market (see Chapter 12). Research by Duncan and Edwards (1999), however, has illustrated the extent to which women engage with 'gendered moral rationalities' that do not necessarily fit the policymakers' ideal. Some women identify themselves primarily as mothers, some primarily as workers, and others as both. More generally, Hilary Graham (1983) has argued that many women accept economic dependency as the price they must pay for the hidden dependence of their families on them as carers.

Britain's New Labour government has sought to temper its aim of maximizing labour force participation by promoting the idea of 'work–life balance': of making it easier for people to combine paid work and family life. This has been pursued through the extension of in-work benefits or tax credits, the development of a National Childcare Strategy (that, as yet, falls a long way short of achieving the levels of childcare provision to be found in most other European countries), and policies to promote 'family-friendly employment'. While it may be argued (see Dean 2002a) that the government's current approach favours the needs of business over the needs of families, the concept of 'work–life balance' creates an opening, in theory at least, for reconceptualizing the boundaries between paid employment and unpaid caring; for the renegotiation of gendered moral rationalities and identities; and 'in which to argue for an ethics of care' (Williams 2001: 488).

ETHNICITY

Just as an awareness of gender has challenged the assumptions on which social policy is made, so 'the concepts, assumptions and direction of policy debates over questions of racial equality and ethnicity are increasingly coming into question' (Law 1996: ix).

The social construction of 'race'

The human species is genetically diverse. We are all born with an observable set of characteristics that we share—albeit in different measures—with our immediate forebears, but which may differentiate us from other members of our species. At the same time, the history of the human species has entailed processes of migration and settlement, of competition as well as cooperation between different social groups, and the building of nations and empires. Human societies have constituted themselves through notions of common identity, but also through the exclusion or subjugation of those who are, or are believed to be, different.

Biological theories about the human species led in the nineteenth and the first part of the twentieth century to what has been called 'scientific' racism, though the term is a misnomer. It was believed that the human species was divided into several sub-species or 'races', and that certain races were physically, intellectually, and morally superior to others. The scientific basis for such understandings has since been largely discredited, but this did not prevent its influence upon the rise of Nazism, for example, nor upon a more general spread of racist thinking. Although the idea that there are biologically distinct races is a myth, **racism** is a real social phenomenon. Racism may be understood both as an ideology that '**racializes**' (Fanon 1967) the relations of power by which social groups and the boundaries between them are defined, and in terms of the outcomes of social and institutional processes that disadvantage racialized social groups.

Racism, therefore, is far more than the result of a scientific misconception. Theorists such as Miles (1989) suggest that racism has roots in the very beginnings of what we understand as 'modern' civilization. When Enlightenment thinking first suggested that civilized human beings are not descended from god(s) but risen from savages, it became possible to ground the fears that citizens of the civilized West had of unknown peoples in a belief in the superiority of civilization over barbarism. Racism grew out of a mistrust of the 'otherness' of people deemed not to be civilised. Other theorists such as Sivanandan (1990) and Callinicos (1993) suggest that racism is more than mere 'heterophobia' (fear of difference), but must be historically situated in relation to processes of economic exploitation: not only slavery in the pre-capitalist era, but specific class conflicts set in train as a result of colonialism, imperialism, and global labour migration. Racism, therefore, has relevance not only in a global context—in relation to the disadvantages systematically visited by rich nations upon poor nations and, for example, the various violent inter-ethnic conflicts that are continuing around the world—but also in the context of domestic social policy, specifically related to the 'racial' differences introduced to British society as a result of immigration.

Williams (1989) suggests that mainstream approaches to issues of 'race' and domestic welfare have been characterized by two approaches derived from 'race relations' studies. The first supposes that social harmony depends on the assimilation or integration of immigrants: immigrants should be helped to assimilate to the way of life of the 'host' community, while the 'host' community should rid itself of racial prejudice. The second embraces cultural pluralism: immigrants should enjoy equal rights of opportunity and the 'host' community should tolerate the cultural differences they exhibit. To an extent, a measure of consensus has been achieved between these approaches inasmuch that 'multiculturalism' has become the orthodoxy of community relations policy. Policy is directed to supporting minority groups within a wider 'British' community. Services for minority groups, it is believed, should be culturally sensitive and the institutions that deliver them must be alive to the dangers of racism. All of this, however, is pursued in the context of policies of immigration control (see Box 8.3 and discussion below).

In response to mainstream approaches, there has been a variety of challenges, including those advanced by the Centre for Contemporary Cultural Social Studies (1982). Recent theories have stressed that racism is not a psychological but a sociological phenomenon: it is not so much about individual fears or prejudices as about social relations of power, institutional structures, professional and organizational ideologies, and the perpetuation of everyday 'commonsense' cultural assumptions. Some theorists have argued specifically for a concept of 'cultural racism' that can account for the quite different experiences of racism to which different minority ethnic groups are subject, and the obstacles to such groups' demand for rights to cultural recognition. Tariq Modood, draws an important parallel between ethnicity and gender:

> Minority ethnicity . . . has traditionally been regarded in Britain as acceptable if confined to the privacy of family and community, and it did not make any political demands. However, in association with other socio-political movements (feminism, gay rights, etc.) which challenge the public-private distinction or demand a share of the public space, claims are increasingly made today that ethnic difference is not just something that needs 'mere' toleration but needs to be publicly acknowledged, resourced and represented. (1994: 7)

The problem with the multiculturalist orthodoxy accepted by policy-makers is that it regards cultural differences and practices as a private matter. At best this trivializes ethnic identity. At worst it may compound the process by which **ethnicity** is racialized. Ethnicity is not a synonym for 'race', nor is it an uncontested concept (see Box 8.2).

Experiences of disadvantage

Just as some commentators identify a feminization of poverty, it is also possible to speak of the racialization of poverty. Minority ethnic groups in Western countries like Britain are especially vulnerable to poverty, and they can be especially stigmatized by welfare

Box 8.2 Reflections on ethnicity

- Ethnicity, like gender, is a matter not of biology but of individual identity. As Ian Law has put it, 'We are all ethnically located in that our subjectivity and identity are contextualised by history, language and culture' (1996: 44).
- Ethnic identity can include religious identity. The concept of cultural racism attempts to accommodate discrimination or persecution on the grounds of religion and would include, for example, the effects of the 'Islamophobia' (Runnymede Trust 1997) that is experienced by Muslims as a religious minority.
- Ethnicity does not, or need not, entail a fixed or ascribed identity. Ethnicity is by nature fluid and dynamic. It may even provide sites of resistance insofar as it is possible for diasporic communities (or, for example, youthful minorities within established ethnic communities) to forge radical new or 'syncretic' ethnic identities that may challenge dominant public discourses and values (e.g. Hall 1992; Gilroy 1993).

provision. There is an association between poverty and minority ethnicity. A recent report by the government's Social Exclusion Unit has observed:

> In comparison to their representation in the population, people from minority ethnic communities are more likely than others to live in poor areas; be poor; be unemployed, compared with white people with similar qualifications; suffer ill health and live in overcrowded and unpopular housing. They also experience widespread racial harassment and racial crime and are over-represented in the criminal justice system, from stop and search to prison. (SEU 2000: ch. 2, summary)

Whereas the SEU goes on to conclude that 'Racial discrimination plays an important role in the disproportionate social exclusion experienced by people from minority ethnic communities', from a more encompassing anti-racist perspective it may be argued that poverty should be reconceptualized as a feature of a global 'xeno-racism' that is implicated in impoverishing developing countries while systematically disadvantaging minority ethnic groups in the developed world. According to this version of the racialization of poverty thesis, 'poverty is the new black' (Sivanandan 2001).

There are nonetheless, in Britain, considerable differences between minority ethnic groups (as well as controversy about the basis of their definition). The minority ethnic population of Great Britain represents around 7.6 per cent of the total population. Evidence from the fourth national survey of minority ethnic groups published by the Policy Studies Institute in 1997 (Modood et al. 1997) has demonstrated that African-Caribbean and particularly Pakistani and Bangladeshi minorities—who together make up almost half the minority ethnic population—are particularly prone to unemployment and low pay, to benefit dependency, and to income poverty. Indian and other non-white minority ethnic groups (such as African-Asians and Chinese), while often suffering certain disadvantages in relation to the white population, nonetheless fared somewhat better. The overall picture, however, is complex (see Table 8.2 for a selection of recent statistical data).

Crude statistics can mask the differences between minority ethnic groups and, for example, between men and women and between younger and older people within ethnic groups. So, for example, men from minority ethnic groups are disproportionately concentrated in the lower-paying sectors of the labour market. Pakistani and Bangladeshi women are especially likely to remain (ostensibly voluntarily) outside the labour market, while young African-Caribbeans are especially likely to be (involuntarily) unemployed. The household and age structures of different minority ethnic groups are diverse, which can affect the risk of poverty to which they are exposed and the likelihood that they may have to depend on means-tested social security benefits: though the age profile of minority ethnic groups tends to be younger than that of the white population, their older members tend to have fewer educational qualifications and shorter and less well-remunerated working lives, and to be less likely to have access to occupational pension coverage. Minority ethnic groups may also be subject to disadvantage in housing, healthcare, and education (see Case Study 8.2).

The key issues for minority ethnic groups have been access to the labour market on the one hand but also access to resources, including the resources of the welfare state, such as public housing. Theorists such as John Rex (see particularly Rex and Moore 1967) had

Table 8.2 Ethnicity, labour market participation, and poverty

	White	African-Caribbean	Indian	Pakistani/Bangladeshi
Economic activity of 16–64-year-olds, 2001 (%)				
In employment	75	62	63	41
Unemployed[a]	4	10	6	8
Outside labour market[b]	22	29	31	51
Earnings from employment, 1997 (mean weekly male earnings in £ p.w.)[c]	336	306	287	209
% in receipt of income support, 1999/2000[d]	2	19	14	22
% in bottom income quintile, 1990/2000 (after housing costs)[e]	18	35	32	61

[a] Unemployed by International Labour Organization definition, although the figures shown here do *not* reflect the official ILO unemployment rate but the proportions of those meeting that definition as a percentage of *all* members of the group—i.e. including those outside the labour market.
[b] Sometimes also referred to as 'economically inactive'.
[c] Adapted from data in Modood et al. (1997).
[d] Based on Family Resources Survey data drawn from Howard et al. (2001: ch. 6).
[e] Based on Households Below Average Income data drawn from Howard et al. (2001: ch. 6), with some calculations by author.
Source: based on Labour Force Survey data drawn from EOC (2002), with some calculations by the author.

argued that it was conflict over such resources, and the unequal outcomes of such conflicts, that had constituted minority ethnic groups as an **underclass**. Though the underclass concept has since been much criticized (see Chapter 5), Rex's analysis was important for the way in which he demonstrated how material, rather than behavioural, factors were implicated in a process that has since been characterized as 'ghettoization' (Wilson 1989). If we are to understand the tendency for minority ethnic groups to be concentrated in poor neighbourhoods and poor housing we must have regard not simply to discriminatory practices but to the preferences and defensive strategies of minority ethnic groups and the wider social context with regard to competition for scarce resources. As Law has put it:

> in the provision of council [i.e. public sector] housing, much attention has been given to eradicating inequalities in allocations with little concern for the influence of racism on patterns of housing choice or for overall patterns of housing finance and investment. . . . it is important that strategies to tackle *racial* inequalities need to be embedded in wider programmes to tackle *social* inequalities for this [i.e. tackling racial inequalities] to be effective. (1996: 24, emphasis added)

Case Study 8.2 Minority ethnic groups' experiences of housing, health, and education

One way to understand the realities of the lives of people from minority ethnic groups is through statistical sources. In the 1990s, for example, according to data from a variety of sources summarized in Howard et al. (2001), it could be seen that the minority ethnic population was disproportionately concentrated in the most materially deprived parts of the country. In England, over half were to be found in the forty-four poorest local authority areas. Minority ethnic households were over seven times more likely than white households to live in overcrowded conditions. African-Caribbean households were almost twice as likely and Pakistani/Bangladeshi households and were two and a half times as likely as white households to live in housing that was in poor condition. What is more, minority ethnic households in general were three times more likely than white households to have experienced homelessness during the past ten years.

Similar insights can be obtained by looking at health statistics. In the 1990s, for example, Pakistani and Bangladeshi people were one and a half times more likely and African-Caribbean people were a third more likely than white people to report ill health. Turning to education statistics, it could be seen in the 1990s that African-Caribbean children were six times more likely to be excluded from school than other pupils. Pakistani and African-Caribbean pupils were a third less likely than white pupils (and twice less likely than Indian pupils) to gain five or more GCSEs at grades A–C.

This is not to say that the discrimination experienced by minority ethnic groups is of no account. There is evidence from a variety of sources that often in the past minority ethnic social security claimants have received unfavourable treatment by benefits administrators, minority ethnic children have been stereotyped by teachers, the needs of minority ethnic patients have been misinterpreted by health professionals, and minority ethnic clients have been treated with cultural insensitivity by social workers. Paradoxically, perhaps, members of minority ethnic groups are themselves disproportionately represented amongst the lower-paid employees of the welfare state. Williams has argued that the control of social expenditure during the development of the welfare state—particularly the National Health Service—in the post-Second World War period depended on the use of 'a reserve army of cheap labour' (1989: 179) drawn from minority ethnic immigrants. Though some of these were skilled, large numbers were employed in menial jobs, for example, as domestics and catering workers. Finally, minority ethnic groups are poorly represented in the democratic process. Currently, only 1.8 per cent of Westminster MPs and only 2.5 per cent of local government councillors are from minority ethnic groups (Ali and O'Cinneide 2002).

Policies and their impact

Policies that address racial inequality or ethnic disadvantage can only be understood in the context of Britain's Immigration and Asylum legislation (see Box 8.3). For over a century Britain has sought to control immigration, and Solomos (1989/1993) has illustrated how the politics of immigration control have themselves been racialized. Historically speaking, Britain as a nation has been constituted through successive waves of immigration, but the motives behind legislative attempts to regulate immigration during the era of the welfare state have been informed by two concerns. The first has been 'race', or rather racism. The second has been a desire to prevent immigrants from becoming a charge on public funds.

While initial measures to control the entry of 'aliens' were developed while the welfare state was in its infancy, later measures were seen as vital in order to protect the integrity of the post-Second World War welfare state settlement. Following the Second World War deliberate steps had been taken to encourage the immigration of cheap labour from New Commonwealth countries whose subjects had been afforded rights of UK citizenship. Subsequent attempts to reign back this process were selectively tailored to curtail 'coloured' immigration (i.e. by black and brown people) from the Caribbean and South Asia, until eventually in the 1980s the basis of British citizenship was redefined so that only those of direct British descent could thereafter settle in Britain without restrictions, including—and particularly—on their right to work, to welfare benefits, and public housing. In the current era of 'globalization' (see Chapters 20 and 22) the focus of immigration control has shifted—as indeed it has across Europe—towards the deterrence of refugees and asylum seekers from global trouble spots of the world (for example, in central Europe, the Middle East, and parts of sub-Saharan Africa). Special welfare arrangements have been set up for refugees while decisions are made as to their rights of entry.

As attempts were being made to regulate minority ethnic immigration, policy-makers also began to seek ways of ameliorating the ethnic inequalities and racial tensions to which immigrant communities were subject. The argument during the 1960s was encapsulated by Roy Hattersley, a prominent Labour Party politician, when he claimed that 'Integration without control is impossible, but control without integration is indefensible' (cited in Solomos 1989: 73). In essence, there were then, as now, two elements to the strategies pursued. The first, responding to the concentration of minority ethnic groups in deprived areas, has focused largely on area-based policies, including urban or neighbourhood regeneration. The second has focused on combating discrimination.

Starting with Education Priority Areas and Section 11 of the Local Government Act of 1966, by which special funds were directed to local authorities to meet the special needs of minority ethnic groups within their areas, policies were developed through the 1970s and 80s, including Urban Aid and Inner-City Partnership and City Challenge schemes, culminating in the introduction of the Single Regeneration Budget, all of which emphasized the need for locally based intervention in deprived areas, with special reference to the support of minority ethnic communities. Several local authorities—most notably the (now defunct) Greater London Council—developed proactive anti-racist policies, concerted attempts were made in some areas of policy provision to publish information in minority ethnic languages and/or to introduce ethnic monitoring to ensure the equitable distribution of locally delivered services, including housing, education, and health. As the turn of the twenty-first century approached, after what have been described as 'thirty years of pilot projects', a New Labour government added 'its own profusion of pilot programmes' (Benington and Donnison 1999: 62), including Education

Box 8.3 The development of British immigration and asylum legislation

Restrictions on 'aliens' (before 1948)	The Aliens Order of 1905 (passed under powers orginally intended to curtail the influx to Britain of Jewish immigrants from Eastern Europe) provided powers to exclude any non-UK subject (or 'alien') who did not have access to the means of adequate subsistence and sanitary accommodation, or who was adjudged 'undesirable'. Powers of exclusion were further extended (on the grounds of 'national security') by the Aliens Restrictions Act of 1914, and subsequently renewed and modified by a series of legislative amendments/orders by which to regulate the entry, residence, and employment of aliens.
The post-colonial immigration regime (1948–1981)	The Nationality Act 1948 granted rights of residence in Britain both to citizens of the UK and Colonies and to citizens of independent Commonwealth countries. However, in an attempt to curtail a wave of immigration from the Caribbean and South Asia in the 1950s and by East African Asians in the 1960s, a series of Immigration Acts between 1962 and 1971 sought to restrict such rights, initially to the holders of UK-issued passports, the dependants of settled immigrants, and those to whom special employment vouchers had been issued. Subsequently, immigration controls were extended to anyone who was not themselves, or who did not have a parent or grandparent who had been, born in the UK or a naturalized or registered UK citizen.
Responding to global migration (since 1981)	The Nationality Act 1981 'rationalized' nationality and immigration law by restricting British citizenship *and* the right of residence to those of direct British descent. However, in instances in which non-UK nationals may still claim a right of residence (and the opportunity to become UK citizens)—such as the foreign spouses of British citizens or people claiming political asylum under international law—immigration controls have sought to exclude the claims of those adjudged not to be 'genuine'. As global economic and political crises resulted through the 1990s in growing numbers of refugees from around the world, a series of Immigration and Asylum Acts have subjected refugees coming to Britain to ever harsher regimes of scrutiny and deterrence by which to distinguish 'economic' migrants with no right of entry from 'genuine' asylum seekers. At the time of writing, these arrangements are under review (see Home Office 2002).

Action Zones, Health Action Zones, Sure Start, and the New Deal for Communities. The fundamental thinking behind such initiatives has been to target intensive assistance on deprived areas but, in the process, to seek 'joined up' solutions through partnerships between government (both central and local) and local communities and their representatives. Significantly, the recommendations of the government's Social Exclusion Unit for further, more specific measures to address minority ethnic issues are framed as part of this National Strategy for Neighbourhood Renewal (SEU 2000).

The other aspect of policy intervention has been anti-discrimination legislation (see Box 8.1). Early attempts to legislate in the 1960s not only laid the foundations for the current legal framework but also provided for a Race Relations Commission (later incorporated with the Race Relations Board to create the Commission for Racial Equality) and a network of local community relations councils charged generally with promoting good 'race relations'. Although its scope has recently been extended by the New Labour government in an attempt to commit all public authorities to remedying systemic racial inequalities, the legislation remains premised principally on individual rights of redress, and is hampered by problems of legal definition and the inherent difficulties of proving racial motivation.

Critics of such policies have suggested that they entail little more than 'coat of paint' solutions (Gilroy 1987) that fall short of addressing the true nature of racism in British society. Nonetheless, the recent inquiry into the violent death of black teenager Stephen Lawrence (Macpherson 1999) and, for example, a report, by the Runnymead Trust on the future of multi-ethic Britain (Parekh 2000) have clearly commanded the attention of both the public and the government, and *possibly* may yet help to change certain 'critical dimensions of the relationship between "race" and British public culture' (Clarke 2001: 16).

DISABILITY

The provision of social care for disabled people has been a feature of the welfare state, and will be discussed later in this book in Chapter 15. However, the purpose of this section is to articulate issues of disability to conceptual debates about identity and the life course, to examine some of the particular disadvantages faced by disabled people, and to touch upon the broad range of policies that bear upon disability.

The social construction of disability

Disability is something that may be experienced when people are born with a genetic **impairment**, if they suffer illness or injury that limits their functioning, or if they suffer from degenerative conditions as they grow older. The impairments associated with disability may be physical or mental and may, for example, include mental health problems or learning difficulties. Disability does not necessarily imply a permanent or static status. Recent research (Burchardt 2000) has explored how people may become more or less disabled in the course of their lives.

While the impairments or functional limitations to which human beings are subject generally have biological causes or effects, disability—like gender and ethnicity—is socially constructed. Disability can, however, be constructed in different ways. Mike Oliver (1990) has argued that two broad understandings or conceptual models may apply (see also the discussion in Chapter 15). The first is an individual model, which regards disability as a personal tragedy that has befallen the individual or as an individual medical problem, susceptible to medical explanation and management. The second is the social model, which regards disability in terms of the consequences of a hostile social environment that does not, or will not, accommodate the particular needs, or recognize the particular abilities, of people with impairments or functional limitations.

The application by policy-makers of individual models of disability has led in various directions. On the one hand, during the first part of the twentieth century, according to Williams (1989) elements of the care provided for disabled people were implicitly **eugenicist**: that is, in order to maintain the genetic purity of the British national 'stock', disabled people—or those adjudged physically, mentally, or morally defective—were maintained in institutions or colonies that segregated them from the 'normal' population and prevented them from having procreative relations. On the other hand, the post-Second World War welfare state developed policies and systems that were intended to ensure that disabled people should no longer be segregated from non-disabled society, but which succeeded nonetheless in excluding disabled people through the creation of dependency. Oliver and Barnes have argued that provision

> was shaped by the traditional assumptions that people with impairments are unable to make basic decisions about their own individual service needs. This has had far-reaching negative implications since logic dictates that if they cannot assume responsibility for organizing their own lives, they cannot assume the responsibilities of citizenship. (1998: 44)

Disabled people, therefore, were construed no longer as a threat, but as a burden on society. Their needs were defined for them by welfare professionals and policy-makers.

Social models of disability, while challenging the orthodoxies of professionals and policy-makers and seeking to give voice to the demands of disabled people themselves, have also led in different directions. The global disability movement—as a movement *of* rather than *for* disabled people—began to mobilize in the 1970s. One strand of that movement, informed amongst other things by the United Nations Declaration on the Rights of Disabled Persons of 1975, has sought to develop disability as a human rights issue. It has largely been through pressure from this lobby that anti-discrimination legislation relating to disability was belatedly introduced in Britain (see Box 8.1 and discussion below). Another strand has engaged with debates about the realities of 'care in the community' and the attempts by policy-makers since the 1980s to achieve a shift away from institutional forms of social care. While feminists provided critical accounts of the way these changes had reconstituted informal carers, the disability movement sought to raise issues concerning disabled people as the *receivers* of care. There is potential conflict between the interests of informal carers and disabled people and there is a parallel here, perhaps, with the conflicts that exist between ethnic groups: just as 'racial' equality can only be secured under conditions of broad social equality, so interdependency between disabled people and other family members can only be fairly negotiated if all families and all family members have access to adequate resources. A similar logic has driven commentators like Jenny Morris (1991) to contend that disabled people should celebrate their differences and should demand opportunities for '**independent living**'. The concept of independent living is here taken beyond the confines of liberal individualism, since independence is equated not with the ability, for example, to get oneself dressed each morning but with the capacity to control one's life. The relative success of the independent living movement, which began with the development of special Independent Living Centres in the USA, is reflected in the institution by some local authorities in Britain of direct payments to disabled people to allow them to purchase, not 'care', but the personal assistance that they require to pursue independent lives.

Whereas once, in the 1970s, there was 'a split between the social policy academics of the Disability Alliance and the grass roots radicals of the Union of Physically Impaired Against Segregation' (Shakespeare 2000: 52), more recently there has been an emerging debate between 'Two alternative theoretical models for reforming care . . . one is based on the independent living principles which have been developed by the disabled people's movements. The second: is the feminist ethic of care' (p. 59). The first seeks actively to reconstruct the identities of disabled people through struggle against the oppression of a disablist society. The other contends that our identities are to be realized not as 'equal rights holders', but as 'selves-in-relationship' (Sevenhuijsen 1998). There is a tension here, and the task for social policy now, it has been suggested, 'is one of redefining *autonomy* to fit with a notion of *interdependence*' (Williams 2001: 481, emphasis added).

Experiences of disadvantage

Disabled people's experiences of poverty have been shaped by the nature of welfare state capitalism. Industrialization and the wage labour system made it more difficult for disabled people to play a productive part in society and turned them, under the Poor Laws, into paupers. The modern welfare state has failed to promote anything more than rather limited labour market participation by disabled people, while sustaining them as benefit and care recipients.

Definitions of disability for statistical purposes are controversial not only because—as we have seen—there are different ways of understanding what constitutes disability, but also because of the diversity of the impairments and functional limitations which disabled people experience. Official disability surveys have employed different definitions that generally rely on self-reporting of long-standing conditions that limit either a person's day-to-day activities (a definition adopted by the Disability Discrimination Act) or the kind or amount of work s/he can undertake. The most recent national survey—conducted in 1996–7 (Grundy et al. 1999)—claimed that around a fifth of the adult population is to some extent disabled, while recent data compiled by the Disability Rights Commission demonstrates that long-term disabled people of working age are nearly five times more likely than non-long-term disabled people to be on state benefits and out of work (see Table 8.3). Disabled people who are in employment are less likely to work full-time and, on average, receive lower earnings than non-disabled people.

It is hardly surprising, therefore, that household incomes tend to be 20–30 per cent lower for disabled than for non-disabled adults, and that households containing disabled adults or children are more likely than other households to experience below-average incomes (Howard et al. 2001). However, disabled people's poverty—and the difficulty of measuring it—is compounded by the higher costs they face: both the costs of the goods and domestic services required for their personal support and the additional spending that may be associated with heating, laundry, and transport. Such costs,

Table 8.3 Disability, labour market participation and personal income in Great Britain

	Not long-term disabled[a]	**Long-term disabled**
Economic activity of men aged 16–64 and women aged 15–59, 2001 (%)		
In employment	81	48
as full-time employees	47	7
as part-time employees	23	28
as self-employed	11	13
Unemployed[b]	4	4
Outside labour market[c]	15	47
Average hourly earnings from employment, 2001 (£ per hour)	9.80	8.70
On state benefits and not in work, 2001 (%)	9	42

[a] Meeting either the Disability Discrimination Act definition *or* the 'work-limiting disability' definition.
[b] Unemployed by International Labour Organization definition, although the figures shown here do *not* reflect the official ILO unemployment rate but the proportions of those meeting that definition as a percentage of *all* disabled/non-disabled people—i.e. including those outside the labour market.
[c] Sometimes also referred to as 'economically inactive'.

Source: based on Labour Force Survey data drawn from DRC (2002).

it has been estimated, could amount on average to £50 per week (Berthoud 1998), though this is probably a conservative estimate.

In addition to the difficulties they experience accessing employment and income, disabled people are systematically disadvantaged in a host of other ways (see, for example, Case Study 8.3)

Policies and their impact

It would appear that welfare policies sometimes contribute to the disadvantages experienced by disabled people rather than alleviating them. This may seem a harsh conclusion, since the post-Second World War welfare state attempted to provide for disabled people. The problem, however, was that:

> despite the establishment of a comprehensive legal framework for the provision of inclusionary services to disabled people, these services somehow do not get delivered. The main reasons for this were first, services had been provided on the basis of professional definitions of need; second, governments of all political persuasions had consistently resisted pressure to force local authorities to meet their statutory obligations; and third, those services that have been provided have locked people into dependency on them. (Oliver and Barnes 1998: 40)

The Employment (Disabled Persons) Act 1944 was intended to promote the employment of disabled people by way of a system of registration and the setting of employment

Case Study 8.3 Disabled peoples' experiences of disadvantage in health, education, and housing

The affects on the lives of disabled people of the social processes and policy outcomes discussed in this chapter can be explored through the analyses of commentators such as Oliver and Barnes (1998), who make a number of contentions.

They suggest that in the realm of health provision disabled people are disadvantaged by the complex and often contentious nature of the boundary between healthcare and social care, the effects of which often compromise the quality of the long-term care arrangements that are available to them (see also Chapters 14 and 15). Additionally, because health care is dominated by a medical model of disability, it is often premised on the idea that disabled patients' 'rehabilitation' must entail their psychological adjustment to impairment, rather than an understanding of the adjustments that may be required to their social and physical environment if patients are to realize or regain their full potential.

In the realm of education, say Oliver and Barnes, disabled people are disadvantaged by the nature of the education that is made available to disabled children and young people. Although it has been estimated that around 20 per cent of pupils may at some time require special educational assistance, only 2 per cent require separate specialized facilities (Warnock 1978). In spite of this, over a third of disabled children (and nearly two-thirds of those living in residential homes) are educated in segregated environments, such as special schools or special classes. The quality and substance of such education has often been informed by individualistic and stereotypical assumptions about disability and the capacities of disabled people.

In the realm of housing, Oliver and Barnes demonstrates the extent to which disabled people are disadvantaged by the poor design and inaccessible nature of most housing provision and much of the built environment. It has been estimated that whereas there are in Britain over four million disabled people with mobility-related impairments, there are fewer than a million accessible homes suitable for their occupation. What is more, partly because of their low incomes, disabled people and their families are twice as likely to live in public housing than their non-disabled peers.

quotas that employers were supposed to observe, but it was never effectively enforced. This forgotten legislation has been superseded, in part, by the Disability Discrimination Act 1995 (see Box 8.1, and discussion below) and, in part, by the New Labour government's New Deal for Disabled People.

The NDLP was part of the government's 'welfare-to-work' strategy which arguably (see Dean 2002b) has signalled a fundamental change in the nature of the British social security system. The post-Second World War System had recognized certain disabled people's claims to citizenship, namely those who had been disabled serving in the armed forces or by injuries at work, who were entitled to pensions and allowances under special schemes. For other disabled people, however, entitlement to benefits was an all-or-nothing affair and depended upon whether or not they were adjudged incapable of work. People who, having entered the labour market, became incapable of work through illness could claim national insurance benefits. Disabled people who had had little or insufficient engagement in the labour market and were incapable of work, initially, could only claim means-tested benefits, although a small non-contributory allowance (that has since been absorbed into a reformed incapacity benefit) was eventually introduced for those adjudged 'severely' disabled. Change came in the 1970s when additional benefits—the contemporary versions of which include disability living allowance and attendance allowance—were introduced not to provide disabled people with the kind of income they might expect to 'earn' in the labour market, but specifically to compensate them for some element of the additional living costs associated with disability. At the same time, a means-tested in-work benefit—the contemporary version of which is the disabled person's tax credit—was introduced to try and encourage disabled people to take up low-paid employment. This emphasis—on enabling disabled people to seek employment rather than persuading employers to employ them—has been developed by New Labour initially through the NDLP pilot projects, which have since been rolled out nationally as part of the Job Centre Plus regime (under which disabled people may be compelled to attend interviews for advice and assistance about labour market opportunities). Aspects of what New Labour have been doing to emphasize disabled people's capacity for work, rather than their incapacity, and actively to assist them to engage with the labour market are to be welcomed; but Thornton (2000) has pointed to the inherent contradiction that remains between a system based around tests of individual capacity and the need to ensure that barriers to labour market participation can be tackled *before* disabled people are pressed into the labour market.

The Education Act 1944 had specified that disabled children should be educated alongside their non-disabled peers, but in practice an extensive system of segregated educational provision was developed for children with various kinds of 'handicap'. In spite of the Education Act 1981, which provided a framework for assessing and meeting the special educational needs of disabled children within mainstream schools, the evidence suggests that the extent of segregation that disabled children experience both between and within schools has changed little. Similarly, the National Assistance Act 1948 had specified that local authorities should provide a range of services for disabled people, but the provision that actually emerged was confined largely to residential care in segregated facilities. The Chronically Sick and Disabled Persons Act 1970, which required local authorities to maintain a register of disabled people, was proclaimed by its supporters as a new charter of rights for disabled people, but imposed no new substantive duties in practice. The NHS and Community Care Act 1990 finally ushered in the age of care in the community. Means and Smith (1998) have pointed out that the new regime, though needs-led in theory, remained cash-limited in practice, and the underlying balance of power between professionals and service users did not change.

The Disability Discrimination Act 1995, which at the time of writing has still to be fully implemented, should make important opportunities available to disabled people individually to enforce their rights as employees and as the consumers of goods and services. It does require employers to make 'reasonable adjustments' to ensure that disabled people are not at a disadvantage in the workplace compared to non-disabled people. Its critics still argue, however, that the legislation does not address the fundamentally 'disablist' nature of society.

One of the most important policy innovations in recent years has been the development of direct payments—cash payments to enable disabled people to purchase care or personal assistance for themselves. A discretionary Independent Living Fund, with a limited budget, was established by the government in 1988, and extended in a more restricted form in 1993. However, legislation in 1996 empowered local authority social services departments to make direct payments to disabled people. The government has taken powers to make direct payments mandatory, but at the time of writing has not exercised those powers. In the meantime, local authorities will not usually make direct payments that exceed the cost they would incur if they were to provide services themselves and not all local authorities operate direct payments schemes (see Chapter 15). The significance of direct payments is that they give disabled people a degree of autonomy and some measure of control.

AGE

The aphorism 'Youth is wild, and Age is tame' (attributed to Shakespeare) encapsulates an apparently timeless set of assumptions about the significance of chronological age for the human **life course**. Aspects of policy relating both to 'Youth' (as a term associated with growing up) and to 'Age' (as a term associated with growing old) are considered throughout this book. Our concern in this chapter, however, is with the part that social policy plays in defining and **problematizing** transitional stages of the life course.

The social construction of youth and old age

Conventional sociological approaches to the life course had tended to regard youth and retirement implicitly as functional processes of engagement and disengagement with the social system. Youth is a transitional stage between childhood and independent adulthood, while retirement marks the transition from independent adulthood to old age. More recently, it has been argued that 'The idea of "youth" . . . like that of "retirement" is not simply a reference to some objective natural state of being, it is a social construction that has its origins in the capitalist division of labour' (Lawrence 1982: 55). In other words, our understanding of youth and retirement is conditioned by the changing political economy of the household and the labour market.

In the pre-modern era childhood, as a stage of dependency on parents, would have ended at or around the age of 7 (Gittins 1993: 8), after which most young people would become full participants in the productive activities of their own household or servants or apprentices in other households. The wage labour system created new and different demands on young people's labour power from without the household. However, it was the social policies of the nineteenth century—factory legislation and the introduction of compulsory education—that curtailed the exploitation of young people's labour and extended the period during which they must remain dependent on their parents. Concerns for young people's social welfare served to extend their childhood, while the meaning of 'youth', as a period following childhood, became more ambiguous. For much of the twentieth century the effect of rises in the school leaving age on the one hand and the development of social security and housing provision on the other further compressed the period in which the transition from childhood dependency to adult independence could occur.

Similarly, in the pre-modern era, when life expectancy in any event was much shorter, people did not retire unless or until they either died or became too infirm to work. Later, the unforgiving pace and rhythms of the wage labour system made it difficult for people to carry on working as they grew older, and it was not until the introduction of old age pensions in 1908 and the retirement pension in 1946 that it became possible for people—other than the wealthy middle classes—to retire. As Anthea Tinker (1997) explains, the age at which people became eligible for a pension has become widely accepted as the point at which 'old age' begins. The vast majority of people over state pension age do indeed retire from the labour market and, as longevity has increased and labour markets have tightened, retirement has become in Townsend's words 'a kind of mass redundancy' (1991: 6). Social welfare provision has provided protection and new freedoms for people as they grow older, but it has also contributed to the way we think about and define old age.

From a social welfare perspective the needs of young people and old people are very different, but from a liberal perspective, one might suppose, their rights should be no different from anybody else's. However, liberal democratic notions of entitlement rest upon the assumption that the individual citizen is fully competent and responsible. If Youth is too 'wild' (and therefore irresponsible) and Age is too 'tame' (and no longer fully competent), then it might be supposed that they should not count as full citizens.

The objective of early welfare provision had been to protect the destitute *children* of the 'perishing' classes, while simultaneous developments in the criminal justice system aimed to punish the delinquent *youth* of the 'dangerous' classes (Morris 1994). The debate about 'welfare' versus 'justice' and about the age at which, and circumstances in which, young people may be held responsible for their actions continues to this day (see Chapter 18). The term 'childhood' was appropriated to refer to the needy and disturbed, whereas 'youth' became the epithet associated with the potentially disruptive and dangerous. The ambivalence of policy-makers towards the rights of young people (see below) reflects conflicting interpretations of young people's status: are they incompetent children or irresponsible youth? Some have argued that at the close of the twentieth century social policies targeted specifically at young people were informed by moral panics about the irresponsibility of youth and, in particular, the imagined threat posed by an emerging 'youth underclass' (MacDonald 1997).

So far as old people are concerned, the replacement of the Poor Law by state pensions and the development of social care provision were supposed to ensure they could play their part as full citizens. However, the **demographic transition** that has been experienced during the twentieth century has raised the 'spectre of old age' (Phillipson 1991) as another imagined threat to developed democracies. Having allowed people some measure of dependency in old age, it is now popularly supposed that we confront a 'demographic time bomb', and that the combination of falling birth rates and increased longevity makes such dependency unsustainable (see Chapter 5). Old people, because of their dependency on the working-age population, have become a burden.

The idea that young people are a threat and old people a burden has been challenged by social policy commentators. Bob Coles (1995) has demonstrated that it is not the inherent nature of youth, but the socially and politically constructed nature of the transitions that young people experience, that place some of them at risk of failure, social exclusion, and alienation. Pat Carlen (1997) suggests that young people are not inherently irresponsible, but they do face a raft of contradictory and confusing expectations such that the responsibilities demanded of them are often out of symmetry with the limited rights they enjoy. Old people's dependency, as Townsend puts it, 'is not the inevitable outcome of a natural process of ageing, but is socially structured, and hence potentially open to change' (1986: 21). What is more, most old people—especially younger old people, aged 60–75—do not make extensive demands on health and social services, but live active and fulfilling lives: many exercise vital roles within their families and communities as grandparents, informal carers, and volunteers, and those with financial resources often make a significant financial contribution towards the wellbeing of younger generations within their families.

Experiences of disadvantage

Although there are no set stages in the human life course, there are nonetheless patterns that many people tend to share, and different risks and costs are characteristically associated with certain points in the life course. When we are children, if we ourselves become parents, and should we in time grow old, we are demonstrably more vulnerable to poverty. As may be seen from Table 8.4, while working-age couples without children are least at risk and lone parents are most at risk of poverty, almost a quarter of working-age single people without children (the group that includes most young people) and a similar proportion of pensioner couples are (according to one standard definition) living in poverty. Single pensioners—who are more likely to be older and to be women and therefore less likely to have accrued occupational pension entitlements—have a higher risk of poverty than pensioner couples.

Although child poverty features as a major issue in the social policy literature (see Chapter 5), youth poverty does not. Nonetheless, the poverty rate for 16–24-year-olds is higher than that for older people of working age (see Table 8.4). The unemployment rate for under-25-year-olds is characteristically twice as high as that for older working-age adults. The effects of labour market restructuring in the last quarter of the twentieth century led to the virtual collapse of the youth labour market, and to youth unemployment rates of over 20 per cent in the 1980s. Analyses of official data (e.g. O'Higgins 2001) show that, although youth unemployment now stands at around 12 per cent in the UK, this is still more than four times higher than in the 1960s, when two out of every three young people would go straight from school into a job (compared with just one in ten now). At the same time, there is evidence that young people are over-represented among

Table 8.4 Risk of poverty across the life course

	% of individuals in households having less than 60% median equivalized[a] income
By family type, 2000/01 (Great Britain)[b]	
Pensioner couple	22
Single pensioner	27
Working-age couple with children	19
Working-age couple without children	11
Working-age single person with children	54
Working-age single person without children	22
By age, 1997 (UK)[c]	
0–15	39
16–24	25
25–49	14
60–64	12
65+	29

[a] i.e. income adjusted for household composition.
[b] Department of Work and Pensions (2002: table 3.5) (Crown copyright). Based on income after housing costs, and excluding the self-employed.
[c] EC (2001: annex table 3a).

the street homeless (SEU 1998b) and those living in hostels and bed-and-breakfast accommodation (Anderson et al. 1993). Young people are systematically disadvantaged in terms of their access both to the labour market and to the housing market.

The experience of old people is rather different. As a group, their vulnerability to poverty is not as great as it was in the post-Second World War period, but this should not mask the fact that there is now greater inequality between older people than before. Since the number of old people—both as a proportion of the total population and in absolute terms—has grown, this means that pensioner poverty is still a substantial issue (see Case Study 8.4).

The employment of older people, like that of young people, can be especially sensitive to changes in labour market conditions. People over pensionable age—and, increasingly, even those approaching pensionable age—may be shut out of the jobs market by employers when demand for labour market falls. Additionally, as Age Concern argue (see McEwan 1990), older people are frequently subject to discrimination if they choose to remain or to re-enter the labour market—often on the basis of unfounded assumptions about their reliability and adaptability. Additionally, old people when they do

Case Study 8.4 Pensioner poverty

Official statistics can provide certain insights into the nature and extent of the inequality experienced by older people. According to data from a variety of sources summarized in Howard et al. (2001) between 1979 and 1997 the median income of the richest fifth of pensioners increased by 80 per cent, compared with only 34 per cent for the poorest fifth. Not all old people are poor, by any means, but the incomes of the richest and poorest have become more polarized. More to the point, perhaps, pensioners are more likely to be persistently poor in relative terms than people of working age. Between 1995 and 1998, 29 per cent of pensioner couples and 38 per cent of single pensioners spent at least three years in the poorest 30 per cent of the population, compared with just 14 per cent of the working-age population.

eventually become frail can be subject to all the problems of disability that we have already discussed.

Policies and their impact

One of the functions of the welfare state has been to smooth the vicissitudes of the life course: to provide for periods when people cannot provide for themselves. In practice the welfare state in the UK functions less like Robin Hood (redistributing resources from the rich to the poor) and more like a savings bank (redistributing resources over time during the course of individual people's lives). According to Falkingham and Hills (1995) only about a quarter of what the welfare state achieves amounts to a Robin Hood effect, while three-quarters amounts to a savings bank effect.

Insofar as social policy is concerned with redistribution over the life course, there is an obvious difference between the resources that are provided for education and training (see Chapter 13) as an initial 'investment' in young people at a time when most will be supported by their families or beginning to support themselves, and those provided for pensions, health, and social care as a 'return' to older people in their retirement.

According to Bob Coles (1995) most young people in modern capitalist societies face a threefold process of transition: from school to work; from their family of origin to a household of family of their own; from their family home to a home of their own. Whereas the post-Second World War welfare state made these transitions in some ways easier, recent policy developments would seem to be making them more difficult. In response to global economic challenges, British governments since the 1980s have declared themselves to be in favour of increasing the proportion of young people who participate in further and higher education, but at the same time support for young people through the benefits system and through student grants has been curtailed. Recent proposals for the extension of Education Maintenance Allowances may signal a reverse in this trend, but for many young people the transition from school to work entails difficult and often unattractive choices (not least because the National Minimum Wage does not apply to 16- and 17-year-olds and has been set at a lower rate for people aged 18–21). Changes since the 1980s in the social security and housing benefits system have made it all but impossible for 16- and 17-year-olds to leave home, and more difficult for 18–24-year-olds to establish independent households. The consensus in housing policy during the last thirty years (see Chapter 17) has strongly favoured owner-occupation over rented housing, while at the same time according childless single people no priority for social sector housing: the effect quite plainly disadvantages young people.

New Labour's 1997 election manifesto and several of the reports produced by the New Labour government's Social Exclusion Unit have clearly focused not only on young people's needs but also on the threat they represent. Two out of the five main manifesto promises of 1997 bore directly on young people: New Labour committed itself to getting young people off welfare and into work (through the New Deal for Young People—see Chapters 12 and 13), and to establish fast-track punishment for young offenders (see Chapter 18). Four of the first six main SEU reports were focused on, or had particular salience for, deviant youth, whether school truants, rough sleepers, teenage mothers, or 16–18-year-olds not in education, training, or employment (SEU 1998a; 1998b; 1999a; 1999b). Youth continues to be constructed through policy and policy discourse as a problematic phenomenon.

Social policies towards older people express a different kind of ambivalence. Although social attitude data (see Taylor-Gooby 1990) show that old people are regarded in the public imagination as more deserving than young people of state support, there is a firm political consensus that the costs of state-funded pensions and social care in particular are unsustainable. It has been the very success of the welfare state that has brought us to this pass. Increased longevity and rising expectations of the quality of life that may be enjoyed in retirement have resulted from the development of pensions and advances in healthcare provision. However, the cost of state pensions, in spite of retrenchment, still represents one of the biggest calls on public spending. The explicit ambition of the present government is to shift the balance of expenditure from the public to the private sector and to encourage working-age people to save more for their retirement through occupational and private pensions schemes—to accept responsibility in advance for the time when they may cease to be economically active. According to many commentators, the likely effect will be to increase the inequalities and uncertainties that people experience in old age, while leaving many dependent on means-tested social assistance benefits (see Chapter 12). While substantial additional resources are being directed to the National Health Service, there are fears that new mechanisms for controlling costs might result in a second-class service for older people (see Chapter 14). The question of whether access to state-funded long-term social care should be available to all without a means test remains controversial, with different policies applying in different parts of the UK (see Chapter 15).

Policy-makers' concerns about the 'burden' that old people place upon our social welfare systems have lately been counterbalanced by moves towards establishing legislation—such as that which has applied for some years in the USA—to outlaw discrimination against elderly people (see Box 8.1). Although this is in some ways consistent with a shift from a social welfare to a liberal equal opportunities approach, it is in fact a development precipitated by a European Union Employment directive. At the time of writing, it is not clear whether the new legislation will go so far as to prevent employers from setting mandatory retirement ages.

Janet Finch (1989) has demonstrated that the development of state pensions and other policies has been important in giving old people a sense of independence and identity: far from increasing their dependency, it has to some extent freed them from dependency on families and kinship networks, or at least enabled them to negotiate the nature of their interdependency. Alan Walker (1996) contends that, at the policy level, we are currently in the process of negotiating a new 'generational contract': both in terms of the way that resources are redistributed between older and younger generations and in terms of the way that caring relationships are brokered within families.

CONCLUSION

One of the purposes of this chapter has been to demonstrate that social policy is concerned not just with social divisions between economic classes or between rich and poor, but with the consequences of other socially and culturally constructed differences that determine our identity. This does not imply that class analysis has no place in social policy. Though some post-modern theorists go so far as to declare that class as a concept is dead, Westergaard (1995), amongst others, has argued that the significance of class and its effects have actually become sharper as society becomes more unequal. But the point for now is that class is one of several ways in which human beings identify themselves in relation to each other.

We have seen that the nature of the human life course is such that we all have multiple identities. We are defined by our gender (and our sexuality), our ethnicity (and, sometimes, our religion), sometimes by disability and usually by our age. Our identities are not merely biologically determined or autonomous, but are largely socially constructed. The nature of identity is not static but dynamic, and will change during the life course: partly because we grow older; partly because of the relationships we form with other people; partly because of the material contingencies or 'risks' we face. Our identities arise out of the nature of our dependency on others and the roles we fulfil, in relation not only to work (both paid and unpaid) and our consumption patterns (or 'lifestyle'), but to the care that we provide for those who depend on us: roles that change, for example, when we enter or leave education or employment, when we establish new households or become parents, and as the circumstances of the people with whom we have relationships change.

Conventional social policy approaches have not been entirely oblivious to these dynamics. On the contrary, they have been implicated in shaping them. What we characterized in the introduction to this chapter as the social welfare approach is preoccupied with identifying and meeting substantive human needs, but tends in so doing to prescribe the identity of the welfare subject in a top-down fashion. The equal opportunities approach is preoccupied with observing formal rights, but tends in so doing to ascribe fixed, individualized identities. Recent thinking has challenged both approaches and has called, on the one hand, for the identification of individual needs to be negotiated from the bottom up, on the other, for substantive rights to the recognition of oppressed or systemically disadvantaged social groups. These calls do not always sit easily with each other. In thinking about identity, however, it is important to acknowledge the distinction made by Taylor (1998) between categorical identity and ontological identity. Categorical identity stems from belonging to a social group or category (or rather a variety of groups and categories); from sameness in difference; from the interests we share with others of the same class, gender, ethnicity, etc. Our ontological identity defines our uniqueness as human beings; it brings coherence and unity to our sense of 'self' in spite of the multiplicity of categorical identities that we have; it is the essential prerequisite of our wellbeing as individuals. While it is often contended that the function of social policy is to address social problems, Paul Hoggett makes the point that it must also, surely, be about wellbeing, and that 'well-being refers to the totality of an individual's social relations' (2000: 145). To put it another way, social policy needs to find ways of addressing simultaneously *particular* claims to recognition by a variety of social groups and *universal* claims to wellbeing by unique individuals.

The current trends in social policy described throughout this book—for example, towards greater welfare pluralism and self-provisioning—have particular implications for the way in which individuals can meet their diverse needs and establish their respective identities in the course of their lives.

REFERENCES

Ali, R., and O'Cinneide, C. (2002), *Our House? Race and Representation in British Politics*. London: Institute for Public Policy Research.

Anderson, I., Kemp, P., and Quilgars, D. (1993), *Single Homeless People*. London HMSO.

Benington, J., and Donnison, D. (1999), 'New Labour and social exclusion: the search for a third way, or just gilding the ghetto again? In H. Dean and R. Woods (eds.), *Social Policy Review 11*. Luton: Social Policy Association.

Berthoud, R. (1998), *Disability Benefits: A Review of the Issues and Options for Reform*. York: Joseph Rowntree Foundation.

Burchardt, T. (2000), 'The dynamics of being disabled', *Journal of Social Policy* 29(4): 645–68.

Callinicos, A. (1993), *Race and Class*. London: Bookmarks.

Carlen, P. (1997), *Jigsaw: A Political Criminology of Youth Homelessness*. Buckingham: Open University Press.

CCCS (Centre for Contemporary Cultural Studies) (1982), *The Empire Strikes Back: Race and Racism in 70s Britain*. London: Hutchinson.

Clarke, J. (1999), 'Coming to terms with culture'. In H. Dean and R. Woods (eds.), *Social Policy Review 11*. Luton: Social Policy Association.

—— (2001), 'Who are we? New Labour, "race" and a modern British people', *SPA News* (May/June): 16.

Coles, B. (1995), *Youth and Social Policy*. London: UCL Press.

Dean, H. (2002a), 'Business *versus* families: whose side is New Labour on?', *Social Policy and Society* 1(1): 3–10.

—— (2002b), *Welfare Rights and Social Policy*. Harlow: Prentice-Hall.

Department of Work and Pensions (DWP) (2002), *Households Below Average Income: A Statistical Analysis 1994/95–2000/01*. London: Corporate Document Services.

Derrida, J. (1978), *Writing and Difference*. London: Routledge.

Donzelot, J. (1979), *The Policing of Families*. London: Hutchinson.

DRC (Disability Rights Commission) (2002), *DRC Disability Briefing: May 2002*. London: DRC.

Duncan, S., and Edwards, R. (1999). *Lone Mothers, Paid Work and Gendered Moral Rationalities*. Basingstoke: Macmillan.

EC (European Commission) (2001), *Draft Joint Report on Social Inclusion*. Brussels: European Union.

Eisenstein, H. (1984), *Contemporary Feminist Thought*. London: Allen & Unwin.

EOC (Equal Opportunities Commission) (2001), *Women and Men in Britain: The Lifecycle of Inequality*. Manchester: EOC.

—— (2002), *Facts about Women and Men in Great Britain*. Manchester: EOC.

Esping-Andersen, G. (1999), *The Social Foundations of Post-Industrial Society*. Oxford: Oxford University Press.

Falkingham, J., and Hills, J. (1995), *The Dynamic of Welfare: The Welfare State and the Lifecycle*. Hemel Hempstead: Prentice-Hall/Harvester Wheatsheaf.

Fanon, F. (1967), *The Wretched of the Earth*. Harmondsworth: Penguin.

Finch, J. (1989), *Family Obligations and Social Change*. Cambridge: Polity Press.

Fraser, N. (1989), *Unruly Practices*. Cambridge: Polity Press.

—— (1995), 'From redistribution to recognition: dilemmas of social justice in a "post-socialist" age', *New Left Review* 212: 68–93.

Giddens, A. (1994), *Beyond Left and Right*. Cambridge: Polity Press.

—— (1998), *The Third Way*. Cambridge: Polity Press.

Gilligan, C. (1982), *In a Different Voice: Psychological Theory and Women's Development*. Cambridge, Mass.: Harvard University Press.

Gilroy, P. (1987), *There Aint No Black in the Union Jack*. London: Hutchinson.

—— (1993), *The Black Atlantic: Modernity and Double Consciousness*. London: Verso.

Gittins, D. (1993), *The Family in Question*, 2nd edn. Basingstoke: Macmillan.

Glendinning, C. (1992), ' "Community care": the financial consequences for women'. In C. Glendinning and J. Millar (eds.), *Women and Poverty in Britain: The 1990s*. Hemel Hempstead: Harvester Wheatsheaf.

Graham, H. (1983), 'Caring: a labour of love', In J. Finch and D. Groves (eds.), *A Labour of Love: Women, Work and Caring*. London: Routledge & Kegan Paul.

Grundy, E., et al. (1999), *Disability in Great Britain*. DSS Research Report 94. London: Stationery Office.

Hall, S. (1992), 'New ethnicities'. In J. Donald and A. Ratansi (eds.), *'Race', Culture and Difference*. London: Sage.

Halsey, A. (ed.) (1988), *British Social Trends since 1900*. Basingstoke: Macmillam.

Hoggett, P. (2000), 'Social policy and the emotions'. In G. Lewis, S. Gewirtz, and J. Clarke (eds.), *Rethinking Social Policy*. London: Sage.

Home Office (2002), *Secure Borders, Safe Haven: Integration with Diversity in Modern Britain*. Cm. 5387. London: Stationery Office.

Howard, M., Garnham, A., Fimister, G., and Veit-Wilson, J. (2002), *Poverty: The Facts, 4th edn*. (2001), London: Child Poverty Action Group.

Joshi, H. (1992), 'The cost of caring'. In C. Glendinning and A. Millar (eds.), *Women and Poverty in Britain: The 1990s*. Hemel Hempstead: Harvester Wheatsheaf.

Kiernan, K. (1992), 'Men and women at work and at home'. In R. Jowell et al. (eds.), *British Social Attitudes: The 9th Report*. Aldershot: Gower.

Law, I. (1996), *Racism, Ethnicity and Social Policy*. Hemel Hempstead: Harvester Wheatsheaf.

Lawrence, E. (1982), 'Just plain common sense: the "roots" of racism'. In CCCS (1982).

Lewis, G., Gewirtz, S., and Clarke, J. (eds.) (2000), *Rethinking Social Policy*. London: Sage.

Lewis, J. (2000), 'Work and care', in H. Dean, R. Sykes, and R. Woods, R. (eds.), *Social Policy Review 12*. Newcastle: Social Policy Association.

—— and Piachaud, D. (1992), 'Women and poverty in the twentieth century'. In C. Glendinning and J. Millar (eds.), *Women and Poverty in Britain: The 1990s*. Hemel Hempstead: Harvester Wheatsheaf.

Lister, R. (1994), ' "She has other duties": women, citizenship and social security'. In S. Baldwin and J. Falkingham (eds.), *Social Security and Social Change*. Hemel Hempstead: Harvester Wheatsheaf.

—— (2000), 'Gender and the analysis of social policy'. In Lewis et al. (2000).

MacDonald, R. (ed.) (1997), *Youth, the 'Underclass' and Social Exclusion*. London: Routledge.

McEwan, E. (ed.) (1990), Age: *The Unrecognised Discrimination*. London: Age Concern.

Macpherson, Sir W. (1999), *The Stephen Lawrence Inquiry*. Cm. 4262-I. London: Stationery Office.

Mann, K. (1992), *The Making of an English Underclass: The Social Divisions of Welfare and Labour*. Buckingham: Open University Press

Marshall, T. H. (1950), 'Citizenship and social class'. Repr. in T. H. Marshall and T. Bottomore (1992), *Citizenship and Social Class*. London: Pluto Press.

Means, R., and Smith, R. (1998), *Community Care: Policy and Practice*, 2nd edn. Basingstoke: Macmillan.

Miles, R. (1989), *Racism*. London: Routledge.

Modood, T. (1994), *Racial Equality: Colour, Culture and Justice*. London: Institute for Public Policy Research.

—— Berthoud, R., Lakey, J., Nazran, J., Smith, P., Virdee, S., and Beishon, S. (1997), *Ethnic Minorities in Britain*. London: Policy Studies Institute.

Morris, J. (1991), *Pride against Prejudice*. London: Women's Press.

Morris, L. (1994), *Dangerous Classes*. London: Routledge.

O'Higgins, N. (2001), *Youth Unemployment and Employment Policy: A Global Perspective*. Geneva: International Labour Organization.

Oliver, M. (1990), *The Politics of Disablement*. Basingstoke: Macmillan.

—— and Barnes, C. (1998), *Disabled People and Social Policy: From Exclusion to Inclusion*. Harlow: Longman.

Ortner, S. (1972), 'Is female to nature as male is to culture?' extract repr. in M. Humm (ed.) (1992), *Feminisms: A Reader*. Hemel Hempstead: Harvester Wheatsheaf.

Parekh, B. (2000), *The Future of Multi-ethnic Britain*. London: Runnymede Trust.

Pascall, G. (1997), *Social Policy: A New Feminist Analysis*. London: Routledge.

Pateman, C. (1989), *The Disorder of Women*. Cambridge: Polity Press.

Phillipson, C. (1991), 'Challenging the "spectre of old age": community care for older people in the 1990s'. In N. Manning and R. Page (eds.), *Social Policy Review 4*. Canterbury: Social Policy Association.

—— and Walker, A. (eds.) (1986), *Ageing and Social Policy*. Aldershot: Gower.

Rex, J., and Moore, R. (1967), *Race, Community and Conflict*. London: Institute for Race Relations/Oxford University Press.

Runnymede Trust (1997), *Islamophobia: A Challenge for US All*. London: Runnymede Trust.

Scott, H. (1984), *Working your Way to the Bottom: The Feminization of Poverty*. London: Pandora Press.

SEU (Social Exclusion Unit) (1998a), *Truancy and Exclusion*. Cm. 3957. London: Stationery Office.

—— (1998b), *Rough Sleeping*. Cm. 4008. London: Stationery Office.

—— (1999a), *Teenage Pregnancy*. Cm. 4342. London: Stationery Office.

—— (1999b), *Bridging the Gap: New Oportunities for 16–18 year olds not in Education, Employment, or Training*. Cm. 4405. London: Stationery Office.

—— (2000), *Minority Ethnic Issues in Social Exclusion and Neighbourhood Renewal*. London: Cabinet Office.

Sevenhuijsen, S. (1998), *Citizenship and the Ethics of Care*. London: Routledge.

Shakespeare, T. (2000), The social relations of care'. In Lewis et al. (2000).

Sivanandan, A. (1990), *Communities of Resistance: Writings on Black Struggles for Socialism*. London: Verso.

—— (2001), 'Poverty is the new black', *Guardian*, 17 Aug.

Solomos, J. (1989/1993), *Race and Racism in Britain*. Basingstoke: Macmillan.

Taylor, D. (1998), 'Social identity and social policy: engagements with postmodern theory', *Journal of Social Policy* 27(3): 329–50.

Taylor-Gooby, P. (1990), 'Social welfare: the unkindest cuts'. In R. Jowell et al. (eds.), *British Social Attitudes: The 7th report*. Aldershot: Gower.

Thornton, P. (2000), ' "Work for those who can, security for those who cannot"? Welfare reform and disabled people'. In H. Dean, R. Sykes, and R. Woods (eds.), *Social Policy Review 12*. Newcastle: Social Policy Association.

Tinker, A. (1997), *Elderly People in Modern Society*, 4th edn. Harlow: Longman.

Titmuss, R. (1955), Lecture at the University of Birmingham in honour of Eleanor Rathbone, repr. in P. Alcock, H. Glennerster, A. Oakley, and A. Sinfield (eds.) (2001), *Welfare and Wellbeing: Richard Titmuss's Contribution to Social Policy*. Bristol: Policy Press.

Townsend, P. (1986), 'Ageism and social policy'. In C. Phillipson and A. Walker (eds.), *Ageing and Social Policy*. Aldershot: Gower.

—— (1991), 'The structured dependency of the elderly: a creation of social policy in the twentieth century', *Ageing and Society* 1(1): 5–28.

Walker, A. (ed.) (1996), *The New Generational Contract*. London: UCL Press.

Waltzer, M. (1983), *Spheres of Justice*. Oxford: Blackwell.

Warnock Report (1978), *Special Educational Needs*. London: HMSO.

Webb, S. (1993), 'Women's incomes: past, present and prospects', *Fiscal Studies* 14(4): 14–36.

Westergaard, J. (1995), *Who Gets What?* Cambridge: Polity Press.

Williams, F. (1989), *Social Policy: A Critical Introduction*. Cambridge: Polity Press.

—— (1992), 'Somewhere over the rainbow: universality and diversity in social policy'. In N. Manning and R. Page (eds.), *Social Policy Review 4*. Canterbury: Social Policy Association.

—— (2001), 'In and beyond New Labour: towards a political ethics of care', *Critical Social Policy*, 12(4): 467–93.

Wilson, W. (1989), *The Truly Disadvantaged: The Underclass, the Ghetto and Public Policy*. Chicago University Press.

Wollstonecraft, M. (1792), *A Vindication of the Rights of Women*. Repr. 1982, Harmondsworth: Penguin.

FURTHER READING

An important text that touches on many of the key issues in this chapter is Williams (1989). A more recent edited collection, Lewis et al. (2000), provides an excellent selection of chapters that broach several of the theoretical challenges associated with identity and the life course. For basic introductory social policy texts on gender, see Pascall (1997); on ethnicity, see Law (1996); on disability, see Oliver and Barnes (1998); on youth, see Coles (1995); on elderly people, see Tinker (1997).

GLOSSARY

biological determinism The belief that human beings' differences and their individual identities are primarily determined by their biology: by their genetic make up; by their natural, sexual, 'racial' and physical characteristics; by the age and condition of their bodies.

demographic transition A long-term process that has transformed the age profile of the population in developed societies, in which fertility declines (i.e. we have fewer babies) while life expectancy increases (i.e. we have longer lives).

divisions of welfare A sociological term used to describe the way that society may be divided into different groups according to the different ways in which people satisfy their needs for social security and pensions, housing, education, health, social care, etc.

equality of opportunity The conditions under which each individual in society has the same formal rights as any other in relation to employment and access to goods and services (including services such as education and housing). Equality of opportunity is not the same as, and does not guarantee, equality of outcome.

ethic of care A set of values that embraces the nature of human interdependency and the importance of caring relationships for the maintenance of the moral and social order.

ethnicity A term used to describe the specific but shared historical, linguistic, and cultural context that defines a human being's identity, the society from which they come, and/or the community to which they belong.

eugenics/eugenicist Terms used to describe policies intended to improve the physical, social, and moral wellbeing of society by the regulation of the genetic composition of the population.

feminization A process through which women, women's roles, women's disadvantages, and/or women's perspectives may acquire greater prominence.

formal An adjective to describe something that has form, rather than (or as well as) substance. An individual may have a formal status or entitlement that is guaranteed in an abstract or procedural sense, but which it may be difficult substantively (that is, in reality) to achieve or enforce.

identity/identities The sense(s) of self by which individuals define who they are—both in terms of belonging to a society or social group and in terms of having integrity as a unique being.

impairment The absence of, limitation of, or damage to a bodily organ or physical or mental function, that may (or may not—depending on the nature of the social context and physical environment) result in disability.

independent living A term pioneered within the disabled people's movement to define arrangements by which disabled people can exercise direct control over their own living arrangements (for example, by directly employing personal assistants) and fully participate in society.

life course A holistic term used to describe the development and experiences of an individual, cohort, or social group though a lifetime. (Unlike the term 'lifecycle', it does not imply that the processes of a human life are necessarily fixed or recurring.)

new social movements The term is usually applied to the kind of globally oriented campaigns—such as second-wave feminism, pacifism, and environmentalism—that developed during the last half of the twentieth century and challenged the existing boundaries of institutional politics.

patriarchy A term to describe political, social, and economic systems, institutions, and practices that are based on male domination and the oppression of women.

problematize An expression often used by social scientists to denote the process by which everyday occurrences or phenomena may come to be recognized or reconstituted as a social problem through changing social, political, or academic discourses.

racialization A process through which racial definitions and racist ideologies are actively promoted or may acquire prominence.

racism A set of ideological beliefs or assumptions concerning the existence of racial differences within the human species and the supposed superiority of certain 'races' over others.

social solidarity An expression relating to the extent of mutual support within a society or social group. It is a concept that has greater resonance within continental European welfare regimes, but is critically important in any debate about the functions and purposes of social welfare systems.

substantive An adjective to describe something that has substance, rather than (or as well as) form. An individual may seek or receive substantive recognition or benefits that are concrete and real, regardless of whether these are things to which a formal right has been properly defined or legally prescribed.

underclass A contested concept that is sometimes used to define a class or stratum that is morally different and/or socially excluded from mainstream society. Right-wing theorists have blamed the welfare state for creating an underclass of welfare dependents, while some left-wing theorists blame the forces of global capitalism for creating an underclass of the permanently excluded.

PART THREE

PLANNING, FINANCING, AND IMPLEMENTING WELFARE POLICIES

9

Professions and Bureaucracy

Andrew Gray and Bill Jenkins

CONTENTS

INTRODUCTION: PROFESSIONS UNDER PRESSURE

Do the words Bristol, Shipman, and Alder Hey mean anything to you? If not, the more recent case of Victoria Climbié may ring a bell. Each represents a failing on the part of professionals in public services. The first three relate to medical practice. Bristol refers to the Bristol Royal Infirmary, where in the 1990s mortality in child surgery was found to be unacceptably high as a result of shortcomings of both surgeons and systems of care

(Cm. 5207, 2001). Harold Shipman was a general medical practitioner who was convicted for the serial murder of fifteen patients under his care. It is probable that he killed hundreds (Baker 2001). Alder Hey is a Merseyside hospital where organs from the bodies of deceased children were removed without parental consent. An inquiry found failings by individual doctors and by the management of the hospital (Department of Health 2001). Victoria Climbié was a child murdered by her neglectful and abusive carers (her aunt and boyfriend). Hers is perhaps the most damning of all recent failures of professional public services, for it reveals not only shortcomings by individual practitioners and managers but also by the systems through which they are supposed to work together for the benefit of clients. Her death was the subject of an extensive inquiry chaired by Lord Laming, a former Chief Inspector of Social Services. Its report revealed that Victoria was known during the terrifying period leading to her death by four social service departments, three housing authorities, two child protection police teams, two hospitals, and a specialist centre managed by the National Society for the Prevention of Cruelty to Children (Cm. 5730, 2003). She might have been rescued on at least fourteen occasions if social workers, medical staff, and police had discharged their responsibilities properly.

These are all dreadful cases not only for the victims and their families but also for the indicted professions. Together with other cases (including in transport and education), they have challenged the values, competence, and even legitimacies of professional practitioners of public goods and services. Each case has been followed by more calls to subject the professions and their practitioners to more regulation (as in quality audits) and their activities to more systematic management (as in clinical governance).

At the same time professionals have also been obliged to recognize that their decisions in individual cases are also resource decisions and vice versa. A quarter of a century of resource constraint has obliged medical practitioners, for example, to accept that a treatment for one patient might be a treatment withheld for another. This rationing is of course a fact of professional life, as there will never be sufficient financial, human, or organizational resources to support every possible treatment. But governments over the past couple of decades have increasingly imposed more non-professional criteria onto the decisions about who receives what care when and how. Governments justify this imposition on the grounds that they are guardians of public policy and resources. Some professions have attempted to fight back. Ian Bogle, chairman of the British Medical Association (the doctors' trade union), warned that government targets to reduce hospital waiting lists were forcing doctors to treat low-priority cases at the expense of patients with more serious conditions and pain. He advised that 'professionals are sick to death of being shackled in this way and having their feelings about clinical priorities overridden by government targets' (*Guardian*, 10 May 2002).

There is no question but that professions in the public sector, especially the caring professions, feel that their essential professional values are under an intensifying threat from government bureaucracy and managerialism. The tension is represented in Fig. 9.1, drawn from a campaign by the Royal College of Nurses against the Conservative health service reforms of the 1980s. The tableau pitches Florence Nightingale—lamp holder for the values of health care—against Sir Roy Griffiths—chairman of a 1983 report championing

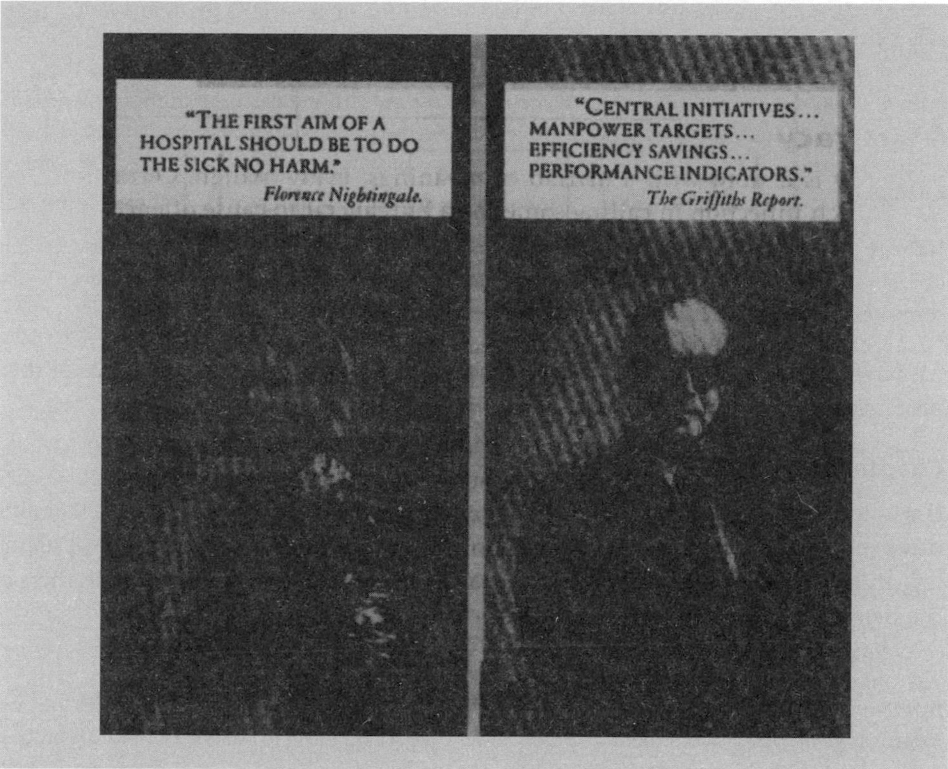

Figure 9.1 White coats and grey suits: Florence Nightingale vs. Sir Roy Griffiths

more general management in health care, doyen of private sector retail management (he was a senior executive with Sainsbury's), and fixated on nostrums of management mantra which, stereotypically, he is unable to express in continuous prose! The implication is that the white coats are losing out to the grey suits.

For the Conservative government of 1979–97, for whom Griffiths was a totem, the imperative was to bring resource issues to bear on social policy decisions. Its campaign was designed to break up restrictive practices perpetrated by monopoly providers with little regard to public costs or desires. The 1980s and 1990s were thus punctuated by a series of reforms of education, healthcare, housing, police, social services, and related public services. The Labour governments since 1997 have reinforced much of the thrust of the reforms although, importantly, they have committed greater public finances to the services. The common intention has been, in a piece of early 1990s jargon, to *reinvent* the professions as *providers* of public services committed to comprehensive management.

For the advocates of reform, the benefits have been both welcome and visible: greater efficiency and more responsiveness. For its detractors, schemes such as increased competition, quality enhancement, performance targeting, and regulation have not only subordinated professionals but also built up powerful and expensive new bureaucracies, with the public as the loser.

Professionals themselves have adopted a variety of positions in relation to these changes. Some have been hostile:

> I did not join the profession to push paper but treat patients (Hospital consultant resisting pressure to be a clinical director, i.e. manager of clinical colleagues in a department.)[1]

Others have been more accommodating:

> If the senior police officers of [this area] don't get stuck in and learn to manage our resources and operations more efficiently and effectively, then some fairy boy in head quarters, or even worse some berk in the Home Office, will take over. (chief superintendent)

All have had to deal with changing contexts and relationships in the practice of their professions.

Chapter aims

It would be easy to engage in a knockabout on the gains and losses in all this. Our aim, however, is to elaborate the changing nature of professional life in public and social policy, and the relationship of professionals to organizational arrangements and others in the delivery of services.

We may begin with Socrates:

> Interference by the three classes [businessmen, auxiliaries and guardians] with each other's jobs and interchange of jobs between them, therefore, does the greatest harm to our state and we are entirely justified in calling it the worst of evils. (Plato, *The Republic*, 434)

By extension, we might suggest that attempts to turn professionals into bureaucratic managers or to invite the bureaucrats to take professionals' decisions may be counterproductive. Yet the past couple of decades in British government have been predicated on precisely this notion; mixing up the 'classes' and bringing their functions closer together has been regarded as exactly what the state needs.

Has it worked? What do we mean by 'bureaucracy' and 'profession'? How have public management reforms affected the relationship between bureaucrats, politicians, professionals, and publics in a new mixed economy of public service? As these are all significant questions, this chapter presents some conceptualizations of bureaucracy and professionalism, offers a comparative analysis of relationships over the past thirty years or so, and draws out some issues.

MODELS OF BUREAUCRACY AND PROFESSION

Bureaucracy

Bureaucracy is a word with a myriad of meanings, many malign. Certainly it does not take much inflection in calling someone a bureaucrat to cause offence. Like other

[1] All anonymous quotations are taken from the Durham Study (Gray et al. 1999) and other seperate research by the author.

social science terms used extensively in social and political debate (such as democracy), it has become attached to particular ideologies and suffered from conceptual vandalism.

Social science itself has compounded the difficulties in that, as Beetham notes (1996), there are at least two major conceptualizations of bureaucracy: those in the sociology of organizations and in political economy. Moreover, any elaboration of a model of bureaucracy has to deal with the term 'model' as a defining, explaining, or prescribing device. Our purpose is limited to helping you to recognize bureaucracy, or more exactly bureaucratic characteristics, as a prelude to an examination of how well professional practice fits in with this traditional organizational arrangement in public services. Thus we seek to elaborate the defining characteristics of bureaucracy and provide some explanation of their effects in practice.

Weber's characterization Since the early years of the twentieth century, any discussion of bureaucracy has begun with the work of Max Weber, a German sociologist (1864–1920). The son of a liberal politician and a dominating and puritanical mother, Weber took up an academic career and rose meteorically to become a professor at the tender age of 31. Following a decade of emotional and mental disorders, he began to readjust to life, and in this period until his death he wrote much of the work by which we now regard him as a leading sociologist, such as *The Protestant Ethic and the Spirit of Capitalism* (written in 1904–5) and *The Theory of Economic and Social Organization* (1910–18). In these we can see ideas about society and bureaucracy underpinned by an interest in the origins, manifestations, and exercise of authority. His sources are eclectic in time and across societies, drawing on ancient civilizations such as China, Egypt, and Greece as well as industrial Europe.

Authority, for Weber, is legitimate power. The basis of legitimation has three distinctive forms. *Traditional authority* is derived from the customs and practices of a particular social group as they pass through generations. Typical are the dynastic traditions of rulers. *Charismatic authority*, on the other hand, is derived from the possession of leadership characteristics. Originally a term used to describe fanatical religious leaders, it has come to embrace qualities such as oratory and vision. Of course, Weber died before the twentieth century provided its most graphic examples of such authority at work through dictators and their cult-generating machines. Had he experienced these he might have taken a less historical view of the decline of this authority in preference to his third category, *rational-legal authority*. For Weber regarded this type as the distinguishing vehicle of legitimate power in the organizations of industrial society. This is the authority that comes from the rights and responsibilities of office, appointment to which has followed laid down procedures, and is recognized by subordinates. Thus the authority does not derive from the individual or the traditions of the office but from the designated responsibilities and procedures of the position itself.

The striking feature of rational-legal authority for Weber was the way it had become institutionalized in modern industrial society. In contrast to organizations and societies governed by elites and citizens (autocracy and democracy), he described this as bureaucracy (government through office). Bureaucracy is thus the organizational arrangement through which rational-legal authority is institutionalized.

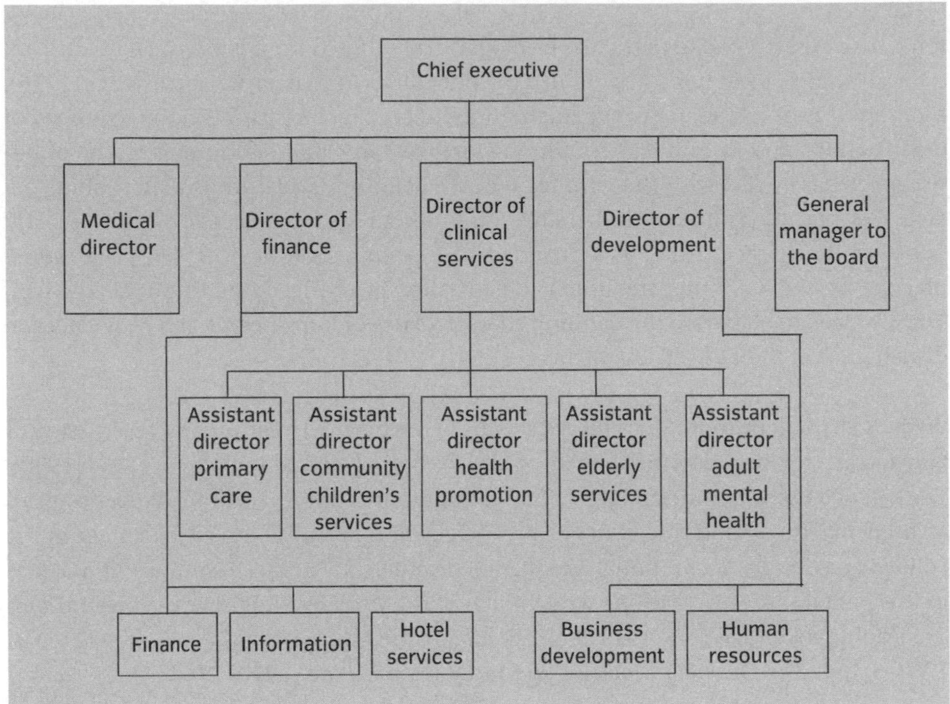

Figure 9.2 A health trust is it bureaucratic?

Figure 9.3 is an abstraction of Weber's ideas for, despite his central concern with this defining form of industrial organization, he nowhere systematically codified his elements of bureaucracy in a single framework. Rather, they emerge from fragmented elaborations. As a result, different commentators may present as few as four main features while others list a dozen or so (see Beetham 1996). However, most agree on a core set of defining characteristics. First, bureaucracies are characterized by a division of labour into *formal jurisdictional areas*: that is, functions are allocated to specified units (sometimes called departments or sections) and the designated responsibilities and authorities are limited by boundaries. Second, authority is transmitted through the organization through a *hierarchy*, i.e. a scalar chain in which the authority of one superior is then subordinate to another. Third, the activities of bureaucracy are carried out according to *rules*, i.e. laid down regulations and procedures for the conduct of activities, whose rationality lies in their promotion of functions. Of particular note here is, fourth, the *recording* of activities against these rules, thereby creating file-based narratives of transactions which subsequent officials may follow.

If these characteristics apply to structure and process, others relate to the bureaucrats themselves. Their performance of tasks according to the distinct jurisdictional areas requires organizational *training*. In the English medieval military, soldiers were part-timers usually commandeered by their landowners under an obligation to the monarch. When the monarch summoned them they just turned up. When such an arrangement became a shaky basis on which to conduct campaigns against increasingly sophisticated enemies who, very un-Britishly, practised beforehand, a standing bureaucratic army

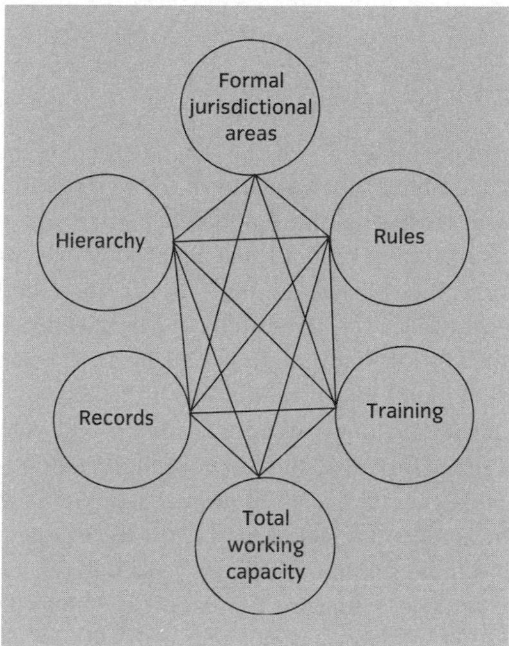

Figure 9.3 Weber's characteristics of bureaucracy

developed in which training was a distinguishing feature for soldiers who also devoted *full working capacities* to the organization.

These elements taken together have been described as constituting bureaucracy as an ideal type. A word of caution here: by 'ideal type' we mean belonging to ideas rather than to states of idyll. Weber's characteristics of bureaucracy are abstractions of what he observed. Thus it may be more useful to treat them as frameworks for analysing the bureaucratic tendencies in organization rather than as prescriptions for or descriptions of actual organizations.

Bureaucracy today: empirical, theoretical, and ideological The empirical pervasiveness of bureaucratic tendencies in the modern world is well documented. Much of it, but by no means all (consider the giant commercial corporations), is found in public service provision. Highly developed and formalized division of labour, extensive hierarchies of command, rules and procedures, with transactions duly noted and recorded by specifically trained dedicated officials, are dominant features of the organizations through which our public services are provided.

For Weber, the growth of bureaucracy was associated with the growth of legal and technical rationality as a response to arbitrary governance and the industrial revolution. In today's world, developments in the technology of work and the increasing pressure by publics for standardized services demand organizational characteristics which combine specialization (to combat the technical complexity) and integration (to give effect to coordinated direction often determined by political masters). Bureaucracy has the potential to provide these, and its predominance in government (and private organizations too) is testament to its power to deliver.

Bureaucratic tendencies, however, are not without their problems. Many researchers have identified the contrast between the formalism of Weber's model and the paradox of the pervasive informal features in organizations which sustain them. Much of this informal behaviour, i.e. that which is not prescribed by the organization, arises as a way of handling the inherent contradictions of different bureaucratic characteristics. Rule use is a particularly striking example. Rules are shown to be greatly functional to the provision of public services. In processing large numbers of transactions, rules help to promote standardized outcomes (like cases being treated alike). Moreover, they execute this with considerable efficiency as they obviate the need for decision criteria to be invented on each occasion. But at least fifty years of research has identified three informal 'Rs' of rule use (and unlike the three 'Rs' of education they actually do all begin with that letter!).

The first two are often found together. *Ritualism* is the habitual use of a rule even in circumstances for which it is no longer appropriate. Box 9.1 provides an illustration. You have probably heard officials defend such literal interpretations of rules with 'Don't blame me, I did not make the rules' and 'It's more than my job's worth to do what you want' disclaimers. These constitute *retreatism*, i.e. the use of rules to protect or defend oneself. *Reductionism* is more subtle: it is the perverse way rules can reduce as well as enhance standards of behaviour. Imagine a situation in which a lack of rules has been identified as contributing to poor performance, perhaps even discrimination in the provision of public services. The remedy, the setting out of a rule, makes explicit the standard of behaviour required. This has the desired effect of putting pressure on poor performers to raise their level. However, for those who are performing above the standard and perhaps being innovative and progressive, the setting of the new standard will not only make them aware of the extent to which they have been performing

Box 9.1 Pensioner refused mature student's grant

In the golden days when university students received grants to support their attendance at university, there lived a pensioner who had retired from work three years earlier and was becoming bored with doing nothing. As with many of his generation, he had missed out on the developing opportunities for further and higher education but had heard about the brave new world it offered. With a 'I'll have some of that' response, he duly applied for and was accepted at his local university. His place secure, the next stop was his local educational authority to obtain one of these mature student full grants he had also heard about. To his surprise he was turned down. Why? Apparently on the grounds that the eligibility rules at the time stated that an applicant for such an award had to be gainfully employed for three years prior to the application. Our pensioner had not been so; he had been retired. A nonsense? Certainly, but it had arisen because the rules had been drawn up to prevent young people (perhaps encouraged by parents who were reluctant to fork out for their share of the grant) from making an application with the appearance of independence from their parents. However, in this case an official in the education authority applied the rules ritualistically to a situation to which they could not adapt. (Fortunately, rules can be changed—though it can be difficult—and our hero got his money!)

Box 9.2 A reductionist tendency of performance indicators

2002 saw the publication of the first comprehensive performance assessments under which local authorities were classified as excellent, good, fair, or poor. The year also saw a revision of the award to social service departments of stars from three (the highest award, in which case the department was likely to be less regulated in future and receive funds for innovative ventures) to zero stars (where departments were likely to be much more closely regulated and not receive additional funding). It is hoped that these broadly based assessments will ameliorate the dysfunctional effects of the Audit Commission's annual publication of league tables of local authority performance in selected services. Some local authority sources reported that for a service to be at the top of a service list was by way of an invitation for resources to be taken away and redeployed in favour of the much more public worst-performing services. In other words, the publication of the standard and performance could help to bring unacceptable performance up to the standard (a formal and desired effect) but also promote reduction of standard amongst the highest performers (an informal and presumably undesired effect).

unnecessarily above it but make their resources the target of those with the poorest performance so that they can improve (see Box 9.2).

A further consequence is *bureaucratic politics*. You will know that political activity derives from differentiation. All differentiation in an organization (as in society) has the potential to lead to political activity, but it takes specific challenges to the interests arising from the differentiation to translate into politics. As we have seen, a central bureaucratic characteristic is division of labour reflected in the differentiation into sections and units. The formal functionality of these arrangements is again evident: effectiveness through specialization, concentration of effort, and discipline. The organizational units thereby created develop group loyalties. In circumstances where the interests of the units are supported (as in resource or policy growth) this differentiation remains tacit politically; however, when these interests are threatened, units may engage in political competition which may not only divert resources in themselves but undermine the concentration of effort towards formally prescribed activities.

Bureaucracy as a theoretical construction (rather than as an empirical reality) is based on certain premises about society and human behaviour and the way in which these are expressed in organizations. Weber conceived bureaucratic characteristics as value-free, i.e. neutral instruments or mechanisms amenable to the promotion of any ordained values irrespective of context. However, this denies the value of bureaucracy itself. After all, an instrument for embodying or promoting a rational-legal authority (or any other) cannot by definition be value-free. Second, for bureaucratic mechanisms to be culturally neutral would imply that the norms and values of organizational members displaying bureaucratic characteristics have no influence on its realization. This seems illogical, given that most of our predictive theories of society are based on exactly the opposite notion.

So, bureaucratic characteristics are intrinsically value-laden. This makes them ideological, and many have been quick to challenge bureaucracy on this ground. You may have

Box 9.3 The deadening hand of bureaucracy?

Joyce Brand, a social worker for twenty-five years (and incidentally the mother of Jo Brand the comedienne), complained in 1997 that professionals had been forced to submit their values to a bureaucratic norm. She attributed the loss of social service departments 'rooted in humanity and professionalism' in part to the relentless march of the market. But she added: 'it is from within the organization that the greatest threat comes. We now have MBA managers so preoccupied with *systems, recording and checking*, that they have stopped valuing their most precious resource, their staff . . . These managers have devised sophisticated and time-consuming *assessment procedures* . . . They have set up *procedures and instructions* . . . while they translate human distress into *recordable statistics*.'

(*Independent*, 10 April 1997; emphasis added)

- Does this strike a chord with you? Does the systematization of professional work thwart or support professional effectiveness?

noticed that these challenges come from both the right and left of the political spectrum. First, there have been arguments against the conservatism of bureaucracy, that is, its inbuilt protection through formal and rigid structures and rules of the status quo or, put another way, its resistance to change. Second, there have been protestations of the inherently undemocratic quality of bureaucratic life. On the other hand, others have advocated bureaucratic characteristics as effective command structures in circumstances where consistency and predictability are a requirement, and as accountability structures through which officials are accountable for not only the quality of public goods and services but also the means by which they are provided. Jaques (1990), for example, described how:

> At first glance hierarchy may be difficult to praise. Bureaucracy is a dirty word even among bureaucrats, and in business there is a widespread view that managerial hierarchy kills initiative, crushes creativity, and has therefore had its day. Yet 35 years of research have convinced me that managerial hierarchy is the most efficient, the hardiest, and in fact the most natural structure ever devised for large organizations. Properly structured, hierarchy can release energy and creativity, rationalize productivity, and actually improve morale.

Interestingly, as Box 9.3 shows, members of public service professions have been amongst the most vociferous complainers about the deadening hand of bureaucracy on their ability to provide services to their clients. But what is a profession and what are the characteristics of professional life? The next section seeks to elaborate these prior to a comparison with those of bureaucracy.

Profession

Weber saw professionalization in society as a manifestation of the same force driving bureaucratization—rationality. Indeed, for classical sociology many of the characteristics of profession are similar to bureaucracy: formal jurisdictions, specialization, training, and full-time commitment. However, we have seen that professionalization is often represented as conflicting with bureaucracy. We shall examine the extent and nature of this conflict in the next section. But first, we must seek some understanding of professionalism.

Profession as a victim of a conceptual tug of war Unfortunately, **profession** as a concept is no easier to elucidate than bureaucracy. Perhaps because in industrial society the status of professional has been prized (with or without financial gains), the concept has become elastic. In fact, not all of its connotations are favourable (consider 'the oldest profession' and the 'professional foul'), and some are selective (professional in contrast to amateur). But, in an occupational sense, the concept has been at the centre of a tug of war between those who regard their vocations and marketplace positions as protectable through a professional label and others who aspire to this status and position without attracting widespread public recognition (see Case Study 9.1). Thus it is hard to deny

Case Study 9.1 Public sector recognition of social policy professions: relative pay

A 2002 survey ('Public Voices', *Guardian*, 21 March) reported the following salaries of public service professionals:

Social worker: £19,000
Senior charge nurse: £24,000
Community care manager: £24,000
Science teacher: £25,000
Further education lecturer: £25,000
Community midwife: £26,000
Youth worker: £26,000
Probation officer: £26,000
University librarian: £30,000
Senior youth officer: £31,000
Educational psychologist: £33,000
Primary school head teacher: £35,000
Speech and language therapy coordinator: £36,500
Education adviser, local education authority: £41,000
University professor: £43,000
Police inspector: £43,000
General medical practitioner: £55,000
Assistant director, social services: £55,000
Chief probation officer: £55,500
Specialist registrar in anaesthetics: £57,000
Consultant in palliative care: £66,000
Coroner: £66,000
Chief executive, housing association: £80,000
Circuit judge: £103,000

- Do these salaries reflect their worth to the public?
- Would you alter this ranking? If so how and why?

that profession is 'an intrinsically ambiguous, multifaceted folk concept, of which no single attempt at isolating its existence will ever be generally persuasive' (Freidson 1994: 25). Nevertheless, as with bureaucracy, our analysis requires some elaboration.

During the 1950s and 1960s there was a concerted interest in defining the characteristics of professions. In an early expression, Greenwood (1957) sought on the basis of a functional analysis to provide a taxonomy of professions. In this the 'established' professions (medicine, law, clergy, and academia) were seen as possessing a set of attributes including specialist knowledge, autonomous judgement, self-regulation, codes of ethics, and a distinctive culture (see Box 9.4). These attributes have been cited in many subsequent collections of readings on professions, and have proved useful in empirical studies in establishing the extent to which different occupational groups can be classified as professions or indeed as semi-professions, a term used to depict some public service occupational groups.

From such studies, specialized knowledge and autonomy emerged as critical defining qualities of professionalism and became the basis of a search for absolute classes of professional groupings. However, it soon emerged that professionalism might be relative. Specialization, for example, was seen to be limited by situation and time while autonomy appeared as at least two-dimensional (i.e. autonomy from client and from employing organization). Further, it became fashionable to ask how far social behaviour was constructed in situations rather than determined by social forces. Thus there developed an increasing recognition of the importance in understanding the way in which the term 'professional' is actually made and used by practitioners in their everyday interactions.

A Durham University study sympathetic to this approach observed professionals working together in local government to ascertain their defining characteristics as professionals and ask professionals about their work (Gray et al. 1999). In adopting a list of self-defining professional groups (e.g. accountants, engineers, environmental health officers, librarians, planners, social workers, solicitors), the study sought to establish from each respondent what it meant to be a professional. The responses revealed that

Box 9.4 Attributes of a profession: a functionalist analysis

- systematic body of theory: 'the skills that characterize a profession flow from and are supported by a fund of knowledge that has been organized into an internally consistent system';
- professional authority: 'the layman's comparative ignorance' leaves the client 'no choice but to accede to professional judgement';
- sanction of the community: 'by granting or withholding accreditation' a professional body is authorized by the state to control entry to and training in the profession;
- regulatory code of ethics: an 'explicit, systematic, and binding' code 'which compels ethical behaviour on the part of its members' in relation to clients and colleagues;
- the professional culture: 'a social configuration unique to the profession' which 'consists of its *values*, *norms* and *symbols*'.

(Greenwood 1957)

professionalism meant one or more of the following: a specialist knowledge and expertise, a position, and an ethos promoting the values of professionals (including against corporate bureaucratic managerialism).

Profession as specialist knowledge and expertise In the Durham study, as in earlier work, individuals identified the professing of specialist knowledge or expertise as a central element of being a professional. Thus for one social worker:

> the purpose of being a professional is to ensure that comprehensive knowledge is available to be applied to various presenting issues.

Moreover, specialism remains central, even though the circumstances of how, when, and where this specialism is used varies between different groups and contexts, while public service reforms are seen as eroding professionals' rights to exclusive exercise of the specialism. For example, local authority architects resent others less qualified taking on an increasing share of their tasks:

> Clients like housing don't want to pay our fees . . . They try to cut corners by employing someone themselves who's a . . . jack of all trades, who thinks he can do it.

Yet practitioners also take on parts of other roles in order to help out and get work done as part of a flexible team approach, or because of staff shortages elsewhere.

Profession as position Professionals see the way this knowledge and expertise is used as furnishing them with a distinctive position. In essence this is about autonomy, i.e. the freedom of both clients and employing organizations to define and determine the application of their work. As we have seen already, autonomy has long been regarded as another central element of professionalism. However, practitioners recognize that its practice is related to context. Indeed, professionals employed in public service organizations have to manage an inherent tension between their obligations to clients, the profession at large, their employing organization's objectives, and their own conception as a professional practitioner.

How this tension is managed is clearly set within the democratic process in general, and the statutory obligations of public agencies and their professions in particular. After all, professionals in public service have to recognize that ministers and councillors are at liberty to ignore the soundest of their professional advice and to accept that legislation (e.g. in community care and housing) shapes the demands on and limits of their professional practice. This suggests that the exercise of autonomy is set by an internal political process of its own. Moreover, this process encompasses collaboration (an increasingly common term in the New Labour dictionary) across disciplines in order to provide services. Thus for a social worker:

> Co-operation with other professional groups is vital in order to give good service to users . . . Health and social services must work more closely together. District nurses, health professionals must 'trust' each other more and understand where they stand.

The position of professionals will also depend on how they are structured in their organizations. Professional groups may be self-contained within discrete units to provide cohesion for professional discipline or, as is increasingly the case, merged with others to give effect to the need to collaborate and focus activities on specific client groups or sets of services. Thus, in bringing (say) housing and social services together into one new department, new professional positions may be forged which, although still dependent on specialist knowledge and expertise, may structure a particular position from which it may be applied.

Profession as ethos To profess a specialist knowledge and expertise is also to espouse a set of values which are to be promoted for the benefit of the profession and its clients. There is a moral element here which, as Weber noted, is a source of political power, and thus subject to opposition by those opposed to the professionals' claim to status. Yet what are its elements? Certainly this ethos imposes a hierarchy of duty on the professional: priority is given to client and profession over other claimants. Thus the specific client is the consumer, and client relationships are sacrosanct. Relationships with other professional practitioners are collegial rather than hierarchical. This collegial and client-oriented ethos is realized through service, professional maintenance, and innovation.

Of course, this ideal of the professional ethos tends to reflect original sole practices, i.e. individual professionals acting directly with clients without outside mediating influences—perhaps as you might find if as a private individual you sought professional advice from a lawyer or accountant. This situation is relatively rare in the context of today's industrial and collectivized society. Moreover, we are concerned with public service professions. These may have a broader conception of the commitment to the client which incorporates obligations to the service department and the employing organization as a whole (e.g. hospital, school, or local authority).

If this commitment to client wellbeing is a defining element of a professional ethos, so is an obligation to the profession as a whole. The codification of specialist knowledge and expertise is set out by the profession through its corporate body (usually an institute or association such as the British Association of Social Work or the Chartered Institute of Public Finance and Accountancy). This explication will usually be supported by codes of conduct and ethical practice which guide members' relations with clients and employing organizations. Such professional associations gain the allegiance of members if only through their control of registration, i.e. the award (or removal) of a licence to practise as a professional. But such bodies are also seen by members as standard-bearers of the values of the profession, so much so that members may be as critical of them for not protecting the profession against external challenges as they are of those challenges themselves.

One set of such threats to professional ethos comes from the bureaucratic tendencies of large organizations. As we shall see in the next section, public sector reforms have intensified these for many public service professions. As one housing officer explained:

> The increased emphasis on performance targets, pleasing political masters to obtain finance etc., have all served to decrease the emphasis and value placed on professional work; professional views/opinions are often not appreciated or welcomed by senior management or members.

Health professionals and social workers have also expressed concern that 'having customers not clients' (i.e. paying punters with sets of service demands rather than recipients of a professionally determined treatment) has undermined their professional ethos.

From the literature on the conceptualization of profession and the reflections of professionals themselves we can draw out elements of the professional experience. At its heart, profession appears to be about the professing of specialist knowledge and expertise, a distinctive autonomous position from which to practise them, and a culture or ethos which emphasizes the commitment both to clients and the collegiality of professional colleagues at large. However, some of these elements coincide with bureaucratic characteristics and some are in direct conflict with them. The next section attempts to provide a comparative framework before providing a history of their relationship in the post-1945 public services in the UK.

Command and communion

We have so far established something of the defining elements of both bureaucracy and profession. Yet how can we compare them so that we are clear about the distinctive qualities and modes of governance? The following paragraphs provide a framework of comparison based on three dimensions: legitimation, accountability, and integration.

By *legitimation* we refer to the basis on which the actions of those in bureaucratic or professional contexts are justified. This is, in effect, the source of the authority by which bureaucratic or professional decisions are made and taken. Etzioni, in a seminal contribution on semi-professionals, argued that 'the ultimate justification for an administrative [i.e. bureaucratic] act is that it is in line with the organization's rules and regulations, and that it has been approved directly or by implication—by a superior rank' while the justification for a professional act is that 'it is, to the best of the professional's knowledge base, the right act' (1969: x–xi). Note that the importance of this distinction is that the legitimation of the bureaucratic act is internal to the organization, with not only the codification of authorized and unauthorized activity but the allocation of praise and blame conducted hierarchically. The legitimation of the professional act is external; the codification of appropriateness and the allocation of praise and blame is carried out externally by a collegial body. Clearly, the potential for conflict is high as professionals working through public bureaucracies face different sources of authority and different mechanisms by which their actions will be judged.

This brings us to the second comparative dimension: *accountability*. Professionals see themselves as accountable to at least three sets of accountees: the client, the profession, and the organization through which they practice (see Fig. 9.4). Thus for the professional there is an accountability in any one set of actions which is subject to these three sets of forces, some of which are external to the organization. For any individual professional, the immediacy of these forces varies. Doctors and social workers, for example, may have day-to-day contact with the public while others, such as accountants and lawyers in public organizations, may have greater contact with their employing organization or even other public agencies including central government departments. In bureaucracy, however, accountabilities are resolved through the managerial hierarchy *within* the organization.

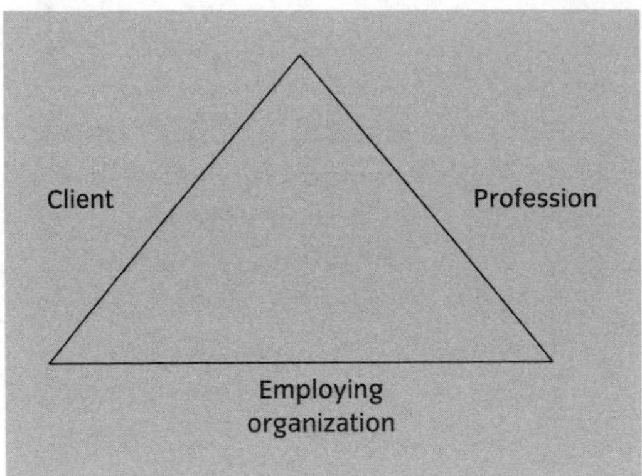

Figure 9.4 Accountabilities in professional modes of organization

These differing accountability patterns are a pointer to another distinction: *integrating mechanisms*, i.e. the means by which differentiated organizational activities are coordinated. Bureaucratic characteristics such as formal rules lead to coordination through the *standardization of work* tasks. With the hierarchical internal authority, these provide a strong integrating capability. The professional organization, however, leaves much of the decision-making and taking to the professional operators on the ground, relying on the *standardization of the skills* of the professionals. As Mintzberg notes in a useful discussion of different coordinating mechanisms available to organizations (1979), this is a loose instrument, dependent on external agents to provide the necessary capability. It also can run into difficulties as attempts by the organization to impose unity on a myriad of individual decisions are resisted by professionals seeking to protect their freedom of action. In these circumstances the integration is a negotiated political process rather than one of command.

We can now summarize the contrasts between the bureaucratic and professional organization by elucidating the dominant mode of governance associated with each. By governance we do not mean here one particular type of government arrangement such as the use of networks (Rhodes 1997). Rather, and more fundamentally, governance comprises the allocation of authority and function and the establishment and maintenance of rights and obligations. Different patterns or modes of governance reflect different types of relationship. Bureaucratic characteristics of organization are associated with a **command mode of governance**. This mode is based on the rule of law emanating from a sovereign body and delivered through a scalar chain of superior and subordinate authority. Legitimacy for public service decisions and behaviours lies in their being within the bounds prescribed through due process by the institutions charged with the provision. The strength of the command mode of governance lies in the efficiency and effectiveness of control and accountability; its weakness is in rigidity and conservatism in the face of changing environments.

Professional characteristics are associated with a **communion mode of governance**, i.e. a set of shared values and creeds. Thus in the delivery of a service the legitimacy for actions lies in their consistency with the protocols and guiding values of the group's shared frame of reference. The strength of communion lies in the guidance afforded by its shared values through different environments; its weakness is its insularity from those environments and a consequent failure to adapt its normative order.

Thus command is associated with the line management of traditional bureaucracy, communion with service decisions in professionalized sectors. As we wish to know whether the public service reforms have effected changes in these modes of governance and in the issues raised for social policy and its beneficiaries and providers, the next section provides an account of these reforms.

CHANGING PATTERNS OF SERVICE DELIVERY

Bureaucracy and professions in traditional public administration

Traditionally, the organization and delivery of government services in the UK has been characterized by the development of a career-based public bureaucracy, and by the organization and delivery of services by established professionals. Established by the reforms of the Victorian Northcote Trevelyan report, the neutral career service developed into a foundation of British central government. In a different way, UK local government has also been based on a career service, but in this case one of professional groups in associated departments (e.g. engineers, social work, housing, education).

In this traditional system of public administration, politicians (ministers, Members of Parliament, local councillors) were separated from service delivery by an administrative cadre that neutrally implemented their policies and in many instances acted as a conduit between politicians and the professional groups who delivered services to the public. Thus, in broad terms, education was left to educators, healthcare to health professionals, policing to police officers, and social work to social workers. In traditional public administration, therefore, professional, political, and administrative domains were relatively segregated (see Fig. 9.5). Command was the dominant mode of relationship between politicians and administrators, while communion was a strong element in

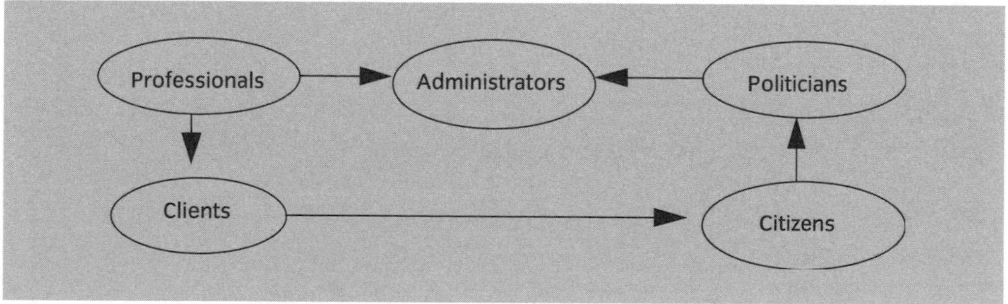

Figure 9.5 Bureaucracy and professions in traditional public administration[2]

[2] Figs. 9.5–9.7 are based on an idea in Richards (1992).

the professional domain (including in the relations with service beneficiaries such as patients).

Bureaucracy and professions in public resource management

From the 1960s, but especially in the mid-1970s, a number of factors undermined this traditional model. Long-held criticisms of UK central administration, not least the lack of coordination in public expenditure planning and control, and campaigns for more rational strategic planning, decision-making, and policy evaluation were exemplified in the Fulton Committee on the Civil Service (Cmnd. 3638, 1968). This was a time of interest by both politicians and administrators in introducing more rational criteria into the allocation of expenditures. These interests were given political momentum by the election of Edward Heath's government in 1970, whose commitment to rational management in government led to the introduction of reforms such as a think tank, the Central Policy Review Staff (CPRS), designed to assist the Cabinet's strategic thinking. In local government there were also attempts to coordinate and integrate local authorities via systems of corporate management, and the creation of policy and resource committees to develop council strategies, while in the health service planning systems also became fashionable.

By the middle of the decade, however, attention shifted sharply in response to a public expenditure crisis. The Treasury's view was that generalist administrators and professionals alike left financial management to others; as a consequence the use and consumption of resources was neglected. The solution was not some complex planning system but rather firm financial *control*. As a result, systems of cash limits introduced from 1976 were followed, after the election of the Conservatives in 1979, by efficiency reviews, financial management initiatives, and resource management regimes. Hence it can be argued that from the mid-1970s resource management replaced traditional public administration, with a consequent shift in the relationships between politicians and professional groups (see Fig. 9.6).

The characteristics of this model clearly vary between and within areas (civil service, local government, health services), but the overall logic of the reforms was undoubtedly to effect a change in the political control of public services. Politicians sought to extend command into professional domains by empowering the administrators (now

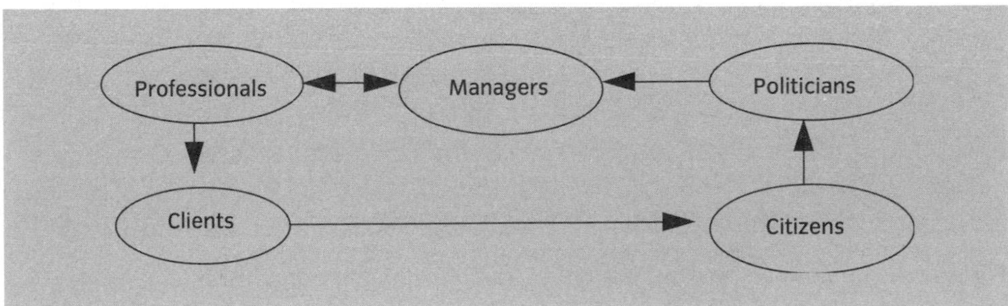

Figure 9.6 Bureaucracy and professions in public resource management

managers) to introduce more line management into their relations with professionals. In some professionalized services such as police and social work this proved possible within the existing structures (in some local authorities, for example, generalist managers became directors of social services and social workers took on management responsibilities in area teams). In health and higher education, however, this proved more difficult and gave rise to the development of parallel structures: general management in health, and a structure of planning, resource, and other committees to bypass the senate–faculty–department professional authority in universities.

The emphasis on resource management shared with traditional public administration a set of value-free arrangements for delivering public services. Resource management, however, was seen as appropriate to the more complex economic and social environment. It emphasized economy, efficiency, and effectiveness, delegated financial management, decentralized personnel management systems and a strengthening of audit (through the National Audit Office and Audit Commission). The first of these strategies was established in 1979 with the Prime Minister's Efficiency Unit and its oversight of departmental efficiency reviews (still called Rayner scrutinies after the first efficiency adviser, Derek Rayner, the Chief Executive of Marks & Spencer plc). Rayner's ambition was not just to make savings. His wider brief was to initiate a cultural change amongst administrators where management in general and resource management in particular would become seen as a valued activity, if not part of the golden road to the top. His schema was later transferred to the NHS and higher education, and spawned an altogether more ambitious programme known as the Financial Management Initiative (FMI). Driven by the logic of management accounting, the FMI was a reform programme that set out to make managers at all levels (the word 'managers' was deliberately used in its publicity) accountable for the resources they used, and to develop and install systems through which performance could be measured. In giving managers devolved budgets and operational targets, the new accountable management sought on the one hand to install greater control and accountability over resource use and on the other to liberate entrepreneurialism.

These changes also introduced a new system of decentralized and results-driven personnel management. Traditional public administration was organized as a career service, with rewards tied to the position of individuals on hierarchical grading structures linked to incremental pay spines. For professionals, advancement was generally on the basis of criteria elaborated and even applied directly by professional peer groups. Any resulting distortions of the pay bill (e.g. as a result of high numbers of merit awards for hospital consultants) would have to be accommodated. The world of accountable management, however, ushered in different possibilities, including a link between reward and performance (as measured by meeting targets) and the local setting of pay and conditions.

Practitioners responded with varying degrees of enthusiasm. If some were sceptical, others, including some professionals, had no difficulty adapting (such as veterinary surgeons, who had experienced such regimes in private practice). Most public service professions, however, found themselves having to reconcile their traditional communion relations with an encroaching command regime and increasingly significant contractual implications.

If in terms of its effects on Whitehall the FMI was only a limited success, the influence of the philosophy that drove it was considerable. Forms of accountable management quickly spread throughout the public sector. In education, healthcare, police, and social work, budgets were delegated, targets set, and professionals designated as 'managers' with responsibilities for delivering activities and services within them. More importantly, these changes made a change in the discourse of administration and professional life inevitable, with the language of financial management colonizing that of administrative and professional groups.

Bureaucracy and professions in the mixed economy of public services

For many reformers at the time these consequences did not reach far enough. The Conservative government, supported by protagonists of free-market economics, was committed to raising the status and profile of management (and a concept of business-style management at that) as a valued activity in its own right. This determination provided the political impetus to drive through more fundamental reforms that embraced privatization and competition, deregulation, and a commitment to customers. Above all, it entailed a subjection of the private world of public service professional monopolies to competition, however that could be contrived. Thus structural reforms sought to institutionalize the separation of service provision from political decision-making, the creation of commissioning mechanisms and competition, and consumer-focused initiatives to orient services outwards to their clients as well as, in certain circumstances, empowering customers themselves. These aims were often entwined rather than separate, but they also found practical expression in a series of reform initiatives that have affected social policy throughout central and local government and the NHS.

The New Labour governments since 1997 have strikingly altered the context of these new arrangements by investing considerably more financial resources than their predecessors and explicitly dissociating themselves from the Conservatives' antipathy to the public sector. They have also removed the apparatus of internal markets and compulsory competitive tendering. However, their actions have in most respects reinforced the mixed economy of public service provision. Guided by a pragmatic doctrine ('what matters is what works') the governments have renewed commitments to schemes such as the Private Finance Initiative (PFI, but formally renamed as Public Private Partnerships), under which private capital is used to build social facilities such as hospitals, schools, and prisons, strengthened the performance regime under which services are increasingly obliged to meet government set targets in return for resources ('earned autonomy'), and increasingly relaxed prohibitions on using private organizations as agents of government.[3] Foundation Hospitals are a clear example of the government's thrust. In return for evidence of past adherence to government targets, they will be granted greater financial and operational freedoms. Supporters of the idea claim the hospitals will act as centres of excellence and innovation; opponents, including at least one former Secretary of State for Health under Mr Blair's first government, argue that they will create a two-tier health service.

[3] You might, as a little research project, find out the government services provided under licence, for example, Capita plc or an American company called EDS.

So what are the main developments in this mixed economy of public services? In structural terms there have been two, perhaps contradictory, developments. The first has been the creation of executive agencies to provide discrete services within central government departments. Within five years of the Efficiency Unit report (1988) that launched the reform, over four-fifths of the home civil service was converted to agency form, a considerable organizational achievement. Headed by chief executives on short-term contracts and performance-related reward systems, these agencies were intended (*pace* the Prison Service and the Child Support Agency) to be run at arm's length from ministers under quasi-contractual framework documents of operational targets and budgets agreed with departments and the Treasury. Many, especially those in health and safety or research and development, are essentially professional services. Others depend on considerable professional inputs (not least the Meat Hygiene Service!).

An extensive structural change in the other direction, and one very much associated with New Labour, has been the development of joined-up government. This seeks to counter the fragmentation of services that accompanies the provision of often discrete activities (including by the agencies described above) by creating, obliging, or encouraging the development of delivery arrangements that seek to integrate different facets of care to the public either as individuals or communities. Primary Care Trusts (PCTs), for example, are new statutory bodies that provide primary and community health and social care and also commission acute health services for their communities. Their executive committees include doctors, nurses, health visitors, social workers, and lay persons to bring an integrating purpose to their activities. Sure Start is a central government-sponsored service that brings together in designated geographical deprived areas education, social services, health, and housing to ensure that pre-school children are not disadvantaged when they reach school age.

This emphasis on the service for those who receive it is also reflected in what is now known as Service First. Launched by the Conservatives in 1991 as the Citizen's Charter (Cm. 1599, 1991), its aim has been to oblige public service monopolies to attend more directly to the needs of their service consumers. Under the scheme, charter marks are awarded to organizations as recognition of the quality of service they provide.[4] New Labour has also reinforced this quality thrust by developing an extensive (its critics call it 'Stalinist') regime under which it publishes league tables of the performance of schools, social service departments, and hospitals. And the privatized utilities are subject to government regulation that sets the framework of service quality and prices in industries such as energy and telecommunications.

These changes are prominent parts of today's public management in which policy and management are seen as distinct and separate activities, there is a corresponding new internal managerial environment where managers are given freedoms within pre-set frameworks and held accountable against agreed targets, and new organizational arrangements are designed to facilitate employees' identification with their organizational purposes, a concern with quality and customer needs. This is a new order of decentralized management within an overall system of central control. For its supporters it

[4] Details of the scheme and the awards made can be found on the Cabinet Office website.

offers scope for the liberation of organizational energy, encouraging local initiative and entrepreneurship and enhancing greater customer or client awareness. It provides a complex overlap and set of interactions between the political, professional, managerial, and customer environments and spheres of responsibility. This in turn has led to new sources of legitimation in service delivery, and to new sets of relationships between politicians, providers, and authorizers.

Perhaps most significant in these relationships is the way the managers have derived (initially at least unintended) power and influence from their pivotal position at the interface of the participants, both representing and communicating with them. Moreover, further government reforms, most notably the recent delegation to health trust chief executives of the responsibility for clinical governance, have become more interventionist in professional areas. It is also noticeable how the client and citizen have become fused with the customer, each with sets of distinctive rights which makes it difficult for traditional professional–client relationships to be maintained (see Gray and Jenkins 2002). It is thus not an exaggeration to describe all this as a transformation of the public sector.

Figure 9.7 represents the consequent profoundly different interactions of the political, professional, and managerial worlds. It is a world not only considerably removed from that of traditional public administration (Fig. 9.5) but also from the simple model offered by market theorists. In this a number of characteristics are clear. First, the professional nature of many public services is often seen in a wholly negative light or as something that needs to be controlled or managed by enhancing the contractual nature of relationships and diminishing the force of communion. Second, any form of decentralization or empowerment changes the nature of power and politics in the system. The consequences depend on the sources of advantage and disadvantage within the new regime. If it is managers who have gained most influence in this new regime, the reasons are not hard to determine. They arise from the centrality of contract and the managers' ability to act

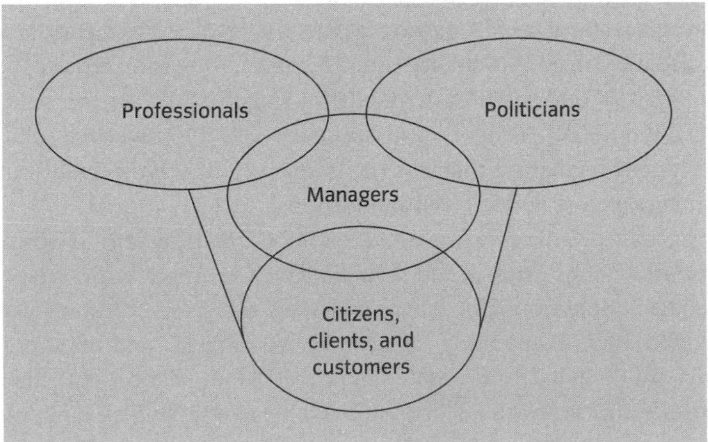

Figure 9.7 Bureaucracy and professionals in today's mixed economy of public management

as brokers to it. Politicians and professionals still wish to maintain some discreteness to their domains; they prefer to deal with each other and the (paying) customers through intermediaries. This is reinforced by the development of contracting as the managers' stock in trade, to the relative disadvantage of other parties.

THE GOVERNANCE OF PROFESSIONS AND BUREAUCRACY: COMMAND, COMMUNION, AND CONTRACT

How have the public sector reforms described in the previous section affected the bureaucratic characteristics of public service organizations and the professions which work through them? The remaining task of this chapter is to provide an answer to this question.

We have conceptualized bureaucracy as characterized by formal jurisdictional areas of function, hierarchy of authority, rules for governing decisions and activities, records of transactions conducted under these rules, dedicated training to assist performance, and the commitment to the organization of members' full working capacities. These characteristics were defined as associated with a command mode of governance. Professionals have been conceptualized as distinguished by their specialist knowledge and expertise, their position (or autonomy) in relation to clients and employing organizations, and their ethos (i.e. the values which vocation demands are to be promoted for the benefit of the profession and its clients). These characteristics were seen as associated with a communion mode of governance.

Both 'models' of bureaucracy and profession are ideal types, i.e. abstractions belonging to the world of ideas rather than expressions of actual organizations. However, the previous section suggests that in traditional public administration the distinctiveness of the domains of bureaucracy and professional meant that the elements of each ideal type were likely to be visible in actual organizational contexts, and that the association of bureaucracy with command and profession with communion was empirically observable.

But what of the effects of the public sector reforms since 1970 on bureaucracy and profession? We suggest that the bureaucratic character of public organizations has been moderated by the extension of discretion in the management of service delivery (e.g. by more freedom to allocate resources and choose alternative forms of service provision), but that this discretion has been governed increasingly by more formal contractual arrangements encompassing both service and financial targets. Thus jurisdictions are a little less rigid, hierarchies a little flatter, and regulations have shifted their emphases. Interestingly, at least two traditional professional groups—accountants and lawyers—have found their positions within public organizations significantly enhanced as the managers of these contractual regimes.

At the same time, the reforms have brought an increase in the bureaucratic tendencies of public service professions. Specialist knowledge, for example, is increasingly determined by the context of practice. This was always true for some professions that grew up indigenously with the welfare state (including social work), but now others, including teachers and accountants, find that the elements of their expertise are defined not only through their organizational situation but often by it. One professional response to this trend has been for professional associations to increase the extent to which acceptable professional practices are elaborated in formal statements (e.g. codes of ethics) which can guide the conduct of members in the new contractual and regulated regimes (see Banks 1995; 1998).

Similarly, professional position and ethos have been affected. If in more traditional models of professional practice (e.g. health) the autonomy from employing organizations was regarded as extensive, nowadays professionals have to reconcile their professional judgements increasingly with the organization's priorities. Thus in a famous televised case, a hospital chief executive (now managing London Underground) warned that clinical consultants who continued to disregard the directions of their clinical director 'would feel the organization's full force' (Channel 4 1993). As we saw earlier, such challenges to professional position have met some restatement of a professional ethos endorsing professional values against the developing power of managers. In the Durham study of local authorities (Gray et al. 1999) there was a tendency for social workers and others to express a reinvigorated professional ethos against the 'men in grey suits'. However, some had clearly accommodated the new order with a professional vocation: '[my profession provides] a challenging position in an agency constantly in the 'eye' of the public' (social worker)—a fact recognized by at least one councillor:

> I see local government officers as having a more independent and impartial role than colleagues in private practice; making decisions on behalf of the community, i.e. quality of life, needs the highest level of professional/democratic partnership. Maybe the local authority has and needs a special kind of professional.

These changes to bureaucracy and professions suggests that the intensification of contract arrangements has weakened both the command mode of governance of traditional bureaucracy and the communion mode of traditional professionalism. Instead, interactions in the new mixed economy of the public service delivery have been governed increasingly by a **contract mode of governance**. Here relationships are effected through an inducement–contribution exchange agreed by both parties, often today reflected in performance targets. Legitimacy for actions under such a mode lies within the terms of the agreed exchange, i.e. the contract or target, or at least its interpretations. The strengths of contract lie not only in the predetermined life of the contract but, more significantly, in the motivation to perform to contract and target expectation (in order to gain the rewards) and the consequent high probabilities that planning assumptions will be acted on. Weaknesses can be traced both to the reductionist tendency of contracts and targets (see Box 9.2), i.e. in the absence of other inducements the parties will limit their actions to those explicitly elaborated in the target, and to the difficulty in the face of changing circumstances in effecting alterations to specification without undue cost. Such weaknesses can be seen in the way teachers have been reducing their commitments to those essential to the classroom, doctors in general practice are withdrawing from the provision of out-of-hours services, and hospital consultants have been unwilling in their negotiations of new national contracts with the NHS (2002–3) to commit themselves to anything other than core medical care as they define it.

ARE THE REINVENTED PROFESSIONS THE WORST OF DEVILS?

In practice, public service management inherently relies on combinations of all three modes of governance. But the balance has altered without much chance of a return to the old order, for good or ill. This would imply a definitive change in the role of public service professionals, even their reinvention in the new contract state. What can we conclude on the relations of professionals and bureaucracy in the present context of public policy?

First, to recapitulate, there has been a shifting emphasis in the modes of professional relations with public service delivery, from differentiated command and communion to more integrative contract. The increasing emphasis on contract as the basis of organizational relationships (purchasers and providers, departments and agencies) is affecting not only the macro relationships of professional organizations with other agencies in the service supply chain but even relationships within organizations (e.g. the development of performance regimes in local authorities, hospitals and universities). The consequent increase in the transaction and opportunity costs of managing such service relationships has led to expressions of considerable professional resentment. But more significant perhaps is the implicit shift in the basis for service rationing and related choices ('is it in the contract?'), the drawing of accountability away from general notions of conduct to explicit terms and conditions which accounts must address, and the professions' tendency to generate more codes of ethics, rather than concentrate on providing the conditions for ethical behaviour.

Second, within this general shift, the reforms have met with differentiated rather than uniform responses in the professionalized public services. Logically, there are distinctions to be drawn both between the different services and between different practitioners within the same profession. How and why these distinctions arise (including why some leave the service and why some stay) is still not properly understood.

Third, the public service professions are increasingly fragmented. Some public service professions have traditionally been characterized by differentiated internal organization (e.g. specialties in medicine and their institutionalization in the Royal Colleges) and have found the reforms reinforcing this. Others appear to have reached a desired integration, only to find that the transition from public administration to today's public management has undermined it (from social work to child protection, community care, etc., each with different levels of self-regulation).

Fourth, some reforms, notably the increase in external audit and evaluation, have brought a shift from opaque to transparent professional work. Perhaps combined with the decline of a deferential culture in today's society, there is a notable questioning of the value of the professional contribution and more access to the answers. Schoolteaching seems particularly to have been affected by this, with even public statements in the recent past by Ofsted (the Office for Standards in Education) on the numbers of unsatisfactory practitioners. Similarly, the transformation of the Commission for Health Improvement, already an agency responsible for the very public inspection of the clinical governance of health trusts, into the Commission for Health Audit and Inspection will put clinical as well as managerial practices even more in the public spotlight from 2004.

Fifth, some de-skilling is in train. The contract and framework regimes are reinforced by increasingly detailed professional and management protocols. In some areas, including health and social services, the effect is to narrow the areas of professional discretion, with the result that non-professionals may be employed at the margins of hitherto professional work. This may not universally lead to a proletarianization of professional work, but it challenges professional hegemony. Thus we observe reluctance by some hospital doctors to see nurses take on clinical work such as prescribing or minor surgery, by police to the role of community wardens, or by paramedics to firefighters taking on more of their role.

Sixth, professionals have reacted to the reforms with different degrees of engagement with the management process. At one extreme are those who have sought to maintain a segregation of their activities from those of management. Thus a sensitive complaint of clinical directors in heath trusts can be that they become more managerial than clinical. But even in medicine, perhaps the most reluctant profession to embrace the management process, there are those who argue that the management of resources and activities is an extension of professional vocation, and who are actively engaging, for example, in the new Primary Care Trusts. And other professionalized services, notably those based in local government, have clearly taken or been obliged to take this view.

Seventh, some of the reforms, notably the development of service charters, have brought more attention to service processing at the expense—certainly as measured by effort if not by quality—of service content and substance. Entering some district general hospitals, for example, one is bombarded with phosphorous electronic screens informing you how many accident and emergency patients were triaged within five minutes of reception, the average wait in the fracture outpatient clinic, and so on. Perhaps the exception is policing, in which the emphasis on targeting crime patterns appears to have changed the substance of detection, but only at the expense of more public complaints about lack of police attention to reported minor offences. However, even here this may force police authorities to focus more on clear-up rates rather than on the general enhancement of pubic security.

Finally, but only in the context of this list, the professions' responses display characteristics both of strategic choices and of contingent responses to strategic imperatives. We would have thought that in 1979 Ladbroke's would have given short odds for social work being at the top of the incoming Conservative Government's hit-list of public service professions. Yet it took at least a decade and a half before social work found itself threatened. Indeed, parts such as child protection managed to secure at least some moral high ground despite continuing public concern with child abuse cases, a concern that may yet, in the aftermath of the Climbié case set out in our introduction, undermine the profession. Nevertheless, social work has shown and may continue to show adaptive behaviour, responding where it must and influencing its environment where it can. Schoolteaching, on the other hand, has responded to each assault (regardless of merit) as though it were a pay and conditions issue, and through this failure to distinguish between imperative and choice has forfeited much of the professional discretion it enjoyed formerly.

These conclusions seem to raise even more questions than they provide answers. You may like to consider at least the following as you continue your reading of this text and other studies:

- Are professions reacting differently to these changes depending on their relationships with different client groups (e.g. individual members of public compared to a local authority as client)?
- Is the problem in the professional–bureaucrat relationship one of maximizing effectiveness and efficacy versus efficiency?
- Are professionals inevitably being drawn into managerial and bureaucratic roles by the commissioner–provider split (e.g. by the need to market themselves or otherwise engage with those who commission their services)?
- Can bureau managers be professional as well as professionals managerial?
- Is it inevitable that, if professionals wish to succeed to the strategic and most senior positions, they will have to cease practising as professionals (in which they may still be needed) in order to become managers?

We need to know much more about current developments before we can answer these questions fully. However, in the new order we may certainly identify members of professions as managers, as marketers, and as entrepreneurs as well as practising providers. These roles undoubtedly fuse rather than keep separate the elements of the state (after Socrates), but do they threaten the public weal? We note that in the increasingly contractual nature of relationships between the professionals and their services there has been a diminution of traditionally espoused (even if rarely realized) values such as equity of treatment and public accountability. Indeed, insofar as the public management reforms have produced a struggle between the reformers and the professions, there is a sense in which the 'public' in public services is often forgotten in a rush to impose or resist 'good business practice'. In this sense Socrates has a point.

REFERENCES

Baker, R. (2001), *Harold Shipman's Clinical Practice 1974–1998: A Clinical Audit Commissioned by the Chief Medical Officer*. London: Department of Health.

Banks, S. J. (1995), *Ethics and Values in Social Work*. Basingstoke: Macmillan.

—— (1998), 'Codes of ethics and ethical conduct: a view from the caring professions', *Public Money and Management* 18(1): 27–30.

Beetham, D. (1996), *Bureaucracy*. Buckingham: Open University Press.

Channel 4 (1993), *Operation Hospital*.

Cm. 1599 (1991), *The Citizen's Charter: Raising the Standard*. London: HMSO.

Cm. 5207 (2001), *Learning from Bristol: The Report of the Public Inquiry into Children's Heart Surgery at the Bristol Royal Infirmary 1984–1995*. London: Stationery Office.

Cm. 5730 (2003), *The Victoria Climbié Inquiry* (Chairman Lord Laming). London: Stationery Office.

Cmnd. 3638 (1968), *Report of the Committee on the Civil Service* (Chairman Lord Fulton). London: HMSO.

Department of Health (2001), *Report of the Royal Liverpool Children's Inquiry*. London: Stationery Office.

Du Gay, P. (1999), *In Praise of Bureaucracy*. Buckingham: Open University Press.

Efficiency Unit (1988), *Improving Management in Government: The Next Steps*. London: HMSO.

Etzioni, A. (1969), *The Semi-Professionals and their Organization*. New York: Free Press.

Exworthy, M. and Halford, S. (eds.) (1999), *Professionals and the New Managerialism in the Public Sector*. Buckingham: Open University Press.

Flynn, N. (2001), *Public Sector Management*, 4th edn. Hemel Hempstead: Prentice-Hall.

Freidson, E. (1994), *Professionalism Reborn: Theory, Prophecy and Policy*. Chicago: University of Chicago Press.

Gray, A. G., Banks, S. J., Carpenter, J. W. S., Green, E., and May, T. (1999), *Professionalism and the Management of Local Authorities*. London: Improvement and Development Agency.

—— and Jenkins, W. I. (2002), 'Government and administration: reasserting public services and their consumers', *Parliamentary Affairs* 55(2): 235–53.

Greenwood, E. (1957), 'Attributes of a profession', *Social Work* 2(3): 44–55.

Griffiths, R. (1983), *NHS Management Inquiry*. London: Department of Health and Social Security.

Horton, S. and Farnhan, D. (1999), *Public Management in Britain*. London: Macmillan.

Jaques, E. (1990), 'In praise of hierarchy', *Harvard Business Review* (Jan.–Feb.): 127–33; repr. in G. Thompson, J. Frances, R. Levacic, and J. Mitchell (eds.), *Markets, Hierarchies and Networks*. London: Sage, 1991.

Mintzberg, H. (1979), *The Structuring of Organizations*. Hemel Hempstead: Prentice-Hall.

Plato (*c*.380 BC), *The Republic*, trans. with an introduction by H. D. P. Lee. Harmondsworth: Penguin, 1955.

Rhodes, R. A. W. (1997), *Understanding Governance: Policy Networks, Governance, Reflexivity and Accountability*. Buckingham: Open University Press.

Richards, S. (1992), *Who Defines the Public Good? The Consumer Paradigm in Public Management*. London: Public Management Foundation.

Wilson, D. and Game, C. (2002), *Local Government in the United Kingdom*, 3rd edn. London: Macmillan.

FURTHER READING

For further discussion of bureaucracy a good general text is Beetham (1996) while a reappraisal of bureaucracy in the UK context is Du Gay (1999). Remember that it is always useful to go back to original sources such as Weber (plenty of edited collections include extracts of his writings). For further discussion of professionals in the context of public service see Exworthy and Halford (1999), and Banks (1995). An excellent general review of professions, including in relation to social policy, is Freidson (1994) but it is written in the context of the USA and is not an easy read. For general accounts of public service reforms in the UK see Flynn (2001), Horton & Farnham (1999) and in local government see Wilson & Game (2002).

GLOSSARY

bureaucracy An abstract organizational form characterized by formal jurisdictional areas of function, hierarchy of authority, rules for governing decisions and activities, records of transactions conducted under these rules, dedicated training to assist performance, and the commitment to the organization of members' full working capacities.

command mode of governance Interactions and relationships regulated through the rule of law emanating from a sovereign body and delivered through a scalar chain of superior and subordinate authority, with legitimacy for public service decisions and behaviours defined by the bounds prescribed through due process by the institutions charged with the provision.

communion mode of governance Interactions and relationships regulated through a set of shared values and creeds under which legitimacy for service actions is defined by their consistency with the understandings, protocols, and guiding values of the group's shared frame of reference or way of interpreting and managing the world.

contract mode of governance Interactions and relationships regulated through an inducement–contribution exchange agreed by both parties. Legitimacy for actions under such a mode lies within the terms of the agreed exchange, i.e. the contract, or at least its interpretations.

profession Occupational groups distinguished by their specialist knowledge and expertise, their position (or autonomy) in relation to clients and employing organizations, and ethos (i.e. the values which vocation demands are to be promoted for the benefit of the profession and its clients).

10

Public Expenditure Decision-Making

John Baldock, Andrew Gray, and Bill Jenkins

CONTENTS

INTRODUCTION: AN OUTLINE OF PUBLIC EXPENDITURE DECISION-MAKING IN BRITAIN

We believe the Treasury has become more powerful in two significant respects in recent years. Firstly, its influence over the strategic direction of the government has grown. The Treasury's role in leading the welfare reform programme and introducing stakeholder pensions and tax credits has led to the Treasury taking a greater role in social security policy. Secondly, Public Service Agreements have substantially increased the Treasury's influence over the affairs of spending departments. (House of Commons Treasury committee Third Report para.19, HC 73.1, 2001)

Public expenditure may appear both esoteric and complex, best left to economists and those few politicians who understand it. On the contrary. As citizens we subscribe to public expenditure when we pay income tax, buy a drink in a pub (paying value added tax (VAT) and excise duty), or fill up with petrol (petrol tax as well as VAT). We are affected as recipients when we attend school, use a university library, or visit a doctor. More specifically, most welfare and social programmes depend on public financial support, with government either acting directly as provider or perhaps indirectly as purchaser of services on behalf of its citizens. These factors, and its growth and scale in recent times, have made it difficult to separate public expenditure from the role of the state. Debates over public spending thus focus on the scope of governmental activity, the management of the economy, and the range and impact of taxing and spending powers.

In Chapter 1 of this book we defined social policies as the intentions and activities of governments that are broadly social in their nature. We suggested that these social intentions are of three main kinds: the redistribution of resources, usually services or cash, to meet identified needs; the management of at least some of the risks to which citizens are exposed; and the prevention or reduction of forms of social exclusion. Fulfilling these social intentions generally involves spending large amounts of money. The ways in which governments decide how much to spend, and how they control and manage that expenditure, is the central focus of this chapter.

What makes the processes of public expenditure decision-making particularly important to an understanding of social policy is that decisions about how much to spend can rarely be separated from decisions on what it should be spent on. In other words, public expenditure decisions are also policy decisions. They reveal the intentions and priorities of governments in the very basic sense of how much they are prepared to spend on those intentions and priorities. The range and types of service provided by governments have, of course, changed over time, influenced by factors such as shifting emphases on **individualism** and **collectivism**, changing needs (e.g. of an ageing population), or new ways of delivering services (e.g. information technology).

The role of the Treasury

In the United Kingdom, primary responsibility for the management of public expenditure rests with the Chancellor of the Exchequer and the Treasury. Both have a long history in managing the finances of the state. In medieval times the Exchequer was the office within which the king's treasurer guarded and accounted for the royal revenue. The exchequer was literally a chequerboard, used by the treasurer to audit the accounts of local sheriffs who collected and spent money on behalf of the Crown. In 1833 parliament passed legislation formally creating the Treasury as a ministerial department under the Chancellor of the Exchequer.

While it is Parliament that must vote annually to approve the expenditure of governments, it remains a principle that ministries can only make payments that have been authorized by the Treasury. The process by which this authorization is negotiated is called the spending round, and the announcements of the results of this process are key points in the social policy calendar. To some extent this process remains an annual one. The round begins each November when the Chancellor gives a pre-Budget report designed to raise some of the key issues to be addressed in the budget of the following spring. Politically important changes may be signalled at this point. In 2001 the Chancellor of the Exchequer, Gordon Brown, announced substantial increases in spending plans for the NHS. In the spring, usually late March or early April, the Chancellor announces the budget. This is essentially about the income side of public spending plans: the taxes that will be levied and borrowing required to pay for them. Between the spring budget and the summer, negotiations take place between the Treasury and the spending ministries over their allocations and these are generally announced in July. However, since 1998 the more significant announcements have been those of the **Comprehensive Spending Reviews**, which set spending plans for the next three years, and the annual round has become less important. Instead, in 1998, 2000, and 2002 announcements were made of spending plans for the subsequent three years, including an overlap with the last year of the previous plan.

The comprehensive spending reviews

This new approach sought to break with the old culture of annual spending rounds. Departments are given three-year budgets. This is intended to set a longer-term horizon for planning, re-prioritization, and investment in reformed ways of delivering services. The weakness of the system of the annual spending rounds that had existed since the early 1960s was that it had led to:

> an annual cycle of year-on-year incremental bids by departments; settlements reached by bargaining over inputs rather than analysis of outputs and efficiency; excessive departmentalism; a split between public and private provision; and a bias towards consumption today rather than investment in our future. (Cm. 3978 2001: 3)

Under the system of three-year plans, current and capital spending are disentangled:

> a key part of this approach is the two strict fiscal rules, first proposed in the Government's election Manifesto, that will govern policy over the course of this Parliament:
>
> - the golden rule: over the economic cycle, the Government will borrow only to invest and not to fund current spending;
> - and the sustainable investment rule: net public debt as a proportion of GDP will be held over the economic cycle at a stable and prudent level. (Cm. 3978 2001: 3)

Under the new system, decisions about spending are linked to defined outputs and to investments that will improve the efficiency or quality of services. Departments are set, after negotiation, targets for efficiency and performance that they are expected to meet and upon which the release of further funding is in principle dependent. These are the Public Service Agreements (see Boxes 10.1 and 10.2) and they are the central instrument in a substantial system of audit and inspection to which central and local government departments have become subject in recent years. In addition to the Treasury's own assessments of how well PSA targets are being met, the public services are now regularly examined by, amongst others, the National Audit Office, the Audit Commission, the Health Inspectorate, the Social Services Inspectorate, a range of inspectorates for different parts of the criminal justice system (for each of the police, prisons, probation service,

Box 10.1 Public Service Agreements

Public Service Agreements were introduced following the 1998 Comprehensive Spending Review. They are published documents which are agreements between the Treasury and spending departments. They set out the broad objectives of the policies of the departments and specific targets that will be delivered over the next three years. Progress in meeting these targets is monitored and reported in annual departmental reports. For example, the 2002 Spending Review PSA White Paper sets out around 130 outcome-focused commitments together with the government's priorities and its strategic agenda for public services for the three years 2003–6. PSAs are supported by more detailed Service Delivery Agreements, which explain how the departments will reach the targets. 'Technical Notes' explain the data sources against which PSA targets will be measured, and are published on departmental websites. Details of PSAs can be found at www.hm-treasury.gov.uk/Spending_Review

magistrates' courts, and crown prosecution service), the Office for Standards in Education, and the Housing Inspectorate, which is located within the Audit Commission. Although the use of inspectorates and auditors goes back to Victorian times (the first HM Inspector of Schools was appointed in 1840), most of those in the list above have been created since the election of the Labour government in 1997. Their growing importance, and particularly their use to test whether government departments are meeting specific targets, is captured by the concept of an 'audit society' in which public servants focus on meeting defined targets rather than simply interpreting policies in terms of their professional standards.

As the quotation at the beginning of this chapter shows, there is some concern amongst politicians and academics as to whether the Treasury is using performance targets to become too involved in the detail of government. The same inquiry by the House of Commons Treasury Committee reported:

> Several witnesses warned of the dangers of the Treasury exerting too much influence over policy-making. Sir Alan Bailey wrote that the Treasury's concern for ensuring that public expenditure achieves value for money could lead to 'detailed second-guessing of each department on all its systems and policies, which clogs departmental discretion and blurs the accountability of spending Ministers'. Sir Michael Partridge thought that the Treasury's involvement in detailed policy making could make the department less effective at undertaking its core work on financial management and the control of public expenditure and would also take responsibility away from managers in other departments. Sir Peter Kemp argued that the Treasury was moving 'into a position of power which is dangerous in our society' in which it was acting as judge and jury of a range of policy matters. (HC73-1 2001 para.17)

A counter-argument to this view is that the Treasury's role in negotiating three-year spending plans and clear performance targets is the opposite of close involvement in the detail of government departments. Rather, it is a way of setting out the objectives that should be met and the sums of money that will be available to achieve them, but then

Box 10.2 Public Service Agreement 2003–2006 for the Department of Health

AIM: Transform the health and social care system so that it produces faster, fairer services that deliver better health and tackle health inequalities.

OBJECTIVES AND PERFORMANCE TARGETS

Objective I: improve service standards.

i) Reduce the maximum wait for an outpatient appointment to 3 months and the maximum wait for inpatient treatment to 6 months by the end of 2005, and achieve progressive further cuts with the aim of reducing the maximum inpatient and day case waiting time to 3 months by 2008.
ii) Reduce to four hours the maximum wait in A&E from arrival to admission, transfer or discharge, by the end of 2004; and reduce the proportion waiting over one hour.
iii) Guarantee access to a primary care professional within 24 hours and to a primary care doctor within 48 hours from 2004.
iv) Ensure that by the end of 2005 every hospital appointment will be booked for the convenience of the patient, making it easier for patients and their GPs to choose the hospital and consultant that best meets their needs.
v) Enhance accountability to patients and the public and secure sustained national improvements in patient experience as measured by independently validated national surveys.

Objective II: improve health and social care outcomes for everyone.

vi) Reduce substantially the mortality rates from the major killer diseases by 2010: from heart disease by at least 40 per cent in people under 75; from cancer by at least 20 per cent in people under 75.
vii) Improve life outcomes of adults and children with mental health problems through year on year improvements in access to crisis and CAMHS services, and reduce the mortality rate from suicide and undetermined injury by at least 20 per cent by 2010.
viii) Improve the quality of life and independence of older people so that they can live at home wherever possible, by increasing by March 2006 the number of those supported intensively to live at home to 30 per cent of the total being supported by social services at home or in residential care.
ix) Improve life chances for children, including by: improving the level of education, training and employment outcomes for care leavers aged 19, so that levels for this group are at least 75 per cent of those achieved by all young people in the same area, and at least 15 per cent of children in care attain five good GCSEs by 2004; narrowing the gap between the proportions of children in care and their peers who are cautioned or convicted: and reducing the under-18 conception rate by 50 per cent by 2010.
x) Increase the participation of problem drug users in drug treatment programmes by 55 per cent by 2004 and by 100 per cent by 2008, and increase year on year the proportion of users successfully sustaining or completing treatment programmes.

xi) By 2010 reduce inequalities in health outcomes by 10 per cent as measured by infant mortality and life expectancy at birth

Value for Money

xii) Value for money in the NHS and personal social services will improve by at least 2 per cent per annum, with annual improvements of 1 per cent in both cost efficiency and service effectiveness.

WHO IS RESPONSIBLE FOR DELIVERY?

The Secretary of State for Health is responsible for the delivery of the targets set out in this PSA.

Public Service Agreements White Paper, (Cm. 5571), The Stationary Office 2002.

allowing a substantial period of defined funding within which the ministers and departments are able to deliver the policies in the ways they think best.

THE SIGNIFICANCE OF PUBLIC EXPENDITURE

Decisions about public spending on social policy account for some 25 per cent of UK GNP (see Fig. 1.1 in Chapter 1) and even more substantial proportions of the economies of other European Union nations. These decisions are essentially political, and reflect the priorities of the politicians in power at the time. However, they are much more than decisions about how much should be spent on particular social objectives. Four main kinds of judgement are involved:

- *Allocation.* While it is impossible for governments to raise the overall level of public expenditure faster than the growth of the economy without either increasing borrowing or taxes, they do have discretion over the allocation between policy areas. This is why increased expenditure in a politically sensitive area, such as health, may be accompanied by reductions in less popular or noticed areas such as local government services.
- *Control.* It is much more difficult to contain or reduce public expenditure than it is to increase it. At key points in the histories of welfare states expenditure has slipped out of control and expanded faster than planned.
- *The balance between consumption and investment.* Public spending on social welfare is necessary to meet the current needs of citizens (expenditure on pensions and income support for example) but it is also an investment in the future productivity of the society (some aspects of education and training and some health care for example) and of public services themselves (new technologies, more modern methods of using public servants). It is both difficult to assess when spending is investment and when it is consumption (a university education, for example), and tempting to sacrifice the future to satisfying present demands.

Box 10.3 Social policy and economic efficiency

It is almost a universal axiom of economics that a government should not intervene in an existing economy unless doing so will produce an efficiency gain or achieve some other goal that is valued above efficiency, such as some criterion of social justice. It follows from this that any proposed state activity, such as a social policy, or even any continuing activity, should be carefully evaluated for its likely costs and outcomes. Included in this evaluation should be some estimate of the **opportunity cost** of the proposed activity. That a social policy achieves its goals is not a sufficient reason to support it. The resources used might have produced even more valued gains in some other area of government policy had they been left to the market to allocate. Economics provides a considerable armoury of concepts and analytical tools that can be used in policy evaluation and it is a source of considerable frustration to economists that these are so rarely or so cavalierly used. For example, Nicholas Barr states firmly:

> The central argument of this book is that the proper place of ideology is in the choice of aims, particularly in the definition of social justice and in its trade-off with economic efficiency; but *once these aims have been agreed* the choice of method should be regarded as a *technical* issue rather than an ideological one.
>
> (Barr 1993: 100, emphasis orginal)

However, anyone with even only a passing interest in the way in which social policies are initiated or changed will know that this simply does not happen. Technical questions, particularly the evaluations of economists, play very little part in the political processes that change social policy. One reason is to be found in the quotation above. Barr speaks of 'once these aims have been agreed'. Unfortunately, they never are. There are always competing definitions of 'social justice and its trade-off with economic efficiency'.

- *Efficiency*. Expenditure by the state is often, though not always, expenditure forgone by the taxpayer. It may be that the taxpayer would have spent the money in a way that added more to social welfare than the choice the state is making. The overall effect of public expenditure on the efficiency of an economy is hard to judge (see Box 10.3), but it is critical to the longer-term growth of the economy and the welfare of citizens. Economic criteria involve questions of **market failure** and **opportunity cost**, as well as the provision of **public goods** (such as defence and police) and the management of **externalities** (pollution).

WHAT IS PUBLIC EXPENDITURE?

Public expenditure is the result of money raised by the state to further its objectives. In any country, however, public spending hides a complex history of values and commitments shaped by political ideology, economic theory, interest group pressure, and changing political and social forces.

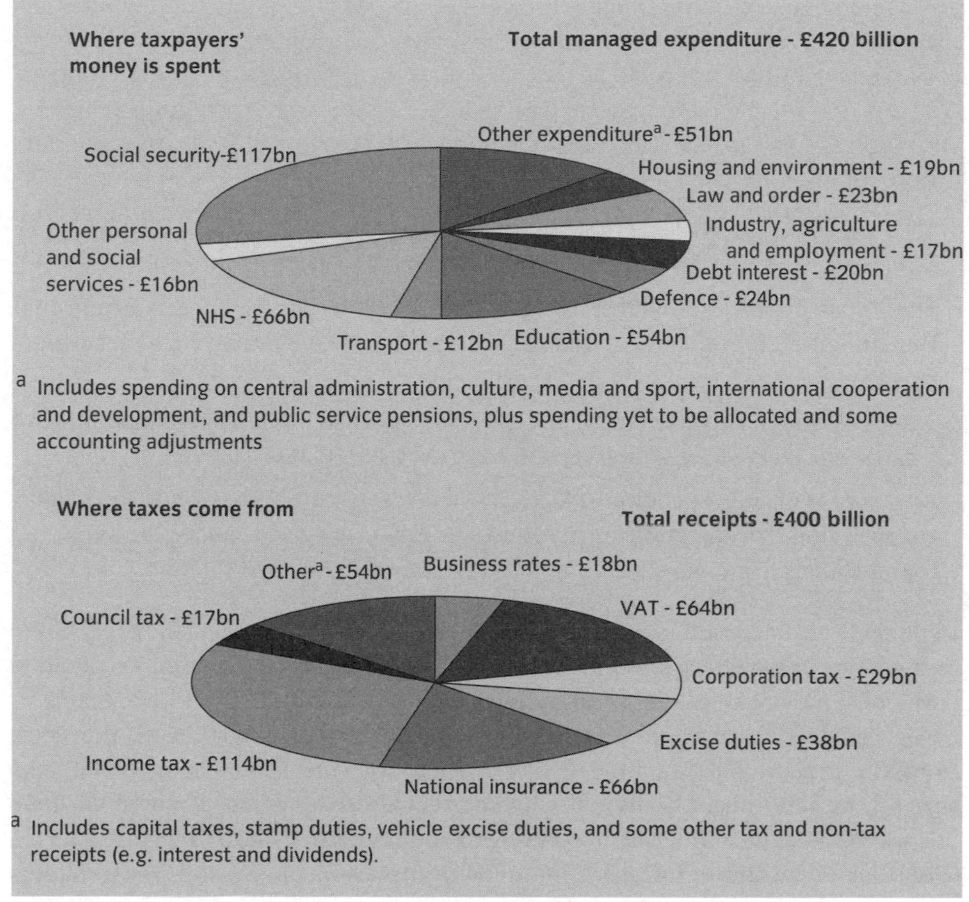

Figure 10.1 Total Managed Expenditure and total receipts, 2004–5

Source: HM Treasury, 2002–3 figures.

Where does the money come from and where does it go? Fig. 10.1 shows the variety of sources of UK public expenditure expected in 2004–5 and its planned application to services. Note the relatively low proportion that income tax constitutes of total revenue, the massive nature of the expenditure sums involved, and the dominance in these of social security, the NHS, and education as well as the cumulative debt interest. Perhaps more important, however, is how and why these spending totals have changed and on the revenue side, how the 'burden' of taxation is distributed. First, however, we turn to the problem of defining public expenditure.

It is an unfortunate fact of political life that UK public expenditure can be defined and measured in a variety of different ways (see e.g. Corry 1997c; Likierman 1988; Mullard 1993); significant changes to both definitions and measurements have taken place over time and were, for example, an integral part of Gordon Brown's 1998 reforms (Cm. 3978). As Watson notes, 'most of the definitions of public expenditure are biased, in one way or another, to suit the objectives of those who seek to promote them'. This is because 'public expenditure policy bridges the gap between politics, economics and social policy. It links the government's involvement with social policies with the resource cost of this approach, as well as indicating the wider cost to the economy' (Watson 1997: 41–2). Yet to understand the debates over public expenditure we need to know how the government calculates and presents its accounts and what the important features of these are.

The UK Government's spending plans for 2002–4 and beyond are shown in Table 10.1. The important terms that emerge are:

- The Departmental Expenditure Limit: a sum agreed by the Cabinet in advance for Departmental spending in a particular year (and post-1998 over a three-year period) effectively setting a ceiling on public expenditure.
- Totally Managed Expenditure (TME): the actual planned public expenditure total for a particular year or at least one version of it (see Table 10.2).
- Annually Managed Expenditure (AME): a new category introduced from 1998 to indicate spending that the government considers cannot be given multi-year limits and that is subject to annual review e.g. social security benefits, debt interest.

Two points are important here: first, debates over the actual totals of public expenditure in the UK over time have often involved consideration of Total Managed Expenditure (TME) or some variant of this; second, crucial indicators for successive UK governments have been less the absolute total of public spending but its relation to the Gross Domestic Product (GDP) or the Public Sector Borrowing Requirement (PSBR), the amount the government needs to borrow to balance revenue and expenditure (in 1998 this was retitled **the Public Sector Net Cash Requirement**). Indeed, for many years the PSBR took on an almost totem-like status, with the test of almost all policy initiatives being 'Will it increase the PSBR?' This obsession assumed that the PSBR provided an indication of the fiscal stance of a government, and that it gave important signals to international financial markets. However, it was often argued that the PSBR was flawed as an economic indicator, and its use as a guide to government finances was out of step with most other European countries. The Labour government's reforms of 1998 made some effort to address such criticisms, and until 2002–3 the government actually succeeded in paying off a substantial proportion of the national debt and so reducing the annual interest charge required to finance it (see Fig. 10.2).

Although the changing terminology seeks to clarify what is and is not included in calculating public expenditure totals, it is still dealing with a situation of considerable complexity. For example, for many years, the *cash* totals made no distinction between *capital* spending such as on the building of roads, *current* spending (e.g. on teachers' salaries), and *transfer payments* (e.g. welfare benefits). As a consequence, cuts in capital expenditure were often made to counter short-term fiscal pressures elsewhere. The 1998 reforms sought to address this by making a sharp distinction between current and capital spending. Second, the accounting process is based on Treasury rules regarding what may be included in the accounts and how they are treated. As will be discussed later, the Treasury has historically seen its role as the guardian of the public purse, and has therefore sought to define

Table 10.1 Departmental expenditure limits in real terms,[a] 1998–9 to 2003–4

	resources, £ million					
	Outturn 1998–9	Outturn 1990–2000	Outturn 2000–1	Estimated Outturn 2001–2	Plans 2002–3	Plans 2003–4
Education and Skills	13,091	13,529	15,810	18,941	22,168	23,689
Health	40,669	41,658	44,971	49,323	53,062	56,909
of which: NHS	*39,557*	*40,850*	*44,065*	*47,958*	*50,805*	*54,576*
Transport and Regions	8,807	9,234	9,642	10,643	12,879	14,386
Local Government	34,133	34,821	35,326	36,002	35,755	37,402
Home Office	7,599	7,659	8,923	10,169	9,845	9,694
Lord Chancellor's Departments	2,896	2,177	2,617	2,839	2,690	2,670
Attorney General's Departments	352	341	376	431	420	421
Defence	24,733	24,570	24,979	23,881	23,359	23,036
Foreign and Commonwealth Office	1,100	1,149	1,311	1,373	1,390	1,223
International Development	2,334	2,594	2,663	3,034	3,172	3,296
Trade and Industry	3,120	3,098	3,376	4,465	4,276	4,077
Environment, Food and Rural Affairs	1,561	1,780	1,849	2,771	2,086	2,124
Culture, Media and Sport	1,011	1,021	993	1,070	1,200	1,162
Work and Pensions	5,063	5,237	5,306	6,350	6,670	7,002
Scotland	13,587	14,065	14,568	16,048	16,880	17,536
Wales	7,112	7,041	7,583	8,310	8,820	9,264
Northern Ireland Executive	4,615	4,731	4,978	5,581	5,822	5,993
Northern Ireland Office	1,028	1,000	952	1,094	1,094	955
Chancellor's Departments	3,420	3,536	3,377	4,047	4,064	3,974
Cabinet Office	1,344	1,521	1,422	1,634	1,513	1,543
Welfare to Work[b]	556	789	1,371			
Invest to Save Budget					28	41
Capital Modernization Fund					321	720
Policy Innovation Fund					38	37
Reserve					400	2,000
Allowance for shortfall				−1,958		
Budget 2002 Addition						**1,500**
Departmental expenditure limits	**178,132**	**181,552**	**192,394**	**206,049**	**218,000**	**230,600**
Total education spending[c]	*40.7*	*41.7*	*44.1*	*49.4*	*51.0*	*53.8*

[a] At 2000–2001 prices, using GDP deflators consistent with those used in the April 2002 Financial Statement and Budget Report.
[b] Spending funded by the Windfall Tax.
[c] Central government spending on education falling within DEL plus locally financed education spending (in AME).

Table 10.2 Total Managed Expenditure, 1998–9 to 2003–4

	Resources, £ million					
	Outturn 1998–9	Outturn 1999–2000	Outturn 2000–1	Estimated outturn 2001–2	Plans 2002–3	Plans 2003–4
Total Departmental Expenditure Limits	**170,829**	**178,284**	**192,394**	**211,818**	**229,500**	**249,000**
Annually Managed Expenditure						
Social security benefits	91,988	96,983	99,129	105,218	109,170	114,177
Housing Revenue Account subsidies	3,486	3,285	3,096	4,549	4,530	4,422
Common Agricultural Policy	3,239	2,747	2,594	2,667	2,598	2,640
Export Credits Guarantee Department	−154	925	1,315	249	352	−207
Self-financing Public Corporations	709	1,387	1,374	1,119	1,198	1,210
Net public service pensions	4,981	4,991	5,016	5,125	5,020	5,411
National Lottery	1,831	1,908	1,855	1,700	2,300	2,300
Other programme spending	263	1,191	299	2,174	145	−33
Non-cash items						
Depreciation	7,345	7,619	9,647	9,696	9,986	10,722
Cost of capital charges	11,947	12,401	13,488	14,323	14,689	15,531
Provisions and other charges	593	2,389	6,275	−643	1,490	1,744
Total departmental AME	**126,228**	**135,827**	**144,089**	**146,177**	**151,478**	**157,917**
Other AME						
Net payments to EC institutions	3,590	2,807	3,696	776	2,163	2,364
Locally financed expenditure[a]	16,865	18,611	18,444	19,354	20,656	21,919
Central Government gross debt interest	29,512	24,927	25,945	22,160	21,132	23,192
Accounting and other adjustments	−13,773	−16,113	−17,413	−8,156	−7,527	−1,854
Total other AME	**36,194**	**30,231**	**30,673**	**34,134**	**36,423**	**45,621**
AME Margin					1,000	2,000

Table 10.2 (contd.)

	Resources, £ million					
	Outturn	Outturn	Outturn	Estimated outturn	Plans	Plans
	1998–9	1999–2000	2000–1	2001–2	2002–3	2003–4
Total Annually Managed Expenditure	**162,423**	**166,059**	**174,762**	**180,312**	**188,901**	**205,538**
Total Managed Expenditure	**333,252**	**344,343**	**367,156**	**392,130**	**418,400**	**454,600**
of which						
Current expenditure	314,724	326,883	348,751	367,373	389,900	420,300
Net investment	5,861	4,615	5,705	11,955	14,400	19,700
Depreciation	12,667	12,845	12,699	12,802	14,000	14,600

[a] Net payments to EC institutions exclude the UK's contribution to the cost of EC aid to non-Member States (which is attributed to the aid programme). Net payments therefore differ from the UK's net contribution to the EC Budget, latest estimates for which are: £3.3 bn in 1998–9, £3.3 bn in 1999–2000, £4.3 bn in 2000–1, £1.5 bn in 2001–2, £3 bn in 2002–3, and £3.2 bn in 2003–4. Figures from 2002–3 are trend estimates.
Source: Cm. 5401: table 1.1.

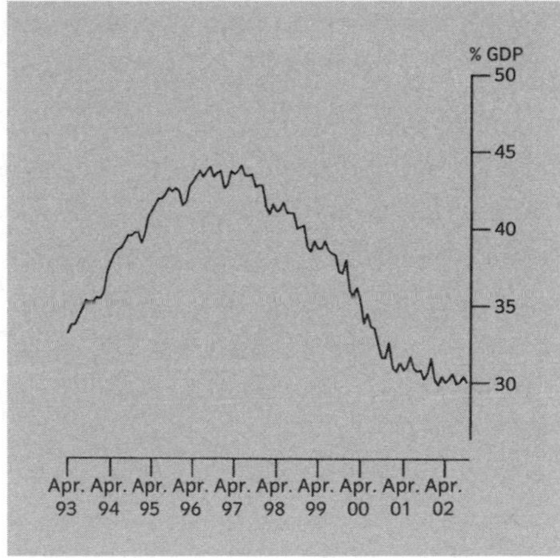

Figure 10.2 Net debt as % of GDP
Source: ONS (2002).

public expenditure in such a way as to protect government and taxpayers from what it perceives as over-commitment now and in the future. Such a role may be laudable, but it is unbalanced if it contributes to a system of public accounts that fails to deal adequately with changes in the way the public sector operates and discriminates against particular types of activity (e.g. public sector investment). Again, the changes made by Gordon Brown in 1998 sought to address part of this problem.

But is the growth of public expenditure by national governments something to be welcomed or viewed with suspicion and horror? Two economists from the **International Monetary Fund** (IMF) have charted public expenditure growth and its consequences for a selection of industrial economies over a period of 125 years (Tanzi and Schuknecht 1995). Their findings (see Fig. 10.3) show similar patterns especially after 1945. Thus, by 1990, most major industrialized nations committed over 30 per cent of their Gross Domestic Product to public expenditure with some (France, Germany) spending in the region of 50 per cent.

Have such increases delivered important social and economic gains, such as declines in infant mortality and increases in life expectancy, educational achievement, and economic growth? Tanzi and Schuknecht argue that before 1960 increased public spending delivered appreciable results; subsequently, however, achievements have been more modest and economies with lower increases have been more innovative. They argue further that smaller-scale government (as in the 'tiger' economies of south-east Asia) do not necessarily perform worse when compared with nations with larger social programmes. This analysis needs to be treated with caution, not least because it neglects causation and overlooks the difficulties of comparing different social and political systems. Yet it indicates both the almost inexorable growth in public expenditure in industrial countries (including those with a small state welfare system such as the USA) and some of the puzzles surrounding these developments.

Even if definitional difficulties and the need to take into account changes in the value of money imply that long-term analysis of public expenditure trends should be viewed

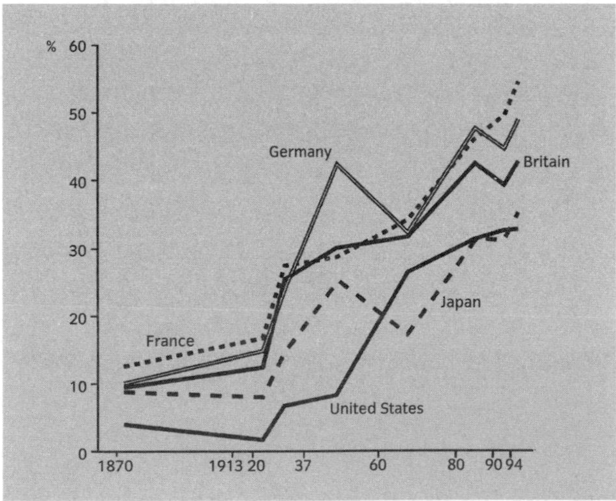

Figure 10.3 Government spending as % of GDP (UK, Germany, France, Japan, USA)

Source: *Economist*, 6 Apr. 1996; Tanzi and Schuknecht (1995).

with caution, it appears that the trend of public expenditure growth in the UK has been steadily upwards. Hogwood (1992), for example, offers evidence of a pattern of increasing expenditure up to and including the Second World War and even more so thereafter. In the immediate aftermath of 1945 increases in social expenditure were balanced by declining defence spending, but after 1950 social expenditure rose both in absolute terms and relative to GDP under all governments.

These trends can be analysed. Figure 10.4 shows General Government Expenditure (GGE) and General Government Revenue (GGR) since 1900 as a percentage of Gross Domestic Product (GDP). This data shows that share of public expenditure was low and falling before the First World War, when it rose steeply, only to fall back to a new peacetime level in the 1920s and 1930s. The Second World War was responsible for another sharp rise, followed by a fall after the war to a new and gently rising plateau of public expenditure which is explained by the steadily growing welfare state. The small peaks at the end of the 1970s, the mid-1980s, and the early 1990s show the effects of recession and rising expenditures on unemployment benefits and income support. Looking at public expenditure as a share of the whole economy tends to exaggerate change. Figure 10.5, which describes the rise in public expenditure in real terms, shows a much more even, incremental pattern.

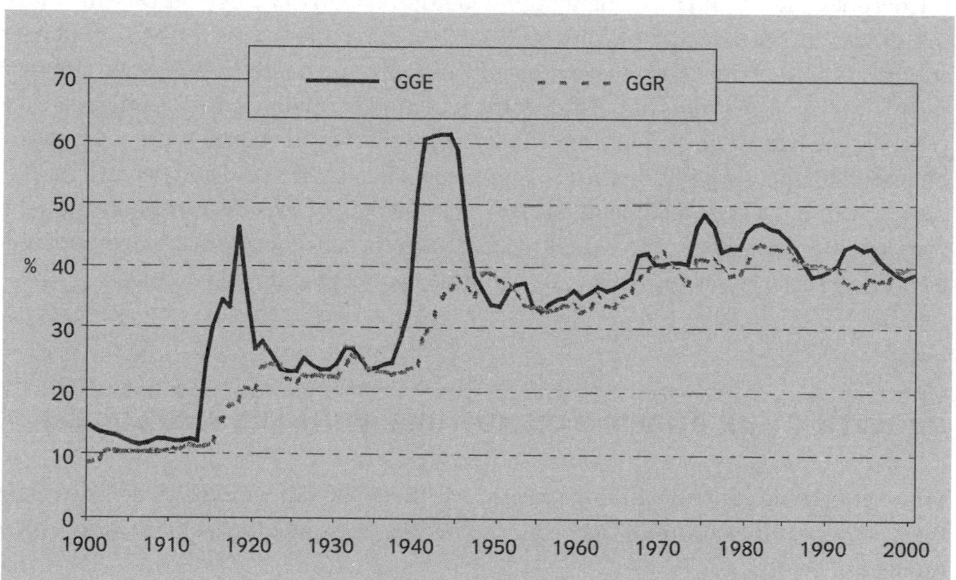

Figure 10.4 Government spending and revenues as % of GDP since 1900

GGE = general government expenditure; GGR = general government revenue.

Notes: For years after UK accession to the European Community, both revenue and expenditure totals have been adjusted to include European income and spending. Numbers on the European System of Accounts 95 basis are available only back to the 1940s, before which time they are measured differently. All series change in 1948, so there is only one major discontinuity in the graph.

Source: authors' calculations, based on data from Feinstein (1976), until 1947, and from the ONS from 1948 onwards.

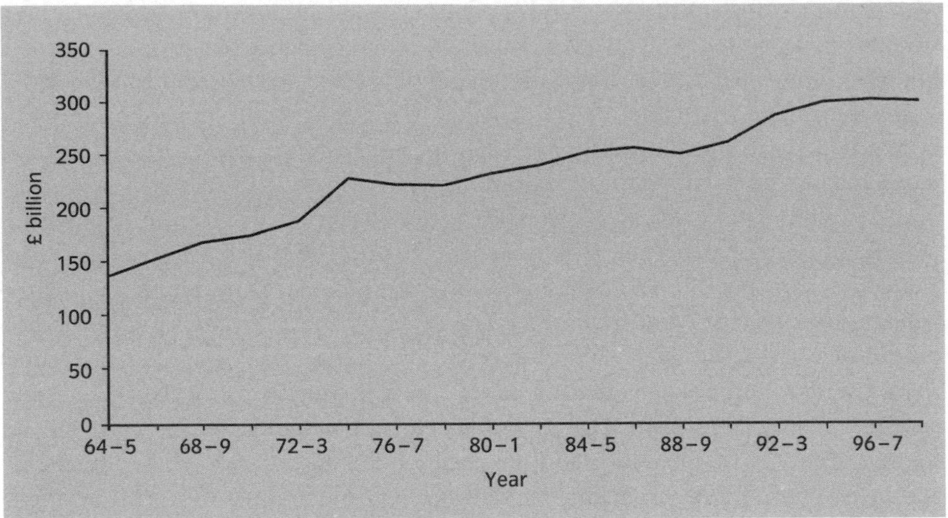

Figure 10.5 Public spending (GGE) in real terms, 1963–1998

Source: Cm. 3901 (1998).

How does one explain this? Some commentators point to a lack of political will against the power of bureaucratic self-interest. Yet, whatever one's view of Mrs Thatcher's administrations of the 1980s, a failure of political will could hardly be numbered amongst their faults. So were events out of government control or unanticipated? Corry and Gray (1997) argue that what remains unrecorded is the effect of the business cycle, especially on unemployment, and its financial consequences for benefits paid and tax revenue forgone. We might add developments such as the widening of income distribution and the consequent triggering of other benefits (e.g. housing benefit). Some unanticipated consequences of social policy initiatives can significantly affect public expenditure.

GROWTH OF UK PUBLIC EXPENDITURE: WINNERS AND LOSERS

The overall trend conceals shifting patterns within public expenditure totals. To explore these, it is worth examining the detail of changes in expenditure by function over a number of years.

Table 10.3 shows how social security expenditure is the largest category, and that it was rising fast until the early 1990s, when various reforms began to reduce its growth rate. NHS and education expenditure were very similar in volume until 1990, after which the effects of a rising number of older people and a relatively constant number of younger people began to show. The table does not show the very substantial increases in health expenditure planned in the 2002 Comprehensive Spending Review (Cm. 5570), and readers are recommended to go to the relevant websites to check how this has

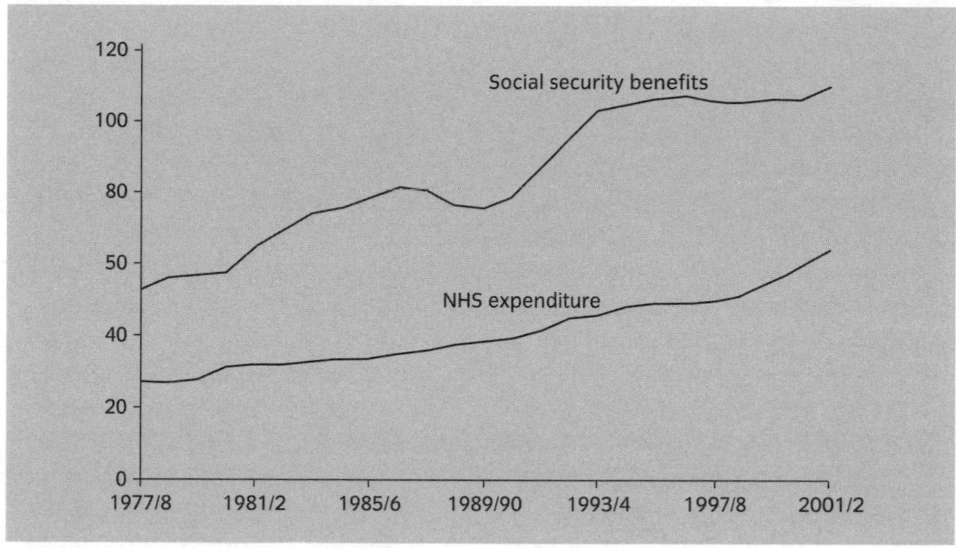

Figure 10.6 Real growth in social security benefits and gross NHS expenditure, UK (£ billion at 2001/2 prices[a])

[a] Adjusted to 2001/2 prices using the GDP market prices deflator (second quarter 2002).

Source: Department of Health; Department for Work and Pensions; Department for Social Development, Northern Ireland.

turned out since the publication of this book. The relative 'losers' over the last twenty years have been housing and defence expenditures. Since the turn of the century there have been substantial proportional increases in international development assistance. Figure 10.6 shows the different trajectories of NHS and social security spending. The first is supply-led, governments deciding how much to spend and the growth being steadily incremental. Social security spending, on the other hand, is more demand-led and rises and falls with the **business cycle**.

Do these changes reflect deliberate policy choices? In part, certainly, but not in whole. Social security spending, for example, has been influenced by the rise in eligible claimants (e.g. pensioners), casualties of downturns in the economic cycle (e.g. the unemployed), and changes to eligibility (e.g. housing benefit). Similarly, health spending has been affected by the upward pressure of demography (ageing population), increased sophistication and cost of medical technology, and greater expectations of and demands for services.

A significant long-term loser in the recent history of public expenditure has been investment. Chancellors find it politically easier to spend less on investment than on consumption. As an analysis by the Institute of Fiscal Studies points out:

> Total gross public investment . . . as a percentage of GDP has fallen almost continuously since the mid-1970s. It comprised 8.9% of GDP in 1975 and fell to 1.7% in 2000. The decline was therefore 7.2 percentage points of GDP, which in 2000 represented around £67 billion.
> (Clark et al. 2001: 20)

Table 10.3 Total Managed Expenditure by function in real terms, 1984–5 to 2001–2 (£ billion)[a]

Function	Outturn																	Estimated outturn
	1984–5	1985–6	1986–7	1987–8	1988–9	1989–90	1990–1	1991–2	1992–3	1993–4	1994–5	1995–6	1996–7	1997–8	1998–9	1999–2000	2000–1	2001–2
Education	30.2	29.5	31.5	32.8	33.2	34.4	34.6	36.0	37.6	38.6	39.9	39.8	40.2	40.1	40.7	41.7	44.1	49.4
Health and personal social services	36.1	36.2	37.8	39.5	40.8	41.6	43.2	46.0	48.9	50.1	53.1	54.6	56.2	57.1	58.4	62.3	66.0	70.4
of which: Health	*30.7*	*30.9*	*32.0*	*33.3*	*34.4*	*34.8*	*36.1*	*38.7*	*41.2*	*41.7*	*43.3*	*44.0*	*45.0*	*45.6*	*46.6*	*49.6*	*52.6*	*56.7*
Transport	12.4	12.0	11.5	10.9	10.5	11.4	12.7	13.5	15.1	13.7	13.9	12.9	11.1	9.9	9.1	8.8	8.7	9.8
Housing	8.4	7.3	6.9	6.7	4.9	7.3	6.4	7.1	7.5	6.1	6.1	5.6	5.1	4.0	3.8	2.9	3.2	4.9
Other environmental services	7.1	6.9	7.9	7.8	7.4	8.3	8.6	9.0	9.3	8.8	9.4	9.5	9.0	9.0	8.7	8.6	10.2	10.5
Law, order, and protective services	11.8	11.6	12.2	13.1	13.6	14.4	15.0	16.0	16.9	17.2	17.6	17.6	17.9	18.1	18.1	19.1	20.1	22.5
Defence[b]	31.9	31.7	31.1	30.3	28.9	29.2	28.2	28.1	27.2	26.3	25.8	24.2	23.5	22.4	23.6	23.1	24.9	23.6
International development assistance and other international services	2.7	2.9	2.9	2.8	3.0	3.1	3.1	3.4	3.6	3.6	3.7	3.7	3.3	3.1	3.3	3.5	3.7	4.6
Trade, industry, energy, and employment	14.4	14.0	13.6	10.6	12.1	10.7	11.5	11.4	11.6	11.8	11.0	10.2	9.5	9.0	9.0	9.2	10.0	11.6
Agriculture, fisheries, food, and forestry	4.5	5.1	3.8	3.9	3.3	3.1	3.8	3.8	3.8	4.8	4.3	4.7	6.7	5.5	5.3	4.9	5.1	7.7

Culture, Media, and Sport[c]	2.9	3.0	3.1	3.3	3.4	3.7	3.7	3.6	3.6	3.5	3.8	3.9	4.1	4.5	5.2	5.7	5.5	5.6
Social security	73.2	75.8	79.0	78.3	75.2	74.4	77.2	86.4	94.8	100.8	102.0	103.6	106.5	104.4	103.6	105.1	105.4	109.1
Central administration and associated expenditure[d]	8.9	8.2	9.1	10.5	9.3	11.8	11.1	7.4	9.8	9.7	8.5	11.0	9.0	9.0	10.9	10.7	12.1	10.4
Total expenditure on services	**244.6**	**244.3**	**250.4**	**250.6**	**245.6**	**253.3**	**259.2**	**271.7**	**289.8**	**295.0**	**298.7**	**301.1**	**302.1**	**295.9**	**299.7**	**305.6**	**319.2**	**340.1**
Public sector debt interest	32.2	33.8	32.6	32.4	30.9	29.7	26.9	22.9	22.9	24.3	27.2	30.0	31.4	32.6	31.2	26.1	25.9	21.6
Other accounting adjustments[e]	17.3	12.8	9.2	10.5	9.3	10.9	8.2	15.6	12.8	12.2	16.0	15.0	16.9	18.3	16.7	19.1	22.1	22.7
Allowance for shortfall													0.0	0.0	−0.1	−0.1	0.0	−2.0
Total Managed Expenditure	**294.2**	**290.8**	**292.2**	**293.5**	**285.9**	**293.9**	**294.3**	**310.2**	**325.4**	**331.5**	**341.9**	**346.2**	**350.4**	**346.8**	**347.5**	**350.7**	**367.2**	**382.5**

[a] For years prior to 1996–7, the effects of transfer and classification changes have been imputed.

[b] The outturns for Defence for 1996–7 and 1997–8 include receipts from the sale of Ministry of Defence married quarters.

[c] Includes expenditure financed from the National Lottery.

[d] Includes net payments to the European Communities and activities such us tax collection and the registration of the population.

[e] Includes net public service pensions.

Source: Cm. 5401 (2003).

Some of this decline is accounted for by privatization. Private suppliers of gas, water, electricity, telecoms, and rail services now make investments outside the public accounts. However, the substantial real reductions remain. This loss of spending affects the basic infrastructure on which much social policy depends; the quality of the public housing stock, of schools, hospitals, police stations, courts, and public buildings of all kinds, as well as the equipment available to civil servants when they seek to deliver efficient services. These problems have been recognized to a degree in the Comprehensive Spending Reviews, and they make investment expenditure much clearer. Another response has been to draw private-for-profit investment into the public sector through Private Finance Initiatives (see Box 10.4). While these allow investments which do not increase public sector borrowing, they commit government to future current expenditure to pay for the use of the schools, hospitals, transport infrastructure, and other facilities that private investors have built. It is suggested that this unnecessarily guarantees future profits out of the public purse. The 2000 review promised investment as a proportion of GDP, growing from 2.7 per cent in 2001–2 to 3.2 per cent in 2003–4. Even if this was achieved, and governments tend to underspend planned investment, it will still have been at half the levels of the 1970s.

Despite the sophistication of their analyses, economists have not yet provided governments with precise levers for managing their economies. Booms and recessions come and go just as they have always done. **Keynesian economics** taught politicians that expenditure on social policies could be used to smooth the consequences of the business cycle. In the 1920s and 1930s it was thought that recessions required governments to cut their budgets and raise taxation. Now it is understood that if consumer demand falls in a recession, it is necessary to stimulate the economy by reducing taxation and interest

Box 10.4 The Private Finance Initiative

Since 1992 the **Private Finance Initiative** (PFI) has sought to provide opportunities for private investment in public services. Under the PFI, private organizations and consortia are encouraged to enter into contractual relations with public sector bodies to provide facilities such as hospitals, student accommodation, prisons, schools, colleges, and a variety of public buildings. By 2002 there were over 400 PFI contracts in force, committing the public sector to future expenditure of about £100 billion. The contracts are generally long-term arrangements involving public expenditure for up to thirty years. Many of the contracts are with local authorities, and the House of Commons Public Accounts Committee reported in 2002 that it was 'very concerned that over one in five authorities consider that value for money from their PFI contracts has diminished, with high prices for additional services an area of concern' (HC 460: para. 5). The incentive for private sector participation is access to a revenue stream in return for a sharing of the risk. The attraction of such strategies to government departments and local authorities is that public expenditure constraints, particularly on capital investment, can be avoided by spreading costs over current expenditure many years ahead.

rates or to replace the lost demand with government spending funded out of borrowing. When unemployment rose in the early 1980s even Mrs Thatcher's administrations accepted that increased expenditure on benefits and reduced tax receipts would raise the share of GDP going to public expenditure. Similarly, from 2002 Labour's Chancellor of the Exchequer, Gordon Brown, had to accept that the recession meant that tax receipts would be less than expected and public expenditure would again have to be funded from borrowing.

GROWTH OF PUBLIC EXPENDITURE: SOME INTERNATIONAL COMPARISONS

How do the UK's patterns of public expenditure compare with other countries? As was noted earlier, in historical terms the growth of public expenditure in the UK has a similar cyclical profile to several other major industrial countries (Tanzi and Schuknecht 1995). Data covering 1979–97 (Fig. 10.7) indicates the relative movement of General Government Expenditure for the UK compared with an average for the European Union (EU) and countries who are members of the **Organization for Economic Cooperation and Development** (OECD) (this group includes the USA, Canada, most west European countries, and Japan). Fig. 10.8 shows social protection expenditure amongst European Union countries through the 1990s. Fig. 10.9 positions EU countries in relation to each other in 1999 in terms both of their expenditure on social protection and of their GDP per capita (see Box 10.5 for the content of 'social protection' as used in European Commission data sets.) Spending on pensions is the largest component of social protection in Europe

Box 10.5 Defining social expenditure in the European Union

Social expenditure in comparative data issued by the European Commission is formulated in terms of the Esspros (European system of integrated social protection statistics). Social protection is defined as 'all interventions from public or private bodies intended to relieve households or individuals of a defined set of risks or needs'. It includes both the financing and direct provision of benefits (benefits in kind and cash transfers) and the related administrative costs. 'Social protection' thus includes the bulk of public support for health, social services, and social security, but does not include education expenditures. The main functional areas covered are: sickness and healthcare; financial and direct support for those with disabilities; services and income support for retired and older people; widows' and other survivors' pensions; family benefits in cash and kind to assist with pregnancy, childbirth, adoption, and bringing up children; support in cash and kind for those defined as unemployed or in publicly supported vocational training; expenditures to provide or assist with the cost of housing. The quality of this data has become better over time as European nations have adapted their national accounting methods to fit better with the EU methodology, but comparative data must always be treated with caution.

(44 per cent of the total in 1999) followed by healthcare (22 per cent of the total). Half of the spending on healthcare goes to those aged 65 and over.

Figure 10.7 gives some indication why Conservative governments in the 1990s often proudly boasted that they were doing better in economic terms than other European counties, and did not wish to be burdened with 'socialist policies' such as the **EU Social Chapter**. During this period the UK moved close to the average for OECD countries,

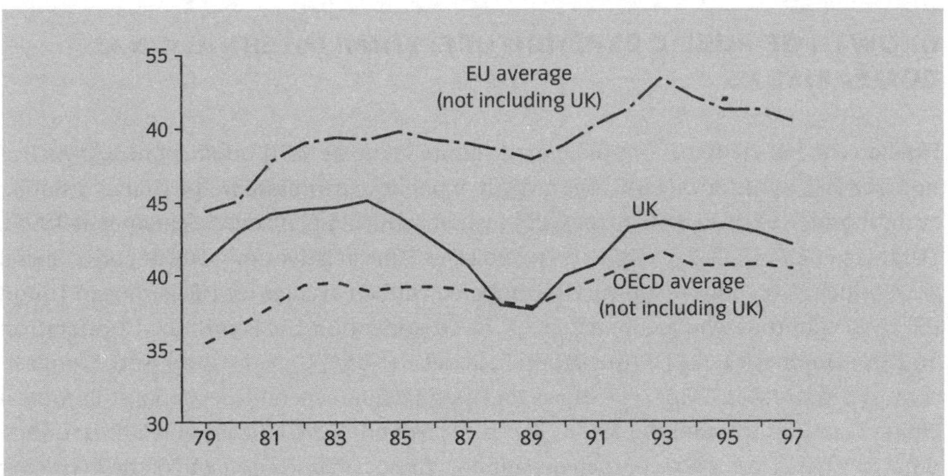

Figure 10.7 General Government Expenditure as % of GDP: EU, UK, and OECD, not including UK

Source: Monck (1997); Treasury (1996b).

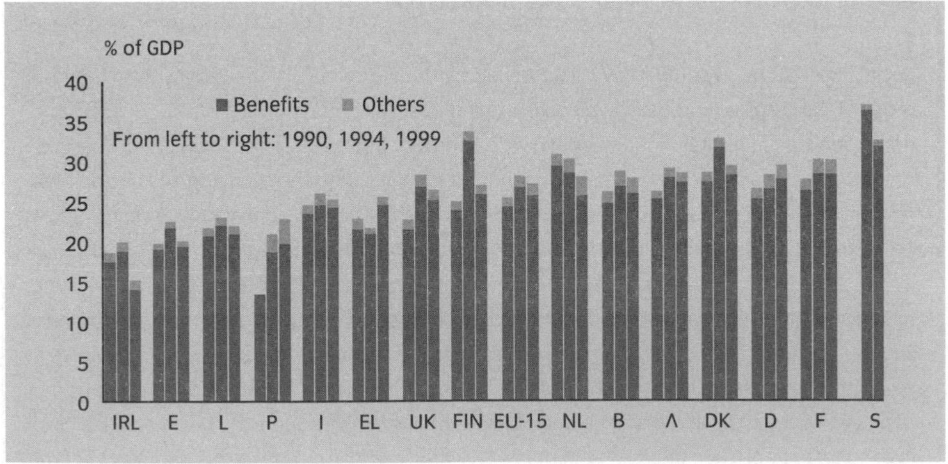

Figure 10.8 Social protection expenditure as % of GDP in the Member States, 1990, 1994, and 1999

Source: EC (2002).

a figure kept low by economies with low social policy budgets (relative to GDP), in particular the USA and Japan. The New Labour government maintained this stance, committing itself to a 'sustainable investment rule' where new public debt as a proportion of GDP will be held, over the economic cycle, at 'a sustainable and prudent level' (Cm. 3978 2001: 5). However, as Figs. 10.8 and 10.9 show, this has meant that the UK does not feature amongst the more 'generous' of the EU nations in terms of social protection expenditures. It is important to consider these comparisons in terms of the overall levels of economic output of nations. Richer nations may 'need' to spend less on social protection, though in practice they tend to spend more. Fig. 10.9 reveals that in 1999 the EU nations could be placed in four broad groups:

- Greece, Spain, Ireland, and Portugal with social protection expenditures of about €3,500 per head (adjusted to affect purchasing power differences between the nations);
- Italy, Finland, and the UK at €5,500–5,900 per capita;
- Belgium, Germany, France, and Austria at €6,400–6,700 per capita;
- Denmark, Luxembourg, the Netherlands, and Sweden, above €6,900.

The UK's relative position may improve during the period, 2003–6, covered by the 2002 Comprehensive Spending Review because of substantial planned growth in health expenditure. As part of the decision-making process Gordon Brown, the Chancellor of the Exchequer, had commissioned a wide-ranging review of health expenditure under the former chief of the National Westminister Bank, Derek Wanless. The review (Wanless

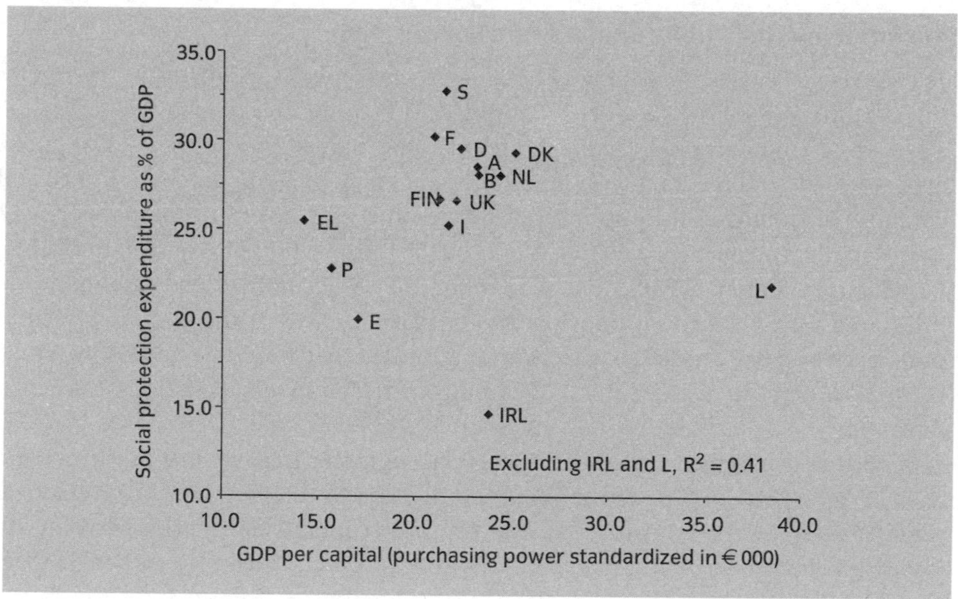

Figure 10.9 Social protection expenditure and GDP per capita in the member states, 1999

Source: EC (2002).

2002) found that no new methods of financing, such as the use of social insurance or private funding, would deliver the required improvements to match the average of EU spending on health. Only increased public expenditure would be cost-effective. As a result, the Chancellor used the 2002 budget to announce 'the largest ever sustained increase in health resources' of 7.5 per cent in real terms each year for five years. These reforms are tied to a major modernization agenda (see Box 10.2), and will be funded by increases in national insurance contributions, which rose by 1 per cent from April 2003.

PUBLIC EXPENDITURE: THE SEARCH FOR CONTROL

All governments have to balance spending with the taxes and borrowing needed to pay for it. The process for making the necessary decisions was traditionally conducted annually, yet the provision of facilities such as hospitals, schools, and roads have long-term expenditure implications. Sustained and adequate social policies require the planning of public expenditure. Different countries approach this in different ways. In the UK, the management and control of public expenditure is the responsibility ultimately of the Cabinet and specifically the Chancellor of the Exchequer, who with the Chief Secretary of the Treasury, another Cabinet minister, stands as guardian of economic policy against the spending claims of departmental ministers. This system is mirrored at the administrative level by Treasury officials, who are in constant dialogue with civil servants in spending departments. In this small, closed community, public expenditure policy is forged and fought over on a continuous basis.

Plowden and the Public Expenditure Survey (PES)

The present system of managing UK public expenditure has its origins in the recommendations of the 1961 Plowden Committee. This committee, established to explore a perceived failure in public expenditure planning, argued that in the annual public expenditure round the long-term implications of many programmes were ignored and commitments entered into by ministers were often not linked to the development of the economy. Plowden therefore proposed the introduction of a system, the **Public Expenditure Survey** (PES), to allow spending to be determined and assessed in an integrated way. The central principle was to plan in terms of the resources (such as numbers of schools, hospitals, teachers, and nurses) that would be needed by public services in order to achieve the desired outcomes. The money costs were calculated separately.

Departments engaged in annual discussions with the Treasury first at official and then at ministerial level to agree their spending plans in the short (annual) and longer term (three to five years) consistent with planned economic policy. This annual cycle was the cornerstone of the public expenditure process for decades, although there were significant changes both in procedure and emphasis from its initiation in the 1960s onwards, while in 1998 Gordon Brown introduced further significant changes, perhaps in an effort to restore the long-lost strategic vision that Plowden sought to impose.

In its first decade PES evolved into a set of regularized and systematic routines, yet public expenditure continued to rise. Initially this was thought to be due partially to inaccurate projections of economic performance and partially to the fact that there was little evaluation of the effects of public spending. The system encountered a crisis in the mid-1970s, when high levels of inflation meant that the resource-based plans turned out to cost much more than expected in money terms. **Cash limits** were introduced in 1975 and refined in the period up to 1979 to set ceilings on departmental budgets, including a fixed limit for inflation as reflected in price increases and wage rises. If circumstances pushed costs up, then departments faced an effective resource cut. These brought greater financial discipline and ensured that departments kept to published economic projections, but they could not be applied to areas where spending was demand-led, in particular the largest area of spending, social security.

Part of the Plowden vision was to impose some economic rationality on political decision-making: to encourage ministers through PES to take a collective view and assist them to prioritize programmes. However, the introduction of cash limits meant that the PES process had, by the 1990s, become little more than a short-term method of expenditure control. In this respect it was relatively successful—hence the falling share of public expenditure within the economy during the 1990s shown in Fig. 10.7.

Assessing the history of PES, Hulme (1997) and Thain and Wright (1995), amongst others, argue that it exhibited a number of strengths and weakness. The former include:

- responsiveness to political leadership;
- the capacity to agree budgets on time;
- sufficient control over expenditure totals to contain inflation;
- containment of public spending as a proportion of GDP equal to if not better than other European countries;
- an increased focus on efficiency and value for money.

In contrast, weaknesses include:

- frequent failure to meet public expenditure targets;
- too much emphasis on short-term factors;
- a lack of 'transparency' regarding information provided by the system and a lack of open debate over choices;
- a lack of objective evaluation of existing policies or new initiatives.

CONCLUSION: CAN CONTROLLING AND PLANNING BE COMBINED?

Gordon Brown suspended the annual round of the PES process and introduced the Comprehensive Spending Reviews described at the beginning of this chapter. However, the effects of this reform were limited during New Labour's first term of office, from 1997 to 2001, because of a reluctance to expand public expenditure beyond the tight constraints designed to prevent it from growing faster than the economy as a whole. It was only with the third Review, announced in July 2002, that the Chancellor began to use the new system to plan a substantial expansion in spending on government services. There is an essential tension in seeking to combine the control of public expenditure with planning it over the longer term. The Comprehensive Spending Reviews are an attempt to restore the link between these two functions. Describing the new system to a conference of local government finance managers in 2002, Ed Balls, the government's chief economic adviser in the Treasury, described its main characteristics in the following way:

> The new approach to public spending, introduced in 1997, makes it possible to plan for the long-term with a clear distinction between current and capital spending as we steadily tackle the back-log of under-investment. Spending decisions are based on in-depth policy review, not simply on last year's figures, and on informed interdepartmental reviews to strengthen coordination across government. We have devolved spending power to departments with a three-year, not a one-year, cycle and there is full end-of-year flexibility for departments to move their budgets from one year to the next. (Balls 2002)

Readers of this chapter will have to judge whether the promise of the new system has been achieved.

REFERENCES

Balls, E. (2002), 'The new localism'. Speech made to the CIPFA annual conference, Brighton, June.

Barnett, J. (1982), *Inside the Treasury*. London: Deutsch.

Barr, N. (1993), *The Economics of the Welfare State*, 2nd edn. Oxford: Oxford University Press.

Blackstone, T., and Plowden, W. (1988), *Inside the Think Tank*. London: Heinemann.

Clark, T., and Dilnot, A. (2002), *Long Term Trends in British Taxation and Spending*. London: Institute for Fiscal Studies.

—— Elsby, M., and Love, S. (2001), *Twenty Five Years of Falling Investment? Trends in Capital Spending on Public Services*. London: Institute for Fiscal Studies.

Clarke, K. (1995), 'The future of Conservatism', Speech. London: Conservative Party Central Office.

Cm. 1867 (1992), *Budgetary Reform*. London: HMSO.

Cm. 3901 (1998), *Public Expenditure: Statistical Analysis, 1998–9*. London: Stationery Office.

Cm. 3978 (1998), *Stability and Investment for the Long Term: Economic and Fiscal Strategy Report 1998*. London: Stationery Office.

Cm. 4011 (1998), *Modern Public Services for Britain: Investing in Reform: Comprehensive Spending Review and New Public Spending Plans 1999–2002*. London: Stationery Office.

Cm. 5401 (2002), *Public Expenditure Statistical Analyses 2002–3*. London: Stationery Office; or www.official-documents.co.uk

Cm. 5570 (2002), *Opportunity and Security for All: Investing in an Enterprising, Fairer Britain: New Public Spending Plans 2003–2006*. London: Stationery Office.

Cm. 5571 (2002), *Public Service Agreements White Paper*. London: Stationery Office.

Cooper, Y. (1997), 'The key public expenditure issues of the future', in Corry (1997a).

Corry, D. (ed). (1997a), *Public Expenditure: Effective Management and Control*. London: Dryden Press.

—— 1997b, 'Introduction: improving public expenditure', in Corry (1997a).

—— 1997c, 'The role of the public sector and public expenditure', in Corry (1997a).

—— and Gray, S. (1997), 'Recent history of public spending', in Corry (1997a).

Dilnot, A. (1997), 'Magic required', *Guardian*, 23 Jan.

Donaldson, C., Scott, T., and Wordsworth, S. (1996), *Can We Afford the NHS?* London: Institute of Public Policy Research.

EC (European Commission) (2002), *Social Protection in Europe 2001*. Luxembourg: EC.

Feinstein, C. H. (1976), *Statistical Tables of National Income, Expenditure and Output of the UK, 1855–1965*. Basingstoke: Macmillan.

Glennerster, H. (1992), *Paying for Welfare: The 1990s*. London: Harvester Wheatsheaf.

Gray, A. G. (1997), 'Editorial: the Private Finance Initiative', *Public Money and Management* 17(3): 3–4.

—— and Jenkins, W. I. (1982), 'Policy analysis in British central government: the experience of PAR', *Public Administration* 60(4): 429–50.

—— —— 1997, 'The management of central government services', in W. D. A. Jones, A. G. Gray, D. Kavanagh, M. Moran, P. Norton, P. and A. Seldon (eds.), *Politics UK*, 3rd edn. Hemel Hempstead: Prentice-Hall.

Hall, J., Preston, I., and Ridge, M. (1997), 'How public attitudes to expenditure differ', in Corry (1997a).

HC 460 (2002), *Managing the Relationship to Secure a Successful Partnership in PFI Projects: 42nd Report of the Committee of Public Accounts, Session 2001–2*: London: Stationery Office.

HC 73 (2001), *House of Commons Select Committee on the Treasury, Third Report*. London: Stationery Office.

Heald, D. (1997), 'Controlling public expenditure', in Corry (1997a).

Heath, A., Jowell, R., and Curtice, J. (1994), *Labour's Last Chance*. Aldershot: Dartmouth.

Heclo, H., and Wildavsky, A. (1974), *The Private Government of Public Money*, 2nd edn. London: Macmillan.

Hills, J. (1993), *The Future of Welfare: The Guide to the Debate*. York: Joseph Rowntree Foundation.

—— (1996), 'Tax policies: are there still choices?', in D. Halpen et al. (eds.), *Options for Britain*. Oxford: Nuffield College.

Hogwood, B. (1992), *Trends in British Public Policy*. Buckingham: Open University Press.

Hulme, G. (1997), 'How public expenditure priorities are determined', in Corry (1997a).

Kellner, P. (1997), 'What does the public think?', in Corry (1997a).

Lawson, N. (1992), *The View from No. 11*. London: Corgi.

Le Grand, J. (1996), 'The thinkable', *Prospect*, July.

Likierman, A. (1988), *Public Expenditure: Who Really Controls it and How?* London: Penguin.

Monck, N. (1997), 'The need for a strong treasury, and how to make it work', in Corry (1997a).

Mullard, M. (1993), *The Politics of Public Expenditure*. London: Routledge.

ONS (Office for National Statistics) (1996), *United Kingdom National Accounts*. London: HMSO.

ONS (2002), *Public Sector Finances* (Oct.). At www.statitics.gov.uk

—— (2003), *Social Trends No. 33*. London: Stationery Office.

Pallot, J., and Ball, I. (1997), 'What difference does resource accounting make?', in Corry (1997a).

Parry, R., Hood, C., and James, O. (1997), 'Reinventing the Treasury: economic rationalism or an econocrat's failure of control?', *Public Administration* 75(3): 395–416.

Tanzi, V., and Schuknecht, I. (1995), *The Growth of Government and the Reform of the State in Industrial Countries*. Washington, DC: IMF.

Taylor-Gooby, P. (1995), 'Comfortable, marginal and excluded: who should pay higher taxes for a better welfare state?', in R. Jowell et al., *British Social Attitudes*. Aldershot: Gower.

Thain, C., and Wright, M. (1992a), 'Planning and controlling public expenditure in the UK, Part I: The Treasury's Public Expenditure Survey', *Public Administration* 70(1): 3–24.

—— —— (1992b), 'Planning and controlling public expenditure in the UK, Part II: the effects and effectiveness of the survey', *Public Administration* 70(2): 193–224.

—— —— (1995), *The Treasury and Whitehall: The Planning and Control of Public Expenditure 1976–93*. Oxford: Oxford University Press.

Treasury (1995), *Better Accounting for the Taxpayer's Money: The Government's Proposals—Resource Accounting and Budgeting*. Cm. 2929. London: HMSO.

—— (1996a), *The Budget 1996: In Brief*. London: HMSO.

—— (1996b), *Public Expenditure Statistical Analysis 1997–8*. Cm. 3201. London: HMSO.

—— (1998), *Public Expenditure: Statistical Analysis 1998–9*. Cm. 3901. London: Stationery Office.

Wanless, D. (2002), *Securing our Future Health: Taking the Long-term View*. London: Stationery Office.

Watson, S. (1997), 'What should count as public expenditure?', in Corry (1997a).

Willman, J. (1998), *A Better State of Health: A Prescription for the NHS*. London: Profile.

Wright, M. (1995), 'Resource accounting and budgeting and the PES system', *Public Administration* 73(4): 580–90.

FURTHER READING

The best introduction to the management of public expenditure and its significance for social policy are Howard Glennerster's *Paying for Welfare: Towards 2000* (3rd ed., 1996, Hemel Hempstead: Prentice Hall) and his more recent and very accessible *Understanding the Finance of Welfare: what welfare costs and how to pay for it* (2003, Bristol: The Policy Press). A more complex research-based account of the detailed mechanics of the relationships between the Treasury and spending departments is Howard Glennerster, John Hills, Tony Travers and Ross Hendry (2000) *Paying for Health, Education and Housing: How does the Centre Pull the Purse Strings* (Oxford: Oxford University Press). Nicholas Deakin's and Richard Parry's *The Treasury and Social Policy: The Contest for Control of Welfare Strategy* (2000, Basingstoke: Macmillan) is almost the definitive recent history of the Treasury's role in social policy but it is difficult to obtain copies of the book except from good university libraries. An excellent but complex account of the 'audit society' is Christopher Hood, Colin Scott, Oliver James, George Jones and Tony Travers, *Regulation inside Government: Waste-watchers, Quality Police and Sleaze-Busters* (1999, Oxford: Oxford University Press). The term was invented by Michael Power in *The Audit Society: Rituals of Verification* (1999, Oxford: Oxford University Press) This is a rapidly changing area in which books become out of date quickly so students should look at recent issues of the journals *Public Administration, Public Money and Management, The Journal of Social Policy and Talking Politics*. The weekly magazine, *The Economist*, also often carries short news articles on public expenditure issues. In addition you should not that H.M. Treasury (www.hm-treasury.gov.uk) and indeed most government departments can be accessed on the internet as can many other organizations of relevance in this area (e.g. Institute of Public Policy Research, Institute of Fiscal Studies). These sites are rich in documents and articles that can be downloaded.

GLOSSARY

business cycle The tendency of an economy to move in waves between periods of growing output and employment and falling output and greater unemployment.

cash limits Term used in central and local government budgeting to indicate the monetary ceiling on expenditure for particular activities or categories of expenditure in any one financial year.

cash planning Linked with a system of cash limits, this is a system of planning (brought in by UK governments in the 1980s) where public expenditure planning is done in cash terms; e.g. service level is determined by money available (how many books can we get for £10,000) rather than the previously used volume planning system (we will plan to purchase 1,000 books whatever they cost).

collectivism A system that favours collective or common provision and ownership in contrast to a system of individual provision and reliance on free markets.

Comprehensive Spending Reviews (CSR) Introduced by the 1997 Labour government of Tony Blair, these are the latest of several efforts by recent British governments to review public provision item by item, asking whether any particular service needs to be provided by the state and, if the answer to this is yes, to explore whether it might be possible to deliver it in alternative ways (e.g. more economically, efficiently, and effectively). The CSR is seen as a mechanism through which public expenditure can be redistributed between departments to further the government's priorities (see further Cm. 4011, 1998).

contracting out When the responsible (state) organization contracts out the performance of a task (e.g. refuse collection) or the provision of a service (e.g. nursing home care) to another, often private or voluntary, agency.

European Union (EU) Social Chapter An initiative taken by European Community members in 1989 to begin to harmonize social policy in particular in the area of labour market and employment relations, due to a concern that workplace conditions and arrangements might suffer as a result of the competitive single market. The Conservative government of John Major secured the UK an 'opt-out' from this arrangement; however, one of the first acts in the EU of Tony Blair's Labour government in 1997 was to waive this 'opt-out' and accept the Social Chapter's terms.

externalities (external costs and external benefits) Either the costs or the benefits that economic behaviour bestows on those who are not parties to the bargain; for example, the damage done to a house by passing lorries or the 'gain' from living close to a perfume factory.

Financial Management Initiative (FMI) Initiative introduced into UK government departments by the Treasury in 1982 aimed at improving the management of resources by a variety of strategies, including delegated budgeting and increasing the accountability of individual managers for the management of resources.

fiscal crisis Term used to indicate a projected crisis for states with large public expenditure programmes, especially in areas such as health, welfare benefits, and pensions, where it is argued (but also disputed) that a combination of rising public demand, entitlements, and falling tax revenue will place governments under an increasing, if not intolerable, economic strain.

General Government Spending (or Expenditure) The international definition of general government expenditure (or public expenditure) includes the spending of central government, of local authorities and in the case of most counties, regional government.

globalization In its economic sense, the tendency for the world to become one market in which goods will be produced where costs are lowest and sold where prices are highest.

GNP and GDP Gross national product is all of a country's output of goods and services (usually in a calendar year) plus income from assets abroad but with no deduction (i.e. gross, not net) for depreciation in the value of the country's assets. Gross domestic product is GNP minus income from assets abroad.

individualism In contrast to **collectivism**, a set of beliefs that puts paramount importance on the rights and freedoms of individuals and the power of free-market mechanisms.

internal markets Pseudo- or **quasi-markets** within an organization or a service system where one part plays the part of purchaser and the other of provider. Real money transfers or merely shadow prices may be used.

International Monetary Fund (IMF) International body established (together with the **World Bank**) as a result of the 1942 Bretton Woods meeting of forty-four countries to create and stabilize the world monetary order, including exchange rates, balance of payments deficits, and the operation of the system as a whole. The IMF can advance credit to countries with serious balance of payments deficits, but has the right to demand economic compliance with its suggestions. Hence it has the power to intervene in the domestic policy-making of countries it assists

Keynesian economics An approach to national economic management named after the British economist and political adviser **John Maynard Keynes** that places strong emphasis on governmental intervention in economic management and, traditionally, on an associated goal of full employment.

long-run efficiency Obtaining economic efficiency over a variously specified longer term, usually several years, and contrasted with short-run efficiency. Long-run efficiency usually requires saving, investment, and innovation.

lumpy goods Those products that cannot be bought in small amounts, for example a house or primary education. This means that many people may not be able to afford them.

macroeconomic management The management by a government of the overall performance of the economy using such controls as interest rates, taxes, and government spending.

marginal benefit The satisfaction or utility gained by the consumption of the last unit of a product, for example the last mouthful in a meal or the last day of a holiday.

marginal cost The cost, measured either in money spent or the effort of work, required to obtain or produce the last unit of output, for example the last car off the production line or the last working hour of the week.

market failure When the market fails to produce what is most wanted at the lowest possible price: usually reflected in unemployed resources, unconsumed output, or unmet demands.

merit goods Goods and services where individual consumption also produces a more general community benefit, e.g. a child's consumption of education.

New Right Term used in the 1980s to describe the intellectual and political influences on conservative-inclined governments such as those of Margaret Thatcher in the UK and Ronald Reagan in the USA. The intellectual basis of New Right thinking is often associated with writers such as the political economist and philosopher Friedrich Hayek and the economist Milton Freedman and the development of free market or 'public choice' economics. New Right thinking is also heavily influenced by ideas of **individualism**, and advocates social and governmental systems based on this.

opportunity cost Refers to the value of all possible lost opportunities to consume resources in other ways from the current or proposed one.

Organization for Economic Cooperation and Development (OECD) A Paris-based international organization financed mainly by the leading international industrial countries set up in the wake of the US Marshall Plan of the 1940s. The OECD is engaged in a variety of research and similar activities in areas ranging from economic forecasting and studies of comparative economic performance to science policy, environmental policy, and the growing importance and effects of information technology.

Political legitimacy Term used to indicate the likely necessity that policy initiatives and spending decisions should match the values and expectations both of voters and of those making such proposals. For example, while the economic case for reforming the welfare state may be strong, the political legitimacy of many proposals for this may be challenged by the public.

Private Finance Initiative (PFI) A scheme introduced by John Major's Conservative government and continued with Tony Blair's Labour government that seeks to finance public sector projects (e.g. bridges, hospitals, student accommodation) by schemes that involve the injection of private-sector capital in return for an income stream from such investments to the financing organization (e.g. through tolls or rents).

progressive taxation Taxation, usually of income, that takes a larger proportion of whatever is taxed the more someone has of it; e.g. a tax rate that starts at 10 per cent of income and rises in stages to a higher rate such as 40 per cent.

Public Expenditure Survey (PES) Annual system of public expenditure planning in UK government involving bilateral bargaining between the major Whitehall spending departments and the Treasury, culminating in Cabinet agreement on public expenditure objectives over the next (and subsequent) financial years. Formerly conducted on an annual basis, this process was moved to a three-year cycle from 1998/9 (see further Cm. 3978, 1998).

public goods Products from which people cannot be excluded from consumption (e.g. fresh air) and where one person's consumption does not reduce what is available to another. There is no possible profit in the production and marketing of such goods.

Public Sector Net Cash Requirement/Public Sector Borrowing Requirement (PSBR) The amount the government needs to borrow at any one time to bridge the gap between income and expenditure. In 1998 this was retitled the Public Sector Net Cash Requirement in line with other changes to the organization and operation of the public expenditure planning system introduced by the Labour government (Cm. 3978, 1998).

purchaser–provider splits The separation of a state welfare bureaucracy into one part that commissions the provision and another part that 'contracts' to provide it.

quasi-markets Where internal markets or contracting out are limited by regulations that mean the arrangements are not fully exposed to market competition.

short-run efficiency Obtaining the maximum satisfaction at the lowest cost in the very immediate term. Unlike **long-run efficiency**, this is usually obtained by using up all resources as fast as possible, for example in a war.

technical change Inventions and innovations that allow cheaper ways of producing existing goods or which create new goods.

World Bank. An agency of the United Nations, based in Washington. It has 184 member countries and its main function is to manage a large trust fund, made up of contributions from the richer nations, which is used to lend money, interest-free, over long periods to poorer countries for specific programmes, including poverty reduction, social services, protection of the environment, and promotion of economic growth. In 2002 the Bank provided loans totalling $11.5 billion in support of ninety-six projects in forty countries.

11

The Role of the Voluntary and Non-governmental Sector

Duncan Scott

CONTENTS

INTRODUCTION: FROM THE MARGINS TO THE MAINSTREAM

The voluntary and **non-governmental** sector is currently considered to be part of 'mainstream' social policy discourse and practice (Kendall 2000). From the early 1980s, with the collapse of a consensus concerning the central and dominant role of the state in all areas of welfare provision, there has been increasing research, policy debate, and practice reflecting the importance of a 'mixed economy' approach to social need. Part of this has involved the promotion of private, for-profit approaches in fields such as health, housing, education, and the care of older people. Alongside some of these for-profit developments have been a range of voluntary sector initiatives. For example, across the OECD countries voluntary sector, service-delivery organizations grew by nearly 25 per cent in the early 1990s and now provide between 6 and 7 per cent of employment in those countries (Anheier et al. 2001: 1–3). In the transition societies of central and eastern Europe, the voluntary sector is considered a major element in social development; large amounts of foreign investment have been dedicated to the 'deepening' of civil society. In Northern Ireland, the European Union 'Special Support Programme for Peace and Reconciliation' has (since 1994) served a similar purpose.

Increased prominence has brought increased scrutiny. As the voluntary sector has become a more common feature of the policy landscape, some traditional assumptions—about the alleged 'uniqueness' of its characteristics (innovative seed-bed, economic service delivery mechanism, home of egalitarian cultures)—have been questioned. Indeed, the idea of common characteristics across a range of organizational types and sizes, is now treated with such scepticism that the concept of a single **voluntary sector** is no longer taken for granted, at least by academic commentators.

Perhaps the central contradiction resides in increased policy prominence alongside increased critical scepticism. It will be argued that the mainstreaming of the voluntary sector has depended more upon assumptions and rhetoric than on a critical understanding of empirical data. Not surprisingly, therefore, the development of key voluntary sector issues has been uneven; Box 11.1 provides five illustrations of this.

Box 11.1 The uneven development of voluntary sector (VS) issues

Issues	Strongly developed	Weakly developed
1. Government policy	Central government 'mainstreams' the VS in policy discourse	Local government VS policy/practice still marginal
2. Academic perspectives	Increased academic interest	Narrow conceptual/theoretical range
3. Government–VS relationships	State–VS 'partnerships'	Endemic instabilities
4. Worker–Volunteer status	Formalization and professionalization of VS workers	Marginality of volunteers
5. Prominence of other stakeholders	Rise of user groups	Weak conceptualization of non-professional

The chapter explores these examples first by considering the central conceptual and explanatory puzzles involved in thinking about the voluntary sector. A case study is then used to introduce descriptive detail of three of the central policy/practice issues—service delivery, regulation, and citizenship. This is followed by a consideration of the significance of unequal resources (both financial and human) for voluntary organizations. Three different examples, at different levels of scale, reinforce the general details, before a final section returns to examine the key policy dilemmas. A concluding note argues the case for comparative and critical approaches to the role of the voluntary sector.

THINKING ABOUT THE VOLUNTARY AND NON-GOVERNMENTAL SECTOR

Popular perceptions

One of the central features of the increased policy significance of the voluntary sector has been the role played by ideas and assumptions about the alleged characteristics and potential of different organizations and sub-sectors. Moreover, the strength of these ideas/assumptions can be gauged to the extent that key decision-makers (in the voluntary sector and within government departments) appear to subscribe to them. Box 11.2 presents eight common perceptions (left-hand column), alongside alternative descriptions. The discussion that follows clearly indicates that even whilst perceptions are powerful, there are multiple realities within the many different organizations included in the term 'voluntary sector'.

Perhaps the most common perception is that *volunteers* are the dominant or only human resource, whereas the larger, so-called voluntary agencies are often entirely peopled by paid workers (Russell et al. 1996). In addition, there are increasing moves to pay

Box 11.2 Popular perceptions and alternative descriptions of the voluntary sector

Voluntary	Paid
Charitable	Rich charities
Non-profit	Non-profit distribution
Independent	Quasi-statutory
Small	All sizes
Non-formal	Formal
Egalitarian	Hierarchic
Marginal	Central

volunteers both as trustees and as service deliverers; in most cases payment is not as a wage, but either for expenses (e.g. travel, childminder, or nursery provision) or as a token, symbol, or honorarium. More subtly, it has been argued that even some full-time, paid workers are 'partial volunteers', in the sense that the ethos of their agency encourages contributions of an unpaid kind, e.g. working late or at weekends to help provide a service. When attempts are made to estimate the economic significance or 'value' of the voluntary sector or sub-sectors within it, these distinctions and subtleties need to be recognized, (Blacksell and Phillips 1994).

The core meaning of '**charity**' or 'charitable' derives from the idea of caring for those in need. But several centuries of British charity laws have created anomalies: many fee-paying public schools (e.g. Eton and Harrow) enjoy charitable status (e.g. relief from certain taxes) despite having assets which make them as wealthy as large commercial organizations. All of which reminds us that any discussion of the voluntary sector must be located within explicit models of society; models stressing wider social inequalities can be expected to suggest comparable inequalities within the voluntary sector (Burt 1998).

A major contributor to inequality at any level in society is uneven income. Traditional perceptions of voluntary sector agencies frequently single out low income and a non-profit ethos—the image of the jumble sale or street collection updated to T V 'children in need' spectaculars. In practice, *all* voluntary agencies seek to generate profits, not for distribution to shareholders, but to be ploughed back into the maintenance and development of their activities. Current policy enthusiasms for 'social enterprise' ('trading for social purposes') seek to bridge the extremes of profit and non-profit; it is suggested that social goals (e.g. responding to the needs of homeless people) can be sustained by economic ones (e.g. by the income-generating activities of *Big Issue* vendors) (Westall 2001).

Whenever there is talk of income, it isn't long before someone trots out the old cliché 'he who pays the piper, calls the tune'. It is asserted that the prominent role of different government sources of funding (e.g. directly via the Department of Health, New Deal programmes, local government contracts for services, and indirectly via a series of tax reliefs) is likely to lead to decreased organizational independence for the recipient agencies involved. In practice, the degree of 'funding dependence' will be mediated by (i) the nature of the overall funding portfolio—a mix of sources being associated with weak dependence; (ii) the overlapping influence of charity laws which prescribe the boundaries of charitable activity (e.g. how much campaigning should 'Oxfam' undertake if such activities bring it into alliance/opposition with the main political parties?) (Burnell 1992).

It is worth noting at this point that much of the discussion about the implications of economic, political, and legal structures for voluntary organizations is peripheral to the everyday concerns of a majority of them. About two-thirds of registered charities have incomes of less than £10,000 per annum; this means that they do not employ full-time workers because the levels of income and expenditure are simply too low (Halfpenny and Scott 1996). In addition, although there will be some basic formal structures such as a written constitution, an annual general meeting, and elected officers, most of the processes in small organizations will be non-formal. On the other hand, the occupational cultures of the larger *minority* of organizations will exhibit degrees of formality and hierarchy; for example, the uniformed youth agencies (Scouts and Guides) and the Women's Royal Voluntary Service. Similarly, the smaller, more informal settings appear more cooperative and egalitarian than their larger, more formal counterparts. However,

> Research into membership of voluntary agencies' management committees suggests little competition for places and selective recruitment procedures. If one is talking about democracy, then the statutory sector may be closer to popular control than many voluntary organisations. (Marshall 1996: 50)

Given the similarity, in formal organization and occupational culture, between larger voluntary agencies and statutory sector bodies (e.g. departments of local authorities), such a conclusion discourages monolithic generalizations about the former. The traditional policy marginality of the voluntary sector may no longer be the case, but 'mainstream' status applies to the more formal, larger agencies rather than to the non-formal, smaller, community-based organizations; even then, being part of the mainstream is often a fragile, uncertain experience, as subsequent paragraphs on policy and practice will demonstrate.

The 'invention' of a sector

Popular perceptions remain surprisingly powerful, but the simplest of them cannot stand up to close scrutiny; the voluntary sector is clearly not homogeneous, and may be at best characterized as full of 'ambiguities', 'an amalgam of several sub-sectors' (Marshall 1996: 58), a 'terminological mire' (Lewis 2001: 33), even 'creative chaos' (Dahrendorf 1997). Despite conclusions that the task of defining and classifying the voluntary sector is 'inherently impossible' (Kendall and Knapp 1996: 16–17), these same authors do just that (c.f. Osborne 1998: 5–19) via their adoption of what has been labelled a 'structural operational definition' (Kendall and Knapp 1996: 17–18). Four themes constitute the heart of this definition, i.e.

- Formality—so many community groups and informal networks are excluded.
- Independence—but many agencies heavily dependent on state funding are included.
- Non-profit distribution—so co-operatives and mutual aid agencies may be excluded.
- Voluntarism—although many organizations have marginalized the voluntary contributions of time and money by their members.

Perhaps the strongest impetus behind the adoption of 'sectoral' terminology is political and economic; being able to turn to a definable voluntary sector allows politicians to make policy promises. Some wish to signal a partial retreat of the state (e.g. the governments of Margaret Thatcher in the 1980s), whilst others talk of **partnership** (New Labour since 1997). Both ideological positions 'need' a sector to legitimize changes in state policy, to advocate new and expanded care roles by voluntary agencies, and to be able to work in relatively flexible ways, visibly and quickly. Underpinning the political and economic influences have been a growing number of academic researchers and policy entrepreneurs. Examples of the former include the various teams involved in the Johns Hopkins University research project (Kendall and Knapp 1996; Anheier and

Kendall 2001), whilst Deakin (Commission on the Future of the Voluntary Sector in England 1996) is depicted as an example of the latter; indeed, the commission he chaired is alleged to have completed a process of sectoral 'invention' begun in a similar reviewing exercise under Lord Wolfenden (Wolfenden 1978): 'What Wolfenden invented, Deakin has consolidated as a field of policy' (Perri 6 and Leat 1997: 33).

'Invention' has led to a more critical scrutiny of the very concept of sector (Kramer 2000), and a more differentiated understanding of sub-sectors and their boundaries; inevitably, the outcomes of such scrutiny have been mixed—a sounder basis for policy initiatives together with an increasing awareness that much of the so-called voluntary sector 'uniqueness' is without empirical foundation. Figure 11.1 outlines the basic 'sectoral geography', and identifies some central definitional dilemmas.

Four sectors are depicted: state, for-profit, voluntary (sometimes labelled 'third'), and informal—the latter not always being deemed coherent enough to deserve sectoral status, because of the mesh of changing networks and associations which are to be located there. The voluntary sector has been differentiated (a) into three unequal-sized layers (which will be described and discussed in the section on financial resources) and (b) into more and less formal sub-sectors represented by solid and broken lines respectively.

Where the voluntary sector overlaps with the other sectors, there are more likely to be hybrid organizations, combining sectoral characteristics, for example:

- **'Quangos'** reflect a *political* gradient with the state: quasi-autonomous (more or less independent) non-governmental organizations (e.g. health service trust), although not directly accountable to Parliament or local government, are responsible for the administration of public services previously directly provided by the state.
- 'Social enterprises' reflect an *economic* gradient with the for-profit sector: organizations (e.g. furniture recycling, *Big Issue*, cooperatives) which attempt to reconcile the discipline of the market with a commitment to social purposes.
- 'Community groups' reflect a *social* gradient with the informal sector (e.g. preschool playgroups), where most of the key actors are volunteers whose relationships are shaped, not by political or economic influences, but by social exchanges.

Classifying, mapping, and interpreting

It is now commonly accepted that the concept of a single monolithic 'sector' is largely unhelpful and that 'the only common feature is . . . [a] mediating character . . . the voluntary sector provides the market-place for negotiating social values and social relationships.' (Marshall 1996: 58) Some commentators go so far as to suggest that the values and relationships are derived not so much from the voluntary sector as from its structural location between the other three sectors (see Fig. 11.1). This location is likened to a 'tension field' in which the inter-organizational relationships are more often precarious and contingent (i.e. dependent on context and issue rather than so-called unique values and characteristics) than stable and predictable (Evers 1996). Instead, therefore, of trying to explain the various roles of voluntary agencies in terms of their values and their functions, it will be important to take a wider view. The 'tension field' approach draws attention to the following ingredients.

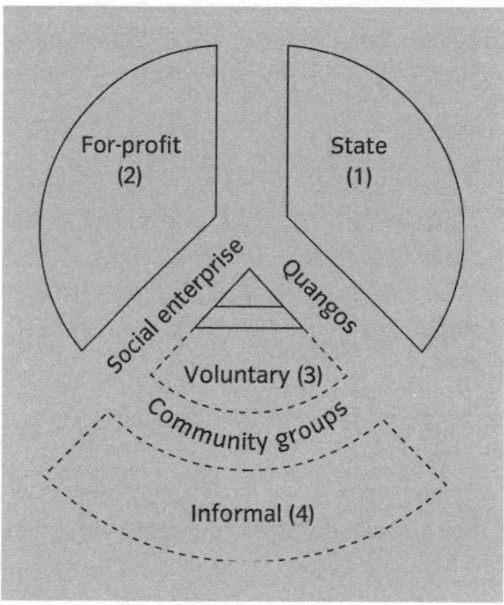

Fig. 11.1 A sectoral geography

- interaction;
- brokering;
- gap-filling;
- challenging;
- dynamics.

Critics of the 'tension field' perspective argue that it cannot be universally applicable; many voluntary organizations are relatively stable and can be understood by reference to their particular functions. The concept of a tension field may be most relevant along sectoral boundaries and in cases of innovation, but it is not the sole explanatory paradigm. What is clear is that, until recently, accounts of the voluntary sector were largely descriptive and uncritical of normative assertions; one reviewer concluded that most commentaries were 'largely atheoretical and leave the study of the voluntary sector in something of a ghetto' (Cameron 1997: 84).

Despite criticism of functional approaches, one of the most useful classificatory tools has emerged from their empirical work. The International Classification of Non-profit Organisations (ICNPO) provides a usable framework within which to compare and contrast voluntary sectors in different societies. Box 11.3 illustrates the key categories, and indicates something of the complexity of sub-categories through the example of social services. Even the most basic category/sub-category classification, comparable to ICNPO, is likely to result in more than seventy functional variations. In addition, it is clear that not all the main functional categories carry the same meaning; there are obvious differences between service delivery (health, social services) and advocacy or politics, between business associations and trade unions. Furthermore, the particular interpretation put on service delivery or politics will, in turn, be dependent on the

Box 11.3 International classification of non-profit organizations

1. Culture and recreation
2. Education and research
3. Health
4. Social services*
5. Environment
6. Development and housing
7. Law, advocacy, and politics
8. Philanthropic intermediaries and voluntarism promotion
9. International activities
10. Religion
11. Business and professional associations, trade unions
12. Others

* children; youth; families; disability; older people; self-help; multi-purpose social service; support, standards, governance.

(Kendall and Knapp 1996: 269–73)

perspective or value system which underpins it. For example, a Marxist might perceive inequality and the need for class struggle, whereas a liberal view of the same circumstances might conclude in favour of individual competition in the marketplace. (Deakin 2001: 8). Voluntary organizations concerned, for example, about the position of racial and ethnic minorities or women in British society will, therefore, not necessarily take one view; the assumption that voluntary and community action is somehow inevitably 'progressive' is a false one.

POLICY AND PRACTICE ISSUES

Service delivery, regulation, and citizenship

In each of the sites in the welfare mix (state, for-profit, voluntary, and informal), three related policy/practice issues arise:

- What minimum standards of *service delivery* exist as bench-marks?
- How is service delivery *regulated* and *developed*?
- What opportunities arise for the exercise of *citizenship* in the sense that different degrees of involvement by different citizen categories are encouraged?

Can it be assumed that the unofficial and official childminders are 'naturally' competent at looking after other people's children? In view of what is known about uneven standards of parenting across social classes and ethnic groups, cosy assumptions about the

Case Study 11.1 A local welfare mix

It is just getting light when a young woman pushes her child in his buggy past the window; two minutes later the scene is repeated. A few minutes go by and two women walk briskly back without buggies. One hour later and the human traffic intensifies as primary and secondary school pupils straggle off to their respective destinations. Then, at about 9.15 a.m., there is another, smaller tidal wave of young mothers tugging 3- and 4-year-olds to preschool. The final episode in all these 'outward' journeys occurs when some preschoolers are shunted from one side of the Community Centre to the other; from voluntary, non-profit preschool to commercial, for-profit 'Tumble Tots'. The welfare mix, for one sub-category of the classification system, is at work.

The earliest buggies are *en route* to paid childminders; some 'hidden' from officialdom, others inspected, supported, and regulated by local authority social services departments. The pre-school group will normally be managed by a committee of parents (usually mothers) on an entirely voluntary basis; the committee will employ paid part-time workers as circumstances allow, and these will be helped by a rota of volunteers from the mothers with children in the group. 'Tumble Tots' is typical of for-profit play/nursery provision and will be owned and managed as a small business. Both forms of pre-school provision (voluntary and commercial) will need to meet certain statutory requirements concerning health and safety and insurance; there will also be regulations relating to the criminal records (or their absence) of all who have direct contact with children. In circumstances where paid workers negotiate differential rates of pay, the possession of approved certificates in childcare will be beneficial.

informal sector's caring capacity cannot be left unquestioned. At the same time, the concept of care has to include physical features such as the size, cleanliness, warmth, and safety of rooms, the quality of toilet, bathroom, and kitchen facilities, and levels of risk in relation to both internal (e.g. stairs) and external (e.g. protection from traffic flow) factors. Playschool contexts add in questions about the appropriateness and safety of equipment and toys as well as the competence of paid workers. Again, the very act of asking questions is seen as unnecessary, even insulting, by those who have traditionally accepted certain normative pictures of informal and voluntary provision. But the new mainstream policy status of the latter, combined with increased academic study, have led to different degrees of scepticism.

Standards are worth little without the capacity to regulate and develop them; in many cases there simply are not the workers or infrastructures to ensure this happens. So, even as the voluntary sector is being asked to play more prominent service delivery roles, serious questions about the uniformity of standards remain.

Finally, there are questions about which social categories become involved as workers and volunteers and which are included or excluded. Women, for example, are unevenly involved in voluntary action in two main ways; first, in terms of content—they are outnumbered by more than two to one by men in sports and recreation, whereas they predominate in welfare fields such as health, education, and social services. A second difference can be identified in terms of the roles undertaken; men are more prominent as treasurers, chairpersons, and committee members, whilst women dominate interpersonal caring, visiting, and befriending (Lowndes 2000: 534). Although there is little data available on the applicability of these findings about women's participation—for example in relation to black and minority ethnic (BME) organizations—it does appear that other dimensions of exclusion affect the work of the latter. For example, particularly outside the large conurbations, it appears that BME involvement in strategic policy issues has been both limited and stereotyped.

> Even where they have been included, the likelihood is that one representative is still, inappropriately, expected to act as the sole voice for diverse minority ethnic communities with divergent interests and experiences; a practice which reinforces exclusion processes. (Craig and Taylor 2002: 141)

Service delivery, regulation, and **citizenship** have become both more important in themselves and more interrelated, as voluntary organizations have assumed greater policy significance. During the early 1990s, service delivery voluntary agencies witnessed a

Cartoon 11.1 Differential citizenship

period of rapid growth, as the 1990 NHS and Community Care Act was implemented; by the mid 1990s it was estimated that over 6 per cent of total employment was located in the voluntary sector. Whilst this might appear of great significance, it is below the average for industrial societies; both Eire and the Netherlands show figures nearly double the UK percentage (Donoghue et al. 1999: 134).

Three related explanatory perspectives attempt to account for the recent growth; these can be broadly termed 'economic', 'political', and 'ideological'. In the first instance, it is argued that voluntary agencies are cheaper, because they use unpaid volunteers and employ paid workers at lower rates than their for-profit counterparts. Secondly, the voluntary sector option allows central governments to initiate policy programmes relatively quickly (there being a general absence of strong trade union and organizational infrastructure), even—in the case of housing associations—appearing deliberately to disempower local authorities. Finally, it is argued that references to 'voluntary' have been used in contradictory, ideological ways both to reinforce the caring roles of women and to open up new opportunities for citizenship—an example is the impact of women's refuges since the 1970s.

General conclusions are probably impossible, given the complexity of what is known as the voluntary sector, but two key questions, with particular reference to service delivery voluntary organizations, can be identified.

- Is there any consensus about the appropriate roles for voluntary agencies in the delivery of publicly funded services?
- In the event that some voluntary agencies do undertake a greater role in delivering public services, what are the impacts?

Partial answers to the above questions will be explored in a consideration of two of the most central resource issues, finance and people.

Financial resources and their consequences

Most people experience requests for donations to voluntary agencies, whether on the street, or via direct mailings or different media; not surprisingly, it is popularly believed that voluntary sector agencies depend on the financial contributions of individuals more than any other source. In reality, the picture is a more mixed one; small, entirely voluntary (i.e. no paid workers) organizations do exist primarily on individual gifts and small-scale fundraising of the jumble sale, sponsored-walk kind. But, as soon as paid workers are a central feature of agency life, the funding pattern changes, and a majority of direct income comes from a range of central and local government departments. It should also be noted that this government dominance is replicated in more indirect ways by various forms of tax relief; despite the continued imposition of Value Added Tax on voluntary organizations, about £1.72 billion of relief was given in the 1999/2000 tax year (Jas et al. 2002: 46). Fig. 11.2 illustrates the income patterns of a sample of voluntary agencies in the north-west of England; the relative importance of individual and government sources of income is clear.

Estimates of the total income of the voluntary sector depend on definition: one of the narrower definitions (using a 'low' figure of UK general charities) resulted in a 1999

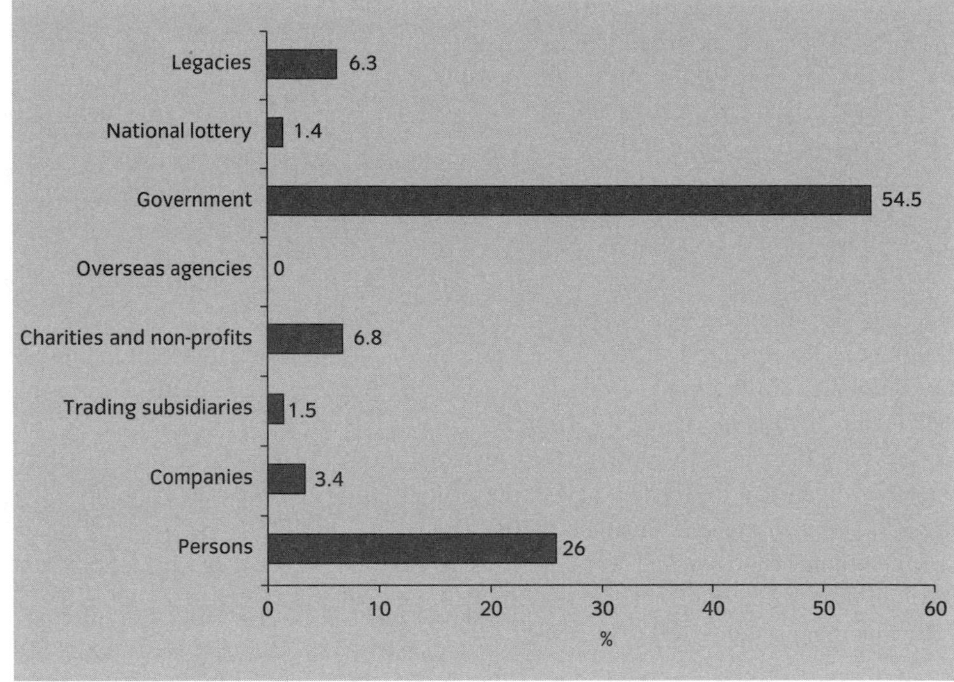

Figure 11.2 Income streams of voluntary agencies in north-west England

Source: Wilding and Passey (2000).

income of £14.2 billion. Broader definitions triple this figure (Hems 2001). Various estimates (by costing volunteer hours) of the different unpaid/volunteer contributions (service delivery, fundraising, administration) produce an additional £11–£12 billion alongside the narrow definition (Hems 2001)

The most striking feature of the real income is its uneven distribution: a third of it is concentrated in the largest organizations, where these are defined in terms of annual incomes over £10 million. Figure 11.3 presents a simplified version of income inequality.

The consequences of income inequality are difficult to summarize; three broad trends have been suggested (Halfpenny and Scott: 1996)

- high-income agencies — increasing number of paid, professional workers; high dependency on funding sources;
- middle-income agencies — organizational uncertainty, with changing mixtures of paid workers and volunteers;
- low-income agencies — increasing reliance on volunteers.

Human resources

The previous section has indicated that large, relatively rich, so-called voluntary organizations are literally so full of paid workers that the roles and contributions of volunteers

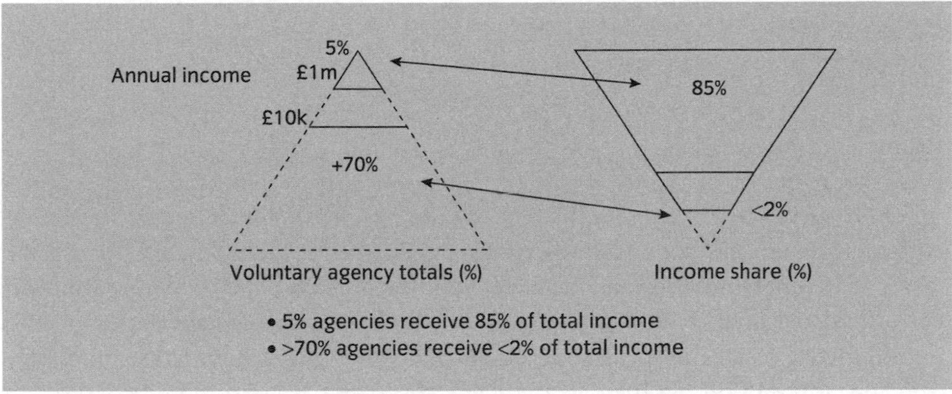

Figure 11.3 Income inequality in the voluntary sector (measured as registered charities)

Table 11.1 Voluntary sector and paid workers: some comparisons

	Overall total	FTE	Part-time (%)	Female (%)
Voluntary sector	514,000	386,000	38	66
For-profit sector			22	40
State sector			30	62

Source: Hems (2001).

are hard to find; the organizational imperatives become those of managerialism and leadership rather than a primary concern with the recruitment, support, and development of volunteers and users. These are the two poles of human resource policy in the voluntary sector. The first pole has, until the recent growth in the policy significance of the sector, been underdeveloped. Indeed, 'parts of the third sector have expressed hostility towards the whole idea of management, which it has seen as belonging to another, alien set of ideologies and concerns' (Lewis 2001: 8).

Despite the hostility, it is apparent that an increasing amount of attention is now being given to the training, support, and development both of voluntary sector managers and the many different levels of workers for whom they are responsible. Table 11.1 summarizes the numbers of paid workers and makes some comparisons with the state and private sectors.

Much greater attention has been paid to volunteers, because there are more of them (3 million supplying 1.5 million full-time equivalents, or FTEs), because voluntary sector ideologies assert their centrality, and because governments are enthusiastic about their policy uses. Recent research has identified the different motivations, roles, and contexts of volunteers and volunteering. Whilst there may be purely altruistic people, who genuinely give their time for selfless purposes, it is becoming generally recognized that individuals volunteer for a mix of personal, social, and economic reasons. Recognition of the mix is vital because policy-makers need to learn how to recruit different categories of volunteer (e.g. young people, newly retired, ethnic minorities); we know enough about the social correlates of changing patterns of volunteering to confirm this. For example, one 1997 survey concluded that the highest rates of *formal* volunteering were associated with increased socioeconomic status, regular employment, and middle age (Davis-Smith 1997: 3). Recent trends indicate that larger numbers of active older people are modifying the age-related finding; similarly, young people are showing a sharp decline in their involvement. When the focus shifts to *informal* voluntary action, larger numbers of African-Caribbean people (particularly men) are recorded; Asian minorities show the lowest rates of both formal and informal volunteering (Prime et al. 2002: 3–6), although relevant empirical data is limited in relation to the latter groups.

The roles and contexts of voluntary effort are equally important, because they often influence both the quality and length of the contribution. Box 11.4 makes a distinction between context and degree of formality; it is useful because it emphasizes the importance of volunteering *outside* the voluntary sector, as well as signalling a distinction between worker-defined volunteering (formal) and volunteer-defined contexts (informal).

Many appeals for volunteers, by voluntary sector and government alike, often fail to recognize these distinctions; the corporate employee who irregularly contributes one or two hours a month (e.g. auditing financial records) is experiencing very different circumstances from a contracted volunteer operating several hours a day, several days per week, or the Women's Royal Voluntary Service (WRVS) shop or trolley in a hospital.

The overall significance of volunteering has become heightened in recent years, not just because of government programmes such as 'Make a Difference' and 'Millennium Volunteers' (Davis-Smith 2001), but also because changing levels of voluntary association membership have been used as indicators in the debates surrounding the concept of **social capital**. Although the concept of social capital has been debated since the early twentieth century (Smith 1998: 51), theoretical and policy interest has increased in the last thirty years via the work of Bourdieu (1972), Coleman (1990), and Putnam (2000). Despite increasing attention, there are still different conceptual approaches; Bourdieu allows social capital (defined as resources derived from active membership of social networks) to be individual or group-based, whereas other writers (including Putnam) argue

Box 11.4 Contexts of volunteering

	Sectoral context	
Degree of formality	*Voluntary sector*	*Other*
High	Contracted day care	WRVS shop/trolley
Low	'Lending a hand'	Irregular corporate help

Box 11.5 Human and social capital

	Human	Social
Key ingredient	The individual	The collective
Indices	Qualifications	Relationships
Impact	Economic output	Social cohesion and trust
Policy response	Education and training	Capacity-building

that the essential ingredient of social capital is collective action. Box 11.5 summarizes the basic distinctions between human and social capital, and their policy implications.

Putnam's thesis argues that the United States has experienced a relative decline in social capital as measured in terms of membership of voluntary organizations. He presents two related dimensions of social capital: first, he talks of *bonding* capital, where social relationships are close-knit and local. This is similar to the concept of communal solidarity depicted in countless studies of poorer urban groups in inner urban neighbourhoods (Smith 1998: 53, 54). On the other hand, *bridging* capital refers to those relationships which stretch out of the intensely local solidarities and connect either with other neighbourhoods or with such institutions as local government departments.

More theoretical approaches have sought to explain the uneven distribution and changing nature of both forms of social capital. Typical questions revolve around origins—does bonding occur mainly in response to group disadvantage, such as poverty or racial discrimination, or can it be located in more affluent sections of society? For example, after race-related disorders in a number of northern English towns in 2001, a series of policy reports prioritized the concept of 'social or community cohesion'; it has been asserted that a reduction of disorder can best be achieved if ways are found to encourage greater social interaction between white and non-white British citizens. At the centre of this policy conclusion are community groups and voluntary associations; how different groups can be encouraged to become more socially interactive (and, therefore, more trusting) is, as yet, less defined (Cantle 2001; Denham 2001). In addition, the same reports which argued for greater social cohesion reluctantly admitted that within some neighbourhoods and groups, considerable social capital could be identified, but that this often took an exclusive, even malign, form. This has been described as the 'dark side' of social capital (Wright 2001: 182).

When policy enthusiasms attempt to become operational, and seek to implement programmes for the development of social capital, two linked questions are central: First, how can before and after measurements confirm that real progress is being made? second, what institutional forms can best assist this?

Measurements, of both a quantitative and qualitative kind, range from the use of single to multiple indicators on the one hand to statements, stories, and case studies on the other (Channan 2002: 34). Present understanding suggests that social capital measurement (levels of voluntary association membership and trust) should be combined with a small number (<10) of other variables such as cohesion, inclusion, and effectiveness. Development of quality measures has been more uneven; Putnam's data has been identified as very male and as neglecting qualitative approaches such as life-history material (Lowndes 2000). In addition, the relatively detached survey approaches have been criticized because of their neglect of local perspectives; the argument being that '. . . there are no robust practical ways of assessing social capital behind people's backs' (Macgillivray and Walker 2000: 201).

When attention shifts to how social capital might be promoted, and particularly to the British context, Putnam's thesis appears to be at least partially contradicted. A key ingredient appears to be government policies (Hall 1999). More local studies confirm and qualify this; for example, 'the institutional aspects that supported people's voluntary action have come at least as much from the general infrastructure of local government as from specific volunteering measures' (Locke et al. 2001: 42; see also Smith 1998: 69).

In short, economic and political reforms are likely to go hand in hand with any increases in social capital. These are crucial rejoinders to those who would prioritize the social at the expense of lifting both the standards of living and the level of democracy; to rely on purely social measures may well amount to a subtle form of social control. Poor and excluded groups would be encouraged to *bond* and *bridge* without sufficient regard for those fundamental inequalities which underpin social interaction.

Much of the policy attention in relation to social capital has focused on the traditional service delivery areas of health, education, and social services. As discussion about indicators and institutions has developed, it is clear that a wider view is needed. For example, much less is known about cultural voluntary organizations—witness the title of what remains a leading work in this area, *The Hidden Musicians* (Finnegan 1989). Yet one of the central ingredients of responses, to disaffected or unemployed young people, is a cultural one—music, theatre, and the arts all proving attractive alternatives to the traditional talk therapy or social or youth work.

At the end of the day, the vital policy connection between voluntary sector organization and the social capital/cohesion discourse has to do with doubts about the concept of 'capital'. In an economic sense capital can be banked or invested, then utilized at a later date. It is not yet clear how far and in what ways social capital can be similarly regarded. Some commentators argue that, unless the social capital is maintained in use (e.g. by active membership in a voluntary organization), then it will fade away like an unused muscle.

ILLUSTRATIONS

Generalizations frequently come to light and make sense to the reader or listener when they are grounded in particular details; the case study or story provides geographical or narrative shape to social action. Instead of a series of static and disembodied statements, there can be movement best interpreted and understood in a specific context. Although there is always a danger of thinking that what can be almost literally touched and seen, in the case or story, is all there is, the following three illustrations are presented to give a degree of substance to the previous sections and to prepare the ground for the final section on policy dilemmas. All three examples are, at local, regional, and national level, broadly typical of those voluntary organizations which attempt to act strategically and provide a space for other activities to come and go. None of them has a central mission to provide direct welfare services; all of them help others to do that, by campaigning and informing and by subletting their resources. They are **intermediary** or 'go-between' **organizations** and, as such, illuminate some of the key dilemmas involved in understanding voluntary sector policy and practice.

A local community association

Oughtrington Community Association (OCA) is a registered charity, founded by local residents in 1979 to prevent the demolition of the former primary school, a Victorian building of some elegance. The village is three miles from a mesh of motorway junctions and fifteen miles south-west of Manchester. In the last thirty years it has grown rapidly from a nineteenth-century core into a dormitory for commuters.

The former school is now a busy community centre used by uniformed youth organizations such as the Guides and Scouts, a preschool, a commercial play organization, a luncheon club for older people, and a set of dancing classes attended by over 120 girls and women per week. A small committee of volunteers coordinates use, deals with physical maintenance, and mediates between users when minor conflicts erupt. Income at the end of the 1990s had risen above £20,000 per annum; donations, grants, hire charges, and the sale of meals were the main sources of income for the association. Each of the user groups maintained their own smaller budgets and operated with proportionately smaller management committees.

Two central issues dominate: finance and volunteers. In the first instance, the 125-year-old centre, which was originally valued at £42,000 in 1979 and is now insured for nearly £500,000, requires increasing capital expenditure for its maintenance, but the potential sums involved are beyond the reach of the local people. Secondly, the number of regular volunteers has not kept pace with the increased usage, which has followed waves of new house-building, prompted by nearby motorways.

OCA is at the bottom of the 'care chain'; it provides a window into local voluntary action for local primary and secondary pupils, a potential site for education in citizenship. It is a first step for those volunteers who subsequently become paid welfare workers, and it offers crucial services for young mothers and older people. But its volunteer resources (largely composed of what are termed 'the active elderly') are caught between rising demand and limited income. As government and charitable foundations increasingly focus on areas and groups in greatest need (inner city, outer overspill, refugees, ethnic groups), lower middle class, white, 'rurbia' (i.e. those rural areas near enough to large urban centres to be increasingly affected by commuting and retirement patterns) becomes a lower priority. Yet, one of the most important population shifts in the twentieth century has been a deconcentration of people from both urban and suburban areas to small towns and rural settlements. This process, known as 'counter-urbanization', has been particularly marked in areas of lowland England easily accessible to larger towns and cities (Phillips 1999: 27).

The social and economic contexts of local voluntary action are clearly important influences which shape both the size and nature of needs and the extent to which voluntary sector responses can effectively meet these. 'Middle England' locations do not figure at the cutting-edge of voluntary sector initiatives, yet they represent a majority of the UK population. The question that has to be posed, therefore, is the same one that must be directed at social policy as a whole: to what extent are social policy/the voluntary sector concerned with the needs of the whole population, or must they be largely preoccupied with those social needs deemed to require the most urgent attention?

A regional 'umbrella' agency

Greater Manchester Centre for Voluntary Organization (GMCVO) is a regional local development agency (LDA) which, with its city-based peer agencies (Councils of Voluntary Service, CVS), attempts 'to support and foster voluntary and community action in their own communities and who operate at the interface between the voluntary sector and government' (Osborne and Ross 2001: 81). GMCVO was established in the mid-1970s to support and coordinate voluntary sector activities (the umbrella function) across the ten local authorities which formally constituted (until dissolution in the early 1980s) the Greater Manchester Metropolitan Authority. It is based in a converted Georgian church in an inner-city area of Manchester and staffed by between twenty and twenty-five full/part-time paid workers; At the end of the 1990s GMCVO had an income of nearly £500,000, from government, lottery, European Union, and charitable trusts. Apart from the volunteer trustees (about fifteen), most of the administration, training, communication, research, lobbying, etc. which constitute the core business is delivered by paid workers; volunteers are notable by their absence.

Whereas the local community association coordinated about ten different groups serving a population of a few thousand, GMCVO lists over 100 'members', i.e. voluntary organizations (some similar to OCA) across a large metropolitan area with over 2 million people. Membership of GMCVO involves much looser relationships, based largely on the changing mix of services provided; individual organizations are not obliged to take up offers of help and so much of GMCVO's everyday work is responsive and episodic. Even the more strategic and pro-active elements in the GMCVO portfolio, such as its coordinating and training roles within a New Deal for Young People scheme (see Scott et al. 2002), depend on intensive negotiation, and even then last usually only for two to three years.

Councils of voluntary service such as GMCVO have begun to play increasingly important roles in the initiation and development of high-profile government responses to urban need. New Deal for Communities as well as for Young People, Millennium Volunteering, Sure Start programmes for young children and their families, initiatives on drugs and the environment are just a few contemporary examples which have involved intermediate voluntary organization intervention. In the case of GMCVO, its regional brief has provided an added tier of activity, as it attempts to service a regional network of voluntary organizations in the north-west and liaise with the North West Development Agency.

The key issues for GMCVO concern the tension between its increasing strategic importance and its inability to obtain sufficient funding over at least the medium term. Without the latter it is unable to develop its information, training, and development roles in such a way as to offer both voluntary and state sector agencies a tailored digest of policy issues. As a recent report on its New Deal activities concluded, truly joint work (with state agencies) will require much greater levels of investment (Scott et al. 2002: 44).

A national centre

The National Council for Voluntary Organizations (NCVO) is the main voluntary sector umbrella agency for England; it was founded in 1919 to promote a greater awareness of the sector's potential among the public, member organizations, and central government. In addition, it carries out research, training, and developmental activities. For example, in 1999 it obtained nearly half a million pounds from what was then the **National Lottery Charities Board** (now the Community Fund), to extend the work of a Quality Standards initiative concerned with more effective organizational development. Whereas OCA might ask its committee to spend one or two mornings a year engaged in a training event (about health and safety or the role of trustees), and GMCVO might facilitate these events at regional and local level, NCVO would be engaged across the sector more strategically.

At the end of the 1990s NCVO, from its modern canal-side offices near King's Cross Station, had an income of £3.7 million, primarily obtained from central government, charitable foundations, and the leasing of its conference facilities. NCVO's public documents list professional staff (about twenty) but none of their administrative and secretarial colleagues. The Queen is its patron, and there are lords, ladies, and 'be-medalled' persons among its trustees. Membership is defined in terms of 'National' (e.g. Age Concern, England) and 'Affiliate' (e.g. Age Concern, Bournemouth); the 1999 Annual Report listed over 800 of the former and about 500 of the latter.

One advantage of NCVO's position at a national level is its ability to take strategic overviews of specific policy issues (e.g. unemployment and the role of the voluntary sector), as well as ensuring that underdeveloped issues (e.g. the impact of devolution on the different UK voluntary sectors (see Jas et al. 2002: 122–41)) are covered. One major set of geographical territories which are largely overlooked in social policy discussions are those areas described as 'rural'. However 'rural' is defined, it is clear that a combination of location, population sparsity, small-scale settlement, and ideology (assumptions about the countryside) do provide a variety of characteristics and needs sufficiently different from most urban-based ones to warrant special attention. A recent NCVO report concluded that 'the support needs of rural organizations . . . are not being met to the same degree as the support needs of voluntary organizations working in more urban areas' (Yates 2002: 24).

This conclusion emerged from research in two contrasting rural areas, Teesdale and East Northamptonshire. Particularly striking was the finding that the numbers of rural voluntary organizations were up to three times greater (per 1,000 people) than average figures for urban areas (Yates 2002: 5).

Two issues for NCVO derive from its strategic location

- in relation to government: critics argue that it may run the risk of exchanging a critical voice for access to policy-makers (c.f. Perri 6 and Leat: 1997 commenting on the NCVO-sponsored 'Deakin report'—Commission on the Future of the Voluntary Sector in England: 1996a; 1996b);
- in relation to other more specialized 'umbrellas' such as Age Concern England or The National Youth Agency: here the dilemmas have to do with reconciling the limited resources of NCVO with the variety (even territoriality) of the voluntary sector.

The three illustrations clearly demonstrate the differentiated nature of the voluntary sector, not just in terms of values, function, or scale but also with respect to the changing significance of financial and human resources. Low-income, volunteer-led agencies experience the financial–human resource tension in ways which are different from the larger organizations led by paid workers.

POLICY DILEMMAS

The fundamental dilemma for policy-makers (assuming they have some sense of the variegated organizational terrain which is the voluntary sector) has to do with being clear(er) about what achievements can be expected from the different levels and types of agency. Academic commentators are only just coming to terms with the complexity of the evaluative task (Kendall and Knapp 2000). There are:

- a range of functions—from service delivery through advocacy and campaigning, from innovative to conservative roles and from leadership building to **community development**;
- a range of perspectives—from normative and rhetorical accounts to deepening scepticisms;

Box 11.6 Policy dilemmas

Policy issue	Example	Dilemma	
Service	Contracting	Formalization of work	Marginalization of some volunteers
Regulation	Charity law	Accountability	Political neutering
Citizenship	Compacts and partnerships	Strategic inclusion	Practical contradiction

- a range of strengths—from committed service and a **social inclusion** tendency to space for personal and political growth; human and social capital;
- a range of weaknesses—from endemic resource problems to a repertoire of exclusions (social class, gender, 'race', and ethnicity all influence personal and institutional relationships); from the persistence of casual approaches to management to divisive elitism between some traditional leaders/workers and volunteers.

Three examples can provide some illuminative detail—not comprehensive, but representative enough of key policy dilemmas.

Service delivery: the costs and benefits of contracting

One of the most significant changes of the 1990s, for voluntary organizations involved in the delivery of welfare services in the UK, was the implementation in 1993 of the 1990 NHS and Community Care Act. This legislation encouraged

- a shift from institutional to community (day and domiciliary) care;
- an emphasis on needs-led rather than supply-led services;
- a decentralization of strategic policy responsibility from central to local government;
- the development of a **mixed economy of care**, involving for-profit and non-profit providers as well as or instead of the state (Scott and Russell 2001: 49–50).

The consequences were mixed: more bureaucracy brought improved administrative and legal skills, greater financial security, and the upskilling of certain (more instrumental and career-oriented) volunteers; these were positives. But greater financial dependence on the local state brought new and narrower roles, mission drift, if not shift; the upskilling of one category of volunteers was paralleled by the incipient exclusion of many traditional volunteers, who brought social rather than technical knowledge.

Wherever the balance lies, it is clearly the intention of New Labour to deepen and widen the service delivery role of voluntary agencies. In the report of the Treasury's cross-cutting review of relations between the voluntary sector and government, published on 10 September, 2002, emphasis was given to core costs, joint planning, training, and (to a lesser extent) leadership (Benjamin 2002; Public Enquiry Unit). The professional managerialist tendency, in the larger voluntary agencies, appears to be in the ascendancy; there is much less attention given to different volunteer issues.

From the perspective of the 'big battalions' all this makes sense; but middle- and low-income agencies, affected by government urging to extend their service delivery contributions, may wish to point to the exclusionary tendencies of such a policy. More professionals, more paid workers, more career volunteers may mean fewer non-professionals and a diminution of the social and developmental significance of voluntary action in favour of a more instrumental orientation.

Regulation: whose voluntary sector?

Parallel to the NHS and Community Care Act of 1990 were a pair of Charities Acts in 1992 and 1993; the Conservative government wanted to achieve greater accountability within the field of registered charities. Given the huge sums involved in both tax relief and the rapid rise in incomes associated with contracting, this was understandable. But as the Charity Commission attempted to respond to government concerns, several dilemmas became more evident. First came the hardy perennial question 'What defines a charity'? The traditional markers of this debate derive from wealth and politics: in what senses are the activities of a public school such as Eton responding to public (in the literal sense) need, and to what extent can charitable status be granted to agencies campaigning politically against poverty? More progress appears to have been made with the latter, in that the relief of unemployment plus urban and rural regeneration were included as charitable in March 1999.

A second area of concern emerged during a period of parliamentary scrutiny: it became clear that charity legislation and regulation were being weakly implemented. A majority of charities did not comply with Charity Commission reporting requirements; even the decision to concentrate attention on the richest charities and double the number of review visits appeared to be scratching the surface (Public Accounts Committee 1998). The enormity of the regulatory task emerged as the voluntary sector became part of both policy and academic attention; radical alternatives then began to be suggested, albeit in an uncoordinated way; these related to a third set of dilemmas concerning the intended and unintended purposes of regulation. At one extreme was the demand to scrap charitable status and save taxpayers' money, particularly if much of the relief could be identified with relatively high-income charities or with those who spent large amounts on administration. At the opposite end of the spectrum were those who wanted to widen the remit of the Charity Commission (or some sister agency) to include the large number of quangos or non-departmental public bodies, such as arts councils, boards of prison visitors, and NHS trusts. It was argued that the higher profile of charity legislation and the work of the Charity Commission displaced attention from the 4,000–5,000 quangos responsible for huge sums of public expenditure, but operating off the regulatory radar screen.

Greater, more complex regulation (albeit with a narrow focus on registered charities of a certain size, rather than with a broader sweep which would include quangos) is likely. Moreover, other regulations concerned with health and safety, the monitoring and audit of grants and contracts, and so on may convince state institutions that different elements of risk are being minimized, but their consequences may be harmful. With particular reference to smaller agencies, the question that must be asked is:

> where is the balance to be struck between the encouragement of spontaneous and freely undertaken informal voluntary action in local communities and the need to ensure that those involved are accountable for their actions? (Rochester 2001:77)

The Strategy Unit report on charity law in England and Wales (Strategy Unit 2002) emphasized the need for changes in charitable status, but it will be important not to become so immersed in legal details as to lose sight of two related issues:

- how the boundaries and mechanisms of regulation are determined;
- the extent to which the actual practice of regulation is shaped more by state bureaucrats and voluntary sector professionals than by local volunteers.

Regulation is not a neutral, technical matter enacted by a benevolent state upon an undifferentiated voluntary sector: the ways in which statutory decision-makers and voluntary sector elites confirm certain patterns of control can have very unequal consequences (J. Lewis 1999). In that majority of voluntary agencies where cash is not the central nexus, and where formal organizational frameworks are substantially integrated with informal, social relationships, regulation may be a very mixed blessing.

Citizenship: compacts in civil society

Traditional assumptions **civil society** and citizenship emphasized inclusion, whereas feminist critics identified an opposing tendency: women were so often excluded. Therefore, 'The idea of citizenship has come to represent a key site of struggle for a range of different interests—from across the political spectrum' (Shaw 2000: 1). These polar conceptions of citizenship provide an organizing framework within which to examine one of the most significant recent strategic policy initiatives involving the state and the voluntary sector: compacts—a family of documents outlining the principles of intersectoral partnerships. Their origins lay in the Deakin report (Commission on the Future of the Voluntary Sector in England 1996a); and their subsequent adoption (from 1998) by the newly elected Labour government represented a break from Conservative policies in two important respects. First, Labour was not deterred by the sheer variety of the voluntary sector; secondly, it was quick to accept a distinction between the former term and the idea of a **community sector**, an amalgam of smaller groups and less formal networks.

Early reviews of the progress of *local* compacts have emphasized a number of critical ingredients for successful development; for example, Time, Fit (i.e. a template for a range of partnerships), Trust, Champions, Resources, Diversity, and Reviewing (Craig et al. 2002: 27–30). Similar points have been made about other government programmes such as New Deal for Communities; the common themes are of optimism and progress. Even when progress is dramatically slow, a positive gloss remains. For example, by mid-2002 only 16 per cent of the 388 English local authorities had signed up to compacts; the target of 58 per cent by April 2003 was just a 'steep climb' (Compact Working Group 2002: 1). At least two structural issues deserve greater attention: first, the need for a greater recognition of the political and organizational contexts of Compact/Partnership development; and second, much greater sensitivity to the differentiated nature of relatively excluded social categories such as black and minority ethnic groups.

Compacts have been described as 'the new "front-room" of statutory/voluntary relationships' (Alcock and Scott 2002: 124), but unless the continued relevance of 'back-room' relationships is identified and discussed in a transparent way, erosion of partnership may quickly follow. This conclusion emerged from a case study which revealed the systematic disruption of formal partnership by pressures external to the local political arena (ibid p. 125).

Black and minority ethnic voluntary organizations frequently don't even make the front-room. An admittedly small-scale study revealed considerable marginality in relation to local policy debates and an almost complete lack of awareness (on the part of black and minority ethnic respondents) of compact initiatives specifically directed at black and ethnic minorities. (Craig et al. 2002: 17–19). Undoubtedly, one factor in all of this is a general lack of knowledge and understanding, on the part of welfare professionals, of the different characteristics and development needs of the 5,500 black and ethnic voluntary and community organizations currently operating in England and Wales (Britton 1999; McLeod et al. 2001; Smith 2002).

The evidence, from three examples of policy dilemmas, is that the voluntary sector's variegated characteristics (in such terms as scale, function, professional–non-professional divisions of labour) allow no simple generalization. Yet in the very territory where New Labour appears to have made the greatest break with previous administrations, compacts, and public–voluntary partnership, there is greatest scepticism. One reason for this may well be a function of initial 'boosterism', as each partner talked up the prospects; the realities have been all the harsher for the early optimism. The main conclusion, however, is that when voluntary sector experiences are described and explained in relation to grounded examples, and when these are analysed with reference to structured inequalities, the conclusion is that 'Partnership working New Labour-style benefits powerful partners' (Rummery 2002: 243). However, what this author does not do is move beyond the dichotomy of *state–voluntary: Powerful–less powerful*; closer attention to the differentiation within the voluntary sector itself would reveal more subtle gradients of power and influence.

CONCLUSIONS

The mainstreaming of the voluntary sector, in relation both to social policy implementation and to the pursuit of academic research, has led to a more differentiated yet incomplete understanding of its characteristics, policy potential, and impact. For example, UK governments have demonstrated increasing commitment to a more positive role for voluntary sector service delivery agencies, and to the deployment of voluntary sector partners in flagship policy programmes such as New Deal. But this commitment appears to have increased despite an emerging consensus among academic commentators that many of the claims for the voluntary sector's social policy potential are at best oversimplified and at worst dangerous. Whilst the time-lag between policy enthusiasms and more sober analyses is not unusual, it will be important to promote a more balanced appraisal during the first decade of the twenty-first century. Such an appraisal will require policy elites and decision-makers in both the state and voluntary sectors being prepared to adopt a less uncritical approach—one which will involve greater realism and humility on the part of all those involved.

The ingredients for reappraisal will include greater recognition of:

- the differential characteristics and potential of the voluntary sector;
- the value of comparative study, both within and beyond the UK;
- the incompleteness of existing interpretative frameworks;
- the inherently contested nature of the prevailing assumptions and values within and about the voluntary sector.

Differentiation has begun with primary attention to functional variety, and with belated concerns about the inconsistent response of many voluntary organizations to social exclusions derived from 'race' and ethnicity, gender, and disability. Moreover, although there are numerous examples of voluntary sector responses to income inequalities, the extent to which the organizational structure and content of voluntary organizations reproduce inequalities (particularly class-based ones) has been much less explored.

Other dimensions of differentiation yet to be seriously considered include the roles of less visible, even secret forms of voluntary organization; these would include, respectively, the ubiquitous Rotary/Round Table associations, which knit together much of the white, middle-class, business, and professional world, and the even less visible networks of freemasonry. Just behind the private and secret curtains of these agencies, considerable useful welfare-related activity may be found; how far and in what ways the private/secret voluntary sector reproduces social inequality and exclusion is a more complex issue.

Comparative perspectives have emerged as responses to such influences as, first, the UK's deepening connections with both the European Union and the transition societies of central and eastern Europe since 1989. Since the passing of the Single European Act in 1986, an increasing number of both statutory and voluntary agencies have proactively sought advice, funds, and relationships from within European Union frameworks. Most of the contacts with peer organizations (e.g. women's groups, disability organizations, families, and children) have been between the UK and Ireland, the Netherlands, with France and Germany also being popular. At the same time, stronger links with the EU have encouraged a 'Europeanization' of sectoral-level policy initiatives across a wide field, from urban and rural regeneration to environmental and traditional social services specialisms. But the overall effectiveness of these moves remains an open question, because of the complex bureaucratic procedures involved. An 'early days' verdict remains the safest one.

Second, global pressures such as the increasing economic interdependency of developed and less developed societies (and the concomitant population movements of poor and professional labour) have facilitated new connections between the UK voluntary sector and those non-governmental organizations (NGOs) with an international development focus. Nevertheless, one of the first systematic attempts to share perspectives and understandings between the UK *domestic* voluntary sector and its international development counterpart only emerged at the end of the 1990. (D. Lewis 1999). Despite this, the linked concepts of 'global civil society' and 'global citizen action' have emerged. There clearly are international and transnational voluntary organizations which work more or less together depending on the issue. But there is not yet strong empirical evidence for global citizen action in the sense of relatively formally coordinated groups. The protests about world trade and environmental issues must be seen, therefore, as very loose movements, capable of convergence at particular events (Edwards and Gaventa 2001: 276–7).

Finally, academic commentators have begun the task of identifying and explaining the extent to which voluntary sectors vary between states. One such approach (the 'social origins' perspective) has attempted to relate voluntary sector characteristics to a range of historical, economic, political, and social influences (Salamon and Anheier

Table 11.2 Voluntary sector employment as % of overall totals

	Culture	Education	Health	Social Services
Ireland	9.9	40.6	22.0	12.3
UK	22.2	20.5	6.5	12.9
W Europe av.	19.0	17.6	15.2	22.7
Czech Republic	33.3	9.9	11.1	12.2
Central Europe av.	31.1	14.1	7.0	17.3

Source: Salamon et al. (1999a: 482).

1998). Table 11.2 presents figures for the overall significance of voluntary sector employment (paid and volunteers) across different functions and states.

Examples include:

- the Irish voluntary sector's high involvement in education—a reflection of the Roman Catholic Church's influence;
- the UK voluntary sector's low involvement in health—a reflection of the strong National Health Service;
- the central Europe percentages in culture—a reflection of pre-1989 strong central state control in education and health and a more open approach to culture.

This use of the ICNPO classification for comparative purposes has been a useful first step away from narrower ethnocentric approaches, but it raises as many questions as it answers, particularly when applied to developing societies. Nevertheless, comparative perspectives on voluntary action are now beginning to develop a multi-layered international literature. An introductory overview (utilizing the ICNPO) is provided by the Johns Hopkins Comparative Nonprofit Sector project (Salamon et al. 1999b: 3–39). Working outwards from the UK, a brief UK comparative study (Kendall with Almond 1998: 8–10) can take the reader on a journey to (1) Northern Ireland and Eire (Donnelly-Cox et al. 2001); (2) eastern Europe (Kuti 2001); (3) Hungary (Deakin 2001: 112–37); and (4) a specific non-governmental organization, studied in the context of international, national, and local social policy environments (Pinnock 2002).

Interpreting voluntary sector activity in its relationship to social policy has been helped by the 'structural-operational' definition and its use of ICNPO data. But, inevitably, these same pioneering comparative studies have exposed explanatory weaknesses. So much stress is placed on formal organization and function that two main lacunae remain under-explored. First, the structural inequalities of any one society (and their impact on sectoral/organizational processes) appear to be treated more as dependent variables, rather than as relatively independent influences on the values, structure, and content of voluntary action. Second, the emphasis on categories and survey-led data underemphasize the dynamics and contradictions associated not just with so much voluntary sector experience but also with the whole post-modern interpretive paradigm; there is less sense of contingency and uncertainty in the apparently reassuring percentages.

At the end of the day, all the differentiated understanding and sensitive policy-making in the world has to come to terms with the question: what is voluntary sector activity for? For some people, the recent mainstreaming of sectoral activities is the best answer: New Labour and new partnerships represent an optimistic future, however flawed (see Deakin 2001: 204). Others are less sanguine. There is a need, all the more urgent *because* of mainstreaming, to restate basic values which assert that voluntary action is 'The expression of free will for a moral purpose for which materialist factors are supporting and not leading . . . An independent force, and not a resource-led force' (Knight 1993: 295).

Pragmatists insist that reality is more complex. The most that can be attempted is a heightened awareness that the voluntary sector contains *contested* values, not just consensual ones, that some (often larger, formal, professional) agencies provide valuable services in the name of voluntary action, when their whole ethos suggests they are more of a hybrid between state and for-profit. Meanwhile, in other parts of the voluntary sector, materialist influences are often less relevant; the small democracies, no less flawed than their bigger brothers and sisters, are providing a different set of experiences. The voluntary sector, as a space for the development of citizenship in addition to or instead of the delivery of public services, appears to be alive and well.

KEY LEGISLATION AND POLICY DOCUMENTS

Charities Acts 1992 and 1993 These Acts prepared the way for clearer accounting systems by registered charities, in particular the regulations concerning a Statement of Recommended Practice (SORP), which became operational from 1 March 1996. There were also sections on investment, fundraising, and the regulatory functions of the Charity Commission.

Compact on Relations between Government and the Voluntary and Community Sector in England 1998 (Home Office) The first of six related documents (three on general issues and three on specific constituencies: (i) black and minority ethnic voluntary and community organizations, (ii) volunteering, (iii) community groups), published between 1998 and 2002. Although not legally binding, this first document implied a degree of authoritativeness because of the subsequent commitment shown by government. At its heart were 'key undertakings' involving lawful voluntary action, standards of governance, quality criteria, cross-sector relations, user involvement, and an annual review.

National Health Service and Community Care Act 1990 This Act stressed the role of the local authority as an enabler rather than as a provider. Local authority departments such as social services were to actively promote a mixed economy of welfare provision by contracting with both the private, for-profit and voluntary sectors for the delivery of such services as residential and day care for older people. From its full implementation in 1993, the Act was given extra force by the provision of a Special Transitional Grant, at least 85 per cent of which was to be spent on community care.

REFERENCES

Alcock, P., Erskine, A., and May, M. (2002). *The Blackwell Dictionary of Social Policy*. Oxford: Blackwell.

—— and Scott, D. (2002), 'Partnerships with the voluntary sector: can compacts work?', In Glendinning, et al. (2002).

Anheier, H. K., Carlson, L., and Kendall, J. (2000), 'Third Sector policy at the crossroads: continuity and change in the world of non-profit organisations'. In Anheier and Kendall (2001).

—— and Kendall, J. (eds). (2001), *Third Sector Policy at the Crossroads: An International Non-profit Analysis*. London: Routledge.

Baron, S., et al. (eds.) (2000), *Social Capital: Critical Perspectives*, Oxford, Oxford University Press.

Benjamin, A. (2002),'Barrier breaker: a helping hand for the charity sector', *Guardian*, 11 Sept.

Billis, D., and Harris, M. (eds). (1996), *Voluntary Agencies: Challenges of Organisation and Management*. London: Macmillan.

Blacksell, S., and Phillips, D. (1994), *Paid to Volunteer*. Berkhamsted: Volunteer Centre UK.

Bourdieu, P. (1972), 'The forms of capital'. In A. H. Halsey et al. (eds.), *Education: Culture, Economy, Society*. Oxford: Oxford University Press.

Britton, N. J. (1999), 'Recruiting and retaining black volunteers: a study of a black voluntary organisation', *Voluntary Action* 1(3): 9–23.

Burnell, P. (1992), 'Charity law and pressure politics in Britain: after the Oxfam inquiry', *Voluntas* 3(3): 311–34.

Burt, E. (1998), 'Charities and political activity: time to rethink the rules', *Political Quarterly* 69(1): 23–30.

Cameron, A. F. F. (1997), 'In search of the voluntary sector: a review article', *Journal of Social Policy* 26(1): 79–88.

Cantle, T. (2001), *Community Cohesion: A Report of the Independent Review Team*. London: Home Office.

Chanan, G. (2002), *Measures of Community*. London: Active Community Unit, Home Office.

Chaney, P., and Fevre, R. (2001), 'Inclusive governance and "minority" groups: the role of the third sector in Wales', *Voluntas* vol 12(2): 131–56.

Coleman, J. (1990), *Foundations of Social Theory*. Cambridge, Mass.: Harvard University Press.

Commission on the Future of the Voluntary Sector in England, (1996a), *Meeting the Challenge of Change: Voluntary Action into the 21st Century* (the Deakin Report). London: National Council for Voluntary Organizations.

—— (1996b), *Meeting the Challenge of Change: Voluntary Action into the 21st Century: Summary of Evidence and Selected Papers*. London: National Council for Voluntary Organizations.

Compact Working Group (2002), *Compact: What's New*? London: National Council for Voluntary Organizations.

Craig, G., and Taylor, M. (2002), 'Dangerous liaisons: local government and the voluntary and community sectors'. In Glendinning, et al. (2002).

—— and Wilkinson, M. (2002), *Contract or Trust? The Role of Compacts in Local Governance*. Bristol: Policy Press.

Dahrendorf, R. (1997), *Speech reported in Parliamentary Debates (Hansard), House of Lords*, Nov. 1996, cols. 315–317

Davis-Smith, J. (1997), *The 1997 National Survey of Volunteering in the UK*. London, Institute for Volunteering Research. (NB The page reference is from www.ivr.org.uk/nationalsurvey.htm/)

—— (2001), 'Volunteers: making a difference?', In Harris and Rochester (2001).

Deakin, N. (2001), *In Search of Civil Society*. Basingstoke: Palgrave.

Denham, J. (2001), *Building Cohesive Communities: A Report of the Ministerial Group on Public Order and Community Cohesion*. London: Home Office.

Donnelly-Cox, G., Donoghue, F., and Hayes, T. (2001), 'Conceptualising the third sector in Ireland, North and South', *Voluntas* 12(3): 195–204.

Donoghue, F., Anheier, H. K., and Salamon, L. (1999), 'Ireland', In Salamon et al. (1999a).

Edwards, M., and Gaventa, J., (eds.) (2001), *Global Citizen Action*. London: Earthscan.

Evers, A. (1996), 'Part of the welfare mix: the third sector as an intermediate area between market economy, state and community', *Voluntas* 6(2): 159–82.

Finnegan, R. (1989), *The Hidden Musicians*. Cambridge: Cambridge University Press.

Glendinning, C., Powell, M., and Rummery, K. (eds.) (2002), *Partnerships, New Labour and the Governance of Welfare*. Bristol: Policy Press.

Halfpenny, P., and Scott, D. (1996), 'Future developments in funding for the voluntary sector'. In Commission on the Future of the Voluntary Sector in England (1996).

Hall, P. (1999), 'Social capital in Britain', *British Journal of Political Science* Vol 29(3): 417–61.

Harris, M., and Rochester, C., (eds.) (2001), *Voluntary Organisations and Social Policy in Britain: Perspectives on Change and Choice*. Basingstoke: Palgrave.

Hems, L. (2001), *The organisational and institutional landscape of the UK wider non-profit sector: An Interim Report for the Performance and Innovation Unit Review of the Legal and Regulatory Framework for Charities and the Voluntary Sector*. London: Centre for Voluntary Sector Policy, University College London.

Jas, P., Wilding, K., Wainwright, S., Passey, A., and Hems, L. (2002), *The UK Voluntary Sector Almanac 2002*. London: National Council for Voluntary Organizations.

Kendall, J. (2000), 'The mainstreaming of the third sector into public policy in England in the late 1990s: why's and wherefore's', *Policy and Politics* Vol 28(4): 541–62.

—— with Almond, S. (1998), *The UK Voluntary (Third) Sector in Comparative Perspective: Exceptional Growth and Transformation*. Canterbury: Personal Social Services Research Unit, University of Kent.

—— Anheier, K. (2001), 'Conclusion: the third sector at the crossroads? Social, political and economic dynamics'. In Anheier and Kendall (2001).

—— and Knapp, M. (1996), *The Voluntary Sector in the UK*. Manchester: Manchester University Press.

—— (2000), 'Measuring the performance of voluntary organisations', *Public Management* Vol 2(1): 105–32.

Knight, B. (1993), *Voluntary Action*. London: Home Office.

—— Smerdon, M., and Pharoah, C. (1998), *Building Civil Society: Current Initiatives in Voluntary Action*. West Malling, Kent: Charities Aid Foundation.

Kramer, R. M. (2000), 'A third sector in the third millennium?', *Voluntas* 11(1): 1–24.

Kuti, E. (1999), 'Different European countries at different crossroads', *Voluntas* 10(1): 51–60.

Lewis, D. (ed.) (1999) *International Perspectives on Voluntary Action: Reshaping the Third Sector*. London: Earthscan.

—— (2001), *The Management of Non-Governmental Development Organisations*. London: Routledge.

Lewis, J. (1999), 'Reviewing the relationship between the voluntary sector and the state', *Voluntas* 10(3): 255–70.

Locke, M., Sampson, A., and Shepherd, J. (2001), 'Bowling along: community leaders in east London', *Voluntary Action* 3(2): 27–45.

Lowndes, V. (2000), 'Women and social capital: a comment on Hall's *Social Capital in Britain*', *British Journal of Political Science*, 30: 533–7.

Macgillivray, A., and Walker, P. (2000), 'Local social capital: making it work on the ground'. In Baron, et al. (2000).

McLeod, M., Owen, D., and Khamis, C. (2001), *Black and Minority Ethnic Voluntary and Community Organisations: Their Role and Future Development in England and Wales*. London: Policy Studies Institute.

Marshall, T. F. (1996), 'Can we define the voluntary sector?' In Billis and Harris (1996).

Murphy, C., and Shucksmith, M. (eds.) (1999), *Rural Audit: A Health Check on Rural Britain*. London: The Rural Group of Labour MPs.

Osborne, S. P. (1998), *Voluntary Organisations and Innovation in Public Services*. London: Routledge.

—— and Ross, K. (2001), 'Regeneration: the role and impact of local development agencies'. In Harris and Rochester (2001).

Perri 6 and Leat, D. (1997), 'Inventing the British voluntary sector by committee: from Wolfenden to Deakin', *Non-Profit Studies* 1(2): 33–46.

Phillips, M. (1999), 'Migration and social Change'. In Murphy and Shucksmith (1999).

Pinnock, K. (2002), 'The impact of the NGO sector and Roma/Gypsy organisations on Bulgarian social policy-making 1989–1997', *Journal of Social Policy* 31(2): 229–50.

Prime, D., Zimmeck, M., and Zurawan, A. (2002), *Active Communities: Initial Findings from the 2001 Home Office Citizenship Survey*. London: Active Communities Unit, Home Office/Stationery Office.

Public Accounts Committee (1998), *The Charity Commission: Regulation and Support of Charities*. London: HMSO.

Public Enquiry Unit (2002), The Role of the Voluntary and Community Sector in Service Delivery: A Cross Cutting Review. London: HMT

Putnam, R. (2000), *Bowling Alone: The Collapse and Revival of American Community*. New York: Simon & Schuster.

Rochester, C. (2001), 'Regulation: the impact on local voluntary action'. In Harris and Rochester (2001).

Rummery, K. (2002), 'Towards a theory of welfare partnerships'. In Glendinning et al. (2002).

Russell, L., Scott, D., and Wilding, P. (1996), 'The funding of local voluntary organisations', *Policy and Politics* 24(4):

Salamon, L., and Anheier, H. (1998), 'Social origins of civil society: explaining the non-profit sector cross-nationally', *Voluntas* 9(3): 213–48.

—— and Associates (1999b), 'Civil society in Comparative Perspective'. In Salamon et al. (1999a).

—— R. List, S. Toepler, S. W. Sokolowski, and Associates (eds.) (1999a), *Global Civil Society: Dimensions of the Non-profit Sector*. Baltimore: Johns Hopkins Centre for Civil Society Studies.

Scott, D., Alcock, P., Russell, L., and Macmillan, R. (2000), *Moving Pictures: Realities of Voluntary Action*. Bristol: Policy Press.

—— and Russell, L. (2001), 'Contracting: the experience of service delivery agencies'. In Harris and Rochester (2001).

—— Faulkner, M., and Nugent, M. (2002), *New Deal, High Stakes: An Evaluation of the Impact on the Voluntary Sector*. Manchester: Greater Manchester Centre for Voluntary Organization.

Shaw, M. (2000), 'Community, citizenship and the market: dilemmas in the voluntary sector'. Unpublished paper, International Society for Third Sector Research, International Conference, Dublin.

Smith, G. (1998), 'A very social capital: measuring the vital signs of community life in Newham'. In Knight et al. (1998).

—— (2002), 'Religion and the rise of social capitalism: the faith communities in community development and urban regeneration in England'. *Community Development Journal* 37(2): 167–77.

Strategy Unit (2002), *Private Action, Public Benefit: A Review of Charities and the Wider Not-For-Profit Sector*. London: Strategy Unit.

Westall, A. (2001), *Value-Led, Market-Driven: Social Enterprise Solutions to Public Policy Goals*. London: Institute for Public Policy Research.

Wilding, K., and Passey, A. (2000), *The Northwest Voluntary Sector Almanac 2000*. London: National Council for Voluntary Organisations.

Wolfenden, Lord (1978), *The Future of Voluntary Organisations*. London: Croom Helm.

Wright, K. (2001), Review of Putnam (2000), *Voluntas* 12(2): 181–4.

Yates, H. (2002), *Supporting Rural Voluntary Action*. London: National Council for Voluntary Organizations and the Countryside Agency.

FURTHER READING

Active Community Unit, Home Office. See www.homeoffice.gov.uk/inside/org/dob/direct/ accu.html for an overview of current government initiatives concerning the voluntary sector and urban regeneration.

Alcock et al. (2002). A useful introduction to the key terms (and some of the most important people) in social policy. Nearly all the Glossary entries in this chapter are to be found at greater length in this *Dictionary*.

Anheier and Kendall (2001). An introduction to some of the leading international commentators, particularly those associated with the Centre for Civil Society, London School of Economics and Political Science, and ISTR (see *Voluntas* below).

Deakin (2001). An accessible guide to the different interpretations of 'civil society', and their relevance for social policy.

Glendinning et al. (2002). The concept of partnership links voluntary sector issues to wider questions of social policy and governance. A good introduction to New Labour's enthusiasm for the '**third way**' and communitarian approaches.

Harris and Rochester (2001). The most comprehensive and contemporary collection of essays with a British (largely English) focus.

Jas et al. (2002). The 4th edn. (since 1996) of a strongly quantitative compilation of basic data. Innovative in containing separate sub-sections on Wales, Northern Ireland, and Scotland. Further information from www.ncvo-vol.org.uk

Kendall and Knapp (1996). The definitive overview of the UK voluntary sector. Although much of the data is now nearly a decade old, it is still the leading work of its kind. To be read alongside the CVO Almanac: see Jas et al. (2002).

Salmon et al. (1999). A comprehensive analysis of the non-profit sector (using a common framework) of twenty-two countries throughout most of the world (none from Africa, only Japan from Asia).

Scott et al. (2000). Using qualitative case studies of eight key policy and practice issues, this text attempts to portray the dynamics and contradictions inherent in much voluntary action.

Voluntary Action. A British-based journal specializing in articles on volunteers and volunteer organizations. Associated with the Institute for Volunteering Research. See www.volunteering.org.uk

Voluntas. An international journal containing a wide range of academic articles and reviews about voluntary and non-governmental issues. Associated with the International Society of Third Sector Research (ISTR: see www.istr.org).

GLOSSARY

charity A concept containing two, partially divergent, interpretations: open, unlimited love; and caring which discriminates in favour of 'true' need and the work ethic. Since the 1601 Poor Law Act, the state has defined, registered, and monitored charitable organizations. There are about 185,000 registered charities in England and Wales, 25,000 (an overestimate?) in Scotland, and 5,000 in Northern Ireland. Charitable status is granted to organizations promoting the relief of poverty, the advancement of education, the advancement of religion, and other purposes beneficial to the community. Such status brings advantages (e.g. significant tax exemptions and privileges) and disadvantages (e.g. limitations on political activity).

citizenship Legal membership of a nation-state, together with political and social rights and obligations; often there are social categories (e.g. women, ethnic minorities) excluded from full citizenship.

civil society The 'spaces' between the market and the state where individuals and institutions can campaign for, and further develop, social and political rights. NB 'active citizenship' is used to label project-based schemes, mainly targeted at young and long-term adult unemployed, which promote volunteering and community activity.

community action Issue-based campaigning by local groups concerned to improve the quality of, for example housing, environmental conditions, or crime patterns.

community association A local group with formal purposes of a non-profit distributing kind; examples include preschool playgroups, youth clubs, and day centres for older people, as well as educational and leisure pursuits.

community development Aims to improve the capacity of local citizens to join voluntary organizations; often supported by local authorities as part of urban regeneration and neighbourhood renewal programmes.

community sector Refers to locally based associations and groups mainly dependent on voluntary support, e.g. preschool playgroups, youth organizations.

compact A formal agreement about the principles that should govern relationships between government and the private or voluntary sectors; established since 1998 at both central and local government levels, with both general and specific (black and minority ethnic groups, volunteering and community groups) publications.

contract culture The assumption that quasi-legal agreements ('contracts'), between local authorities (purchasers) and service delivery voluntary organizations (providers), promote more formalized procedures in the latter. Advocates of such approaches welcome the specificity and cost-effectiveness, whereas critics point to a loss of agency independence and the marginalization of volunteers.

intermediary organization Acts as a link between local and national voluntary agencies and other sectors, especially the state. General examples include Councils of Voluntary Service (CVS) in urban areas and Rural Community Councils (RCC). Specialist examples exist in most welfare fields, e.g. Age Concern (with reference to older people) and Community Relations Councils (with reference to black and minority ethnic groups).

mixed economy of care Refers to service provision by combinations of sectors (private, state, voluntary, and informal).

National Lottery Charities Board (renamed the Community Fund) One of six boards or committees charged with distributing the 28 per cent of overall lottery income allocated to them.

non-governmental organization (NGO) The term traditionally used to identify those agencies dedicated to economic and social development in the third world; they can be broadly divided into (i) northern—NGOs in the more developed societies; (ii) southern—NGOs in the developing societies; (iii) international—NGOs which cut across national boundaries. NB The term 'non-governmental' in this chapter is mainly synonymous with 'voluntary'.

partnership A generic term for any systematic set of relations between at least two organizations. More recently, it has become increasingly formalized to refer to inter-sectoral agreements.

quango A quasi-autonomous non-governmental organization, operating at arm's length from the central state and local authority, but authorized to oversee aspects of public administration such as health service trusts.

social capital Refers to those relationships between individuals which are based on reciprocity and trust rather than contract and payment. Further conceptualized as of two types: (i) bonding, where the emphasis is on close, dense relationships usually within a locality, and (ii) bridging, where the emphasis is on extended, thinner relationships between localities or groups (Locke et al. 2001).

social exclusion A term, first developed in continental Europe, for the conditions and causal processes which characterize a broader range than income poverty; so social and political exclusion are included as well as limited financial resources. The term can be applied to individuals, groups, and localities.

social inclusion Refers to those conditions and responses designed to ameliorate or remove exclusion; this includes individual and collective capacity-building, improved access to services, and better service delivery (see Chaney and Fevre 2001).

third sector This term attempts to avoid debate about the relevance of 'voluntary', 'nonprofit', and 'independent' as alternative labels; it does not imply lower rank or status in relation to other sectors.

Third Way A term adopted by New Labour to describe policy initiatives combining state, for-profit, and voluntary sector values and institutions rather than reflecting any single sector.

voluntary sector A generic term for the total field of non-profit distributing organizations, which have varying numbers of volunteers on their management and in their workforce. Use of 'sector' does not imply a particular degree of common identity and organization.

volunteer People who feel they are freely contributing their time to help an individual or group outside the immediate circle of family, neighbours, and friends.

PART FOUR

DELIVERING WELFARE

12

Cash Transfers

Tony Fitzpatrick

CONTENTS

CASH, THE WELFARE STATE'S MOST DISPUTED TERRITORY

The benefit system attracts perhaps more controversy than any other welfare institution. One of the reasons for this is obvious: in 2000–1 benefits cost £101 billion in total, and at the present rate of growth this figure is expected to reach at least £110 billion by 2005–6. This represents about one third of all government spending, or about 12–13 per cent of **Gross Domestic Product**.

There are two points to bear in mind, however. First, approximately 47 per cent of the benefits bill is typically spent on the elderly, 27 per cent on sick and disabled people, 20 per cent on families, and just 6 per cent on the unemployed. Therefore, the idea that there are substantial savings to be made by either encouraging or forcing people into employment is a popular misconception. Secondly, the UK's spending on benefits has long been below the European Union (EU) average, with only Spain, Portugal, Ireland, and Greece spending less. On one level, then, we are required to analyse the economics of the subject and examine issues relating to cost and redistribution. However, this kind of analysis does not, by itself, reveal why the subject of cash transfers attracts such controversy.

The real reason lies in the essential difference between this system and the others which are dealt with throughout Part Four. With goods such as health and education we are dealing with services in kind and, as you will see in the following chapters, these services have generated a great deal of debate and disagreement. Nevertheless, when we examine services in *cash*, by comparison, we have to take into account a level of normative and prescriptive commentary that arguably exceeds that of any other welfare system. There are several reasons for this greater intensity of debate, but the most significant concerns the fact that a cash transfer can be spent in whatever way the benefit claimant chooses: in other words, in-cash services offer a degree of freedom, and demand a degree of self-responsibility, which surpasses that of in-kind services.

THE ORIGINS OF THE BRITISH SYSTEM

By cash transfers we mean the benefits which are paid out by the system of **social security**, but the meaning of the term 'social security' changes depending upon the context. Ginsburg (1992: 101–2) notes how in the United States a distinction is made between welfare and social security: the former refers to the means-tested assistance for the very poor which carries a considerable social stigma; the latter refers to the non-means-tested benefits, which are more highly esteemed. In continental Europe, however, social security has a very broad meaning which may encompass health care and which sometimes even substitutes for terms such as the 'welfare state' and 'social welfare'. In Britain, we tend to occupy a midway point between these positions. Therefore, we can define social security as referring to the benefits and cash transfers which are provided, financed, and regulated by the state for the purpose of income maintenance in particular and social welfare in general.

The history of social security can be traced back to the Germany of the 1870s. Rimlinger (1971) has observed how Chancellor Bismarck responded to the rising influence and importance of the industrial working class by trying to reduce the appeal of socialist ideas. He introduced various benefits inspired by the **social insurance principle** where people contribute to a collective pool during their periods of economic activity and draw benefits from that pool when they become economically inactive. Social insurance benefits are therefore intended to provide the individual with a collective form of protection, and Bismarck imagined that such benefits would therefore make the working class less likely to challenge the existing social order. Over the course of time, however, the German socialists and social democrats came to adopt the social insurance principle as their own, as something which could empower the powerless. Therefore, the social insurance principle has been of central importance to twentieth-century welfare systems because it has offered conservatives a means of defending the existing order and has offered socialists and social democrats a means of changing it.

The German experience convinced the British Liberal government of 1905–15, partly under the influence of William Beveridge, to adopt a scheme of social insurance and so laid the foundations for the benefit system of the interwar years. As we shall see below, the insurance system offers various advantages and disadvantages. On the publication of the Beveridge Report (1942), however, at the height of the Second World War, it was the advantages which were stressed, setting the tone for the widespread postwar belief that the welfare state was an essential part of a just society.

THE AIMS AND ROLES OF SOCIAL SECURITY

The basic aim of Beveridge's system was the prevention of 'want', or poverty; he believed that an insurance-based system would do this by guaranteeing a decent minimum income for those who either (a) lost their earning-capacity, e.g. due to unemployment, sickness, and accident, or (b) lacked earning capacity, e.g. due to retirement. However, as well as insuring the incomes of earners the Beveridge system was concerned to meet the needs of households that depended upon them: in particular, the costs of a family and the important events that might affect it, e.g. birth, death, and marriage. The prevention of poverty, argued Beveridge, would be brought about by reducing to a bare minimum the numbers of people relying upon means-tested assistance, and he anticipated that a scheme of compulsory social insurance, in the context of full employment, would be sufficient to achieve this. However, in addition to benefiting from full employment there was also the expectation that social security would contribute to the creation of full employment itself. Jose Harris (1997) records how enthusiastic Keynes was for Beveridge's proposals because he believed that they would assist in the management of the demand for goods and services and so for high levels of employment (see Chapter 6).

The politicians and policy-makers who followed Beveridge throughout the next few decades held to this expectation that an insurance model of social security would prevent poverty. Gradually, however, as unemployment began to rise, the emphasis shifted away from poverty prevention to poverty relief. More and more households either exhausted their rights to insurance benefits or, because of rising unemployment, could not amass the contribution records needed to entitle them to such benefits in the first place. In other words, the aims of cash transfers became more modest than Beveridge had orginally envisaged: increasingly, the explicit aim was to keep claimants' heads above water rather than to imagine that social security could free them from poverty altogether. By the 1960s it was admitted that a large-scale reliance upon means-tested assistance was not going to disappear when National Assistance benefit became Supplementary Benefit, and reliance upon means-testing has grown rapidly ever since (see the section on the categories of cash transfer).

Critiques of social security

As the postwar welfare state began to experience the pressures of rising unemployment, the Right became ever more critical. Milton Friedman (1962) criticized social insurance schemes as forms of state compulsion which infringe upon the freedom of individuals and which are less efficient than a market-based system. As an alternative, he advocated that social security should become a purely means-tested system which aims to relieve the proven need of those whose income falls below a certain level. Also on the Right, F. A. Hayek (1976: 87) argued that there was a need for an 'assured minimum income' to be provided outside the market, and was not averse to the principle of social insurance (Hayek 1960: 285–97). However, he was opposed to the monopolization of such schemes by the state which, he thought, should provide only for those who experience absolute destitution.

By contrast, many on the Left have interpreted social security not so much as a system for poverty prevention or relief but as a system of social control. Marxists have argued that cash transfers function according to wider socioeconomic requirements: they help to camouflage the exploitative nature of capitalism and they enforce the values and behavioural norms which enable capitalism to function more effectively. For instance, according to Norman Ginsburg (1979), the social security system can be charged with having three repressive functions. First, it depresses wage levels because benefits are so low that people are effectively forced into low-paid jobs. Second, it maintains the labour supply because in order to claim benefits people are expected to be capable of, and actively looking for, employment, so providing a cheap pool of labour where people can be hired and fired at will. Also, since eligibility for insurance benefits requires the kind of long-term employment histories which women are less likely to have, they are thrown back onto their domestic roles as carers, 'reproducing' the present and future generations of (male) workers. Finally, the system disciplines claimants and workers alike: the former are rendered powerless, the latter are effectively disciplined into accepting the capitalist labour market since, for all its faults, being a wage-earner is demonstrably better than being a claimant.

Some feminist theorists have argued, along similar lines, that social security reinforces gender divisions. Beveridge may have talked about equality between men and women, but this did not square with his assumption that most women would be dependent upon a husband so that their entitlements to benefits could reasonably be determined by the employment records of their spouses. What this has done, feminists argue, is to weaken women's independence within marriage and to restrict their freedom to leave an unwanted partnership. Howard et al. (2001: 38) show that women and children are more likely to be in poverty than men and that 61 per cent of lone parents (90 per cent of whom are women) were in poverty in 1999–2000.

Of the above critiques it was those from the political Right which were to be the most influential in actual policy-making. By the 1980s the Thatcher government was explicit in its belief that social security should aim to relieve destitution rather than to prevent poverty—a concept which they disputed anyway. Therefore, the benefit system should have three aims: the system must meet genuine need, i.e. those of the deserving poor; it should be consistent with the general aims of the economy; it must be simple to understand and administer. The benefit reforms of the Thatcher government consequently introduced into the system more means-testing, more targeting, more discretion and greater enforcement of the work ethic. As we shall see below, New Labour's reforms have been largely continuous with these aims.

Overall, the experience of the last fifty years has shown that the basic and fairly simple aims of the Beveridge social security system need to be understood in the context of the more complicated realities that emerge in trying to fulfill those aims. Barr and Coulter (1990: 274–6) summarize the strategic aims of the social security system as: *income support*, which encompasses poverty relief, the protection of living standards, and redistributing an individual's income throughout the lifecycle; *the reduction of inequalities*, i.e. class, racial and sexual inequalities; *social integration*, so that benefits permit social participation without stigma. However, they argue that these will only be achieved if a transfer system can adhere to certain operational principles: *efficiency*, so that incentives to work and save are not adversely affected; *equity*, which implies providing an adequate minimum income to those who need it the most; and *administrative simplicity*.

From the above arguments, we can see that the aims of the actual cash transfer system are complex and even contradictory. In some respects it seems to have a benign aspect to it (fulfilling basic needs and relieving poverty) whereas in others it may appear less than benign (controlling behaviour and reproducing underlying social disadvantages).

DIRECT AND INDIRECT FORMS OF TRANSFER

One of the earliest and still the most influential analyses of the postwar social security system was provided by Richard Titmuss (1958). According to Titmuss, the Beveridge system enshrines a 'social division of welfare' where we fail to appreciate the extent and the generosity of an indirect and hidden welfare state. First, Titmuss distinguished between state welfare and **fiscal welfare**: the former refers to the attempt to improve wellbeing by delivering goods and resources *to* people; the latter refers to the wellbeing which derives from a deliberate failure to collect resources *from* people. Cash transfers may therefore be classified as state welfare, whereas tax reliefs and allowances can be classified as fiscal welfare. Titmuss's distinction is important because the former is defined as expenditure (money that governments pay out) while the latter is merely forgone revenue (money that the government never receives), and so the former tends to attract a level of attention that the latter avoids. In short, our reactions to state welfare are different from our reactions to fiscal welfare: we easily become obsessed with the costs and the 'burdens' of the poor because they are seen as draining the public purse, whereas the fiscal welfare state, from which the non-poor mainly benefit, is conveniently overlooked. As Dee Cook's (1989) study has shown, this is reflected in the different responses which society makes to benefit fraud and tax evasion, with the former receiving much more government attention and public disapproval than the latter. And as we shall see below, New Labour's approach to benefit reform has consisted of trying to extend the advantages of fiscal welfare to the poorest households also.

Titmuss also drew attention to **occupational welfare**, or the advantages which people may derive from their employment, e.g. subsidized canteens, housing and gyms, company cars, life assurance policies, and private health insurance. These can be thought of as 'indirect wages' because they help to boost employees' disposable incomes but are more tax-efficient for the employer than simply raising salaries. State and occupational provision now interact in ways which are more complex than when Titmuss was writing, due to the introduction of things such as Statutory Sick Pay, which is administered by employers, and the growth of occupational pension schemes. For millions, the latter have gradually replaced the state pension as the main source of post-retirement income; these schemes are administered by employers but they are also a form of fiscal transfer, since people paying into an occupational scheme pay fewer insurance contributions to the state and benefit from certain tax advantages.

Titmuss argued that once all of these forms of provision are taken into account the transfer system is far less redistributive and egalitarian than it might at first appear. Later research by Julian Le Grand (1982) seemed to confirm Titmuss's worst expectations about the non-poor benefiting disproportionately from welfare provision because class-based inequalities have remained more or less intact. However, Powell (1995) points out that the welfare state was always concerned with a more modest form of citizenship which did not necessarily require the massive transfer of wealth and income to the worst-off.

An important revision of Titmuss's categories was provided by Hilary Rose (1981). According to Rose, although Titmuss showed far more sensitivity to the social position of women than most of his contemporaries, he too neglected what she called the 'sexual division of labour'. This sexual division refers to the fact that because it is women who still perform most of the unpaid work in the home, and because it is men who gain the highest wages, as well as the wage-related benefits which go with them, then women could be thought of as being net contributors to the wellbeing of men by boosting their disposable incomes. Indeed, the research of Jan Pahl (1989) demonstrated how the distribution of income within the household is skewed in favour of men. For instance, women are more likely to spend their money on their children, whilst men are more likely to spend their money on themselves.

Titmuss's distinctions have been further refined by Kirk Mann (1992), who insists that the social division of welfare exists because both policy-makers and the affluent have observed and exploited social divisions within the working class. He finds that the

Box 12.1 The racial division of welfare

- Black people are two to three times more likely than white people to experience poverty.
- Black people are twice as likely to be unemployed.
- Black people are more likely to be in low-waged jobs, with the average hourly pay of black men being 88 per cent that of white men
- Black people are less likely to qualify for insurance benefits, due to factors such as low and irregular earnings, short working lives in the UK, and absences abroad.
- Black people are two to three times as likely to be dependent upon means-tested benefits and less likely to claim benefits to which they are entitled in the first place.
- There is evidence of direct and indirect discrimination within the benefit system, both in the conditions imposed on benefit eligibility (e.g. not relying upon public funds is a condition of immigration into the UK) and in the administration of transfers (e.g. both direct and institutional racism).

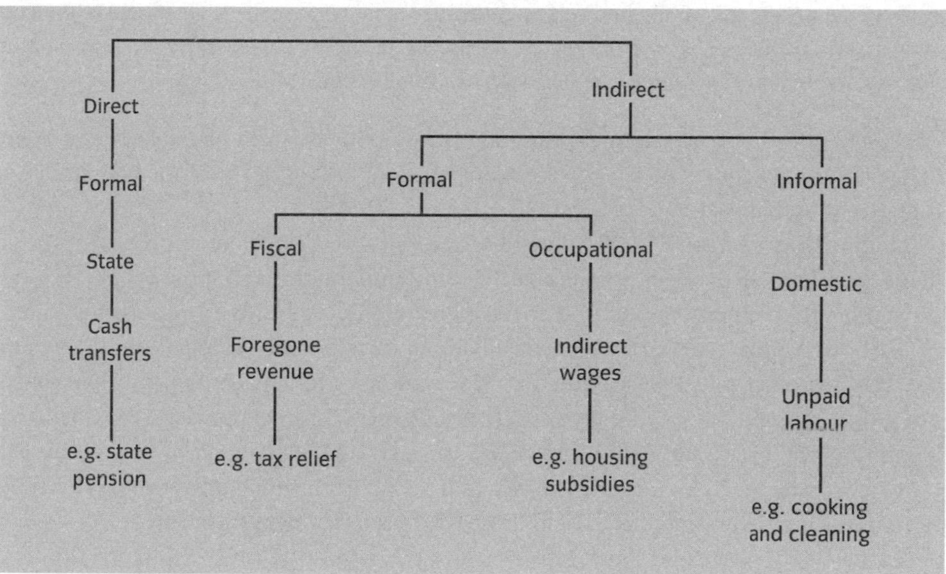

Figure 12.1 Transfer systems

organized labour movement failed to address racial discrimination, and sometimes exacerbated it, ensuring that poverty would have a substantial racial dimension and so giving rise to what Mann calls the 'racial division of welfare', where black people are more likely than their white counterparts to experience the most draconian and least generous aspects of welfare provision. For some reason, there has been far less research conducted into ethnicity and social security than into any other welfare institution (Craig 1999; Berthoud 2002), but Mann's thesis (as summarized in Box 12.1) seems to be confirmed.

The distinctions drawn by Titmuss suggest that any discussion of cash transfers has to be receptive to the indirect as well as direct forms of welfare, as illustrated in Fig. 12.1.

Throughout the rest of this chapter we shall be mainly discussing the direct cash transfers of the social security system but we will have to make some reference to indirect transfers also.

UNIVERSALISM AND SELECTIVISM

A debate about the relative merits of universalism and selectivism has shadowed the last fifty years of social policy research, although many authors have come to dismiss it as redundant, e.g. Spicker (1993: 94) insists that the 'debate is moribund and has been for years'.

According to Titmuss, the principle of universalism refers to:

> the aim of making services available and accessible to the whole population in such ways as would not involve users in any humiliating loss of status, dignity or self-respect. There should be no sense of inferiority, pauperism, shame or stigma in the use of a publically provided service; no attribution that one was being or becoming a 'public burden'. (Titmuss 1968: 129)

This principle therefore seems an admirable one upon which to base a benefit system. However, the defenders of selectivism point out that universalism is not as desirable as it might at first appear.

Imagine that we have £1,000 to distribute among 100 people. The universalist would demand either that every person receive the same amount or that if some people are to receive more than others (because their need is greater) then this should be done humanely, i.e. without having to reveal personal details about their income, savings, possessions, and so forth. However, selectivists argue that without tests of income and means then we are not going to target our £1,000 very effectively. Those who are in need are those who are genuinely not able to look after themselves through no fault of their own, and this can only be ascertained by examining the personal details from which universalists shy away. As such, universalism may fail to help those who need that help the most.

The debate does not end there, however, as selectivism works less well in practice than it does in theory. Means-tested targeting implies four basic stages. First, we have to *identify* those to be targeted; but since means-testing involves a certain amount of stigma (see the section below on 'Stigma, take-up, and fraud') then people may not come forward to be identified in the first place. Second, we have to *aim* at our targets; but this may not be easy since people's circumstances change rapidly, i.e. the nature of the target may be constantly shifting, and this may put us off our aim, especially where a great deal of discretion is involved. Third, we have to *hit* our target; but this may not be easy either, since those who receive the benefits (usually men) may not be those who need the resources the most (usually women and children). Finally, we have to hit our target *without disabling it*; as we shall see in the section on unemployment and poverty traps, means-testing is often very poor at doing this.

In short, selectivism implies means-testing or charging at the point of use, whereas universalism implies the absence of means-testing and charging. Yet given the nature of the debate, why do some regard the debate as 'moribund'? After all, the distinction does seem to apply to many benefits. Child Benefit is a universal benefit, not because it is provided to absolutely everyone—obviously, childless couples do not receive it—but because entitlement to it is triggered by the birth of a child. By contrast, Housing Benefit is selective because the amount which an individual does or does not receive depends ultimately on his or her level of earnings, savings, or other forms of income. However, the reason why some regard the debate as outdated is because many cash transfers are both universal and selective. Unemployment Benefit, for example, has been universalist in that it is payable on an interruption of earnings and yet it is also selectivist because it is payable only to those who have previously amassed the required level of contributions through wage-earning activity. Commentators point out, therefore, that the defenders of one principle invariably make room for the other, and Titmuss (1968), for instance, recognized the need to combine both universalist and selectivist provision.

The debate has revived in recent years, although the terms of the debate have altered. This is, first, because both Conservative and New Labour governments have placed a great emphasis upon means-testing, forcing the defenders of universalism onto the defensive. Second, Deacon et al. (1997: 17–19) point out that the debate has reappeared on the supranational stage and continues to fuel a large amount of controversy with the supranational agencies that currently oversee global capitalism, e.g. the International Monetary Fund and the World Bank, encouraging the dismantling of social insurance and the creation of means-tested safety nets in both developed and developing countries.

SIX CATEGORIES OF CASH TRANSFER

The six types of benefit are illustrated in Table 12.1 and explained in the following subsections.

Social insurance benefits

In order to qualify for insurance benefits in the event of unemployment, sickness, or retirement, employees must previously have paid a certain amount of contributions into a compulsory state-managed fund. Such benefits, therefore, are 'earned entitlements' which go to workers rather than to citizens per se. According to Clasen (2001) about 46 per cent of all social security expenditure in the UK was allocated to social insurance transfers in 1999, considerably less than was allocated in the 1960s though still approximating to the European average. Social insurance was once the foundation of social security in the form of Unemployment Benefit and the State Pension. However, the

Table 12.1 Types of benefit

Type of transfer	Principles	Examples
Social insurance benefits	Contributory	Contribution-based Jobseeker's Allowance Retirement pension
Social assistance benefits	Means-tested	Income-based Jobseeker's Allowance Housing Benefit
Categorical benefits	Non-contributory and non-means-tested	Child Benefit Disability Living allowance
Discretionary benefits	Rules and judgements	Social Fund
Occupational benefits		
Statutory	Employment status	Statutory Sick Pay
Non-statutory	Employment record	Occupational Pension
Fiscal transfers	Tax concessions	Personal allowances Tax Credits

former, which was previously payable for twelve months, has been incorporated within the Jobseeker's Allowance and is now payable for a maximum of six months, while the relative value of the latter has been steadily eroding because since 1980 it has been uprated annually in line with inflation rather than earnings. Relative to average disposable incomes (or general living standards) the basic state pension is worth approximately 15 per cent of average earnings, slightly less than it was in 1948 (Hills 1997: 45); and if it continues to be indexed to inflation, by the year 2040 it will be worth just 7.5 per cent of average earnings. In 2000–1 10.8 million people were receiving a state pension (including the earnings-related pension) at a total cost of £37.8 billion.

Hills (1997: 44) identifies five problems with the insurance system:

- The link between contributions and entitlement is obscure.
- Beveridge assumed an economy of full-time full (male) employment; but women (and other disadvantaged groups) have always been less likely than men to accumulate the necessary contributions, and Beveridge's ideal economy no longer exists anyway.
- Insurance benefits have been so low that many more people than Beveridge anticipated have had to rely upon means-testing.
- The insurance fund is more symbolic than real, since contributions are really a de facto form of taxation.
- Widening the coverage of insurance benefits means that certain groups have to be 'credited' into the system, which undermines the contributory principle.

However, there are also four main advantages:

- There is both a real and a perceived link between contributions and entitlements, even if the link is somewhat obscure.
- Insurance contributions can be thought of as a 'hypothecated tax', i.e. tax revenue which is earmarked for specific purposes.
- The take-up of insurance benefits is high because, as earned entitlements, there is far less stigma than with means-tested benefits.
- Social insurance contributes to the functioning of the labour market, e.g. by reducing the costs associated with risks.

Social assistance benefits

These benefits provide a residual safety net for those who do not qualify for insurance benefits, and they are paid out to those whose income and assets have fallen below a prescribed amount, the level of which depends upon family size and other circumstances. Entitlement to assistance benefits is basically worked out by (a) calculating the amount the claimant is assumed to need, (b) calculating the income, savings, or capital assets which the claimant has access to, and (c) subtracting (b) from (a). The main assistance benefits are: Income-based Jobseeker's Allowance, Income Support (which used to be the main means-tested benefit but can now be claimed only by those who do not need to look for work in order to qualify for benefit), Housing Benefit, and Council Tax Benefit. In 1948, 2 per cent of the population were claiming National Assistance; by 1979 17 per cent of the population were claiming means-tested benefits, and this had risen to 25 per cent by 1999. According to Clasen (2001), in 1999 means-tested benefits accounted for 33 per cent of total transfer payments.

According to Spicker (1993: 141–2) the main arguments for means-tested assistance are that it enables resources to be targeted to those most in need and that, because it is financed out of taxation, resources are **vertically redistributed** from rich to poor. However, as already indicated above, there are also three problems with means-tested benefits: first, they create a poverty trap where any increase in earnings is largely cancelled out by the withdrawal of benefit (see next section); second, they do not reach everyone in need because the take-up of such benefits is typically lower than for insurance benefits (see later section); finally, because they are not provided on a universal basis they are complex and expensive to administer.

Categorical benefits

These are paid to specific groups, or categories, so long as certain criteria are met. The most obvious example of a categorical benefit is Child Benefit, which is provided automatically on behalf of all children under the age of 16. In 2001 12.7 million children received Child Benefit, a total cost of £8.8 billion. Also, Disability Living Allowance goes to those who either find it difficult or impossible to walk or who require constant supervision and care from another person. The Invalid Care Allowance is paid to the carers of those in receipt of the Disability Living Allowance.

Discretionary benefits

This refers to the Social Fund, which was created in 1988 and provides help for those on means-tested assistance who have urgent or exceptional needs. Strictly speaking the Social Fund is not entirely discretionary, since it contains a regulated element which provides a legal entitlement for maternity expenses, funeral expenses, and cold weather payments to those who satisfy the eligibility conditions. However, there is also a substantial discretionary element to the Fund: each benefit office has an annual budget which it must not exceed, there is no legal entitlement to payment as officials decide who receives money and who does not, most payments are in the form of loans which have to be repaid to the Benefits Agency, and there is no right of appeal to an independent tribunal.

Occupational benefits

These benefits can be either statutory or non-statutory. The former refers to Statutory Sick Pay and Statutory Maternity Pay, both administered by employers. The category of non-statutory occupational benefits now refers largely to the occupational pension schemes which are run by employers and into which employees contribute a certain percentage of their earnings. Occupational pensions are an increasing source of income for elderly people as the value of the state pension dwindles.

Fiscal transfers

Governments have always used tax allowances and reliefs for this purpose, but recent years have seen the increased coordination of fiscal transfers within the benefit system. In America the Earned Income Tax Credit boosts the income of low-earning families and is generally popular because it is regarded as a 'hand up' and a reward for work rather than a handout. Taking its lead from America, what has made New Labour's benefit reforms most distinctive is the increased use of fiscal transfers, and so we will look at this in more detail in the section on New Labour below.

UNEMPLOYMENT AND POVERTY TRAPS

The **unemployment trap** and the **poverty trap** should not be confused although they both occur because of the ways in which social security interacts with the labour market.

The phenomenon of the unemployment trap was noted by Beveridge in his 1942 Report:

> it is dangerous to allow benefit during unemployment or disability to equal or exceed earnings during work . . . It has been experienced in an appreciable number of cases under unemployment benefit and unemployment assistance in the past. The maintenance of employment . . . will be impossible without greater fluidity of labour . . . than has been achieved in the past. To secure this the gap between income during earning and during interruption of earning should be as large as possible for every man. (Beveridge 1942: paras. 411–12)

Michael Hill (1990: 104–5) describes the unemployment trap as the disadvantage which arises when a person's income in employment is not significantly greater than, and may even be less than, their income when on benefit. This is known as a high **replacement ratio**, and describes the situation where benefits establish a 'wage floor' below which paid work is either not financially worthwhile or only marginally so. A narrow gap between earnings and non-earnings provides the unemployed claimant with a significant disincentive to look for a job. We can therefore define the unemployment trap as the situation where a move into paid employment leads to no significant increase in overall income due to a high replacement ratio, i.e. a narrow gap between earnings and benefits.

In his history of the period Hill notes how the unemployment trap became of increasing concern to policy-makers in the 1960s. The National Assistance scheme had a provision known as the 'wage stop' to prevent individuals from receiving benefits which were more generous than the wages they were likely to earn when in work. In short, the gap between earnings and non-earnings was maintained by reducing benefits under certain circumstances. However, by the 1960s policy-makers preferred to pursue an alternative route: introducing benefits which people could receive whilst in employment in order to tackle the disincentive effect of the unemployment trap. This kind of approach involves a system of earnings disregards, where a person can earn a certain amount without it affecting their benefit entitlement, thus boosting their overall income. It was decided to introduce a scheme of income-tested rent and rate rebates for the lower paid and Family Income Supplement (FIS) for families with children. While this approach went some way to tackling the unemployment trap, however, it had the additional effect of creating a poverty trap.

This refers to the situation faced by the low-paid worker claiming in-work benefits: as their earnings increase that person not only has to pay tax and insurance contributions but also experiences a withdrawal of their benefits. For instance, an increase of £1 in earnings might lead to £0.80 of that £1 being effectively taken away again due to taxation and benefit withdrawal; this would imply a 'marginal tax rate' (the amount of income lost for every extra pound earned) of 80 per cent. We can therefore define the poverty trap as the situation where an increase in earnings leads to no significant increase in overall income due to the combined effect of taxes and transfers (see Box 12.2).

Box 12.2 The poverty trap in action

Piachaud illustrates this disincentive effect using the example of a married couple with two children who live in council housing. In April 1995 gross earnings of £50 per week would have left this family with a net income of £127 once transfers had been taken into account; however, if their gross earnings were to rise to £210 per week then, because of the combined effects of taxation and benefit withdrawal, their net income would only be £137, i.e. they would be just £10 better off than previously. In short, they would face a marginal tax rate of 94 per cent and, in 1995, one quarter of all employees were earning less than £210 per week.

This poverty trap was first described by Frank Field and David Piachaud, and received an extended analysis by Alan Deacon and Jonathan Bradshaw (1983). They found that in the early 1980s the low-paid could face marginal tax rates of more than 100 per cent so that an increase of earnings could actually leave people worse off than before. Therefore, although those on low wages had slightly higher incomes than they would otherwise have had on benefits alone, they were effectively trapped at this level of income unless their wages rose significantly. The social security reforms of the 1980s were partly designed to address the poverty trap: Housing Benefit was introduced in 1982 and Family Credit replaced FTS in 1988. The explicit intention of the Conservative government was to improve the incentives of the low-paid (without the affluent having to pay more tax), but to what extent has this happened?

According to Piachaud (1997), the incentives for large numbers of people worsened during the period from 1979 to the mid-1990s, when reliance upon means-testing exploded. The problem with marginal tax rates reaching 100 per cent or more was dealt with: in 1985, 70,000 people faced rates of 100 per cent plus whereas by 1995/6 this had fallen to 10,000. However, the numbers facing rates of 60 per cent or more rose from 450,000 to 630,000 over the same period, and the numbers facing rates of 80 per cent or more rose from 290,000 to 420,000. Some, like Frank Field (1995), have therefore identified a new 'poverty plateau' where families can remain on low incomes for an extremely long time.

Pete Alcock (1997: 229) points out that this increase in means-testing has also introduced another form of trap: a savings trap. Because most means tests now take into account both the capital holdings of claimants and the interest that collects on savings (above a specific amount), then those with savings can either lose their entitlement to means-tested support altogether or have their level of benefit reduced. This savings trap particularly affects those pensioners who are on low incomes but who have saved or invested money 'for a rainy day'.

As we shall see below, New Labour has also been wrestling with the poverty and savings traps.

STIGMA, TAKE-UP, AND FRAUD

Stigma implies the possession of a low status in the eyes of society: to occupy, and to be seen to occupy, an inferior social rank. According to Paul Spicker (1984), five forms of stigma can be identified. First is the stigma engendered by poverty and social exclusion. Second is the stigma to which a physical disability or a disease can lead. Third are stigmas associated with things such as mental illnesses and drug addictions. Fourth are moral stigmas which certain actions or patterns of behaviour can give rise to, e.g. criminal behaviour. Finally, there is the stigma which a dependency upon welfare-services can create.

An important question to ask is why this final form of stigma has continued to exist. Is it due to a failure of the welfare state? As the quotation from Titmuss on p. 336 suggests, he believed that the universalization of social rights would eliminate the sense of inferiority which accompanied, and was intended to accompany, the use of public services under the Poor Law. People would be able to use and to claim welfare services as of right, without experiencing shame or dishonour. On this reading, the continuance of stigma might be attributed to the failure of modern policy-making. However, such universalism was not the only objective of state welfare. For T. H. Marshall (1981), one of the aims of the welfare state should be to eliminate stigma without thereby eliminating social inequality per se, i.e. to create a society of equal citizens who could possess unequal amounts of wealth and income. Yet could this maintenance of social inequality undermine attempts to eliminate stigma? If inequality is needed to make people respond to incentives, then perhaps those who do not respond properly may be legitimately stigmatized. Such was the conclusion of Beveridge himself:

> Assistance . . . must be felt to be something less desirable than insurance benefit; otherwise the insured persons get nothing for their contributions. Assistance therefore will be given always subject to proof of needs and examination of means; it will be subject also to any conditions as to behaviour which may seem likely to hasten the restoration of earning capacity. (Beveridge 1942: para. 369)

So, although Beveridge desired the gradual reduction of means-testing he believed that it must always be 'felt to be something less than desirable'. These arguments suggest, therefore, that some of the architects of state welfare effectively saw a valuable and continued role for stigma in maintaining people's incentives to better themselves.

One way or another, stigma has always been most closely associated with cash transfers. The association is weakest in the case of insurance benefits, since these are defined as earned entitlements, and strongest in the case of assistance benefits. Carol Walker (1993: 146–68) notes how, as Beveridge's goal of reducing means-testing has been abandoned, successive governments have tried to make assistance benefits look more attractive while those who depend upon them have been simultaneously demonized as scroungers. She argues that this mixed message has led to a poor record on the **take-up** of assistance benefits, with significantly fewer people applying for them than are actually entitled. There are undoubtedly other factors at work with the non-take-up of benefits, e.g. a general lack of knowledge about entitlements, or a wariness of the complexity of the benefit system; but Walker insists that the take-up of assistance benefits is lower than it should be largely because potential claimants can see the stigmatizing effects. These effects can be difficult to quantify, however. For instance, the Social Security Advisory Committee (1997: 7) notes that 70 per cent of those who apply to the Social Fund are successful in their application (and by 2000 the number of successful applications had risen); but this figure takes no account of those who do not apply in the first place for what is the most discretionary and stigmatizing form of cash transfer. A report in 2001 found that even Social Fund loans can force the poorest families deeper into poverty (Bennett with Jones 2002: 308). According to the Department of Work and Pensions the most recent figures for the take-up of means-tested benefits are shown in Box 12.3.

By and large, governments tend to be more concerned with the amount of benefit being fraudulently claimed than they are with the amount going unclaimed. There are two aspects to this issue: the economic and the moral. First, how much is being

Box 12.3 The take-up of benefits

- In 1999–2000 the take-up of Income Support was 77–87 per cent. This means that somewhere between 520,000 and 1 million people were not claiming that to which they were entitled, a total of between £720 million and £1.6 billion in unclaimed benefits.
- In 1999–2000 the take-up of Housing Benefit was between 89 per cent and 95 per cent, with between 200,000 and 530,000 people not claiming that to which they were entitled, a total of between £290 million and £840 million in unclaimed benefits.
- In 1999–2000 the take-up of Council Tax Benefit was between 73 per cent and 80 per cent, with between 1.2 million and 1.8 million not claiming that to which they were entitled, a total of between £460 million and £710 million going unclaimed.
- In 1999–2000 the take-up of income-based jobseeker's allowance was between 67 per cent and 78 per cent, with between 250,000 and 420,000 people not claiming that to which they were entitled, a total of between £490 million and £900 million in unclaimed benefits.
- Overall, in 1999–2000 between £2 billion and £4 billion in income-related benefits went unclaimed, a take-up of 78–86 per cent.
- In the winter of 2001–2, 700,000 elderly people did not claim the winter fuel payment to which they were entitled.

(www.dwp.gov.uk/asd/statistics.html)

defrauded? Claim and counter-claim is made in answer to this question. The Conservative government was particularly extravagant in its claims and some of the wilder estimates were based upon rumour and conjecture rather than solid evidence, as the government itself occasionally admitted (DSS 1996: para. 4). Unfortunately, these make-believe estimates have long since leaked into popular consciousness via the media, with a figure of £2 billion in annual Housing Benefit fraud still doing the rounds. Roy Sainsbury (1998) points out that the estimates of how much is being fraudulently claimed correspond closely to the amount of fraudulent activity which the Benefits Agency claims to have terminated. Is this because the Agency is remarkably efficient or is it because estimates regarding fraudulent activity and detection are systematically over estimated in an institution where performance-related pay is so important? Since the National Audit Office found that local authorities had overestimated the amount of fraud in Housing Benefit and Council Tax Benefit by 30 per cent, Sainsbury insists that it is 'difficult to lend any credence at all to official measures'. Guesswork and wishful thinking tend to predominate, with officials calculating how much fraud *is* being conducted by estimating how much *would* have been conducted had defrauders not been caught.

Second, why do people engage in fraud? The popular image of the defrauder is of a selfish, criminally motivated individual stealing resources from those who genuinely need them. Research by Hartley Dean and Margaret Melrose (1996; 1997), however, found that this image bears little correspondence to reality. People were often motivated out of sheer desperation, genuine confusion (about what they were and were not entitled

Box 12.4 Defrauding who?

When asked about it in quite general terms, most people condemn benefit fraud. Think of the following vignette, however. Peter is on benefits when his neighbour, Paul, asks him whether he would like to spend some of his spare time mending Paul's garden fence. To make it worth his while Paul offers to pay £20 to Peter. What should Peter do? Should he do the work and then declare his £20 to the Benefit Agency? But if he does that then the Agency will withdraw some of his benefits so that most of his £20 effectively disappears (remember the poverty trap). Or should he do the work and not declare it? But that would be fraudulent, strictly speaking. Or should he simply decline Paul's offer? Whenever I put this scenario to a classroom of students a surprising number of those who originally condemned fraud end up recommending that Peter should do the work and not declare his earnings. Why? Because they believe that the benefit system should not penalize Peter for doing something of value and improving his income. The object of the exercise is to suggest that benefit fraud is a far more complicated issue than we might gather from hysterical headlines and moralizing politicians.

to), a sense that they had been betrayed by the welfare state, or economic necessity in response to a system which seemed to want to keep them in poverty. Equally, the government could be said to derive an advantage from fraud: because fraud assists the operation of a flexible, low-wage economy, because people who work unofficially in the 'informal' economy are contributing to national output, and, finally, because politicians can make political capital out of condemning fraud at periodic intervals. Box 12.4 illustrates why fraud is a more complex issue.

DEPENDENCY CULTURE AND THE UNDERCLASS

The debate concerning the underclass is a very old one which continually reappears in new guises. Lydia Morris (1994: 10–32) traces its roots from the nineteenth century, finding a succession of theorists expressing concern about those, the undeserving poor, who were believed to threaten the stability and prosperity of society: for Malthus they were the 'redundant population', for Marx they were the semi-criminal lumpenproletariat, for Mayhew, Booth, and Stedman-Jones they were the residuum of decent society. Therefore, Morris argues that when we discuss the underclass we are merely continuing a debate which has lasted, on and off, for two centuries.

In our day the debate has been revived on two separate occasions. In the America of the 1960s Oscar Lewis (1968) published the findings of his research into poor Puerto Rican families. Lewis had concluded that these families had successfully adapted to their poverty and deprived social environments by repressing their expectations of better times to come, by abandoning any hope of secure, well-paid employment, and by developing a culture which enabled them to cope with being poor in an affluent society.

Lewis had merely set out to describe what he called a 'culture of poverty', but his thesis was picked up by those who were critical of the recent expansion of social security and welfare programmes. Some of these criticisms focused upon the poor as victims of a welfare system which trapped them in poverty, while others identified the poor as responsible for their own social conditions due to a failure of moral character on their part. Daniel Moynihan (1965: 5), for instance, attributed poverty amongst black Americans to the 'disintegration of the negro family'. From a Marxist perspective, Piven and Cloward (1971) interpreted these debates as a camouflage for America's unwillingness to abolish poverty and as an attempt to further regulate the poor.

Concerns about the underclass and what came to be called the 'culture of dependency' revived in the early 1980s and flourished in a fertile political climate with the Reagan administration in America and the Thatcher government in Britain. The commentator Charles Murray (1984) alleged that over-generous benefits in America had led to the emergence of a significant underclass of several million people. By encouraging neither marriage nor independence within the labour market, the American equivalent of assistance benefits had created a generation of unemployed and unemployable black youths, as well as a generation of lone mothers who expected to be 'married to the state'. Murray's empirical research was subsequently challenged by many, but the gist of his argument proved to be highly influential. Lawrence Mead (1986) argued that in the future the welfare state in general and the benefit system in particular would have to stress the obligations rather than the rights of citizenship. These kinds of arguments have given a theoretical justification for the expansion of **workfare** programmes in the USA where claimants are compelled to work or train in return for their benefits.

For those such as Murray, therefore, the term 'underclass' does not refer to an extreme of poverty, i.e. the poorest of the poor, but to a different *type* of poverty: the value system (the culture) possessed by those who expect society and the state to do everything for them without having to contribute anything in return. Murray's thesis has come to wield a certain amount of influence in this country, certainly on the Right but also on the Left. Dennis and Erdos (1992) argued that the benefit system had helped to break up the traditional family, with catastrophic social effects. Frank Field (1989) was initially sceptical regarding Murray's account of the dependent underclass, arguing that he had ignored 'structural' factors beyond individual control, but argued subsequently that means-testing failed precisely because it panders to the inherent selfishness of human nature:

> Means tests sanction inaction, non-saving and lying. These powerful messages, relayed through the system which gives basic income support to the poorest, play a part in cutting the poorest off from mainstream Britain. (Field 1996: 17)

Field's recommendations for a 'socially authoritarian' benefit system that sets out to enforce obligations has wielded some influence on New Labour.

The research of those such as Dean and Taylor-Gooby (1992) and Walker with Howard (2000) represents the best response to the above claims. They conclude that terms such as 'underclass' and 'dependency culture' indicate a widespread tendency to blame the victims for the very disadvanages (unemployment, social exclusion) which have been perpetrated against them. Claimants are not culturally separate from 'normal' society: if anything, claimants cope with their situation by adopting and internalizing what they see as the norms and values of non-claimants. Edwards and Duncan (1997) found that lone mothers who rely upon state benefits, a group often vilified as irresponsible, hold views broadly in line with dominant British norms about motherhood. So far from requiring additional motivation to work, claimants might actually have unreal expectations about what the job market can deliver. What the underclass debate does is to depreciate state dependency in order to make dependency upon employers/wages and upon the traditional family look natural, moral and inevitable. As a consequence, even more pressures are now being loaded upon benefit recipients than in the past.

NEW LABOUR

I have already indicated that New Labour has been wrestling with some old problems (poverty and savings traps) by using some of the Conservative's methods (means-testing and the enforcement of work obligations) and some new methods (tax credits).

Principles and strategies

It is possible to summarize the government's basic approach according to the following three principles. First, it has emphasized merit and the idea that people must be helped to help themselves: a 'hand up, not a handout'. This individualistic doctrine assumes that the idea of aspiring to a better standard of living, for oneself and one's family, is people's primary motivation. Second, however, this is not to imagine that New Labour has ignored the importance of social cohesion. It has repeatedly stressed the importance of social inclusion and integration into the norms and mainstream of society. However, although it has wanted to improve the position of those at the bottom (assuming they can demonstrate they deserve such improvement) this does not necessarily translate into social equality per se. New Labour has been concerned with the height of the social floor but not necessarily with the height of the social ceiling. Finally, then, without much of an egalitarian emphasis it has spoken more in terms of community and has associated community with notions of desert, duty and reciprocity. By its motto that 'rights imply responsibilities' New Labour argues that what you put into society must be broadly proportionate to what you take out.

These principles (merit, social inclusion, community) converge around an employment-centred approach, with waged work being regarded as the principal means through which people can escape from poverty, hence its slogan: 'Work for those who can, security for those who cannot' (DSS 1998). (And in 2001 the Department of Social Security became the Department of Work and Pensions.) Employment is thought to be the means by which people get on in life and the means of ensuring that all participate in the activities of the social community.

Cartoon 12.1

© Bill McArthur, *Glasgow Herald*, 11 February 1999

As such, these principles have given rise to some clearly identifiable strategies:

- A stick-and-carrot emphasis upon 'labour market activation'. The post-Second World War welfare state has been repeatedly (and misleadingly) described as passive, as paying people for doing nothing, and as therefore redundant for the flexible markets that we allegedly need in a global economy. An 'active' welfare system is therefore required, one that will help the 'deserving' (through Personal Advisers assisting with job searches, for instance) but will clamp down on those who shirk their social obligations.
- Like its Conservative predecessors, New Labour has rejected universalism as too wasteful and blunt an instrument and has preferred selectivist measures. Social insurance benefits have therefore been allowed to wither, with New Labour signalling as far back as 1996 that it had no intention of scrapping the Jobseeker's Allowance.
- New Labour has wanted to 'make work pay'. It is aware that employment is not per se the route out of social exclusion since wages may be low. Therefore, it has sought to raise the floor below which wages cannot fall and to improve the system of in-work transfers.
- New Labour has emphasized value for money as a way of reassuring Middle England regarding its economic competence. This has meant that it has been generally silent about its more traditional social democratic aims and has effected 'redistribution by stealth' in the hope that affluent households would not notice some of the redistributive measures being introduced. Not until the budget of April 2002 did it dare to raise

taxes (in the form of National Insurance contributions), and even then the redistributive intention was modest.

- The government has repeatedly emphasized the importance of private provision. It has sought a Third Way between a purely market-based system and one where the state controls each and every aspect of income maintenance. As social insurance has declined so people have been encouraged (though not yet compelled) to take out private forms of insurance.
- New Labour has addressed the culture or the psychology of social security. For instance, in 1999 it replaced Family Credit (a means-tested benefit for working families with children) by the Working Families Tax Credit (WFTC), claiming that the latter was more generous and superior in terms of incentives. However, the fact that such changes could also have been introduced by reforming Family Credit indicates that the real change was psychological: Family Credit was a benefit, whereas WFTC was paid through the wage packet. In other words, state welfare (bad) was being shifted towards fiscal welfare (good).

Policies

If these are the broad strategies of New Labour, what are the actual policies to which they have given rise? We can identify the following main areas: the **New Deal**, tax credits, value-for-money measures, pension reform.

First, the **welfare to work** philosophy of the New Deal stresses that receiving benefits for 'doing nothing' is no longer an option, and that to continue receiving benefits claimants must accept one of the following: subsidized employment, full-time education or training, a job in the voluntary sector, work with an environmental task force. There are a range of penalties, i.e. having your benefit stopped, attached to non-compliance. Such compulsion was initially applied only to those aged 24 or less but have gradually been extended to others, with lone parents and disabled people increasingly required to attend interviews with benefit officers. The government has hailed the New Deal as a success, especially in reducing youth unemployment, but no overall picture yet exists. Evidence suggests that activation policies work well in areas of high employment but are much less effective where there are few jobs available (Peck 2001). In other words, 'employability' is of little help where the jobs simply do not exist. And even the success stories may need qualifying, since those who find work through activation policies are more likely to enter low-waged, insecure, part-time jobs with few opportunities and to leave those jobs again in the short term. It may also be that those who find work would have done so anyway (Standing 1999).

Second, the government has tried to 'make work pay' by introducing a minimum wage (see Chapter 6) and tax credits. Tax credits (of which the WFTC was the most prominent) were introduced in 1999 and the various strands are now in the process of being systematically integrated (Treloar 2002). Essentially, 2003 will see the introduction of a Child Tax Credit (CTC) and a Working Tax Credit (WTC); there are additional plans to reform Housing Benefit, Council Tax Benefit and pensions along similar lines. The CTC will be paid to the main carer and is intended to integrate the existing streams of support for low-income families with children; the WTC will be paid via the employer and makes financial support available to workers without children as well as those with—though an additional Childcare Tax Credit will also be available for working parents with childcare needs. What this will do is separate out the credits provided for children and those provided for adults.

The potential advantage of tax credits is that they provide a more secure minimum income floor than that offered by benefits; they smooth the transition of people into work and up the incomes ladder; and they are less stigmatizing than means-tested benefits. The potential disadvantages are that, although tax credits may alleviate the poverty trap, they do not eliminate it: tax credits are a different form of means-testing, not an alternative to it. Further, by stressing the moral superiority of waged work, non-employment forms of activity are consequently devalued. Finally, employers are tempted to offer low wages in the knowledge that these will be topped up by the state—indeed, evidence from America suggests that tax credits invite some employers to defraud the system (Wiseman 2000). At present the effects of the 1999 reforms are still working their way through, but we will review the latest evidence on UK poverty in the next section.

Third, the government has also adopted a variety of value-for-money measures that, as noted above, often seem designed to appease taxpayer anxieties. This tendency appeared early on when at the end of 1997 it abolished lone-parent benefits and premiums. After a massive outcry the value of the cuts was subsequently and quickly restored, but the episode left a bad taste despite the welcome increases in Child Benefit that the government has introduced. Disabled people have also been affected. Access to benefits has been gradually tightened, including the extension of compulsory measures and a crackdown on fraud that, especially in its early days, was widely perceived as an attack on disabled people; a variety of New Deals have been implemented with the intention of encouraging and facilitating the entry of disabled people into the labour market; finally, measures to combat discrimination have been introduced.

This macho stance has affected asylum seekers particularly badly. Asylum seekers have few entitlements, and between 2000 and 2002 they were subjected to a voucher system where they received from the state, not cash, but vouchers that could only be spent at designated stores and could not be exchanged for money. Compounding the other problems that asylum seekers face this stigmatizing measure does not seem to have been based on anything other than prejudice and misconception (see Case Study 12.1). Although the scheme was eventually scrapped, the government's social policies towards them continue to reflect popular fears about immigration (see Case Study 12.2).

New Labour claims success in cracking down on benefit fraud but, as noted already, this issue usually gets lost in a political and statistical fog. For example, it has launched frequent initiatives against benefit fraud to remind taxpayers constantly that their money is not being wasted. These initiatives are punctuated by even more frequent ad campaigns and press releases that are targeted at affluent areas and social groups, i.e. precisely the people who are *not* claiming benefits. The government claims that between 1997 and 2002 it reduced the annual cost of fraud from £1.38 billion to £1.2 billion. However, it does not just talk of fraud, but of fraud *and error*. Over the same period it clamns to have halved the number of cases where Income Support and Jobseeker's Allowance was paid out 'without sufficient evidence'. How much of the reduction in

Case Study 12.1 'Good riddance to vouchers' (Raekha Prasad, *The Guardian*, 5 April 2002)

At last, vouchers for asylum seekers are to be tossed into the grave of political U-turns.

Since their introduction in April 2000, vouchers have banished their users from all but a few state-approved stores and marked them out in the few shops where they could be spent. The Home Secretary, David Blunkett, has said that the new method of payment will be 'less socially divisive'. But while cash-in-hand payments may diminish the stigma, the systemic mess which has caused asylum seekers such hardship continues unabated.

Getting hold of the subsistence support to which they are entitled—a mere £37.77 a week for those aged 25 or over, compared with the £53.95 which British citizens on income support get—will, for thousands of asylum seekers, still present challenges of Kafkaesque proportions. Under the voucher system, many desperate people went without food, while others could not travel or buy clothes because of administrative errors. Too often, the book of receipts needed to pick up the vouchers at post offices failed to arrive, or there were no vouchers waiting once they got there. Dumping vouchers for cash is unlikely to improve things, because the same bungling machinery responsible for the delays and errors in processing vouchers will now process cash.

One adviser in a Citizens' Advice Bureau in the north of England was told by a Nass (National Asylum Support Service) official that the pregnant Somali woman sitting next to her, who had received no vouchers for a week, 'had left the country'. Further calls to Nass met with a constantly engaged line, being put on hold for an hour, and a claim that the agency had no record of previous calls. Six months later, the woman is still awaiting the unpaid vouchers and is supported by family members who are themselves struggling to make ends meet.

In another case, a frightened and desperate woman sought help from an adviser in Yorkshire after being racially harassed by local residents. Nass had not responded to her request to move. A letter was faxed reiterating the request, but two weeks later they had still received no response. Meanwhile, the accommodation complaints number had changed and after 10 minutes waiting to be put through to the right department, the line went dead.

Bureaux have also seen numerous asylum seekers called to obligatory Home Office interviews or appeal hearings without receiving travel warrants. An adviser in Staffordshire, when contacting the agency on behalf of a man who had been called for an interview but had no means of getting there, was told by a Nass official that non-receipt of a warrant was not a valid reason for failing to attend an interview.

Even those who have been granted refugee status or exceptional leave to remain face long delays in receiving benefits. If proof is needed of the indifferent, if not callous, treatment of asylum seekers, then it may be found at the bottom of the standard letter sent out by Nass: 'If you have not received this letter you should contact Nass immediately on the number above.' What other agency would so comprehensively fail to meet the needs of the people it serves?

fraud is actual and how much is due to a more stringent (and possible more unjust) administrative system? All applicants are now processed through the same 'gateway' of interviews, etc. regardless of their work history—another indication of how far the social insurance principle has fallen. Moreover, New Labour's rhetoric on this issue is

Case Study 12.2

'Asylum cheats to get boot' (George Pascoe-Watson, The Sun, 24 April 2002)

Asylum cheats who come 'shopping' in Britain for higher benefits are to be kicked straight out. Thousands of immigrants will be sent packing as soon as they arrive under changes in the law unveiled today.

Home Secretary David Blunkett is determined to root out bogus asylum claims as he bids to stop the racist BNP gaining a foothold in town hall elections next week.

Tens of thousands of immigrants enter the EU each year claiming they are fleeing persecution. They receive benefits while their cases are processed, but many shop around and find they will get bigger handouts here. Many drift away to work on the UK black market. But town hall chiefs are legally obliged to give them food, a place to live and £37.77 cash expenses a week.

'We come here for work, not to live on handouts' (Ben Summerskill, *The Observer*, 29 April 2001)

A major study of illegal immigrants has found that almost all of them come to Britain with the intention of finding work, contrary to the popular image of new arrivals in search of generous benefits. 'Not a single illegal immigrant we examined thought that benefits was a reason for coming to Britain,' said Professor Bill Jordan of Exeter University, who carried out the government-funded project. 'A key reason people gave for coming here was that they expected to be able to work,' said Jordan, whose work was based on interviews with more than 150 illegal immigrants. 'It's a reflection of our economic conditions.'

Asylum seekers, who are registered on arrival, are largely prevented from working. But illegal immigrants find work, the survey discovered, because they are highly motivated, presentable and—above all—prepared to accept low pay. Many were also better educated than their British counterparts. Half the immigrant workers doing manual jobs were graduates or had diplomas.

frequently dangerous. For example: 'We want people to recognise that the right to benefit comes with a responsibility to the society that supports them. That is why we are tackling benefit fraud on all fronts' (DWP press release, 29 Nov. 2001). Since they also stress the responsibility to earn, this comes perilously close to suggesting that those who are not employed and those who defraud are part of the same problem group.

Finally, New Labour's attempt to reform UK pensions has led it into extremely complex and controversial waters. All welfare states face some hard choices when it comes to pensions, owing to the rising numbers of those above working age. The demographic time bomb is not as explosive as is usually claimed, but the options for defusing the bomb include raising the retirement age, raising more revenue through higher taxes and contributions, or lowering the generosity of pensions. In the early 1980s the Conservative government decided on the third of these options, indexing the state pension to inflation rather than earnings, disabling the state's earnings-related scheme, and encouraging the growth of occupational and private pension schemes (leading to a massive mis-selling of the latter). As a result the UK is not facing a particularly high pensions bill, but the price has been paid by those pensioners who either did not or could not buy into private schemes. Consequently, Britain has higher levels of pensioner poverty than most EU countries.

New Labour has refused to re-index the state pension and has preferred a patchwork of reforms. First, it has introduced a Minimum Income Guarantee, a means-tested top-up to the basic state pension. Second, it has introduced a system of privately managed stakeholder pensions for those on just-below-average incomes. Finally, for those at the very bottom of the incomes ladder it has introduced a second state pension. The government insists that such reforms are the only way to relieve the poverty of today's pensioners while ensuring that younger generations are able to provide for themselves without loading too much on the state. Critics (Ward 2000) allege that New Labour is overestimating the cost of a properly funded state scheme, underestimating the costs of its approach, and so failing to make the hard decisions all countries face. (The twist in the tail is that in 2002 many employers started to reduce the value of their pension schemes and even to urge their workers to opt back into the state system. In short, the private market may not be the panacea that the Conservatives and even New Labour have imagined.)

INEQUALITY

Social security and redistribution

There are basically two main forms of redistribution: vertical and lifecycle. **Vertical redistribution** implies redistribution from net losers to net gainers. Assistance benefits, for instance, are intended to redistribute from high-income to low-income groups. **Lifecycle redistribution** implies the redistribution of resources from one part of a person's lifecycle to another: most people of working age pay taxes and contributions to fund the services, e.g. pensions, which they expect to receive during the non-working periods of their lives.

What happens if we look at the figures on taxes and transfers for any one year (Hills 1997)? Households in the bottom half of the income distribution receive 2.4 times as much from cash benefits as those in the top half. The poorest tenth receives four times as much as the richest tenth, and, because the poorest derive less of their income from the market, cash transfers make up 69 per cent of their gross income whereas they account for only 2 per cent of the gross income of the richest. Direct income tax takes a greater proportion of higher incomes than of lower ones, but once all taxes, including indirect ones like VAT, are taken into account, the effects of taxation are evened out. In fact, those in the poorest tenth actually pay out more of their gross income in the form of taxes than any of the other nine income groups (Hills 1997: 85). Overall, though, the bottom five tenths are net gainers from the tax and transfer system, whilst the top five are net losers. However, this does not necessarily mean that vertical redistribution has taken place, since it might well be that people in the bottom five tenths are basically funding their own benefits.

In fact the research of John Hills confirms that the combined effect of taxes and transfers does redistribute income from those parts of our lives when our earning capacity is greatest (early 20s to late 50s) to those when it is weakest. The difference is in the distribution of self-financed benefits, with those in the bottom tenths less likely than those in the top to pay for their own benefits out of their own taxes. Based upon data from the early 1990s, he concludes:

> The system does therefore redistribute quite successfully from 'lifetime rich' to 'lifetime poor'. However . . . *most* benefits are self-financed over people's lifetimes, rather than being paid for by others. Of the £133,000 average gross lifetime benefits from the system, an average of £98,000 is self-financed. Nearly three-quarters of what the welfare state does looked at this way is a 'savings bank'; only a quarter is 'Robin Hood' redistribution between different people. (Hills 1997: 19)

In other words, when we look at the total amount of redistribution effected by the welfare state 75 per cent is of the lifecycle form and 25 per cent is vertical.

Recent trends

What effects have the governments benefit reforms had upon the distribution of income in the UK? Obviously, income distribution is influenced by a range of taxation and labour market changes as well, but transfers certainly play a key role in determining levels of poverty and inequality.

At the time of writing the latest data is available in the form of a Households Below Average Income (HBAI) report published by the government in April 2002 and covers the period up to 2000–1. The HBAI reveals the following headline figures. Between 1996–7 and 2000–1:

- The number of people in households with below 60 per cent of average income after housing costs fell from 14 million to 13 million between 1996–7 and 2000–1
- There were 500,000 fewer children in poverty by the end of the same period, a fall from 4.4 million to 3.9 million

Effectively, by 2000 there were somewhere between 13 million and 14.5 million people living in poverty (23 per cent–26 per cent of the UK population).

In short, New Labour has reduced the numbers of those living below the poverty line, but not to a substantial degree. Of particular disappointment is the statistic concerning children. In 1999 Tony Blair set the brave target of eliminating child poverty within twenty years (by 2019, in other words). In pursuit of this aim the government was once claiming that by the end of its first term it would have brought between 1 million and 1.2 million children out of poverty; as HBAI shows, it actually achieved about half of this interim target.

New Labour continues to argue that the full effects of its 1999 reforms have yet to be felt, and that its plans for future reform (especially tax credit integration) will produce the effects that it wants. Critics, though, continue to allege that its reliance upon means-testing, its preference for compulsion based upon a distinction between the deserving and undeserving, its emphasis upon the supply side of the economy rather than the demand side, its general reluctance to raise benefit levels (especially in line with earnings), and its reluctance to tax high earners means that poverty is unlikely to reduce by great amounts, and so its record up till 2001 is no great surprise. Some estimate that real improvements will require a rise of 4 per cent in the rate of income tax (Elliott and Carvel 2002).

EUROPEAN AND GLOBAL DIMENSIONS

A useful overview of the changes in European cash transfer systems between 1985–95 has been provided by Mary Daly. Daly (1997: 133) identifies four trends in European reform over this period: a restriction in the access to benefit through a tightening up of eligibility criteria; the increased use of means-testing; movement towards privatization; and a shift towards more active employment measures where benefits are closely tied to things such as job search and training. Overall, European countries tried to reduce the costs of transfers to employers, to emphasize taxation rather than contributions as the source of funding, and to alter the division of responsibility for funding between national, regional, and local levels. Daly discusses three areas where reform is tending to occur: pensions, unemployment benefits, and benefits related to caring.

She detects something of a convergence in European pension systems over this period. First, there was a lengthening of the period which people have to spend in employment. In fact, whereas in 1960 thirteen years was the average contribution period, by 1985 this had risen to twenty-six years, and by the mid-1990s the period ran from a minimum of thirty-five years in Spain and Greece to a maximum of forty-eight years in Ireland. Second, there was an increased use of means-testing and income-testing in addition to changes in the rules which mean that the pension levels are now more likely to be calculated on the basis of a person's entire working life rather than the years in which earnings, and therefore contributions, were highest. Daly (1997: 134–6) concludes that people now have to work longer in order to qualify for less generous pensions.

Unemployment benefits were also reformed to reflect labour market incentives and disincentives more closely. Eligibility rules were usually made more restrictive and the level of benefits made less generous. Finally, the most significant development in the benefits associated with caring for children was in the area of parental leave, with greater subsidy by the state. By 1995, ten out of sixteen European nations were prepared to make payments towards parental caring. There was also a trend towards the state subsidization of private and personal care for the elderly, the ill and the disabled. An interesting attempt to rank unemployment programmes against one another has been made by Dixon (2001), who concludes that the best system is to be found in Australia—with the UK in thirtieth position and the USA in forty-third.

Gough et al. (1997: 24–7) demonstrate that assistance benefits have been of most importance in those 'neoliberal' countries in which markets play the greatest role. In most of these countries the group which is largely dependent upon assistance is that of elderly people, whereas in other countries they are largely catered for through insurance benefits. Women and lone parents also make great demands on these nations' assistance schemes. Neoliberal countries also experienced the greatest rises in the numbers of recipients and in expenditure on assistance benefits. Based on data from the mid-1990s Gough et al. (p. 33) found that after housing costs the most generous benefits are in Austria, Italy, Luxembourg, the Netherlands, the Nordic countries, and Switzerland; the least generous are in the USA and southern Europe.

Since the mid-1990s Clasen (2001) identifies a trend towards the strengthening of social insurance across many EU countries. Overall, then, since the early 1990s there has been something of a convergence: those countries with a strong social insurance tradition have weakened the contributory base and those with a weak social insurance tradition have allowed more scope for earnings-related contributions (usually at the expense of universal forms of redistribution). No great innovations or extensions to social assistance have been made, except in those countries where a reliance upon social assistance was already firmly entrenched: Australia, Canada, New Zealand, UK, and USA (Ditch and Oldfield 1999).

It is in the USA that some of the most dramatic recent changes can be found. In 1996 President Clinton ended the system that had been in place since the 1930s.

- Social assistance is now no longer available to an individual for more than five years in total.
- Workfare schemes have been extended and strengthened.
- The Aid for Families with Dependent Children scheme was replaced by the less generous Temporary Assistance for Needy Families.
- There has been a greater reliance upon tax credits.
- Federal funding has been cut, with what was an open-ended contribution replaced by a block grant that tempts individual states into cutting their benefit bills.

On the positive side, there is now more money available for childcare, and social security pensions (from which middle-income households benefit) remain healthy. Essentially, though, the USA has moved towards a more punitive system, exemplified by Wisconsin's replacement of welfare by an employment assistance programme whereby mothers are required to return to employment, as a condition of receiving benefit, when their children are just twelve weeks old. Early research suggests that these reforms have led to a fall in the number of people drawing benefits (Wiseman 2000). But is this because people are finding employment (as defenders of the changes insist) or because millions are disappearing into the shadow economies of family dependency, hand-to-mouth existence, and criminality? No clear picture has yet emerged.

Finally, how might all of the changes sketched above have affected the distribution of income? Between the mid-1980s and the mid-1990s inequality fell in Finland, Ireland, Italy, Portugal, and Spain, rose slowly in Belgium, France, (West) Germany, Japan, and the USA, and rose most significantly in Australia, Britain, the Netherlands, New Zealand, Norway, and Sweden. Indeed, Hills (1995: 65) reports that because income inequality rose so rapidly in Britain between 1977 and 1990, a pace matched only by New Zealand between 1985 and 1989, it had become one of the most unequal countries in the developed world by the mid-1990s. The data given at the end of the preceding section suggests that the UK's trend towards greater inequality has been halted but not reversed to any great extent.

CONCLUSION

It may well be that no social security system can achieve all of the aims that benefits are called on to achieve, because those aims are themselves often contradictory. Any system inevitably involves trade-offs of one form or another. If so, this would indicate that, despite the technical nature of social security and the fact that few are expert in each and every aspect of what is a very complicated system, decisions about those trade-offs are primarily political, cultural, and ethical. For instance, if society decides that it wants a highly targeted system, it will have to accept the continuance of the poverty trap. If, however, society wants to improve the work incentives of the poorest, it will have to accept that resources may consequently 'spill over' to those higher up the income ladder who do not need them. In short, as technically complex as the transfer system is, reforming and improving it is ultimately a question of which values and principles we collectively regard as important. To a large extent, cash transfers mirror and reflect the society within which they operate.

KEY LEGISLATION

So far as social security is concerned New Labour's most important piece of legislation remains the Welfare Reform Bill enacted in February 1999 and based substantially upon DSS (1998). More recent policy initiatives and legislative acts continue to refer back to the general principles encapsulated in the Bill.

REFERENCES

Alcock, P. (1997), *Understanding Poverty*, 2nd edn. London: Macmillan.

Barr, N., and Coulter, F. (1990), 'Social security: solution or problem?' In Hills (1990: 274–337).

Bennett, F., and Jones, K. (2002), 'Social policy digest', *Journal of Social Policy* 31(2): 307–37.

Berthoud, R. (2002), 'Poverty and 'prosperity among Britain's ethnic minorities', *Benefits* 10(1): 3–8.

Beveridge, W. (1942), *Social Insurance and Allied Services*. London: HMSO.

Clasen, J. (2001), 'Social insurance and the contributory principle: a paradox in contemporary British social policy', *'Social Policy and Administration* 35(6): 641–57.

Cook, D. (1989), *Rich Law, Poor Law*. Milton Keynes: Open University Press.

Craig, G. (1999), '"Race", social security and poverty'. In Ditch (1999: 206–26).

Daly, M. (1997), 'Cash benefits in European welfare stales', *Journal of European Social Policy* 7(2): 129–46.

Deacon, A., and Bradshaw, J. (1983), *Reserved for the Poor: The Means-Test in British Social Policy*. Oxford: Basil Blackwell & Martin Robertson.

Deacon, B., with Hulse, M., and Stubbs, P. (1997), *Global Social Policy: International Organisations and the Future of Welfare*. London: Sage.

Dean, H., and Melrose, M. (1996), 'Unravelling citizenship: the significance of social security benefit fraud', *Critical Social Policy* 16(1): 3–31.

—— (1997), 'Manageable discord: fraud and resistance in the social security system', *Social Policy and Administration* 31(2): 103–18.

Dean, H., and Taylor-Gooby, P. (1992), *Dependency Culture: The Explosion of a Myth*. Hemel Hempstead: Harvester Wheatsheaf.

—— Sykes, R., and Woods, R. (eds.) (2000), *Social Policy Review 12*. London: Social Policy Association.

Dennis, N., and Erdos, G. (1992), *Families Without Fatherhood*. London. Institute for Economic Affairs.

Department of Social Security (1996), *Housing Benefit Fraud: Reply by the Government to the Third Report from the Social Security Select Committee. Session 1995–96*. London: HMSO.

—— (1998), *New Ambitions for Our Country*. London: HMSO.

Department of Work and Pensions (2001), press release, 29 Nov.

Ditch, J. (ed.) (1999), *An Introduction to Social Security*. London: Routledge.

—— and Oldfield, N. (1999), 'Social assistance: recent trends and themes', *Journal of European Social Policy* 9(1): 65–76.

Dixon, J. (2001), 'A global perspective on social security programs for the unemployed', *International Social Work* 44(4): 405–22.

Edwards, R., and Duncan, S. (1997), 'Supporting the family: lone-mothers, paid work and the underclass debate', *Critical Social Policy* 17(4): 29–49.

Elliot, L., and Carvel, J. (2002), '4p on Tax "Needed to Halve Child Poverty" ', *Guardian*, 12 Apr.

Field, F. (1989), *Losing Out*. Oxford: Blackwell.

—— (1995), *Making Welfare Work: Reconstructing Welfare for the Millennium*. London: Institute of Community Studies.

—— (1996), *Stakeholder Welfare*. London: Institute for Economic Affairs.

Friedman, M. (1962), *Capitalism and Freedom*. Chicago: University of Chicago Press.

Ginsburg, N. (1979), *Class, Capital and Social Policy*. London: Macmillan.

—— (1992), *Divisions of Welfare*. London: Sage.

Gough, I., Bradshaw, J., Ditch, J., Eardley, T., and Whiteford, P. (1997), 'Social assistance in OECD countries', *Journal of European Social Policy* 7(1): 17–43.

Harris, J. (1997). *William Beveridge: A Biography*, 2nd edn. Oxford: Clarendon Press.

Hayek, F. A. (1960), *The Constitution of Liberty*. London: Routledge & Kegan Paul.

—— (1976), *Law, Legislation and Liberty*, vol. ii: *The Mirage of Social Justice*. London: Routledge & Kegan Paul.

Hill, M. (ed.) (1990), *Social Security Policy in Britain*. Aldershot: Elgar.

Hills, J. (1995), *Joseph Rowntree Inquiry into Income and Wealth*, vol. ii. York: Joseph Rowntree Foundation.

—— with Gardiner, K., and the LSE Welfare Programme (1997), *The Future of Welfare: A Guide to the Debate*, rev. edn. York: Joseph Rowntree Foundation.

Howard, M., Garnham, A., Fimister, G., and Veit-Wilson, J. (2001), *Poverty: The Facts*. London: Child Poverty Action Group.

Le Grand, J. (1982), *The Strategy of Equality*. London: Alien & Unwin.

Lewis, O. (1968), *La Vida*. London: Panther.

Lodemel, I., and Trickey, H. (eds.) (2000), *'An Offer You Can't Refuse'*. Bristol: Policy Press.

Mann, K. (1992), *The Making of an English 'Underclass'? The Social Divisions of Welfare and Labour*. Milton Keynes: Open University Press.

Marshall, T. H. (1981), *The Right to Welfare*. London: Heinemann Educational.

Mead, L. (1986), *Beyond Entitlement*. New York: Free Press.

Morris, L. (1994), *Dangerous Classes: The Underclass and Social Citizenship*. London: Routledge.

Moynihan, D. (1965), *The Negro Family: The Case for National Action*. Washington, DC: Department of Labor.

Murray, C. (1984), *Losing Ground: American Social Policy 1950–80*. New York: Basic Books.

Pahl, J. (1989), *Money and Marriage*. London: Macmillan.

Peck, J. (2001), 'Job alert! Shifts, spins and statistics in welfare-to-work policy', *Benefits* 9(1): 11–15.

Piachaud, D. (1997), The growth of means-testing. In Walker and Walker (1997: 75–83).

Piven, F., and Cloward, R. (1971), *Regulating the Poor: The Functions of Public Welfare*. London: Tavistock.

Powell, M. (1995), 'The strategy of equality revisited', *Journal of Social Policy* 24(2): 163–85.

Rimlinger, G. (1971), *Welfare Policy and Industrialization in Europe*. New York: Wiley.

Rose, H. (1981), 'Re-reading Titmuss: the sexual division of welfare', *Journal of Social Policy* 10(4): 477–502.

Sainsbury, R. (1998), 'Putting fraud into perspective', *Benefits* 21: 2–6.

Social Security Advisory Committee (1997), *Eleventh Report 1997*. London: HMSO.

Spicker, P. (1984), *Stigma and Social Welfare*. Beckenham: Croom Helm.

—— (1993), *Poverty and Social Security*. London: Routledge.

Standing, G. (1999), *Global Labour Flexibility*. London: Macmillan.

Titmuss, R. (1958), *Essays on the Welfare State*. London: Allen & Unwin.

—— (1968), *Commitment to Welfare*. London: Allen & Unwin.

Treloar, P. (2002), 'New tax credits', *Benefits* 10(1): 49–52.

Walker, A., and Walker, C. (eds.) (1977), *Britain Divided*. London: Child Poverty Action Group.

Walker, C. (1993). *Managing Poverty: The Limits of Social Assistance*. London: Routledge.

Walker, R., with Howard, M. (2000), *The Making of a Welfare Class*? Bristol: Policy Press.

Ward, S. (2000), 'New Labour's pension reforms'. In Dean et al. (2000: 157–83).

Wiseman, M. (2000), 'Making work for welfare in the United States'. In Lodemel and Trickey (2000: 215–48).

FURTHER READING

Benefits A journal now published 3 times a year by the Policy Press and which probably represents the best single source of information on recent developments within the benefit system and on recent research.

W. Beveridge, *Social Insurance and Allied Services* (London: HMSO, 1942). The original report itself which should be read not only for its historical significance but because it still represents an insightful analysis into social security issues.

Department of Work and Pensions website: http://www.dwp.gov.uk/ The department created out of the old Department for Social Security in 2001. The website offers a useful overview of UK benefits that is largely intended to assist claimants.

J. Ditch (ed.), *An Introduction to Social Security* (London: Routledge, 1999). An invaluable source of information covering a wide range of subjects and debates.

J. Hills with K. Gardiner and the LSE Welfare Programme, *The Future of Welfare: A Guide to the Debate*, rev. edn. (York: Joseph Rowntree Foundation, 1997). For data up until the mid-1990s this is still an indispensable source of information for those interested in welfare issues generally.

International Social Security Review published four times a year by Blackwell, this provides an international overview of recent debates and research provided by the key figures in the field.

S. McKay and K. Rowlingson, *Social Security in Britain* (London: Macmillan 1999). A user-friendly guide through the intricacies of social security that is intended mainly for social policy students.

J. Millar (ed.) (2003), *Understanding Social Security* (Bristol: Policy Press, 2003). An accessible, learning-based text.

R. Walker *Social Security and Welfare* (Milton Keynes: (Open University Press, 2003)). An important introductory text by one of the foremost experts in the subject.

R. Walker with M. Howard, *The Making of a Welfare Class*? (Bristol: Policy Press, 2000). A mine of information focusing upon the issue of benefit dependency and reviewing the relevant arguments in a way that is accessible but statistically rigorous.

GLOSSARY

fiscal welfare Refers to the distribution of welfare which comes through the deliberate policy of not collecting revenue from people, e.g. due to tax reliefs and allowances.

Gross Domestic Product The value of all goods and services which are produced by those British citizens who are resident in Britain.

Lifecycle redistribution Also known as 'lifecourse' redistribution, this refers to the redistribution of resources from the more affluent periods of a person's life, i.e. the years of labour market activity, to the less affluent periods, e.g. childhood and retirement.

New Deal The specific name given to a range of schemes designed to ease the transition into paid work through the coordination of social security, taxation and employment policies.

occupational welfare The benefits which a person receives by virtue of their occupation or career, e.g. from employers, trade unions or other workplace associations.

poverty trap The situation where an increase in earnings does not leave an employed individual much better off, and possibly even worse off, due to the combined effects of taxes and benefit withdrawal.

replacement ratio The difference between earnings and benefits when out of work. A high ratio implies a narrow gap between the two and a low ratio implies a wide gap.

social insurance principle The principle that individuals should be collectively insured against the risks, e.g. unemployment, which they face within the labour market, through the payment of contributions into a fund during periods of employment.

social security The system of benefits and transfers for income maintainence which are funded out of taxation and insurance contributions.

stigma The feeling of shame and rejection which accompanies low status, e.g. the lack of self-respect which long-term dependency upon benefits may induce.

take-up Refers to the percentage of those who receive the benefits to which they are entitled, e.g. a take-up of 80 per cent indicates that eight out of ten of those eligible for a benefit actually receive it.

unemployment trap The trap faced by the unemployed and those in low-waged jobs where, due to a combination of benefit withdrawal, taxation and low wages, the earnings received while in work are hardly greater than, and may even be worse than, the income received while out of work.

vertical redistribution Typically refers to redistribution from rich to poor, but can also imply redistribution from poor to rich.

welfare to work Describes New Labour's general approach to welfare reform and the notion that all who can work should work for a variety of financial and moral reasons.

workfare The more punitive aspect of a welfare to work approach whereby claimants are required to engage in some form of employment or training scheme in order to qualify for benefits. Emphasis upon compulsion and penalties for non-compliance.

13

Education and Training

Sarah Vickerstaff

CONTENTS

INTRODUCTION

In most industrial societies, state involvement in education pre-dates the development of other comprehensive services such as healthcare. As a universal state service, education has always been a core interest of social policy students and researchers. Inequalities in access to education and variations in educational outcomes, particularly social differences in educational attainment, have been of central concern. It has been much less typical for standard social policy texts to consider the structure of training provision and the policy implications of access to training opportunities. This is largely because training was seen as a labour market or economic issue rather than a social policy issue. However, this is changing: in addition to the traditional concern with the social impact of education, policy debates since the 1970s have focused primarily upon the economic outcomes of education and training provision, namely on their effects on employment, earnings, and economic growth.

It has been argued with increasing force since the late 1970s that the quality and capacity of a country's education and training systems (these will be referred to by the acronym ET, the accepted term in the literature) are a critical element in the performance of whole economies. The distinctive differences in ET from one country to the next are thought to be a factor which helps to explain the differential performance and success of national economies. It is argued further that this economic effect of ET may be becoming more significant in the rapidly changing economic and technological environment that prevails in the new century.

THE SOCIAL AND ECONOMIC FUNCTIONS OF EDUCATION AND TRAINING

The fact that governments typically became involved in mass education before the development of other comprehensive services of the welfare state poses the question of why **education** is thought to be so important. Education has always been seen as providing individual, social, and economic benefits. For the individual, education is supposed to provide opportunities for personal development and growth, scope to realize potential, and hence the basis for progress into work and careers. On a more social level, education is characterized as a civilizing force, with the potential to reduce social inequality and contribute to social unity. A traditional liberal view of education has tended to stress the value of education for its own sake, eschewing the idea that education should perform an explicitly preparatory function for employment. However, it has always also been argued by some that education should fulfil a role in preparing each generation for employment, by inculcating habits of time-keeping and discipline and providing abilities and skills relevant for the world of work.

What the functions of **training** should be have been much less debated. Traditionally, there has been both a philosophical and an institutional split between education and training. They have been seen as fulfilling distinct functions, and in Britain, historically, they have been provided by different institutions and agencies. For much of the last century training has been viewed as primarily providing economic benefits for particular employers, and therefore something best left to private individuals to provide. Although training is typically seen in this more instrumental light as providing specific skills and abilities for, or in, employment, it is also recognized as providing advantages to the individual in terms of their employability, their earning potential and future career prospects, and hence their welfare. More recently it has been argued that a highly skilled workforce is also a more flexible, creative, and innovative one, so that in addition to the immediate benefits of enhancing someone's specific skills there is the broader advantage of a more adaptable pool of labour for the economy as a whole. This is taken one step further in the argument that people must become **lifelong learners** in a learning society and be willing and able to continue with education and training throughout their lives.

For these reasons it is, in practice, difficult to separate the individual, social, and economic advantages and disadvantages of access to ET. Levels of ET contribute to an individual's and—it seems—a nation's earning capacity, and hence make a great contribution to welfare. It is not surprising, therefore, that debates over the 'proper' function of education and the right balance between the individual, social, and economic functions of ET has been a linking thread of policy reform since the 1970s. From that time the view has grown that schools are failing to provide young people with the basic education and kinds of skill they needed for the world of work. As Wolf (2002: 13) has put it:

> For twenty years, British politicians have been obsessed with education—convinced that it is in a uniquely parlous state, and that this matters as never before . . . this passion for education rests on the belief that the world's whole economy has changed. It is now so 'knowledge-driven' that only those nations committed to 'lifelong learning' in a 'learning society' can hope to thrive. Lip-service may still be paid to learning for personal enrichment and development, but in politicians' speeches the emphasis is unremittingly on what education can do for the economy of the UK.

Before considering what implications these developments have had for policy in the ET field we will briefly consider the history and legacy of ET policy in the UK.

THE EDUCATION AND TRAINING LEGACY

The capacity of national ET systems to respond to the rapidly changing social and economic conditions in the new century is obviously built, in part, upon the education and training legacy in each country. Britain's education and training system is often seen as inferior to those of her competitors.

> Britain's failure to educate and train its workforce to the same levels as its international competitors has been both a product and a cause of the nation's poor relative economic performance: a product because the ET system evolved to meet the needs of the world's first industrialized economy, whose large, mass-production manufacturing sector required only a small number of skilled workers and university graduates; and a cause, because the absence of a well educated and trained workforce has made it more difficult for industry to respond to new economic conditions. (Finegold and Soskice 1988: 21–2)

Education policy

A national system of mass schooling developed relatively late in England in comparison with other European countries. Throughout the nineteenth century the development of education was characterized by **voluntarism**, and provision was neither directed nor co-ordinated by government. The model for the curriculum was derived from the traditional independent **public schools**, in which a classical education was prized over science or anything of a vocational or practical bent. As Green comments:

> One of the principal casualties of the tradition of laissez-faire in education was scientific and technical instruction. With the exception of pure science which developed largely independently of formal educational institutions, England was, by the mid [nineteenth] century, incomparably backward in most areas of scientific and technical education. For the working class, elementary education was largely absent. State-organized trade schools for artisans and engineers, which were common in Europe, had not developed in England where received opinion regarded the workshop as the only fit place for learning a trade. (1990: 292)

This tradition of elite education left vocational and practical education and training to industry, and has continued to have effects on the ET system to the present day. With the development, in the last century, of a national education system, the split between education and training was rigidly maintained, and resulted in the failure to develop a comprehensive and integrated system that catered not merely to the needs of an academically oriented minority but also to those of the mass of people destined for skilled and unskilled manual and routine clerical work. The 1944 Education Act recommended the creation of a schooling system composed of three types of secondary school catering for different abilities and aptitudes: the grammar school for a traditional academic curriculum, technical schools for more practical or vocational studies, and secondary modern schools for a less academic route. The Act also provided for some compulsory education for the post-school 15–18 age group. In practice, the technical schools were never widely introduced and provisions for post-compulsory school education were weak. The failure to create the system outlined in the 1944 Act was due in part to the decentralized nature of education administration in which local government had practical management control over education (Aldcroft 1992: 30–1). In education, meanwhile, over the long period from the end of the Second World War to the middle 1970s, change in policy was gradual.

As Taylor-Gooby has argued, the period can be characterized by four key features: the decentralized nature of education management in the hands of local education authorities; the dominance of teachers and other education professionals in defining and determining the content of education; the gradual replacement of the division between grammar schools and secondary moderns with the extension of the comprehensive schooling model; and lastly, the persistent primacy, culturally and in resource terms, given to academic curricula and qualifications over more vocational education (1993: 102–3). This pattern met with increasing criticisms from both Left and Right as the 1970s progressed.

Industrial training policy

Until the end of the 1970s the apprenticeship system was the mainstay of industrial training in Britain. Originally a legally regulated system dating back to the medieval guilds, the apprenticeship had become, over the long haul of industrialization, a self-regulated system administered by the two sides of industry. The apprenticeship system was built on work-based, practical, hands-on learning, as much a process of socialization into a trade as a process of skills acquisition. Divorced from education, this system reinforced the gulf between theoretical learning in education and practical training in industry.

The lack of a national framework for the regulation of training also meant that the apprenticeship model was never systematically extended to cover the broad range of emerging occupations in the new modern industries and services, but remained concentrated in traditional industries and manufacturing such as shipbuilding, construction, and engineering. The apprenticeship system reinforced the split between education and training. A byproduct of this differentiation was the higher status and desirability of education, and the identification of vocational education or training as a second best option.

Prior to the 1960s British governments were willing to intervene in training matters only in times of war or as part of what have been called elsewhere Poor Law measures to provide training for the unemployed. However, by the 1960s wider concerns about economic performance, and the pressures of foreign competition, put the industrial training issue back on the political agenda. Skill shortages and the then current vogue for economic planning and tripartism led to the first major attempt to reform the training system, through the 1964 Industrial Training Act. The French example of an apprenticeship tax was an important model, and the 1964 Act introduced a levy on firms administered by tripartite Industrial Training Boards (ITBs) representing employers and trade unions. Firms paid the levy to the ITBs and could then be reimbursed if they had undertaken appropriate training. The aim was to spread the costs of training more equally across industry (Vickerstaff 1992: 250). Subsequently, the tripartite Manpower Services Commission (MSC) was created in the early 1970s to coordinate policy in the training and employment areas. This was the first time that a single body was commissioned with a strategic capability to oversee and plan policy.

Although these developments were a departure from the voluntarist past, it was still relatively weak regulation by European standards. There was no individual legal entitlement to training as a right; the MSC in practice had very little power to change what happened at the level of the individual firm; and the separation of education and training remained largely intact. These changes did move Britain closer, however, to other models of ET provision in Europe. With the change of government in Britain in 1979 the previous period of reform towards a more interventionist approach, in which the role of the social partners (trade unions and employers) were institutionalized in agencies like the MSC, began to be challenged.

This potted history of ET in the last century in Britain indicates the specific legacy of institutions and approaches from which current policy reform has had to build. Developments up to the 1970s had resulted in a hybrid system with a bias towards keeping government's role confined to broad overall direction rather than detailed intervention or control. Today ET is offered by five main groups of providers in Britain: the school system (both public and private), further education colleges, higher education in universities, government-sponsored schemes based on work experience and training with employers, and on-the-job training in employment. This mixed system of provision has tended to be poorly integrated, with the status of academic qualifications and routes overshadowing the vocational stream; movement between academic and vocational streams has traditionally been limited.

THE ROLE OF SOCIAL AND PUBLIC POLICY

Much recent debate on ET in Britain (as with other areas of social policy) has been dominated by arguments about the relative roles of the state and the market (or the public and private sectors) in delivering the quantity and quality of services needed. The case for state intervention in ET is usually built around two main lines of argument: economic arguments about market failure and social arguments about equity and equality of opportunity. The economic justification for state involvement in ET revolves around an assessment of the relative benefits that accrue from ET to society as a whole (the public good), to individuals and to employing organizations (the private good) the argument being that the balance of gains should determine who pays. The question immediately becomes complicated, however, because of course not all education and training have the same benefits or advantages. It is necessary to distinguish between **basic education** and **higher education** and to analyse the nature of different skills gained through training (see Box 13.1). It is apparent that the more general the education or training the more difficult it is to apportion the relative benefits to society, to the individual, and to employers. It is now taken for granted that the state should provide access to education, funded through general taxation, and that a basic level of education should be compulsory. Although the individual is the prime beneficiary, the public

Box 13.1 What are skills?

Core skills now more usually referred to as 'key skills'. These are very general skills needed in almost any job. They include basic literacy and numeracy and a range of personal transferable skills such as the ability to work well with others, communication skills, self-motivation, the ability to organize one's own work, and, often, a basic capability to use information technology.

Vocational skills. These are needed in particular occupations or groups of occupations, but are less useful outside these areas. While these skills are less general than core skills, they are nonetheless highly transferable between jobs in a given field. An example is a basic ability to use common computer packages, such as a broad understanding of computer-aided design packages.

Job-specific skills. The usefulness of these is limited to a much narrower field of employment. Often these are forms of knowledge rather than skills as traditionally defined. They could be specific to individual firms. An example could be using a specific computer-aided design package to produce designs to a style and format required by an employer.

(DFEE 1996: 40)

goods or gains are also clear: the democratic, cultural, and creative benefits of an educated citizenry and the economic advantages, in terms of productivity, flexibility, and innovation, of a well-educated workforce.

The same argument is less transparent for other aspects of ET. Table 13.1 shows that whereas the public good argument is relatively easy to make for compulsory education, it becomes progressively more difficult with training. The more firm-specific training is (i.e. the extent to which the training is not transferable to other work situations) the less justifiable it appears to be to finance it from the public purse through general taxation. In response to these issues we can distinguish theoretically between three ideal types of ET regulation: the **market model**, the **social partnership model**, and the **state model** (Sheldrake and Vickerstaff 1987: 55; see also Finegold and Crouch 1994: 276).

Paying for ET

The market model argues that if individuals or firms perceive a commercial advantage in acquiring skills or skilled employees they will undertake training. For example, the return on the investment in adding skills will be recouped either in higher wages for the individual or in higher productivity for the employer. The role of policy here is to ensure the smooth operation of the market but to allow the quantity and quality of training provided to be market-driven. However, for various reasons the market may produce sub-optimal outcomes in terms of the quantity and quality of training desirable for the economy as a whole. For the employing firm, the problem is that in a free labour market the trained employee can take her skills to the highest bidder. This is usually known as the 'poaching' problem, and has often been used by companies as a justification for not investing in training: they spend money on training someone only to see that employee poached by another firm which free-rides on the benefit. There are thus incentives for firms either to poach already trained labour or to restrict training to firm-specific skills, which have less value in the labour market. In practice, however, it may be very difficult for training to be sufficiently firm-specific. In the case of many vocational and job-specific skills, the obvious beneficiary is the individual whose employment prospects are enhanced. Nonetheless, from the individual's perspective there is a risk that investing in skills, either by not earning or by taking lower wages whilst undergoing education or training, will not be repaid by a better-paid job in the future. There is also an information problem for the individual in knowing which skills would make a sound investment. It may also be the case that the individual cannot currently afford to acquire desirable skills. (For a full discussion of these market incentives and failures see Layard 1994; Finegold 1991.)

Another way of looking at these issues, which has become prominent in education policy debates, is by reference to **rates of return** on spending on ET. By calculating the cost of education and training, for an individual in terms of forgone earnings and for society in respect of public expenditure, we can attempt to determine the rate of return to the individual and to society as a whole in terms of extra earnings and output (see Glennerster 1998: 54–7). This approach was very significant in the 1990s in the debates about higher education. The proven pay premium for graduates (expected extra earnings

Table 13.1 Benefits accruing from different aspects of education and training

Aspect of ET	Provider	Public good	Individual benefit	Employer benefit
Foundation and key skills	Compulsory education in schools	Social and cultural benefits; flexible workforce	Access to further and higher education; foundation for life; career opportunities	Core skills of workforce; trainability of employees
Vocational preparation	Schools, further education (FE) colleges, and employers	School-to-work transition facilitated	Access and entry to workforce improved	Work role socialization; pre-recruitment screening
Intermediate vocational skills	Employers/FE colleges	Skills base for the economy; economic competitiveness	High market value of transferable skills; earnings/career prospects	Vocational skills provision; impact on productivity, innovation, and quality
Higher education	Universities and FE colleges	Cultural and creative life; research and development	Career prospects; individual development	Preparation of future managerial and professional staff; research and development
Job-specific skills	Employer	Healthy economy	Career progress within the company	Return on training investment in terms of employee retention, quality, productivity, and innovation

as a result of having a degree) have been seen as a justification for expecting students to contribute more to the direct costs of their education:

> The costs of higher education should be shared among those who benefit from it. We have concluded that those with higher education qualifications are the main beneficiaries, through improved employment prospects and pay. As a consequence, we suggest that graduates in work should make a greater contribution to the costs of higher education in future. (National Committee of Inquiry into Higher Education (NCIHE) 1997: 28–9)

Nevertheless, the social rate of return in the form of social, economic, and cultural benefits are seen still to justify continued, and even expanding, public expenditure in higher education (NCIHE 1997: 29). For an extended discussion and a critique of social rates of return arguments, see Wolf (2002: 13–55).

These problems of quantifying who benefits from ET, and the market failures and perverse incentives that result, imply that public policy must seek solutions either by providing ET directly (the state model) or by developing mechanisms for sharing the costs of training amongst the main beneficiaries (the social partnership model). In practice, many countries use a combination of approaches depending upon the particular area of ET.

Access to ET?

In addition to the policy issue of who pays for ET there is also the question of whether governments should become involved in determining the structure and contents of ET to ensure that its benefits are evenly spread and that the curricula are 'appropriate'. If ET has an impact on an individual's welfare, in terms of earning capacity and participation in the cultural and social life of the society, then public policy faces questions of equality of access to ET opportunities. In practice, evaluations of educational opportunities and outcomes show that the experience of education varies significantly from one social group to another. Rather than being a force for liberation, many writers have argued that schooling reinforces social divisions and serves to perpetuate or reproduce class, race, and gender divisions (see Box 13.2 and, for further discussion, Halsey et al. 1997). Access to education and rates of success, as measured by qualifications, are highly correlated with socio-economic background, gender and race (see Table 13.2). It is also the case that those with the poorest education are least likely to receive substantial post compulsory education and training, being confined to unskilled work in which little or no training is offered.

Since the beginning of the 1980s the pressures on public expenditure (see Chapter 10 in this volume), the growth and persistence of unemployment, changes in the abilities and skills needed in the economy, and growing fears about the social implications of a poorly educated and increasingly unemployable underclass have put all these issues of the role of government in overseeing and providing an 'appropriate' ET system into sharp relief.

Box 13.2 Social class and education

If the industrial working class was the driving force behind social change in the nineteenth and early decades of the twentieth century, it is the middle class who are now seen to determine the destiny of post-industrial societies. During the period of economic nationalism [1945–72] the burgeoning middle class benefited most from the expansion of the welfare state, employment security, and the opportunities afforded by comprehensive education and the expansion of post-compulsory provision. Accordingly, within the sociology of education it was the question of working-class access and opportunity which dominated debates . . . Now, it is not working-class resistance to education which represents the primary sources of class conflict as predicted by neo-Marxist analysts, but the exclusionary tactics of the middle classes at a time of profound personal and social insecurity. With the breakdown of economic nationalism, the demise of bureaucratic careers and the attendant risks of downward mobility have led the middle classes to reassert their vested interests in an attempt to maximize the reproduction of their class advantage.

. . . cultural capital in the form of academic credentials is essential to the reproduction of middle-class privilege. This, it can be argued, has led to intense class conflict over the question of educational selection, when concerns about ensuring 'equality of opportunity' have been superseded by primarily (although not exclusively) middle-class claims for greater 'choice' over the education of their children . . . This is clearly reflected in buoyant demand for access to higher education. Therefore at the same time that the 'new' middle class have been demanding increasing access to higher education for their children, the 'old' professional middle class is concerned to preserve its monopoly of access to elite universities.

(Brown et al. 1997: 14–15)

RECENT POLICY: SCHOOLING

Much has been done since the early 1980s to try to upgrade vocational education and provide a coherent system in which the traditional academic routes and the newer vocational schemes are integrated. Governments have taken a far more centralized approach to the development of both the academic and vocational curricula. This has been part of a wider debate about the extent to which schools were accountable for their methods, were delivering acceptable standards, and were meeting the needs of industry (Dale et al. 1990: 13). Thus, the development of government policy had two dimensions: the desire to change the content of education, to make it more vocational and hence 'relevant' to the world of work; and the urge to change the processes of educational reform by taking tighter centralized control. The key piece of legislation in the process of change was the 1988 Education Reform Act.

The government, through this Act, instituted for the first time a **National Curriculum** for all schools in England and Wales. This continued a trend for more central government

Table 13.2 Highest qualifications held,[a] by gender and ethnic group, Great Britain, 2000–2001(%)

	Degree or equivalent	Higher education[b]	GCE A Level or equivalent	GCSE grades A–C	Other qualifications	No qualifications	All
Males							
White	17	8	31	18	13	14	100
Black	16	9	20	17	22	16	100
Indian/Pakistani/Bangladeshi	20	4	16	15	24	20	100
Other groups[c]	23	5	18	12	30	12	100
All	17	7	30	18	13	15	100
Females							
White	13	10	17	28	14	18	100
Black	14	11	18	22	21	15	100
Indian/Pakistan/Bangladeshi	13	5	14	16	23	29	100
Other groups	18	10	14	13	30	15	100
All	14	9	17	27	14	18	100

[a] Males aged 16–64, females aged 16–59. [b] Below degree level. [c] Includes those who did not state their ethnic group.

Source: ONS (2002: 62).

control over the school curriculum and the breaking up of the teaching professions' monopoly over curriculum design. An earlier policy, the Technical and Vocational Education Initiative (TVEI), created in 1982, had begun this trend by aiming to involve business people more in the development and delivery of school education. TVEI provided extra funds for schools to develop projects in different subject areas, which gave students experience of how industry worked, and skills relevant to work and new technologies.

This focus on the curriculum also reflected the growing belief that educational standards in Britain were falling; as has often been the case in the history of ET policy, comparisons with other countries were influential in seeming to prove that Britain was not educating its children as well as some other countries. However, evidence on Britain alone suggests that standards, as measured by examination results, have been improving, Interpretation of such data raised the question of how to define standards in education, which, as we will see, continues to be a major focus of educational policy debate.

The Education Reform Act of 1988 allowed schools to opt out of local education authority (LEA) control and become **grant-maintained** from central government; those remaining under LEA control moved to local school-level management. The development of **Local Management of Schools** introduced five new elements to the management of schools: delegated responsibility for the school budget; formula funding, in which most of a school's delegated budget is based on pupil numbers; new admissions regulations; devolved responsibility for staffing matters; and performance indicators in the form of league tables of pupil performance (Thomas and Bullock 1994: 41). The Act attempted to increase parental choice: by open enrolment, in which parents could 'choose' schools for their children outside their local authority area, some choice had been available before the Act but had been hindered by the operation of LEA quotas on admission numbers. The aim of these reforms was to create a managed market system of education, which encouraged schools to compete for pupils.

The 1988 Act has been a controversial intervention in education, not least for its particular definition of educational standards as something that can be measured primarily by examination results and performance indicators such as rates of truancy. Under the Act such results are published nationally in the form of league tables. This information is supposed to help parents in making a choice of school for their children. Critics of the Act have argued that the league tables merely measure the social class backgrounds of the children and do not give any indication of **value added**, that is, the extent to which the school has had an impact on individual pupil's progress and achievements during their schooling (see Box 13.3). The new Labour government which came to power in 1997 remained committed to the publication of league tables, but discussion continues as to whether measures of value added could be incorporated in some way.

The 1988 Act has also been challenged for its vision of parental choice. Research by Ball et al. (1997) has indicated that, in practice, the degree of choice may be profoundly circumscribed by parents' social circumstances:

> In the case of the working class respondents' choice of secondary school was a contingent decision rather than an open one. . . . School has to be 'fitted' into a set of constraints and expectations

Box 13.3 What do the league tables measure?

'. . . the position of a school in a league table of this kind is influenced by many factors which have little to do with whether it is a good school. A selective school will normally show up well, just because it is selective . . . . It is well established, for example, that the children of parents with post-compulsory schooling are likely to do well at schoolwork. Conversely poverty is liable to impact on a home in a way that holds a pupil back. Accordingly, it is not surprising if a school which draws many of its pupils from a relatively prosperous neighbourhood figures higher in a league table than one in a deprived working-class area . . . . There is no telling, however, whether it is a better school on that account.

. . . if schools come to believe that their position in a league table is vital to their prestige and to their future success, they may adopt practices, which are not in the best interests of children, in order to maintain or improve their position. If more children apply for places than are available, schools may be tempted to select covertly on ability or on the basis of parental attitudes. They may be wary of accepting pupils who they fear will prove hard to teach, and too ready to exclude those who prove disruptive.'

(National Commission on Education 1993: 64–5)

> related to work roles, family roles, the sexual division of labour and the demands of household organisation. . . . it is not simply a matter of education being of less importance for working class families, our interviewees were very concerned that their children get a good education. Rather the competing pressures of work and family life made certain possibilities difficult or impossible to contemplate. (Ball et al. 1997: 411)

In addition, the cost of travel and the difficulties of resourcing childcare may make the local school the only real 'choice' for the poor family.

The Labour government which came to power in 1997 fought the election campaign with education policy as one of it main priorities. The first major piece of education legislation of the new government was the School Standards and Framework Act of 1998 which included the following policy developments: the abolition of the **assisted places scheme**; measures to reduce class sizes for 5–7-year-olds; a new framework of community, foundation, and voluntary schools; and action to raise school standards (Tomlinson, 2001: 85–111). The focus on infant class sizes has shown some results (see Table 13.3).

The New Labour government has continued the trend towards tighter prescription of the curriculum, introducing the literacy hour and the numeracy strategy in primary schools and revising the National Curriculum with effect from September 2000 (Tomlinson 2001: 89, 108). The main innovations to the National Curriculum are the introduction of citizenship teaching and a stronger focus on information and communications technology (ICT).

Overall the emphasis on raising standards, publishing school results, and targeting poor performing schools, which had been developed by the previous government, remains a central plank of policy, along with the commitment to centralized control of

Table 13.3 Percentage of pupils in infant classes, taught by one teacher, having thirty-one or more pupils, England, September 1998–2001

1998	22.0
1999	11.0
2000	2.0
2001	0.5

Source: www.dfes.gov.uk/trends

the curriculum. Given the cost of schooling to the public purse (see Chapter 10), the debates about how public policy can best ensure value for money and provide the kind of schooling which people desire for their children will inevitably continue, as will debates about the balance between the social and economic functions of education.

THE TRANSITION FROM SCHOOL TO WORK

There have been major changes since the late 1970s in the traditional routes from full-time education into work. In the past many school leavers went straight into employment at 15 or 16 (the school leaving age was raised to 16 in 1973) and some into apprenticeships—the latter were mainly young men. In the mid-1970s youth unemployment began to rise and there was a debate about the role of education, with employers arguing that schools were failing to meet the needs of industry and many educationalists arguing that schools were still failing the majority of students who were not destined for higher education (Blackman 1992). In addition during the 1970s the old apprenticeship system was beginning to collapse, through a combination of declining employment in traditional industries, where apprenticeship was the accepted route into skilled trades, and the continuing recession, which was causing a reduction in employers' expenditure on training. Both factors speeded up the decline in apprenticeship that had been apparent for some time.

A long-held criticism of the British ET structure was the complicated qualification system, which had developed incrementally and in an uncoordinated fashion over a long period. A major set of developments in the 1980s attempted to overcome this problem by establishing frameworks for the ET system as a whole, in addition to the National Curriculum for schools, there was the development of **National Vocational Qualifications** (NVQs), and the framing of National Targets for Education and Training (NTETs). In 1986 the Government established the National Council for Vocational Qualifications (NCVQ) to institute a framework of qualifications to cover all occupations in England, Wales, and Northern Ireland. Scotland is covered by parallel developments overseen by the Scottish Vocational Education Council (SCOTVEC). This was the

Table 13.4 Levels of qualification

National level of qualification	General		Vocationally related (applied)	Occupational (purely vocational)	Expected job destinations
5	Higher-level qualifications those qualifications at or above NVQ Level 4 or HE equivalent, including HNDs, first degrees, and postgraduate			Level 5 NVQ	Professional, senior management
4				Level 4 NVQ	Junior managerial, technician
3 Advanced Level	A Level	Free-standing mathematics units Level 3	Vocational A Level (AVCE)	Level 3 NVQ	Junior white-collar, skilled manual, service, craft
2 Intermediate Level	GCSE Grade A*–C	Free-standing mathematics units Level 2	Intermediate GNVQ	Level 2 NVQ	Semi-skilled, clerical, manual
1 Foundation Level	GCSE Grade D–G	Free-standing mathematics units Level 1	Foundation GNVQ	Level 1 NVQ	Unskilled, routine manual, service-sector jobs
Entry Level	Certificate of (educational) achievement				

first major attempt in the twentieth century to create a unified system of vocational accreditation linked to academic qualifications. The standards for NVQs in each industry have been established and accredited by the Industry Lead Body for that sector. A General National Vocational Qualification (GNVQ) has also been developed as a vocational qualification for those not in training or employment.

A contrast is often made between a state-led system of ET provision, such as is found in Sweden where initial vocational education and training is provided in the education system, and the **dual systems** typical of Germany, Austria, and Switzerland. In the latter, vocational education and training is primarily provided by employer-based apprenticeships, with requirements for off-the-job training and restrictions on firms employing school leavers without providing further ET. In Britain there is a hybrid system. This is shown in Table 13.4, which illustrates the connections between the traditional educational qualifications and S/NVQs, the institutions that provide them, and the typical labour market expectations associated with different levels of ET.

Britain traditionally had a low rate of 16- and 17-year-olds staying on in full-time education and a low proportion of 16- or 17-year-olds undertaking any further education compared with other industrial countries. However, the situation has changed over the last decade and a half for a number of reasons: the introduction of the Youth Training Scheme (YTS) meant that a majority of school leavers received some further training and education, and youth unemployment encouraged young people to stay on at school or go to college.

The increases in staying on rates indicated in Table 13.5 have been largely stabilized in the years since 1995, but with some shifts towards more young people undertaking vocational courses (see Table 13.6).

The YTS was introduced in 1983 as a publicly funded one-year scheme for school leavers. Most YTS places were with employers, but had to include some off-the-job training. In 1986 the scheme became two years in duration, and in 1987 a change in policy meant that young people who refused a YT (the scheme also changed its name to Youth Training) were ineligible for unemployment benefit. In some industries the YT scheme took over as the first year and then two years of an apprenticeship. However, it is generally agreed that the relatively low level of most YT schemes did not compensate for the loss of traditional apprenticeships. Perhaps the key enduring legacy of YT is the breaking of the assumption that young unemployed people are entitled to benefits. Since YT the policy assumption has been that young people are expected to take up their entitlement

Table 13.5 Percentage of 16- and 17-year olds in education and training, England

1985	1986	1987	1988	1989	1990	1991	1992	1993	1994	1995
66.7	69.1	72.7	74.8	75.7	77.1	80.6	81.7	83.6	83.6	82.7

Source: DfEE (1997: 52).

Table 13.6 Percentage of 16-year-olds in full-time education by type of course, England, 1992–2000

	1991	1992	1993	1994[a]	1995	1996	1997	1998	1999	2000
Academic qualification	45	45	44	40	40	40	40	39	40	40
Vocational courses	21	24	28	30	29	29	29	30	31	31

[a] Change in data source

Source: www.dfes.gov.uk/trends

to further education or training, as Gordon Brown, Chancellor of the Exchequer, said in 1997: there is 'no option to stay at home in bed watching television' (*Financial Times*, 26 June 1997; see also Chapter 7 above).

With the collapse of traditional apprenticeships, intermediate and technician level skills have been identified as some of the key areas of skill shortages (Skills and Enterprise Network 1993: 51; Ryan, 1991). In partial response to this, the government announced the introduction of a new programme of **Modern Apprenticeships** (MA) in 1993. Modern Apprenticeships are available at two levels, Foundation leading to an NVQ Level 2 and Advanced leading to an NVQ Level 3. The training has to conform to a model for each sector developed by the relevant **sector training organizations**. There is a 'pledge' or training contract between the apprentice and the employer. The reintroduction of apprenticeships has the potential significantly to improve the quality and quantity of post-compulsory education and training that the average young person who is not going on to higher education receives. However, there is still considerable uncertainty for the young school leaver as to the best likely route into work; the 1980s and 1990s have seen the proliferation of different routes and qualifications. The Labour government announced in 2002 the target that by 2004 one quarter of school leavers would enter apprenticeships. A major problem with the policy so far has been the large numbers of young people who enter an MA but do not achieve the NVQ. There are also concerns about the variability in the quality of training that young people receive in different sectors of employment.

Nevertheless, far fewer British school leavers now go straight into employment or unemployment than was the case in the 1970s. Over three-quarters of 16-year-old school leavers went into work in 1978; for most young people at the turn of the millennium the transition from school (or college) to work has been elongated and no longer typically occurs at 16. This trend for more young people to continue in education after the compulsory school-leaving age, although initially a response to youth unemployment, has become established now and there is not the same expectation amongst 16-year-olds that they will go straight into paid work on leaving school. However, the significance of

Case Study 13.1

In comparison to young people leaving compulsory education in the 1950s and 1960s, young people today face a broader range of further education and training opportunities. Government policy has increasingly set targets for certain percentages of young people to take particular routes, e.g. 25 per cent doing apprenticeships, 50 per cent undertaking degrees. It is not always easy however, for young people, their parents/guardians, teachers, or careers advisers to know which is the best route. This is compounded by the fact that a number of institutions are effectively in competition with each other to attract these young people, so they have a vested interest in selling their route as the best one.

Look at the scenarios below and discuss in groups what your advice to each of the young people would be, give reasons for your recommendations.

Lucy

Lucy is soon to take her GCSEs. She doesn't expect to do brilliantly but hopes to get at least four at grade C or above. She is not sure what sort of work she would like—something in an office environment is where her ideas have gone so far. She is not sure whether to stay on at school as her school suggests and do AS Levels, which she thinks will be a struggle, or to go to college and do some more vocational qualifications, perhaps a GNVQ in Business Administration. She has also heard about Modern Apprenticeships and wonders whether this might be an option. On the other hand, she could endeavour to get an office job to try it out for a while and take a bit more time to work out whether she wants to go for more qualifications.

Carl

Carl is about to sit for his A Levels and has an offer of a place at university to study fashion design conditional on achieving three Cs. He is expected to achieve these grades without any great effort. However, more recently he has been wondering whether a university degree is really the best route into what he wants to do: bespoke tailoring. He has been thinking about trying to find an apprenticeship, perhaps in Savile Row. Then he could be earning a little, not building up a great debt, and actually getting on with learning and doing the job he really wants to do.

these increased staying-on rates is mitigated by the relatively low levels of qualification of many of these young people.

HIGHER EDUCATION AND TRAINING FOR ADULTS

The funding and role of higher education became major policy issues in the 1980s and 1990s. An influential committee chaired by Sir Ron Dearing was commissioned in May 1996 to make recommendations on 'how the purposes, shape, structure, size and funding of higher education, including support for students, should develop to meet the needs of the United Kingdom over the next 20 years' (NCIHE 1997: 3). The report indicated that more young people were going into higher education than ever before: 32 per cent of the 18+ age cohort in 1995 compared to just 12.4 per cent in 1980 (p. 40). The target set by the New Labour government in the new century is for 50 per cent of the age cohort to have a higher education experience.

This expansion in the numbers of people in higher education resulted in a change in intake, with increasing numbers of mature students, growth in the number of part-time students, and a greater diversity of educational background and experience amongst undergraduates. Nonetheless, young people from the upper and middle classes are still far more likely to go on to university than their working-class peers. The Dearing report recommended the continued expansion of higher education and most contentiously, recommended that students should be expected to contribute more to the cost of their education by paying a proportion of the tuition fees. The report adhered to a traditional liberal view of the functions of education whilst acknowledging the 'rate of return' arguments discussed above:

> Over the next 20 years, the UK must create a society committed to learning throughout life. That commitment will be required from individuals, the state, employers and providers of education and training. Education is life enriching and desirable in its own right. It is fundamental to the achievement of an improved quality of life in the UK. (NCIHE 1997: 8)

The argument is that, as individuals who undertake a degree and the organizations which employ them benefit most from university education, they should be expected to contribute more to the cost of it. The expansion of higher education places has been achieved without a proportionate increase in the funding which universities receive; this has led to debates about whether universities should be allowed to charge **top-up fees** to students in order to increase their revenue. In January 2003 the Department for Education and Skills published a White Paper, *The Future of Higher Education*, which proposed a new set of funding arrangements for universities that may allow the more prestigious institutions, whose courses potentially generate the largest gain to individuals, to charge higher fees. This would be subject to regulation requiring them to demonstrate that they were encouraging access from less advantaged applicants (DfES 2003).

Despite the growth in the number of mature student entrants into universities over the last decade (NCIHE 1997: 12), the wider continuing education and training for adults has traditionally been the weakest area of ET. Government, through general taxation, funds considerable initial training for young people and schemes for the adult unemployed, and in addition there is a range of training, education, and enterprise programmes. However, in Britain there are no specific taxes levied for training. The majority of job-related training is paid for by private industry. Governments have been prepared to intervene with schemes for the long-term unemployed, but continuing training and retraining for employed adults has generally been seen to be industry's responsibility, and has thus been subject to the market failures and perverse incentives described above. The Labour government of 1997 introduced a New Deal for 18–24-year-olds as part of the wider programme of Welfare to Work policies (see Chapter 7). The **New Deal** was aimed initially at young adults who have been unemployed for six months or more, and involves four options, each of which includes an element of continuing education and training: a subsidized job with an employer; full-time education or training; work on the Environment Task Force; or work with the voluntary sector (DfEE 1997: 2). Progressively the New Deal model has been extended to unemployed adults, lone parents, older workers, and the disabled.

As with other areas of ET provision, international comparisons of employers' policies and expenditure on training for adults have been influential in the policy debate in Britain. Studies in the middle 1980s argued that British employers spent significantly less than their German, American, French, and Japanese competitors. However, it is difficult to compare adult training expenditure either within Britain or across economies because of the problems of how training has been defined and measured from case to case (Ryan 1991). In addition, it has proved difficult to quantify the volume of training actually done, as companies are not obliged to record their expenditure on training.

Most of this in-work training is of relatively short duration, undertaken either on an employer's premises or at a college of further education (Skills and Enterprise Network 1993: 60; Department of Employment 1993: 23–58). More adults are returning to education and training, either because of unemployment or because of employers' demands for new skills. Nevertheless, there are still concerns about the skills and qualification levels of the British workforce in comparison to other countries. As a government publication concluded:

> the task is not just one of training, but of constant updating and improvement of skills to meet the demands of the jobs of today and tomorrow. There is also clear evidence of deficiencies in the qualifications of people across the whole economy and, most notably, in the key intermediate level occupations. (DfEE 1996: 55)

This suggests that in the future more and more people will have to learn new skills in order to keep their jobs and that adults will be an increasingly significant group within ET provision. This is heralded as the need for a 'learning society' in which people expect, and are enabled, to continue updating their education throughout life (see e.g. Commission on Social Justice 1994: 141–5; DfEE 1996: 69–82). The creation of a learning society and encouragement of lifelong learning would challenge the traditional focus of ET public policy and funding on schooling, higher education, and the unemployed, and would raise anew the issue of whether the social return on investment in continuing education and training for adults justifies support from the public purse.

CONCLUSIONS

This chapter has provided an introduction to some of the key policy issues and debates in the area of education and training (ET). It is clear that the pace of change in British ET has quickened considerably since the early 1980s, and that the state's role in terms of funding, regulation, and provision has come under increasing public scrutiny. Belatedly, the ET system is encouraging more young people to stay on in education and more school leavers to continue in some further education and training than ever before. Compulsory education must be the foundation for any strategy to improve the skills profile of the workforce as a whole. Training builds upon the base which education has laid down, and often in the past too many young people left full-time education bored, poorly qualified, and thoroughly ill-disposed towards the idea of education. Not only for economic but also for social reasons, a continuing improvement in the number of young people staying on in education must be desirable, assuming that the curriculum is able to meet all their needs, aspirations, and aptitudes.

Recent policy developments in Britain have gone some way to mitigating the historical legacy of a weak and fragmented ET system. Moves to develop a national framework of academic and vocational qualifications offer the promise of upgrading the image of training and of facilitating moves between vocational and academic streams which were so difficult in the past. Nevertheless, academic qualifications remain the 'gold standard' against which the newer S/NVQs and GNVQs are measured.

In the twenty-first century most young people will continue with some education and training after compulsory schooling. It may also be that employers taking on school leavers are increasingly expected (or even required) to provide some further ET. There is much rhetoric about the desirability of a 'learning society' in which everyone is enabled to continue with the education and training necessary for work or simply to pursue their own interests and development. It is now much more accepted that ET should be a continuing process throughout life. A key problem for policy debate is how expansion and improvements can be financed, and in particular, how public financing should be spread more evenly across different parts of ET provision. The policy developments discussed above suggest an increasing recognition of the need for some kind of social partnership model of funding for ET in which the costs are shared more equally amongst those who benefit. A mixed economy of ET provision, combining public expenditure, individual finance, and employers' contributions, has always existed, but the relative costs to the different sectors are likely to remain centre stage, as are concerns about the balance between the social and economic functions of ET.

REFERENCES

Aldcroft, D. H. (1992), *Education, Training and Economic Performance*. Manchester: Manchester University Press.

Ball, S. J., Bowe, R., and Gewirtz, S. (1997), 'Circuits of schooling: a sociological exploration of parental choice of school in social-class contexts'. In Halsey et al. (1997: 409–21).

Blackman, S. (1992), 'Beyond vocationalism'. In P. Brown and H. Lauder (eds.), *Education for Economic Survival*. London: Routledge, 203–25.

Brown, P., Halsey, A. H., Lauder, H., and Stuart Wells, A. (1997), 'The transformation of education and society: an introduction'. In Halsey et al. (1997: 1–44).

Commission on Social Justice (1994), *Social Justice Strategies for National Renewal*. London: Vintage.

Dale, R., Bowe, R., Harris, D., Loveys, M., Moore, R., Silling, C., Sikes, P., Trevitt, J., and Valsecchi, V. (1990), *The TVEI Story*. Milton Keynes: Open University Press.

Department of Employment (1993), *Training Statistics 1993*. London: HMSO.

DfEE (Department for Education and Employment) (1997), *Design of the New Deal for 18–24 Year Olds*. London: DfEE

—— (1996), *Labour Market and Skills Trends 1996/7*. London: DfEE.

DfES (Department for Education and Skills) (2003), *The Future of Higher Education*. London: Stationery Office.

Finegold, D. (1991), 'Institutional incentives and skill creation: preconditions for a high skill equilibrium'. In Ryan (1991: 93–116).

—— and Crouch, C. (1994), 'A comparison of national institutions'. In Layard et al. (1994: 251–81).

—— and Soskice, D. (1988), 'The failure of training in Britain: analysis and prescription', *Oxford Review of Economic Policy* 4(3): 21–50.

Glennerster, H. (1998), 'Education: reaping the harvest'. In H. Glennerster and J. Hills (eds.), *The State of Welfare*. Oxford: Oxford University Press, 27–74.

Green, A. (1990), *Education and State Formation*. Basingstoke: Macmillan.

—— and Steedman, H. (l993), *Educational Provision, Educational Attainment and the Needs of Industry: A Review of Research for Germany, France, Japan, the USA and Britain*. London: National Institute of Economic and Social Research.

Halsey, A. H., et al. (eds.) (1997), *Education, Culture, Economy, and Society*. Oxford: Oxford University Press.

Hodgson, A., and Spours, K. (1999), *New Labour's Educational Agenda*. London: Kogan Page.

Layard, R. (1994), 'The welfare economics of training'. In Layard et al. (1994: 31–49).

—— Mayhew, K., and Owen, G. (eds.) (1994), *Britain's Training Deficit*. Aldershot: Avebury.

National Commission on Education (1993), *Learning to Succeed*. London: HMSO.

NCIHE (National Committee of Inquiry into Higher Education) (1997), *Summary Report*.

ONS (Office for National Statistics) (2002) *Social Trends* London: HMSO.

Roberts, K. (1995), *Youth Employment in Modem Britain*. Oxford: Oxford University Press.

Ryan, P. (ed.) (1991), *International Comparisons of Vocational Education and Training for Intermediate Skills*. London: Falmer Press.

Sheldrake, J., and Vickerstaff, S. (1987), *The History of Industrial Training in Britain*. Aldershot: Gower.

Skills and Enterprise Network (1993), *Labour Market and Skills Trends*. Sheffield: Employment Department.

Taylor-Gooby, P. (1993), 'The new educational settlement: National Curriculum and local management'. In P. Taylor-Gooby and R. Lawson, *Markets and Managers*. Buckingham: Open University Press, 102–16.

Thomas, H., and Bullock, A. (1994), 'The political economy of local management of schools'. In S. Tomlinson (ed.), *Educational Reform and its Consequences*. London: IPPR/Rivers Oram Press, 41–52.

Tomlinson, S. (2001), *Education in a Post-Welfare Society*. Buckingham: Open University Press.

Unwin, L., and Wellington, J. (2001), *Young People's Perspectives on Education, Training and Employment*. London: Kogan Page.

Vickerstaff, S. (1992), 'Training for economic survival'. In P. Brown and H. Lauder (eds.), *Education for Economic Survival*. London: Routledge, 244–67.

Wolf, A. (2002), *Does Education Matter?* London: Penguin.

FURTHER READING

For a history of the British education system, see A. Green (1990) *Education and State Formation*. For a detailed account of developments in education since 1945 see S. Tomlinson's (2001) *Education in a post-welfare society*. A good edited collection of readings on education, covering the history, sociology, and politics of the educational process, policy, and practice is A.H. Halsey, H. Lauder, P. Brown and A. Stuart Wells (eds.) (1997) *Education, Culture, Economy and Society*. Two books which look at the impact of ET on young people, their experiences and the effects of ET on employment prospects are L. Unwin and J. Wellington (2001) *Young People's perspectives on Education, Training and Employment* and K. Roberts (1995) *Youth Employment in Modem Britain*. A standard social policy approach to education can be found in H. Glennerster (1998) 'Education: reaping the Harvest' in H. Glennerster and J. Hills (eds.) *The State of Welfare*. There is a wide ranging literature on training policy but an edited volume by R. Layard, K. Mayhew and G. Owen (1994) *Britain's Training Deficit* provides a good overview of current issues and the article by D. Finegold and C. Crouch in this volume 'A comparison of national institutions' introduces some of the key themes in cross-national comparisons of training policy. For a review of the New Labour Government's approaches to ET issues see A. Hodgson and K. Spours (1999) *New Labour's Educational Agenda*.

USEFUL WEBSITES

www.dfes.gov.uk/index.htm The website for the Department for Education and Skills provides considerable information on existing policies, White Papers, and consultation documents. It provides one of the best ways to keep up to date with policy developments.

www.lsc.gov.uk/index.cfm The website of the Learning and Skills Council, which is responsible for funding and planning all education and training for over-16-year-olds in England except higher education. A good place to look for developments in work-based learning such as apprenticeships.

www.lsda.org.uk The website for the Learning and Skills Development Agency, previously known as the Further Education Development Agency, which acts as a strategic national resource for the development of policy and practice in post-16 education and training. Another good place to look for developments in work-based learning.

www.ofsted.gov.uk The website for Ofsted (Office for Standards in Education), a non-ministerial government department which inspects and regulates standards in education and childcare. The site provides access to inspection reports undertaken by Ofsted.

www.gca.org.uk The website of the Qualifications and Curriculum Authority, which works to develop the school curriculum and associated assessments and to accredit qualifications in schools, colleges, and at work. Good site for information on the qualifications framework and curriculum and assessment issues.

GLOSSARY

assisted places scheme Under the 1980 Education Act, local education authorities could give financial assistance on a means-tested basis to enable young people who would otherwise be unable to, to attend private schools.

basic education This term usually refers to the basic skills of reading and writing, literacy, and numeracy that should be acquired during compulsory schooling. In recent years, especially since the development of the National Curriculum (see below), there has been considerable debate over what constitutes these basic elements of education, for example whether physical education and music are as much a part of basic education as are English and mathematics.

dual systems This is a system of vocational ET which combines work-based training with school- or college-based education. The German apprenticeship system is one example.

education This can refer both to the institutions, e.g. schools, colleges, universities, and to the process—that is, what is learnt in educational institutions or indeed in other contexts. The issues of what education is for or what it should contain are much debated, as was seen in this chapter.

grant-maintained school Under the 1988 Education Reform Act, schools were enabled to opt out of local authority control and become self-governing schools run by their head teachers and governors funded (grant-maintained) directly by central government. Under the New Labour government's 1998 School Standards and Framework Act many of these schools will become Foundation Schools.

higher education This refers to degree-level and post-degree-level education.

lifelong learners Traditionally, education and schooling was associated with learning at the outset of life. It is argued that to face the fast pace of change in contemporary society, and especially in the world of work, individuals will have to continue to learn and update their knowledge and skills throughout their lives.

Local Management of Schools Under the 1988 Education Reform Act, the budgets for schools were devolved from the local authority to individual schools. The board of governors for each school became responsible for managing the budget.

market model The market model of training provision is where government provides little or no direct training provision nor imposes any requirement on companies to train. The amount of training is left to the market to decide. In theory, if the company needs a particular skill in order to compete, it will acquire it through either training or recruitment. An individual may invest in their own training because they can see a future labour market advantage in doing so.

Modern Apprenticeships these were announced by the then government in the autumn of 1993. Modern apprenticeships have now been established in many different sectors of employment, and are designed to achieve a NVQ level 2 (Foundation MA) or NVQ level 3 (Advanced MA) qualification according to a model of training for each sector developed by the relevant sector organization.

national curriculum This was introduced by the 1988 Education Reform Act; it applies to all children of compulsory school age in state schools, with a few exceptions such as hospital schools. The curriculum specifies subjects to be taken and levels of attainment to be achieved at different ages.

national vocational qualifications (NVQs) In 1986, the National Council for Vocational Qualifications (NCVQ) was set up to establish a system of national vocational qualifications (NVQs). These NVQs are work-based assessments of competence and skill at five levels. The standards for each level were developed by leading bodies in industry, the public sector, and commerce.

New Deal See Chapter 11.

public schools These are independent schools, which charge fees; they do not have to provide the National Curriculum.

rates of return This refers to extra earnings gained by an individual who invests in extended education. For example, a university student may forgo some earnings now in expectation that a degree will subsequently increase earnings. This is a private rate of return, but there can also be social rates of return, although there is more debate about these. In the latter case it is argued that, for example, the extra earnings accruing from extended education translate into a measure of the society's economic gain overall.

sector training organizations Industrial training organizations (ITOs) were established as voluntary, sector-based training organizations when most of the statutory Industrial Training Boards (ITBs) set up under the 1964 Industrial Training Act were abolished in 1981. These in turn were replaced by National Training Organizations (NTOs) in 1998 and by Sector Training Organizations in 2002.

social partnership model This refers to joint public and private funding of training provision through tripartite (government, industry, trade unions) delivery systems within a framework of nationally agreed procedures and standards.

state model This model of training is when public funding via taxation and delivery through public institutions predominates, within a context of legal training rights and duties.

top-up fees Fees that higher education institutions may charge above the standard fee paid by the state for lower income families (£1,100) in 2003. The government has proposed that up to £3,000 may be charged from 2006.

training There is no single agreed definition of training. A definition used by the Department of Employment in 1993 is not untypical: training is an 'intentional intervention to help the individual (or the organization) to become competent, or more competent, at work' (Department of Employment, 1993: 8).

value added In relation to education, this refers to the extent to which schooling has affected the rate of learning or improvement of an individual child. Whereas league tables measure outcome in terms of examination or test performance, a value-added measure would need to assess how much a child had progressed, regardless of whether or not they achieved a particular test outcome.

voluntarism This is the belief that industry is best left to manage its own employment affairs free of government intervention or legislation.

14

Health and Health Policy

Gillian Pascall

CONTENTS

INTRODUCTION: HEALTH, SOCIETY, AND SOCIAL POLICY

Health is very unequal in Britain, related to key variables such as gender and race, and deeply patterned in particular by social class. What lies behind these patterns of health and disease in society? It is widely assumed that the **National Health Service** (NHS) produces health, and that improving health is a result of improving medical care. But what impact does the National Health Service have on health? The chapter will start with a discussion of health, to examine its social features, and to underpin thinking about health services and the needs they may be thought to address. By contrast to these patterns of inequality in health, the NHS appears to offer a model of healthcare that is very egalitarian, offering care—broadly—on the basis of need rather than ability to pay, membership of scheme, or contribution record. Health policy in the UK rests on the National Health Service Act of 1946, the key parliamentary Act of the postwar Labour government. The NHS itself began in July 1948. Health debates even now revolve around the decisions made at that time (see Box 14.1).

Social, economic and political change since 1948 has challenged all these ideas and ideals. After its review of health, the chapter will take each of the key policy decisions embedded in the 1946 National Health Service Act, and ask how it has stood up to these changes. How fit is the NHS for the twenty-first century? And how does it compare with other systems of health provision?

Box 14.1 The National Health Service 1948

Set up to provide:

- a system of medical care to individuals;
- with ideals of comprehensive service covering all health needs;
- free at the point of use, paid for by general taxation;
- nationally owned and planned from the centre, through regional and local bodies;
- on a **universal** basis, equally to citizens.

HEALTH AND HEALTH INEQUALITIES

'Instead of exposures to toxic materials and mechanical dangers, we are discovering the toxicity of social circumstances and patterns of social organisation' (Wilkinson 1996: 23).

Why study health inequalities?

Why do health inequalities matter? Three reasons can be put forward for making these a priority in an understanding of health that is relevant to social policy:

1. The intrinsic significance of issues of life and death, health and disability, and how these are distributed in society.
2. Relationships of health with social variables—such as social class and race—give clear evidence of the significance of society, social science, and social policy to health: health does not belong wholly to medicine, however appropriate medicine might be to people who are ill.

3. A better understanding of the ways that health relates to social disadvantage may provide a basis for better policy. Perhaps the most promising strategy for improving the national health is to improve the health of the most disadvantaged.

What are the key social features of health?

Social class, gender, and ethnicity can all be related to people's experience of health, sickness, and disability. Powerful evidence of these inequalities has been collected in the UK. A government-commissioned report by Sir Douglas Black (DHSS 1980) was particularly influential in collating, analysing, and publicizing evidence of health inequalities. The Black report also stimulated new research that has subsequently elaborated the picture it drew of social class as a key determinant of people's life chances. More recently, another government-commissioned report, Sir Douglas Acheson's Independent Inquiry into Inequalities in Health, gathered and analysed the data anew, for a New Labour government, in 1998 (Acheson 1998).

Some measures of health have improved dramatically during the twentieth and twenty-first centuries. For example, life expectancy has increased from around 45 years for men and 49 years for women in 1901 to over 75 and 80 years respectively in 2000 (ONS 2002: chart 7.1). **Infant mortality rates** have declined too: the chances of surviving the first year of life have become much greater (Fig 14.1). But people have not shared equally in this improvement. For example, life expectancy at birth for social class I, the 'professional' class, increased almost six years over the last quarter of the twentieth century, while the rise for social class V, 'unskilled manual workers', was less than two years. The gap between these two classes stood at almost ten years by the end of the century (ONS 2002: 120). There is a wide gap in 'infant mortality too, with the rate for social class V now double that for social class I (Department of Health 2002). These measures suggest that improving health over the population as a whole has been accompanied by widening differences between experience of health, life, and death in different social groups.

Very different sources of data show very similar pictures of social class differences in health, illness, and death. Table 14.1 shows the social class differences in **standardized**

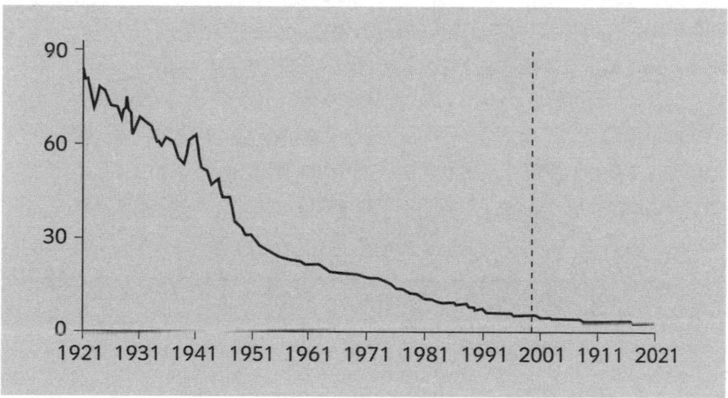

Figure 14.1 The decline in infant mortality, UK

Source: Office for National Statistics.

Table 14.1 European standardized mortality rates, by social class, selected causes, men aged 20–64, England and Wales, selected years

All causes
rates per 100,000

Social class	*Year*		
	1970–2	*1979–83*	*1991–3*
I—Professional	500	373	280
II—Managerial & Technical	526	425	380
III(N)—Skilled (non-manual)	637	522	426
III(M)—Skilled (manual)	683	580	493
IV—Partly skilled	721	639	492
V—Unskilled	897	910	806
England and Wales	624	549	419

Lung cancer
rates per 100,000

Social class	*Year*		
	1970–2	*1979–83*	*1991–3*
I—Professional	41	26	17
II—Managerial & Technical	52	39	24
III(N)—Skilled (non-manual)	63	47	34
III(M)—Skilled (manual)	90	72	54
IV—Partly skilled	93	76	52
V—Unskilled	109	108	82
England and Wales	73	60	39

Coronary heart disease
rates per 100,000

Social class	*Year*		
	1970–2	*1979–83*	*1991–3*
I—Professional	195	144	81
II—Managerial & Technical	197	168	92
III(N)—Skilled (non-manual)	245	208	136
III(M)—Skilled (manual)	232	218	159
IV—Partly skilled	232	227	156
V—Unskilled	243	287	235
England and Wales	209	201	127

Stroke
rates per 100,000

Social class	*Year*		
	1970–2	*1979–83*	*1991–3*
I—Professional	35	20	14
II—Managerial & Technical	37	23	13
III(N)—Skilled (non-manual)	41	28	19
III(M)—Skilled (manual)	45	34	24
IV—Partly skilled	46	37	25
V—Unskilled	59	55	45
England and Wales	40	30	20

Table 14.1 (contd.)

Accidents, poisoning, violence rates per 100,000				**Suicide and undetermined injury** rates per 100,000			
Social class	*Year*			*Social class*	*Year*		
	1970–2	*1979–83*	*1991–3*		*1970–2*	*1979–83*	*1991–3*
I—Professional	23	17	13	I—Professional	16	16	13
II—Managerial & Technical	25	20	13	II—Managerial & Technical	13	15	14
III(N)—Skilled (non-manual)	25	21	17	III(N)—Skilled (non-manual)	17	18	20
III(M)—Skilled (manual)	34	27	24	III(M)—Skilled (manual)	12	16	21
IV—Partly skilled	39	35	24	IV—Partly skilled	18	23	23
V—Unskilled	67	63	52	V—Unskilled	32	44	47
England and Wales	34	28	22	England and Wales	15	20	22

Note: Social Class I Professional (doctors, lawyers) II Managerial and technical/intermediate (nurses, teachers), III Non-manual skilled (clerks, cashiers), III Manual skilled (carpenters, cooks), IV Partly skilled (guards, farm workers), V Unskilled (building labourers, cleaners).

Source: ONS (2002: chart 7.10).

mortality rates, which are the measures generally used to compare death in different population groups. These show that for all causes of death, mortality rates for unskilled manual workers in 1991–3 were 806 per 100,000, compared with 280 for professional workers, around two and a half times higher. They also show—broadly—that each decrease in social class brings an increase in mortality. The patterns are replicated across different diseases, with accidents, poisoning, and violence showing the sharpest differences between social classes. These figures also show the sharpening of differences between social classes over time, in every category of disease. A very different idea of health is found in data from the General Household Survey. This is a government-sponsored survey in which people are asked about their experience of long-standing illness and how much it limits their capacities in comparison with people of their own age. These data show unskilled manual men reporting over twice as much limiting long-standing illness as professional men, with a similar pattern between women in different social classes (ONS 2001: table 7.2).

Gender differences in health and death can be shown too, but are less marked than social class differences. Women tend to live longer than men: there is currently a five-year gap in life expectancy. But women experience poorer health: longer life brings a heavy burden of chronic sickness and disability in later years, with 48 per cent of women of 75 and over experiencing limiting long-standing illness according to current General Household Survey data (ONS 2001: table 7.1).

Ethnic differences have been less well documented than class or gender differences. Health and mortality differences between ethnic minority and white groups have little to do with experience in country of birth: they appear to be more strongly connected with experience in Britain. Differences in socioeconomic status of different ethnic minority groups, rather than biological or cultural differences, are the key to their different experiences of health and death (ONS 1996).

Social class does not encapsulate all variations in health. There are differences between men and women, between different ethnic groups, and even between areas—the **north–south divide**—which cannot be wholly understood in terms of class. But social class is a strong component of health variations. This can be illustrated by thinking about the relationships between class, gender, and race. For example, married women's health varies according to their partners' occupations. Despite all the changes in work and family, women's lifetime earnings are about half men's, on average. Their living standards are still determined more by their partner—or lack of one—and by the household income rather than their individual earnings: women's health is thus clearly patterned by social class. Ethnic minorities' health fits socioeconomic patterns, with those highest in socioeconomic terms—Chinese and African-Asian—having the best health experience, and poorer groups—Pakistani, Bangladeshi, Caribbean—having the worst experience of health. Social class is the most powerful predictor of health.

The environmental movement has made us more aware of manmade risks, produced by nuclear energy, pesticides, genetically modified food. Such risks may appear to threaten us all. Do these developing environmental threats change the traditional relationship between poverty, ill health, and early death, making us equally vulnerable? The evidence offered so far suggests not. Patterns of inequality associated with social class are persistent, even increasing.

How can health inequalities best be explained?

It is easy to think of reasons for social inequalities in health: perhaps people have different patterns of smoking, eating, exercise, and these lead to social class differences? Perhaps health services are unequally distributed? Perhaps the tobacco companies are too free to sell damaging products? Perhaps unemployment or low benefits are the problem? It is much easier to propose theories than to decide which theories offer the most powerful explanation. And explanation is a crucial foundation for understanding policy and the failure of policy.

Mapping factors that affect health—and may produce health inequalities—is a first step to unravelling a complex picture. Figure 14.2 offers a useful aid to figuring out how different factors may fit into the picture. It fits individuals into their social and environmental context. In this figure, individuals—with their age, sex, and genetic makeup—are in the centre of the picture. A **biomedical model** of health and disease starts in the middle, with understanding disease processes in individuals. But individuals affect their own health by their lifestyle choices: asking why disease processes start might lead us to behavioural factors such as smoking and food choices. Asking why people smoke or eat

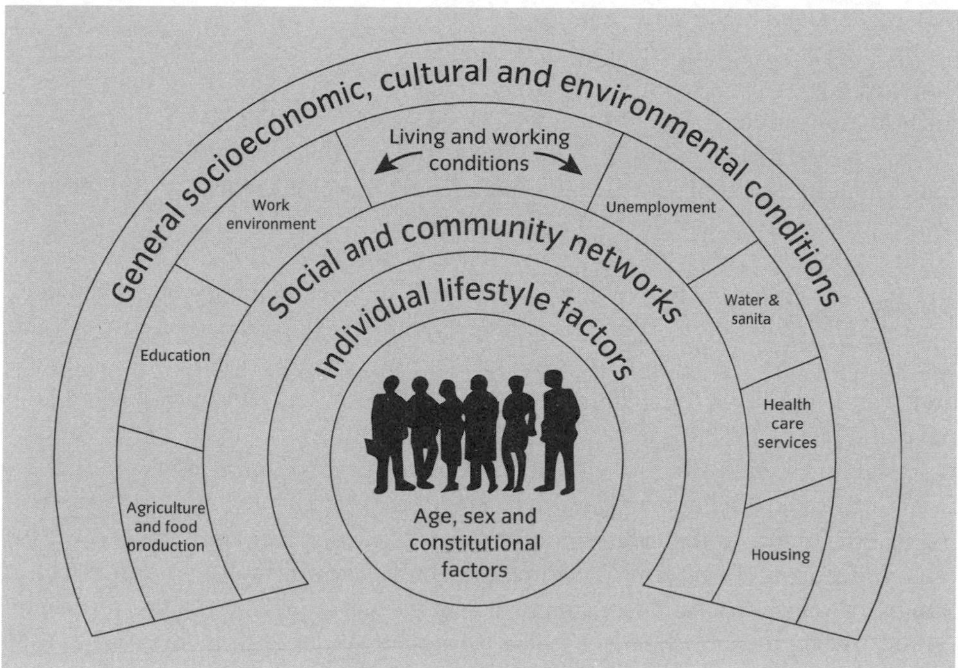

Figure 14.2 The main determinants of health

Source: Acheson (1998), Citing Dahlgren and Whitehead (1991).

unhealthy food might lead us to social and community influences. Asking why some social groups are more likely to smoke or eat unhealthily might lead us to ask about their living and working conditions. But what lies behind living and working conditions? Wider economic and political factors, such as national government policies on benefits and asylum seekers, tobacco companies and markets, international agencies such as the World Bank and International Monetary Fund, are important in the distribution of resources that are significant to health.

Three of the most important questions to arise out of the debates and research on health and health inequalities are addressed below. The first question is about the relationship between health and medical care. How important is unequal access to medical care and health services in explaining differences in health? But more debates in the health literature are about how much people can choose better health by improving their lifestyles or whether health is largely determined by social and economic circumstances. Could we all equally improve our life chances by following health advice about smoking, exercise, and diet? How much are the choices and health of people in poorer social circumstances constrained by factors over which they have no control? A third set of questions in this next section is about policy, about the policies of UK governments and other national governments, and about what approaches to health and health inequalities may work best to improve health and reduce health inequalities.

Medical care and health First, how important is access to medical care in determining health? McKeown's thesis is a focus for debates here (McKeown 1976). McKeown argued that the biggest improvements in health in the UK took place before there were effective medical interventions to address them. He investigated population data from the beginning of the registration of deaths, in the 1830s, and examined the trends for the various causes of death that contributed to the major trend of declining mortality over the nineteenth century. The example of TB is given in Fig. 14.3.

The graph suggests that TB was already in decline when records started to be collected, and shows a great reduction in deaths during the nineteenth and twentieth centuries, when no effective medical or public health interventions were available. The first scientific understanding of TB came with the identification of the tubercle bacillis in 1882. Effective drug treatment came in the 1940s, and BCG vaccination in the 1950s. Thus, medical treatment and prevention have come rather late to give assistance to a trend that was already well established. McKeown showed that this pattern was replicated for most of the key diseases, and argued that improving health had more to do with improving nutrition and living standards than with medical interventions. McKeown may have understated the importance of public health measures in the nation's improving health—measures such as improving water supply and sanitation which were brought to Britain by the nineteenth-century public health movements (these debates are discussed in more detail in Gray 2001b: 123–130). We cannot read directly from this account of medicine in the nineteenth and twentieth centuries to the uses of medicine in the twenty-first. But these debates suggest that we should not take the importance of medicine to health for granted.

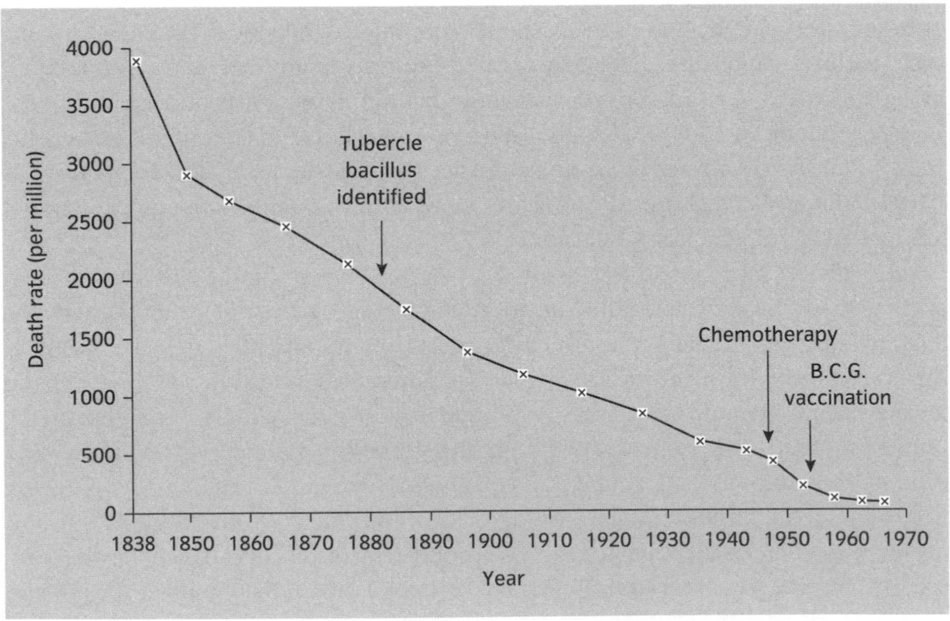

Figure 14.3 Respiratory tuberculosis: death rates, England and Wales

Source: McKeown (1976: 93). Reproduced by permission of Hodder Arnold.

Access to medical care in the UK has not been entirely equalized, despite the NHS aim of delivering care in relation to need rather than ability to pay (Department of Health 1980). Access is more equal than in the more market-oriented service in the USA—no payment at the time of use, free prescriptions for lower-income groups—and the more obvious obstacles to equal treatment are thus removed. There are less obvious obstacles—the cost of journeys and time off work. But if equal medical care could produce equal health we might expect to see greater equality of health in the UK than the statistics (Table 14.1) show at present. We might also see more differences between different diseases. The same patterns of inequality show for cancer, heart disease, and accidents: these suggest that something—perhaps to do with living conditions—lies behind the medical situation of people dying from these diseases.

These debates suggest that medicine should take its place as one among many factors that influence health and survival.

Individual behaviour v. social circumstances? Figure 14.2 may help us to make sense of a complex set of factors and explanations and how they may fit together. But how can we assess the importance of individual behaviour and how do individual choices relate to social circumstances? There is evidence for the impact of individual behaviour on health, and on inequalities in health. The clearest example is smoking, which brings risks of heart disease and cancer and is related to social circumstances, with people in poorer circumstances more likely to smoke. Exercise and healthy eating are also related to socioeconomic patterns, with better-off people more likely to do regular exercise and to eat a diet rich in fibre, fruit, and vegetables that conforms to the government's health advice.

Should we blame poor people's health on their smoking and food choices? If so, how much of the blame for health inequalities lies here? The Whitehall study has been tracking 18,000 government employees in London—from top civil servants to caretakers and other manual workers—since 1967, reporting most recently in 2000. It offers evidence that smoking plays a part in differences between people in different positions. But it also shows that smoking and other known risk factors can only account for a third of the difference in mortality between the highest and lowest grades (a more detailed account of this study and other studies on the explanation of health inequalities is given in Gray 2001a: 240).

Have poorer people not understood the official messages? There is research on people's knowledge of health advice. But studies have failed to show major differences in knowledge about food between different socioeconomic groups. They do indicate that poor mothers have as much desire as better-off ones for healthy food for their children.

And why have better-off people responded more and more quickly to health warnings? The key to these differences lies primarily in the social context. People cannot make choices that are wholly divorced from their environment. There are many obvious material constraints on choices when people live in poor environments. Budgeting studies showing the difficulty of affording healthy food are reviewed by Spencer: 'Far from being able to afford a healthy diet, many members of low income families frequently go without any food, healthy or unhealthy. Children are less likely to go without food because they are protected by their mothers, but . . . 10 per cent of children said they had gone hungry in the preceding month because of lack of money (Spencer 1996: 156). Access to fresh food may be improving for those with cars, but car-based out-of-town shopping diminishes access for those who have to add bus fares to the price of food. Food choice may be hampered by the inability to risk waste.

Low incomes may also lead to disconnections of essential services of water, gas, and electricity, especially since privatization, making people vulnerable to cold, respiratory infections, and gastro-intestinal infections. Damp housing, poor heating/insulation, traffic pollution, and unsafe play spaces for children are among the problems people face trying to make a healthy environment for their children on low incomes. These add up to formidable material limitations which are the social and economic context for people's health choices. Higher incomes bring the choice of housing, avoiding many kinds of environmental threat: traffic pollution, nuclear power stations, electricity pylons, and agricultural chemicals.

A major study of health and social circumstances aimed to compare the impact of healthy living behaviours—lifestyles over which people have some control—and social circumstances, over which they do not. Generally social circumstances were found to be more powerful explanations than personal behaviours. But the study also found differences in what different social groups could achieve by healthy living. People in good social circumstances could improve their health by exercise, non-smoking, good diet. But people in poor social circumstances who made healthy choices did not gain as much benefit. There was a lower return from healthy choices, with health overwhelmed by factors they could not control. These findings may help to explain why poorer people are less likely to make healthy choices. If there is less health gain to be had from giving up smoking while living in a polluted area, then the rational choice may be to make less effort (Blaxter 1990).

Material limitations are likely to be part of any account of health inequalities in Britain. But the damage of social exclusion may go beyond this. Unemployment and debt create psychological damage; smoking may be used as a—damaging—refuge from social stress. Exclusion from choice in a consumer society is damaging to self-esteem. Wilkinson argues that the damage lies in unequal access to society even more than in unequal access to material resources. It is social circumstances that are toxic, rather than material ones. The evidence for this argument is not conclusive: it lies in comparisons with other societies at similar economic levels, with more equal societies having more equal health. If it is equality that makes the difference, then it will not be enough to wait for economic growth to improve the material circumstances of people in poverty: we would need to redistribute resources, not simply lift socioeconomic levels for everyone (Wilkinson 1996).

Policies for health and to reduce health inequalities Approaches to understanding health and health inequalities are clearly connected to approaches to policy. From the middle of the twentieth century, UK governments have tended to adopt strategies that first emphasize the distribution of medical care and second persuade people to adopt healthy lifestyles. So the NHS was developed in the 1940s to give everyone access to treatment when they became sick. When ministers of health argued for preventing ill health, they published *Prevention and Health: Everybody's Business* (DHSS 1976), stressing people's ability to look after themselves rather than the conditions that might damage health and make healthy living difficult. Research at the end of the twentieth century found that advice about healthy living tended to increase health inequalities: it was more readily adopted by advantaged people than by disadvantaged. These studies preferred policies to improve the conditions under which people lived, which would improve health directly and materially and would also make it easier to adopt healthy lifestyles and to lower psychological stress. The recommendations from this literature were, for example, for changes in housing policy to produce quality social housing and reduce homelessness, raising child benefits, and control over tobacco advertising and sponsorship (Benzeval et al. 1995; Acheson 1998).

Current UK government policy is for: 'striking a new balance . . . a **third way** . . . linking individual and wider action' (Department of Health 1999). The emphasis on individuals improving their own health remains, but governments now acknowledge the difficulties arising from poverty, poor housing, pollution, low educational standards, unemployment, and low pay, as well as the link between health inequality and social inequality. Policies across this wide agenda have in practice been uneven, but increased levels of child benefits are among the most significant of policy developments aimed at reducing poverty, social inequality, and the roots of health inequality.

What is to be learnt from comparison with other countries? There is a strong relationship between health measures such as infant mortality and socioeconomic development. In general, poverty goes with high infant mortality rates (IMRs), which are the number of infant deaths during the first year of life for every 1,000 births. In 1998, industrialized countries had an average IMR of six deaths per 1,000 births, while low-income countries had an average of 80 deaths. But there are poor countries with good records as well as rich countries with poor records. Evidence from those poorer countries that have achieved good health suggests that going for economic growth alone may not be the best way. A UNICEF study chose ten high-achieving countries which had better health than might be expected given their levels of national wealth. These included Kerala State in India, with an IMR of seventeen, Cuba with seven, and Korea with five. The study emphasized the role of public action and balanced economic growth, spending on basic services and on education, especially women's education, and fairness in public spending. The overarching principle was that 'these countries did not give priority to achieving economic growth first, while postponing social development' (Mehrotra 2001).

Comparison with countries more similar to the UK in economic development shows that the high-achieving countries in western Europe from this point of view are Luxembourg, Sweden, and Finland, where deaths of children in the first year of life were 1997 were 4 per 1,000 compared with six in the UK and in Ireland (Eurostat 2000). The policy regimes of these highest achievers in Europe emphasize high levels of government intervention to reduce poverty and social inequality and to increase social cohesion. The **social democratic regimes** of Finland and Sweden may be contrasted with the USA, where governments promote a **liberal, free-market-based approach to social policy**. Here infant mortality rates are higher, at seven per 1,000, despite high levels of economic development and spending on health care (www3.who.int/whosis).

HEALTH POLICY

The NHS in 1948

Governments had already intervened in health and health policy, with public health legislation in the nineteenth century, hospitals under the Poor Law, National Health Insurance early in the twentieth century, and the Emergency Medical Service during the war. But the Second World War brought a qualitative difference in assumptions about what governments could and should do. It also brought experience of the confusion of existing health services and their inadequacy. William Beveridge was commissioned to make plans for social security after the war (see Chapter 1). His plan for the nation's social security assumed that there would be 'comprehensive health and rehabilitation services'. The wartime government did indeed plan for a major extension of health and medical services. But the first election after the war brought a Labour government to power and Aneurin Bevan to the Ministry of Health. The plans for reform acquired a more radical twist. It was already assumed in the wartime plans that the new health service would be universal (available to all), comprehensive (including all services, both preventative and curative), and free (involving no payment at the point of delivery)' (Webster 1998: 22). Bevan's plan also nationalized the hospitals and reorganized them into a system that would be managed on a regional basis. He aimed to '**universalize the best**' health care, in contrast to a Poor Law, minimum-level approach which favoured means-tested services for the poor, and which stigmatized those who used it. The service would not only be free at the point of use; it would also be funded mainly through general taxation, rather than through insurance contributions. This meant that people would pay according to how much they could afford, through taxes which Bevan believed should be progressive, taking a higher proportion from higher earnings. Thus the NHS was built on explicitly egalitarian and **redistributive principles**. The NHS Act was passed in 1946 and the service inaugurated in 1948, with a leaflet, 'The New National Health Service', on everyone's doormat at the start of the NHS, declaring:

> It will provide you with all medical, dental, and nursing care. Everyone—rich or poor, man, woman or child—can use it or any part of it. There are no charges, except for a few special items. There are no insurance qualifications. But it is not a charity. You are all paying for it, mainly as taxpayers, and it will relieve your money worries in time of illness. (quoted in Webster 1998: 24)

While the legislation and establishment of the NHS evoked fierce opposition, the service did in fact become popular, for the freedom from medical bills and the anxiety that surrounded them. Not only was the NHS popular with the public, it also gained loyalty and support from those who worked in it. More surprising, perhaps, is the degree of support it commanded, from politicians of different political colours, including Conservative governments with very different ideals from those of Bevan and the postwar Labour government. There have been many opportunities to move from the principles of the NHS, to introduce market-oriented systems of healthcare, but over the years politicians—including Thatcher and Blair—have continued to express broad loyalty to NHS ideals.

Bevan's proposals for the NHS can be seen as a 'mixture of audacity and prudence' (Webster 1998: 15). If nationalizing the hospitals, universalizing the best, and funding through taxation were the audacious part, there were prudent elements in the NHS mixture. The NHS held onto systems of administration that already existed, making a 'tripartite' system whose lack of coherent planning structure revisited later health ministers. The system was also conservative in the services that it offered. The system took over hospitals and general practitioner services and drew local authority public health services under its umbrella. The Appointed Day for starting the NHS brought no chaos of new systems, rather the same services as delivered the previous week, albeit to far more people. 'Comprehensive health and rehabilitation services' dominated by medical services to individuals lay at the centre of this most collectivist system of health service delivery.

The next sections discuss what has become of these NHS principles in practice over the fifty-five years since the service began. Social, political, and economic changes during this period have made in many ways a different world. Family change has changed the assumptions we can make about how much we care for each other. Demographic change has brought a much older population, with much heavier needs for health care. Consumerism brings patients who have more expectations and make more demands than their predecessors. Economic growth brings new resources, but also globalization and less confidence in interventions by national governments. Technical development brings new possibilities, mainly more expensive possibilities, for all kinds of therapeutic intervention. How has the NHS responded to all these changes? And how well is it placed to adapt to the twenty-first century? Each of the following sections takes a key issue that was part of the decisions that established the NHS and asks how it has fared and whether the principles of 1948 are still recognizable in the service that exists today. The chapter also discusses the extent to which the principles of the NHS are relevant to health and healthcare today.

The NHS in the twenty-first century: contesting medical dominance?

A biomedical model of health was the dominant model at the beginning of the NHS, rooted in assumptions about the value of medical science in the treatment of individuals. Doctors' authority was central to the operation and management of hospitals, primary care, and community health, including authority over other professionals and health workers. Patients had little role in NHS decision-making, and were seen as having little role in their own healthcare. There were few 'alternative' practices such as chiropractic or acupuncture. As we have seen in earlier sections, medicine's role in health has been challenged by social science. The dominance of medicine in the NHS has also been contested from several directions. We may ask whether patients have been turned into consumers, how much doctors' authority has been contested by other professionals in the NHS as well as outside—lawyers for example—and whether a more **social or environmental model** has gained ground over the medical perspective.

The development of consumerism is a key social change. If people using health services were once assumed to be patients, they may now have greater expectations of choice and control as consumers of services. Patient groups have developed around

Box 14.2 The NHS now: a snapshot

On a typical day in the NHS:

- Almost a million people visit their family doctor
- 130,000 go to the dentist for a check up
- 33,000 people get the care they need in accident and emergency
- 8,000 people are carried by NHS ambulances
- 1.5 million prescriptions are dispensed
- 2,000 babies are delivered
- 25,000 operations are carried out including 320 heart operations and 125 kidney operations
- 30,000 people receive a free eye test
- District nurses make 100,000 visits

On a typical day in the NHS, there are:

- 90,000 doctors
- 300,000 nurses
- 150,000 healthcare assistants
- 22,000 midwives
- 13,500 radiographers
- 15,000 occupational therapists
- 7,500 opticians
- 10,000 health visitors
- 6,500 paramedics
- 90,000 porters, cleaners, and other support staff
- 11,000 pharmacists
- 19,000 physiotherapists
- 24,000 managers
- 105,000 practice staff in GP surgeries

(Department of Health 2000: 23)

chronic health conditions, such as Parkinson's disease, and carers' groups to support those who have responsibility in the community. These operate as foci of information for the many NHS users who have long-term illness or impairment. The Internet enhances the sharing of information for such groups and for individuals. People now frequently choose alternative therapies rather than medicine or as well as medicine. The transformation of people from patients into medical consumers is partial: illness makes people vulnerable, and they may still be seen as patients needing expertise and services. But these social changes may be seen as bringing some elements of consumerism into relationships between doctors and patients, making the authority of medical decisions less taken for granted.

A more political aspect of these changes is the development of **new social movements**, which have challenged the assumptions on which medical authority rested. The women's movement and environmental movement both developed during the last quarter of the twentieth century. The green movement has drawn attention to the environmental aspects of health in contrast to the medical ones. The women's health movement challenged medicine's masculinity and its relation to other professions, in particular nursing and midwifery. Women were denied access to medical schools in the nineteenth century, and not admitted equally with men until nearly the end of the twentieth. Nursing and midwifery were established as female professions under medical authority. Gender divisions and power relations in health work have been changed—though not wholly transformed—by the challenges of the women's movement and legislation such as the Sex Discrimination Act (1975). While medicine's relation to other professions was under scrutiny, so was its relation to women as patients. Contraception, abortion, childbirth, and new reproductive technologies such as in vitro fertilization bring issues of choice into sharp focus. In the last quarter of the twentieth century the women's movement fought for—and to some extent achieved—more autonomy for women in making decisions about whether, when, and how to have babies (Doyal 1995; 1998).

Medical authority has also increasingly been challenged in the courts, and in public inquiries. Litigation is increasingly seen as a way for individuals to gain redress when they are dissatisfied with the quality of care. But confidence and trust in medicine has been the subject of high-profile investigations into poor-quality care, the ability of individuals to expose it and of health systems to deal with it. An increasingly open environment—in which the media play a key role—makes public issues of medical decisions which might earlier have remained within the privacy of doctor–patient relationships.

But while medical authority has been increasingly challenged, it has not died. The description of the National Health Service as a National Illness Service or a National Medical Service appears in every textbook. NHS spending has always been dominated by

Box 14.3 Evidence-based medicine

Growing interest in evidence-based medicine (EBM) can be seen as one response to these challenges to medical science. Doctors and medical researchers want to ensure that clinical practice is informed by up-to-date research findings in order to preserve the credibility of medicine. Managers have an interest in eliminating ineffective treatments, in order to make the budget go further and raise the quality of care. Variations in the introduction and use of effective treatments are also seen as inequitable by patients and organizations representing patients. Systems to make sure that new research findings are implemented in clinical practice have developed from within clinical professions as well as from managers and governments.

Clinical guidelines have been produced by the professional bodies, such as the Royal Colleges, setting out agreed standards.

Government initiatives include the National Institute of Clinical Excellence, to produce guidelines on clinical and cost effectiveness of services. There is also a Commission for Health Improvements in clinical services (Baggott 1998: 56–7).

spending on hospitals, with primary care and public health lagging behind. Health ministers are always centrally concerned with hospital beds, waiting lists, and standards of care. If these concerns fitted with the 1948 ideas about the role of medical science and treatment in health, they may be seen as increasingly at odds with research and debates about the sources of health and ill health at the end of the twentieth century. There have been attempts by recent governments to push public health up the agenda. For example, the World Health Organization has encouraged governments to work on strategies to bring health rather than treat disease. The UK government has responded with White Papers such as *Saving Lives: Our Healthier Nation* (DoH 1999) and a Minister with responsibility for Public Health. Ministers of Health and government documents, even HM Treasury, now make references to the need for prevention and the need to reduce health inequalities. The agenda has changed and broadened to include a health perspective as well as a medical one. The priorities in practice are more persistent. The NHS Plan set out ten core principles for the NHS (see Box 14.4) These include providing a universal service based on clinical need (1), shaping the services around the needs and preferences of individual patients, their families and their carers (3), and working to improve quality services and minimize errors (5). The ninth principle is that 'The NHS will help keep people healthy and work to reduce health inequalities'. But it is the only principle that reflects the agenda of social change rather than the agenda of medical care (Department of Health 2000: 3–5).

Box 14.4 NHS core principles, 2000

1. The NHS will provide a universal service for all based on clinical need, not ability to pay
2. The NHS will provide a comprehensive range of services
3. The NHS will shape its services around the needs and preferences of individual patients, their families and their carers
4. The NHS will respond to different needs of different populations
5. The NHS will work continuously to improve quality services and to minimize errors
6. The NHS will support and value its staff
7. Public funds for health care will be devoted solely to NHS patients
8. The NHS will work together with others to ensure a seamless service for patients
9. The NHS will help keep people healthy and work to reduce health inequalities
10. The NHS will respect the confidentiality of individual patients and provide open access to information about services, treatment and performance

(Department of Health 2000: 3–5)

The medical model of health may no longer be unchallenged. Consumerism, new social movements, especially the women's movement and the environmental movement, growing litigation and public inquiries, social science research: these diverse changes in society make medicine's authority and dominance now much more open to question than it was at the start of the NHS. But perhaps the statement of ideals in the

NHS Plan, as well as practice on the ground, in particular spending, suggest these have undermined trust in medicine and trust in doctors less than may at first appear.

The NHS in the twenty-first century: comprehensive care?

Rationing If comprehensive care was part of the 1946 promise, delivering comprehensive health services brings dilemmas. The possibilities of medical intervention already seem limitless, yet they grow all the time. We have not, as a society, decided to spend more than a fraction of our resources on healthcare, and few would wish for a society and economy consumed by meeting health needs. Increasing the resources spent on healthcare would solve some problems, meet more needs, but would not meet them all. Comprehensive care, meeting all health needs, whether defined by professionals or by people as patients, parents, sons or daughters of patients, may best be seen as an ideal that cannot be realized in practice. Perhaps this ideal may also be seen as a measure against which to assess what the health system does achieve and to compare it with others. These problems emerge internationally in different health systems. The NHS commitment to comprehensive care, free at the time of use, poses the dilemma in a particular form in the UK, but every health system generates debates about rationing and priorities.

Prioritizing or **rationing** in fact takes place. Some services have been withdrawn from the NHS in some areas—cosmetic operations, infertility treatment, long-term care of the elderly. Some groups of patients are less likely to receive services than others. There is evidence of discrimination against older patients, or smokers may be deemed less likely to benefit from treatment. Mechanisms for rationing include those set out in Box 14.5.

More demanding health consumers make these issues more contentious. There was never a golden age in which all possible health needs were met, but patient questioning about priorities defined by professionals has probably grown, as patients have become more ready to complain (Powell 1997: 107). The more overt debates about rationing that have ensued have raised the question about who should take such decisions and how. Community participation in developing priorities is one kind of solution, scientific calculation of **cost–benefit or cost effectiveness** another. Public participation in decision-making may bring advantages, but may also tend to exclude unpopular groups/needs from health treatment. The scientific approach—calculating costs and benefits—is more defensible in comparing different treatments for the same problem than in the infinitely complex problem of making systematic comparisons of costs and

Box 14.5 Rationing mechanisms

- waiting lists;
- deterrence through charges;
- deflecting demand to other services;
- diluting (e.g. using cheaper drugs);
- denial of some services (Hunter 1997: 22).

benefits across different health needs. The question of which different treatment is most cost-effective for kidney disease can be addressed by accounting the costs of each in relation to the effectiveness of the treatment. But more fundamental difficulties are raised by attempting to count the costs and benefits of drugs to ease multiple sclerosis against those of, say, infertility treatments.

Central governments have aimed to diffuse the blame attaching to hard decisions, with professionals and health authorities having in practice to decide questions such as whom treat and how much, how much to spend, what to leave out. There is therefore variation around the country in these decisions and how they are made. The accusations of 'postcode lottery', in which treatment depends on where you live, has brought efforts to bring more coherence to these decisions. The National Institute for Clinical Excellence was established in 1999 'to provide patients, health professionals and public with authoritative, robust and reliable guidance on current 'best practice'. Advice will cover specific treatments, such as drugs, techniques and procedures, and clinical management of specific conditions (NICE 2002). NICE (the National Institute for Clinical Excellence) has reported on many contentious issues, such as the value of drug treatments for Alzheimer's disease or multiple sclerosis. At present the guidance from NICE does not give patients the right to receive particular treatments unless these are prescribed or offered in their area. NICE is therefore an aid to more coherence in the professional decision-making process rather than a new rationing agency. But this could change. Participation in NICE decisions is being implemented, through a Citizens' Council: ordinary members of the general public have been invited to join this and discuss the questions on which NICE will report.

Box 14.6 on long-term care offers illustration of these issues too. It shows a shift of care from health authorities to social care agencies and families which represents a shift in what is defined as healthcare. While the coverage of the NHS has in many ways widened over time—to include contraceptive services, and many drug treatments as they have become available—this is an instance of the narrowing remit of the NHS.

The NHS in the twenty-first century: from state finance to mixed economy?

One idea of the transformation of social welfare provision in the UK during the latter part of the twentieth century is that it went from domination by the state to a more variegated mix of public, private, voluntary, informal care—a **mixed economy of welfare**. This section examines the mix of state and private finance in the UK, as well as the mix of state and family care, to ask how true this picture is in relation to health care.

State and private finance Do we spend too much or too little on health? Freedom from payment at the point of use gives rise to fears that people will ask too much. Right-wing critics have argued the need for a price mechanism to regulate demand: people may want more at the point of need than they are prepared to pay for in taxes. Defenders of the NHS have argued for its efficiency in keeping costs down as well as its humanity in meeting needs. As an experimental system, the NHS did overspend in its first two years, an experience which brought a long period of stringency and constraint, with spending

Box 14.6 Long-term care

'The policy thread that binds all these official attempts to promote community care has been a concern to shift the responsibility for care from one agency to another—from the NHS to local authorities, from local authorities to families' (Lewis and Glennerster 1996: 2).

The issue of long-term care gives an example of changing policy over what should be deemed to be health needs and included as part of the health service. Policy has, in effect, changed, so that people who might once have occupied hospital beds are now more likely to be in nursing homes or residential care, or in their own homes with support from community services. Care that would have been free at the point of need within the NHS may be charged by social services or nursing homes, or may be delivered by relatives without charge or count.

The NHS inherited many long-term beds from the Poor Law, warehouses for older people, some of whom needed hospital or nursing care, but many whose need was for an alternative place to go. Movements in mental health and geriatric medicine towards enabling people to support themselves in their own homes as long as possible have contributed to this decline in long-stay hospital beds. These developments have produced a wider range of community and smaller home provision and enriched the choice for people needing long-term care. But the desire to move costs, from fully funded NHS beds to means-tested local authority responsibility, and from local authority to unpaid care at home, has been a major power behind these changes. An element of privatization has been involved, as the government has fostered development of an industry of care homes, as well as pushing costs onto families and unpaid carers.

At the start of the NHS there were eleven hospital beds per 1,000 population. By 1989/1990 this had dropped to 6.2 per 1,000 and by 1999/2000 to 4.1 per 1,000 (Office of Health Economics 2002). There are many reasons for this decline, which affects acute hospital beds as well as long-term ones: the remaining beds are used much more intensively, with quicker patient turnover, shorter hospital stay, and keyhole surgery allowing patients home. But this huge decline in hospital beds, at a time of ageing population, gives some indication of the shift from NHS to local authorities, and from local authorities to families, described above by Lewis and Glennerster.

A Royal Commission Long Term Care for the Elderly was established by the new Labour government in 1997, and published a report in 1999. Scotland decided to follow its recommendations for a comprehensive package of care for people with long-term needs. But people in England and Wales have been offered less. There is a new agreement to include the costs of nursing care within the NHS. But a new boundary has been created, which may be difficult to defend, between those whose needs are deemed to be for nursing and those whose needs are for personal care. Personal care remains outside the NHS.

settling at around 3.5 per cent to 4.1 per cent of GDP during the first 25 years (Webster 1998: 30–4).

Currently, both public and policy analysts are more concerned about the low levels of NHS spending—and low levels of service—in comparison with other European countries (Fig 14.4). After long periods in which governments have argued for small government and low taxation, there is official support for higher government spending, especially on

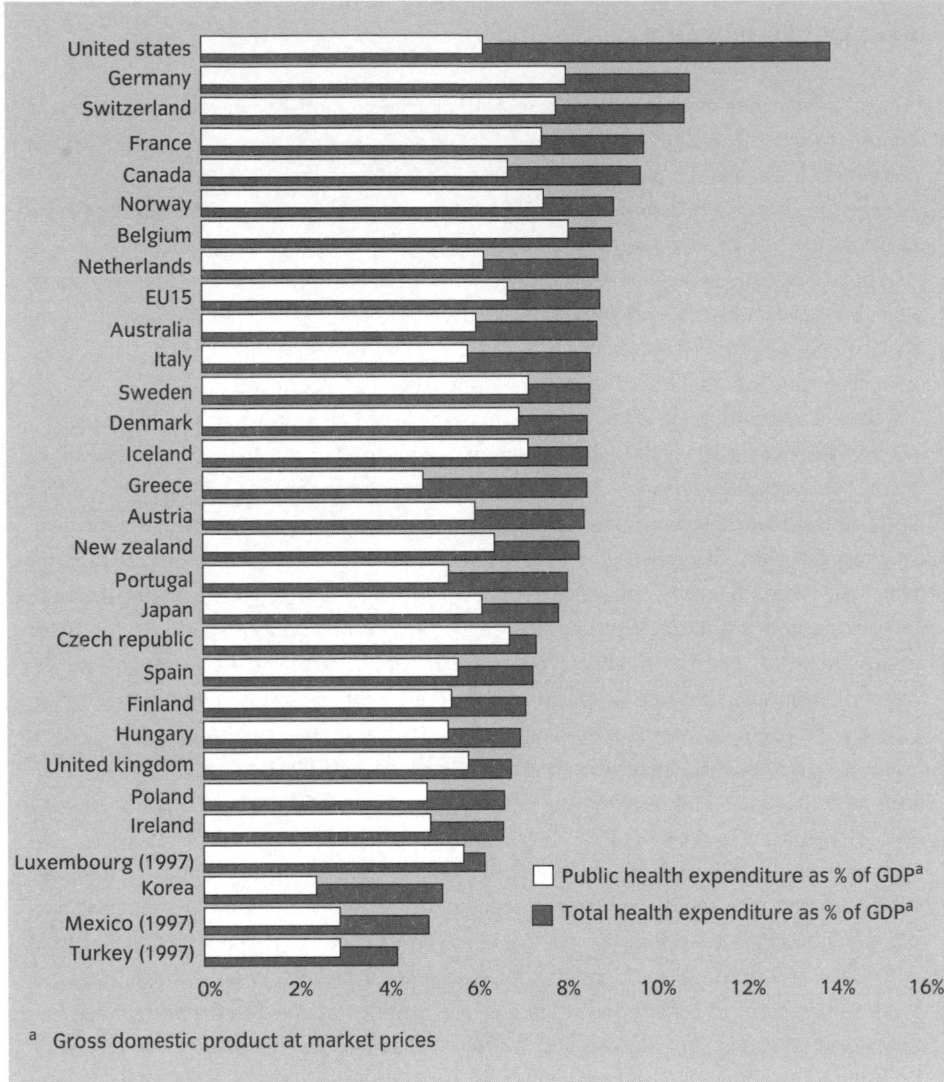

Figure 14.4 Total health expenditure as a percentage of GDP* in OECD countries, 1998

Source: Office of Health Economics (2002).

health. The NHS plan acknowledges that 'in part the NHS is failing to deliver because over the years it has been underfunded' (Department of Health 2000: 1). The Treasury has commissioned a report to quantify 'the financial and other resources required to ensure that the NHS can provide a publicly funded, comprehensive, high quality service available on the basis of clinical need and not ability to pay' (Wanless 2002). This includes counting the cost of many years' underinvestment in NHS staff and buildings, in order to bring them up to contemporary expectations and comparable countries in Europe.

Increasing living standards have tended to bring higher health care spending. Now Turkey is spending about 4 per cent, but the US is spending nearly 14 per cent of its GDP on health. The EU average is just over 8 per cent, and UK spending appears low by comparison with countries at a comparable economic level. Promises to lift public spending on health and close the gap with the rest of Europe begin to show in the figures, with 6.1 per cent of GDP spent on the NHS in 2000 (Office of Health Economics 2002).

Debates about the source of payment for healthcare also persist. Bevan's ideal at the start of the NHS was for a service that would be funded through taxation, reflecting ability to pay, with an element of contribution through national insurance. Private practice would continue, but universalizing the best in the NHS would give people little incentive to pay privately. Challenges to these ideals started early, with the introduction of prescription charges proving the first crack in the ideal of a service free at the point of use. Political differences around public funding—and political change from the collectivism of the postwar era—have made more room for charging, as well as for developing alternatives to the NHS such as private health insurance: 11.5 per cent of the UK population were covered privately in 2000. However, every country shown in the graph of health spending (Fig. 14.4) has private health spending as well as public. In comparative terms, the UK's private/public share resembles the social democratic countries of Scandinavia, with very high proportions of spending coming from public sources, rather than the USA, whose public spending is less than half its total health spending.

The key debate about the merits of public vs. private funding is about how redistributive the system is between different income groups. Public funding is mildly 'progressive' in the sense that national systems of taxation take a higher proportion from higher income groups than from lower. The system is less progressive than it seems at first sight because indirect taxes such as VAT hit lower-income groups harder; but overall, public funding means that funding comes disproportionately from higher-income groups. Currently NHS finance is financed 80 per cent from taxation, with 12 per cent from National Insurance contributions and 4 per cent from charges (Dixon and Robinson 2002). Public funding tends to be associated with better population health outcomes. And, from the point of view of the economy, 'private health spending has no advantages over public health spending. The most obvious consequence of shifting from public to private spending is to shift the burden from the relatively rich to the relatively poor' (Normand 1998, quoted in Wanless 2002: 141).

While UK health funding remains distinctly public, the mixture of public and private within the system has grown, and changed the character of the NHS (Box 14.7). The NHS has always purchased drugs and equipment from the private sector. Contracting out hospital cleaning and catering services introduced contracting with private companies from the 1980s, and has expanded to involve agencies supplying nursing staff. The private finance initiative brings private investment capital to major investment projects in general practice and in hospitals. Contracts with the private sector to undertake operations and with overseas health services mean that healthcare itself may be contracted out. NHS contracting with private companies continues to grow.

State and family care The idea of a National Health Service taking care of its citizens from cradle to grave always missed one crucial component of care: to a large extent

Box 14.7 Private finance in the NHS

The Private Finance Initiative (PFI) was introduced in 1992 to bring the private sector into public sector developments, including the design, building, financing, and operation of hospitals and other health facilities. In practice PFI started slowly, with only one major hospital development signed by 1996, to build a major district hospital in Norwich.

Labour governments have reaffirmed their commitment to the use of private-sector capital for funding major projects, accepting that 'private finance might complement public funds, as long as schemes were compatible with NHS priorities' (Baggott 1998: 171). For the government, PFI projects are a way to increase public sector building projects quickly without big increases in government borrowing or spending. They are also seen as transferring risk to private companies.

PFI has grown under New Labour, with 105 health projects signed by 1 September 2001, worth £2,502 million (Allen 2001: 11).

Critics point to longer-run costs, with today's public buildings costing tomorrow's taxpayers, a growing stream of public payments to private companies, and some evidence of risks falling on the public rather than the private sector when costs escalate. Finally, some critics wonder whether this is a route to privatizing the NHS.

people have taken care of each other, without intervention from governments or services. Feminist writing in the 1980s began to identify unpaid care, and women's work as unpaid carers, as a crucial component of health and social systems, albeit one that was not quantified (Pascall 1997). Counting it, understanding the work, who does it and why they do it, have grown into a very significant body of research. This work spans cradle and grave, in its concern with parenting as well as with care for disabled people and the frail elderly. Parents' core concerns with raising healthy children, protecting them from injury, may be seen as health work; responsibility for the interface with public services—taking children to services and managing treatment—put parents at the centre of healthcare for young children. Where children are disabled it is not unusual for parents to do specialized nursing work. And older people, especially spouses, often meet and manage each other's health and care needs.

Feminist investigation began with the gendering of care work. While parenting has become a more fashionable idea, research continues to show mothering as a more common practice. The picture of care for elderly people is more complicated, as it is common for spouses to care for each other, and such care involves husbands as well as wives. But it has become clear that women are more likely to have responsibility for heavy nursing care and to have a wider set of responsibilities, in and beyond the immediate family (Finch 1989; Morris 1990). Since feminist work drew attention to the importance of unpaid work, it has become much more common for researchers to count it, to develop accounts of time use, which include paid and unpaid work. The evidence accumulates across many countries that women's joining the labour market has not been matched by men's joining family work, though there is some convergence of working patterns between men and women (Gershuny 2000).

If one crucial argument about care work is about its distribution between men and women, another is about its distribution between state and family. Box 14.6 on long-term care looks at the recent history of health and community care for frail elderly people who may need personal and/or nursing care. There is no straightforward way to count a shift from state care to family care, but there is evidence that it has happened. First, the reduction in hospital beds—now just over a third of the provision in proportion to population that existed in 1948—suggests that some care has shifted from hospital to home. Second, the elderly population has grown, especially the very elderly, whose healthcare needs are greatest (see Chapter 15). And third, governments concerned with the numbers of frail elderly and with public finance have shifted policy to ensure that more older people, and more frail older people, are in need of support and living at home.

Does the evidence support the idea of a trend from state provision to a more mixed economy of care in UK health policy? There is clearly an increase in the extent to which governments have turned to the private sector and to the family. There has been a growth in private insurance outside the NHS, and a growth of private-sector contracts in the NHS. There is little quantitative evidence about what families did in the postwar period, but the implications of changing policy and changing needs are that the health and care work of families has been growing, especially in relation to older people. But the UK continues some of its postwar tradition. Its NHS is more collectivist, more dominated by public spending than the more liberal USA, and in this respect retains a more social democratic style in relation to health than in relation to other social provisions.

The NHS in the twenty-first century: planning for health care—top down or bottom up?

Who should have power over the development of health services? What kind of mix should there be between governments and professionals, service providers and service consumers, managers and professionals? And how should that power be exercised? Should central government take decisions that apply nationwide? Or should local communities participate in decision-making about local services, even if it means diversity in the way services are provided? How can health service planning be integrated with social service planning? If governments have tended—ultimately—to take the same line about public funding for a national health service, they have tended to take different lines about how to manage it. Problems of organization have sometimes taken the blame when the level of funding was a more likely culprit. The resulting organizations and reorganizations have been many.

Top-down planning for health care The 1948 model was essentially a top-down one, with the Minister of Health in at least theoretical control of a health service managed through regional boards and local management committees and, to a lesser extent, local government authorities. There was a new integrated structure for delivering hospital services, but the first design for the NHS owed as much to the need to placate entrenched interests, to get a health service started, as it did to any ideals about how services should be managed.

The first organization of the NHS was much criticized for its tripartite nature, with no integration of hospital, general practitioner, and local authority public health services. But the NHS in this period did develop integrated local services, domiciliary services for health and social care under Medical Officers of Health. Reorganization to make more coherent planning structures for health, implemented in 1974, created a much more difficult environment for integrating local health and social services. It also took the management of health entirely away from local government. Critics see problems of public accountability in health services, with decision-making by non-elected authorities and a lack of public participation in decision-making.

If the 1948 model appeared to critics to be top-down, it did not always appear so to Ministers of Health. Ministers enunciated policies, to move resources to 'Cinderella' services for elderly and mentally ill patients, but spending continued in established patterns, with acute hospitals receiving more money. From the point of view of Ministers of Health it appeared that medical consultants controlled spending rather than themselves, with resources following medical decisions rather than ministerial ones.

The NHS came to be criticized as a bureaucratically managed system, lacking flexibility and unresponsive to patients, protecting entrenched interests, especially the professionals delivering the services. General management was introduced in 1985, as a solution to these problems: managers—never mind whether their background was in industry, financial services, or nursing—would be responsible to government for delivering policy.

This produced a radical change in the management of health services, but a more radical one was to come. Right-wing critics saw in the health service a command-and-control style of management that bore an uncomfortable resemblance to discredited Soviet systems. Markets were seen as more dynamic, with incentives and freedom to innovate, and responsive to consumers, who could take their custom elsewhere if not satisfied. After a brief flirtation with the idea of exchanging the NHS for alternative systems—especially market-based systems—the Thatcher government decided to keep the NHS but import market principles into its management. Hence the 1989 White Paper *Working for Patients, and the NHS* and Community Care Act of 1990, which introduced the **internal market** into the NHS.

The internal market The government aimed to bring the virtues of markets to the NHS while keeping the promise of public funding for a public service. The top-down bureaucracy of NHS authorities would be dismantled. Instead of authorities using government funds to provide services, purchasing authorities would have funds to buy services and providing authorities would produce and sell them and compete for a market share. Purchasers could pick and choose between providers, and contract for the best services available. General practitioners could become fund-holders, purchasing services from hospitals and other providers. Hospitals could become NHS Trusts, with independence from health authorities, and freedom to develop in their own way, subject only to winning enough custom. The internal market offered a very radical reorganization. All provider units in fact became trusts, including hospitals and ambulance and community health services. GP fund-holding also spread widely.

Critics of markets looked for inequalities in the NHS internal market. Would the service continue to offer service on the basis of need, or would some patients get turned off GP lists? Would patients of fund-holders get better service than others (Le Grand et al. 2001)? There were many other questions around the costs and efficiency of the internal market. Would the high transaction costs of the internal market, the managers and computers needed to operate it, bring efficiency benefits to outweigh their costs? But perhaps the most politically pressing issue for a new Labour government in 1997 was whether the internal market would generate the kind of inequalities that the NHS was founded to eliminate. The incoming government offered a new solution.

Primary care trusts: a primary care-led NHS? Primary care trusts (PCTs) are being introduced, to provide a 'third way' between top-down management and the fragmentation of the internal market: 'integrated care, based on partnership' (Department of Health 1997: 5). These aim to bring key decision-making to local-level groups based on primary care.

PCTs will be funded directly from central government according to their population size, weighted according to measures of health need. They will provide primary care and community health services and become the new purchasers for hospital services. They can also purchase primary care services such as physiotherapy, counselling, and alternative therapies. The government claims an intention to produce a more collaborative arrangement than the internal market, but there will still be contracts between one part of the health service and another, as well as contracts with outside providers. The internal market is being softened, but perhaps not abolished, with these developments.

The government appears to intend two shifts of power in these new arrangements. First is to enhance a shift that has already taken place, from hospitals to general practitioners and others who work in primary care. Since the 1990 NHS and Community Care Act, fund-holding GPs have purchased services from hospitals, and the primary care trusts will extend the resources and power at primary care level. The second shift is a devolution of power to the local level, with patients and citizens having a greater say in the service. But ideas of participation and local decision-making are in tension with ideas about quality control, spreading best practice, monitoring and setting standards, productivity, efficiency, and performance, which are also a strong part of central government rhetoric. Local decision-making seems likely to be ring-fenced by central government control.

A universal NHS in the twenty-first century: do other systems work better?

Has the NHS become out of date? Towards the end of the twentieth century it was criticized for everything, from its waiting lists to its standards of hygiene. The argument gained ground that there was something wrong with the NHS as a system, that there was a flaw at the centre of its collectivist ideals: a product of the post-war period could not meet the demands of the late twentieth century. The alternative interpretation of NHS ills was that they were mainly a product of a struggle to survive in a hostile climate. The

Cartoon 14.1 Steve Bell, 1998. 'Superstankers is Turning at last.' © Steve Bell.

collectivist NHS could not survive without taxation, but taxation for public expenditure was seen only as a burden. All health systems have problems, but the NHS seemed particularly deeply troubled as the end of the twentieth century.

The most different system of health care in a developed country is in the USA. A much stronger market operates, with less than half the spending coming from governments. Private funding systems bring many problems: they tend to be 'inequitable, regressive (those with greater health needs pay the most), have weak incentives for cost control, high administration costs and can deter appropriate use' (Wanless 2002: 141). In the USA a tiered system has emerged, with the best health services for people with occupational coverage and their dependants. There are middle tiers of people with 'bare bones' coverage such as Medicaid, and there is a growing uninsured population at the bottom, who have only limited access to public hospital clinic and emergency rooms. Health spending levels far above European countries omit 40 million Americans from health insurance cover. One American author advises his European readers:

> First, cherish your universal coverage and relatively lower costs. You may not realize how good your systems really are. Second, cherish your commitment to solidarity and equity. Your systems may lack efficiency from the point of view of health economists who are concerned with moral hazard and cross-subsidization from the young and healthy to the old and sick, but that is the price for a sense of community and social justice. Third, be very careful about the creation of a large upper tier of people who purchase all of their care privately . . . Support for the public system could decline, and with it funding for the public system. (Kirkman-Liff 1997: 42)

European systems all use public funds as the main source of funding for healthcare. Some have tax-based systems similar to the NHS, while others use social insurance. Insurance gives a narrower base for funding, as people pay only during their working lives, and countries are shifting from this model. Comparison with European and other countries shows that, despite differences in organization and funding, a number of challenges are shared. These include: 'ensuring equity of access to health services; raising quality; improving health outcomes; sustainable financing; improving efficiency; greater responsiveness; citizen involvement in decision-making; and reducing barriers between health and social care' (Dixon and Mossialos 2002). So not all problems can be put down to the NHS as a system.

Public support for the NHS has remained high, with 80 per cent thinking that the NHS is critical to British society and must be maintained (Wanless 2002: 137). The beginning of the twenty-first century has seen a new commitment to the principles of the NHS from government departments. The NHS Plan in 2000 examined other forms of funding healthcare, and concluded that the systems used by other countries do not provide a route to better healthcare: 'The way that the NHS is financed continues to make sense. It meets the tests of efficiency and equity. The principles on which the NHS was constructed in 1948 remain fundamentally sound, (Department of Health 2000: 40). This new commitment is not just to universal principles, but also to a level of funding that will make a universal service work, 'universalizing the best' health care.

The Treasury plans unprecedented increases in public spending to bring the NHS up to modern European standards. The Department of Health plans increases the number and standards of hospital beds, the NHS workforce, equipment, and IT systems. It also aims to reduce waiting times, and to produce national standards to replace the uneven quality or 'postcode lottery'. The positive uses of taxation, enabling state action, are to the fore in these plans to improve the quality of care.

CONCLUSION

If we look back to the ideals and ideas of those who began the NHS in 1948, there are obvious changes in all the elements identified at the opening of the chapter. The management of the health system is the most changed, when top-down planning was blamed for bureaucratic inertia and insensitivity to local needs. But perhaps more surprising is how much has survived through to the twenty-first century, through changes of government, economy, and society. Governments have turned to a more mixed economy of care involving markets and families as well as state provision, and charges for items such as prescriptions have increased. But the major part of NHS funding comes from taxation, as it has since 1948. The traditional commitments of the NHS to a universal service for all based on clinical need, not ability to pay, and a comprehensive range of services have been reasserted in the NHS Plan (Department of Health 2000), where they are declared as the plan's first two principles. There is a new commitment to defend the NHS in argument, and to support it with levels of funding to compare with other countries of Western Europe.

It can be argued that social and economic changes reinforce the need for an NHS based on principles of universal service rather than insurance by those in work or charges to patients at the time of use.

Increases in the elderly population in proportion to the working population mean reducing the capacity of insurance systems based on employment to meet healthcare needs. They also bring an increasing population of vulnerable adults, with large healthcare needs and small incomes. An increasing population of disabled people growing up with significant health needs is another problem that is difficult to meet through any other system. Increasing social inequality and social exclusion are other reasons for the increasing relevance of a system that is not related to ability to pay.

After a period towards the end of the twentieth century when the core ideas of the NHS were under attack from critics who preferred a market-based system, these principles begin the twenty-first century strengthened. Governments and public opinion have acknowledged the value of a service that meets people's health needs mainly through taxation, on the basis of citizenship rather than payment or contribution. These collectivist ideals also continue to support an individualist style of medical care. Medical authority is now more contested by patients, lawyers, and social movements, but the ideals of a public health movement remain on the margin. Perhaps the greatest challenge of the twenty-first century will be to address the problems of health and health inequalities discussed at the beginning of the chapter.

KEY LEGISLATION AND POLICY DOCUMENTS

NHS Act 1946.

NHS and Community Care Act 1990.

Department of Health and Social Security 1980, *Inequalities in Health: Report of a Working Group* (the Black Report). London: HMSO.

Acheson, D. (1998), *Independent Inquiry into Inequalities in Health*. London: Stationery Office.

Department of Health (2000), *The NHS Plan: A Plan for Investment, a Plan for Reform*. Cm. 4818-1. London: Stationery Office.

Wanless, D. (2002), *Securing our Future Health: Taking a Long-Term View*. London: HM Treasury.

REFERENCES

Acheson, D. (1998), *Independent Inquiry into Inequalities in Health*. London: Stationery Office.

Allen, G. (2000), *The Private Finance Initiative (PFI)*. Research paper 01/117. London: House of Commons Library.

Baggott, R. (1998), *Health and Health Care in Britain*. Basingstoke: Macmillan.

Benzeval, M., Judge, K., and Whitehead, M. (1995), *Tackling Inequalities in Health: An Agenda for Action*. London: King's Fund.

Blaxter, M. (1990), *Health and Lifestyles*. London: Routledge.

Dahlgren, P. and Whitehead, M. (1991) *Policies and Strategies to promote Social Equity in Health*. Stockholm: Institute of Futures Studies.

Department of Health (1997), *The New NHS: Modern, Dependable*. Cm. 3807. London: Stationery Office.

—— (1999), *Saving Lives: Our Healthier Nation*. London: Stationery Office.

—— (2000), *The NHS Plan: A Plan for Investment, a Plan for Reform*. Cm. 4818-1. London: Stationery Office.

—— (2002), 'Health inequalities: national targets on infant mortality and life expectancy: technical briefing'. http://www.doh.gov.uk

DHSS (Department of Health and Social Security) (1976), *Prevention and Health—Everybody's Business: A Reassessment of Public and Personal Health*. London: HMSO.

—— (1980), *Inequalities in Health: Report of a Working Group* (the Black Report). London: HMSO.

Dixon, A. and Mossialos, E. (2002), *Health Care Systems in Eight Countries: Trends and Challenges*. London: European Observatory on Health Systems, LSE.

—— and Robinson R. (2002), 'The United Kingdom'. In Dixon and Mossials (2002). LSE, London.

Doyal, L. (1995), *What Makes Women Sick: Gender and the Political Economy of Health*. London: Macmillan.

—— (1998), *Women and Health Services*. Buckingham: Open University Press.

Eurostat (2000), *The Social Situation in the European Union 2000*. Luxembourg: European Commission.

Finch, J. (1989), *Family Obligations and Social Change*. Cambridge: Polity Press.

Gershuny, J. (2000), *Changing Times: Work and Leisure in Post-Industrial Society*. Oxford: Oxford University Press.

Gray, A. (2001a), 'Explaining inequalities in health in the United Kingdom'. In A. Gray and P. Payne, *World Health and Disease*. Buckingham: Open University Press.

—— (2001b), 'The decline of infectious disease: the case of England'. In A. Gray and P. Payne, *World Health and Disease*. Buckingham: Open University Press.

Hunter, D. J. (1997), *Desperately Seeking Solutions: Rationing Health Care*. London: Longman.

Kirkman-Liff, B. (1997), 'The United States'. In C. Ham (ed.), *Health Care Reform: Learning from International Experience*. Buckingham: Open University Press.

Le Grand, J., Mays, N. J., and Mulligan, J. (2001), *Learning from the NHS Internal Market: A Review of the Evidence*. London: King's Fund.

Lewis, J. and Glennerster, H. (1996), *Implementing the New Community Care*. Buckingham: Open University Press.

McKeown, T. (1976), *The Modern Rise of Population*. London: Arnold.

Mehrotra, S. (2000), *Integrating Economic and Social Policy: Good Practices from High Achieving Countries*. Florence: UNICEF.

Morris. L. (1990), *The Workings of the Household*. Cambridge: Polity Press.

NICE (National Institute for Clinical Excellence) (2000), statement by Sir Michael Rawlins, chair, NICE (www.nice.org.uk).

Office of Health Economics (2002), *Compendium of Health Statistics*. London: OHE.

ONS (Office for National Statistics) (1996), *Social Focus on Ethnic Minorities*. London: ONS.

—— (2001), *Living in Britain: Results from the 2000/01 General Household Survey*. London: Stationery Office.

ONS (Office for National Statistics) (2002), *Social Trends no. 32*. London: ONS.

Pascall, G. (1997), *Social Policy: A New Feminist Analysis*. London: Routledge.

Powell, M. (1997), *Evaluating the National Health Service*. Buckingham: Open University Press.

Royal Commission on Long Term Care for the Elderly (1999), *With Respect to Old Age: Long-Term Care: Rights and Responsibilities*. Cm. 4192-I. London: Stationery Office.

Spencer, N. (1996), *Poverty and Child Health*. Oxford: Radcliffe.

Wanless, D. (2002), *Securing our Future Health: Taking a Long-Term View*. London: HM Treasury.

Webster, C. (1998), *The National Health Service: A Political History*. Oxford: Oxford University Press.

Wilkinson, G. (1996), *Unhealthy Societies: The Afflictions of Inequality*. London: Routledge.

FURTHER READING

R. Baggott, *Health and Health Care in Britain* (Basingstoke: Macmillan, 1998). A comprehensive and detailed account of health and health care issues.

R. Baggott, *Public Health: Policy and Politics* (Basingstoke: Macmillan, 2000) A wide-ranging text which examines a range of health issues, such as the environment, food, and alcohol, within an account of the politics of public health.

M. Benzeval, K. Judge, and M. Whitehead, *Tackling Inequalities in Health: An Agenda for Action* (London: King's Fund, 1995). A collection of essays which discuss the policy options for addressing health inequalities.

A. Gray and P. Payne, *World Health and Disease* (Buckingham: Open University Press, 2001). This Open University text assembles the evidence about health inequalities and their explanations in two accessible chapters: ch. 9 on 'Contemporary patterns of disease in the UK' and ch. 10 on 'Explaining inequalities in health in the UK'. Ch. 6 also includes a useful discussion of explanations for the modern decline in mortality.

C. Ham, *Health Policy in Britain* (London: Macmillan, 1999). An accessible and enlightening study of health policy and policy-making processes.

M. Powell, *Evaluating the National Health Service* (Buckingham: Open University Press, 1997). This study asks how well the NHS has worked, what its successes and failure are, and how it compares with other systems.

W. Ranade, *A Future for the NHS? Health Care for the Millennium* (London: Longman, 1997). An accessible text on the NHS.

C. Webster, *The National Health Service: A Political History* (Oxford: Oxford University Press, 1998). An accessible account of the history of the NHS, which covers its implementation and its first fifty years.

USEFUL WEBSITES

Department of Health: www.doh.gov.uk

HM Treasury : www.hm-treasury.gov.uk

The King's Fund: www.kingsfund.org.uk

National Health Service: www.nhs.uk

National Statistics: www.statistics.gov.uk

Office for Health Economics: www.ohe.org.uk

Organization for Economic Cooperation and Development (OECD): www1.oecd.orga/els/health/sof

World Health Organization (WHO): www3.who.int/whosis

GLOSSARY

biomedical model An understanding of health rooted in the biological and medical sciences. Its orientation is towards treating illness in individuals.

cost–benefit and cost effectiveness analysis Economic tools for assessing the merits of policies or practices. Both involve a broad assessment of the full costs of a decision to individuals, to the health service and to society more broadly. Cost–benefit analysis also attempts to make a full assessment of the benefits, in order to compare treatments for different kinds of problem.

infant mortality rates These count the deaths of children under 1 year old and measure them over time, or in comparison with other countries. They are expressed per 1,000 live births, and are regarded as an indicator of comparative health.

internal market A structure for providing health (or other public services) in which the authorities responsible for making decisions about the availability of services, and for purchasing them, are separate from the organizations which produce and deliver services to patients. They introduce competitive market forces into public services.

liberal, free-market-based approach An approach to social policy which is built on the assumption that individuals should be free to choose their own welfare, buying through markets, rather than having them provided through the state.

mixed economy of welfare A description of the diverse sources of welfare, in state, private, voluntary, and informal family sectors. During the latter part of the twentieth century governments saw it as their role to stimulate and support a wider range of sources of provision, beyond the state. This has largely continued under New Labour, though recent developments have re-emphasized the role of the state in funding and providing services, especially in health and education.

National Health Service (NHS) The system of health service provision established by the NHS Act in 1946. Its system of public funding, with no charges at the time of use, made it a model of the collectivist ideals of the postwar era, when the emphasis was on collective, state action to meet human needs and to regenerate society.

new social movements Started as collective protests and aimed to work through public opinion and civil society. The women's movement and environmental (green) movements have influenced social policy widely, and both have significant health agendas.

north–south divide The evidence of different health experience in different regions in the UK is strong, with the poorer regions of the north having higher mortality rates than the richer south-east.

Primary Care Trusts (PCTs) PCTs in England and Local Health Groups in Wales are now the main purchasers of healthcare services. They receive money from central government, mainly according to their population size. They serve populations of between 50,000 and 250,000 people. PCTs provide primary care services, but purchase hospital and other services—which could include physiotherapy and alternative therapies—from other providers. In Scotland the system of purchasing and providing is more integrated.

Rationing Decisions about allocating resources or setting priorities. These may be decisions about which services to provide as part of the NHS and which not to provide, as well as decisions about who should be treated and who not.

Redistributive A system of taxation and benefits which reduces inequality by taking a higher proportion from higher-income groups and giving a higher proportion of benefits to poorer households.

social and environmental model A social model of health stresses the importance of people's place in society in making them healthy or sick: social class in particular is seen as a key determinant of health. Environmentalists share the concern with factors beyond the individual, but their attention is more to health hazards which may affect everyone: nuclear fallout, agricultural chemicals, air pollution.

social democratic regimes The social democratic belief that capitalism can be reformed by state intervention lies behind the welfare strategies of Scandinavian countries, especially Sweden. Here, social policies are based on government intervention to produce social cohesion, with higher taxation, income redistribution, labour market policies to bring people into work, and more equal outcomes than in most western European countries or the USA.

standardized mortality rates Annual death rates per 100,000 in a population group. They are standardized to enable comparison between groups with different age structures.

Third Way The approach of the New Labour government which came to power in 1997. The Blair government looked for a way between two political traditions, based on the central state (old Labour) and the market (new Right), using a mixture of state and market, according to 'what works'.

universal service, universalizing the best The principle on which the NHS was founded was that of providing to the whole population, according to need rather than ability to pay. The stigma attached to means-tested provision and the poorer quality of services for poorer people which characterized Poor Law systems were to be avoided by providing the highest-quality care for everyone, 'universalizing the best'. Insurance-based systems tend to leave some people out (e.g. those who are disabled, and/or have weak employment records). Such systems may have less than universal coverage, and they may have different levels or tiers of service for different groups of people.

15

Social Care

Julia Twigg

CONTENTS

INTRODUCTION: THE UNCERTAIN BOUNDARIES OF SOCIAL CARE

This chapter discusses social care. By this we mean the support of people with a disability, illness, or frailty, usually living in the community. The term thus overlaps considerably with community care. To a large extent, social care is defined in opposition to medical care: it is about those aspects of life that are not normally thought of as falling under the remit of medicine. The boundary of the medical and the social is, however, uncertain and contested and, as we shall see, where it is deemed to lie has become a political issue, and one that has considerable financial implications for individuals and government.

In the chapter we start with the situations of various client groups—older and disabled people, carers—and then discuss the role of community care in their support. Two final sections explore the care of people with mental health problems and learning disabilities.

OLDER PEOPLE

Most people over 65 live independently and have no major care needs. For many, retirement opens up a period of leisure and new opportunities that is sometimes termed the **Third Age**. Not tied to chronological age, it is generally regarded as running from the mid-50s to mid-70s. Most people in this age group do not suffer from health problems that limit their independence. A significant minority, however, do have problems with physical functioning or mental health, and the likelihood of these increases with age. For example, 9 per cent of people over 65 cannot manage on their own getting up and down stairs, 2 per cent getting in and out of bed, and 7 per cent bathing or washing all over. Among those who are over 75, 11 cannot bathe on their own and 15 per cent cannot manage stairs without being held being supported, or at all (ONS 2000). Some mental health problems are associated with age. Dementia (whether caused by Alzheimer's disease or multi-infarct dementia) affects about one in ten of the population under the age of 80, and about one in five after 80 (Marshall 1990). Though such difficulties present real problems for some older people, and ones with considerable cost implications (older people are the largest consumers of public welfare services), it is salutary to consider the figures in reverse: 80 per cent of those over 80 do not have dementia, and 89 per cent over 75 manage their own personal care.

Problems with health and functioning are often exacerbated by the circumstances in which many older people live, particularly poor housing and poverty, which are both more common the older a person is. The importance of material and social factors in structuring of the experience of old age is the basis of the **political economy perspective** exemplified in the UK in the work of Townsend, Phillipson, and Walker. Their central assumption is that:

> the process of ageing and the experience of old age cannot be understood without reference to the elderly person's location in the social structure and their relation to the economy. (Walker and Phillipson 1986: 2)

They term these connections the 'structured dependence of old age': it is economic and social forces rather than individual functioning that determine the circumstances of older people both as a group (their relative poverty or social marginalization) and as individuals (people carrying into old age the resources—economic, social, and cultural—that they built up and enjoyed in earlier life).

Gender

Women live on average longer than men: life expectancy at birth for British men is now 75 and women 80, and the gender differential has widened this century (ONS 2001: 128). 'The gender imbalance is most marked in advanced old age; over the age of 85, women outnumber men by three to one' (Arber and Ginn 1995: 11). Women suffer from greater material disadvantage, and old women are generally poorer than old men (largely because of the gendered nature of pension provision). The financial dependence of older women is socially created earlier in life by traditional expectations of financial dependence in marriage, so that inequalities in old age are related to the domestic division of labour earlier in life. Arber and Ginn argue that gender is as important as class in determining the situations of people in old age. Building on the political economy approach they point to the way in which:

> a person's role in production and reproduction during working life has a profound influence on the material and health resources they have at their disposal in later life . . . the prejudicial images of older people that underlie discrimination derive from a dominant ideology in which only certain kinds of work are highly valued: production is given priority over reproduction . . . elderly women have been doubly devalued by combined ageism and sexism. (Arber and Ginn 1991: 178)

Ageism

Ageism is a form of social prejudice comparable with racism and sexism. Bytheway defines it as a set of beliefs that:

> legitimates the use of chronological age to mark out classes of people who are systematically denied resources and opportunities that others enjoy, and who suffer the consequences of such denigration,

> ranging from well meaning patronage to unambiguous vilification . . . Ageism generates and reinforces a fear and denigration of the ageing process [stereotyping] presumptions regarding competence and the need for protection. (Bytheway 1995: 14)

Women suffer more from such ageist assumptions than do men. The fact that the old are predominately female subtly detracts from the status of the group as a whole.

This cultural ageism extends into the welfare system, with mobility benefits not available to people of pensionable age, effective health treatments denied and support services closely rationed. Though the new National Service Framework for Older People (Department of Health 2001) includes rooting out such age discrimination amongst its aims, it remains to be seen whether it is possible to effect such a profound change in service culture.

DISABLED PEOPLE

Disabled people under pensionable age, although often treated for planning purposes as a single group (**younger physically disabled** or **YPD**), in fact form a heterogeneous category that includes people born with an impairment (e.g. spina bifida, cerebral palsy); those whose disability results from trauma (e.g. spinal injury, loss of limb); and those suffering from degenerative conditions increasingly common in later life (e.g. arthritis, heart disease). This range affects not just the nature of the impairments but also their meaning and significance for the individuals and society. The politics of disability have largely been driven by the concerns of the first two groups.

The politics of disability

In Britain the disability movement arose in the 1970s and 1980s, spearheaded by individuals, themselves disabled (some of whom had formerly lived in institutions like Cheshire Homes), determined to challenge what they saw as the demeaning and oppressive accounts of disability presented by researchers, policy-makers, and practitioners. It is a civil rights approach that draws on the experiences of other radical social movements. Oliver, one of its main theorists, argues that the dominant account of disability is one of personal tragedy in which the central problem is located in the individual and his/her impairment rather than the socially constructed barriers that create that disability (Oliver 1990). This **social model of disability** sees disabled people not as individual victims of tragedy but as collective victims of an uncaring and oppressive society. Environmental barriers—lack of lifts, steps, narrow doors—are the clearest example of the social construction of disability: they are what handicaps people with functional impairments, not the impairments themselves. But it extends also to assumptions about what is normal or valued. Much medically based rehabilitation, Finkelstein argues, rests on stereotypical ideas of normality, for example forcing disabled people to walk upright, however awkwardly or painfully, rather than accepting that for some people a wheelchair may be their normal mode of mobility—just as shoes or a car are for others (Oliver 1990). This approach has had its greatest success in the Disability Discrimination Act

Box 15.1 Terminology

Oliver and others in the disability movement make a distinction between:

- **impairment**: lacking part or all of a limb, or having a defective limb, organism, or mechanism of the body, and
- **disability**: the disadvantage or restriction caused by a contemporary social organization which takes no account of people who have physical impairments and thus excludes them from the mainstream of social activities (Oliver 1990: 11)

1995, which placed an obligation on service providers to make their services accessible to disabled people.

Though the social model is still dominant in disability theory, it has been subject to challenge from different directions:

- Bury (1995) argues that the majority of disabled people are in fact chronically sick or older people, and that the social model reflects the concerns of a small minority of young, active, and often male wheelchair users.
- Morris (1997), though a supporter of the social model and herself a wheelchair user, critiques its writings from a feminist perspective, noting how it shies away from the subjective experience of disability. This leaves central experiences like pain unacknowledged.
- Hughes and Paterson (1997) argue that the sharp distinction drawn between impairment and disability effectively hands over the subject of the body to medicine, leaving the experience of impairment untheorized.

INFORMAL CARE

Informal carers are people who give substantial amounts of practical and emotional help to frail or disabled people, usually members of their family on an unpaid basis. Though they are often simply called 'carers', the term 'informal' is used to distinguish them from paid carers working in the formal service sector. The popularization of the term 'carer' since the 1980s marked a further stage in the debate about community care, one in which the involvement of families and of the informal sector assumed new visibility.

The rediscovery of family obligation

Although the word 'carer' was new in the 1980s, the reality that underlay it was not. Family care has always been the predominant form of care. That fact, however, was obscured within academic and policy debate by a series of assumptions about the modern family. Sociologists in the 1950s and 1960s—reinforced by popular prejudices—assumed that extended family responsibility had withered away with the rise of modern industrial society and the nuclear family, and that modern families did not 'care' in the way that they had in the past. These assumptions began to be challenged in the 1970s, particularly by feminist scholars who sought to expose the normative assumptions that underlay the old sociology of the family, particularly in regard to women. No longer exclusively focused on the nuclear couple, researchers were able to explore the range of household forms in which people increasingly lived, and this included the households of older people. The conceptual separation of 'family' and 'household' made it possible to see the ways in which households were linked in wider **kin networks** that could involve significant transfers of help. An explosion of research on carers in the 1980s and 1990s explored the nature of these transfers and their importance, particularly in the lives of older people (Finch and Mason 1993; Qureshi and Walker 1989).

As a result, the earlier picture of disengagement and neglect by the family was shown to be wrong. Most help that comes to older and disabled people continues to come from their families, and this applies across households as well as within them. Most older people in Britain do not live with their offspring, but this does not mean that they do not receive substantial amounts of help from them when they are in need.

Carers: the new client group?

The forces that create caregiving derive from the family and kinship obligation, but their operation is shaped by the context of formal provision. What the state does and does not provide affects what families do. Failing to provide alternatives and making assumptions about involvement represents an implicit policy by default. In practice, community care could not continue were it not for the activities of family carers. Their input greatly exceeds that of the formal service sector, a fact that has increasingly been recognized by policy-makers. In 1995 the Carers (Recognition and Services) Act gave carers the right to a separate assessment of their needs.

The new emphasis on carers arose in part from a recognition of the heavy burdens that many of them bear. Caring can be a stressful, lonely, and exhausting task, and carers are people who deserve public recognition and support. But the desire to support carers arose also from more instrumental motives on behalf of government. Supporting carers was seen as a cost-effective strategy, with small amounts of formal support enabling the continuance of large amounts of informal support. Considerations of this sort suggested to government that the state should aim to incorporate carers more effectively into its activities. Exactly on what basis is less clear. Service agencies in responding to carers have to juggle three models of their relationship with them: carers as resources (people whose involvement can be assumed and who form part of the background to formal provision); as co-workers (people with whom the agencies must cooperate and work in order to maximize the input going to the client); and as co-clients (people who in themselves have needs that social care agencies have an obligation to recognize) (Twigg 1989). This means that they cannot focus exclusively on either the disabled person or the carer, but hold their interests in balance. It also means recognizing that there are, at times, significant conflicts of interest between the carer and the disabled person.

There are also tensions between people's roles as carers and the other activities and obligations they may have to carry out, for example as parents, wives, or husbands. A very high proportion of carers are not in paid employment, partly because many are retired people looking after a disabled partner, but sometimes because their caring tasks make it impossible to hold down a job as well. Single parents face this problem particularly. However, many carers do juggle paid work and their functions as carers. This is one aspect of what has come to be called the **work–life balance**, and the trade-offs that are involved affect not only individuals but the health of the economy as well.

Caring as a feminist issue

Caring emerged as a women's issue very clearly in the 1980s. Initially it arose from a concern with the unequal burdens of men and woman in society, and the assumptions made by the welfare state about the responsibilities of women for family care. Whereas women had little option but to care, men could discharge their family obligations through the labour of their wives. This pattern of inequality was reinforced by the state. For example, the **Invalid Care Allowance** (**ICA**), a benefit developed in 1975 to support carers who would otherwise be in paid work, was originally only awarded to men and unmarried women under pensionable age, with the assumption that married women were always 'available' to care and did not merit compensation. This gender bias was later removed after threat of a judgement in the European Court in 1986, but the lobbying that preceded it provided an important focus for the emerging feminist concern over informal care in the late 1970s and early 1980s.

The feminist interest in informal care was never an isolated one: it was always part of a larger project of making the unpaid work of women conceptually and politically visible. In the 1970s this had applied to housework and childcare, but in the 1980s it was extended to the responsibilities for elderly care that many feminists of the second wave were starting to experience in their own lives. Seeing caring as a form of labour, often hard physical labour, undertaken in unrewarding circumstances with little public recognition, was of great strategic importance. It counteracted sentimentalizing discourses of love and family, and showed how caring at home in the private sphere limited women's lives and restricted their access to socially valued roles in the public sphere (Hooyman 1990).

Caring also raises questions about the meaning of care itself. Though feminist work tended to conceptualize caring as labour, the aspect of love was never absent. As Ungerson (1987) and Graham (1983) showed, though caring *for* and caring *about* were conceptually different, they were also often linked. Caring was rarely simply a matter of physical tasks; it also involved feelings, both in that caring takes place in the context of intimate relationships which themselves involve strong feelings, and in that the activity of caring requires the direct deployment of feelings. **Emotional labour**—a term developed by Hochschild (1983) in relation to flight attendants and extended by James (1989) in relation to hospice work—involves close personal attention to the needs of another in which feelings are manipulated and used to support and maintain the well-being of that person. Emotional labour characterizes much of woman's work whether in the paid sector of the formal economy—typically the service sector—or the unpaid world of the family. Caring, whether informal and located in family relationships or formal and paid, is clearly part of this.

Criticism from the disability movement

The disability movement has been critical of the new emphasis on carers. Morris argues that such policies underwrite dependence and divert attention and resources away from the real issue, which is the needs of disabled people. Morris also criticized early feminist research on caring for failing to incorporate the subjective experiences of the recipients of care—in many cases themselves women—and this in a literature that emphasized the ways in which the personal is political. She argues that feminists constituted their subject—women—in ways that excluded disabled women (Morris 1991).

It remains the case, however, that caring takes place in relationships, often ones of long duration, and the dynamics of family and personal life are complex. Though some disabled people may indeed be oppressed by their 'carers', forced into a secondary position in relation to service providers, the reverse can sometimes also be true, and the needs of carers can sometimes be obscured behind those they care for (Twigg and Atkin 1994). So long as carers feel that they are under an obligation to care, whether enforced by the cared-for person or deriving from internalized social norms, Twigg has argued, there should be some recognition of their needs in their own right. It is the fact that carers are obligated by family relationships that means that caring is not simply a voluntary act. Many carers care against their own interests and are not able to give up at will. The issue therefore is how far it is proper in these circumstances to have regard for their needs, *in their own right*, and how these should be balanced against those they care for.

Box 15.2 Who are the carers?

In 1985 a series of questions concerning carers were added to the General Household Survey, and in 1990 and 1995 some were repeated or new ones added (Green 1988; Social Trends 1995; Rowlands 1998). Together these studies have provided reliable basic facts about the numbers involved in caring and the tasks they carry out. They have revealed that more than 6 million people, or one in seven of the adult population, were involved in caring at any one time. For those providing more than twenty hours a week of care, the figures are 1.4 million, or 3 per cent of the adult population. Caring cannot be seen as a marginal phenomenon, but something that most people will be involved in at some stage of their lives.

One of the surprising aspects of the data is that the gender difference is not as great as might have been expected: 17 per cent of women were carers and 13 per cent of men (1990 figures). Partly this reflected the presence of spouse carers, where gender differences are not significant. It is among offspring caring for a parent that the gender imbalance is marked. Intimate care is also more strongly associated with women. Caring is thus **gendered**, but not in the blanket way that is sometimes asserted.

COMMUNITY CARE FOR OLDER AND DISABLED PEOPLE

Social services departments (SSDs) were created in 1971 following the Seebohm Report as part of wider reform of local government. They united under one head the disparate range of services for children, mothers and babies, older and disabled people that had developed piecemeal since the 1880s across the voluntary and local authority sectors. The purpose was to create a 'single door' for those seeking help. They were formed around the idea of **generic social work**. The aim was to overcome the previous plurality of different specialisms and the fragmentation of provision. The departments also represented a new confidence in social work as a profession.

In practice, informal **specialization** soon developed. The political and professional dominance of child protection work (see Chapter 16)—intensified by scandals involving the deaths of children under the supervision of social services—meant that work with older and disabled people was mostly relegated to social workers who were not formally qualified. Though social work has dominated the ethos of social services, only a minority of staff have ever been qualified social workers. Currently about 80 per cent of the social care workforce, mostly careworkers, have no formal training (Department of Health 1998).

SSDs were originally organized either at the county level (e.g. Dorset) or in metropolitan areas at the level of the district (e.g. Lambeth). The reorganization of local government in the 1990s left many of the counties intact, though in some areas, usually urban conurbations, smaller unitary authorities were created (e.g. Medway in Kent), and these took on responsibility for social services.

Changes in community care: the Thatcherite agenda

Though the Thatcher government was not initially much concerned with **personal social services**, by the late 1990s policy interest had moved to the reform of the public sector, and in particular to the injection into it of private-sector values and management techniques, the latter encapsulated in the term **new public management**. The agenda was pursued through quasi-privatization or the creation of quasi-markets across a number of sectors including housing and the NHS. In the case of social services it was largely promoted through the purchaser/provider split and the encouragement of a mixed economy of provision, introduced in the NHS and Community Care Act 1990. One of the driving forces behind the act was the desire of government to cap the ever-expanding residential care budget funded out of social security (see p. 435). The principle features of the community care reforms were:

- Purchaser/provider split: this shifted SSDs from being major suppliers of services to purchasers, later commissioners, of services. SSDs through the 1990s divested themselves of most direct provision in areas like home care and residential care. Such provision was often transferred into trusts or other not-for-profit forms of organization.
- Mixed economy of provision: this involved encouraging a plurality of suppliers across the independent sector (voluntary and private). Local authorities contracted with

various agencies to provide services to particular localities, or on a spot purchasing basis to particular clients.

- Targeting: under the influence of the work of the PSSRU, a critique had developed of social care that suggested that support was poorly targeted, a scattergun of low-level assistance, and that those with complex needs often received insufficient support. Under the resource constraints of the 1990s, this became a rationale for concentrating home care at the heavy end of need, and effectively abandoning public provision for those who only needed a few hours of domestic help per week. Such concentration and withdrawal was widely unpopular, and contributed to the problems over inappropriate admissions, since low levels of home care have a preventative function.

Health and social care: the medical/social boundary

The boundary between health and social care has been a persistent source of conflict and debate. No single criterion defines the division; rather, it is constituted by the sedimentation of a series of boundaries: financial, administrative, professional, cultural. The boundary is not fixed, and significant shifts have occurred. For example, in the last

Box 15.3 PSSRU and the Kent community care experiments

During the 1970s and 1980s, the Personal Social Services Research Unit at the University of Kent, under the direction of Bleddyn Davis, undertook a series of demonstration projects that aimed to show how case managers, particularly if they held their own budgets, could provide better and more closely tailored packages of support, maximizing the effectiveness of resources and ensuring the best mix of services at the keenest prices. It appeared from the Kent experiments that frail older people on the brink of admission to residential care could on average be supported in their own homes at less than two-thirds the cost of a residential place with a case management approach (Challis and Davis 1986). These ideas provided the basis for the development of care management.

The intellectual roots of PSSRU are in economics. Its central analytic framework, the 'production of welfare approach', models welfare activity in terms of various inputs (formal as well as informal) and a range of welfare outcomes. It thus addresses directly the issues of outcomes, efficiency, and effectiveness that have become increasingly central in debates about the reform of the public sector.

For example, Davis makes a useful distinction between **horizontal target effectiveness** (the degree to which individuals in the target category receive the intervention) and **vertical target effectiveness** (the degree to which individuals who receive the intervention fall within the target definition of need). This enables him to assess one aspect of the effectiveness of an authority's provision: how many people who deserve to get the service are not getting it—because, for example, they are unknown to the agency or refused in error—and how many who do get the service are not in the target category—for example, wrongly assessed, or recovered from their previous illness.

decade the long-term care of people with dementia or brain damage used to take place within the NHS; it is now part of social care. A similar transfer has occurred in relation to personal care.

The two sectors, though they are spoken of in parallel, in fact relate to each other in a highly asymmetrical way. Health is the dominant and defining one, drawing on the prestige of scientific medicine. Social care, by contrast, is seen as lesser, defined in a residual way as 'all the rest'. Healthcare needs are regarded as 'real' and important, and this underpins the way they are largely made available free at the point of use. Social care needs are seen as more optional, something that people should be required to pay for themselves if they are able. This different valuation of the two sectors is something that reverberates through policy. All too often policy is driven by the needs of the health sector: for example, the recent development of intermediate care (see p. 431) resulted from difficulties over hospital throughput as much as concern with a gap in social care.

Health and social care: the demise of social services?

The reforms of the 1990s weakened the institutional base of SSDs by reducing their manpower and scope. The growth of managerialism also undermined the professional status of social work within senior management: increasingly, directors of social services were not required to have a social work qualification, and in many authorities their duties were combined with those of other chief officers. Developments in relation to child protection in the wake of yet more scandals reinforced the idea of childcare as a distinct activity and one that might be best managed by a specialist agency.

Table 15.1 Medical/social boundary

Institutional/financial	Health care institutions Free at point of use Social right	Social care institutions Responsibility of individual or Means tested Residual right
Level of government	National	Municipality
Professional orientation	Medicine and professions Ancillary to medicine	Social work
Professional status	Accepted	Disputed
Knowledge base	Bio-science Hard	Social science/therapeutics Soft
Application of technology	High and esteemed	Low and not esteemed
Action	Direct Bodily	Vague Psychosocial
Legitimation and power	'Real', life-and-death needs Necessary	More disputed 'needs' Optional

Box 15.4 **The body and community care: personal care and bathing**

Personal care is a central element in community care. Providing older and disabled people with help with washing, bathing, dressing, going to the toilet, and getting in and out of bed is vital if they are to be enabled to remain living at home. The management of the body is thus an essential activity of social care. This fact, however, has not always been acknowledged in policy-making or research. The body is traditionally regarded as belonging within the remit of medicine, something that is primarily dealt with by doctors or nurses rather than by social workers. It is the case that up until the 1980s bathing in the community was primarily provided within the NHS by the community nursing service. Over the last decade, however, it has been transferred across into social care, where it is now provided by the home care service or by agencies providing home care. It is an example, therefore, of the fluid nature of the boundary between health and social care.

Bathing and washing—involving as they do undressing, nakedness, touch—raise all sorts of sensitivities. For many older and disabled people, receiving help in this area is potentially embarrassing, even demeaning. How it is negotiated and provided is thus very important. It thus provides an example of one of the central truths about community care: that it is in the fine detail of the exchange at the front line between the careworker and the client that the real issue of quality lies.

This raised the question of whether SSDs were still needed, and whether responsibility for social care itself might be transferred. The health and social care interface had long been identified as a source of problems and service irrationalities. One possibility was that social care might be integrated into primary health and that GPs might take it over. What are the pros and cons here?

- GPs are widely known and trusted in the community. Most people are registered with a GP, and health centres are familiar places. Social services, by contrast, are less well understood and can be seen as stigmatizing—only for the poor and needy—or as agents of social control in relation to unsatisfactory parenting.
- Older and disabled people typically have a mix of health and social care needs. Bringing them under one roof seems to make sense and would allow a more seamless service without artificial barriers and discontinuities—e.g. is the wheelchair there to support health or social care needs?
- Doctors already coordinate other services in their practices, so why not social care inputs like home care?
- The reality of medical prestige and specialist knowledge is such that, while doctors can to some degree direct and prescribe the activities of social care providers, the reverse is not the case. Integration has therefore to be centred around the doctor.
- However, the history of social provision suggests that GPs are not good at coordinating social care. They have no training in it, and little interest. General practice is currently overloaded with new functions, and social care would be an unwelcome and probably neglected addition.

- Though individuals vary, many GPs have limited commitment to community care as a value. GPs in the past have often endorsed, and even encouraged, the transfer of older people into residential homes. Doctors often wish to be rid of patients whose frailty and instability create anxiety and take up professional time.
- Doctors have traditionally adopted a more directive, at times authoritarian, approach to patients. This is at odds with attempts to encourage greater autonomy among frail users.
- Articulate users like younger disabled people are in general critical of the medical model of provision (though it should be added that they are scarcely more in favour of the social work one).
- Social work professional values are centred around autonomy, dignity, and self-direction. Though these are not always perfectly realized, the transfer of social care out of social services would weaken their influence in the sector.

Currently government has not chosen to promote this model. Rather, it has pursued the integration agenda by means of joint commissioning and integrated care.

New Labour and community care

New Labour's plans for social services were outlined in *Modernizing Social Services* (Department of Health 1998). These centre on:

- Partnerships and joint commissioning: New Labour has been determined to bring down the 'Berlin Wall' between health and social services. In pursuit of this, legislation passed under the Health Act 1999 allowed for new flexibilities in the use of money and determination of responsibilities at the interface between health and social services. A range of different models of provision have emerged: some based on pooled budgets; others on lead commissioning assigned to one or the other side; others on integrated provision. Umbrella partnerships in the form of Local Strategic Partnerships (LSPs) are being formed to bring together public, private, voluntary, and community sectors. The aim is to improve quality of life and governance in a particular locality through refocusing mainstream services and resources.
- Intermediate care: this is a new range of services aimed at bridging the gap between acute hospital and primary and community care. The principle driver behind their development has been the old issue of delayed discharge, or in health services parlance, **bed blocking**. Work for the National Bed Inquiry suggested that as many as 20 per cent of bed days for older people were probably inappropriate, and would be unnecessary if alternative facilities were available. The Audit Commission Report of 1997 concluded that there had been too little investment in preventative and rehabilitative services, and that there was a group of older people whose functioning could be brought back to levels that would support independence. Health and social services are required in the National Service Framework for Older People (Department of Health 2001) to work together to develop a range of such intermediate forms of support.

The rise of regulation and standard-setting

One of the marked features of New Labour has been its use of regulation and standard-setting as a means to direct and control service provision. This is linked to the wider modernization agenda, aimed at 'driving up standards' in the public sector. As a result, local authorities and other public bodies have been subject to an onslaught of performance indicators, inspections, audits, targets, and reviews. Across a range of services central government is prescribing levels of service and determining detailed standards of performance in a way that has not occurred before.

The trend towards greater control by the centre is not new, but the pace has increased markedly under New Labour. In large measure it has replaced two earlier principles governing the provision of services:

- The idea of local autonomy rooted in the political process. Variations in what is provided locally and in the levels and principles of charging were once seen as legitimate matters for local choice, determined by local democracy. This is no longer the case; and the current expectation is that services will be available and charged for uniformly across the country.
- The Thatcherite idea that market forces and individual consumer choices should guide and shape the pattern of provision. The market analogy was always of limited relevance, since these are services that are not directly purchased by users, who are themselves not always experts in their own needs. At best they are **quasi-markets**, controlled by public-sector agencies. New Labour has moved away from the language of markets and purchasing towards one of commissioning and partnerships.

Funding long-term care

The debate on the funding of long-term care for older people arises from a number of factors:

- Increasing numbers of older people. Though the figures are relatively stable at the moment, between 2011 and 2041 the number of over 85s will double (from 1.15 to 2.21 million).
- The growth in the 1980s and 1990s of scepticism about the welfare state. Thatcherite values encouraged people to seek individual, market-based solutions rather than collectivist ones. Long-term care in old age has always rested on a mix of private and public funding, with some people paying for themselves and others receiving state provision. But growing private affluence meant that expectations began to shift.
- However, private-sector solutions like long-term care insurance have proved insecure and expensive. It is unlikely that they could ever meet the needs of the majority.
- At the same time, public provision also seems increasingly uncertain. There is a widespread belief among the political classes that the population is no longer willing to pay the taxes needed to support the welfare state at a generous or universal level. In the past, tax has been used as a means of redistributing income over the lifecycle and between the generations. The political will to do this appears to have weakened.

- The shifting medical/social boundary. Healthcare has traditionally been provided free at the point of use. Social care, by contrast, has always been means-tested to some degree, so that most people are expected to pay all or part of the cost themselves. Long-term care over the last decade has effectively been transferred out of health and into social care. Hospitals no longer have long stay beds. Long-term care, even where it involves nursing, is increasingly defined as 'social care', and has to be paid for by individuals.

The payment regime resulted in a number of politically sensitive situations:

- Where an older person in residential care is forced, as in the United States, to 'spend down', using up most of their assets before they become eligible for state support. This means that they will not be able to pass on their savings or the value of their house to their children—something that the Thatcherite expansion of home ownership implicitly promised.
- The situation where one spouse goes into residential or nursing care but the other remains at home is insecure, with the possibility that the assets of the house and the pension will be required to fund the long-term care.
- Where someone wishes to remain at home, but has few resources other than the value of the house, and finds it difficult to fund their support. Reverse mortgages, whereby equity is released in advance of an eventual sale, are only offered on highly disadvantageous terms. Current charging regimes for home care are very variable. For example, someone with a weekly income of £115 and receiving twelve hours care per week could pay £13 in one area and £48 in another (Department of Health 1998).
- Where someone, for example with brain damage, is expected to fund the cost of nursing care despite the fact that it is 'healthcare' because it is provided in a social care setting (this anomaly was ended from 2001, when government agreed to pay for such nursing care).

In 1999 the Royal Commission on Long Term Care produced a divided report on the future funding of the sector. The Majority and Minority Reports can be seen as representing two opposing views of how society should approach the issue.

The Majority Report recommended that personal care element in long-term care should be made free for all deemed to need it. This should apply whether the person is living at home, in residential, or in nursing care. The rationale is that:

- Care in old age is just as much a public shared responsibility as healthcare. Indeed for older people, personal care represents a major aspect of their bodily healthcare needs. To refuse public finding for it is an implicit form of ageism. We do not take this attitude for example to maternity care.
- The welfare state is a form of social insurance for all. We pay in during our lifetime in order to be covered against the risks of old age. The need for personal care is one such risk. There is no need for private insurance in this area, and anyway, as we have seen, it is costly and uncertain.
- This represents a universalistic approach to the welfare state.

The Minority Report opposed such an extension of state support. The rationale was:

- It would be prohibitively expensive (they disputed the figures presented in the majority report).
- The net gainers would be the children of the better off, since the assets of their parents would no longer be eroded by care costs.
- It would cost a great deal and bring no new money into a sector that is already seriously underfunded. Better to spend the money on easing the terms under which public support is provided.
- This represents the classic means-tested basis for the welfare state in which people are expected to fund their care unless they are too poor to do so.

New Labour has broadly endorsed the Minority Report view, with the exception of personal care in nursing homes. In Scotland, however, the policy was overturned by the Scottish Parliament, which determined that all personal care should be funded by the state. Two payment regimes thus exist in parallel.

Direct payments

The disability movement has long advocated the replacement of care services by cash payments enabling disabled people to purchase their own assistance. Services in the state and voluntary sector, Morris and others argue, have too long been dominated by the interests and views of professionals, providing limited and patronizing services, with a rigid and over-complicated division of labour.

> When the allocation of resources was placed in the hands of social services organisations and those working for them, [professionals] chose to spend large sums of money on segregated provision—which meant that disabled people had to live restricted and impoverished lives that the professionals concerned would *never* have chosen for themselves. (Morris 1997: 59)

Giving money directly to disabled people frees them to exercise choice over the sort of help they receive, from whom and when. The preferred model within the disability movement is that of the personal assistant (PA), employed and trained by the disabled person and directly accountable to them.

During the late 1980s, the state-financed Disabled Living Fund did provide some money on this basis, though its scope was limited and government was cautious about its extension (Kestenbaum 1996). By the mid-1990s, however, with the development of the purchaser/provider split, the use of direct payments began to be looked on with greater favour by policy-makers. Such payments fitted in with the emphasis on the mixed economy of care and the personal responsibility of individuals for their own care. The Community Care (Direct Payments) Act 1996 allowed local authorities to make direct cash payments to certain individuals under the age of 65 in lieu of the community care services that they had been assessed as needing. *Modernizing Social Services* notes the success of this model and signals the intention to extend it to those over 65.

Residential care

The great majority of older people continue to live at home—this applies even to severely incapacitated people, three to four times as many of whom live at home as do in institutions. Among the population of those aged 65–74 only about 1 per cent live in some form of institutional setting, whether residential or nursing home or hospital; and among those 85 and over, it is about 26 per cent (1994 figures by Laing quoted in Peace et al. 1997).

Certain factors increase the likelihood of going into residential care; living alone is one of the strongest predictors. Cognitive impairment, particularly dementia, is also associated with institutional care, and most residents in residential or nursing homes have some level of confusion, even if slight. Of those with severe cognitive impairment in the general population, about one third are estimated to live in residential or nursing homes (note this means that about two-thirds do not).

Since the 1960s, government policy has endorsed community care as the preferred option, and research supports the view that the overwhelming majority of older people would prefer to stay in their own homes. For those who do go into residential care, it is rarely a positive choice: most make the transition perforce, and few are consulted or have the opportunity to review the options or the provision (Allen et al. 1992). Hospital discharge is often a point of transition when older people move into residential care. Families play a key role in initiating and negotiating the transition; equally, they can play an important role in enabling the older person to remain at home. Carer breakdown or withdrawal is an important cause of institutionalization.

Residential care raises issues about the wider treatment of older people in society. As Peace and her colleagues argue:

> if social policy is one of the important ways in which society is both constructed and managed, then residential care for older people, as a form of social policy, shapes attitudes towards and beliefs about older people and old age. (Peace et al. 1997: 69)

This view is particularly associated with the work of Peter Townsend:

> residential homes for the elderly serve functions for the wider society and not only their inmates. While accommodating only a tiny percentage of the elderly population they symbolise the dependence of the elderly and legitimate their lack of access to equality of status. (Townsend 1986: 32)

The expansion of private residential care in the 1980s

Despite the long-established policy of supporting community rather than residential provision for older people, the 1980s saw an astonishing expansion of residential care funded by the public purse. This was caused by changes in the regulations that allowed social security to meet the costs of private residential care for older people who had very limited personal means. Previously only the better-off could choose to go into a private residential home; those without means had to rely on local authority provision, which was scarce and required an assessment of care needs. Now individuals could choose to enter a private facility and the state would pay. There was no cap on the budget. From about £6 million in 1978, the cost to social security rose to £200 million by 1984, peaking in 1993 at £2,500 million (Peace et al. 1997).

Though the policy that lay behind the extension was unclear (and probably unintended), once embarked upon it was hard to stop, partly because it appeared to be popular with the public, and partly because it was linked to the Thatcherite projects of privatization and support of small businesses. Private residential homes were classic family businesses, typically started by a nurse with her/his partner in a large house bought with a mortgage or family savings. Profitability was closely linked to the capital and property markets, and availability was uneven geographically, clustered in decaying resort towns and other places where property was cheap.

The NHS and Community Care Act 1990 capped the open-ended commitment. Since 1993 local authorities have had the responsibility for assessing an individual's need for care and for contributing to the purchase of appropriate provision. Hard-nosed purchasing by local authorities has driven down the prices that home owners are able to charge, to the limits of profitability. This, together with the increasing raft of requirements imposed by the new national minimum standards for care homes (Department of Health 2000), have led many owners to leave the sector. Nonetheless population pressure, the availability of public financial support, and possibly the rationing of home care services have supported a continuing rise in the numbers of local-authority supported residents in residential and nursing homes (Fig. 15.1)

Sheltered housing

Sheltered housing is sometimes presented as a preferable alternative to residential care. Encouraged in the 1960s partly in reaction against the bleak care regimes revealed in Townsend's classic study of 1962 *The Last Refuge*, which showed how poorly postwar old people's homes had lived up to Bevan's dream of hotel-style accommodation for all classes. It has expanded greatly in the decades that followed, so that by the late 1980s it accommodated nearly five per cent of older people (Mackintosh et al. 1990). Very sheltered housing or close care, with meals and care facilities on the premises, has been a recent area of growth, particularly in the private sector.

Sheltered housing has been criticized by for not being the panacea that is sometimes suggested. Social care needs, Butler et al. (1983) argued, can be provided in the original home of the older person and do not require a move to sheltered housing, which largely

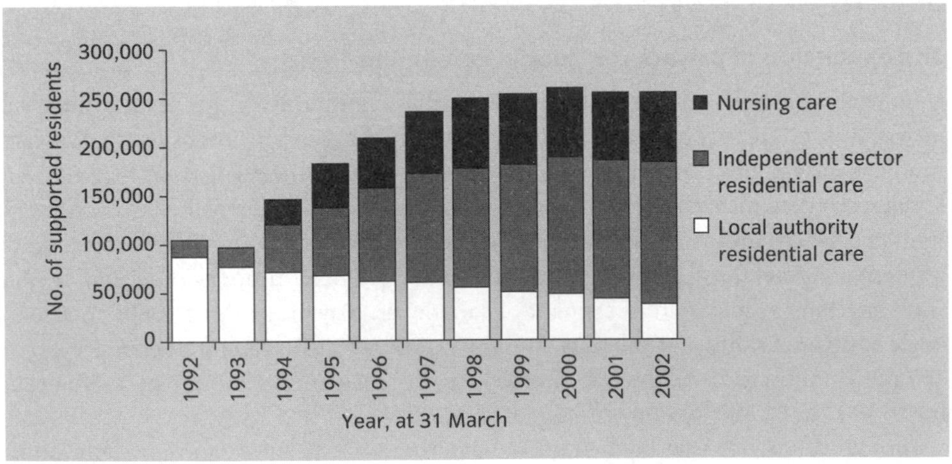

Figure 15.1 Local authority-supported residents by type of accommodation

Source: Department of Health (2002).

solves a housing rather than a social need (many older people are poorly housed). There is little evidence that sheltered housing alleviates loneliness, and it can reinforce a ghetto mentality towards the old. Although people in sheltered housing receive more domiciliary care than those at home (largely as a result of the proactive work of wardens), sheltered housing does not appear to prevent eventual admission to residential care. It is, however, widely popular with families, who value the security it offers.

MENTAL HEALTH PROBLEMS AND SOCIAL CARE

Mental health is an area in which terminology, definition, and understanding are all contested. Within the medical model, mental illness is a condition that can, like any other illness, be diagnosed and classified according to objective symptoms and measurable criteria. It is treated or managed by a medical approach in which physical treatments like drugs (and in the past ECT) play a central role. This mental illness model is most commonly applied to psychotic conditions like schizophrenia or severe depression. Opposed to this is an alternative interpretation that stresses the subjective and meaningful nature of mental health problems, which are regarded as the product of interpersonal, social, and environmental pressures, and as existing on a continuum with the ordinary difficulties of life. This approach is most commonly applied to neurotic disorders like depression, obsessional behaviour, or substance abuse. Some who espouse this second model go beyond looking for social factors in the causation of mental health difficulties to deny the existence of mental illness itself, regarding it as a social construct, the product of medical discourse or other forms of social **labelling**. This view is most commonly associated with the anti-psychiatry movement of the 1960s and the work of R. D. Laing, D. G. Cooper, and, from a different perspective, Thomas Szasz. Most current writers and practitioners adopt a mixed position, accepting some elements of the illness model, at least in relation to schizophrenia, at the same time as recognizing the importance of the subjective experience of difficulties and of social and environmental factors in the causation and exacerbation of mental health problems.

Prevalence of mental health problems

These can broadly be divided into **psychotic** conditions, such as schizophrenia, where the individual lacks insight into his/her condition and where grasp of reality is significantly disturbed (hearing voices, visions), and **neurotic** conditions, such as depression and anxiety where the individual remains broadly in touch with reality, although distressed. Estimates of prevalence suggest that about one in seven adults aged 16–64 living in the community have some sort of neurotic health problem (Fig. 15.2). For those with functional psychosis (schizophrenia, manic depressive psychosis, and schizo-affective disorders) the rates are four per 1,000, though this needs to be supplemented to include those living in long-stay institutions. Alcohol dependency is estimated at 47 per 1,000, and drug dependency 22 per 1,000 (Meltzer et al. 1995).

Environmental factors greatly increase the risk of mental ill health. Stress, loss, and social isolation, together with a variety of social and economic pressures, all contribute.

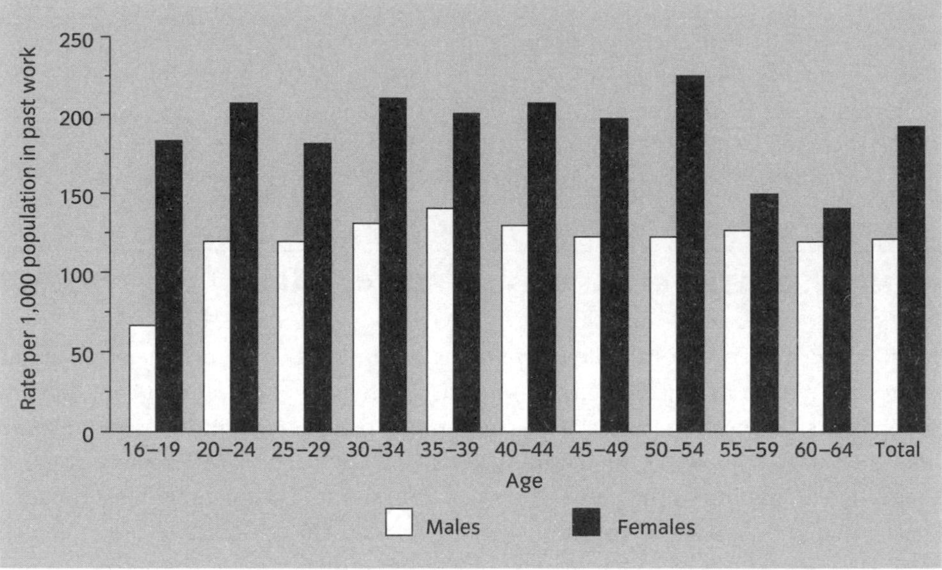

Figure 15.2 Prevalence of any neurotic disorder by sex and age, Great Britain, 1993–1994 (adults aged 16–64; includes anxiety, depression, phobias, panic disorder)

Source: ONS (1995).

For example:

- Anxiety and depression are much more common in separated, widowed, and divorced people.
- Children who are cared for away from home have much higher rates of mental health problems.
- Rates of depression are highest among the unemployed.
- Among those sleeping rough or in night shelters, or in prison, rates of mental illness are very high.
- Depression is increasing among young people in particular. (Department of Health 1999)

In addition, various forms of dementia, including Alzheimer's, are associated with ageing, and differ from other psychiatric problems in that they have an unequivocal physical base in the form of organic deterioration of the brain. Although they are managed within the psychiatric (often psycho-geriatric) service, they are usefully considered in terms of the general difficulties of older people.

Gender and mental health

The links between women and madness have received much attention. Writers like Showalter (1987) and Ussher (1991) have focused on the cultural representations of madness, exploring the ways in which women have been presented as unstable, irrational, nearer to madness than the 'rational' dominant male. They point to the preoccupation in this essentially misogynistic discourse with women's physiology—reproduction,

Box 15.5 Mental health professionals

- *Psychiatrists* are medical doctors who have specialized in mental illness. They emphasize an illness model and drug-based treatment, though many now operate in an eclectic way. They work predominately with more severe cases.
- *Clinical psychologists* are not medical doctors, but have an academic background in psychology, augmented by a professional training. Their practice varies, but many use either *behavioural approaches* in which the aim is to modify outward behaviour (rather than inner thoughts or feelings) through the use of incentives such as token economies within hospitals or self-generated rewards, or *cognitive approaches*, where the aim is to modify maladaptive thought processes, for example irrational negative ideas about yourself or life that may support depression.
- *Psychoanalysts* draw on the work of Freud and Jung and stress the role of the unconscious mind and the experiences of childhood in the formation of later difficulties. Analysis centres on talking, and may last for several years. The majority of analysts are in private practice.
- *Psychotherapists* also use talking as the core of their practice, but their involvement tends to be shorter and more focused on particular forms of change in the patient's life. They draw on a variety of approaches, including psychoanalysis, and many are influenced by the humanistic psychology of Carl Rogers or by Eric Berne's Transactional Analysis. They practice in a variety of settings.
- *Approved social workers (ASW)* have a statutory role in relation to compulsory admission to hospital under the Mental Health Act 1983. Their practice is based on the techniques of social work.
- *Community psychiatric nurses (CPNs)* are psychiatric nurses who are based in the community. They sometimes operate an outreach service from the hospital.

sexuality—as the key to their mental instability. Hysteria becomes the metaphor for all that is ungovernable and threatening in women. As with other radical critiques, definitions of madness are seen as based on value judgements and prescriptions of normality that support existing power structures, in this case those of **patriarchy**. Anger, misery, and frustration are recast and re-experienced as illness and depression.

Women appear to suffer more from mental health problems than men. They are more likely to be admitted to a psychiatric ward, to be prescribed psychotropic drugs for depression and anxiety, to consult a GP for minor mental health problems, or identify themselves as having such in community surveys. This greater tendency to mental health problems applies, however, only to depression and anxiety: the rate for schizophrenic-type illness is the same for men and women (Meltzer et al. 1995).

Some writers explain this pattern in terms of women's socialization into dependence and passivity, resulting in behaviour that turns inwards as depression or self-harm rather than outwards as anger. Others such as Payne (1991) point to material and social factors, for example women's greater likelihood to be in poverty or a lone parent. Being at home

Box 15.6 Brown and Harris and the social origins of depression

Brown and Harris's study of working-class women in London in the early 1970s identified four factors that made women vulnerable to depression: (1) loss of the mother before the age of 11, (2) presence at home of three or more children under 14, (3) absence of a confiding relationship, particularly with a husband, and, (4) the lack of a full- or part-time job. The study was important and influential because of the evidence it gave for the *social* origins of depression, and for its identification—despite not being in any sense a feminist study—of features of traditional domesticity as detrimental to women's mental health. It also has implications for intervention. As some feminists have pointed out, if the sources of vulnerability are being at home with children, what is needed is support with childcare, not a prescription for Valium. The identification of the lack of a close relationship was also important in relation to arguments put forward by Eichenbaum and Orbach (1983) that women within traditional gender relations suffer from lack of nurture: men look to and receive emotional support from women but are not socialized to give it in return.

with a young child and without a job is, as Brown and Harris showed, associated with depression. There is some evidence of a closing of the gender gap in recent years, again pointing to the significance of social factors such as labour market participation.

Men, by contrast, suffer more from problems of alcohol and substance abuse. They are also three times more likely than women to commit suicide; and young men are especially at risk (Fig. 15.3). Suicide is the second most common cause of death for those under 35, and young men are thirty times more likely to die as a result of suicide rather than AIDS or heroin.

Race and mental health services

People from ethnic minorities (including the Irish) are overrepresented in psychiatric admissions. Afro-Caribbeans are detained under the Mental Health Act 1983 at a rate two and a half times that of the local white population (Rogers and Pilgrim 1996). The pattern in relation to people of Asian decent is mixed, with evidence of both greater and lesser involvement (Bhui and Christie 1996).

Some psychiatrists argue that this pattern is a reflection of higher rates of mental illness in certain populations, and some—contentiously—have suggested a genetic link with schizophrenia. Others point to the impact of poverty, deprivation, and the social difficulties—including pervasive racism—that black people face. Such commentators have also explored the racial stereotypes that lie behind the differential responses of mental health workers including doctors, in which black people are presented as threatening. Once within the orbit of psychiatry, black people do appear to be treated differently. They are more likely to be given major tranquillizers or antidepressants, more often as an injection, in higher doses, and accompanied by less in the way of psychotherapy or counselling (Bhui and Christie 1996). The context in which black people receive treatment is thus a highly coercive one, and there are parallels with their treatment in the criminal justice system, where there is a similar pattern of overrepresentation and of harsh and punitive treatment:

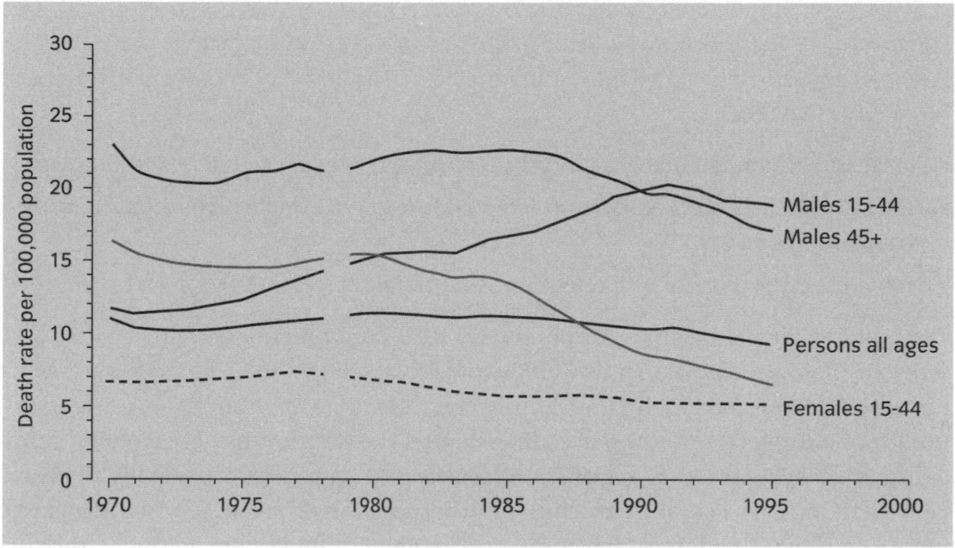

Figure 15.3 Standardized mortality rates from suicide and undetermined injury by age and sex, England, 1969–1996 (three-year average rates; each age group has been separately age standardized, i.e. adjusted for differences in the age structure of the population)

Source: ONS Mortality Statistics (ICD E950–E959, E980–E999 less E988.8).

psychiatry forms part of a larger social control mechanism which regulates and oversees the lives of black people. Since black people, particularly young black men, are over-represented in all parts of the criminal justice system, both the 'criminalisation' and 'medicalisation' of black people may be closely connected processes. (Rogers and Pilgrim 1996: 139)

Not surprisingly therefore, many black people fear and mistrust mental health services and seek to avoid contact (Sainsbury Centre for Mental Health 2002).

The closure of the asylum

In the 1950s and 1960s policy shifted away from the long-stay hospital in favour of community care. The gaunt Victorian asylums, isolated and custodial, no longer seemed appropriate places in which to treat or care for people with mental health problems. New drugs played a part by controlling people's behaviour, though their role has been exaggerated (Rogers and Pilgrim 1996). Long-stay hospitals were increasingly perceived to be expensive and oppressive; and there was a growing desire in psychiatry to reposition acute psychiatric services with other acute specialisms on the main hospital site. Though the policy of running down the long-stay hospitals was established in the 1960s, it was not until the 1980s that the process of closure got under way. Between 1980 and 1990 thirty-five large long-stay hospitals were closed, and the process accelerated through the 1990s (Rogers and Pilgrim 1996).

Care in the community

Hospital closure was meant to be accompanied by the building up of mental health services in the community. This did not always happen. The gains from the sale of hospital sites and the closure of long-stay beds were not always realized, and resources were allowed to leach across into the acute hospital sector. As a result, mental health services have remained underfunded and under pressure. The problem is particularly acute in inner city areas where:

- Social and environmental conditions support high rates of mental health problems.
- There are inadequate numbers of acute beds, often through closure (particularly a problem in London).
- Problems of the recruitment, retention, and morale of staff are endemic.

The issue of mental health and community care was brought before the public by a series of high-profile cases in the 1990s involving killings (the Clunis case) or other bizarre behaviour (one man climbed into the lions' cage at London zoo). These produced something of a **moral panic**. In response, the Conservative government introduced in 1994 **supervisory registers** to identify and keep track of mentally ill people who were most at risk to themselves or others and, in 1996, **supervised discharge** for patients who had at some point been compulsorily detained. Under this the supervisor—usually the key worker—can require the patient to live in a particular place and to attend for treatment (Department of Health 1996).

Reflecting these concerns, the New Labour Secretary of State for Health, Frank Dobson, in 1999 stated:

> Care in the community has failed because, while it improved the treatment of many people who were mentally ill, it left far too many walking the streets, often at risk to themselves and a nuisance to others. A small but significant minority have been a threat to others or themselves. (Department of Health 1999: 6)

It is important in this context to emphasize that care in the community can be, and remains, a successful policy for many. As the Audit Commission report argued, it is, and can be, cost-effective, and is greatly preferred by users and families (Audit Commission 1994).

New Labour strategy for mental health

This is outlined in *Modernizing Mental Health Services: Safe, Sound and Supportive* (Department of Health 1999). Its emphasis reflects the public safety concerns of the previous decade. It focused on four areas in particular.

- Improving links between health and social care services. In line with other developments at the health/social care interface, the government has encouraged the growth of partnerships in commissioning and of multi-disciplinary teams.
- Assertive outreach. This is a more active approach to treatment and care among people with mental illness, who are typically hard to engage because of their negative experiences of statutory services. The approach is characterized by work with clients in their own environment. Staff expect to see their clients frequently and to stay in contact, however difficult that may be. They aim to build up a relationship of trust that can deliver an individually tailored package of health and social care. Assertive outreach workers sometimes work together in a dedicated team, or they can be specialists working out of a generic community mental health team (Sainsbury Centre for Mental Health 2001).

- Treatment in the community. The transfer to community care has raised issues around treatment, or rather exposed ones that had previously been hidden. While patients were living in hospital, it was relatively easy to cajole or force them into receiving medication, and they could if necessary be legally required to do so. But once they were transferred to the community, the lack of legal sanction became apparent. Concerns were raised over patients, typically those diagnosed with schizophrenia, who failed to take or refused their medication. The public order emphasis was prominent: *Modernizing Mental Health* states as the first guiding principle in this area that: 'the safety of the public is of prime concern' (p. 41). Legislative changes were proposed to ensure compliance with appropriate treatment.

  Critics have remained unhappy at this prospect of compulsory treatment. Rejecting medication and help can be a symptom of the mental illness, but this is not always so. Many psychiatric drugs have significant and unpleasant side-effects. They impair concentration and willpower, and their long-term prescription can cause brain damage, producing disfiguring voluntary movements of the body that are distressing and stigmatizing. People in the user movement in particular object to the impersonal and over-zealous manner in which drug therapy has often been applied, and they fear that compulsion in this area will be a substitute for genuinely supportive services.

- Compulsory detention. There are a small group of individuals with severe antisocial personality disorder who can present a danger to the public. Because they are not deemed mentally ill they do not come under the Mental Health Act 1983 and cannot be compulsorily detained. Psychiatrists are reluctant to be involved in their management. Where such individuals commit a crime they can be imprisoned, though they may eventually be discharged. In response to this, New Labour has proposed to create a new form of reviewable detention in cases of people with severe personality disorder who are considered to pose a grave risk to the public.

  The proposal has proved contentious among mental health professionals, who see it as a violation of human rights: these individuals have committed no crime, and will receive no treatment since they are not deemed mentally ill. They also see it as part of a worrying emphasis in government thinking on mental health problems as issues of social order rather than of individual health and wellbeing. Many feel that the government agenda is increasingly driven by populist fears that perpetuate negative stereotypes of mental illness.

LEARNING DISABILITIES AND SOCIAL CARE

Learning disabilities (previously termed 'mental handicap') are lifelong impairments, usually present from birth, involving incomplete development or damage to the brain or nervous system. In the past they were primarily defined in terms of level of IQ, but social development is increasingly recognized as significant, and some individuals with low IQ manage very successfully socially. There are about 210,000 people with severe learning disabilities in England and about 1.2 million with mild or moderate disabilities. Health and social services expenditure for adults with learning disabilities is about £3 billion per year (Department of Health 2002).

The vast majority of people with learning disabilities (89 per cent) live either with their families or in some form of independent supported accommodation. In the 1991 census, about 4 per cent lived in hospital and 6 per cent in community-based residential accommodation.

Normalization

The key concept informing service development in the last three decades has been normalization (Brown and Smith 1992). Originally developed in Scandinavia and extended in the United States through the work of Wolfensberger, normalization aims to ensure that people with learning disabilities share the same lifestyles and choices as non-disabled people. In the Scandinavian work this is rooted in ideas of social rights and citizenship; in Wolfensberger's it is related to sociological concepts of deviance and labelling, whereby people with learning disabilities are socially devalued and excluded (Emerson 1992).

According to the principles of normalization, people with learning disabilities should be integrated with the rest of society—using the same facilities, living in ordinary housing, taking part in social and community life. Their surroundings and clothes should not be marked out as different—second-best, shabby, or demeaningly childish. They should be allowed to progress through the lifecycle with all the normal expectations of adolescence, adulthood, and old age, including personal relationships, marriage, parenthood. The rhythm of the day, week and year, should be the same: getting up and going to bed, enjoying work, leisure, weekends, and holidays, just like other people.

In Wolfensberger's work particular emphasis is placed on **social role valorization**, whereby the negative and demeaning stereotypes projected onto disabled people by society are rejected and reversed through their positive involvement in socially valued activities. Wolfensberger has at times been criticized for a conservative emphasis on what is socially normative. This can involve a denial of individual choice. There is an authoritarian streak in his work: he is willing, for example, in the face of disabled people choosing a devalued option, to coerce them into taking the valued one. Individual choice is thus made secondary to challenging the social status of the devalued individual or group (Emerson 1992).

Within UK service development, O'Brien's reformulation of normalization has been widely influential (Box 15.7). This identifies five accomplishments that services should attempt to achieve (Emerson 1992).

Deinstitutionalization and community care for people with learning disabilities

Up until the 1960s, responses to people with learning disabilities were dominated by the Victorian asylum—large, grim, isolated institutions where people with learning disabilities were expected to spend the whole of their adult lives. Though a series of scandals in the 1960s and 1970s that exposed the squalid and neglectful conditions in these hospitals were the catalyst for change, the shift in policy away from institutions was part of a larger movement of **deinstitutionalization** and decarceration across Western societies (closures also took place in North America and Europe) that encompasses both mental illness and mental handicap hospitals.

Box 15.7 O'Brien's five service accomplishments

- Ensuring that service users are *present* in the community by supporting their actual presence in the same neighbourhoods, schools, workplaces, shops, recreational facilities, and churches as ordinary citizens.
- Ensuring that service users are supported in *making choices* about their lives by encouraging people to understand their situation and the options they face, and to act in their own interest both in small everyday matters and in such important issues as who to live with and what type of work to do.
- Developing the *competence* of service users by developing skills and attributes that are functional and meaningful in natural community environments and relationships
- Enhancing the *respect* afforded to service users by developing and maintaining a positive reputation for people who use the service by ensuring that the choice of activities, locations, forms of dress, and use of language promote the perception of people with leaning disabilities as developing citizens
- Ensuring that service users participate in the life of the community by supporting people's natural relationships with their families, neighbourhoods, and co-workers and, when necessary, widening each individual's network of personal relationships.

The policy of hospital closure only began to take effect in Britain in the 1980s with the Care in the Community Demonstration Projects, which aimed to transfer patients, many of whom had spent decades in hospital, to a new life in the community. Informed by the principles of the Ordinary Life report produced by the King's Fund in 1980, the care in the community strategy was as much about developing new models of community provision as about resettling ex-hospital patients. The new community-based models of care have been overwhelmingly popular with users.

The **Ordinary Life Movement** of the 1980s envisaged provision in small houses where individuals could choose their companions and use local faculties. Funding pressure in the 1990s, however, led to homes getting larger (ten to twenty-five residents), with the increasing use of centralized facilities like laundry and catering. The transfer of staff from hospital to the new community facilities reinforced this trend towards micro-institutions. Ward (1995) argues that the NHS and Community Care Act 1990, far from facilitating individually tailored responses as its rhetoric suggested, in fact undermined them. Competitive contracting reduced rather than encouraged innovative services.

At the same time as service planning moved in the direction of larger and more impersonal units, progressive thinking increasingly abandoned the concept of the group home in favour of **supported living**, whereby individuals choose where and how they live, with a range of supports built around those choices. Supported living separates housing from support—the agency is no longer the landlord—and allows for genuine exploration of how the individual would like to live his/her life and the assistance needed to enable this.

Much of the most effective service planning has been for those with less severe disabilities. One group who have posed problems for the new models of care have been those with

challenging behaviour. These are a diverse group: some with mild or borderline learning disability but diagnosed as mentally ill who may become involved with the criminal justice system through, for example, arson or sexual offences, others with profound difficulties who may injure themselves (head-banging) or behave in ways that pose a challenge to those that care for them. Thirty years ago such individuals were largely in long-stay hospitals. Now many remain living with their families, and this can impose considerable strains upon them, often made all the harder by the unwillingness of services to take them on. In many authorities the solution has been one of seeking specialist placements out of the area.

New Labour and learning disabilities

New Labour has signed its plans for learning disability in the 2001 White Paper *Valuing People*. It aims to give learning disabled people more choice and control over their lives. The key elements are:

- the development of person centred planning;
- the use of Direct Payments to facilitate this. Direct payments have proved successful in relation to people with learning disability, but only a small number have received them—216 in 2000. Government plans to ensure greater availability and take up, with mechanisms to support their use;
- the development of a national advocacy structure in collaboration with the voluntary sector;
- local partnerships, establishing Learning Disability Partnership Boards within the framework of Local Strategic Partnerships. Partnership Boards will be responsible for agreeing plans for the use of the flexibilities on spending created under the Health Act 1999.

Conflict with parents

The new approaches to service provision have at times run into conflict with parents and with organized parents groups who are influential lobbyists in some localities. Parents can be overprotective, and may underestimate the capacity of their child to develop into greater independence. In the past many people with learning disabilities remained in an enforced state of childhood, denied the expression of adult choice or of sexuality. Girls were particularly protected and limited.

For some parents, however, the issue is less one of their child's capacity or potential than of the capacity of service provision. Many parents have had a long 'career' in which social workers and models of care have come and gone (Twigg and Atkin 1994). They can be particularly anxious about securing the future of their offspring, especially beyond their own life, and many lack confidence in the stability of the new services and the agencies that provide them. This is one of the reasons why parents are often attracted to the village community model. These seem to offer an enduring and, above all, safe environment. That they are also isolated, segregated, and that they assume that the countryside is the preference of all, is to them of lesser consideration.

Parents have lost out in the new models in terms of respite. Weekday attendance at a specialist day centre (the old ATCs, Adult Training Centres) did at least offer regular relief to parents, which might also allow them to engage in paid work. The new forms of day provision, using for example the local swimming pool or adult education centre, are more individually tailored and flexible, but they do not offer the same secure respite for parents. For some progressive service providers that idea of respite is itself suspect, suggesting an improper focus on the interests of the parents rather than the disabled person. For those looking after someone with severe challenging behaviour, however, regular respite may be vital to their ability to continue caring.

Abuse

One of the central anxieties expressed by parents concerns abuse. Though this can be a symptom of the overprotectiveness of parents, and while there is no evidence that individuals are more at risk in the new models of service provision, research has revealed that people with learning disabilities are exposed to alarming levels of physical and sexual abuse. Hilary Brown's work estimated that there are about 900 new reported cases a year. Men and women are both at risk, and abusers are mostly men known to their victims—other service users, family members, and staff. It is not a question of stranger danger. Prosecution is rare. It has often proved difficult to persuade the courts to accept the evidence of people with learning disabilities, and so far too little attention has been given to supporting victims through the criminal justice system.

In 2000 the government issued national guidance, *No Secrets*, on developing multi-agency strategies to combat abuse. This established a framework for joint action across local authority, health, police, and independent-sector services to protect vulnerable adults. Though most of the work on abuse has centred on people with learning disability, and these implicitly remain the focus of the guidance, older people and people with mental health problems are also included. Abuse is understood as having a number of possible dimensions: physical, sexual, psychological, financial, neglect, or discrimination.

Self-advocacy

The growth of the self-advocacy movement, in which people with learning disabilities are encouraged and supported in expressing their views and preferences, has been the single most significant development of the last decade (Ward 1995). Through organizations like People First, users have increasingly been involved in service planning and purchasing. The 2001 White Paper *Valuing People* signals the intention of government to invest £1.3 million a year in developing advocacy services in partnership with the voluntary sector.

CONCLUSION

Since the 1960s, the field of social care has been dominated by a single policy, that of community care. This crosses all the client groups, and is advocated by all political parties. It commands wide public support (at least in relation to groups whom the public regard as unthreatening).

And yet the reality of community care is more fragile. Social care remains caught in a secondary relationship with medical and acute hospital provision. To a considerable degree, its services are defined against what the health services do. It has a residual quality, picking up the aspects of care not covered by the medical model. Social care never commands the same status as medical care. Politicians and the public have remained reluctant to recognize professional expertise in these areas, which are assumed to rest on merely common-sense knowledge. Community-based services may be praised in theory, but they are often starved of resources (this is particularly true of mental health services). Their character of being 'out there', provided in the privacy of people's own homes, makes them less visible to planners and policy makers. Services with a clear institutional base tend to have a higher profile in the minds of those who allocate resources. As a result, we have the paradox that although social care is governed by one relatively clear policy—community care—it remains one of the more unstable areas of social policy, subject to cuts and to short-term political change.

KEY LEGISLATION

Mental Health Act 1983: established the current arrangements for the compulsory detention of severely mentally ill people. It reflected a civil rights concern with what was seen as an overly medically dominated approach established by the 1959 Act. The 1983 Act introduced the Approved Social Workers (ASW) who have a role in compulsory detention. The act has been criticized for being overconcerned with detention and of little relevance to the needs of the majority of people with mental health problems who face considerable difficulties in living in the community.

NHS and Community Care Act 1990: this set up the reform of community care carried through in the nineties, introducing care management and giving primary responsibility for community care—lead agency status—to social services.

Carers (Recognition and Services) Act 1995: gave carers the right within community care to a separate assessment of their needs. It was strengthened in the Carers and Disabled Children Act 2000.

Disability Discrimination Act 1995: places requirements on service providers (businesses and organizations). Since 1996 it has been unlawful for them to treat disabled people less favourably than others; since 1999 it required them to make adjustments for disabled people such as providing extra help or making changes to the way they provides services; from 2004 they will have to make reasonable adjustment to physical features of premises to overcome physical barriers to access.

Community Care (Direct Payments) Act 1996: permitted local authorities to make direct cash payments to individuals under 65 in lieu of the community care services that they had been assessed as needing.

Health Act 1999: introduced new partnership flexibilities particularly in relation to finance to enable health authorities and councils to improve services at the interface of health and social care.

Care Standards Act 2000: created the National Care Standards Commission (NCSC), an independent non-government public body to regulate social and health care services previously regulated by local councils and health authorities. It extended the scope of regulation to domiciliary care agencies and foster agencies.

REFERENCES

Arber, S., and Ginn, J. (1991), *Gender and Later Life: A Sociological Analysis of Resources and Constraints*. London: Sage.

—— —— (eds.) (1995), *Connecting Gender and Ageing: A Sociological Approach*. Buckingham: Open University Press.

Audit Commission (1994), *Finding a Place*. London.

Bhui, K., and Christie, Y. (1996), *Purchasing Mental Health Services for Black Communities*. London: HMSO.

Brown, G., and Harris, T. (1978), *The Social Origins of Depression*. London: Tavistock.

Brown, H., and Smith, H. (1992) *Normalisation: A Reader for the Nineties*, London: Routledge.

Bury, M. (1995), 'The body in question', *Medical Sociology News* 21(1): 36–48.

Butler, A., Oldman, C., and Greve, J. (1983), *Sheltered Housing for the Elderly*. London: Allen & Unwin.

Bytheway, B. (1995), *Ageism*. Buckingham: Open University Press.

Challis, D. J., and Davis, B. P. D. (1986), *Case Management: An Evaluated Experiment in Home Care of the Elderly*. Aldershot: Gower.

Central Statistical Office (1995), Social Trends.

Department of Health (1996), *Building Bridges: A Guide to the Arrangements for Inter-Agency Working for the Care and Protection of Severely Mentally Ill People*. London: HMSO.

—— (1998), *Modernizing Social Services: Promoting Independence, Improving Protection and Raising Standards*. London: HMSO.

—— (1999), *Modernizing Mental Health Services: Safe, Sound and Supportive*, London: HMSO.

—— (2001), *National Service Framework for Older People*. London: Stationery Office. Also available at: http://www.doh.gov.uk/nsf/olderpeople.htm#docs

—— (2000), *No Secrets: Guidance on developing and implementing multiagency policies and procedures to project vulnerable adults from abuse*, London: Stationary Office.

—— (2002), *Statistical Bulletin* 2002/19. London: Department of Health.

Eichenbaum, L., and Orbach, S. (1983), *What Do Women Want?* London: HarperCollins.

Emerson, E. (1992), 'What is normalisation?' In H. Brown and H. Smith (eds.), *Normalisation: A Reader for the Nineties*. London: Routledge.

Finch, J., and Mason, J. (1993), *Negotiating Family Responsibilities*. London: Routledge.

Graham, H. (1983), 'Caring: a labour of love'. In J. Finch and D. Groves (eds.), *A Labour of Love: Women, Work and Caring*. London: Routledge.

Green, H. (1988), *Informal Carers: A Study Carried out on Behalf of the Department of Health and Social Security as part of the 1985 General Household Survey*. London: HMSO.

Hochschild, A. (1983), *The Managed Heart: The Commercialisation of Human Feelings*. Berkeley: University of California Press.

Hooyman, N. R. (1990), 'Women as caregivers of the elderly'. In D. E. Biegel and A. Blum (eds.), *Aging and Caregiving: Theory, Research and Policy*. London: Sage.

Hughes, B., and Paterson, K. (1997), 'The social model of disability and the disappearing body: toward a sociology of impairment', *Disability and Society* 12(3): 325–40.

James, N. (1989), 'Emotional labour: skill and work in the social regulation of feelings', *Sociological Review* 1: 15–42.

Kestenbaum, A. (1996), *Independent Living: A Review*. York: Joseph Rowntree Foundation.

King's Fund Centre (1980), *An Ordinary Life: Comprehensive Locally-Based Residential Services for Mentally Handicapped People*. London: King's Fund.

Korman, N., and Glennerster, H. (1990), *Hospital Closure: A Political and Economic Study*. Buckingham: Open University Press.

Lewis, J., and Glennerster, H. (1996), *Implementing the New Community Care*. Buckingham: Open University Press.

Mackintosh, S., Means, R., and Leather, P. (1990), *Housing in Later Life: The Housing Finance Implications of an Ageing Society*. Bristol: School of Advanced Urban Studies.

Mansell Report (1993), *Services for People with Learning Disabilities and Challenging Behaviour or Mental Health Needs*. London: HMSO.

Marshall, M. (ed.) (1990), *Working with Dementia*. Birmingham: Venture Press.

Meltzer, H., Gill, B., Petticrew, M., and Hinds, K. (1995), *OPCS Surveys of Psychiatric Morbidity in Great Britain, Report I: The Prevalence of Psychiatric Morbidity among Adults Living in Private Households*. London: Office of Population, Censuses and Surveys.

Mental Health Foundation (1996), *Building Expectations: Opportunities and Services for People with a Learning Disability*. London: HMSO.

Morris, J. (1991), *Pride against Prejudice: Transforming Attitudes Towards Disability*. London: Women's Press.

—— (1997), 'Care or empowerment? A disability rights perspective', *Social Policy and Administration* 31(1): 54–60.

Nolan, M., Grant, G., and Keady, J. (1996), *Understanding Family Care*. Buckingham: Open University Press.

Oliver, M. (1990), *The Politics of Disablement*. Basingstoke: Macmillan.

ONS (Office for National Statistics) (1995), *Psychiatric Morbidity Survey Report* 1. London: ONS.

—— (2000), *Mortality Statistics*. London: ONS.

Parker, G., and Clarke, H. (1997), 'Will you still need me, will you still feed me. Paying for care in old age', *Social Policy and Administration* 31(2): 119–35.

Payne, S. (1991), *Women, Health and Poverty*. Hemel Hempstead: Harvester Wheatsheaf.

Peace, S., Kellaher, L., and Willcocks, D. (1997), *Re-evaulating Residential Care*. Buckingham: Open University Press.

Qureshi, H., and Walker, A. (1989), *The Caring Relationship: Elderly People and their Families*. Baskingstoke: Macmillan.

Rogers, A., and Pilgrim, D. (1996), *Mental Health Policy in Britain*. Basingstoke: Macmillan.

Rowlands, O. (1998), *Informal Carers: An independent study carried out by the Office for National Statistics on behalf of the Department of Health as part of the 1995 General Household Survey*. London: Stationery Office.

Royal Commission on Long Term Care (1999), *With Respect to Old Age: A Report by the Royal Commission on Long Term Care*. Cm 4192. London: Stationery Office.

Russell, D. (1995), *Women, Madness and Medicine*. Cambridge: Polity Press.

Sainsbury Centre for Mental Health (2000), Breaking the Circles of Fear: A Review of the Relationship between the Mental Health Services and African and Carribbean Communities, London: SCMH.

Showalter, E. (1987), *The Female Malady*. London: Virago.

Thornicroft, G., and Strathdee, G. (1996), *Commissioning Mental Health Services*. London: HMSO.

Townsend, P. (1962), *The Last Refuge*. London: Routledge.

—— (1986), 'Ageism and social policy'. In C. Phillipson and A. Walker (eds.), *Ageing and Social Policy: A Critical Assessment*. Aldershot: Gower.

Twigg, J. (1989), 'Models of carers: how do social care agencies conceptualize their relationship with informal carers?', *Journal of Social Policy* 18(1): 53–66.

—— (2000), *Bathing: The Body and Community Care*. London: Routledge.

—— and Atkin, K. (1994), *Carers Perceived: Policy and Practice in Informal Care*. Buckingham: Open University Press.

Ungerson, C. (1987), *Policy is Personal: Sex, Gender and Informal Care*. London: Tavistock Press.

—— (1997), 'Give them the money: is cash a route to empowerment?', *Social Policy and Administration* 31(1): 45–63.

Ussher, J. M. (1991), *Women's Madness: Misogyny or Mental Illness*? Hemel Hempstead: Harvester Wheatsheaf.

Walker, A., and Phillipson, C. (1986), 'Introduction'. In C. Phillipson and A. Walker (eds.), *Ageing and Social Policy: A Critical Assessment*. Aldershot: Gower.

Ward, L. (1995), 'Equal citizens: current issues for people with learning difficulties and their allies'. In Ward and Ward (1995).

—— and Ward, T. (eds.) (1995), *Values and Visions: Changing Ideas in Services for People with Learning Difficulties*. Oxford: Butterworth-Heinemann.

FURTHER READING

S. Arber and J. Ginn (eds.), *Connecting Gender and Ageing: A Sociological Approach* (Buckingham: Open University Press, 1995).

H. Brown and H. Smith (eds.), *Normalisation: A Reader for the Nineties* (London: Routledge, 1992).

J. Campbell and M. Oliver, *Disability Politics: Understanding Our Past, Changing Our Future* (London: Routledge, 1996).

C. Gilleard and P. Higgs, *Cultures of Ageing: Self, Citizen and the Body* (Harlow: Longman, 2000).

J. Lewis and H. Glennerster, H., *Implementing the New Community Care*. Buckingham: Open University Press, 1996).

S. Peace, L. Kellaher, and D. Willcocks, *Re-evaluating Residential Care* (Buckingham: Open University Press, 1997).

A. Rogers and D. Pilgrim, *Mental Health Policy in Britain* (Basingstoke: Macmillan, 1996).

Twigg, J., *Bathing: The Body and Community Care* (London: Routledge, 2000).

L. Ward and T. Ward (eds.), *Values and Visions: Changing Ideas in Services for People with Learning Difficulties* (Oxford: Butterworth-Heinemann, 1995).

USEFUL WEBSITES

Department of Health: www.doh.gov.uk particularly the Social Care Section at

www.doh.gov.uk/cos/index.htm

Sainsbury Centre for Mental Health: www.scmh.org.uk

GLOSSARY

bed blocking The process whereby discharge from hospital is delayed resulting in the occupancy of a hospital bed by someone not directly in need to it. A health services biased term: delayed discharge preferred term in social care.

care management Introduced by the NHS and Community Care Act 1990, it involves a single worker—not necessarily a trained social worker—taking responsibility for assessing, commissioning, coordinating, and sometimes purchasing support for a client.

challenging behaviour Behaviour that challenges the resources of families or services. Particularly associated with learning disabilities, it can involve violent behaviour that threatens the physical safety of the person or those around them, or distressing and transgressive actions that limit access to ordinary community facilities.

community care The support of older and disabled people in the 'community', usually taken to mean their own homes, or in home-like provision. Defined in opposition to institutional care. Community care has been official policy since the 1960s, though its implementation has been variable.

deinstitutionalization The process of closure of large, long-stay institutions established to care for and contain old people, the mentally ill, and those with learning disabilities.

emotional labour The deployment of emotion as part of paid or unpaid work.

generic social work Provision by an individual worker or by a team of workers who use the common core skills of social work to help meet all forms of individual need. Originally seen as a means of providing a single door for all problems, it is now often considered inferior to specialist social work.

horizontal target effectiveness Term used in relation to service provision to evaluate the degree to which individuals in the target category receive the intervention. Contrasted with **vertical target effectiveness**.

informal carers People who give substantial amounts of practical and emotional help to frail or disabled people, usually members of their family on an unpaid basis. Often simply termed 'carers', the word 'informal' is used to distinguish them from paid carers working in the formal service sector.

invalid care allowance (ICA) Benefit available to people of working age who are out of the labour market. Set at a relatively low level, it represents neither full compensation for wages forgone nor payment for care. Few carers receive it, as it interacts with other benefits.

kin networks Networks of kin that extend beyond the nuclear family and include kin acquired by marriage as well as blood.

labelling A theoretical approach that suggests that people become deviant as a result of the social process of being labelled as such.

learning disabilities Lifelong impairments, usually present from birth, involving incomplete development or damage to the brain or nervous system. Previously referred to as 'mental handicap', and sometimes termed 'learning difficulties'.

moral panic Overreaction by media, police, and wider community to deviant acts that become amplified in their extent or significance.

mixed economy of welfare The way in which welfare is provided by a variety of agencies, including statutory, voluntary, for-profit, and informal (families and friends).

neurotic condition Mental health problems where the individual remains broadly in touch with reality, although distressed, for example, depression and anxiety.

new public management The application to public sector of management theory and techniques from the private sector, associated with Thatcherite reforms.

normalization Currently the guiding principle in relation to services for people with learning disabilities, but extended to other groups of disabled people, aiming to ensure that they share the same life styles and choices as non-disabled people.

Ordinary Life Movement Set of principles outlined in King's Fund Report of 1980 guiding development of services to people with learning disabilities whereby their lives should be enabled to follow as nearly as possible those of the rest of society.

patriarchy The dominace of men over women, usually understood as social rather than biological. The form that it takes varies greatly between differnt societies.

personal social services (PSS) Services provided to a range of clients by **social services**. At the national level they fall under the remit of the Department of Health.

political economy perspective Applied in particular to the situation of older people, it analyses inequalities in resources and life chances as resulting not from individual variation but from the power relations that structure society.

psychotic condition Mental illness where the individual lacks insight into his/her condition and where grasp of reality is significantly disturbed, for example schizophrenia.

quasi-markets Term used to describe the attempts in the 1980s and 1990s to introduce market mechanisms into public sector provision, replacing monolithic forms of service delivery by plural ones in which parts of public sector 'trade' with one another. The internal market in the NHS and the purchaser/provider split in social services are examples.

social model of disability Approach that emphasizes the ways in which disability is created not by impairments but by the expectations of society.

social role valorization Conscious attempt to ensure that negative and demeaning stereotypes projected onto disabled people are rejected through positive involvement in socially valued activities.

social services departments (SSDs) (also known as LASSDs: local authority social service departments) Established in 1971 to coordinate and provide a range of social care, both community-based and residential. Responsible for **personal social services (PSS)**, their main client groups are children and families, older and disabled people, people with learning disabilities, and, to a lesser degree, mental health problems. They also have a remit to support carers.

specialization In social work the tendency for workers to specialize in particular care groups such as children or people with learning difficulties; opposed to generic work.

supervised discharge Introduced in 1996 for certain patients detained at some point under the Mental Health Act 1983, whereby the supervisor—usually the key worker—can require the patient to live in a particular place and to attend for treatment.

supervisory registers Introduced in 1994 to identify and keep track of severely mentally ill people living in the community who are most at risk to themselves or others.

supported living Approach to service planning in which individuals with a disability are supported to live in the way that they choose rather than in specialized and dedicated provision.

Third Age A post-retirement period of extended middle age in which people who are no longer confined by the labour market and are free from direct responsibility for children can pursue leisure interests and enjoy the fruits of later life. The emergence of this new social space is often linked to theories about identity and selfhood in postmodernity, particularly ones that emphasize self-fashioning. It is open to critique that such optimistic accounts of the Third Age are only possible by virtue of projecting the negative aspects of ageing into a dark Fourth Age, a period of declining health and social loss, sometimes also termed 'deep' old age.

user Person in receipt of social services support, adopted in preference to the more traditional 'client' to reflect a less passive approach and one that emphasizes the importance of their interests and views.

vertical target effectiveness The degree to which individuals who receive the intervention fall within the target definition of need. Contrasted with **horizontal target effectiveness**.

work life balance The balance between the time and emotional energy given to work as opposed to family and leisure activities. The issue is particularly acute for women in employment and for households with children.

younger physically disabled (YPD) People with disabilities between the ages of 18 and retirement. Covers a range of conditions including those born with an impairment (e.g. spina bifida); those whose disability results from trauma (e.g. spinal injury); and those suffering from degenerative conditions (e.g. arthritis, heart disease).

16

The Care and Protection of Children

Derek Kirton

CONTENTS

INTRODUCTION: THE CHILD, THE FAMILY, AND THE STATE

As a public issue, the care and protection of children presents something of a paradox. For the most part it remains hidden and marginal, yet it has the emotive capacity to generate some of the most heated discussions in the field of welfare policy. Clearly, this applies especially to child protection—where 'scandal' may arise either from a perceived failure to protect or the 'unnecessary' removal of children from their homes—but also to matters such as the quality of residential care or the suitability of adopters. It might be argued that this situation reflects a deeper paradox within the treatment of children, where general social neglect can live cheek by jowl with self-righteous indignation when things go wrong.

This chapter will look at various aspects of 'the child care system' but it is perhaps appropriate at this point to highlight some of the key factors which help to shape it. The pivot around which the care and protection of children turns is the relationship between state and family. In principle the model is a fairly straightforward one, which sees child-rearing as primarily the responsibility of parents, with the state providing certain supports, setting out certain requirements, and playing a monitoring role. The state is essentially concerned with the question of whether **good enough parenting** is being provided. If not, it should intervene, either to ensure adequate care within the family or to provide alternative care for the child.

In practice, the model is rather more complex. Judgements of the adequacy of parenting raise questions as to whether there is a consensus on what is 'good enough' and what, to use the legal term, causes 'significant harm' to the child. Who is to make such judgements and upon what basis? When intervention does take place, how is the balance to be struck between offering support of various kinds to the family and effectively protecting the child? As we shall see, such matters are strongly influenced by views on the importance of the 'blood tie' between parents and children born to them. A related concern is how far the child's interests can be understood as separate from those of their family. Moves in recent decades to emphasize 'the rights of the child' imply a degree of separation which would have been unthinkable a century ago.

While the care and protection of children is generally perceived as a matter for those directly involved in working with families, it is also important to emphasize the wider social policy context. The focal point for debate is the well-established link between, on the one hand, problems such as child abuse, family breakdown, and youthful offending and, on the other, those of poverty, homelessness, ill health, and school exclusion. For some, this link points to the need for more extensive welfare provision, which by providing greater support to (poor) parents will help reduce the incidence of 'care and protection' issues. For others, the link is largely coincidental, the problems individual, and the need is for targeted intervention to change parental behaviour or to remove the children. Supporters of this position will highlight the fact that only a small minority of poor parents abuse their children, and argue that to suggest a link with poverty is an insult to the majority.

FOUNDATIONS OF THE MODERN CHILDCARE SYSTEM

Although its origins can be traced to the nineteenth-century activities of **child-savers** such as Thomas Barnardo and Mary Carpenter, the modern childcare system took shape following the Second World War. Responding to material and emotional problems associated with evacuation, and Sir Walter Monckton's report (1945) on the death through neglect and beatings of 13-year-old Dennis O'Neill at the hands of his foster carers, the Curtis Report (1946) led to the Children Act 1948 and the establishment of Children's Departments in local authorities. The new departments were significantly influenced by the work of John Bowlby on **maternal deprivation and attachment**, which focused on the importance for children of a consistent relationship with a nurturing figure.

Although the postwar era saw a growing interest in 'preventive' work (i.e. supporting families in order to avoid children requiring substitute care), a more immediate effect was the attempt to reform substitute care to ensure that it corresponded as closely as possible to a family model. This entailed both the promotion of foster care as the 'preferred option' (and one which had the additional merit of being cheaper) and the reform of residential care. In particular, there were efforts to move away from the large so-called 'barrack homes' (described by John Stroud as 'mouldering bastions'), which often accommodated up to 200 or more children, and appeared to embody all the problems of the institution. The drive to create more homely environments was typified by the **family group home**, with at most ten to twelve children, live-in houseparents, and the twin aims of stability and simulation of family life.

Children's departments expanded steadily during the postwar years before they were absorbed into the Social Services Departments (SSDs) in 1971 (see Holman 1996 for an interesting historical account of the Children's Departments). Local authority SSDs have remained central to the provision of child care, although in recent years some authorities have merged services to children and families with education departments with the aim of improving coordination. In 2000 there were an estimated 20,800 local authority social workers working with children and families, of whom roughly 95 per cent were qualified (Department of Health 2000a). Local authority expenditure on children and families totalled £2.9 bn in 1999–2000, representing 23 per cent of all social services expenditure (Department of Health 2000b).

Although the state is the dominant partner, childcare services do operate within a 'mixed economy of welfare'. There are many voluntary providers, including long-established national organizations such as the NSPCC (National Society for the Prevention of Cruelty to Children), Barnardo's, or NCH (National Children's Homes,

Action for Children,) and during the past decade there has been a sharp rise in private providers of foster and residential care.

PROTECTING CHILDREN

As was noted earlier, it is perhaps with issues of abuse and protection that childcare issues come most prominently under the public gaze. This tends to take the form, on the one hand, of death or serious injury which might have been prevented or, on the other, the 'unnecessary' removal of children. Within these scenarios, the professionals (most commonly social workers) are cast somewhat contradictorily, either as 'naive woolly liberals' or as behaving 'like the Gestapo'. Beyond creating what can appear to be a no-win situation for social workers, media coverage and public debate have also had important influences over policy and practice, as we shall see.

It is customary to trace the origins of modern child protection to the late nineteenth century, highlighting the formation of organizations such as the NSPCC in the 1880s and the first protective legislation dealing directly with parents, the Prevention of Cruelty to and Protection of Children Act 1889. The Act made cruelty, neglect, or abandonment of a child an offence, and gave powers for the court to remove the child and place them with another appropriate adult. While policy evolved quite gradually and unevenly, it is possible to locate its development within the context of changing views of childhood. During the nineteenth and much of the twentieth centuries, there was a progressive separation of children from the adult world, with childhood seen as a period of natural innocence and vulnerability, requiring long and careful socialization in readiness for the adult world. An increasingly protected status can be seen as part of this process.

The rediscovery of child abuse

Child abuse had concerned Victorian reformers such as Thomas Agnew and Ben Waugh, and was to an extent seen as having been dealt with by the legislation of that period. It re-emerged into the public domain in the 1960s as 'battered child (or baby) syndrome'. Numerous medical research studies, and especially the work of Dr Henry Kempe in the US, demonstrated (largely through the use of X-ray evidence) that injuries inflicted by parents on children were frequently going undetected. The use of the term 'syndrome' to describe both the patterns of injuries and parental behaviour was important in establishing a medical model (see below) for child abuse. Its principal effect was to heighten awareness of physical harm amongst the medical profession and child welfare agencies. In the UK, the work of the NSPCC's Battered Child Research Unit contributed significantly to a higher public profile during the 1970s, described by Moore (1985: 55) as 'the age of child abuse'. Arguably a greater influence arose from the death of Maria Colwell in 1973 and the public reaction to it. Seven-year-old Maria was returned to her mother and stepfather after several years with foster carers, and subsequently suffered extreme neglect before being battered to death by her stepfather. Parton (1985: 69–99) argues that Maria's death coincided with growing concern about violence in society and breakdown in law and order, permissiveness, and perceived decline in the family. Media coverage of the case saw the birth of the 'naive do-gooder' stereotype for social workers, and pressure rose for a more authoritarian approach to be taken towards child abuse. Formal measures included: the establishment of committees to coordinate policy and liaison between different agencies (now known as Area Child Protection Committees); the requirement that case conferences should be held to bring all professionals together to discuss individual children; tighter procedures for investigation; and the establishment of a register for children 'at risk' of abuse (now termed the Child Protection Register). Informally, there was pressure towards greater use of legal powers to remove children, and the 1970s saw a significant rise in compulsory removal of children from their homes. 'At the beginning of the decade over two-thirds were in care voluntarily and one-third on some sort of statutory order. . . . By 1980 only a quarter of children in care were not on some sort of statutory order' (Parton 1985: 125).

Child abuse inquiries and their consequences

Writing in the 1990s, Doyle (1997: 156–8) noted that since the death of Maria Colwell there had already been over forty formal inquiries into other child deaths; at the time that this chapter was written, one of the largest inquiries, into the death of Victoria Climbié, chaired by Lord Laming, had just reported (www.victoria-climbie-inquiry.org.uk). Its conclusions ('What transpired during this period can only be described as a catalogue of administrative, managerial and professional failure by the services charged with her safety') laid blame on management failures as well as individual Social work judgement. Throughout the period since the Colwell inquiry, the media stereotype of the ineffectual social worker has remained strong—neatly if cruelly captured in a *Daily Mirror* headline (16 January 1980), 'Malcolm Died as He Lived: Freezing Cold, Starving and Surrounded by Social Workers'. It is a matter of some debate as to how useful the many formal inquiries have been in improving child protection practice. In their favour, it can be argued that the death of a child provides the strongest possible force for change, adding weight to any recommendations and being more likely to enter the consciousness of child protection workers. On the other hand, it is questionable how representative any one case, however tragic, can be of practice in general. There is also a danger of hindsight—that *after* a child's death the circumstances leading up to it appear misleadingly 'obvious' (Frost and Stein 1989: 53). Worries have been expressed about the overwhelmingly bureaucratic measures which have been prompted by inquiries. 'In the final analysis, when the parents and children are talking alone with the worker, no amount of procedural guidelines will guarantee that the right things are said and done' (Jones et al. 1987: 66).

UNDERSTANDING CHILD ABUSE

Grasping the nature of child abuse—its causes and effects—is not merely of academic interest. Such knowledge has the potential to aid the prevention and detection of harm, and decision-making following abuse. Apart from assisting judgements made by welfare, legal, and medical professionals, insights into child abuse can also inform wider policy-making—for instance decisions about the use of resources, or cooperation between agencies. Effective understanding, however, is rendered difficult by a number of factors, perhaps the most important of which is definition.

Official classifications identify four categories of abuse: physical, neglect, sexual, and emotional. In the following section, we concentrate on physical abuse and neglect, while sexual abuse is dealt with in a later section. Although registrations for emotional abuse have risen significantly in recent years, there is as yet little in the way of relevant research, and hence emotional abuse will not be discussed in this brief overview.

If abuse sometimes appears self-evident—as in the case of serious injury or young children being left alone at home while their parents go on a fortnight's holiday—at other times it is much less so. One well-known example of this is smacking. For some, it is inherently 'abusive' and should be banned, while for others it is a requisite for effective child-rearing and should be used more widely. More generally, consensus is unlikely as to types and degrees of legitimate punishment, about age and duration for leaving children alone, their staying out, about suitable TV viewing, and so on. In deciding whether acts or practices constitute abuse, their seriousness, frequency, and likelihood of repetition must all be judged.

The prevalence of child abuse

As for any identified social problem, there is an inevitable interest in the scale of child abuse. Measures, however, will depend on both the definition used and the accuracy of the measurement. Official data tell us that in recent years there has been a steady fall in the number of children on the child protection registers, dropping from over 40,000 in the early 1990s to 26,800 (or 2.4 per 1,000 children) in 2001 (Department of Health 2001). Forty-eight per cent of registrations were for neglect, 28 per cent for physical abuse, 18 per cent emotional abuse and 17 per cent sexual abuse (percentages total more than 100 per cent as some children are registered under more than one category). Gibbon et al.'s study (for a useful summary see Department of Health 1995) provides a snapshot of this process and the various filters involved. The researchers found that during 1992 there were 160,000 child protection investigations, of which 40,000 (25 per cent) led to the convening of a case conference, and subsequently to 24,500 (15 per cent) additions to the child protection register. Only 4 per cent of cases investigated resulted in the child being removed from home under a legal order.

While official statistics give crucial insights into the operation of child protection services, their usefulness as a measure of abuse is more open to question. Research studies, often based on (young) adults' reports of their abuse as children, appear to show a markedly higher incidence of abuse (Cawson et al. 2000).

Child abuse may go unrecognized and unreported for a variety of reasons. Referral for investigation, which will usually be from teachers, health workers, neighbours, or police officers, requires both that the 'abuse' is known about and that someone regards it as sufficiently important to be reported. Passage through the various filters will then depend on the information available to professionals and the judgements they make.

A study by Dingwall et al., *The Protection of Children* (1983), gives valuable insights into the world of professional judgements. The authors contend that a **rule of optimism**, in effect the benefit of the doubt, is usually applied to the many situations where abuse might be suspected. This rule tends to be suspended mainly for one of two reasons: either where the parents are judged to be behaving inappropriately (including failure to co-operate with the professionals) or where those professionals directly involved feel that they must refer the matter outside their immediate circle, usually to higher authority.

Issues of policy and practice are also important in shaping whether and how (alleged) abuse is recorded. As in many areas of social policy, there are wide variations across local authorities (Department of Health 1995: 68). For example, different thresholds or workload pressures may mean that similar cases would be investigated in one authority but not in another. The wider policy context also exerts a powerful influence. Since the mid-1990s there has been a concerted effort to refocus childcare work, away from what was seen as a narrow concern with investigating child abuse towards a broader notion of assessing 'children in need'. The rationale for this shift was summarized in the Department of Health (1995) publication *Child Protection: Messages from Research*. Studies appeared to show that concentration on investigating alleged cases of abuse was deflecting attention from key questions of children's development and wellbeing. Investigations were often found to have traumatic effects for families, while in cases where abuse was not found, families tended to receive little in the way of supportive services, even where the child(ren)'s needs warranted them. Yet as Corby (2000: 59) warns, there are dangers that a more 'supportive' approach to families may leave children at greater risk of abuse from their parents, thereby highlighting one of the major tensions within child protection.

Child abuse and social inequality

Information drawn from child protection registers indicates that reported child abuse is overwhelmingly a phenomenon of poorer working-class families, and closely associated with factors such as unemployment and lone parenthood. Observing also an association with incidence of domestic violence and mental illness in families, the Department of Health report (1995: 25) concludes that 'it is the most vulnerable in our society who are most likely to become the object of a [child protection] enquiry'.

These associations have sparked considerable debate between those who take recorded abuse as an accurate measure and those who do not. Those who would question the statistics can point to a number of factors which may lead to underrepresentation of more affluent families. First, such families come to the notice of welfare agencies less frequently, as they are less likely to seek help or to become objects of professional concern. Second, they are more likely to benefit from the 'rule of optimism', because they are viewed as unlikely abusers and communicate more easily with middle-class professionals. Third, they may be better equipped to contest decisions.

No one would dispute that serious child abuse occurs in all social strata, and few would suggest that reporting and processing of abuse cases is entirely without bias. The key question is whether biases can account for the class differences in recorded abuse.

One who believes they cannot is Pelton (1985), who strongly attacks what he calls the **myth of classlessness**. Apart from what he describes as the consistent and overwhelming nature of the evidence linking abuse with poverty and deprivation, Pelton highlights three specific factors in support of his argument: first, that increased awareness and reporting has done nothing to diminish the class gap in recorded abuse; second, that even within classes, levels of abuse correspond with those of deprivation; third, that child abuse fatalities, which are extremely difficult to hide or disguise, also occur mainly in poor families. Gauging the 'real' incidence of abuse is always likely to remain elusive, but, as Pelton has argued, it is difficult to believe that abuse is evenly distributed throughout society. As to why the myth should exist, Pelton suggests that apart from well-meaning concerns not to 'label' poor families, the myth serves the interests of the psychological and helping professions, whose prestige gains from portraying abuse as a disease requiring their diagnosis and curative intervention. Recognizing abuse as a product of poverty would undermine such ambitions and raise awkward questions for politicians and policy-makers. Pelton's broad conclusion is supported by research commissioned by the NSPCC (Cawson et al. 2000) which found higher levels of self-reported abuse from those growing up in Social Classes 4 and 5. However, the study also found that abuse among higher socioeconomic groups was more likely to go unreported.

Child abuse, race, and ethnicity

Summarizing studies in the United States on associations between race and child abuse, Corby (2000: 108–10) notes that minority ethnic families are overrepresented in official child protection statistics. In the United Kingdom, there has been little research or ethnic monitoring and no clear pattern. The seeming absence of any ethnic differences within the UK in recorded levels of abuse may reflect the balancing out of two contradictory trends. Channer and Parton (1990: 110) observe how on the one hand Eurocentric norms may lead to 'inappropriate and heavy-handed treatment' and hence over-readiness to remove children. On the other, however, a belief in **cultural relativism**, the notion that 'cultural' norms and behaviours are equally valid and only to be understood by insiders, may lead workers to 'hesitate to intervene at all and hence put children from black families in real and serious dangers' (p. 111).

Theorizing child abuse: why does it happen?

Corby (2000: 130–55) provides an excellent review of the wide range of perspectives, drawn primarily from psychological and sociological theory, which have been used to cast light on the causes of child abuse. Within the professional mainstream, there has been considerable interest in developing profiles of at risk populations with a view to prediction. Checklists have been developed in order to identify parents most likely to abuse and children most likely to suffer abuse. A well-known example is provided by Greenland (1987), who lists high risk factors as shown in Box 16.1.

The quest for prediction is understandably controversial. Checklists clearly have the potential to improve the protection of children by alerting professionals and policy-makers to pertinent risk factors. Yet there are also dangers with the checklist approach. Listed factors may harden towards a stereotype, and lead to self-fulfilling prophecy, with

Box 16.1 Child abuse and neglect high-risk checklist

	Parents	*Child(ren)*
1	Previously abuse/neglected as a child	Previously abused/neglected
2	Age 20 or less at birth of first child	Under 5 at time of abuse/neglect
3	Single parent/separated Partner not biological parent	Premature/low birth weight
4	History of abuse/neglect or deprivation	Now underweight
5	Socially isolated, frequent moves, poor housing	Birth defect, chronic illness, developmental lag
6	Poverty, unemployed/unskilled worker, inadequate education	Prolonged separation from mother
7	Abuses alcohol and/or drugs	Cries frequently, difficult to comfort
8	History of criminal assault behaviour and/or suicide attempts	Difficulties in feeding and elimination
9	Pregnant, post-partum, or chronic illness	Adopted, foster or stepchild

abuse incorrectly identified among those who score highly on the list, and missed among those who do not.

Medical or social explanation?

The factor-based or checklist approach fits well with what is often termed the **medical model** of child abuse. Typified by the early references to a child-battering syndrome, the key assumptions implicit in the model are that abusive practices are symptoms of a disease, the causes of which must be diagnosed in order to effect a cure. The precise nature of the disease has numerous variants, depending upon the theoretical base utilized—e.g. attachment theory; the psychodynamic, behavioural, or cognitive schools of psychology; family-based theories (see Corby 2000: 132–44)—and the weight given to environmental factors. What is common to all is a relatively narrow focus on individual or family pathology, with external factors serving only as triggers, rather in the way that over-exertion may trigger a heart attack where there is already weakness. As with other medicalized social problems, a central role is given to the professionals in diagnosis and treatment, while their patients or clients are offered the **sick role** as an alternative to direct culpability.

A rather different approach is offered by the **social model** of abuse. Again, there are several variations (Corby 2000: 144–53), but their common ground rests with the claim that social analysis offers better prospects for understanding child abuse than does the individualized medical model. Two rather different strands can be detected within the social model. The first relates to sources of stress. Writers such as Pelton (1985), Gil (1970), and Parton (1985) have underscored the importance of poverty, unemployment, and housing problems, while the 'ecological' theories of Garbarino and others (see Parton 1985: 154–8 for discussion) have pinpointed the role of social isolation and lack of neighbourhood supports in the generation of abuse. These sources of stress are given much greater weight than in the medical model. Rather than simply providing triggers for underlying pathology in individuals or families, they can be seen as creating enormous pressures, under which the parenting in some families will buckle. The second strand involves locating child abuse in a wider social context. This can include examination of the ways in which the notion of abuse is socially constructed—for example, varying views about appropriate punishment, age-related responsibilities, or sexual knowledge—and is thus far from self-evident as implied in the medical model. It may also highlight the links between violence against children and a wider incidence and 'acceptability' of violence in families or society. Strauss et al. (1980: 72) contend that in the United States, 'children are injured and abused because we as a society are committed to norms which approve of and legitimize using violence as a frequent form of training and punishing children'. This wider focus may also facilitate the posing of different questions, such as whether abuse of children reflects their lack of rights vis-à-vis parents/adults, and whether those in power who permit child poverty, deprivation, and racism are not at least as abusive as those who are labelled child abusers.

Among theorists of child abuse, it is widely accepted that no single perspective comes close to offering all the answers. Child abuse undoubtedly reflects a complex mixture of psychological and social factors, and much depends on what type of explanation is being sought. If we are trying to understand abuse as a 'private trouble', then clearly the individual/family-based explanations may have more to offer than a broad brush social theory. If, however, the aim is to cast light on child abuse as a 'public issue', its levels, patterns, and trends, then the reverse is likely to be true. Ideally, both medical and social perspectives can make significant contributions. As noted earlier, these theoretical considerations have important policy implications, notably in terms of the perceived contributions of broad-based welfare services and targeted family interventions to reducing child abuse

CHILD SEXUAL ABUSE

If the 1970s could be described as the 'age of child abuse', then it is probably fair to say that the 1980s were 'the age of sexual abuse'. The latter's emergence is believed to have resulted from work within the women's movement (Frost and Stein 1989: 67). In particular, awareness of the family as a site for violence and the use of sexuality as a form of male domination, for example in rape or harassment, paved the way for greater recognition of child sexual abuse within families. This was further bolstered by the voice given to those who had suffered and survived sexual abuse. Greater recognition was reflected in a dramatic rise in detection, with the number of children placed on the child protection register due to concerns about sexual abuse rising almost six fold between 1984 and 1986 (Corby 2000: 89). Recognition of the particular difficulties for children in telling of sexual abuse and being believed was a significant factor in the establishment of Childline—the free telephone helpline for children experiencing abuse—in 1986.

Yet it was events in Cleveland during 1987 that were to bring child sexual abuse dramatically to the attention of a wider public, and which seemed to symbolize the struggle over its recognition (Campbell 1988). When an unexpectedly large number of children were taken into care largely on the basis of a controversial medical diagnosis known as reflex anal dilatation, opinion was sharply divided between those who were inclined to see this as further uncovering of abuse and those, led by the local MP, Stuart Bell, who believed that certain doctors and social workers had 'gone mad'. The ensuing inquiry (Department of Health and Social Security 1988) was highly critical of many of the professionals involved, both for their kneejerk reactions to medical diagnosis and for their flawed investigative techniques. However, if there was some evidence of a fall-off in referrals for child sexual abuse following the Cleveland affair, there was to be no return to the days when sexual abuse was rarely reported. This was despite other well-publicised cases of 'authoritarianism' on the part of social workers and police, e.g. in Orkney and Rochdale, where subsequent reports found much of the intervention to have been heavy-handed (Social Services Inspectorate 1990). While the climate has remained fairly receptive towards believing children's allegations of abuse, there has also been a significant undercurrent of opposition from those who claim that allegations (including those against teachers or care staff) may be malicious, motivated by desire for compensation, or, in the case of so-called **false memory syndrome**, planted in the mind during therapy (Davies and Dalgleish 2001).

Understanding sexual abuse presents many of the same difficulties as for other forms of child abuse, though with the added problems of secrecy and commonly a lack of any physical evidence to support allegations. Questions of proof and the difficulties faced by child witnesses in legal cases are among the most distressing aspects of sexual abuse. On definitions and judgements, while serious forms of abuse present little difficulty, consensus can be much more elusive around the margins as to what is or is not 'sexual', what is harmful or abusive, what is appropriate to different ages and so on. As the work of Smith and Grocke (Department of Health 1995: 81–3) demonstrates, there is wide variation in families' treatment of sexual matters and what is considered 'normal'. Perhaps their most thought-provoking findings relate to perceived signs of abuse. 'Excessive masturbation, over-sexualised and extensive sexual curiosity or sexual knowledge and genital touching are thought to be indicators of abuse. But since these behaviours were found to be common within a community sample, they were not in themselves sufficient to suggest abuse' (p. 83). Definitions of sexual abuse can also be drawn narrowly or broadly. The former tend to concentrate on serious sexual assaults: rape, intercourse, or forced masturbation. The latter may additionally encompass experiences of indecent exposure, unwanted touching, verbal abuse, and inappropriate watching of sexual activity.

Prevalence figures depend very much upon the breadth of definition used. Kelly et al. (1991) found that 4 per cent of women and 2 per cent of men reported having experienced serious sexual abuse as children, these figures rising to 59 per cent and

27 per cent respectively when the wider definitions were used. The markedly higher rate for abuse of girls has been a consistent finding in both official records and self-report studies. Studies also show that the overwhelming majority of sexual abuse, especially of girls, where the figure exceeds 90 per cent, is carried out by men (Corby 2000: 105; Cawson et al. 2000).

Causes of sexual abuse: family dysfunction or the unacceptable face of patriarchy?

As for other forms of abuse, there has been a range of theoretical perspectives focused on sexual abuse, examining the characteristics of individual perpetrators, family dynamics, or broader social factors. In relation to child sexual abuse, tensions between medical and social models have revolved around gender rather than class (it being more widely accepted that sexual abuse is loosely, if at all, associated with social class).

Within the mainstream of professional intervention in cases of child sexual abuse, family models come closest to an 'orthodoxy'. In general terms, such models focus on relationships and communication within families, the analysis informing therapeutic intervention. In the case of sexual abuse, there is particular concentration upon (step)father–daughter incest. This is generally taken to arise as a response to difficulties in relations between parents, whereupon the (step)father 'turns' to his daughter(s) for sexual gratification. Family models often claim or imply that mothers collude in this process to varying degrees, but are rarely entirely unaware of the abuse.

Not surprisingly, feminists have mounted a very strong critical challenge to this model and its assumptions. For them, the central point is to locate child sexual abuse within a patriarchal society, where both women and children may be seen as male 'possessions', over whom they have rights, and in particular to sex. For feminists, the family-based orthodoxy rests on gender assumptions which ignore the context of power and allow the logic of responsibility for abuse to be turned on its head. 'Male sexuality is seen as driven and uncontrollable', observe MacLeod and Saraga, continuing ironically 'Poor men! It is up to women not only to nurture and care for their men adequately, and to control their own desires, but also to control men's sexuality' (1988: 34). Furthermore, women are also cast as the natural protectors of their children, transforming abuse from male perpetration to female failure to protect. Feminists also challenge the orthodoxy's implication that if only women performed their roles as wives and mothers better, the problem of sexual abuse would disappear. Instead, they highlight the importance of gender and in particular the social construction of masculinity.

Feminist perspectives have had some success in arguing for the value of having women deal with the aftermath of sexual abuse, whether as police officers, social workers, or carers, and in promoting the removal of perpetrators rather than children from the family home. It is, however, also worth noting that greater recognition has also been given in recent years to sexual abuse by women (Elliott 1993).

Beyond sexual abuse?

Following the emergence of child sexual abuse as an issue, there has been considerable, often intense discussion as to the existence of ritualized, sometimes satanic abuse. In some ways this has mirrored earlier debate on sexual abuse, with 'missionaries' preaching belated recognition of a major problem, others dismissing this as fanciful scaremongering. An investigation carried out by La Fontaine found evidence of organized abuse, sometimes involving several families and/or paedophile networks, but only very rarely any links with ritualistic abuse. 'Evidence that adults had performed rituals of recognisably occult significance was virtually non-existent; there was even a scarcity of evidence of vaguer interest in the occult' (Department of Health 1995: 74). Other researchers, however, suggest that a significant incidence of ritualistic abuse is still not being recognized (Scott 2001).

INSTITUTIONAL ABUSE

This term is used most frequently to describe abuse which takes place within the care system, and in particular within children's homes. In the 1980s and 1990s there have been a number of highly publicized cases, often involving many children and occurring over many years (Corby 2000: 51–5). The irony of children, often removed from home for their own protection, then being abused by their protectors is a tragic one. Institutional abuse has taken a wide range of forms, including sexual abuse, physical abuse, or emotional abuse involving degrading treatment. Bullying by other residents has often been identified as a problem in residential care. On occasion, as with the case of 'pindown' (a system of punishment based on isolation and humiliation), it may be the home's regime itself which is deemed abusive (Levy and Kahan 1991). Though less well-publicized, abuse within foster care is not uncommon, as is most clearly shown in the calls to Childline's dedicated 'Children in Care' line (Morris and Wheatley 1994). Sir William Utting's (1997) report into safeguards for children living away from home found continuing cause for concern throughout the care system, and made wide-ranging recommendations to improve children's safety in residential care, foster care, boarding schools, hospitals, and prisons. The report highlighted the need to see safety in terms of the whole system for protecting children and not simply as a matter of dealing with individual perpetrators. Further recommendations emanated from the Waterhouse (2000) inquiry into abuse in children's homes in north Wales. They included measures to strengthen complaints procedures, encouragement of 'whistle-blowing' by staff witnessing abuse, and the appointment of a Children's Commissioner for Wales.

Taken at its broadest, the concept of institutional abuse also alerts us to the possibility of interventions themselves being damaging, perhaps the result of numerous moves within the care system or of poorly conducted child protection investigations.

PLANNING FOR CHILDREN WHO ARE BEING 'LOOKED AFTER'

Research has found that the childcare system is often disorganized and slow in setting and achieving goals for the children it looks after. The higher priority given to planning within the childcare system over the past two decades and more can be traced back to

Rowe and Lambert's (1973) landmark study *Children Who Wait*. In examining the situations of children in long-term care, Rowe and Lambert identified the problem of **drift**, where children lived either in foster care or residential homes often for many years, with no clear plan as to whether they would return home to their families, remain in care, or be adopted. The problems highlighted related both to planning for individual children and to planning services for children.

Concerns about planning were also boosted by a wider focus on the importance of long-term security for children, which came to be encapsulated in the term **permanence**. Maluccio et al. (1986: 5) describe permanence planning as 'the systematic carrying out, within a brief time-limited period, of a set of goal directed activities, designed to help children live in families that offer continuity of relationships with nurturing parents or caretakers and the opportunity to establish life-time relationships'. The philosophy of permanence placed particular emphasis on securing the futures of children both decisively and relatively speedily. If parents could meet the children's needs adequately, without damaging delay and with good long-term prospects, then permanence would be provided within the birth family. If not, then it should be provided through substitute care, most usually adoption, as quickly as possible. Good planning was to provide the means both for ensuring that decisions were soundly based, and that time-scales did not allow drift to occur.

Adoption or return to birth family?

The philosophy of permanence coincided in the 1970s with one of the periodic pendulum swings towards, or in this case away from, the importance of 'blood ties'. The death of Maria Colwell clearly contributed to this, but there were also theoretical influences, notably the emphasis on 'psychological parenting', with parent–child relationships seen to depend much more on the quality of care-giving than on biology (Goldstein et al. 1979). By the late 1970s, with increasing removal of children from their birth families, many critics believed that permanence policies had in effect become adoption policies. Countering what Fox Hording terms the 'state paternalism' lying behind permanence policies, organizations such as the Family Rights Group and later Parents Against Injustice emerged to defend a **family rights** position. While in part this stance was based on giving greater weight to blood ties, it included an important political dimension. In particular, it was argued that at all stages of the process, from children being removed from home to their being adopted, the odds were stacked against birth families, who were for the most part relatively poor and disadvantaged. Not only were judgements often made on the basis of middle-class norms, but there was little acknowledgement of material deprivation and its effects. Furthermore, social work agencies were widely accused of making insufficient efforts to prevent children coming into care and subsequently to return them to their families. Fox Harding (1991: 59–154) provides a very good review of the arguments surrounding permanence and family rights, noting the dangers in their idealizing of substitute and biological families respectively.

In broad terms, the 1980s and early 1990s saw the pendulum swing back towards birth families, while from the mid-1990s there has been growing pressure for substitute care

Table 16.1 Children looked after in England and Wales, 1980–2000

	000		
	1980	1990	2000
Children looked after	95.3	60.5	58.1
No. in foster care	35.2	34.3	37.9
No. in residential care	32.4	10.7	4.8

Source: Department of Health (2001b).

and especially adoption (see below). The initial swing can be detected in the steadily falling 'in care' population, the broad outline of which can be seen in Table 16.1.

Although some of this fall can be explained in economic terms, as authorities sought to control and reduce the costs of providing care, it also reflected the continuing efforts of the family rights campaign, which linked advocacy for individual families with lobbying policy-makers. The primary aims were to make social work practice more accountable—through greater openness and extending the legal protection of families—and to maximize efforts to keep or reunite children with their birth families. Such efforts received significant support from research carried out in the early 1980s and summarised as *Social Work Decisions in Child Care* (DHSS 1985). Three major themes emerged from this research, the first being to show that contact between children and birth parents was vital both to prospects for return home and for the children's wellbeing. A second, however, was that much social work practice appeared neglectful or even obstructive of contact (p. 5). The third theme was that of problems within the care system itself, where moves and instability were found to be common (p. 10). In all, too many children were seen to be losing contact with their birth families while not necessarily being offered the security implied by permanence policies. Social work agencies stood accused of being more concerned with intervention than with what it might achieve. Echoing some of the earlier anxiety about drift, Millham et al.'s (1986) study *Lost in Care* found that if children did not return home within five weeks, there was a strong chance of remaining in care for two years or more, and that levels of contact were the best indicator for return. Importantly, on leaving care the overwhelming majority of young people returned to or re-established contact with their birth families.

Following the report of a government commissioned working party (Parker et al. 1991), efforts have been made to implement a more rigorous and standardized system of planning for 'looked after' children. The impetus came from recognition that alongside planning over the major issues—such as return to birth family or adoption—more attention was needed in areas such as education, health, and social skills, where there was evidence of children's needs being neglected with ultimately damaging consequences. The poor educational performance of many children in care has been of particular concern, given its consequences for later life (Jackson 2001).

Box 16.2 Key features of the Children Act 1989

- more active involvement of courts in decision-making about children;
- welfare of the child to be paramount;
- use of a welfare checklist for decision-making;
- avoidance of delay;
- no order to be made unless better than not to do so;
- ascertaining and taking into account child's wishes;
- specific orders to deal with residence and contact;
- parental responsibility to be maximized, even when the child is in care;
- bringing together public (local authority, police powers, etc.) and private (divorce etc.) law;
- due consideration to be given to child's religious persuasion, racial origin, cultural and linguistic background.

The Children Act 1989

Such acknowledgements coalesced during the 1980s into a greater emphasis on working constructively with birth families, and increased recognition was given to the importance of links with extended family and siblings. Boosted by the events of Cleveland, the Children Act 1989 placed particular emphasis on the importance of support for birth families and the rights of parents, albeit couched in terms of parental responsibilities. The dominant theme was that of 'partnership'. At the same time, pressure for **children's rights** began to exert at least some influence on policy and practice, notably in terms of encouraging their participation in decision-making and attempts to give them a stronger voice (Fox Harding 1991: 155–200). Borrowing ideas from New Zealand in particular, some agencies began to experiment with **family group conferences**, in which family members were brought together and encouraged to draw up their own solutions to problems of childcare and protection with professional involvement being kept to a minimum (Marsh and Grow 1998).

The thinking behind the Children Act is aptly described by Fox Harding (1991) as an 'uneasy synthesis', and many commentators have noted how the Act can be interpreted in quite different ways. For alongside the moves to empower birth families and children, there was to be no easing up on child protection nor a return to drift. Importantly, no additional resources were made available to implement the Act. In turn, this made it difficult to offer the promised support to families, and threatened to overload social work agencies and the courts as they grappled with the competing demands.

RESIDENTIAL OR FOSTER CARE?

We will be looking at both residential and foster care in more detail below, but at this point it is useful to make some brief points about their respective places in providing public care for children. Since 1945, foster care has generally been the favoured option for most children, having, according to Packman (1981: 25), 'the blessing of Curtis, Bowlby and the Treasury'; and as can be seen from Table 16.1 there has been a steady shift away from residential care. While research on the respective merits of foster vis-à-vis residential care (especially for older children) is by no means unequivocal, the majority view tends to support the former as preferable. Colton (1988) summarizes the arguments which suggest that children and young people in foster care benefit from more extensive and personalized adult attention, and that this is generally reflected in their confidence, behaviour, and happiness with their carers. Research and testimony from young people themselves has also highlighted problems in residential care of lack of privacy, study facilities or autonomy in everyday life, and bullying (Fletcher 1993). During the 1990s there was growing acknowledgement of problems of abuse by young people of others, running away, and child prostitution (Department of Health 1998). Against this, however, it must be noted that foster care is not without its problems, and that many young people appear to prefer the range of contacts and activities available in residential care (Fletcher 1993: 84). The move from residential to foster care and to smaller units has been repeated throughout Europe, although taken much further in the UK than in any country except Sweden (Madge 1994). Analysis of foster and residential care is made more difficult by their respective populations and the problem of 'comparing like with like'. For while outcomes, such as in education, often appear better in the former, it is recognized that, on balance, young people in the latter have faced greater difficulties in their lives.

Residential care: a positive choice?

Apart from its dramatic reduction in size, residential care has also undergone significant change in its organization and rationale. With the modern emphasis on planning and permanence, residential care has largely ceased to provide long-term homes for children and has become more 'task-focused'. Placements are likely to be time-limited, in principle at least relatively short-term, and aimed at some particular outcome. This may be return to the family, preparation for foster care or adoption, provision of a therapeutic environment, or for older teenagers, readiness for life after leaving care. Homes, whether run by local authorities or by private or voluntary organizations, have often specialized around such functions, although the specialization has frequently been subverted by the need to find places urgently (Berridge and Brodie 1998). Despite these developments, the perception of residential care as a 'darkened door at the end of the line' (Department of Health 1998: 39) remains widespread, a placement for adolescents perceived as troubled or troubling. With foster care the preferred option, residential care is widely assumed to provide only for those too difficult to foster, whose foster placements are yet to be found or have broken down, or whose abuse is thought to make family life inappropriate.

Staffing has remained a consistent problem in residential care throughout the postwar years, with homes often experiencing high turnover, while low pay and levels of qualification symbolize a lack of expertise and status for residential workers' compared with field social workers. In 2000, only 11 per cent of residential child care workers had the government's preferred qualification although, perhaps optimistically, local authorities expect this figure to rise to 84 per cent by 2004 (Robbins 2001). This situation is often seen as increasing the potential for abuse, not only making it easier for abusers to gain employment but also through lack of coping skills, awareness, or confidence to challenge bad practice. Considerable efforts have been made in the 1990s to iron out many of these difficulties (including the limits of legitimate restraint), with somewhat mixed results. In their follow-up study, Berridge and Brodie (1998) conclude that while residential care is 'safer' in some respects than previously, it is less so in others. If residential care appears to crystallize many of the difficulties inherent in parenting by the state, it remains both an integral part of the childcare system and appreciated by many of its residents. The quest remains one of building upon the undoubted achievements of some homes and some services, such as those offered to children with disabilities, to maximize the sector's contribution to child welfare (Department of Health 1998).

Foster care: the ideal method?

Looking after other people's children on a temporary basis has a long history, both as a formal practice, known as 'boarding out' under the Poor Law, and doubtless longer still as an informal one. As noted above, foster care has been the favoured means of providing care for children since 1945, and now provides for a clear majority of children 'looked after' (see Table 16.1).

Modern foster care has been shaped by the twin concerns of extending 'fosterability' and adaptation to the emphases on planning and permanence. Together, these have fuelled moves towards the 'professionalization' of foster care. Initially, the extension of fosterability entailed finding placements for those regarded as hard to place—on grounds of age, disability, or ethnicity. More recently, similar efforts have been made in relation to survivors of sexual abuse, and children infected with HIV or AIDS. The extension of fosterability has been achieved through a combination of education, training, support, and financial reward. Following the early examples, most notably of Kent, many agencies set up professional foster care schemes during the 1970s and 1980s (Shaw and Hipgrave 1983). Most dealt with teenagers and, formally at least, mainly those who had been involved in crime. In addition to strong emphases on training and support, the schemes involved the payment of a fee to carers in addition to maintenance allowances, the fee being regarded as both a compensation for disruption to home life and reward for the carers' skills. Treatment rather than simply care was to be provided. However, maintaining a clear distinction between 'professional' and 'traditional' foster care has proved awkward, and more complex patterns have developed (Waterhouse 1997: 41–54). This is in part due to problems of distinguishing degrees of difficulty or skills, but also because many of the features of professional schemes, such as training and support, have been extended to all foster carers. Many of the newly formed independent fostering agencies have a strong professional emphasis, including the payment of higher fees to carers offering placements to more 'difficult' children or young people.

Foster care, permanence, and planning

From the 1970s onwards foster care has, like residential care, become increasingly 'task-focused'. The combined emphases on permanence and planning have served to underline the temporary nature of foster care and its role in working towards particular goals, whether return home, readiness for adoption, or independent living, perhaps entailing work on personal and family problems. The shift is well captured in Holman's (1975) distinction between a quasi-adoptive **exclusive foster care** and an **inclusive** model, where foster families can work constructively with birth parents and social workers and accept 'letting go' of the children.

As foster care now provides for two-thirds of children looked after, its quality is crucial to that of the childcare system itself. While not attracting the negative publicity of residential care, fostering has not been without its own challenges. Many of these stem from the uneasy mix of 'professional childcare' and 'normal family life', the ambivalent status of foster carers between workers and volunteers, and whether they are genuinely valued as colleagues by social workers. The tensions are difficult to resolve and regularly surface in debates over payment and motivation, or what might reasonably be expected of foster carers in their work with children and families. **Breakdowns** (some prefer the term 'disruption') of placements have been a worryingly common feature of foster care, with many investigations seeking to identify the factors relevant to success and failure (Berridge and Cleaver 1987). The demands of fostering and the increasing employment opportunities available for female carers have been reflected in difficulties of recruitment and retention of carers. While a national survey found the position surprisingly buoyant, there remained many localized shortages, including those relating to minority ethnic carers, while nationally, 'the most serious carer shortages identified . . . were for older children and sibling groups' (Waterhouse 1997: 47). The problem is not so much one of overall numbers, which have remained fairly constant for many years, but rather of creating a sufficient pool of carers to allow children to be placed in the most appropriate family rather than simply wherever there is a vacancy.

ADOPTION: A SERVICE FOR CHILDREN?

Although, like foster care, it has a very long informal history, adoption as a legal concept in the UK dates only from 1926. It has been organized by both voluntary and statutory agencies, under regulations designed to prevent abuses (such as selling children for adoption), and to ensure that children are appropriately matched with suitable adoptive parents.

Following the Second World War, adoption came to be based on the **clean break**, involving the severance of all legal links with the birth family and identical status to children born to the adopters (the one exception to this being that adoptees cannot inherit aristocratic titles). This 'clean break' was thought to be in the best interests of all members of the **adoption triangle**—namely birth parent(s), child, adoptive parents. During the 1950s and 1960s this was increasingly questioned, with recognition of the need for adoptees to trace their birth family in order to understand their **identity**. Research was to show that total severance often increased the sense of loss experienced by those involved in adoption. The Children Act 1975 allowed adoptees access to their original birth certificate and knowledge of the circumstances surrounding their adoption.

By contrast with the clean break philosophy, more recent thinking has placed greater emphasis on **openness in adoption**. Openness can be seen as a continuum, from greater supply of information to all members of the triangle or perhaps involvement of a birth parent in selecting adopters through to continued face-to-face contact between the child and birth family. Unlike many countries, the UK has no 'simple' adoption, which involves a more limited transfer of parental responsibilities and is therefore reversible. As well as developments in thinking on children's needs, moves towards openness have also reflected the changing nature of adoption. The transformation since the 1960s has been dramatic, with the overall scale of adoption falling sharply and affecting a very different group of children and families.

Having peaked at nearly 25,000 annually during the late 1960s, the number of adoptions has since dropped dramatically (see Table 16.2). The most striking aspect of the change has been the precipitous decline in baby adoptions, which is also indicated in Table 16.2.

The drop in baby adoptions is generally explained as the result of greater use of contraception and termination, and the declining stigma attached to illegitimacy. Adoption is now much more likely to be from the care system, which often means that the children may be older, be the victims of abuse, or have special needs. Importantly, many more adoptions are now **contested**, i.e. opposed by birth parents. Debates over contested adoptions crystallize some of the key differences between the advocates of permanence (and those who would wish to see adoption expanded) and family rights campaigners, both about the form of adoption and indeed about its necessity or desirability. For Ryburn, adoption law still treats children 'as pieces of transportable personal property who can, by a legal fiction, have past links extinguished and join a new family as if they were born to it' (1993: 39). Government policy, however, has become progressively more pro-adoption over the past decade. This shift has been linked to the perceived failings of the care system in two respects. First, adoption is seen as offering children better life chances compared with remaining in care. Second, the care system stands accused of failing to pursue adoption early enough or with sufficient rigour to prevent children languishing in care. In July 2000, Prime Minister Tony Blair (PIU 2000) launched a review of adoption from which came a commitment to increase adoption from care by at least 40 per cent by the year 2004–5. In 2001, 3,067 such adoptions took place, representing an increase of 12 per cent on the previous year. While many welcome the drive to increase adoption, there are also concerns that the setting of targets and

Table 16.2 Adoption orders, 1980–2000

	1980	1990	2000
No. of orders made (thousands)	10.6	6.5	5.0
% of children under 1	24	15	5

Source: ONS (2002).

timescales may interfere with professional judgement in areas such as the child's best interests or the approval of adopters. A further concern is that adoption may be seen, quite unrealistically given its small scale, as a 'panacea' for the ills of the care system, leading to neglect of foster and residential care.

Race, ethnicity, and adoption: political correctness?

Adoption has long been recognized as conferring social mobility upon children: the majority of birth families are poor, while the majority of adopters are more affluent. Far more controversial, however, has been the placement of black and minority ethnic children in adoptive (and foster) families. In 1965, the British Adoption Project (BAP) sought to challenge the prevailing view of the time that black children were unadoptable, due to racial prejudice on the part of white families, and the lack of availability of black families. The BAP was successful in placing over fifty children, most with white families. Thereafter, **transracial adoption** (TRA—in practice the adoption of black or minority ethnic children by white families) became established in many adoption agencies. The rise of black liberation struggles in the 1970s brought increasingly strong opposition to the assimilationist ideas underlying TRA. Its opponents argued that placement in white families had detrimental effects on children's sense of racial identity, knowledge of their culture of origin, and ability to cope with racism. It was also contended that the one-way traffic of black children into white homes was rooted in norms which devalued or even pathologized black families and assumed the inherent superiority of their white counterparts. Moreover, the long-standing notion that there were too few black adoptive families available for children was challenged, being blamed on the inadequate recruitment efforts of adoption agencies. This critique was very influential in the 1980s and led many agencies to apply **same-race placement** policies which sought racial and ethnic matching between adoptees and adopters. The issue has however, remained highly controversial, periodically erupting into the media spotlight, usually when a black child is removed from a white foster family who wish to adopt. The supporters of transracial adoption have argued that the fears expressed are not borne out by research and that the shortage of black families is real, thereby leading black children to remain in care for longer than necessary. They also tend to see the practice of transracial adoption as promoting racial integration and social harmony. By contrast, they characterize same-race policies as 'separatist' or even a form of apartheid (Gaber and Aldridge 1994). Hostile politicians and media pundits have targeted same-race policies, as well as adoption by lesbians and gays, as 'political correctness', and threatened to clip the wings of those who support them. The latter continue to see such measures as important both for meeting the needs of children and for wider moves towards social justice. (For a more detailed discussion see Kirton 2000.)

CHILDREN, YOUNG PEOPLE, CRIME, AND WELFARE

During the 1990s with its more punitive approach to young offenders, it may seem anomalous to include their treatment in a chapter dealing with care and protection. This would, however, be to misunderstand the history of what is now termed youth justice and to assume that recent policy swings are irreversible. The last 100 years has seen a continuing debate about whether young offenders are criminals deserving punishment or the victims of deprivation who need social care. (Note: some of the issues covered in this section are also discussed, from a more criminological perspective, in Chapter 18).

The rise of welfarism

Interest in the 'welfare' of young criminals can be traced to the nineteenth century and the construction of childhood as a period of 'natural innocence', but also of vulnerability to corrupting influences. The programme of Victorian 'child savers' rested on the twin pillars of separation from adult offenders and tutelage from appropriate adults for children involved in, or at risk of, offending. The mid-nineteenth-century creation of the reformatory and industrial schools typified this process, with their emphasis on strict discipline and training for modest but respectable trades (usually domestic service in the case of girls). More generally, children came to be imprisoned less and to have their own separate courts and prisons, the latter known from the early twentieth century as 'borstals'. The trend towards seeing youthful offending as the product of deprivation continued. Initially cast in terms of poor socialization, the link was increasingly clothed in psychological garb. In the postwar years the work of John Bowlby was influential, especially the notion that maternal deprivation (see above) led to various forms of disturbed, antisocial behaviour, often including the criminal. His work also seemed to offer some explanation for the well-documented failure of institutions, approved schools, detention centres, and borstals to curb offending (see Minty 1987 for a summary of relevant research).

The 1960s are often taken to mark the high tide of welfarism, with the Children and Young Persons (CYP) Act 1969 its most potent symbol. Within the **welfare model**, offending was to be seen as a symptom of need, whether social or psychological. The Act sought to 'decriminalize', raising the age of criminal responsibility from 10 to 14, and envisaging a move to 17. Responsibility for young offenders was to be significantly relocated from the criminal justice system to welfare agencies. One of the central measures was the **care order**, where offending provided one of the grounds for transferring parental responsibility to the local authority.

The 1970s and a 'return to justice'

The CYP Act 1969 was born into a changed and hostile political climate. The incoming Conservative government in 1970 decided not to implement the raising of the age of criminal responsibility to 14. There was also opposition from magistrates and police, and more generally from the emerging 'new right', who saw welfarism as undermining both individual responsibility for crime and the workings of the criminal justice system. Above all, it was portrayed as 'soft' and thereby responsible for the rising crime rate. Magistrates appeared to respond by making greater use of custodial sentences in order to ensure punishment and keep control over sentencing.

If welfarism attracted predictable fire from the Right, it was also subjected to considerable critique from the Left, based primarily on civil liberties arguments. It was argued that welfarism had been grafted onto and extended the existing system—thereby 'widening the net'—rather than replacing it. Welfarist assumptions could lead to effectively indeterminate sentences (care orders once made lasting until 18) for often quite minor offences. Furthermore, the making of 'welfare-based' orders could have the effect of harsher sentences if the child should then reoffend. Crucially, the growing harshness of the system was masked by a popular image that it was now hopelessly 'soft'.

These twin pressures led to the development of what was known as a **justice model**, which emphasized the importance of the offence and direct punishment according to its seriousness. This restoration of offending as an act of will, playing down any connection with social circumstances or psychological factors, was reflected in changes to social work and probation practice, with a stronger focus on 'offending behaviour' and less concern with the background of the offender.

The 1980s and the paradox of diversion

Conservative governments from 1979 to 1997, with law and order the dominant theme in criminal justice, endeavoured to make punishment more central to the treatment of young offenders. One of the earliest initiatives involved toughening the regimes in detention centres—to provide a **short, sharp shock**. Yet paradoxically, by the end of the 1980s, the number of young people in custody had fallen dramatically, as indeed had the number sentenced. These falls can be seen from the figures in Table 16.3, which also show the small but significant reversal of the trend on custody during the 1990s.

While the 1980s falls in sentencing and use of custody can partly be accounted for by a small fall in reported crime, they owe much more to the strategy of **diversion**. This term could cover a range of measures, sometimes including community service or reparation, the common element being a desire to divert the young person away from the machinery of the criminal justice system and especially custody. The use of police cautions rose dramatically—from 36 per cent of young male and 60 per cent of young female offenders in 1984, to 59 per cent and 80 per cent respectively in 1994 (Ruxton 1996). Despite declining support for welfarism, the idea that offending was often just a 'passing phase' remained strong, along with awareness that legal measures to 'label' an

Table 16.3 Numbers of young people in custody, 1985–2000, as a proportion of numbers sentenced (in thousands)

Year	Males, 10–17		Females, 10–17	
	Total	Custody	Total	Custody
1985	87.2	11.5	9.8	0.2
1990	40.8	3.6	5.1	0.1
1995	37.2	4.2	5.0	0.1
2000	42.6	5.7	6.7	0.4

Source: Home Office (2001).

offender often made matters worse. Diversion was for the most part pursued away from the public gaze, and stood in sharp contrast to the 'get tough' rhetoric of politicians. It was, however, sufficiently successful to underpin the Criminal Justice Act 1991's emphasis on custody only as a last resort, albeit with the quid pro quo of tougher 'punishment in the community' sentences.

The 1990s and (really) 'getting tough'

Like the CYP Act 1969, the 1991 Act was soon overtaken by events and a changing political climate. The years immediately following were to see the re-emergence of moral panic about young offenders and a pronounced shift in policy. Joyriding, 'bail bandits', and the 'persistent young offender' all emerged as important signifiers in public perception. Yet arguably the most powerful came from a single event, the murder of toddler James Bulger by two boys barely old enough to be legally responsible for their crime. Coinciding with wider concern over youth crime, this offence took on a wider resonance, appearing to herald the demise of 'childhood innocence'. As Jenks remarks (1996: 127) 'it was not just two children who were on trial for the murder of a third but childhood itself. At the same time the long-standing image of a system 'soft on crime' was revived with stories of young offenders being sent on expensive safaris only to reoffend on their return. A series of 'get tough' measures followed, dramatically reversing the effects of the 1991 Criminal Justice Act. Existing custodial sentences for young offenders were extended both in length and scope, while new 'junior prisons', known as **Secure Training Centres**, were introduced for persistent offenders aged 12–14. Custodial regimes were to be toughened, with the introduction of US-style 'boot camps' and the use of the army's 'glass house'. The major political parties vied with each other for toughness in dealing with young offenders in the community, with proposed use of electronic tagging and blanket local curfews.

Following the 1997 election, the new Labour government seemed keen to fulfil its opposition slogan 'Tough on crime, tough on the causes of crime'. Home Secretary Jack Straw attacked the 'excuse culture' surrounding youth crime but also emphasized preventive measures. The Crime and Disorder Act 1998 included provisions to remove the presumption that children under 14 did not 'understand right from wrong', to replace cautions with a system based on two warnings only, to promote reparation and to allow curfews for children under 10, on either an individual or area basis. The Act also introduced an order which would require parents of offenders to attend counselling or guidance sessions to improve their parenting. At the local level, youth offending teams, comprising social workers, probation officers, police officers, and education and health personnel, were created, with the new system overseen by a national Youth Justice Board. The twin-track approach has continued. Toughness is readily apparent in the rising use of custody (Table 16.3) and the extension of community sentences such as electronic tagging and intensive surveillance. Yet the government has also been keen to develop its more preventive policies, focusing on parenting and restorative justice.

Anglo-Saxon youth justice: the only way?

The approach to young offenders in the UK stands in marked contrast to most of continental Europe, being much closer in style to the US. The European model remains more rooted in welfarist ideas, with much lower rates of custody and higher ages of criminal responsibility (the European average age being 14–16 against 10 in England and Wales, 8 in Scotland and Northern Ireland). A stronger emphasis on welfare is also evident in processes based more on investigative enquiry rather than prosecution, though the Scottish hearings system has elements of this approach. This system relies on panels comprising lay volunteers, whose role is to consider whether any compulsory measures—such as statutory supervision or placement in residential care—are necessary to secure the effective care of the young offender. The hearings seek to provide a less formal atmosphere than court, and encourage the participation of the offender's family.

CONCLUSION

Early in the new millennium, the care and protection of children remains a challenging and contentious field. There is no doubt that since coming to office in 1997 the Labour government has demonstrated a strong commitment to the welfare of children, rooted in the idea that they represent 'the nation's future'. Tony Blair declared his initial priorities to be 'education, education, education' and later pledged to 'end child poverty in a generation'. Chancellor Gordon Brown's reform of the tax and benefit systems has seen significant redistribution to families with children, especially through tax credits for the lower-paid. More targeted initiatives such as Sure Start and the Children's Fund have been launched to help families in poverty, while children occupy a prominent place on the social exclusion agenda, including tackling truancy and teenage parenthood. While the (longer-term) success of these initiatives is still uncertain, the Labour government can take credit for allowing the broader view of child welfare to influence policy. Another consistent theme has been to promote more 'joined-up' approaches, both focusing on inter-agency cooperation and in some instances creating new organizations—including the proposed children's trusts—to deliver multidisciplinary services.

In relation to the subject matter of this chapter, the most important government initiative has been 'Quality Protects' (www.doh.gov.uk/qualityprotects) which has followed the formula of providing additional earmarked funding linked to local authorities meeting specific targets. The latter have been wide-ranging: focusing on improving child protection, education, and life chances for children in need and those looked after; services for care leavers, disabled, and minority ethnic children; reducing moves in the care system and promoting permanence, especially through adoption. Central to all these goals has been a drive to improve information systems and management of children's services.

Despite the substantial funds invested in Quality Protects, questions remain regarding the strength of government commitment to child social care services. Recruitment of social workers has deteriorated significantly in recent years, and the government response has been lukewarm compared to its efforts in respect of nursing and teaching. While this can readily be explained in terms of political priorities, the human costs are ultimately borne by those vulnerable children and families who rely on services.

KEY LEGISLATION

Prevention of Cruelty to and Protection of Children Act 1889 The Act's two key measures were first to make wilful cruelty or neglect a criminal offence, and second to allow a child victim to be removed and placed with a relative or other 'fit person'.

Children Act 1948 The Act's main measures were the establishment of Children's Departments within local authorities and clarification of circumstances within which children could be received into care voluntarily or where the local authority could assume parental rights. The Act also placed a duty on local authorities to attempt to return children to their families where possible, and to place them in foster families where this was not.

Children and Young Persons Act 1969 The Act is perhaps best known as the high point of welfare approaches to juvenile crime, with its various measures to decriminalize and to treat crime as a symptom of family problems. The main provision of the Act was the creation of the care order, which could be made by a court where parental care and control were regarded as inadequate and one of a series of conditions was met. These conditions were wide-ranging, from being a victim of abuse or being in moral danger, through being beyond parental control, to non-school attendance and offending behaviour.

Children Act 1975 The Act aimed to prioritize the welfare of the child, especially where this might be seen to conflict with the interests of their family. Its main measures related to facilitating adoption, allowing children to be legally 'freed' for adoption, strengthening the position of foster carers who wished to adopt, and introducing allowances for those who might not otherwise be able to afford to adopt. Adoptees were given rights to their original birth certificates and hence a route to tracing their birth parents.

Children Act 1989 Though the term is not used in the Act itself, 'partnership with parents' is widely taken to be its guiding principle. The Act emphasized the importance of parental responsibility, and laid a duty on local authorities to support parents, including maximization of involvement when children are looked after by the state, even when subject of a care order. A greater role for the courts was seen as a way of strengthening the position of parents dealing with social work agencies. The Act also attempted to strengthen the rights of children to be involved in decisions affecting them, and to place greater emphasis on the extended family.

Criminal Justice Act 1991 For youth justice, the main thrust of the Act was to consolidate the strategy of diversion, avoiding custody wherever possible, while making the community alternatives as 'tough' as possible. The Act also attempted to make parents more directly responsible for their children's offending.

Crime and Disorder Act 1998 Within this wide-ranging Act were some major reforms to the youth justice system. These included the creation of local multi-agency Youth Offending Teams (YOTs) and a national Youth Justice Board. Specific measures included the abolition of *doli incapax* (which required prosecutors to show that children aged under 14 understood that their actions were seriously wrong), and the introduction of parenting orders, local curfews, and measures to promote reparation.

The Protection of Children Act 1999 This act was a response to growing concern about unsuitable people finding their way into organizations working with children. It strengthened the arrangements for maintaining lists of such people and sharing them amongst organizations. It created a new *Protection of Children Act List*: www.doh.gov.uk/scg/childprotect.

REFERENCES

Berridge, D., and Brodie, I. (1996), 'Residential child care in England and Wales: the inquiries and after'. In M. Hill and J. Aldgate (eds.), *Child Welfare Services: Developments in Law, Policy, Practice and Research*. London: Jessica Kingsley.

—— —— (1998), *Children's Homes Revisited*. London: Jessica Kingsley.

—— and Cleaver, H. (1987), *Foster Home Breakdown*. Oxford: Blackwell.

Campbell, B. (1988), *Unofficial Secrets*. London: Virago.

Cawson, P., Wattam, C., Brooker, S., and Kelly, G. (2000), *Child Maltreatment in the United Kingdom: A Study of the Prevalence of Child Abuse and Neglect*. London: NSPCC.

Channer, Y., and Parton, N. (1990), 'Racism, cultural relativism and child protection'. In Violence Against Children Study Group, *Taking Child Abuse Seriously: Contemporary Issues in Child Protection Theory and Practice*. London: Unwin Hyman.

Colton, M. (1988), 'Substitute care practice', *Adoption and Fostering* 12(1): 30–4.

Corby, B. (2000), *Child Abuse: Towards a Knowledge Base*, 2nd edn. Buckingham: Open University Press.

Creighton, S. (1989), *Child Abuse Trends in England and Wales 1983–87*. London: NSPCC.

Curtis, M. (1946), *Report of the Care of Children Committee*. Cmnd. 6922. London: HMSO.

Davies, G., and Dalgleish, T. (eds.) (2001), *Recovered Memories: Seeking the Middle Ground*. Chichester: Wiley.

Department of Health (1995), *Child Protection: Messages from Research*. London: HMSO.

—— (1998), *Caring for Children away from Home: Message from Research*. Chichester: Wiley.

—— (2000a), *Personal Social Services Staff of Social Services Departments in England at 30 September 2000, Statistical Bulletin 16*. London: Stationery Office.

—— (2000b), *Personal Social Services Current Expenditure in England 1999–2000, Statistical Bulletin 11*. London: Stationery Office.

—— (2001a), *Survey of Children and Young Persons on Child Protection Registers, Year Ending 31 March 2001*. London: Stationery Office.

—— (2001b), *Health and Personal Social Services Statistics 2000*. London: Department of Health.

DHSS (Department of Health and Social Security) (1985), *Social Work Decisions in Child Care*. London: HMSO.

—— (1988), *Report of the Inquiry into Child Abuse in Cleveland* [Butler-Sloss]. Cm. 412. London: HMSO.

Dingwall, R., Eekelaar, J., and Murray, T. (1983), *The Protection of Children: State Intervention and Family Life*. Oxford: Blackwell.

Doyle, C. (1997), *Working with Abused Children*. Basingstoke: Macmillan.

Elliott, M. (ed.) (1993), *Female Sexual Abuse of Children: The Last Taboo*. Harlow: Longman.

Fletcher, B. (1993), *Not Just a Name: The Views of Young People in Foster and Residential Care*. London: National Consumer Council.

Fox Harding, L. (1991), *Perspectives in Child Care Policy*. London: Longman.

Frost, N., and Stein, M. (1989), *The Politics of Child Welfare: Inequality, Power and Change*. Hemel Hempstead: Harvester Wheatsheaf.

Gaber, I., and Aldridge, J. (eds.) (1994), *In the Best Interests of the Child: Culture, Identity and Transracial Adoption*. London: Free Association.

Gil, D. (1970), *Violence against Children*. Cambridge, Mass.: Harvard University Press.

Goldstein, J., Freud, A., and Solnit, A. (1979), *Beyond the Best Interests of the Child*. New York: Free Press.

Greenland, C. (1987), *Preventing CAN Death: An International Study of Deaths due to Child Abuse and Neglect*. London: Tavistock.

Holman, B. (1996), *The Corporate Parent: Manchester Children's Department 1948–71*. London: National Institute of Social Work.

Holman, R. (1975), 'The place of fostering in social work', *British Journal of Social Work* 5(1): 3–29.

Home Office (2001), *Criminal Statistics for England and Wales 2000: Statistics Relating to Crime and Criminal Proceedings for the year 2000*. London: Stationery Office.

Jackson, S. (ed.) (2001), *Nobody Ever Told Us School Mattered: Raising the Educational Attainments of Children in Care*. London: British Agencies for Adoption and Fostering.

Jenks, C. (1996), *Childhood*. London: Routledge.

Jones, D., Pickett, J., Oates, M., and Barbor, P. (1987), *Understanding Child Abuse*. Basingstoke: Macmillan.

Kelly, L., Regan, L., and Burton, S. (1991), *An Exploratory Study of the Prevalence of Sexual Abuse in a Sample of 16–21 year olds*. Child Abuse Studies Unit, University of North London.

Kirton, D. (2000), *'Race', Ethnicity and Adoption*. Buckingham: Open University Press.

Levy, A., and Kahan, B. (1991), *The Pindown Experience and the Protection of Children*. Stafford: Staffordshire County Council.

MacLeod, M., and Saraga, E. (1988), 'Challenging the orthodoxy: towards a feminist theory and practice', *Feminist Review* 28: 16–55.

Madge, N. (1994), *Children and Residential Care in Europe*. London: National Children's Bureau.

Maluccio, A., Fein, E., and Olmstead, K. (1986), *Permanency Planning for Children: Concepts and Methods*. London: Tavistock.

Marsh, P., and Grow, G. (1998), *Family Group Conferences in Child Welfare*. Oxford: Blackwell.

Millham, S., Bullock, R., Hosi, K., and Haak, M. (1986), *Lost in Care: The Problems of Maintaining Links between Children in Care and their Families*. Aldershot: Gower.

Minty, B. (1987), *Child Care and Adult Crime*. Manchester: Manchester University Press.

Monckton, Sir W. (1945), *Report on the Circumstances which Led to the Boarding Out of Dennis and Terence O'Neill at Bank Farm and the Steps Taken to Supervise their Welfare*. Cmd. 6636. London: HMSO.

Moore, J. (1985), *The ABC of Child Abuse Work*. Aldershot: Gower.

Morris, S., and Wheatley, H. (1994), *Time to Listen: The Experiences of Young People in Foster and Residential Care*. London: Childline.

ONS (Office for National Statistics) (2002), *Marriage, Divorce and Adoption Statistics*. London: ONS.

Packman, J. (1981), *The Child's Generation: Child Care Policy in Britain*, 2nd edn. Oxford: Blackwell.

Parker, R., Ward, H., Jackson, S., Aldgate, J., and Wedge, P. (1991), *Looking After Children: Assessing Outcomes in Child Care*. London: HMSO.

Parton, N. (1985), *The Politics of Child Abuse*. Basingstoke: Macmillan.

Pelton, L. (1985), 'Child abuse and neglect: the myth of classlessness'. In L. Pelton (ed.), *The Social Context of Child Abuse and Neglect*. New York: Human Sciences Press.

PIU (Performance and Innovation Unit) (2000), Adoption: Prime Minister's Review. London: Cabinet Office.

Robbins, D. (2001), *Transforming Children's Services: An Evaluation of Local Responses to the 'Quality Protects' Programme*. London: Department of Health.

Rowe, J., and Lambert, L. (1973), *Children Who Wait*. London: Association of British Adoption Agencies.

Ruxton, S. (1996), *Children in Europe*. London: NCH Action for Children.

Ryburn, M. (1993), 'The effects of an adversarial process on adoption decisions', *Adoption and Fostering* 17(3): 39–45.

Scott, S. (2001), *The Politics and Experience of Ritual Abuse: Beyond Disbelief*. Buckingham: Open University Press.

Shaw, M., and Hipgrave, T. (1983), *Specialist Fostering*. London: Batsford.

Social Services Inspectorate (1990), *Inspection of Child Protection Services in Rochdale*. London: HMSO.

Strauss, M., Gelles, R., and Steinmetz, S. (1980), *Behind Closed Doors: Violence in the American Family*. New York: Anchor.

Utting, W. (1991), *Children in the Public Care: A Review of Residential Child Care*. London: HMSO.

—— (1997), *People Like Us: The Review of the Safeguards for Children Living Away from Home*. London: HMSO.

Waterhouse, R. (2000), *Lost in Care: Report of the Tribunal of Inquiry into the Abuse of Children in the Former County Council Areas of Gwynedd and Clwyd since 1974*. Cm. 4776. London: Stationery Office.

Waterhouse, S. (1997), *The Organisation of Fostering Services*. London: National Foster Care Association.

FURTHER READING

A good historical overview of the child care system is given in O. Stevenson, *Child Welfare in the UK 1948–98* (Oxford: Blackwell, 1999), while J. Packman, *The Child's Generation*, (Oxford: Blackwell, 1981) provides a very readable account of earlier postwar developments. B. Holman, *The Corporate Parent* (London: National Institute for Social Work, 1996) offers a sensitive and moving account of the work of Manchester Children's Department before reorganization in 1971. Other useful overview texts include L. Fox Harding, *Perspectives in Child Care Policy* (Harlow: Longman, 1997), which outlines four main influences—laissez-faire, state paternalism, birth family rights, and children's rights—on policy development.

Of the many texts on child abuse and protection, B. Corby, *Child Abuse: Towards a Knowledge Base* (Buckingham: Open University Press, 2000) offers a good overview of definitions, debates about causes, and consequences. The second collection of essays by the Violence Against Children Study Group, *Children, Child Abuse and Child Protection* (Chichester: Wiley, 1999), offers a wide range of contributions from leading writers in the field. Though now somewhat dated, N. Parton, *The Politics of Child Abuse* (London: Macmillan, 1985) remains a classic in its application of wider social context to child care. N. Parton, D. Thorpe, and C. Wattam, *Child Protection: Risk and the Moral Order* (London: Macmillan, 1997) deals with some of the debates on risk management, placing them in a broader social context.

As an overview text on child sexual abuse, D. Glaser and S. Frosh, *Child Sexual Abuse* (2nd edn., London: Macmillan, 1996) is probably the most useful. Department of Health, *Child Protection: Messages from Research* (London: HMSO, 1995) provides an excellent summary of research projects undertaken during the 1990s and the key implications to be drawn from them. Among areas covered are the child protection system, partnership between professionals and parents, inter-agency cooperation, defining and researching abuse, and organized and ritual abuse.

A number of studies of residential care are summarized in Department of Health, *Caring for Children Away from Home: Message from Research* (Chichester: Wiley, 1998). The studies address a range of issues including the factors which make for successful homes, the perspectives of care staff, management, and the contribution of private homes. D. Berridge and I. Brodie, *Children's Homes Revisited* (London: Jessica Kingsley, 1998) gives an interesting picture of life in children's homes, and is able to chart some of the changes which have taken place since the 1980s.

For foster care, D. Berridge, *Foster Care: A Review of Research* (1997) offers a comprehensive guide to the relevant literature. J. Triseliotis, C. Sellick, and R. Short, *Foster Care: Theory and Practice* (London: Batsford, 1995) gives a wide coverage of relevant issues and is an excellent textbook for foster care. Along similar lines and equally good for coverage of adoption is J. Triseliotis, J. Shireman, and M. Hundleby, *Adoption: Theory, Policy and Practice* (London: Cassell, 1997). Various adoption studies are summarized in Department of Health, *Adoption Now: Messages from Research* (Chichester: Wiley, 1999).

The following two books both provide good overviews of the youth justice field: K. Haines and M. Drakeford, *Young People and Youth Justice* (London: Macmillan, 1998); B. Goldson (ed.), *The New Youth Justice* (London: Russell House, 2000). For a more radical perspective, see J. Pitts, *The New Politics of Youth Crime* (Basingstoke: Palgrave, 2001). For issues relating to childcare in Europe, S. Ruxton, *Children in Europe* (London: NCH Action for Children, 1996) provides a very useful introduction, while a more analytical account is provided by K. Pringle, *Children and Social Welfare in Europe* (Buckingham: Open University Press, 1998).

USEFUL WEBSITES

The Department of Health and Social Services Inspectorate's combined social care site includes much about current policies and useful links. Children's services are accessed from:
www.doh.gov.uk/cos/childrenandmaternity/index.htm

The Home Office runs a useful Youth Justice Page which contains links to official publications, new legislation and information on projects and organizations working in the area:
www.homeoffice.gov.uk/yousys/youth.htm

The Victoria Climbié inquiry used the Internet to make its deliberations public in a way that has rarely happened before. As the inquiry proceeded, all the paper evidence presented was placed on the site, together with transcripts of the hearings. The full final report is also now available:
www.victoria-climbie-inquiry.org.uk

GLOSSARY

adoption triangle This term, coined by Tugendhadt, refers to the relationships between child, birth parent(s), and adoptive parent(s). It serves as a reminder that adoption is always a triangular affair, and can aid understanding of the relationships involved.

breakdowns Sometimes also known as disruptions, breakdowns describe those fostering and adoption situations where placements end sooner than planned or intended as a result of problems experienced within the foster or adoptive family.

care order A court order which transfers parental responsibility to the local authority, although it does not entirely extinguish the responsibility held by the child's parent. Care orders are made where the court believes this necessary to prevent significant harm to the child.

children's rights The term is used both to describe formal and substantive legal rights held by children and, more broadly, a philosophy which seeks to maximize the involvement of children in decision-making. There are different approaches to children's rights, most notably those which see rights in a more paternalistic way, i.e. as rights to a certain treatment by adults, and those tending more towards 'liberation', emphasizing that children should have greater powers.

child-savers A term coined by Platt to describe nineteenth-century reformers who sought to rescue children from life on the streets and its attendant deviance, and to provide homes which would offer a more constructive upbringing.

clean break An approach to adoption which involves complete severance of ties between the child and birth family, with its proponents arguing that this is in the best interests of the child, adopters, and usually, birth parents. See also **openness in adoption**.

contested adoption Adoption applications where the birth parent(s) does not consent to the child's adoption. In this situation, courts can dispense with parental consent if they think it is being withheld 'unreasonably'.

cultural relativism The idea that norms and behaviour can only be judged in the context of their own culture and that those of different cultures are equally valid.

diversion A strategy in youth justice which seeks to avoid or minimize contact with the courts and custody.

drift Describes a situation where there is either no clear long-term plan regarding a child's future or where the plan is not being effectively implemented.

exclusive and inclusive foster care Terms used to describe foster care, depending on whether the birth family (and sometimes professionals) tend to be excluded from or included in the foster family and actively involved in the foster child's life.

false memory syndrome A memory which is objectively false but strongly believed to be true by the person concerned. The 'syndrome' connotes a situation in which this false memory has a profound influence on personality and lifestyle. In relation to sexual abuse, it has been claimed that false memories can be 'planted' during therapy, leading to false accusations being made.

family group conferences (FGCs) FGCs attempt to maximize the possibility of (extended) families finding solutions to childcare problems, while professional intervention is kept to a minimum.

family group home A residential home modelled on 'family life' with relatively small numbers of residents and consistent parental figures among the staff.

family rights An approach to childcare issues which emphasizes the importance of birth family ties (or blood relationships).

good enough parenting Phrase used to indicate a threshold below which action must be taken to ensure that the child is able to receive appropriate parenting.

identity An important concept in modern adoption, which recognizes the importance of 'origins' or heritage (e.g. familial, social, cultural, racial, religious) in the adoptee's sense of self and wellbeing.

justice model An approach to youth crime which stresses the responsibility of young offenders for their crimes, that punishment is important, and that it should be proportionate to the seriousness of the crime.

maternal deprivation and attachment A theoretical perspective deriving from the work of John Bowlby, which emphasizes the importance of secure attachments between children and their parental figures, and explores the consequences of attachment problems.

medical model An approach to understanding child abuse which treats it as a disease, with abusive behaviour the visible symptom.

myth of classlessness A phrase coined by Pelton which attacks the view that child abuse occurs equally across all social classes, and which highlights the importance of poverty and inequality in generating abuse.

openness in adoption Adoptions where contact (which may take a variety of forms) is continued between the adopted child and the birth family.

permanence A principle of childcare which seeks to avoid **drift** and to resolve the long-term futures of children both decisively and fairly speedily.

rule of optimism A term used by Dingwall which suggests that professionals generally give parents the benefit of the doubt where there might be suspicions of child abuse.

same-race placements A policy under which children from particular racial or ethnic groups will be fostered or adopted by families from the same group.

Secure Training Centres Institutions introduced in the mid-1990s for 'persistent young offenders' aged 12–14, with an emphasis on discipline.

short, sharp shock Used in the early 1980s to describe a toughened regime in Detention Centres, intended to deter young offenders from reoffending.

sick role A feature of the **medical model** which regards abusers as sick and hence less than fully responsible for their actions.

social model An approach to child abuse which emphasizes social factors both in its definition (or 'construction') and in its causes.

transracial adoption Literally the adoption of a child from one racial group by a family from another; in practice, almost invariably the adoption of minority ethnic children by white families.

welfare model An approach to youth crime which sees offending as a symptom of deprivation, whether psychological or social, and hence in need of social work intervention rather than punishment.

17

Housing and Housing Policy

Chris Pickvance

CONTENTS

INTRODUCTION: HOUSING POLICY AND HOUSING PATTERNS

In this chapter we examine the development of the institutions through which housing is provided in the UK, the changing pattern of housing policy, and the present housing situation. It is shown that historically housing policy responded very slowly to housing conditions, and that it was political changes which were the stimulus to advances in housing policy. Similarly, today housing policy is as much concerned with political goals, such as securing votes and expanding the scope for market activity, as with meeting housing need. It is thus argued that housing policy is only partly a social policy. The distribution of households across the housing stock is discussed and the effects of processes such as the expansion of owner-occupation and the residualization of council housing are outlined.

WHAT IS HOUSING?

Housing patterns and ways of thinking about housing vary between countries reflecting their different national housing traditions. As every visitor to continental Europe—east or west—knows, flat-dwelling is a much more common pattern than in England and Wales (see Table 17.1). On the other hand, in Scottish cities in the nineteenth century the 'continental' pattern of flat-dwelling took root rather than the pattern of terraced housing south of the border. The explanation for this is to do with industrialization, wage levels, patterns of land ownership, land prices, the organization of the building industry, and architectural influence. For example, in Scotland in the nineteenth century, working-class wage levels were lower than in England while land prices and building costs were higher, and architects were able to press the flat-dwelling solution more successfully.

A second difference concerns **housing tenure**, which refers to the legal relationship between household and dwelling. As Table 17.1 shows, Spain and Greece, two of the poorest countries in the EU, have the highest level of owner-occupation, and West Germany, the richest country, has the lowest level. This flies in the face of the traditional British idea that owner-occupation is associated with high income. The country in the world with the highest level of owner-occupation is in fact Bangladesh (87 per cent). Clearly this raises questions about the value and quality of what is owned and how it is

Table 17.1 European housing patterns, 1987–1992

	% owner-occupation	% social rented or non-profit	% private rented	Average floor space (m^2)	% flats
Spain	78	2	18	83.6	63
Greece	77	0	23	–	57
UK	66	24	9	79.7	19
(Scotland	54	40	6	–	45)
France	54	17	20	85.4	42
Sweden	43	21	21	92.0	54
West Germany	38	15	43	86.6	50

Source: McCrone and Stephens (1995: tables 2.2, 2.3, and 2.4).

built (self-built, commercially built, etc.) It also emphasizes the contrast between agricultural societies, where owner-occupation is the norm, and urban industrial societies, where industrialization leads initially to the growth of rented housing. Tenure, therefore, like any other single characteristic of housing, conceals as much as it reveals.

Table 17.1 also draws attention to contrasts in the role of social and non-profit housing between countries. This refers to housing whose construction is subsidized. Not only does it vary from nil to 24 per cent, but how it is provided varies greatly. In the UK, apart from Northern Ireland, non-profit housing is provided by local councils and to a small extent by housing associations. In Germany for a long time a trade union organization was the largest social provider. In France subsidies have been given to private providers. Once again the British experience of local political control of subsidized housing provision is very unusual. Within the UK, Scotland has a very high level of council housing—which is linked to its weaker economy and strong working-class tradition.

Average dwelling size does not vary greatly between the countries listed in the Table 17.1, but size in square metres is a much more common matter of discussion about housing in continental Europe than in the UK. This is a product of postwar housing shortages and rent controls which were based on rents per square metre. In eastern Europe households are likely to know the precise size of their dwelling, as rent levels were set on the basis of size.

In the UK, thinking about housing centres on housing tenure, and the following four categories of tenure will be used throughout the chapter:

- owner-occupiers: who own outright or are buying their house or flat with a loan (which is known as a mortgage)
- private tenants: who rent their house or flat from a private landlord
- council tenants: who rent their dwelling from the local council, and
- housing association tenants: who rent from housing associations (also known as registered social landlords, or RSLs)

The latter two categories are often referred to as 'social tenants'. More information on each will be given below. But it should be remembered that tenure gives a partial picture of a housing situation.

Every country, then, has its own way of thinking about housing which relates to a tradition of housing provision, policy debate, and intervention, and in turn to the country's particular economic, social, and political history. In this chapter we explore these in the British case. We examine the development of the main types of tenure, and of housing policy, analyse the present housing situation, and show in detail how the owner-occupation and council housing sectors work. The emphasis is on how far housing policy should be seen as social policy and how the housing 'system' works in practice.

THE EMERGENCE OF DIFFERENT HOUSING TENURES AND THE EVOLUTION OF HOUSING POLICY UP TO 1939

We have already introduced the four main types of tenure. We now examine how and why these have changed over time. This historical account will also explain the emergence of housing policy, and will allow us to introduce the question of how far housing policy is about meeting housing need and how far it has other objectives.

In the nineteenth century the vast mass of urban households were private tenants, and their landlords were middle-class business people and professionals who invested in housing as a safe way of saving. Low average income levels for most meant that anything beyond renting a room or a house was out of the question. Owner-occupation was restricted to the very well-off. It was in this situation that two types of initiative developed which were to have long-term consequences for housing provision in the UK: building societies and state action. There were others, such as philanthropic housing and employer-provided housing, but these had no long-term effects.

Building societies started as a self-help solution to housing conditions. They developed independently of the state, and subsequently became one of the most important institutions of the UK housing scene.

Building societies were created in the early nineteenth century by people who earned enough to be able to save, and who formed societies to enable them to build houses for themselves. The principle was that the members would commit themselves to making regular savings which would be used to build houses once a sufficient amount had accumulated. This meant that once the first house had been built and the first member obtained a house, the members would continue to make payments into the society until a house had been built for the last member. The society would then 'terminate'. Terminating building societies only worked if members trusted each other to keep up their payments until they all had houses. In practice they were vulnerable to members losing their jobs or falling ill. A second variety was the 'permanent' building society, in which savers did not need to be borrowers, and this became the basis for the building society familiar to us today, though until the 1930s they lent mainly to private landlords. Unlike public companies owned by their shareholders, building societies were and are mutual organizations owned by their members. By 2000 most building societies had converted into banks.

In the nineteenth century, building societies could not be a widely used solution to housing provision, since they were restricted to the small minority with high enough incomes to be able to save. However, in the interwar period they expanded considerably. They became a convenient place for investors to save—replacing houses in this respect—and as average incomes rose the fraction of the population which could afford to buy a house with a long-term loan increased. The interwar rise in owner-occupation was thus facilitated by the growth of the building societies. As Table 17.2 shows, by the late 1930s owner-occupation was established as a significant form of housing tenure. The growth of building societies up to the Second World War happened with minimal government

Table 17.2 Housing tenure in Great Britain, 1914–2001

	Home owner	Public rented[a]	Private rented	Other[a]
1914	10.0	1.0	80.0	9.0
1938	25.0	10.0	56.0	9.0
1951	29.0	18.0	45.0	8.0
1961	43.0	27.0	25.0	6.0
1971	50.5	30.6	18.8[a]	
1981	57.1	30.6	10.1	2.1
1991	66.0	21.3	9.6	3.2
2001	69.2	14.4	9.9	6.6

[a] 'Public rented' includes new towns as well as local councils. The 1971 figure does not distinguish between 'Private rented' and 'Other'. From 1981 'Other' includes housing associations only, and other tenures are included with 'Private rented'.

Source: Forrest et al. (1990: 57); Department of Environment (1998: table 9.3); www.odpm.gov.uk/housing/statistics, table 102.

Box 17.1 Urban housing conditions in 1843

These streets are often so narrow that a person can step from the window of one house into that of its opposite neighbour, while the houses are piled so high, storey upon storey, that the light can scarcely penetrate into the court or alley that lies between. In this part of the city there are neither sewers nor other drains, nor even privies belonging to the houses. In consequence, all refuse, garbage and excrements of at least 50,000 persons are thrown into gutters every night, so that, in spite of all street sweeping, a mass of dried filth and foul vapours are created, which not only offend the sight and smell, but endanger the health of the inhabitants in the highest degree. Is it to be wondered at, that in such localities all considerations of health, morals, and even the most ordinary decency are utterly neglected? On the contrary, all who are intimately acquainted with the condition of the inhabitants will testify to the high degree which disease, wretchedness, and demoralization have here reached. Society in such districts has sunk to a level indescribably low and hopeless. The houses of the poor are generally filthy, and are never cleansed. They consist in most cases of a single room which, while subject to the worst ventilation, is yet usually kept cold by the broken and badly-fitting windows and is sometimes damp and partly below ground level, always badly furnished and thoroughly uncomfortable, a straw heap often serving as a bed, upon which men and women, young and old, sleep in revolting confusion.

(Report in an English magazine, *The Artisan*, 1843, quoted in Engels (1969: 69) support. Governments established a regulatory framework to prevent fraud and provide security to savers, but did not provide financial support to them.

The other main development in the nineteenth century was the gradual growth of pressure for state intervention in housing, which led ultimately to council housing.

As the quotation from Engels in the Box 17.1 shows, housing conditions in the nineteenth century were atrocious and aroused moral outrage among observers. If there was a simple connection between housing conditions and housing policy, this would have been a time of dramatic advances in housing policy. In fact it was not. The slow emergence of housing policy shows how ideology, self-interest, and politics are far more important than housing need.

The nineteenth century was a period of laissez-faire in the economic sphere: the market was supposed to work best with minimal state involvement. Those who owned property resented state intrusion into their rights, and in particular central interference in the running of localities. Since only the propertied had the vote until the later nineteenth century, they were able to control local policy. Most local councils were made up of landlords who were unlikely to initiate action that would affect their own housing or increase the local taxes they paid. They therefore did little—until the 1840s, when cholera struck. The desire of the propertied class for self-preservation overcame their resistance to legislation, and an exception to laissez-faire was allowed. Local and central state action on sanitation and urban infrastructure took place where the benefits to the propertied classes were clear. This paved the way for further state action.

Public-health professionals were at the forefront of pressure for reform and had some support from politicians. But the rights of landlords to run their houses as they chose, whatever the resulting housing conditions, were strongly defended. The second half of the nineteenth century saw a gradual acquisition of powers by local councils to regulate new and existing housing in their areas. For example, they gained powers to set minimum standards of lighting, ventilation, sanitation, and structural stability in new houses, and powers to close houses unfit for human habitation and to demolish them. They were also obliged to rehouse the tenants and to compensate owners of such housing. These powers were given under public health legislation. It was only in the 1880s that government realized that housing issues needed to be addressed directly. In 1890 councils were allowed to build working-class housing as long as it was sold within ten years—a restriction later removed.

However, the strength of laissez-faire ideology meant that Parliament would not pass **mandatory legislation**, i.e. laws that required action to be taken. Instead it passed **permissive legislation**, which allowed councils who wished to apply these measures to do so but had no effect on the remainder (Gauldie 1974). Despite these obstacles to public action, a few councils took a pioneering role and built council houses. State intervention in housing became more acceptable in the late nineteenth and early twentieth centuries because of changes in the political situation. The political strength of the working class increased considerably after the vote was given to working-class men in the 1870s, and working-class political parties formed. The embryonic Labour party made winning control of local councils its first objective as a step towards gaining power nationally, and this reinforced the importance of local councils as a means of achieving policy goals.

Public mobilization over the state of working-class housing increased and governments were afraid of disorder. Lastly, government grants to local councils increased so that the financial impact of public action on local ratepayers was partly lifted.

The culmination of this pressure for a new direction in housing policy did not occur until 1919, when councils became legally obliged to build houses to meet housing need, subject to central government approval, and were given a government subsidy. This dramatic step was partly due to government concern about house-building levels: the private sector had been failing to build enough houses before 1914, and war had meant a halt to house-building. But again the crucial stimuli were changes in political conditions:

- the continued growth of the labour movement as a political force (and fear that the Russian revolution might incite workers in the UK);
- the Glasgow rent strike in 1915 which caused government to introduce **rent control** to keep down rent levels; and
- the experience of war, with the huge contribution of the mass of the population and the feeling of solidarity that it created, which led the government to believe that a new policy was necessary. Hence the name for the first council housing programme: 'homes fit for heroes' (Gilbert 1970).

It was this policy that gave councils their prominent role as direct providers of housing and helped maintain the tradition of strong local council action. In other countries subsidies were channelled to private building firms or specially created housing organizations.

This historical background reveals the three main types of state intervention in housing.

- The first is state regulation, mostly of private sector activity. This includes the legislation already referred to concerning overcrowding and the closure of unfit housing, building standards, rent controls, and the regulation of building societies. These all remain important, and have been elaborated in the postwar period. For example, detailed planning regulations now exist to improve the appearance and orderliness of the built environment and achieve social goals, and building regulations have been altered to reflect the new concern with energy efficiency.
- The second is state subsidization: the state provides financial support to private actors such as households, landlords, financial institutions, or building firms. Subsidies increase the resources of private actors and take the form of payments, or reductions in taxes. They include tax relief to house purchasers on the interest paid on mortgages, and housing benefits to poor households to enable them to pay higher rents than they otherwise could.
- The third is direct provision. In the case of housing the clear example of this is council housing. Here, instead of regulating and subsidizing or taxing private agents to achieve policy aims, government acts directly.

The first and third types of state intervention are mainly the work of local councils (or the 'local state') while the second involves central government and local branches of ministries too. It should be noted that in the case of housing the contrast between 'state' and 'market' provision is particularly unhelpful. The concept of state provision, i.e. council housing, is clear enough. But all private provision, whether by private landlords or owner-occupation, is highly regulated by the state and, in the case of owner-occupation, subsidized too. Hence there is no such thing as a pure market form of housing provision.

POSTWAR TENURE PATTERNS AND HOUSING POLICY

In the postwar period, as Table 17.2 shows, there have been three tenure trends: the continuing growth in owner-occupation, the continuing decline in private renting, and the rise and subsequent decline in council renting. These changes are connected with changes in housing policy which have made it far more varied in its aims. In particular it is now less of a social policy and favours middle- and high-income groups as well as low-income groups. This is because housing policy has become an explicit means of winning votes for the main political parties, and housing policies which attracted votes from the better-off have become as important as policies aimed at the badly-off. Let us examine policies towards the various housing tenures.

Council housing

From 1945 housing policy concentrated on reconstruction, and council housing played an important role in this task. Subsequently the massive slum clearance programme of the 1950s and 1960s created space for further building of council houses and flats, including the much-criticized high-rise blocks. The council share of the housing stock continued to rise until a peak in 1977/8 in Great Britain, after which it went into a slow decline. We now examine the political and economic reasons for this evolution.

The rationale for council housing is that it is a way of meeting housing need for those whose ability to pay is so low that they could not afford a reasonable quality of housing on the private housing market. To achieve this aim, council housing rent levels need to be low enough to make it affordable. The difficulty of achieving this had emerged in the 1920s, when the rent levels of the first council houses placed them out of reach of the lowest income groups in the working class. Whether council housing is affordable to poor households depends partly on rent levels and partly on social security benefits (such as housing benefits) designed to help with housing costs. The topic of housing benefits will be referred to briefly below, but generally the impact of social security benefits on households, ability to pay for housing is not considered here.

There are three reasons why rent levels have been lower in council housing:

- because the government subsidizes the production of council housing. For example the rate of interest the government pays when it borrows money to build council housing is a special below-market rate;
- because until 1990 councils could subsidize rents from rates (the predecessor of council taxes); and
- because council housing operates outside the housing market. This difference between council and private rented housing is explained in Box 17.2.

Box 17.2 Council and private rent levels: how being outside the market helps keep council rents low

Rent levels in council housing depend on original building costs (and also on repair/modernization costs and subsidy levels), whereas rent levels in private rented housing depend on current market values.

In a period of rising house values the current market value of a house may be far higher than its original building cost. In the private sector, successive owners each make a capital gain as the house is sold at successively higher prices, and landlords base their rents on the current value. Council houses do not go through this process, but remain outside the market. (They do have a market value, but this is irrelevant as long as they remain council houses. Only when they are privatized is this market value relevant.) It is because council house rents are based on original building cost, not current value, that they can be much lower than private sector rents. Additionally, since most councils own houses built at different periods they generally engage in 'rent pooling' which spreads the advantage of the low building costs of the oldest houses over the whole stock.

Policy towards the council housing sector has changed considerably since the Second World War. Initially there was agreement between the Labour and Conservative parties on its importance. But in the mid-1960s the Labour government argued that the job of postwar reconstruction was completed and that slum clearance should give way to individual house improvement. Hence the level of council house building was reduced. The Conservative party took this further, and felt it should cater only for a small minority of households, while Labour continued to give it a broad role. These debates fed into conflicting positions about the level of government subsidy, rent levels, and the desirability of selling council housing.

In 1972 the Conservative government's Housing Finance Act introduced a major reform which reduced the subsidies paid on council housing. The aim was to force councils to raise rents which the government considered excessively low. Its motivation was to encourage households in the council sector to move into private rented or owner-occupied housing, and to discourage demand from new applicants for council housing. The new rents were called 'fair rents' which meant 'closer to private-sector rent'. The change was an attempt to reverse the traditional advantage of low rents in the council sector by aligning rents with those in the private sector. This measure was reversed by Labour in 1975 but reintroduced by the Conservatives in 1980. The effect was that between 1980 and 1989 council rents rose from £13 to £20 per week in constant prices. Over the same period, subsidies per council tenant fell by two-thirds, while they increased by one-third per owner-occupier household. By 1995 council rents were at a level which required housing benefit to be paid to two-thirds of tenants in England. On average this benefit reduced rents for those receiving it from £40.60 to £18.80, and fuelled an increase in spending on housing benefits—see Table 17.3. Paradoxically, therefore, the price of raising council rents to make the sector less attractive was an increase in housing benefits expenditure which more than made up for the reduction in subsidies paid to councils. This example of the dependence of a market solution on increased government spending emphasizes the obstacles to market solutions in the housing of poorer households.

The second major policy change affecting council housing has been the **right to buy** (or council house privatization) policy introduced by the Conservative government in 1980. This policy gave council tenants the right to buy (or 'privatize') their council house or flat at a discount. Whereas previously councils had had the right to sell housing, only a minority of them had used it. The new act thus gave tenants a new right. The size of the discount was between 33 per cent and 50 per cent initially, the maximum later being raised to 60 per cent for houses and 70 per cent for flats. A maximum discount of £38,000 was in force by 2002. Restrictions were also introduced to penalize resale within three years. The government had several motivations in introducing this policy:

- the pursuit of a property-owning democracy as a political goal;
- the belief that councils have too much power and too many assets, and are inefficient landlords; and
- the belief that the scope for market solutions in housing should be expanded because they are more efficient.

The right to buy policy worked in tandem with the policy mentioned above of reducing subsidies and increasing rents in the council sector to make it less attractive to remain in.

The policy achieved its aims. It was the main factor in the reduction of the stock of council (and New Town) dwellings in Great Britain from 6.5 million in 1979 to 3.6 million in 2001, i.e. 44.6 per cent. As a proportion of all housing, the size of the sector shrank from a peak of 31.7 per cent of all housing in 1977 and 1978 to 14.4 per cent in 2001. At the same time the level of house-building by councils fell to below 10,000 houses per year in 1991 and to under 1,000 houses per year from 1996 to 2001. Councils were only allowed to use a small proportion of the proceeds of the sale of council housing for new building. The result was that the capacity of the council sector to provide housing for the groups most in need in the future has declined.

What were the detailed effects of the right to buy policy? Research by Forrest and Murie (1988) shows that:

- Houses were much more likely to be bought than flats. Between 1981 and 1985 only 5 per cent of sales were of flats whereas they made up 30 per cent of the stock.
- Attractive houses, e.g. postwar houses, with two or more bedrooms and a garden, and houses in attractive areas were most likely to be bought.
- Council housing in areas with higher levels of owner-occupation, higher income levels, and under Conservative control were more likely to be bought. In London, sales levels in outer boroughs were far higher than in inner boroughs.
- The households most likely to purchase were those with a head in employment, with multiple earners, which owned a car, whose adult members were in the 30–59 age group, which had school-age children, and which were white rather than black.

Conversely, there was a low rate of sales in areas with high unemployment and high social deprivation.

This led to two important outcomes:

- Changes in the quality of the council housing stock. As the most attractive council housing was purchased, the housing remaining in the council sector became less attractive, more likely to be in unpopular areas, and more likely to be made up of flats.
- Changes in the social composition of households in the council sector. Council tenants have become more homogeneous and increasingly share characteristics associated with poverty, e.g. having no earners or being female-headed households. This is known as the **residualization** of council housing. For example, between 1962 and 2001 the proportion of households in council housing in England with no earners (i.e. whose members are unemployed, pensioners, or have long-term illness) rose from 7 per cent to 69 per cent, while in the owner-occupier sector it rose only from 19 per cent to 33 per cent. There is therefore a growing gulf between the two tenure sectors, which is discussed further below.

By 2002 some evidence was found of companies (legally) paying tenants to buy their houses and then vacate them. The company would then let the house for three years before selling it once the early resale penalty was no longer payable. This was on a small scale. However, measures were due to be introduced in March 2003 to cut maximum discounts from £38,000 to £16,000 in forty-two areas of high demand in the South East.

Owner-occupation

The continuing rise of owner-occupation, from 29.0 per cent in 1851 to 69.2 per cent in 2001, has been the most striking trend of the postwar period (see Table 17.2). Successive governments have adopted policies favouring owner-occupation, the type of housing tenure favoured by middle- and high-income groups. In 1963 the tax on the imputed rent on the investment value of the house was abolished, in 1965 owner-occupied houses were exempted from capital gains tax, and in 1974 tax relief on mortgage interest was left untouched when it was abolished for most other types of borrowing. Additional government support for owner-occupation has taken the form of tax concessions to building societies to enable them to offer higher rates of interest to savers, guarantees to savers in the case of a building society bankruptcy, and the discreet encouragement of takeovers of failing building societies. Support for owner-occupation through tax relief reached a peak in 1988, after which it declined until it was abolished in 2000. Initially the limit of tax relief was not raised in line with inflation: it was raised once from £25,000 to £30,000 in 1983, and from 1988 it was restricted to one taxpayer per house to prevent unmarried couples claiming relief on mortgages of £60,000. By comparison the average house price in 1998 was £78,000. After 1988 the value of tax relief was further diminished by reducing the tax rate to which it applied, which by 1998 had fallen to 10 per cent, and by the declining rate of interest itself. Whereas until the mid-1990s tax relief on mortgage interest was seen as politically untouchable, its declining value meant that its final abolition was relatively uncontroversial.

The strong growth of owner-occupation has led to a debate about whether this growth is entirely due to the government policies outlined which make it more attractive than other tenures. There are two counter-arguments. The first is that in a period of inflation of the type experienced since 1970 any asset which provided a hedge against inflation would be very popular. Since the value of houses rose faster than inflation until 1988, there is evidence to support this argument. Calculations by Saunders (1990) based on surveys in three towns in 1986 showed average net capital gains of £20,000 per owner-occupier household in 1986 prices. (Net capital gain is gross capital gain less the value of the outstanding mortgage.) The net capital gain was highest in Slough (£26,000) and lowest in Derby (£19,000) and Burnley (£13,000). Taking into account the number of years people had been owner-occupiers, the net real capital gains per year were £2,800 in Slough, £800 in Derby and £900 in Burnley. For most households these gains are paper gains in the sense that they are hard to realize; though this can happen, e.g. through inheritance or by over-mortgaging (when a house buyer moves house and takes out a larger mortgage than needed, releasing cash in the process). Capital gains may nevertheless act as incentives to owner-occupation alongside government policies. Interestingly, in Germany, where owner-occupation is low, it is not regarded as a hedge against inflation, and house prices rose only 0.4 per cent per year between 1972 and 1989, compared with 2.2 per cent per year in the UK between 1948 and 1988 (McCrone and Stephens 1995: 53).

The second counter-argument is also put forward by Saunders, who argues that owner-occupation offers greater security and scope for freedom, control, and self-expression than any other type of housing. He goes further and suggests it may be rooted in a 'natural' desire for possession. Others have argued that rented housing can offer the same attractions, and that what is important is that the dwelling is self-contained.

These counter-arguments are not, of course, mutually exclusive. Hence, for example, from Saunders's point of view the different national levels of owner-occupation indicated

Box 17.3 Tax relief on mortgage interest as an incentive to owner-occupation

This tax relief means the house buyer pays and the government receives less income tax. By cheapening the cost of houses this tax relief increased demand and had the effect of keeping house prices higher than they would otherwise be, since the supply of houses responds very slowly to changes in prices. The effect of abolishing it was to raise government tax receipts and to lower house prices.

However the size of these effects depends on the size of the tax relief, which depends on the rate of interest prevailing, the level of income tax to which the relief applies, and any ceilings in operation. The lower the rate of interest, the lower the income tax rate, and the lower any ceiling, the smaller the advantage to the house buyer of tax relief on mortgage interest (and correspondingly the less the cost to the government.) The abolition of this relief in 2000 came after a period when the value of this tax relief to the individual purchaser had reached an all-time low. (See Table 17.3.)

in Table 17.1 do not imply that there are national differences in the 'natural' desire for owner-occupation. They could equally be due to government policies and to differences in economic incentives to households.

One effect of the rising share of owner-occupation has been the increased significance of owner-occupiers as a bloc of voters. The very success of policies favouring owner-occupation has meant that housing policy is increasingly identified with policy which meets the needs of owner-occupiers. The effect of the rise in owner-occupation on the composition of households in the sector is discussed in the next section.

Finally trends in three other fields of housing will be referred to briefly: the private rented sector, housing associations, and homelessness.

Private renting

The long-standing decline of private renting can be attributed to a number of factors:

- the encouragements to owner-occupation and subsidies for council housing which have not been paralleled by favourable treatment for landlords;
- the attraction to landlords of converting rented housing to owner-occupation;
- the stigma attached to private landlords due to abuses;
- legislation which gave certain tenants security against eviction in the 1960s and discouraged landlords; and
- the past use of rent controls and fear that even after they were removed they might be restored.

By the late 1980s, however, the size of the sector had fallen so much that the government introduced new policies such as new types of tenancy which gave tenants fewer rights, incentives to householders to rent rooms, and the removal of regulation of rents in new rented housing (1980) and in new rental contracts except where the tenant receives housing benefit (1989). These factors, combined with rising house prices and low interest rates on savings, eventually led to an increase in the private rented sector from a low of 2.1 million in 1989 to 2.4 million by 2001. A key factor was the growth in popularity of 'buy-to-let' by which landlordism regained some of its former appeal. Nevertheless, although the popularity of buy-to-let may have peaked for the time being there is still a shortage of housing in this sector, rents are high, and tenants cannot always enforce their rights against landlords. The level of rents in the private sector has been a factor in the rise in spending on housing benefits, since the private rented sector is one which houses a minority of poorer households.

Housing associations

The Conservative dislike of council housing was accompanied by support for housing associations. These are non-profit organizations which generally provide rented housing to groups with particular needs, such as elderly people or young people. Originally they were largely funded by government money—on condition that they kept rents below certain levels in order to appeal to low-income households. Their great attraction to the governments of the 1980s was that they were not councils. By 1990 they were building more new housing in Great Britain than councils (18,800 compared with 15,200 out of a total of 190,500 completions). Their contribution peaked in 1995 (37,400, 19.8 per cent of the total of 189,000), but by 2001 had fallen to 20,700 (12.8 per cent of the 162,100 total).

Their difficulties increased after 1988 when they came under government pressure to expand but also to rely less on government funding and more on private funding. Under this pressure they have diversified their activities considerably into housing management and urban regeneration, and even into providing market housing. They try to use some of the profits from these activities to subsidize their traditional provision of housing for groups with specific needs, but have had to charge higher rents to pay back the higher interest rates on private-sector loans. They are thus less able to provide housing for needy groups than before. The higher rent levels lead automatically to higher housing benefit entitlement, and in 2000 63 per cent of housing association tenants in England were receiving housing benefit. In 1998, the last year for which a comparison can be made, 68 per cent of housing association tenants received housing benefit compared with 66 per cent of council tenants.

Homelessness

Last but not least, there has been a considerable increase in homelessness and a number of government responses to it. The definition of homelessness is a difficult one. The narrowest definition is 'rooflessness'—meaning those sleeping rough. Wider definitions include those who are squatting, and those living in hostels for the homeless run by charities or by local councils. Even wider definitions include those living in insecure private housing at risk of eviction, and those who are concealed because they are living as parts of other households. Clearly the reality is much more complex than the single word 'homeless'.

Government responses have been twofold. In 1977 local councils were given the responsibility of housing 'unintentionally homeless' people, a label which implies a distinction between the 'deserving' and the 'undeserving'. This was the culmination of a long campaign by squatters drawing attention to empty council housing (Bailey 1973) which finally found support from a Labour government. In 1985 the obligation was redefined, and only those unintentionally homeless people who fell into a priority need group, e.g. households with children, pregnant women, or 'vulnerable' persons, were eligible for housing. Single homeless people and couples without children are generally outside this category (Malpass and Murie 1994). From 1997 councils were required to provide temporary accommodation for two years only, and to make homeless households apply for permanent housing through the council waiting list (Peace et al. 1997). In 1978 53,000 people were accepted by councils as unintentionally homeless. This figure reached 175,000 in 1992 before falling to 144,000 in 1994. A similar number was refused because they failed to meet the eligibility criteria. In the early 1990s the government provided funding for a number of shelters for homeless people run by charities. In the late 1990s the Labour government gained publicity by appointing a 'homelessness czar' to drive homeless people off the streets. More concretely, in 2002 a new Homelessness Act was passed. This replaced the two-year duty on councils by an indefinite one which was only ended when certain types of offer are made. In addition, the list of types of unintentionally homeless persons in priority need was extended to include 16- and 17-year-olds, certain types of care leaver in the 18–20 age group, and vulnerable ex-service people, ex-offenders, and people fleeing all kinds of violence. (Students were generally ineligible.)

Public spending on housing

One way of understanding the overall character of housing policy is to examine the pattern of public expenditure on housing. Table 17.3 shows the main categories involved. (The figures are at constant prices so they are comparable.) Column (a) shows the decline in subsidies on existing social housing. Column (b) reflects the fall in social housebuilding, and column (c) the rise and fall of receipts from the sale of social housing. Column (d) shows the net cost of social house-building to the public purse. Column (e) shows the dramatic growth of spending on housing benefits. Finally, column (g) shows the rise and fall of mortgage interest relief.

Ideally one would like to read each column of figures as a yardstick of policy aims. Whether this is possible depends on whether the spending is under government control or is influenced by factors beyond housing policy. Columns (a) and (c) do reflect the explicit policies of reducing subsidies to social housing, and cutting the rate of council house-building, which are largely within the government's control. But column (b) reflects tenants' response to the right to buy social housing, and hence the evolution of spending is partly outside government control. Column (e) is even less influenced by government policy and hence cannot be read as meaning that the government wanted to devote more and more spending to housing benefits. Rather, the growth of spending on housing benefits is an unintended effect of another housing policy, namely the

Table 17.3 Public spending on housing, UK, 1976–2000, at 1995/6 prices (£ million)

	Current	Gross capital	Capital receipts	Net capital	Housing total		Mortgage interest relief
					Benefits	Spending	
	a	b	c	d	e	f	g
1976/7	5,292	12,504	1,152	11,352	2,947	17,314	4,659
1981/2	3,960	6,277	2,387	3,889	4,087	12,399	4,569
1986/7	2,321	6,988	3,748	3,250	5,974	12,063	7,218
1991/2	1,406	7,795	2,658	5,138	8,513	15,342	6,823
1996/7	−115	4,996	2,279	2,717	12,423	15,267	2,634
1999/2000	n.a.	n.a.	n.a.	n.a.	10,645	13,165	1,429

Col. b − col. c = col. d.
Col. a + col. d + col. e + N. Ireland spending = col. f.
Cols. a–d are for Great Britain; cols. e–g are for the UK.
The figure 13,165 includes a UK figure for current and net capital spending of £2,821 million.
Source: Hills (1998: table 5A1; HM Treasury (2002: table 3.6); www.inlandrevenue.gov.uk/statistics, table 5.2.)

raising of social housing rents towards market levels and the reduction of regulation of private sector rents. It is also due to continuing low incomes of the tenants concerned. The result is that two-thirds of social tenants cannot afford to pay the rents they face, and 60 per cent have the whole of their rent paid by housing benefit. Housing benefit spending has expanded to facilitate the shift to market rent levels, and is intricately linked with the financial stability of housing providers such as councils, RSLs, and private landlords. Finally, the rise and decline of mortgage interest relief in column (g) are partly due to the changing policy (where the incentive value of the interest relief peaked in the mid-1980s) but are also influenced by interest rates which are a matter of general economic policy. Paradoxically, then, the largest form of public spending on housing in 1996/7, spending on housing benefits, was not the intended result of housing policy but was due to the social security lifeboat needed to rescue tenants who could not afford market rents. This is a measure of the obstacles to introducing market mechanisms where people's ability to pay is very low.

In 1997 Labour considered radical plans to reduce the scale of spending on housing benefit. There were a number of reasons for considering radical reform. As Table 17.3 shows, spending on housing benefit had more than doubled in real terms between 1986 and 1996. In addition, it was believed to be open to abuse, and allegedly created dubious incentives for both landlords (who might be encouraged to impose large rent increases) and tenants (who might be deterred from 'shopping around' for cheaper rents). Proposals included introducing a flat rate or setting a maximum below 100 per cent of the rent charged (which 60 per cent of recipients receive). In the end the government abandoned its plans. As Kemp (2000) shows, reforming housing benefit would have had knock-on effects for social security, disrupted housing suppliers whose financial stability depended on the boost in 'ability to pay' which housing benefit gave tenants, and created many losers, with unpredictable electoral consequences. The way housing benefit was locked into housing finance, social security, and electoral politics thus prevented radical reform.

Conclusion: housing policy and social policy

It has been shown that housing policy is not simply or even primarily aimed at those in greatest housing need. Housing policy was very slow to develop in the nineteenth century, and the driving forces then and since have been political. Only by the 1920s did it gain a strong 'social' strand. For twenty years after 1945 housing policy was the subject of an inter-party consensus and went ahead 'on two legs', council housing and support for owner-occupation. Since the 1960s it has been increasingly used to pursue party political objectives, even when this meant helping the better off more than those in greatest housing need. The promotion of owner-occupation, especially until the mid-1980s, the demotion of council housing, and the attempt to introduce market rents for social tenants are clear illustrations of this. This could happen because the voices of those in housing need and those representing them are often very weak compared with the voices of financial institutions and builders and the voting strength of the majority. Governments calculate the votes to be won and lost before introducing new policies. Since governments have numerous policy goals, it should not be expected that policy in an area such as housing is driven by a single goal such as meeting housing need.

THE PRESENT HOUSING SITUATION IN THE UK

To understand the present housing situation, we first need to understand what is meant by a household and the housing stock. This will help answer the question whether there is a housing shortage. We then investigate the distribution of households across the different tenures.

The **housing stock** refers to the available housing in the country. This is partly a physical fact, since there are a certain number of physical dwellings available. This number increases if one includes caravans. However, it is also a social fact. The existence of second homes means that not all the housing stock is available to those seeking housing. Some housing is also necessary to facilitate movement, and to allow repair in both private and social sectors. Some housing is unfit or empty because it is 'hard to let' (e.g. because it lacks lifts or is located in a very unattractive neighbourhood).

Turning to **households**, the census definition refers to 'a single person or group of people who have the address as their only or main residence and who either share one meal a day together or share a living room'. (The pre-1981 definition required that household members were catered for at least one meal a day by the same person, a requirement which was abandoned in the face of variability in eating habits.) The number of households depends partly on the size and age structure of the population. But there is no constant relation between the size of the adult population and the number of households. The ratio between the number of households and the adult population is known as the 'headship rate'. This depends on customs regarding young and elderly people living independently, rates of cohabitation, marriage, separation and divorce, women's participation in the labour force, preferences for living alone rather than with partners, etc. For example, in southern Europe it is still unusual for young people to leave home before marriage or setting up home as a couple. In northern Europe the opposite is the case. Between 1971 and 2001 there was an increase in the number of households in England as the mean household size decreased from 2.9 to 2.3.

However, some households contain other potential households. For example, a single adult or young couple sharing with their parents is known as a **concealed household** because potentially they would like to live as a separate household. Whether they can do so depends on the housing situation itself. When the supply of housing increases, or its affordability improves (either because incomes rise or housing costs fall), the number of households increases. For example, young people leave home earlier, or young couples who are living in the parental home can afford to live on their own. For all these reasons the number of households is not simply a demographic fact. It follows that the scale of housing needed by the population can never be expressed in a single figure.

In 2001 it was estimated that in Great Britain there were 24.1 million households and 24.7 million dwellings. Of the latter, 230,000 were second homes and 750,000 were empty, some unfit, some unlettable. Given the need for some empty houses simply to allow for households to move, and given that concealed households are omitted from the 24.1 million figure, it is clear that the housing problem measured in these terms is far from solved. In addition, local variation in housing demand means that local shortages will exist even when the national figures show less of a gap.

Tables 17.4 to 17.6 show the distribution of households with different social characteristics among the different housing tenure categories.

Table 17.4 can be read by comparing each tenure column with the 'All tenures' column. It shows that outright ownership is concentrated in the middle and older age groups and that under-35s make up one quarter of owner-occupiers buying with a mortgage, a very high figure by European standards. The age distributions of council tenants and RSL tenants are very similar to those of all tenures, but with an underrepresentation of 45–64s. This reflects the fact that young households can enter the sector and once within it are likely to stay—unless they buy the dwelling. Private renting is by far the 'youngest' of the tenures, being extremely important for the under 25s with nearly half of private tenants being under 35: this reflects young people's lower incomes, lower priority on housing compared with work, and greater mobility.

Table 17.5 can be read by comparing the row for each tenure with the 'All tenures' row. This reveals whether a tenure group has more or less than the average proportion of households in a particular income group. As might be expected, the table shows that higher-income households are more likely to be buying a house. However, the likelihood of being an outright owner (i.e. having no outstanding loan) is actually higher for lower income groups. This is partly because of the relation between income and age. On retirement, when most owner-occupiers have paid off their mortgages (see Table 17.4), their household income will fall and they will move to a lower-income decile as they rely on pensions. It is also because of ownership of low-value houses among low-income households.

Conversely, low-income households are more likely to be social or private tenants. There is no appreciable difference between the incomes of council tenants and RSL tenants. However, neither of the social housing tenures is absolutely restricted to the lowest two income groups, which account for 40 per cent of all households. First, social

Table 17.4 Age structure of household head by tenure category, England, 2000–2001 (vertical percentages)

	Outright owner[a]	Owner with mortgage	Council rented	RSL rented	Private rented	All tenures
Under 25		1.9	5.4	5.6	15.2	3.5
25–34	2.1	23.0	16.1	19.5	33.4	16.9
35–44	4.0	32.0	17.1	18.6	18.1	19.8
45–64	38.5	40.0	27.1	23.8	19.6	34.6
65–74	30.7	2.2	16.1	13.7	5.3	13.2
75 or over	24.7	0.9	18.2	18.9	8.5	12.0

[a] An outright owner is someone without a mortgage.
Source: OPDM website, table 809, my calculations.

Table 17.5 Household income (net of income tax and National Insurance contributions) by housing tenure category, England, 2000/2001 (horizontal percentages)

Household income	Under 100	100–200	200–300	300–400	400–500	500–600	600–700	700 and over
Outright owner	10	27	21	15	9	5	4	9
Buying with mortgage	2	8	14	18	17	13	9	19
Local authority rented	27	45	17	7	3	1	0	0
RSL rented	24	45	18	6	2	1	0	0
Private rented	18	28	19	11	9	4	3	6
All tenures	11	29	17	14	11	7	5	11

Source: OPDM website, table 809.

housing is not restricted to the very lowest income groups. This may be because, while access depends on need, there is no continuing check on household income and no obligation on a household to leave social renting if its income rises. Households with multiple earners may stay in a council dwelling rather than move out. In recent decades council tenants have been increasingly concentrated among the lowest income groups as the size of the tenure category gets smaller, and it is made up increasingly of people without income from employment.

Since 1980 there has been a sharp decline in council renting across the board, but particularly in the upper income groups. In other words, as those purchasing have become more heterogeneous in income terms, the remaining council sector has become a more homogeneous and lower-income sector. The decrease in the private rented sector has been more even across the income range. Finally, there has been an increase in outright ownership among the middle income groups.

A recent study has pointed out that because of the high proportion of households in owner-occupation, half of the people living in poverty are either outright owners (18 per cent) or people buying their house with a mortgage (32 per cent) (Burrows 2003). This results directly from the growing economic and social heterogeneity of households in owner-occupation. Burrows points out that current policy measures, for example housing benefit, do not recognize the extent of poverty among owner-occupiers.

Table 17.6 can be read by comparing each tenure column with the 'All tenures' column and looking at the differences in socioeconomic group distribution. The table confirms

Table 17.6 Socioeconomic group and economic activity composition of households in each tenure group, Great Britain, 2000 (vertical percentages)

	Outright owner	Owner with mortgage	Council renting	Housing association renting	Private renting unfurnished	Private renting furnished	All tenures
Professional	3	9	1	1	7	16	6
Employers and managers	8	26	2	3	12	15	15
Intermediate non-manual	5	15	3	6	11	13	10
Junior non-manual	4	10	7	8	11	13	8
Skilled manual and own account non-professional	10	22	10	9	10	7	7
Semi-skilled manual and personal service	3	8	10	9	10	7	7
Unskilled manual	1	2	3	4	3	3	2
Economically inactive	67	8	65	59	32	22	38

Source: www.statistics.gov.uk/lib2000/resources/fileAttachments/GHS2000.pdf (Office for National Statistics, *Living in Britain*, 2000 edn., table 4.13).

outright ownership as being very high among the economically inactive (i.e. pensioners, but possibly some unemployed households too.) Owner-occupiers with mortgages show the expected overrepresentation among the four highest socioeconomic groups. However, it is less expected to find that skilled manual households are also overrepresented among owner-occupiers with a mortgage. This shows how far owner-occupation has spread. (These figures may be misleading, since the classification is by the occupation of the head of household, whereas ability to take out a mortgage depends on the incomes of both partners in the case of couples.) Council tenancy shows the concentration of the two lowest-status socioeconomic groups which parallels that of low incomes shown in Table 17.5. However, skilled manual work households are underrepresented in council housing, an indication of the effect of council house sales in residualizing the sector. Housing association tenants show a similar distribution to council tenants.

COUNCIL HOUSING AND OWNER-OCCUPATION IN PRACTICE

As we have seen, the major political debates over housing have concerned the degree to which it should be provided by the state or by the market, and the degree to which it should be subsidized and regulated. To go beyond the ideological debates about market and state alternatives of access to housing, we need to understand how different housing tenures work in practice. The focus here will be on owner-occupation and council housing and how households gain access to them. It will be shown that the normal functioning of both tenures leads to some undesirable results.

It is useful to think of access as controlled by **gatekeepers**, and to see households as possessing varying characteristics and resources which affect their chances of successful entry. In owner-occupation the gatekeepers are the staff of estate agents, banks, and building societies. In council housing they are council officials. The term 'gatekeeper' is appropriate because these groups operate **rules of access** which determine the chance that a household will be able to obtain access via the channel concerned. In owner-occupation, access depends on ability to pay and the security of the house as an asset. In council housing, access depends on meeting rules of eligibility which are mostly non-financial.

Owner-occupation in practice

The first step in considering owner-occupation is to recognize that, for the vast majority, owner-occupation is only possible with the help of a mortgage provided by a building society or bank. It is true that a small minority of people inherit houses or can afford to buy them for cash. It is also true that the mortgage will not cover the whole cost of purchase, and that some reliance on savings or on a family loan will be necessary. The extent of inheritance of houses and family financial help and their correlation with social class are discussed in Boxes 17.4 and 17.5.

Box 17.4 Inheritance of housing

This refers to the inheritance of a house or of the proceeds of the sale of a house. A survey by Hamnett et al. (1991) found that 9 per cent of respondents lived in households where a member had inherited a house or part of the proceeds of the sale of a house. 67 per cent of recipients were 40 or over. Those who were owner-occupiers at the time of inheritance were six times as likely to inherit as council tenants (13 per cent versus 2 per cent), and there was a strong correlation with social class: 17 per cent of households with professional or managerial heads had inherited compared with 5 per cent of semi-skilled and unskilled manual heads. Inheriting on more than one occasion was even more strongly correlated with class. Since the probability of inheriting housing depends on the ownership patterns among the parental generation, the degree of inequality in this respect may become less in the future due to the increasing proportion of all households in owner-occupation. However inequalities in the value of inherited houses are likely to remain.

Box 17.5 Family help with finance for housing

It is difficult to research into how much financial help a household has had from its family, since finance may not have been given explicitly for housing. A study of 16–35-year-olds in south-east England in 1991 found that of those who had left home only 29 per cent had received financial help for any purpose since leaving, and only 12 per cent had received help explicitly for housing purposes (Pickvance and Pickvance 1995). This was correlated with parental social class. The average amount received was £1,900. When asked the purpose of the help, 7 per cent (of those who had left home) said it was to help with purchase of a flat or house. As many as 49 per cent of all respondents thought their parents could provide some help—£2,000 being the median figure—but only 20 per cent agreed that parents should provide financial help with housing. This suggests that even in a region where parental incomes are high and house prices are high—so that both the capacity to provide and the need for financial help are great—the extent of actual financial help was very limited.

The primary concern of banks and building societies—the main source of mortgages—is profit (or 'surplus'). This means they need to match the investments they receive from savers with the loans they make. Originally building societies borrowed only from individuals. Today, like banks, they also borrow on the money markets. Since the deregulation of financial institutions all mortgage lenders have been able to diversify their operations. In some cases they have invested in risky activities which have jeopardized their stability. To operate effectively, financial institutions need to maintain public confidence and control risk. Banks and building societies risk losing their money if borrowers prove unable to maintain their repayments. Building societies are subject to an additional constraint. Because their savings are taken in on a short-term basis but are lent out in long term (e.g. twenty-five-year) house mortgages, they are less able to withstand a 'run on the bank'—when savers descend demanding their money back—a familiar phenomenon in Russia or Latin America. Hence the creation of public confidence in their operation is a prime concern. Their success in achieving this is a reflection of the high degree of social stability in the UK and trust in institutions generally. One form of government support for building societies is that it guarantees the protection of 90 per cent of a person's savings (up to a certain maximum) in the case of a collapse. In passing, it may be added that competition from banks in the provision of mortgages, and the greater reliance of building societies on the money market for funds (a means of avoiding the instability and high cost of collecting savings from individuals), were major influences in the conversion of many building societies into public companies in the 1990s. What had started as self-help mutual organizations became fully-fledged market institutions.

The need of mortgage lenders to maintain confidence and control risk has practical effects on access to housing, since it is translated into a concern for the security of the loan. This means they examine carefully the capacity of the borrower to repay, and the value of the house. They want to be confident about the regularity and level of income of the household. And since the mortgage is secured against the house (i.e. the lender holds the deeds of the house as long as the occupier has an outstanding loan), they are selective about what houses they lend on. This has three consequences.

- *Red-lining*. In some cities whole neighbourhoods are considered risky and are 'red-lined', which means that no loans are obtainable for purchase in them from the main lenders. (The term refers to the line drawn round such neighbourhoods on a map.) For example, in the 1960s Islington, an inner north London district well-known today for its affluent population, was an area in which the main building societies were unwilling to lend (Williams 1976). At this time it contained a large majority of private rented housing. During the 1960s the landlords who owned this housing realized that they could make more money by converting the house for single-family occupation. Moreover, the government made available improvement grants to cover part of the cost of modernization. Ironically, these partial grants were only of use to owners who had savings to add to them or who planned to sell the house when it was renovated. Existing tenants, who were obstacles to renovation and resale, were evicted and the conversion of the area started. The result was that eventually Islington became a very safe area for investment and one in which today all lenders operate.
- *Unmortgageable dwellings*. Just as certain neighbourhoods may be judged too risky by lenders, so individual houses may be avoided. Houses liable to subsidence or flooding, or newly built houses built on polluted land or on former waste sites giving off gases, may prove unsaleable by existing owners. Houses or flats containing asbestos or decaying concrete, or simply with basements, may also fall foul of risk-avoiding lenders.
- *Risky occupations*. Finally, lenders pay attention to the borrower's occupation and are likely to discriminate against borrowers in 'risky' occupations. These include many self-employed occupations. (In 1997 13 per cent of the labour force in employment was self-employed.) Cyclical industries such as building are also considered risky.

One important conclusion is that mortgage lenders are selective in their lending policy, since their aim is to meet their own financial objectives. They only meet the housing need of those who fit these criteria.

However, not all loans for house purchase come from major banks and building societies. Other sources of loans, such as secondary banks and finance houses, are used by some borrowers who are rejected by the main lenders. How is this possible? The answer is that the mortgage market is segmented. Secondary banks offer loans at a higher rate of interest and for a shorter term. In turn they can offer higher rates of interest to savers—who take higher risks in the hope of greater rewards. The result is that loans are available at higher rates of interest and for shorter terms from these lenders. Each segment of the mortgage market involves different types of lender, dealing with different types of borrower and different types of house and offering different terms. Those who are least creditworthy (including the poorest households) pay most for mortgages or do not get one at all, while the most secure borrower pays least. This result may seem bizarre but it is a completely normal effect of market operation. Gatekeepers in market institutions like mortgage lenders create rules of access which have nothing to do with housing need and everything to do with their own solvency. Hence, as a mechanism for ensuring affordable housing for all social groups one cannot say that the housing market works.

Lending institutions generally defend their access rules and deny that red-lining takes place. But however it is described, a refusal to lend in an area by major lenders has inevitable consequences: the area will go 'downhill'. This happens because any mortgages that are available are at a high cost, and to meet these costs the owner has to crowd the house with more households in order to afford the repayments. The result is to worsen the reputation of the district and bring about the decline feared by the initial risk-averse lender.

Marginal owner-occupiers We now examine the impact of owner-occupation on lower-income households. In the 1980s the rising share of households in owner-occupation came about because many households who would previously not have considered owner-occupation began to do so. They included those who privatized their council house or flat, but many others too. The popularity of owner-occupation in the 1980s was due to the following factors:

- the decline in supply of private rented housing;
- the increasing cost and decreasing attractiveness of council housing as privatization proceeded;
- the desire for capital gains: in the 1970s and 1980s house prices rose much faster than inflation and produced 'capital gains' (at least on paper) to owner-occupiers;
- the increasing ability to pay for loans as more women entered the labour force;
- the large supply of funds available to mortgage lenders;
- a relaxation of lending criteria such that households were allowed to borrow a larger multiple of their income, e.g. three or more instead of two and a half. This allowed mortage lenders to lend all the funds they had available. It also enabled households to borrow more, but increased the level of their repayments and made them more vulnerable to any fall in their income;
- tax policy which allowed unmarried couples or groups to borrow more.

This mixture of constrained alternatives, changed access criteria by lenders, and individual desire to translate increasing incomes into capital gains led to the entry of a new swathe of households into the owner-occupied sector. Unfortunately, house prices rose to a peak in 1989 and then fell 15 per cent to 1993, only reaching the 1989 level again in 1998. (If inflation is allowed for, the fall is much greater and the 1989 level had not been reached by 1998.) As a result there was a 'shake-out' in which mortgage arrears and repossessions increased. The fall in house prices meant that some households wishing to sell could only do so at a price which was less than the value of their mortgage. In other words the value of their house, after deducting the mortgage, was negative: hence the term **negative equity** (or 'negative net capital gain', in Saunders's terms). Research showed that in 1993 households affected by negative equity were most likely to:

- have purchased between 1988 and 1991;
- to have been under 25 at the time of purchase;

- to have purchased a house for under £40,000;
- to have had manual or clerical occupations; and
- to have had an annual joint income of between £20,000 and £30,000 (Dorling and Cornford 1995).

In brief, they were precisely the marginal owner-occupiers attracted into the sector in the 1980s.

Other symptoms of the late 1980s and early 1990s were mortgage arrears and repossessions. Any threat to a household's income has an immediate impact on its ability to keep up mortgage payments. The easing of lending criteria in the 1980s, the rise in interest rates in the late 1980s, and the increase in unemployment in 1990 had a direct impact on owner-occupiers' ability to maintain mortgage payments. This was particularly so for those who had bought a house in the late 1980s and whose housing costs were a high proportion of their incomes.

This led first to the increase in households experiencing **mortgage arrears**, i.e. payments which have not been made and which are owed to the lender. Between 1988 and 1991 the proportion of households with mortgage arrears rose from 0.6 per cent to 2.3 per cent. For a mortgage lender this poses a problem. It can either allow a grace period during which arrears build up in the hope that the mortgagee will be able to pay later, or it can repossess the house, forcing the household to give up the house and allowing the lender to sell it, in the hope of recouping the value of its loan. In a significant minority of cases repossession took place, and from 1989 to 1992 the level of repossessions rose from 0.2 per cent to 0.8 per cent of households with mortgages, i.e. 76,000 houses (Bramley 1994).

The fall in interest rates in the 1990s and the recovery of the economy had the effect of reducing mortgage arrears and repossessions. By the mid-1990s the memory of the decline in house prices led to a new mood. The government became cautious about the desirability of expanding occupation any further. It feared that the dream of a property-owning democracy was turning into a nightmare, and that voters would remember this at election time. During the 1991–6 period the proportion of owner-occupied housing rose only from 66.0 per cent to 66.9 per cent (Table 17.2). The lending institutions also showed a new caution: the experience of negative equity, mortgage arrears, and repossessions led them to adopt less generous lending policies. On the demand side, labour market uncertainty made households rethink their attitudes to house purchase. The idea that owner-occupation was a source of security or a way of making large capital gains seemed to belong to a long past age. But by the late 1990s confidence in rising house prices had returned. The low interest rates had a double effect on demand. They made mortgages cheaper and housing more affordable, but also diverted savings from low-interest accounts into house purchase where there was the chance of a capital gain. As a result demand was stimulated and prices were still rising rapidly by 2002.

Areas of high and low housing demand Finally in this section we discuss two recent developments in government policy, key worker housing and housing market renewal, which address two related aspects of an increasingly prominent areal contrast in the UK. Areas of high housing demand are characterized by high housing costs, difficulties in recruiting workers, and workers undertaking long-distance weekly commuting journeys. **Key worker housing** refers to housing which responds to this situation. It is the result of a successful claim to prioritize the affordability problems of specific groups of workers. In 2000 the problems of recruiting (and retaining) health workers, policemen and women, and teachers led the employers and unions concerned to convince government that these 'key workers' needed special treatment in housing provision. As a result, in 2001 the Labour government made £250 million available under its four-year 'Starter Homes Initiative' to build houses for 10,000 key workers in the south-east. In 2002 a further £200 million was allocated for 4,000 more such homes. Although the reality of the affordability problem for these groups cannot be denied, households who share the same affordability problems but are not in public service jobs are ignored.

Conversely, in areas of low demand the symptoms are vacant, deteriorating, or abandoned dwellings. These occur in all tenure categories, and include owner-occupied housing where there is negative equity. These are areas of unemployment and out-migration. However, they are also areas where new housing has been built, and paradoxically this has added to the difficulties of renting or selling less attractive housing. In 2001, in response to lobbying by local governments and house-building interests, the government set up a £25 million 'housing **market renewal** fund' to operate 'pathfinder' projects in nine towns in the Midlands and north. Subsequently, in 2002 a £500 million fund was set up. There is some debate about how such funding is best used. Efforts to improve the conditions of existing housing or to help owners with negative equity will be of limited value if new house-building in the same locality continues to divert demand.

Council housing in practice

Turning to the second major housing tenure, to understand how households get access to housing in the council sector it is necessary to be aware of supply as well as demand. Councils own large and diverse stocks of housing. Council housing differs in age from interwar to modern, in type from flats in low- and high-rise blocks to semi-detached houses, in size (e.g. number of bedrooms), in the attractiveness and location of the neighbourhood (from inner-city to urban periphery), and in condition from unmodernized to renovated. Councils can also make use of bed-and-breakfast accommodation.

The character of this stock reflects past building policy, modernization policy, and council housing sales. The effect of the latter in removing the more attractive housing from the sector has already been discussed. Councils are selective in their modernization efforts, with the effect that differences in quality are preserved. The heterogeneous stock means that councils are gatekeepers to a variety of housing types.

Turning to how councils allocate their housing, they are subject to some national legislation about which groups are eligible. Councils are obliged to rehouse families whose houses were demolished. This was very important in the period of slum clearance in the 1950s and 1960s. Since 1977 they have been obliged to provide housing for the **unintentionally homeless** in priority categories. Finally, the 'waiting list' has been the access channel for those in need who did not fit any specific category. For completeness, one should add that tenancies can also be passed on to children, and transferred to or exchanged with other tenants. Normally, moves by existing tenants take priority over tenancies offered to new tenants.

Councils have considerable discretion about what criteria they use when dealing with households applying through the waiting list. For decades the most common type of allocation system has been the **points system**, in which points are given for various measures of need such as having children, living in damp or overcrowded conditions, or suffering illness. More debatable criteria may also be included, such as years of residence in the area. Having a low income is not a criterion. Those with the highest number of points are offered housing. Other less common schemes rely on the date of application (i.e. 'first come first served') or discretion. There is no obligation to house households on the waiting list within a specific time. The length of time a household waits is dependent on the number of tenancies becoming available, whether they match the household's characteristics, and the number of households with higher positions on the waiting list. Some households fail to apply for council housing because they think the chance of a tenancy is remote. Likewise, some households give up hope but leave their names on the list—it is estimated that 40 per cent of names on waiting lists are 'dead wood'.

In 2002 a new Act allowed councils to abandon single housing registers and widened the groups eligible for council housing. In particular, intentionally homeless people and applicants from outside the area became eligible, but not people 'subject to immigration control'. It might seem surprising that a sector which was shrinking in size should widen the groups eligible to gain access to it. The reason for this was the emergence of large numbers of empty dwellings in certain parts of the country, for example in many parts of northern England. In such areas councils were under pressure to adopting a marketing mentality rather than a restrictive mentality in order to persuade households to occupy these dwellings, a quite new experience on this scale. (Previously there had been 'unlettable blocks' in otherwise popular areas.) The new legislation allowed councils to adopt the appropriate method for their own locality.

Despite the sale of council housing, the number of lettings to new tenants remained remarkably constant from 1983 to 1995. Since then in England it has fallen by 23 per cent, from 422,000 in 1996/7 to 327,000 in 2000/1. Of the latter, 104,000 (32 per cent) were to existing tenants wishing to move within the sector and 222,000 (68 per cent) to new tenants. Of the latter, 72 per cent were drawn from the waiting list and 27 per cent from among homeless households (ODPM website, table 601).

The allocation of tenancies by councils has been extensively studied, and reveals the importance of the diversity of the housing stock. First, councils see themselves as public landlords with a duty to preserve the value of the stock. To do this they match households to 'appropriate' housing. This is partly a matter of matching household size with dwelling size. More controversially, councils make judgements about both the quality of the dwellings and the 'quality' of the households. Again a deserving/undeserving distinction is implicit. Households are classified by their reputation as regular payers, 'problem' families, etc. 'Good' tenants are then offered housing in estates or parts of estates with other 'good' tenants, while 'problem' families are placed together in the least attractive housing. Homeless households are allocated unattractive council housing or placed in temporary housing, e.g. low-quality private rented or bed-and-breakfast accommodation. In practice, although being homeless and on the waiting list are distinct access channels, some homeless households are on the waiting list. By making the housing offered to homeless households unattractive, councils seek to encourage people to use the waiting list rather than take a 'short cut' via the homelessness channel. This practice was later reinforced by legislation, and from 1997 councils had to place homeless households in temporary accommodation and only allow them to obtain permanent council housing through the waiting list. This restriction was removed in 2002.

Secondly, contrary to what is often believed, the allocation of tenancies has often allowed applicants some choice (Clapham and Kintrea 1986). The extent of this varies considerably according to demand. It means that applicants can state a preference for an area, and can receive several offers. They are not obliged to accept the first offer, but the snag is that if they do not they cannot be sure that a second or third offer will be better, and after three offers they may lose their place on the waiting list. Applicants are more likely to express preferences for the most attractive estates and dwellings, but councils need to let all their dwellings. To deal with the problem of how to find tenants for the least attractive dwellings, they offer the least attractive dwellings as 'first offers' to 'problem households' in the hope that they will be accepted. 'Good' households are more likely to be offered attractive dwellings initially. It has been found that households in most desperate need are likely to accept the poor-quality dwellings first offered to them, while those in less need wait and hope for something better. The effect of this is to create and preserve a hierarchy of council estates, and to make it likely that those households in greatest need find themselves in the worst council housing (Pawson and Kintrea 2002).

The way households get access to council housing, therefore, depends on the nature of the stock and on council allocation policies. These allocation policies are determined by national legislation and locally decided priorities. However, they are concerned with the management of the stock as well with meeting housing need.

In conclusion, we have seen that both owner-occupation and council housing operate with rules of access which exclude some households and include but differentially treat others. Two categories of household are excluded from owner-occupation: those whose incomes are too low or too uncertain and those who want to buy 'risky' houses or houses in 'risky' areas. Although the segmentation of the mortgage market means that some households will remain 'included' but have to cope with tough loan terms, others will be totally excluded. The rules of access here are probably resistant to change because they are part of the conventional wisdom of the wider financial system. In council housing the effect of the professional ideologies of council housing managers is to channel households to better or worse housing within the sector. This is differential treatment of the sort normal in a housing market. Exclusion also exists in the council sector. It applied to homeless households who before 2002 did not meet the legal criteria of being unintentionally homeless and in a priority group. But it also occurs because being on the waiting list does not guarantee inclusion, i.e. eventually being offered council housing. This is why some households in housing need do not join the waiting list, while others do so but find their own housing or remain as concealed households. The effects of council housing allocation also depend on the supply situation. In areas of housing surplus, as mentioned above, councils may be in the position of desperately seeking households (though they may channel people to housing of different qualities). It is in areas of housing shortage that the phenomenon of exclusion will be most marked.

Thus, whereas the normal functioning of owner-occupation means it cannot meet all housing need, because access depends on ability to pay, council housing too, which is aimed at those unable to pay, in practice is also unable to do so completely. It would be reassuring to think that the private rented sector and housing associations cope with those excluded from these two sectors. Undoubtedly they do so to some extent, but the other options for those who are excluded from the two large sectors are to be homeless and/or to be a concealed household.

CONCLUSION

In this chapter we have answered the question 'Is housing policy social policy?' by rejecting the idea that it is simply a response to housing need. Rather, we have seen that housing conditions only become a housing problem leading to government action when a successful claim is made following mobilization by interested parties such as political parties, unions, local councils, employers, and housing suppliers and financiers. It is these groups and their mobilization which determines whether state action in response to need takes place, and if so, what form it takes and which groups benefit from it.

The immense level of housing need in the nineteenth century met with minimal response until its last decades. What changed then was the rise of the working class as a political actor. This led to housing policy with a 'social' character and, together with the wartime experience of solidarity, to the post-1918 government's major innovation of council housing. After 1945 there was quite a long period when both major political parties supported the building of both council housing and owner-occupied housing. Only in the 1970s did the inter-party differences become striking. After that the Conservative government defined council housing as an obstacle to increased owner-occupation and took measures against it. The Labour government passed the 1977 Homelessness Act and briefly reversed the Conservative attack on council housing. But in the 1980s it abandoned its traditional identification with council housing and accepted that there was widespread support among council tenants for the right-to-buy scheme. By the 1990s therefore housing policy was partly 'social' (e.g. council housing, housing associations, housing allowances) and partly support for market provision (assistance to owner-occupiers and private landlords). The explanation of this policy shift is that housing policy became a means of winning votes from the middle-income groups. Their interests were therefore advanced at the expense of the low-income groups.

Paradoxically, this shift in the direction of housing policy has not corresponded to a reduction of state intervention. State regulation of housing has continued at a high level, and Table 17.3 shows that while there has been a reduction in the scale of state spending on council housing and that subsidies in the form of mortgage tax relief have ended, there has been a threefold expansion in housing benefit from 1976 to 1999. The latter trend is due to the difficulty of introducing market-level rents in the three rented sectors used by poorer households, and ultimately to the dual (pro-poor and pro-market) character of housing policy in the UK. Thus in the housing sphere it is not the question of whether state intervention is present or absent which is important but rather what forms it takes and who benefits from it. It is likely that the income groups which benefit from housing policy in the future will depend on the same mix of economic, political, and social need considerations which have been evident in housing policy in the past.

KEY LEGISLATION

1972 Housing Finance Act Introduced 'fair rents' for council tenants and allowed councils to make a surplus on council housing. This initiated the rise in council rents.

1977 Homelessness Act Imposed a duty on councils to rehouse unintentionally homeless families and individuals permanently.

1980 Housing Act The 'right to buy' act, which gave council tenants the right to buy their dwelling at a discount. Previously councils had a right to sell but council tenants had no right to buy.

1988 Housing Act Reduced regulation of private rented sector, and forced housing associations to rely more on private finance. Increased rent levels followed, and helped lead to the increase in housing benefit payments

1996 Housing Act Required councils to place unintentionally homeless people in temporary accommodation (either in social housing or private rented housing). Their access to permanent council accommodation to be only through the waiting list.

2002 Homelessness Act Extends the duty on councils to house unintentionally homeless people, extends the list of applicants in priority need, and gives councils more flexibility in allocating their housing.

REFERENCES

Bailey, R. (1993), *The Squatters*. Harmondsworth: Penguin.

Bramley, G. (1994), 'An affordability crisis in British housing: dimensions, causes and policy impact', *Housing Studies* 9: 103–24.

Burrows, R. (2003), *Poverty and Home Ownership in Contemporary Britain*. Bristol: Policy Press.

CSO (Central Statistical Office) (1993), *Family Spending: A Report on the 1992 Family Expenditure Survey*. London: HMSO.

Clapham, D., and Kintrea, K. (1986), 'Rationing, choice and constraint: the allocation of public housing in Glasgow', *Journal of Social Policy* 15: 51–67.

Department of Employment (1982), *Family Expenditure Survey 1980*. London: HMSO.

Department of Environment (1998), *Housing and Construction Statistics 1997–8*. London: HMSO.

Dorling, D., and Cornford, J. (1995), 'Who has negative equity? How house price falls in Britain have hit different groups of home buyers', *Housing Studies* 10: 151–78.

Engels, F. (1969), *The Condition of the Working Class in England* [1845]. London: Panther.

Forrest, R., and Murie, A. (1988), *Selling the Welfare State*. London: Routledge.

—— and Williams, P. (1990), *Home Ownership: Differentiation and Fragmentation*. London: Unwin Hyman.

Gauldie, E. (1974), *Cruel Habitations*. London: Allen & Unwin.

Gilbert, B. B. (1970), *British Social Policy 1914–1939*. London: Batsford.

Hamnett, C., Harmer, M., and Williams, P. (1991), *Safe as Houses: Housing Inheritance in Britain*. London: Paul Chapman.

Hills, J. (1998), 'Housing'. In H. Glennerster and J. Hills (eds.), *The State of Welfare*, 2nd edn. Oxford: Oxford University Press.

H M Treasury (2002), *Public Expenditure Statistical Analysis 2002–3*. Cm. 5401. London: HMSO.

Kemp, P. (2000), 'Housing benefit and welfare retrenchment in Britain', *Journal of Social Policy* 29: 263–79.

McCrone, G., and Stephens, M. (1995), *Housing Policy in Britain and Europe*. London: UCL Press.

Malpass, P., and Murie, A. (1999), *Housing Policy and Practice*, 5th edn. London: Macmillan.

OPCS (Office of Population Censuses and Surveys) (1996), *Living in Britain: Results from the 1994 General Household Survey*. London: HMSO.

Pawson, H., and Kintrea, K. (2002), 'Part of the problem or part of the solution? Allocation policies and social exclusion in Britain', *Journal of Social Policy* 31: 643–67.

Pickvance, C. G., and Pickvance, K. (1995), 'The role of family help in the housing decisions of young people', *Sociological Review* 43: 123–49.

Pleace, N., Burrows, R., and Quilgars, D. (1997), 'Homelessness in contemporary Britain: conceptualization and measurement'. In R. Burrows, N. Pleace, and D. Quilgars (eds.), *Homelessness and Social Policy*. London: Routledge.

Saunders, P. (1990), *A Nation of Home Owners*. London: Unwin Hyman.

Williams, P. (1976), 'The role of institutions in the inner London housing market: the case of Islington', *Transactions of the Institute of British Geographers* 1: 72–82.

FURTHER READING

The References list contains some of the main texts and research monographs in the field. Others include P. Balchin and M. Rhoden, *Housing Policy* (London: Routledge, 2002); C. Hamnett, *Winners and Losers: Home Ownership in Modern Britain* (London: UCL Press, 1999); M. Kleinman, *Housing, Welfare and the State in Europe* (Aldershot: Elgar, 1996); and A. Marsh and D. Mullins (eds.), *Housing and Public Policy: Citizenship, Choice and Control* (Buckingham: Open University Press, 1998). The main sources of government data are: Office of the Deputy Prime Minister, *English House Condition Survey* and *Housing and Construction Statistics*; Office of National Statistics, *Family Spending*, *Living in Britain*, *Social Trends*, and *Survey of English Housing*.

USEFUL WEBSITES

The Office of the Deputy Prime Minister website: www.odpm.gov.uk/housing/statistics/ includes scores of continuously updated tables of housing statistics, including data on historical trends. The only drawback is that they are mostly for England. Data on spending including on housing is on the Treasury website: www.hm-treasury.gov.uk/ Statistical data for the UK or Great Britain such as censuses and surveys is published on the Office of National Statistics website: www.statistics.gov.uk There is a useful website on homelessness: www.homelessnessact.org.uk/

GLOSSARY

affordable housing Housing whose cost is below some threshold, for example 20 per cent, of household income.

building society Financial institution which attracts money from savers and lends it to house purchasers. Today most have been privatized and have become banks.

concealed household A single person or group of people who share a meal a day together or a living room with another single person or group of people. Typically it refers to single persons or couples who are living with their parents but who would like to live independently, i.e. form separate households

gatekeeper In the housing context, the owner or financier whose rules of access control who is able to gain access to a particular type of housing. It applies to mortgage lenders, councils, housing associations, private landlords, etc.

household A single person or group of people who have the address as their only or main residence and who either share one meal a day together or share a living room (definition used in the UK census from 1981).

housing stock The number of available housing units in the country. There are a certain number of physical dwellings available, through the convertibility of buildings between residential and other uses means the size of the stock is not absolute. However, not all units are available to those seeking housing. For example, some housing is unfit or 'hard to let' (e.g. because it lacks lifts or is located in a very unattractive neighbourhood). The concept of housing stock thus has both physical and social dimensions.

housing tenure The legal relationship between household and dwelling. The main types of tenure, owning and renting, involve sets of rights and obligations which depend partly on national legislation and partly on rules applied by mortgage lenders, councils, etc. Hence, for example, the rights of private tenants vary between countries and over time.

key worker housing Affordable housing provided for specified groups of workers, usually in the public sector. A response to the successful definition of their problems as deserving special treatment.

mandatory legislation Legislation which imposes a duty on, for example, a council to undertake certain actions.

market renewal Measures to reinvigorate housing markets in areas of low demand.

mortgage, mortgage arrears Households buying dwellings normally take out loans, or mortgages. The mortgage allows the purchaser to pay the whole cost of the dwelling to the seller, and in exchange the household undertakes to make monthly repayments of the loan to the mortgage lender. When the household fails to maintain these payments the mortgage is said to be in arrears.

negative equity Equity refers to the value of a household's investment in a dwelling. This value is calculated by estimating the value of the dwelling and then deducting the value of outstanding loans. If the result is positive, the household has positive equity; if it is negative, the household has negative equity.

permissive legislation Legislation which allows but does not require, for example, a council to undertake certain actions.

points system System of allocating council housing in which applicants are given points based on criteria of housing need.

rent control Controls imposed by legislation on the level of rents which landlords can charge tenants.

residualization Process of social change in council housing in which the composition of households changes to include more households in great housing need. This happens because households leaving council housing are less deprived than those entering, due for example to the right to buy and homelessness legislation.

right to buy The council house privatization policy introduced by the Conservative government in 1980 under which council tenants were given the right to buy their council house or flat at a discount. This replaced the previous policy under which councils had the 'right to sell' housing, a right which was little used.

rules of access Criteria applied by owners and financiers of housing governing who gains access to housing and under what conditions.

unintentionally homeless Not homeless by their own choice. A concept introduced in the 1977 homelessness act which obliged local councils to provide housing only for those who were 'unintentionally' homeless (and who had a local connection), as opposed to those who were considered to have made themselves homeless by their own choice.

18

Crime, Justice, and Punishment

Tina Eadie and Rebecca Morley

CONTENTS

INTRODUCTION: CRIME—A PERVASIVE SOCIAL POLICY CONCERN

We are surrounded by crime—as a problem and as entertainment—in the media, in novels, in everyday discussion. We have television programmes which implore us, the public, to assist the police in solving crimes in our communities and to help put right miscarriages of justice. The annual crime statistics for England and Wales make headline news. They are offered as key indicators of the moral condition of society. Periodic rises and falls in crime rates provide ammunition for political debate concerning the successes and failures of social policies in the 'fight against crime', as the main political parties battle for the high ground on 'law and order'. Dramatic incidents of crime—the abduction and murder of children, mass killings arising from terrorist attacks, a deranged individual, or even human error—reverberate in the daily conversations of ordinary citizens filling us with outrage, horror, fear, grief. Less dramatic but persistent crime—mobile phone theft for example—results in anger and indignation that crime is not being controlled. Dramatic rises in **recorded crime** during the latter half of the twentieth century have only recently begun to show signs of levelling off. Opinion polls show crime continuing to be a major public concern. Many people have a deep sense of the criminal justice system failing them—as victims of crime and as members of communities in which criminal activities and anti-social behaviour are rife. Clearly crime is a central social policy theme.

In this chapter we touch on the following questions as they bear on social policy concerns: What is crime? How much crime is there? How is it changing? Who are its victims? Who commits it? How is it dealt with? How much does it cost? Why does it occur? Can it be prevented? There are no simple answers to these questions, and debates concerning them are complex and often contradictory. Recognizing that this chapter can only offer a brief overview of some of these questions, we hope that readers will follow up the references and further reading.

WHAT IS CRIME? MEASUREMENT, STATISTICS, AND TRENDS

The impression often given by politicians and the media is that crime is a physical fact, like the air temperature or rainfall, which, with proper techniques, can be accurately measured and assessed. However, closer examination shows that crime is thoroughly socially produced—that it is a **social construction**.

The most common and seemingly straightforward and unproblematic definition of crime is violation of the criminal law—'law-breaking'. But laws are 'man–made', in both the generic and specific sense of the word 'man'. Laws change over time and place. We need therefore to ask how and why certain acts are defined and legislated as criminal in certain places and times (and why others are not). Perspectives on this question vary and are underpinned by differing views concerning the nature of social order: simplistically, whether crime arises from a social consensus about morality and norms of conduct or is the outcome of social conflict and coercion. The first suggests that crime is politically neutral; the second, that we need to examine issues of power and politics—who has the power to define what is criminal, and whose interests do these definitions serve?

Proponents of this second view ask, for example, why property crimes and personal violence are much more likely to be considered crimes than environmental pollution, unethical business practices, and health and safety hazards in the workplace. Marxist-oriented criminologists argue that the criminal law and its operation are biased towards crimes of the poor and powerless, protecting the economic and political interests of the powerful while ignoring acts which are arguably more socially harmful in terms of financial loss and personal injury or death. Feminists argue that the law and criminal justice system ignore the bulk of men's physical and sexual violence against women ('private' violence as opposed to street violence), supporting the interests of men or 'patriarchal' power. Domestic violence, for example, was legally sanctioned until the late nineteenth century and is only now—patchily and falteringly—treated as crime by the criminal justice system; rape in marriage was legal in England and Wales until 1991.

The obvious limitations of **legal definitions** have led some to argue that crime should be defined as actions which are socially harmful or which violate human rights, whether or not they are legally sanctioned. Such **social definitions** would include racism, sexism, poverty, and imperialism as crimes. However, in terms of public and policy debate, the most influential definition of crime is clearly law-breaking, and within this, law-breaking that comes to the attention of the police and media.

Measurement

Crime is not just socially constructed in definition, it is socially constructed in measurement. Official crime rates for England and Wales, compiled from police records and notified to the Home Office, have been published each year since 1876. Comparable statistics are produced for Scotland and Northern Ireland; however, those from England and Wales figure most prominently in policy debates and the media. Police recorded crime is the end-point of a complex series of decisions: crime must be recognized by the victim or someone else, reported to the police, classified as an offence, and actually recorded. Some crimes (such as car theft) are far more likely to survive this process than others (such as marital rape).

Further, police only record certain categories of crime, called 'notifiable offences'. Prior to 1998, these broadly corresponded to 'indictable offences'—supposedly more serious crimes triable only in Crown courts or 'triable either way' in Crown or magistrates courts—as opposed to supposedly less serious 'summary offences' triable only in magistrates courts. Thus, for example, violence which the police classified as 'common assault' (a summary offence) rather than 'actual bodily harm' (a notifiable offence) were not recorded even though these incidents could be as injurious: Edwards (1989: ch. 4), for example, found that police routinely 'downcrimed' domestic violence in order to avoid paperwork and further investigation, which they regarded as wasted effort. In 1998 the Home Office expanded the list of notifiable offences to include some closely related summary offences including common assault, assault on a constable, drugs possession, cruelty to or neglect of children, vehicle interference, and dangerous driving.

Clearly, then, official views concerning the seriousness of various types of crime change over time, and these changes result in rises or falls in the recorded crime rate. Even within the categories of notifiable offences, different police forces may concentrate their efforts on detecting different sorts of crime at different points in time for a wide variety of reasons. These decisions, too, will affect the volume of recorded crime. More generally, police officers traditionally have had a great deal of discretion in deciding whether and how to record incidents which are reported to them. The **British Crime Survey** estimates from 1981 to 2002 indicate that between 38 and 51 per cent of notifiable offences which are reported to the police each year do not get recorded (Simmons 2002: fig. 3.6).

Moroever, rules for counting instances of notifiable offences have changed several times, most recently in 1998 and 2002. The counting changes in 1998, in combination with the expansion of the list of notifiable offences, led to an estimated artificial increase in the total volume of recorded crime in 1998/99 of 14 per cent (Povey and Prime 1999: table A1). Offences of 'violence against the person' were particularly affected, increasing by a massive 118 per cent, due in large part to the inclusion of common assault in the list of notifiable offences. The changes in 2002 were the result of a new National Crime Reporting Standard (NCRS) which aims to take a more victim-centred approach to crime recording—all reports of incidents should be recorded if they amount to notifiable offences in law and there is no evidence to the contrary—and thus to reduce police discretion. This change has increased the 2001–2 recorded crime figures overall by 5 per cent. Again, offences of violence against the person have been particularly affected (13 per cent increase), as have sexual offences (21 per cent increase), while robbery and vehicle crime have been virtually unaffected (Simmons 2002: table 3b). The impact of the NCRS is expected to increase as it moves towards full implementation.

Undeniably, then, recorded crime rates are fragile creatures which require great care in interpretation.

Statistics and trends

At face value, the overall picture of crime from recorded statistics is startlingly clear. Apart from a small sustained decline in the early 1950s, the total volume of recorded crime rose steadily from the 1930s to the early 1990s, and particularly dramatically from the mid-1950s (see Fig. 18.1): in 1950 recorded crime stood at 500,000, or 1 per 100 population; in 1992 nearly 5.6 million, or 11 per 100 population, an elevenfold increase (Home Office 1997a). From 1992 rates have declined modestly, although the changes in coverage and counting rules, which artificially inflated the figures, have muddied the picture since 1998. Moreover, overall trends do not necessarily reflect individual groups of crime. For example, while the recent decline has been mirrored in property offences, crimes of violence have increased. This increase, in turn, is much steeper for robbery (28 per cent from 2000–1 to 2001–2, much of which was mobile phone theft) than for violence against the person (8 per cent), the largest category of violent crime which is also substantially affected by changes in coverage and counting (Simmons 2002: table 3b).

The vast majority of recorded crimes are property offences. Of the 5.5 million crimes recorded in 2001–2, 82 per cent were property offences (see Fig. 18.2). Despite the considerable impact of changes in coverage and counting on offences of violence against

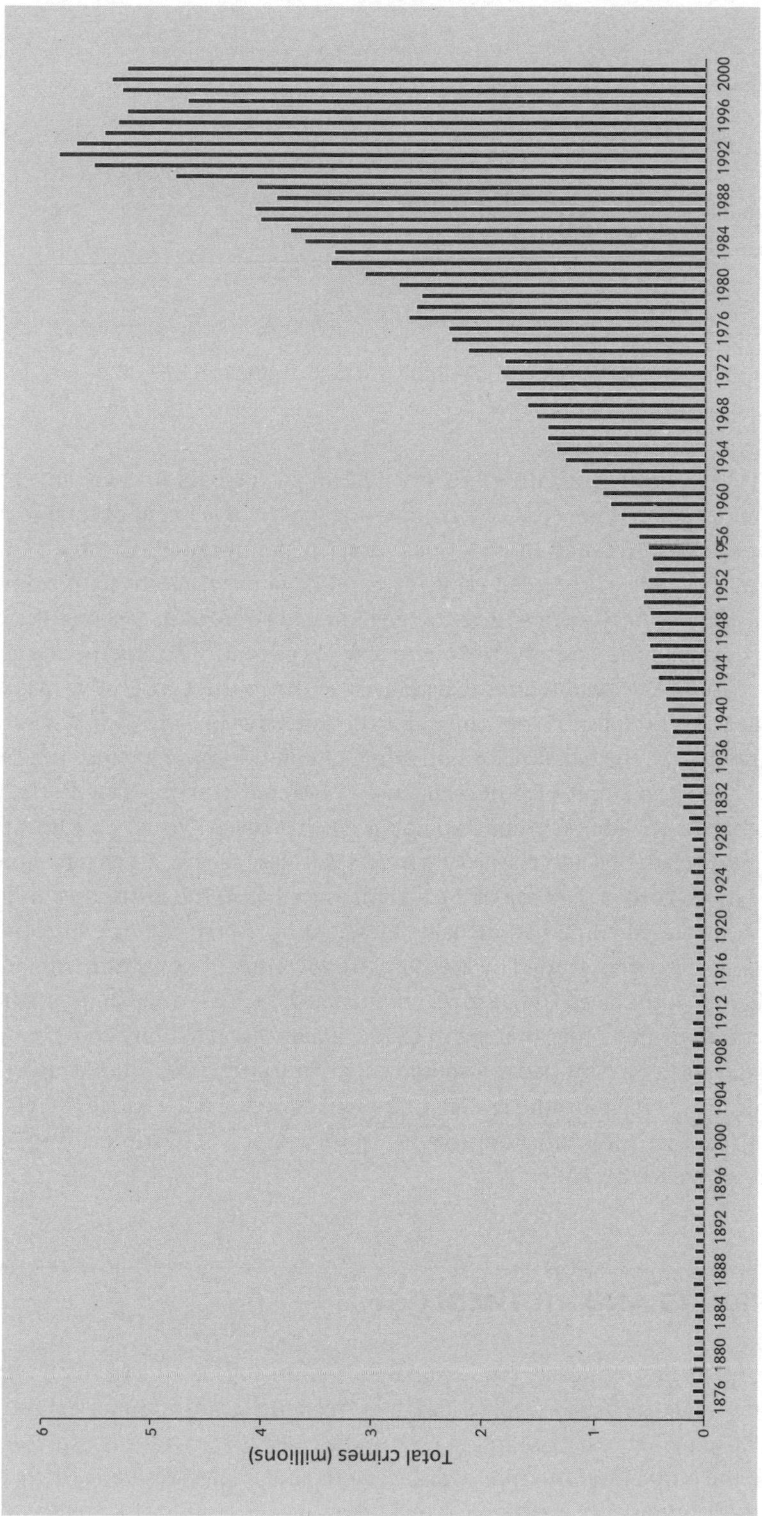

Figure 18.1 Offences recorded by the police, 1876–2000

Source: Maguire et al. (2002: 345).

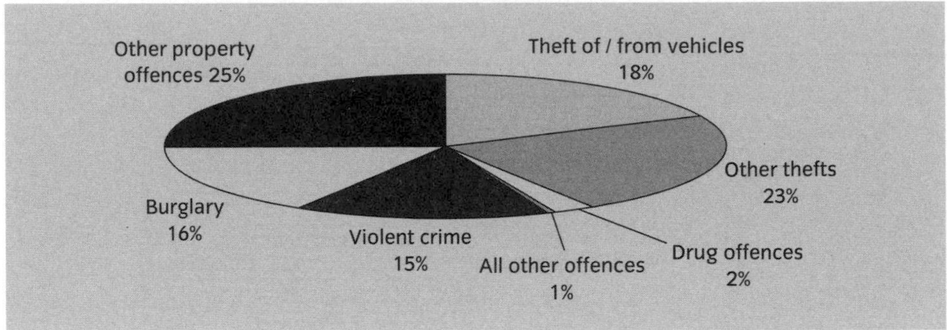

Figure 18.2 Police-recorded crime, 2001–2002 (total all offences 5,527,082)

Source: Simmons (2002: table 3.04).

the person, violent crime including robbery accounted for only 15 per cent of total crime. Further, less than 4 per cent of violent crime (only 0.6 per cent of total recorded crime) was homicide and other 'more serious' violence (Simmons 2002: table 3.04).

Unsurprisingly, trends in recorded crime can and have been selectively presented to support opposing positions concerning the government's record in tackling the crime problem. For example, the Conservatives were able to celebrate winning the war against crime on the basis of the 1996 figures which revealed the fourth consecutive overall fall in crime, while the Labour Party's 1997 manifesto declared that: 'Under the Conservatives, crime has doubled . . . the worst record on crime of any government since the Second World War. . . . Last year alone, violent crime rose 11 per cent' (Labour Party 1997: 22). In 2002, New Labour asserted that crime had stabilized after several years of decline, pointing to the impact of the NCRS in inflating a 'real' increase of just 2 per cent from the previous year to a recorded increase of 7 per cent, as well as to the British Crime Survey finding that comparable crime had actually decreased by 2 per cent. The Conservative Shadow Home Secretary responded by accusing the government of 'statistical manipulation' and, alluding to the steep rise in street crime, stated: 'it is the drugs and gangs rather than the forces of law and order that are in charge' (*Independent*, 12 July 2002). As a general point, there are important debates about the extent to which statistics represent real changes in criminal behaviour (the **realist approach**) as opposed to changes in reporting and recording (the **institutionalist approach**). The development of crime surveys can be seen as one response to this issue.

CRIME SURVEYS AND VICTIMOLOGY

Government-sponsored national crime surveys, comprising interviews with random samples of the population who are asked about their experiences of criminal victimization during a specified period, emerged in the USA in the early 1970s with the expressed aim of addressing the problem of interpreting official crime data. By 1980 researchers in the Home Office were arguing for a national crime survey on the grounds that policy-makers needed a better idea of the extent and shape of crime than that provided by official statistics, and that public misconceptions concerning crime levels and risk needed to be challenged (Mayhew and Hough 1988: 157).

The resulting British Crime Survey (BCS), first undertaken in 1982 and covering crimes committed in the previous year, claims to allow a more complete count of crime by including incidents which are not reported to and/or recorded by the police. In practice, the two sources cannot be directly compared since they do not count exactly the same things. For instance, the BCS counts offences which are not 'notifiable', but does not count homicide, since the victims of homicide cannot talk to the interviewer about their victimization. (Box 18.1 compares the main features of the two sources.) However, for the subset of crimes which are comparable, estimates of the so-called 'dark figure' of unreported and unrecorded crime can be made. Further, the BCS collects other information such as the distribution of risk across different population groups, the impacts of victimization, and the public's fear of crime.

The BCS is now a source of major importance to policy-makers, rivalling police recorded statistics. Indeed, it has played a crucial role in the general shift in government policy since the 1980s from crime prevention towards 'victimization prevention'. More generally, crime surveys have transformed the field of **victimology**—the study of victims—which originated in the 1940s as a concern with the relationship between the victim and offender, and which was much criticized for its preoccupation with victim typologies and notions of victim precipitation of crime. National crimes surveys have now been carried out in many countries, and there have been several international victimization surveys producing comparable data across a range of countries.

The picture of crime from the British Crime Survey

As expected, the BCS uncovers many more crimes than recorded statistics—just over 13 million, as compared to 5.5 million, in 2001–2 (Simmons 2002). However, trends since 1981 are broadly similar, though BCS rates increased less steeply and continued to rise after 1992 until 1995, albeit at a much slower rate than before 1992. Since 1995 BCS crime has fallen in every survey, though negligibly from 2000 to 2001–2. Under half (42 per cent) of all comparable BCS crimes uncovered in 2001–2 were reported to the police, and only one quarter of BCS crimes were recorded by the police (Simmons 2002: table 2.01). The 'dark figure' of unreported and unrecorded crime is thus considerable, though it varies substantially by type of offence (see Fig. 18.3). Nonetheless, the broad similarity in shape of crime uncovered by the BCS and crime recorded by police indicates that changes in police statistics represent more than simply changes in institutional practices.

Although the first BCS, measuring crime in 1981, confirmed the view that much more crime exists than is officially recorded, the tone of the report was overwhelmingly reassuring: 'the real message of the BCS is that it calls into question assumptions about crime upon which people's concern is founded. It emphasises the petty nature of most law-breaking' (Hough and Mayhew 1983: 33). Indeed, the authors calculated (p. 15) that:

> assuming that rates remain at 1981 levels . . . a 'statistically average' person aged 16 or over can expect:
>
> - a robbery once every five centuries (not attempts)
> - an assault resulting in injury (even if slight) once every century

Box 18.1 Comparison of the British Crime Survey and police-recorded crime

The British Crime Survey	Police-recorded crime
• Starting in 1982, it measures both reported and unreported crime. As such it provides a measure of trends in crime not affected by changes in reporting, or changes in police recording rules or practices	• Collected since 1857. Provides measure of offences both reported to and recorded by the police. As such they are influenced by changes in reporting behaviour and recording rules and practices
• In recent years measured crime every two years. From 2001 the BCS moved to an annual cycle	• The police figures are published annually. For the first time in 2002, published together with the BCS
• For the first time in 2002, published together with police recorded crime	• Only includes 'notifable' offences which the police have to notify to the Home Office for statistical purposes
• Measures based on estimates from a sample of the population. The estimates are therefore subject to sampling error and other methodological limitations	• Provides an indicator of the workload of the police
• Has not measured crime at the small area level well, but more reliable regional information is available from 2001 sweep onwards	• Provides data at the level of 43 police force areas and for Basic Command Units (similar in size to Local Authorities)
• Does not include crimes against: • Those under 16 • Commercial and public sector establishments • Those in institutions, and the homeless	• Includes crime against: • Those under 16 • Commercial and public sector establishments • Those in institutions, and the homeless
• Does not measure: • Victimless crimes • Crimes where a victim is no longer available for interview • Fraud • Sexual offences (due to the small number of incidents reported to the survey and concerns about willingness of respondents to disclose such offences, estimates are not considered reliable)	• Measures: • Victimless crimes • Murder and manslaughter • Fraud • Sexual offences where these have been reported to the police
• Collects information on what happens in crime (e.g., when crimes occur, and effects in terms of injury and property loss)	• Collects information about the number of arrests, who is arrested, the number of crimes detected, and by what method
• Provides information about how the risks of crime vary for different groups	• Does not show which groups of the population are most at risk of victimization

(Kershaw et al. 2001: table 1.1, amended to include changes in 2002)

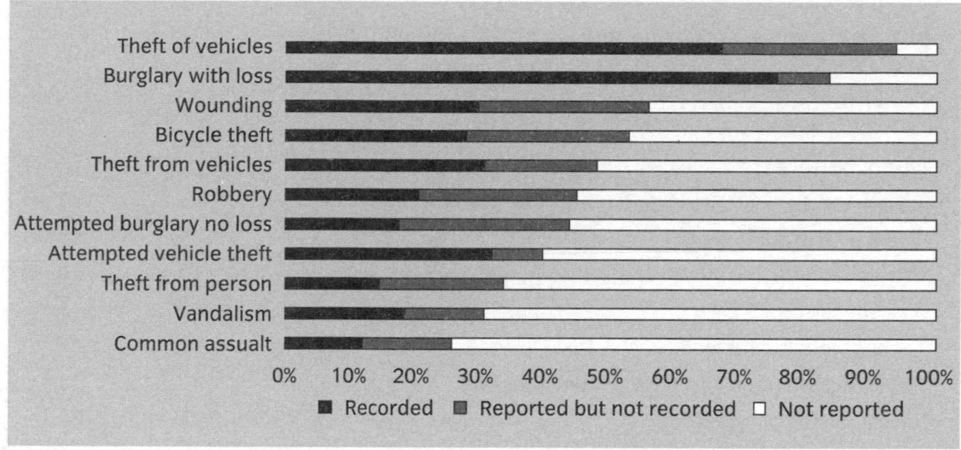

Figure 18.3 Reported, recorded, and unreported crime, 2001–2002

100% = total number of incidents estimated by BCS.

Source: Simmons (2002: table 2.01).

- the family car to be stolen or taken by joyriders once every 60 years
- a burglary in the home once every 40 years

. . . and a very low rate for rape and other sexual offences.

The authors offered further reassurance through an analysis of the differential risk of serious victimization. For example, the typical victim of assault was found to be a young, single male who spent several evenings a week out, drank heavily, and assaulted others (like himself) (Hough and Mayhew 1983: 21). In contrast, and seemingly paradoxically, fear of crime—measured by questions such as feelings of safety on the street at night—was found to be highest amongst those least at risk of victimization—women and the elderly. In addressing the paradox, the authors hinted at the possibility that fear is in part 'irrational or excessive', and concluded that 'in some areas, fear of crime appears to be a serious problem which needs to be tackled separately from the incidence of crime itself (Hough and Mayhew 1983: 27). Fear reduction policies, aimed particularly at women and the elderly in the inner cities, were advocated (Maxfield 1984), and a number of policies emerged in the 1980s aimed at educating and reassuring the public concerning the 'reality' of crime.

Critical responses to the BCS

This optimistic picture of the reality of crime was contested, in particular by Left realists (see Young 1988) and feminists (see Stanko 1988), who argued that the BCS provided a distorted picture of the distribution of risk, failing to uncover the disproportionate victimization of those most disadvantaged in society—the poor, ethnic minorities, and women—and thus misinterpreting the meaning of fear of crime. Since the mid-1980s, a number of local crime surveys have been conducted in order to elucidate the victimization experiences of these groups.

For example, a survey of an inner city area of London—the first Islington Crime Survey (Jones *et al.* 1986)—found that a total of one third of all households had experienced

Box 18.2 The Wandsworth Violence Against Women Survey: proportion of 314 women experiencing various forms of men's violence during previous twelve months

Type of violence	%[a]
Violent attack	44
Threatened in public place	13
Threatened/attacked by stranger in their home	10
Obscene telephone call	11
Sexual harassment at work	38
Threatened/attacked by men they were living with	12
Total assaulted or harassed	89

[a] Percentages are not additive. Many women experienced more than one type of violence.

(Radford 1987:35)

a burglary, robbery, or sexual violence within the previous year; that women were more likely than men to be victims of assault; and that while older people suffered less crime than younger, assaults against them were more likely to be serious in terms of level of violence, injury, and impact.

Feminist surveys have not only uncovered much higher levels of serious violence to women than the BCS, but have also documented the pervasiveness of women's experiences of acts which are not classified as crimes—for example, sexual harassment, being touched up, leered at, followed, and so on—which constitute an ever-present climate of threat in women's lives. Radford's (1987) survey of women in Wandsworth, London, for example, found that 89 per cent had suffered some form of assault or harassment during the previous twelve months, covering a wide range of type of incident (see Box 18.2). Most women had experienced more than one incident; some as many as thirteen (personal communication, Jill Radford, 1998).

Findings such as these have affected the conduct of the BCS, and have undoubtedly been crucial to the recent reassessment by BCS researchers of the relationship of risk to fear of crime. Moreover, alterations in the BCS survey design have been made in response to criticisms regarding its weaknesses in uncovering differential patterns of victimization. For example, in the 1996 and 2001 surveys, a computerized self-completion module was included to improve estimates of domestic violence. In addition, two booster samples have become a permanent feature of the BCS—an ethnic minority booster and a youth booster—which will allow analysis of crime experienced by these groups.

THEORIES ABOUT CRIME

Theories about the nature and causes of crime are not just academic exercises. They serve both as stimuli to, and as rationalizations of, policy. Theories are thus crucial to understanding policy positions concerning crime control and prevention, although in practice political declarations and policy outcomes often represent a—sometimes muddled—coalescence of varying and potentially contradictory theoretical presumptions.

Traditional paradigms of crime

The two competing traditional paradigms of crime are classicism and positivism. **Classicism** emerged from eighteenth-century enlightenment thought which views humans as rational, self-interested, and exercising free will. It follows that crime is rationally motivated (freely chosen) by self-interest, and that offenders are fully responsible for their actions. What is required is punishment aimed at deterring (rational) individuals from committing crime. Punishment should be systematically applied, based on the nature and seriousness of the criminal act rather than the characteristics of the offender. In short, criminals should get their **just deserts**—proportional punishment with determinate (or fixed) sentences.

Positivism is rooted in nineteenth-century empiricist science, searching for the causes of phenomena through objective observation and measurement. In contrast to classicism, positivist theories of crime focus on the offender as determined rather than possessing free will. Crime is thus non-rational, caused by forces beyond the criminal's control. The earliest versions of positivism (still in evidence) focused on individual determinants—defects in the person's biological or psychological make-up which predispose him/her to crime. Because the problem is essentially a pathology or sickness, the appropriate response is treatment (not punishment) aimed at rehabilitation. Since appropriate treatment requires responding to individual needs, sentences should be indeterminate, taking into account not only the seriousness of the crime but the individual's diagnosis and prognosis.

The rise of social positivism

Individual positivism dominated thinking about crime during the first half of the twentieth century. However, by the late 1950s a group of theories—originating in American sociology from the 1920s onwards—were coming to prominence which stressed the social causes of crime. Although these theories can be described as varieties of **social positivism** (see Box 18.3), most are more accurately viewed as theories which credit humans with certain freedoms within a determined social framework.

One strand focuses on the relationship between the propensity towards criminal behaviour and social norms and values. 'Social disorganization' theory suggests that crime is most likely to occur in specific urban areas where traditional norms and values have broken down due to immigration and migration. Alternatively, in 'strain theory', people at the bottom of the social structure—the working class and poor—are viewed as particularly susceptible to criminal behaviour precisely because they accept dominant norms and values but are denied legitimate means to achieve socially valued goals: crime is a meaningful solution to the disjunction between socially induced goals and the opportunity structures of society. 'Subcultural theory' maintains that these disjunctions are not solved by individuals in isolation, but by groups of people in similar structural positions who form deviant subcultures which may, over time, develop alternative, deviant norms and values. 'Differential association' examines the processes through

Box 18.3 Varieties of 'social positivism' and their policy implications

Theory	*Argument*	*Policy implications*
Social disorganization	Breakdown of moral order of a community	Community development; urban renewal; stamp out extreme criminal elements, e.g. drug pushers
Strain theory	Poverty, deprivation, blocked goals	Anti-poverty programmes; equal opportunity
Subcultural theory	Criminal behaviour socially valued	Social mobility through economic growth; equal opportunity; education policies
Differential association	Local peer/gang cultures	Removal of gang leaders; breakup of peer groups
Labelling	People defined as criminal become criminal	Decriminalization; diversion of first-time offenders to non-penal treatments
Marxist	Inequalities of power and class conflict	Collective ownership of means of production and control; redistribution of resources according to need
Feminist	Patriarchy, women's economic and social subordination	Social empowerment of women through economic, social, and political equality

which criminal behaviour is learned through acquiring skills, meanings, motives, and traditions in association with peer groups involved in criminal activity. All of the above imply that the solution to the problem of crime lies in social programmes designed to alleviate the precipitating social conditions of poverty, deprivation, unemployment, urban decay, and disorganization; in promoting equality of opportunity in education and employment; and through interventions to break up organized criminal groupings.

For labelling theorists, it is not that the poor are more deviant than other people, but that they are more likely to be labelled deviant by those who have the power to label. Once labelled, the person may take on a role or identity commensurate with the label, thus engaging in further deviant activity and seeking out the company of others with similar labels. The impact of labelling is potentially the creation of a criminal career, fuelled by a **deviancy amplification spiral**. Hence, it is argued, criminal justice policy should be geared towards decriminalization and keeping offenders out of formal justice systems as far as possible—radical non-intervention.

While labelling theory begins to question the assumption that there exists a social consensus of norms and values, it does not really challenge fundamental social structures. In contrast, Marxist theories focus centrally on issues of power and conflicts of interest in society: crime arises out of class divisions. The state, including the law and criminal justice system, is viewed as a tool used by those who own and control the means of production—those with power—to protect their interests; hence the criminal justice system targets crimes of the less powerful which threaten the powerful—property crime and public order offences. Unlike the other perspectives discussed so far, Marxist perspectives are interested not only in crimes of the less powerful but also in crimes of the powerful. The latter (such as fraud, environmental destruction, and corruption) are caused by a desire to increase wealth or to gain competitive advantage, while the former are a result of economic necessity—ensuring subsistence—or are acts of alienation. Ultimately the solution of crime requires annihilating inequalities through overthrowing capitalism, collective ownership and control of the means of production, and redistribution of resources according to need. However, lesser demands—for public accountability, for democratization of institutions, and for social programmes to eliminate poverty and deprivation—have all been made in the name of Marxist thinking.

Feminist perspectives are also concerned with power and structural inequalities, but focus primarily on their relation to gender. Feminists argue that women are structurally disadvantaged; society is patriarchal, based on male domination and female subordination. Women's unequal position in society is key to understanding both female offending and victimization. Women who kill men, for example, have often been subject to repeated violence from their victims; female property crime tends to be petty thieving and fraud carried out to support children. Women are vulnerable to sexual violence because of men's power over women, constructed through double standards of masculinity and femininity. The solution to both lies in eradicating patriarchy—empowering women economically, socially, and politically. Feminist perspectives have also raised questions concerning male offending: what is it about men and masculinity that results in their greater involvement in crime?

The theoretical climate from the late 1970s

Many commentators have pointed to a postwar consensus on crime, strongly based on the social positivist notion that improving social conditions and reducing inequalities through social policies would alleviate the crime problem. This consensus had fractured by the end of the 1970s for two interrelated reasons: first, the impact of the recession which resulted in calls for cuts in public expenditure, and second, the apparent failure of rising living standards to halt the rise in crime. Both were accompanied by a questioning of the ability of the welfare state generally, and social programmes specifically, to alleviate social problems.

'New Right' approaches gained prominence in this climate, the implications of which are explored in the following sections. These approaches stress individual responsibility, law and order, and punishment and control of offenders, and include both revitalized classicism and positivism. They also have historical links with 'control theory', which holds that human nature is not naturally conforming but inherently anti-social, and that all people would commit crime if they were not subject to internalized and/or externalized controls.

'Rational choice theories' suggest that people make decisions to engage in criminal activity, and choose specific times and places, when economic benefits outweigh costs.

Rather than focus on the causes of crime and motivations of the offender, the solution is deterrence, which requires increasing the cost of criminal behaviour by making it riskier or more difficult to carry out, the policy emphasis being on victimization prevention. 'Situational crime prevention' embraced by the Home Office in the 1980s stresses the effectiveness of 'target hardening' (locks and bolts and other devices), surveillance, 'target removal', and the like in deterring criminal behaviour. At the other extreme are theories which either find biological defects in criminals or imply that human nature is inherently anti-social and blame crime on the 'permissive society', especially lack of discipline in the family (read single parents) and schools.

Particularly influential on the right has been the 'bio-social' thinking of James Q. Wilson (Wilson 1975; Wilson and Herrnstein 1985), for whom crime is caused by a combination of constitutional factors which determine the ease with which an individual's conscience can be conditioned, the quality of conditioning of conscience and self-control provided by the family and community, and the costs and benefits of crime. Though the larger constitutional and socialization causes of crime may be difficult to tackle, Wilson suggests that marginal gains can be made. These tend to prioritize enforcing order over social justice. This thinking has fed into 'zero tolerance' policies advocating heavy-handed policing of sub-criminal behaviour at one extreme and calls to get 'tough on criminals' through lengthy prison sentences at the other.

An important challenge to New Right thinking has come from Left realist approaches to crime. These emerged in the mid-1980s as an attempt to reclaim the law and order terrain for the Left by acknowledging public anxieties about the rise of crime and disorder in society. A key cause of crime is seen to be relative deprivation—the belief that one's allocation of society's resources is unfair. Thus crime is not confined to those in absolute deprivation—the poor. However, 'it is among the poor, particularly the lower working class and certain ethnic minorities, who are marginalized from the "glittering prizes" of the wider society, that the push towards crime is greatest' (Young 1997: 488). While longer-term social change in the direction of social justice is clearly important in solving the crime problem, Left realists emphasize the importance of more immediate interventions to control crime—for example, more responsive policing, community involvement, and support of victims.

Somewhat counter-intuitively, New Labour's understanding of crime, underpinned by its central notion of social exclusion, owes more to the legacy of New Right thinking than to the left. Crime is seen to be concentrated in a minority of the socially excluded underclass populated by inadequate families living in a dependency culture due to excessive welfare provision. The ultimate solution is social inclusion through policies such as welfare to work and neighbourhood regeneration, while controlling crime in the short term through tough criminal justice and zero tolerance policies.

Looking overall at the range of theoretical perspectives on crime, we can see that they are underpinned by a variety of contrasting views about human nature, the nature of social order, and resulting policy requirements for dealing with crime. It is also clear that the influence of certain theories and their underlying presumptions at certain historical periods is very much bound up with the larger economic and political climate of the time.

THE POLITICS OF LAW AND ORDER

As will have been clear from the discussion so far, crime, justice and punishment do not exist in a vacuum: political values determine definitions of crime; political beliefs about crime causation are reflected in the criminal justice response to crime and public disorder; and political decisions determine the social conditions which impact on crime. An illustration of this is the different strategies towards law and order taken by the Labour and Conservative parties in the second half of the twentieth century—the former citing structural factors such as unemployment and social deprivation as contributing towards crime, the latter placing the blame on individuals. Helping offenders with problems created or at least exacerbated by external causes (**welfare model**), as opposed to punishing them in proportion to the seriousness of the offence committed (**justice model**) became the parties' respective responses to crime until the early 1990s. Since then there has been increasing party political consensus on law and order, specifically in relation to the centrality of the victim to the criminal justice process, and on the prioritization of policies to protect the public from both dangerous and persistent offenders. As noted in the previous section, this has resulted in an apparent overall shift to the Right as each party attempts to 'out-tough' the other in the battle to manage—and be seen to be managing—crime effectively. This, from New Labour, has been one of the most striking shifts in their overall policy direction and is a far cry from Labour's welfare perspective in the 1960s.

The rise and demise of the welfare approach

Policy in the mid-twentieth century had become focused on the offender rather than the offence. Rehabilitation through treatment highlighted the role of probation officers, social workers, therapists, and counsellors whose task was to provide diagnostic and curative services for offenders. The approach was at its height in the 1960s in relation to juvenile offenders. (For further discussion of this period see the section 'Children, young people, crime, and welfare in Chapter 16.) The **welfare model**, with its focus on rehabilitation through treatment, was challenged from a number of sides during the 1970s. Most damning was research claiming that no penal sanction, treatment or punishment, was more successful than any other in reducing recidivism (Martinson 1974). Lack of evidence to demonstrate the model's effectiveness in preventing reoffending, and the fact that the previous twenty years had witnessed steadily increasing crime rates, bolstered the right-wing assertion that it was time to bring back punishment.

The 'party of law and order': Conservative policy

In their 1970 General Election manifesto, the Conservatives argued that the continued rise in the crime rate was related to policy, specifically Labour policy. They also pointed to Labour's increasingly hostile and confrontational clashes with the trade unions as evidence that Labour, with its affiliation to the trade union movement, not only was incapable of controlling crime but also promoted civil disobedience. By the 1979 general

Box 18.4 **'Justice on Trial: what Conservative Home Secretaries have said about the wisdom of jailing more offenders' (*Guardian*, 13 October 1993)**

William Whitelaw (1979–83): 'On the evidence it would appear there could be a substantial fall in our use of imprisonment without any significant rise in the threat to individual safety' (1981).

Leon Brittain (1983–5): 'I shall continue to support the use and development of non-custodial penalties where the courts consider them appropriate' (1983).

Douglas Hurd (1985–9): 'For those convicted of the common less serious and non-violent offences, which comprise the majority of all offences, the argument that custody should be used sparingly . . . seems to me entirely persuasive' (1985).

David Waddington (1989–1990): 'Prison is an expensive way of making bad people worse . . . I am moving with the tide of public and judicial opinion in seeking to reduce the jail population while cracking down on violent offenders' (1990).

election, the Conservative manifesto brought 'law and order' to the fore as a major election issue and, in contrast to the Labour strategy, set out clear policy proposals.

Elected on a 'law and order' ticket, the Conservative government under Margaret Thatcher set about implementing these policies, beginning with the strengthening of police powers, sentencing reform, and expanded budgets for criminal justice agencies at a time when other departments were experiencing cuts. Prison numbers rose but, unfortunately for new Right ideologues, so too did official crime rates.

Alongside, and in contradiction to, the punitive rhetoric, successive Conservative Home Secretaries throughout the 1980s were persuaded by senior civil servants that alternatives to imprisonment could and should be sought (see Box 18.4 above). This serves as a reminder that the party political context is not the only influence on this complex and contentious area of policy. What subsequently emerged, in the Criminal Justice Act 1991, was a so-called 'twin-track' approach to sentencing. Custody was to be reserved for more serious—specifically violent and sexual—crimes, while persistent but less serious offenders were to be punished in the community by means of a range of **community sentences** and a new system of **unit fines**.

The 1991 Act was an attempt to introduce a sentencing framework in which proportionality between sentence severity and offence seriousness would guide sentencing decisions—so that convicted criminals would get their '**just deserts**'. However, the approach also enabled sentencers to go *beyond* desert, as set out in the preceding White Paper, 'Crime, Justice and Protecting the Public' (Home Office 1990):

> . . . the legislation which the Government proposes will allow the Crown Court to send [violent offenders] to custody for longer than would otherwise be justified by the seriousness of the offences they have committed, if this is necessary to protect the public. (1990: 2)

Public protection was to eclipse both the **welfare** and **justice models** as rationales for sentencing from this point onwards. In what marked a complete U-turn in the previous decade's penal policy, Michael Howard, Home Secretary 1993–7, in a speech to the

Conservative Party Annual Conference in October 1993, stated:

> Prison works. It ensures that we are protected from murderers, muggers and rapists—and it makes many who are tempted to commit crime think twice . . . This may mean that more people go to prison. I do not flinch from that. (Howard 1993).

As a result the prison population, which had begun to show signs of decreasing in the early 1990s, soared. Further incarcerative measures were introduced in the Criminal Justice and Public Order Act 1994 (for example the introduction of **secure training orders** for persistent young offenders aged 12–14 and restrictions on the granting of bail), and through planned legislation for mandatory sentencing. The fact that these went largely unopposed by New Labour highlighted the party's sea-change on law and order.

The 'party of law and order': New Labour policy

As part of Labour's attempt to lose the 'soft on crime' label, Tony Blair as Shadow Home Secretary stated in 1993, 'We will be tough on crime and tough on the causes of crime', an imaginative compromise of matching the Tory rhetoric of toughness while seemingly holding onto a commitment to tackle structural inequalities. The slogan was later cited in the Labour Manifesto of 1997, along with a new emphasis on personal responsibility and in punishing crime. Labour now claimed to be the party of law and order, setting the seal on its ideological rebirth as 'New Labour'.

Following New Labour's landslide victory in May 1997, Jack Straw as Home Secretary announced that securing the safety of the public was his overriding priority and tough policy initiatives have been taken subsequently towards youth crime, street crime, repeat offending, sex offending, and drug offending. Certain of the measures would have been unrecognizable as Labour policy twenty years ago:

- implementing the Crime (Sentences) Act 1997 drafted by the previous government;
- pursuing policies with the potential to criminalize non-criminal populations—for example, **anti-social behaviour orders** to combat 'neighbourhood nuisance' and policies relating to immigration and asylum seekers;
- making extensive use of advances in technology to electronically monitor the whereabouts of offenders supervised in the community—including provision for offenders aged under 16;
- adopting New Right concepts of a 'war against drugs and crime' and 'zero-tolerance';
- piloting proposals to punish non-compliance with community sentences—for example suspending benefits of offenders in breach of an order.

Other polices, however, have represented a bold response to contentious issues, and demonstrate that New Labour has not lost all of its former credentials in relation to civil liberties and human rights:

- the pursuit of legislation to tackle racist and racially motivated crime;
- the acceptance of the Macpherson Inquiry's definition of institutionalized racism in the police force (see Case Study 18.1);

Case Study 18.1 Institutionalized racism

The Macpherson Inquiry (1999) into the racist murder of Stephen Lawrence, an 18-year-old African-Caribbean man, by a gang of young white men in south-east London in 1993 was instigated by Jack Straw in 1997, three months after taking up office. The Inquiry found that institutional racism played a part in the flawed investigation by the Metropolitan Police Service, defining this as:

'The collective failure of an organization to provide an appropriate and professional service to people because of their colour, culture or ethnic origin. It can be seen or detected in processes, attitudes and behaviour which amount to discrimination through unwitting prejudice, ignorance, thoughtlessness and racist stereotyping which disadvantage minority ethnic people' (Macpherson 1999: 6.34)

The Inquiry acknowledged that institutionalized racism was likely to be prevalent in other institutions and organizations in society, not just the **criminal justice system**, serving as an important reminder that good anti-discriminatory policies on paper must be put into practice in order to be effective.

- the decision to declassify cannabis from a Class B to a Class C drug—the least harmful—and relax the law on possession;
- the incorporation into domestic law of the European Convention on Human Rights in the Human Rights Act 1998.

New Labour continues to be 'tough on crime'. It has been suggested (Downes and Morgan 2002: 293) that 'tough on the causes of crime' has produced noticeably less hard-hitting policies than the ones being persued against criminals. Despite record numbers in prison and recognition from the Home Secretary of the need to reduce short custodial sentences in particular, most of the new sentences proposed in the White Paper *Justice for All* (Home Office 2002a) involve the use of imprisonment, including weekend imprisonment. If new initiatives by the **National Probation Service**—including **drug treatment and testing orders** and **cognitive-behavioural programmes**—fail to reduce reoffending, less serious but persistent offenders, as well as those committing more serious crimes, will continue to fill prison cells. This has implications for how young offenders are managed. Statistics indicating 26 per cent of known offenders are under 18, including a small number of persistent offenders committing a disproportionate number of crimes (Audit Commission 1996), persuaded the incoming Labour government to prioritize young offenders and the tackling of youth crime. It is to this group that we now turn.

POLICY IMPLICATIONS: YOUNG OFFENDERS

Nowhere in the criminal justice system are the tensions between competing philosophies and approaches to crime and its control more explicit than in relation to young offenders aged 10–17. Disentangling help or treatment from punishment has, in

Box 18.5 Sentencing Jolie

Jolie experienced years of physical and sexual abuse from her stepfather between the ages of 4 and 11. After repeatedly running away from home, she was accommodated by the Local Authority. Fostered by a couple with teenage sons, Jolie was bullied and sexually molested by the 15-year-old and began self-harming. She was placed in a residential home for adolescents, where she was introduced to prostitution as a means of obtaining money. Disaffected and rarely attending school, she began to experiment with drugs. Soon she was addicted to crack cocaine, and started shoplifting to fund her habit. At the age of 15 she became involved with a group of lads who used her to solicit men whom they then attacked and robbed at knifepoint. Eventually, following the serious assault of a 40-year-old man, she and two of the group were caught and prosecuted. In relation to sentencing Jolie:

- Should she be given help with problems associated with her offending in the hope of reducing or preventing future offending (**reductive punishment**)?
- Should she be punished in proportion to the seriousness of the offence to deter her from further offending (**retributive punishment**)?
- Do members of the public need to be protected and should the sentence ensure this (**incapacitative punishment**)?
- Can one sentence achieve all of the above?
- What approach should be taken if Jolie persists in offending in this, or in any other way?

practical terms, never been straightforward, but is particularly difficult when the welfare of the child must be considered alongside his or her punishment (see 'Children, young people, crime, and welfare' in Chapter 16). The increasing emphasis on public protection and the punishing of persistence has added further layers of complexity, as Box 18.5 demonstrates in relation to sentencing.

In addition to tensions between care, control, and public protection, criminal and anti-social behaviour by young persons tends to be used as a barometer for the moral climate of the nation. When high, the resulting **moral panic** (Cohen 1972) often leads to policy responses that are tougher than are warranted by the original incident—for example, the disproportionately heavy deterrent sentences imposed for mobile phone theft as part of a crackdown on street crime. Whittock's cartoon (see over) links this to another major policy concern, repeat offending. Conflicting attitudes towards young offenders can be tracked through policy responses over the past thirty years.

Systems management: diverting young offenders

The election of a Conservative government back into power in 1970, combined with growing right-wing antagonism and legal criticism towards welfarist policies, set the stage for a more punitive, justice-based approach towards young offenders. Throughout the 1970s and 1980s, however, a counter-initiative was developed to divert large

Cartoon 18.1 Moral panics and young offenders: how far will policy makers go?

numbers from both custody and the criminal justice system altogether. Innovative attempts by social work practitioners (known collectively as **systems management**) successfully influenced police and court responses towards young offenders. These included:

- inter-agency diversion panels set up to decide whether young persons arrested by the police could be cautioned rather than prosecuted—resulting in high numbers cautioned;
- credible alternative sentences proposed by pre-sentence report writers for young persons at serious risk of custody (for example, **Intermediate Treatment**)—resulting in a fall in numbers of 14–16 year olds receiving a custodial sentence.

These diversionary tactics were based on the belief that youth rather than criminality was the problem and that, with support and encouragement, the young person would 'grow out of' crime (Rutherford 1992). Crucial to this policy, based on labelling theory and radical non-intervention, is a means of identifying those young persons who demonstrate more serious delinquent tendencies—for which more formal intervention is required. Failure to do this opened the door to the more punitive lobby's accusations that young people were being 'let off' and allowed to continue offending.

Moral panics: punishing young offenders

The deepening of the recession from the late 1980s coincided with the publication of official crime statistics showing increased crime figures. An already disillusioned electorate sought a scapegoat. Crime, particularly that of young people, was an easy target. Tabloid newspapers reflected (or shaped?) a moral panic of inadequate official responses to public disorder, crime in general, and persistent offending by young people in particular (see Brown 1998: 37–53). At the height of the media attack, the 2-year-old James Bulger was abducted and killed by two truanting 10-year-old boys.

The public outrage and 'demonization' of children that followed allowed the Conservative government under John Major to justify an increasingly punitive 'law and order' approach to young offenders. A package of measures was announced which included the introduction of the **secure training order**, a restriction on cautioning young offenders, and US-style 'boot camps' (see Cavadino and Dignan 2002: 298–300). Predictably, sentencers responded by locking up more young people.

No more excuses: managing young offenders

The shift in New Labour's approach towards young offenders was set out in the White Paper *No More Excuses* which preceded its flagship legislation, the Crime and Disorder Act 1998:

> An excuse culture has developed within the youth justice system. It excuses itself for its inefficiency, and too often excuses the young offenders before it, implying they cannot help their behaviour because of their social circumstances . . . This White Paper seeks to draw a line under the past and sets out a new approach to tackling youth crime. (Home Office 1997b: 2)

The Crime and Disorder Act 1998 attempted to completely reshape existing provisions in relation to youth crime. It was influenced by the Audit Commission report, *Misspent Youth: Young People and Crime* (Audit Commission 1996). The report highlighted inefficiencies in the system and recommended shifting resources from processing young offenders to dealing with their behaviour—both post- and pre-conviction. Central to the Act was the development of the Youth Justice Board and Youth Offending Teams—made up of representatives from probation, social services, police, health, and education to ensure partnership between the key agencies involved with young people. Their overarching aim was defined as 'preventing offending by children and young persons'. New Labour thinking towards young offenders can be traced through the measures introduced in the legislation.

This emphasis on early intervention to prevent escalation of criminal behaviour ('nipping crime in the bud') was demonstrated by the introduction of the child safety order—designed for children under the age of 10 thought to be at risk of becoming involved in crime, and enabling them to be placed under the supervision of a social worker or youth justice worker. Criticism of repeat cautioning of persistent young offenders was addressed by the introduction of a new system of police reprimand and final warning scheme. Only one reprimand can be given, and a final warning triggers a package of measures from the youth offending team designed to help prevent re-offending.

The theme of 'taking responsibility' was demonstrated through the abolition of the common law presumption of *doli incapax* (that children under the age of 14 do not understand right from wrong), and the introduction of the reparation order requiring young offenders to make reparation to the victim of their offence or to the wider community. The latter reflected growing interest in **restorative justice** approaches for young offenders. Parental responsibility was emphasized by the introduction of a parenting order consisting of counselling or guidance sessions for up to three months to help the parents of young offenders turn their children away from crime.

The Act introduced a new community punishment for young offenders—the action plan order—combining punishment, reparation, and rehabilitation. It offers programmes to address offending behaviour, specifically cognitive-behavioural programmes similar to those being developed with adult offenders. A new detention and training order was introduced for those whose offending has not been prevented by community intervention or is of a serious nature. Combining custody and rehabilitation, it aims to both punish and rehabilitate young offenders.

The Crime and Disorder Act 1998 was followed swiftly by the Youth Justice and Criminal Evidence Act 1999. This created a new sentence of 'referral to a youth offender panel', to be restricted to first convictions in the first instance. The referral order is intended to replace the conditional discharge with the addition of a package of interventions designed to prevent reoffending (see Haines 2000 for a critique of this new order).

Overall, the pace of youth justice legislation and changes in relation to youth offending has been staggering. While the emphasis on early intervention is an attempt to prevent the escalation of offending by children and young persons, there are signs that increasing numbers of those who persist in offending are being incarcerated, reflecting the situation in the adult system.

IMPLICATIONS FOR POLICY: COSTS, NUMBERS, AND OUTCOMES

Costs

Crime imposes costs on victims, offenders, their families, and society as a whole. Two types of cost occur—the direct financial loss incurred by victims and the 'opportunity costs' to the general public when resources are diverted to making good the damage caused by the criminal act. The highest of these is expenditure on the criminal justice system (see Box 18.6).

Other costs to the general public include resources used for the treatment of victims of personal injury, and mitigating victims' losses through insurance and compensation. Attempts have been made to quantify the physical and emotional costs of crime for compensation purposes—for example, a standard award for minor injuries requiring treatment by a medical practitioner is £1,000, rising to £40,000 for the loss of an arm (Home Office 1999: 75). In addition, the government spends a considerable amount of money on crime prevention.

Box 18.6 Criminal Justice System expenditure 1999/2000 (£ billions)

Police	£7.5
Prison Service	£1.9
Criminal Legal Aid	£0.9
Probation Service	£0.5
Crown Prosecution Service and Serious Fraud Office	£0.3
Magistrates' courts	£0.3
Other	£0.2
Criminal Injuries Compensation and Victim Support	£0.2
Crown Court	£0.2
Total expenditure	£12.056

(Home Office 1999: 70)

Punishment also incurs costs. Comparisons of the annual cost of a custodial sentence with a community sentence will always show custody to be more expensive. Figures for 2000–1 demonstrate this (Home Office 2001: 4; 2002: 42)

- custody £27,090
- community rehabilitation order £1,970
- community punishment order £1,730

It is important to remember that these figures are based on actual costs—the marginal cost of sending one more person into a prison at or near capacity is actually much smaller than the above figure suggests.

What is not included in official Home Office figures is any attempt to put a price on the human costs of imprisonment. It was famously stated (Sir Alexander Paterson in Ruck 1951: 13), 'Men [*sic*] come to prison *as* a punishment, not *for* punishment.' The loss of liberty is the punishment. Nevertheless, the experience continues to be punishing—see Box 18.7.

In addition to cramped and unhygienic physical conditions in many prisons in the UK, prisoners face bullying and physical attack, including racist and sexual assaults. Illegal drug use thrives in prison, encouraging non-drug-takers to start using. Prisoners under 21 accounted for 18 per cent of self-inflicted deaths in 2001 (Liebling 2002: 140). When imprisoned, even for a short time, people stand to lose homes, jobs, partners, children, and social ties, militating against successful rehabilitation into the community. Unquantifiable costs are suffered by children separated from mothers and fathers.

Box 18.7 Prison Conditions: a view from the Chief Inspector

'Every so often in life, everyone has an experience that will stay with them for ever. I had one of those in December 1995 when, as the newly appointed Chief Inspector of Prisons, I joined my inspectors in an unannounced inspection of Holloway, the largest women's prison in England. It was overcrowded, filthy dirty, its staff overstretched and demoralised and the vast majority of its prisoners locked up in their cells all day, doing nothing. There were wholly inadequate arrangements for caring for the large numbers of mentally disordered women. Rates of self-harm were alarmingly high. In the Mother and Baby Unit new mothers asked me whether it was right that they had been chained to prison officers while they were in labour. . . . The Prison Service's attitude was exemplified by the fact that injuries to women were recorded on a diagram of a man's body.'

(Sir David Ramsbotham, GCB, CBE, HM Chief Inspector of Prisons: Carlen (2002: ix))

Numbers

Prisons in England and Wales were declared full on 13 July 2002, with overflow prisoners being diverted to police cells. The official prison population on this day was recorded as 71,480, including a record 4,428 women. The increasing numbers of women prisoners is believed to be in part related to high numbers of foreign nationals being convicted of drug-trafficking offences. Ten years before, the prison population had actually decreased to 40,000 following the 'talking down' of imprisonment by successive Home Secretaries (see Box 18.4) and emphasis on 'punishment in the community' for less serious offenders in the Criminal Justice Act 1991. Following Michael Howard's 'Prison works' speech, numbers increased steadily, with a slight levelling off between 1999 and 2001 following the introduction of the **home detention curfew** in January 2001.

In March 2002, 12,400 of a total 69,780 prisoners were on **remand** rather than **sentenced.** Many of these would have subsequently been found not guilty or received a community sentence.

While foreign nationals contribute to the disproportionate numbers of Black African-Caribbean, Asian, and other minority ethnic groups compared to white in both male and female prisons (8 and 15 per cent of total prison populations respectively), statistics routinely show this occurring also at earlier stages of the criminal justice process (see Home Office 2000). Reasons are complex, but various studies suggest these include (see Bowling and Phillips 2002):

- the social construction of ethnicity and criminality;
- intensive policing of minority ethnic communities, especially African-Caribbean;
- stop and search, caution and arrest practices by the police;
- bail and remand decision-making;
- higher numbers of minority ethnic defendants being sentenced in the Crown Court;
- judicial discretion in sentence length.

Minority ethnic communities continue to be underrepresented as employees of criminal justice agencies. Although 'milestone targets' are now being set in prisons, police, and probation, only probation met (and surpassed) their 2002 targets.

Outcomes

Assessing the impact of different types of sentencing on future behaviour is by no means straightforward, but the most viable means is by comparing reconviction rates. Statistical data show that 58 per cent of prisoners released from prison in 1997 were reconvicted within two years (Home Office 2001), with particularly high rates (76 per cent) for young male offenders. Those sentenced to shorter sentences (under twelve months) had a higher reconviction rate—raising even more concerns about high numbers of short prison sentences. While comparative data regarding community penalties has been disappointing, the revival of rehabilitation and treatment through the **'what works'** movement and the development of **cognitive-behavioural programmes** is aiming to demonstrate more positive results (McGuire 2000).

VARIETIES OF EUROPEAN EXPERIENCE

Countries throughout Europe have very different historical and cultural experiences of crime control. In France, transportation to the French colonies only ended in 1938. Spain did not begin its transition into democracy until after the death of Franco in 1975. Scandinavian countries' longstanding welfare-based social systems are reflected in their humane and often radical penal policy—for example, Norway in the mid-1970s introduced a 'waiting system' for less serious offenders sentenced to imprisonment, and in the early 1980s Denmark reduced maximum sentences for property crimes and liberalized the rules concerning drunken driving. Holland has been highlighted for its 'culture of tolerance' (see Downes 1988), although increased use of imprisonment as a response to the country's growing drug problem has since resulted in a prison population comparable with neighbouring countries. The opening up of eastern European countries to the West, and the ending of strict state control, is having an impact on crime and its management in those countries.

Varieties of crime control

Comparing statistics across national boundaries, each with different legal definitions and measurement of crime rates, is difficult. Evidence suggests, however, that rates of recorded crime have risen throughout most western European countries since the Second World War, and in eastern Europe since capitalist economies replaced socialism at the end of the twentieth century. In Europe, as in Britain, increased crime and media representations of crime have increased the public's fear of it along with demands for an effective and robust response from criminal justice agencies. A shift to the right in countries such as Austria, the Netherlands, and France has resulted in deterrence-based crime control policies and calls for uncompromising policies on immigration, asylum, and crime.

In contrast, many eastern European countries are looking to the West for ways of managing high levels of incarceration through the development of alternatives to custody. Case Study 18.2 highlights one such project in Ukraine.

Varieties and types of prison population

More than 8.75 million people are held in penal institutions throughout the world. About half (4.32 million) of these are in the United States, Russia, or China, with the United States having the highest prison population rate in the world (700 per 100,000 of the national population) (Walmsley 2002). By contrast, the median rate for southern European countries is 65, for central and eastern European countries it is 210, and for the UK it is 125.

Prison populations reflect criminalization processes, with large numbers of unemployed, poor, homeless, and immigrant persons routinely incarcerated throughout Europe. Women and minority ethnic groups, both indigenous and from different countries of origin, warrant particular mention. While the conviction and prosecution of women is still far below that of men, there are indications throughout Europe that increasing numbers are being sentenced to imprisonment and for longer (Ruggiero et al. 1995: 13–15). There is evidence of similar controls being applied to minority ethnic groups, with heavy policing and imprisoning of those whose lifestyles are believed to threaten order and stability—specifically immigrants (legal and illegal), asylum seekers, refugees, guest workers, and foreigners (Ruggiero et al. 1995: 10–13).

Case Study 18.2 The development of alternative sentences of imprisonment in Ukraine

Ukraine, with a prison population rate of 435 per 100,000, holds many more people in prison than neighbouring eastern European countries, many of whom are serving sentences of one year or less. In consultation with several project partners, a need to develop alternatives to custody was identified—both as community sentences in their own right and to support mechanisms for the early release of prisoners. While there was already considerable scope for the application of non-custodial penalties within the existing legal and institutional framework (conspicuously, the suspended sentence of imprisonment), these were being underused. The judiciary and the public needed to be persuaded on two counts:

1. that these measures were associated with very low levels of reconviction;
2. that they could be used without compromising public safety.

Through the establishment of two small demonstration projects in Ukraine, training of existing staff, and a series of high-profile seminars, the project has, over a period of three years, contributed to the increased confidence in and use of alternatives to imprisonment.

(The authors are grateful to Rob Canton, author of the Concept Paper which informs the above, and member of the Project Team (comprising representatives of the University of Nottingham Human Rights Law Centre and Inner London Probation Service). Further information is available at www.nottingham.ac.uk/law/hrlc.htm)

Rates of imprisonment are not determined by factors wholly beyond government control—they are ultimately a matter of political choice. Policy-makers in Europe, as in the UK, must decide whether the huge costs of an incarcerative penal policy for both the most serious *and* less serious but persistent offenders can be sustained. Also how, if they decide they cannot, decarcerative strategies can be introduced which will be acceptable to those who voted them into power (see Christie 2001). Ultimately, in a democratic society, it is the electorate who will influence government policy. The challenge, then, for politicians is to ensure that members of the public are fully aware of the costs—to themselves as taxpayers as well as to victims and offenders—of a continued dependence on imprisonment to control crime.

KEY LEGISLATION

Criminal Justice Act (CJA) 1991 Representing a major development in sentencing law and practice, the Act endeavoured to establish a coherent sentencing framework for the use of financial, community, and custodial punishments by introducing proportionality, or just deserts, as the guiding principle for sentencers. Amongst its provisions were new categories for the early release of prisoners, two new community orders (the **combination order** and the **curfew order**), **national standards** to tighten up probation officers' enforcement of community orders, and the renaming of the Juvenile Court the 'Youth Court'.

Criminal Justice Act 1993 The Act made statutory amendments to the CJA 1991 within a year of its implementation which moved sentencing further away from the new desert-based framework. The assessment of offence seriousness now took into account all current offences, previous convictions, and any failure to respond to previous sentences. Offences on bail were to be treated as an aggravating factor—increasing overall seriousness.

The Criminal Justice and Public Order Act 1994 In part a response to moral panics of the early 1990s, the Act's provisions included the secure training order for 12–14-year-olds, and the doubling (twelve months to twenty-four) of the maximum sentence of detention in a young offender institution for 15–16-year-olds. Provisions relating to public order increased police powers to remove trespassers from land—'squatters', 'new age travellers', 'unauthorized campers', those organizing or attending 'raves', 'hunt saboteurs', and other protesters.

The Crime (Sentences) Act 1997 The central provision of the Act was to introduce mandatory life sentences for certain second-time violent and sexual offences and minimum prison sentences for third-time drug dealers and burglars similar to the 'three strikes and you're out' policy being pursued in the United States. The Act abolished the need for the court to seek an offender's consent to a **community sentence**.

The Sex Offender Act 1997 The Act required designated sex offenders to notify the police of their name and address, and any subsequent changes, in order to establish a sex offender 'register'. Despite concerns about non-compliance, by the end of 1997 88 per cent of offenders had notified police of their whereabouts as required (see Thomas 2000).

The Crime and Disorder Act 1998 The Act aims to prevent crime and disorder through a tranche of new provisions—anti-social behaviour orders, sex offender orders, parenting orders, child safety orders, and child curfew schemes—to reduce delays in processing offenders through the system.

The Youth Justice and Criminal Evidence Act 1999 The Act establishes a new approach to the sentencing of first-time young offenders—the referral order—and introduces measures to protect vulnerable witnesses and support them in giving evidence.

Criminal Justice and Court Services Act 2000 The Act created a unified National Probation Service, one that is directly accountable to the Home Secretary, renamed certain community orders (see **community sentences**), strengthened sanctions for failure to comply with probation supervision, and extended the use of electronic monitoring.

REFERENCES

Audit Commission (1996), *Misspent Youth: Young People and Crime*. London: Audit Commission.

Bowling, B., and Phillips, C. (2002), *Racism, Crime and Justice*. Harlow: Pearson Education.

Brown, S. (1998), *Understanding Youth and Crime: Listening to Youth?* Buckingham: Open University Press.

Carlen, P. (ed.) (2002), *Women and Punishment: The Struggle for Justice*. Cullompton: Willan.

Cavadino, M., and Dignan, J. (2002), *The Penal System: An Introduction*, 3rd edn. London: Sage.

Christie, N. (2001), *Crime Control as Industry: Towards Gulags, Western Style*, 3rd edn. London: Routledge.

Cohen, S. (1972), *Folk Devils and Moral Panics: The Creation of the Mods and Rockers*. Oxford: Martin Robertson.

Downes, D. (1988), *Contrasts in Tolerance: Post War Penal Policy in the Netherlands*. Oxford: Oxford University Press.

Downes, D., and Morgan, R. (2002) 'The Skeletons in the cupboard: the politics of law and order at the turn of the millenium'. In M. Maguire, R. Morgan and R. Reiner (eds.), *The Oxford Handbook of Criminology*. Oxford: Oxford University Press.

Edwards, S. S. M. (1989), *Policing 'Domestic' Violence: Women, the Law and the State*. London: Sage.

Haines, K. (2000), 'Referral orders and youth offender panels: restorative approaches and the new youth justice'. In B. Goldson (ed.), *The New Youth Justice*. Lyme Regis: Russell House.

Home Office (1990), *Crime, Justice and Protecting the Public: The Government's Proposals for Legislation*. Cmnd. 965. London: HMSO.

—— (1997a), *Criminal Statistics England and Wales 1996*. Cmnd. 3764. London: HMSO.

—— (1997b), *No More Excuses: A New Approach to Tackling Youth Crime in England and Wales*. London: Home Office.

—— (1999), *Information on the Criminal Justice System in England and Wales: Digest 4*. London: Home Office.

—— (2000), *Statistics on Race and the Criminal Justice System 2000*. London: Home Office.

—— (2001), *The Prison Population in 2000: A Statistical Review*. London: Home Office.

—— (2002a), *Justice for All*. London: Home Office.

Home Office (2002b), *Probation Statistics England and Wales 2000*. London: Home Office.

Hough, M., and Mayhew, P. (1983), *The British Crime Survey: First Report*. Home Office Research Study No. 76. London: HMSO.

Howard, M. (1993), 'Speech by the Rt. Hon. Michael Howard QC MP, the Home Secretary, to the 110th Conservative Party Conference, 6 October'. London: Conservative Party Central Office.

Jones, T., MacLean, B., and Young, J. (1986), *The Islington Crime Survey: Crime, Victimization and Policing in Inner-City London*. Aldershot: Gower.

Kershaw, C., Chivite-Matthews, N., Thomas, C, and Aust, R. (2001), *The 2001 British Crime Survery*, London Home Office.

Labour Party (1997), *New Labour: Because Britain Deserves Better*. London: The Labour Party.

Liebling, A. (2002), 'Suicide and the safer prisons agenda', *Probation Journal* 49(2): 140–50.

Macpherson, Sir W. (1999), *The Stephen Lawrence Inquiry*. Cm. 4262-1. London: Stationery Office.

Maguire, M. (2002), 'Crime statistics: the 'data explosion' and its implications'. In Maguire et al. (2002).

McGuire, J. (2000), *Cognitive-Behavioural Approaches: An Introduction to Theory and Research*. London: Home Office.

Martinson, R. (1974) 'What works? Questions and answers about prison reform', *Public Interest* 35:

Maxfield, M. G. (1984), *Fear of Crime in England and Wales*. Home Office Research Study No. 78. London: HMSO.

Mayhew, P., and Hough, M. (1988), 'The British Crime Survey: origins and impact'. In M. Maguire and J. Pointing (eds.), *Victims of Crime: A New Deal?* Milton Keynes: Open University Press.

Povey, D., and Prime, J. (1999), *Recorded Crime Statistics England and Wales, April 1998 to March 1999*. Home Office Statistical Bulletin 18/99. London: Home Office.

Radford, J. (1987), 'Policing male violence: policing men'. In M. Maynard and J. Hanmer (eds.), *Women, Violence and Social Control*. London: Macmillan.

Ruck, S. K. (ed.) (1951), *Paterson on Prisons*. London: Muller.

Ruggiero, V., Ryan, M., and Sim, J. (eds.) (1995), *Western European Penal Systems: A Critical Anatomy*. London: Sage.

Rutherford, A. (1992), *Growing Out of Crime*, 2nd edn. Winchester: Waterside Press.

Simmons, J. (2002), *Crime in England and Wales 2001/2002*. London: Home Office.

Stanko, E. A. (1988), 'Hidden violence against women', In M. Maguire and J. Ponting (eds.), *Victims of Crime: A New Deal?* Milton Keynes: Open University Press.

Thomas, T. (2000), *Sex Crime: Sex Offending and Society*. Cullompton: Willan.

Walmsley, R. (2002), *World Prison Population List*, 3rd edn. London: Home Office.

Wilson, J. Q. (1975), *Thinking About Crime*. New York: Basic Books.

—— and Herrnstein, R. (1985), *Crime and Human Nature*. New York: Simon & Schuster.

Young, J. (1988), 'Risk of crime and fear of crime: a realist critique of survey-based Assumptions'. In M. Maguire and J. Ponting (eds.), *Victims of Crime: A New Deal?* Milton Keynes: Open University Press.

—— (1997), 'Left realist criminology: radical in its analysis, realist in its policy. In Maguire et al. (1997). Maguire, R. Morgan and R. Reiner (eds.), *The Oxford Handbook of Criminology*, 2nd edn. Oxford: Oxford University Press.

FURTHER READING

Blackstone Press (Oxford) publish comprehensive guides to the legislation discussed in this chapter (including a copy of the Act)—see *Guide to the Criminal Justice Act 1991* (2nd edn. incorporates Criminal Justice Act 1993 amendments); *Criminal Justice and Public Order Act 1994; Crime and Disorder Act 1998; Youth Justice and Criminal Evidence Act 1999*.

B. Bowling and C. Phillips, *Racism, Crime and Justice* (Harlow: Pearson Education, 2002) offers a comprehensive and critical analysis of racism and the criminal justice process from a number of perspectives.

J. Simmons, *Crime in England and Wales 2001/2002* (London: Home Office, 2002) combines and replaces, for the first time, the previously separate publications of the British Crime Survey and police recorded statistics. (For a free copy telephone Communications and Development Unit, 020 7273 2084).

M. Maguire, R. Morgan, and R. Reiner (eds.), *The Oxford Handbook of Criminology* (Oxford: Oxford University Press, 1994, 1997, 2002). All three editions contain a number of stimulating articles relating to numerous aspects of crime, justice, and punishment. See in particular David Garland, Lorraine Gelsthorpe, David Downes and Rod Morgan, Mike Maguire, Lucia Zedner, Jock Young, Frances Heidensohn, and Tim Newburn.

C. Murray (ed.), *Does Prison Work?* (London: IEA Health and Welfare Unit, 1997) includes Murray's own provocative essay on the subject, alongside three critical responses.

J. Reiman, *The Rich Get Richer and the Poor Get Prison*, 4th edn. (Needham Heights, Mass.: Allyn & Bacon, 1995) is a classic Marxist-oriented account of the American penal system.

USEFUL WEBSITES

Criminal Justice System	http://www.criminal-justice-system.gov.uk
Home Office	http://www.homeoffice.gov.uk
Police Service	http://www.police.uk
Prison Service	http://www.hmprisonservice.gov.uk
Victim Support	http://www.victimsupport.com
Youth Justice Board	http://www.youth-justice-board.gov.uk

GLOSSARY

anti-social behaviour order Introduced in the Crime and Disorder Act 1998 and implemented in April 1999, these are civil orders which can be applied for by the police or local authority against an individual aged 10 or over whose behaviour is deemed to be 'anti-social'. Orders last for two years and breach makes it a criminal (and imprisonable) offence.

attendance centre order Requires a young person (aged 10–20) to attend a local centre run by the police for a maximum of three hours per day where s/he receives 'appropriate occupation and instruction'. Length of orders range between twelve and thirty-six hours depending on age.

British Crime Survey (BCS) A series of large household surveys of people's experiences and perceptions of crime in England and Wales. The first one was undertaken in 1982.

classicism A traditional, punishment-oriented approach to crime emphasizing clarity in the law and due process in criminal procedure, combined with certainty and regularity of punishment. Classicists see human beings, including offenders, as having free choice and as individuals who will therefore be deterred from certain acts prohibited by the law by the anticipation of swift and certain punishment.

cognitive-behavioural programmes Groupwork (and sometimes individual) intervention based on a synthesis of methods drawn from behavioural and cognitive psychology which aim to change the way people think about themselves and their environment. Applied to offenders, the programmes attempt to change offender's attitudes towards their offending behaviour and hence the behaviour itself.

community punishment order (CPO) Requires an offender aged 16 or over to perform unpaid work on behalf of the community. Orders involve a minimum of forty and a maximum of 240 hours to be completed within twelve months. Managed by the Probation Service.

community punishment and rehabilitation order (CPRO) Combines elements of both CPO and CRO. Offenders aged 16 or over can be required to perform between 40 and 100 hours of community punishment and be subject to probatia supervisia for between twelve months and three years commuity rehabilitation.

community rehabilitation order (CRO) Requires an offender aged 16 or over to be supervised by a probation officer for a specified period of between six months and three years. Requirements can be added to orders regarding accommodation, supervised activities, and treatment (mental health/substance misuse)

community sentences Introduced by the Criminal Justice Act 1991 as a penalty in their own right rather than an 'alternative to custody', the term describes the tier of sentences between financial penalties and custodial sentences. A 'community sentence' is composed of one or more 'community orders' which include (post Criminal Justice and Court Services Act 2000): a **community rehabilitation order (CRO)**, a **community punishment order (CPO)**, a community punishment and rehabilitation order (CPRO, combining the CPO and CRO), a **curfew order** (with **electronic monitoring** attached), a **supervision order**, and an **attendance centre order**.

criminal justice system The term most commonly used to refer to the group of agencies responsible for various aspects of the work of maintaining law and order and the administration of justice. Key agencies are the Police Service, the Crown Prosecution Service, the Court Service, the Prison Service, and the National Probation Service. Sometimes referred to as the criminal justice process.

curfew order Powers given to criminal courts by the Criminal Justice Act 1991 to impose a curfew requirement of between two and twelve hours for no longer than six months on offenders aged 16 and over. Implementation was delayed until **electronic monitoring** was working successfully. The Crime (Sentences) Act 1997 made it possible to make an electronically monitored curfew order on a young person below the age of 16.

detention and training order (DTO) Introduced by the Crime and Disorder Act 1998 and implemented nationally from 1 April 2000, this order replaced Detention in a Young Offender Institution for those aged 15 to 17, and Secure Training Orders for those aged 12 to 14. Orders are made for terms between four and twenty-four months, and are served half in custody and half in the community under the supervision of a probation officer or social worker.

deviancy amplification spiral A process whereby a certain type of deviance arouses public attention and is focused on by, for example, the police and the media. The activity then appears to increase (and may actually increase) through heightened awareness, reporting, recording, and research.

drug treatment and testing order (DTTO) Introduced in the Crime and Disorder Act 1998 and implemented in October 2000, these orders are aimed at those aged 16 and over who are convicted of crimes committed to fund their drug habit and who show a willingness to cooperate with treatment and subsequent testing. The orders last between six months and three years.

electronic monitoring Piloted extensively throughout the 1990s and available nationally since December 1999, the offender's whereabouts are 'electronically monitored' through the wearing of a 'tag' working in combination with equipment located at the offender's address. Managed by a private-sector company, it is used in relation to bail, early release from prison, and as a community sentence attached to a curfew order.

home detention curfew (HDC) Introduced in the Crime and Disorder Act 1998, the scheme began operating on 28 January 1999. It allows prisoners serving sentences of between three months and four years to be considered for early release subject to a home curfew enforced by **electronic monitoring**.

incarcerative punishment Punishment which ensures an individual is unable to reoffend through some form of constraint—the physical constraint of the prison walls being the most obvious form.

institutionalist approach An approach to interpreting crime statistics which suggests that they are more a product of the institutions that define and measure crime than 'real' phenomena.

Intermediate Treatment (IT) schemes A new form of treatment for children and young persons made possible by the Children and Young Persons Act 1969. Schemes enable young persons to remain at home while attending supervised activities designed to have a positive impact on their behaviour, rather than their having to enter a residential establishment.

just deserts The classical notion that wrongdoers should be punished in proportion to the harm done—literally that they receive their 'just deserts'. Desert-based sentencing is based on this principle.

justice model An approach which seeks to reduce official discretion in the justice system, and to ensure that like cases are treated alike—punishment to fit the crime, not the criminal.

legal definitions (of crime) The definition of a crime simply as an act defined as criminal by the law, irrespective of how current social values define the act.

moral panic The term used by Stanley Cohen in *Folk Devils and Moral Panics* (1972) to indicate a process of collective overreaction to a form of apparently widespread deviance. The media initially 'identify' the 'crisis', and the inevitable societal reaction is to demand greater control through increased policing and more retributive law.

National Probation Service (NPS) The Criminal Justice and Courts Services Act 2000 renamed the Probation Service for England and Wales 'the National Probation Service for England and Wales', and set out its aims as being to protect the public, to reduce offending, and to provide for the proper punishment of offending.

national standards Introduced into legislation by the Criminal Justice Act 1991 and implemented in 1992, the standards provided guidelines on the circumstances in breach of which action should be taken by probation officers supervising offenders in the community. Successive Standards in 1995 and 2000 have limited officers' discretion considerably.

positivism Most commonly associated with the Italian Cesare Lombroso, the positivist school of criminology views crime as caused by factors and processes that can be discovered by observation and scientific investigation. Positivists often subscribe to the doctrine of determinism: that human beings, including criminals, do not act from their own free will but are impelled to act by forces beyond their control.

realist approach An approach to interpreting crime data which suggests that they reflect 'real' trends in criminal behaviour, as opposed to the practices of the institutions that produce this data.

recorded crime Crime which is recorded by the police and notified to the Home Office. Includes all 'indictable' and 'triable either way' offences together with some closely related 'summary offences'.

reductive punishment Punishment which seeks to reduce the incidence of the types of behaviour prohibited by the criminal law, whether committed by the person punished (individual deterrence) or by others (general deterrence).

remand prisoners Unconvicted persons committed to custody rather than released on bail pending a further stage of criminal proceedings. The defendant is said to be 'on remand' during the adjournment.

restorative justice A new way of thinking about responding to crime, aiming to make offenders aware of the harm they have caused and encouraging them, in consultation with victims and members of their community, to seek to make reparation (direct or indirect) for the harm.

retributive punishment Punishment which sets out to impose an amount of pain proportionate to that caused by the criminal act. The criminal receives his or her **just deserts**.

secure training order (STO) A new and controversial custodial sentence for young offenders aged 12–14 made available to the courts in the Criminal Justice and Public Order Act 1994. To be served half in custody and half in the community under the supervision of a probation officer or social worker. Replaced by the **detention and training order**.

sentenced prisoners Persons committed to custody following conviction of a criminal offence in a court of law.

social construction The notion that a phenomenon—in this case crime—is not an objective, observable entity in the world waiting to be discovered, but rather is created (constructed) by social values and preconceptions.

social definitions (of crime) Definitions which are based not on whether or not an act is against the law (legal definitions) but on the basis of broader social criteria; for example, social values and norms or social justice.

social positivism The positivist belief that the main cause of crime is to be found in social conditions rather than in the biological or psychological make-up of the individual.

Supervision Order Requires a young person aged 17 years or under to be supervised by a member of a youth offending team for between three months and three years. Specified activities to help them address their offending behaviour can be attached as a condition of the order.

systems management The collective term for methods developed throughout the 1970s and 1980s to affect positively rates of juvenile custody, juvenile prosecution, and juvenile crime itself by attending to the mechanics of the criminal justice process. Methods included cautioning panels, discontinuance from prosecution, and **Intermediate Treatment**.

unit fines A system of fines introduced by the Criminal Justice Act 1991 which attempted to achieve 'equality of impact' amongst offenders—the poorer the offender, the less s/he would pay as a proportion of disposable income. Sustained criticism during the first few months of implementation resulted in the system being abolished seven months after its introduction.

victimology The study of the relationship between victims and offenders. The academic 'discipline' of victimology was founded in the late 1940s.

welfare model Most commonly referred to in the context of juvenile justice to describe a 'positivistic' approach which holds that young offenders should be helped rather than punished. Transferable to the young adult offender and adult context.

'what works' A research-led agenda leading to increased optimism about the ability of **community sentences** to rehabilitate offenders and demonstrate reduced reconviction rates. As the latter are not an accurate measure of reoffending (measuring only those who get caught), measures of attitude and behavioural change are also used to evaluate the effectiveness of different sentences.

19

The Environment and Green Social Policy

Michael Cahill

CONTENTS

INTRODUCTION

The environment has ceased to be the sole concern of the political and academic fringe and become an important policy area. It is widely acknowledged today that environmental considerations need to be built into all government policies, the work of business and the management of the economy. This chapter surveys the rise of environmental and green thinking, shows the ways in which the concept of **sustainability** has been utilized and its connections with social policy, and reviews some policy proposals which could be said to have been informed by green thinking.

THE LEGACY OF INDUSTRIALIZATION

Modern social policies first emerged as responses to the social problems produced by industrialization, a process which simultaneously was making a profound impact upon the natural environment. Industrialization promised to take humankind out of a period of scarcity, where life was precarious and short, and into an age of plenty. In general this was achieved in the advanced industrial societies of the north, where even the poor today live in relative and not subsistence poverty. Nonetheless, the industrial and urban activities of the past 250 years have led to insupportable burdens for the planet. Beneficial advances in science, medicine, and telecommunications have been gained at the expense of the natural world. In order to achieve the levels of economic growth witnessed over the last 250 years, the environment has been pillaged: millions of hectares of forests have been removed, the seas and rivers have been used as dumps for chemicals, waste, and other pollutants, and this in turn has meant that the habitats of marine life, birds, and most mammals other than man have been seriously damaged. The continuing world population growth, consequent upon the vast expansion in material wealth, has in turn produced yet greater pressures on the natural environment, leading to increasing demands for food and living space.

During the last half-century the damage to the natural environment wrought by humankind has accelerated. Advances in science and technology have meant that manufactured consumer products are now universally used by people in the industrialized West. Some of these have quite catastrophic impacts upon the natural world: the motor car, for example, symbolizes the consumer society, in that it is privatized and endows its driver with the freedom to travel; but in its manufacture, use, and disposal it consumes vast quantities of water, minerals, and petroleum, and is a major source of environmental pollution This is in addition to the estimated 3,000 deaths a day on the world's roads (Whitelegg 1997).

The first major realization of the impact of humankind's unsustainable activity was the fear in the early 1970s that minerals and natural resources were being depleted at such a rate that the Western way of life would become insupportable. Although the more dire predictions have not yet been borne out, it remains a real probability that resource depletion will just take longer to occur; it is expected that reserves of oil, for example, will be depleted by the middle of the twenty-first century rather than, as was earlier forecast, by the end of the 1990s. The risk from environmental hazards, from nuclear waste, from genetic engineering, from contaminated food has led some social scientists to define ours as a **risk society** (Beck 1992; Giddens 1991). Uncertainty, insecurity, and hazard abound for individuals in a society where traditional ways of life have come to an end, while the advance of science and technology has meant that nuclear power and genetic engineering, to take two examples, pose risks on a global scale. **Globalization** is ensuring that industrialization and urbanization continue to transform the lives of millions, with China set to become the world's leading industrial power by 2020.

SUSTAINABILITY

Sustainability is an end-state that no society has yet reached. Sustainable development is the process whereby societies can move towards that end. It would be utopian to think that the end state of sustainability can ever be reached in the same way, as it is utopian to think that a society with perfect equality could be attained. Jacobs has identified six themes that are important in the contemporary discussion of sustainability and sustainable development:

- integration of environmental considerations into economic and social planning;
- futurity: concern about the impact of contemporary decisions on future generations;
- environmental protection: policies to limit environmental damage;
- equity: commitment to meeting the basic needs of the poor today and in the future;
- quality of life: economic growth does not necessarily equate with human well being;
- participation: sustainable development requires as much involvement as possible by individuals and groups if it is to work. (Jacobs in Dobson 1999: 26–7)

Leaving aside environmental protection, all of these have relevance to social policy. How they will be put into policy and practice depends on the political ideas of those in power. The impact of green ideas on political thought requires some brief attention.

GREEN IDEOLOGIES

There are many varieties of green ideologies, with a continuum in green thinking from the **ecocentric** to the **technocentric** (Pepper 1996), from **dark green** to **light green** (Porritt 1984; Dobson 2000), from **deep ecology** to shallow ecology (Naess 1988), or, as the German Greens say, from fundamentalist to realist positions (Hulsberg 1987). The realist, technocentric view of our environmental problems holds the dominant position in the world of UK government policy-making.

Ecologism

Ecologism holds that the environmental crisis is the most urgent concern for humankind and all other considerations should be subordinated to this. Existing forms of economic and social arrangements which contribute to the ecological crisis should be replaced or superseded. There are limits to economic growth, and the current forms of industrialization and urbanization are contributing to the environmental crisis. Furthermore, ecologism contends that even in the consideration of the environment too much has been designed thinking only of humans and not the rest of nature. Ecologism posits a future society where the structures of the policy and the economy will be transformed so that the natural and the human world can live in greater harmony. For its future thinking of this kind it draws upon a tradition of anarchist and decentralist thought. (The best account is to be found in Dobson 2000: ch. 3.)

Survivalism

Survivalists believe that the environmental crisis is so pressing that normal forms of democracy and the market are unable to deal with the impending crisis. They advocate a series of authoritarian measures to protect the planet. They are to be found mainly in the USA, where a significant body of opinion is concerned to protect the wilderness areas.

Population size is a major concern for many environmentalists and especially the survivalists. Garrett Hardin developed one of the best-known arguments—'the tragedy of the commons'—around the theme of population and environmental pressures. The simple but effective analogy is with the practice before the enclosure movement, when common land was used for grazing. The common land was intended to be shared by a small number of cattle. It was in the interests of each individual to bring as many cattle as possible onto the land; but the net result of this was overgrazing and the decline in quality of the land. Hardin argues that we have the same problem today, but on a world scale. There are too many people in the world, and by extension we are overburdening not just the land but also the sea and the air. His arguments are neo-**Malthusian**, in that he believes that we have to stop giving a lifeline to people in the poorer world, and allow them to starve to death. The 'tragedy of the commons' highlights the immense strains that we are putting on our planet; but an obvious rejoinder is that the industrialized countries, particularly in their consumer capitalist phase, are putting much more strain on the resources of the planet than the people of the south (Hardin 1968). Hardin's writings and those of Ehrlich (1968) are notable for their authoritarian conclusions, which prioritize the needs and the aspirations of the rich world. They are open to the objection that per head it is the people of the rich world who produce the greatest burden on the planet through the orgy of consumption engaged in by the mass of the population in affluent societies.

Ecofeminism

Ecofeminism makes a strong connection between the exploitation of the natural world and the exploitation and undervaluing of women. Ecofeminists share the belief that the natural world is but one, and that human beings are a part of nature. Arguing that women have always been closer to nature than men, ecofeminists believe that women's subordination is linked with the treatment of nature (Mellor 1997). Ecofeminists argue that 'female' qualities of caring, kindness, and nurturing are suited particularly to an ecological society (Sargisson 2001). All of these positions beg the question as to whether there is a 'male' or a 'female' set of behavioural attributes. Given the long history of women's subordination, we do not know that women, equipped with economic independence and full political and social rights and control over reproduction, would necessarily behave differently towards nature and the environment than men have done.

Ecosocialism

Ecosocialism attributes the parlous state of the world's environment to the depredations of the market system, and suggests that it is capitalism which needs to be overthrown if the planet is to be saved from destruction. In many ways it is the successor to the revolutionary movements that were so popular among students in the 1960s: it offers a goal for the future rooted in an implacable opposition to contemporary capitalism. Its best-known exponents were to be found among the West German Greens, principally within its fundamentalist tendency, and in the writings of the late Rudolph Bahro (Bahro 1982; 1986). The German Greens since their inception in 1980 have been an alliance between the non-aligned Left, peaceniks, and feminists: 'Ecology is only a factor in their identity' (Jahn in Jacobs 1997: 175). Many ecosocialists draw upon Marxism for their understanding of environmental problems, believing that it is within the social relationships of capitalist society that change must be effected, rather than focusing on lifestyle change among the mass of the population. They argue that industrial progress can go further without damage to the environment, but only if it is within the context of a society organized around the common ownership of the means of production (Ryle 1988; Pepper 1993).

Conservatism

Green conservatism is not an especially prominent aspect of contemporary thinking on the environment. Conservative ideas, however, pervade much thinking about the environment, although this is in the sense of conservation rather than political conservatism with a large C. The form of conservatism which has most points of connection with the environment is traditional conservatism, as opposed to the free-market variant which triumphed under Mrs Thatcher and has been the dominant strand in the Conservative Party subsequently. Traditional conservatives place a high value on continuity, preservation, and the protection of the countryside from urban encroachments. Change should be gradual and organic. (For an argument which links environmentalism and traditional conservatism, see Gray 1993.) Having said this, the dominant conservative response to environmentalists in the UK is often to see them as radicals who would damage the structure of society.

GREEN PARTIES, GREEN PRESSURE GROUPS, AND SOCIAL WELFARE

The Green parties which emerged in western Europe in the 1980s claimed that they were 'neither left nor right but in front'. They offered a political programme which embraced far more than the environmental agenda, having policies on health services, income maintenance, and the other traditional areas of political controversy. Although Greens achieved some limited success in countries which have a proportional representation system, in the UK the Green Party has never polled more than 1 per cent of the vote at general elections. As Carter has noted, the environment has not become an issue of party political conflict, so that there is an absence of widespread debates as to the direction of environmental policy. (Carter, N. 2001: 318). As the environment has now become part of mainstream politics, it is noticeable that neither Labour or the Conservatives accords the environment a leading place in its policy plans, although the Liberal Democrats have, it is true, a much harder-edged approach. Much of the detailed work of critique of government policy comes from think tanks and from environmental pressure groups. Friends of the Earth and Greenpeace, both radical environmental groups, have moved from a position of being outsiders to insiders in the policy networks. Friends of the Earth has shifted its stance to include discussion of broader social as well as environmental policies (Lamb 1996).

SUSTAINABLE DEVELOPMENT IN UK POLITICS

Any picture of consensus across the political spectrum on sustainability would be misleading. There is much debate as to the meaning and consequent priorities of sustainability: should primacy be given to state or market in achieving sustainability; can sustainability coexist with the present national degree of commitment to the consumer society and the existing distribution of income and wealth? 'Sustainable development', defined by the Brundtland Commission as 'development which meets the needs of the present without compromising the ability of future generations to meet their own needs' (World Commission on Environment and Development 1987: 8), became a popular term in the 1990s because it embraced aspirations for conservation with an apparent acceptance of the importance of economic growth. Within the concept lies the important commitment to 'inter-generational equity'. Given this expansive, all-embracing definition it could not fail to win favour. Since then employers, government agencies, and pressure groups have all sprayed 'sustainable' onto policies and titles. But this often hides a different reality; as Carter cautions, 'policy continues to emerge from a sectoral administrative structure where economic growth is the priority, producer interests prevail and environmental considerations remain an afterthought' (2001: 282).

In 1992, following the Rio Summit, the UK government headed by John Major committed itself to sustainable development across all policy areas. Since then Conservative and Labour governments have published an annual statement on progress towards sustainable development (see e.g. DEFRA, 2002). The Department of the Environment, Transport and the Regions formed by the New Labour government in 1997 was designed to give environmental considerations a much greater prominence in the work of the merged department. In the event this proved to be an unworkable mega-ministry and following the 2001 general election there was a de-merger, with a separate Department of the Environment Food and Rural Affairs (DEFRA) and a Department for Transport (DfT) being created, with some significant responsibilities for urban regeneration being transferred to the Office of the Deputy Prime Minister (ODPM)

Constitutional change in the UK has meant that self-government for Scotland, Wales, and Northern Ireland has created new bodies which have endorsed sustainable development for their countries. Equally, the creation of regional assemblies has added another actor to the sustainable development debate.

In all of this work it is **ecological modernization** which is an increasingly influential theme in the politics of environmental problems and represents the stance of the Labour government. Proponents of this viewpoint believe that the environmental restructuring necessary for sustainability can occur within capitalist economies, but will require widespread industrial change. The tools of industrial management can be utilized to achieve more environmentally benign economic behaviour. These would involve recycling, much greater use of renewable energy sources, and shifts from industrial activity which has a major impact on the environment to that which has a much smaller impact, like the service sector (see Weale 1992; Jacobs 1999). Pollution abatement, renewable energy, and environmental management are all areas where new jobs can be created. Stricter environmental regulations in the UK will ensure that there is a domestic incentive for UK firms to develop the requisite technology which can then be sold abroad (Tindale 1996).

Quality of life

The Labour government has shown a willingness to bring economic, social, and environmental issues together in policy documents since it came to power in 1997. It has headlined its sustainable development strategy a plan for improving quality of life. What has been particularly welcome is the way in which it has made connections between sustainable development and poverty and social exclusion and community development. This is demonstrated in its choice of indicators against which it has asked to be measured by the public. As shown in Box 19.1 economic indicators are present along with environmental and social. But what is lacking is any consideration of the role of consumption in the discussion of quality of life.

Quality of life is a slippery concept, but is used in discussions of sustainability to refer to the environmental and social goods which lie outside market regulation (see Jackson 1995; Offer 1996; Seed and Lloyd 1997). It can embrace the proximity of public libraries as well as bus stops, or even the very existence of public libraries. 'Quality of life' is subjective: it will be interpreted differently from one individual to the next. People in Lancashire were asked to define what they meant by 'quality of life', and they responded by choosing the following: having a more local job, not having to worry about money, better relationships with friends and family, more community spirit, and better amenities, especially for children (Lancashire County Council 1997). Similarly, in Leicester 'quality of life' has been central to Agenda 21 policy (see below), being interpreted as a sense of community which 'supports individuals, supports a diverse and vibrant local economy, meets the needs of food and shelter and gives access to fulfilling work that is of benefit to the community' (Selman 1996: 106). For many people their quality of life is better measured by the number and range of consumer durables which they possess,

Box 19.1 Sustainable development: government's headline indicators

Economic
Economic output
Investment
Employment

Social
Poverty and Social Exclusion
Education
Health
Housing
Crime

Environment
Climate change
Air quality
Road traffic
River water quality
Wildlife
Land use
Waste

(DEFRA 2001: 53–6)

and this is perhaps the dominant view in our society. When questioned, however, people agree that for them public amenities such as parks, libraries, and public conveniences are also part of their quality of life. These are what economists call 'social goods', for they are enjoyed in common and have to be provided collectively, unless one is very rich indeed (Jacobs 1997). The extent to which the mass of the population can be mobilized in support of these social goods, such as when they are threatened by developers or road-builders, is unpredictable because the values of individual self-advancement and private consumption are often stronger. There is nonetheless a widespread perception that there has been an erosion of the 'quality of life' in our society despite the increases in personal consumption.

The New Economics Foundation has attempted to measure the quality of life in the UK over the last 25 years. Their **Index of Sustainable Economic Welfare** (ISEW) uses the volume of consumer expenditure as the main constituent of the Gross Domestic Product (GDP) and then makes additions and subtractions based on such factors as increased traffic congestion, resource depletion, and positive additions such as unpaid household labour. The ISEW measure, unlike GDP, also takes account of environmental factors, for example, by building in a measure for the depletion of North Sea oil and the impact of climate change. The ISEW has fallen by around 22 per cent since 1980 in the UK. The UK's per capita GDP is 2.5 times greater in real terms in 1996 than it was in 1950, an average year-on-year growth of 2 per cent. But the level of the ISEW is only up by 31 per cent on the 1950 figure (Friends of the Earth/New Economics Foundation 1997; Jackson et al. 1998). Clearly the environmental measures used by the New Economics Foundation can be contested, but their arguments also demonstrate weaknesses in conventional measures of the standard of living and social welfare.

These arguments are an example of a growing body of work which attempts to construct a 'new economics' where basic human needs are not measured only by indices of material consumption. In conventional economics, consumption has been seen as a proxy for welfare. Green economists define welfare in terms of the satisfaction of basic human needs and wants, building on the work of Maslow (1954), who argued that material needs have first to be satisfied before the human wants of love, truth, and justice can be met. The Chilean economist Max Neef has expanded on this list to include affection, understanding, participation, identity, idleness, creativity, and freedom (Max Neef 1992; Jackson 1995).

LOCAL AGENDA 21

Local Agenda 21, which emerged from the Rio Earth Summit in 1992, aims to make sustainable development a reality in localities. It is about people and their interaction with the environment, taking as its focus the work of the local authority and the range of responsibilities that it has: for example, environmental health, transport, recycling, and energy are core areas of LA 21 activity. In this way environmental issues are now being integrated with other policy areas, with a stress on how people and their actions can improve or damage the environment. In the UK local authorities have reviewed their activities in the light of the principles of sustainability; many have implemented environmental audits, while others have integrated the Local Agenda 21 process into their system of corporate management. Some councils have drawn up indicators which will measure progress towards local sustainability. These generally cover two areas: those that measure the quality of the environment and the way in which the local authority can respond to the stresses on it; and those which measure environmental efficiency in areas such as transport, industry, and energy (Selman 1996; Buckingham-Hatfield 1998). Local authorities have on the whole been sensitive to the ways in which these indicators can be constructed. There has been an awareness that it is easy to ignore the views of those who do not naturally participate in environmental policy-making, but who are concerned about the environment: that is to say, the great majority of the population! Research has revealed that most people have not even heard of the concept of sustainability (Macnaghten 1995).

The thrust of Local Agenda 21 enables issues of access and inequality to be encompassed in the drive for sustainability. Lancashire County Council has incorporated social objectives in its green audit. One of the indicators that it has used in its review of the population of Lancashire is the percentage who live more than one kilometre from five basic services: post office, primary school, food shop, GP surgery, and bus stop. In this way the concept of accessibility is operationalized.

Box 19.2 Key areas of action in the Local Agenda 21 process

Three areas for action within the local authority

Managing and improving the local authority's own environmental performance

- corporate commitment;
- staff training and awareness raising;
- environmental management systems and budgeting;
- cross-sectoral policy integration.

Integrating sustainable development aims into the local authority's policies and activities

- green housekeeping;
- land use planning, transport, housing and economic development;
- tendering and purchasing;
- tourism and visitor strategies;
- health, welfare, equal opportunities and poverty strategies;
- explicitly 'environmental' services.

Awareness-raising and education

- support for environmental education and voluntary groups;
- visits, talks, and awareness-raising events;
- publication of local information and press releases;
- initiatives to encourage behaviour change and practical action.

Three areas for action within the wider community

Consulting and involving the general public

- public consultation processes;
- forums, focus groups, and feedback mechanisms;
- 'planning for real' and parish maps.

Partnerships

- meetings, workshops, conferences, roundtables, working/advisory groups;
- Environment City model;
- partnership initiatives;
- developing-world partnerships and support.

Measuring, monitoring and reporting on progress towards sustainability

- environmental monitoring and state of environment reporting;
- sustainability indicators and targets;
- environmental impact assessment and strategic environmental assessment.

The Local Government Act 2000 gave local authorities a remit to prepare Community Strategies which would promote the economic, social and environmental well-beings of their area. It remains to be seen whether Community Strategies will give sufficient priority to sustainable development.

WORK, PAID EMPLOYMENT, AND THE GREEN POLICY AGENDA

In pursuing their arguments, Greens and the 'new economists' have also contributed to a reassessment of the value of work and production in the creation of welfare (Robertson 1989). The way in which advanced industrial countries have moved from being primarily manufacturing economies to becoming primarily service-sector economies has meant that many unskilled jobs have disappeared. In our post-industrial society employment has been transformed by the massive restructuring generated by globalization and the technological revolution of the last two decades. In the process millions of jobs have been lost in labour-intensive industries, as machines have replaced people or as jobs have moved to cheaper countries. The decline in manufacturing industry has reduced the number of jobs for unskilled, particularly male workers: the male family breadwinner has been consigned to the dustbin of history. At the same time consumerism has ensured that the attachment to paid work as a source of cash and hence identity has permeated all sections of society.

The crisis of growing unemployment goes right to the heart of the industrial system which has transformed the world in the past two centuries, revealing the attachment to wage labour which lies at the centre of the modern economic system. Job losses affect not only the person who loses his or her job: the wider community loses not only the purchasing power in that area, but often the benefits of the job that was axed. The loss of the park keeper means that there is more vandalism. The loss of the bus conductor means that some older and infirm people cannot use the bus because there is no one to assist them in the (for them) difficult task of getting on and off the vehicle.

One proposal to remedy this position is to distribute work better by limiting the hours of the full-time workers in order to create more jobs in the economy. However, as yet there has been little support for this among the workforce. The obsession with work can mean that other parts of life time spent together with families—hobbies, pastimes, physical recreation, sport—are all downgraded in the individual's priorities. The workaholic culture has reached its high point in the United States of America, where on average workers have fewer holidays and work longer hours than their European counterparts. The fixation with work is part of the consumerism that pervades American society, with people working long hours in order to get more money in order to buy consumer goods and durables (Schor 1992). In dual earner families where both parents are working full-time there is much less time for the children, with the result that caring services have to be bought by the parents in the form of nannies, au pairs, and others. In the USA the amount of time spent in parent–child interaction has decreased (Etzioni 1995). It is argued that similar trends are becoming apparent in the UK (Leach 1994). In 1997 the number of women in the UK workforce overtook the number of men for the first time. Now some contemporary feminist writers have begun to question seriously the feminist strategy of putting emphasis on waged work as a means of achieving sex equality, when it has led to a devaluing of motherhood for women and increasingly frantic lives for both sexes (Benn 1998).

The indices used to track our economy do not measure the amount of unpaid work. Therefore it is not included in the value of the Gross Domestic Product, yet calculations show that it is a considerable amount of labour. The increased role of women in formal employment has meant that their unpaid family labour is more apparent, especially in those households which pay for this work to be performed by purchasing childcare or cleaning services. The market now provides the goods and services which are needed by those with little time. For example, many working people think that cooking meals from fresh ingredients is too lengthy a process after the working day, and there has been a large increase in the amount of convenience food sold.

Given the fact that the labour market will not be able to fulfil the demand for employment either in the present or in the foreseeable future, the arguments of Greens and others for a revaluation of work are coming to be seen as more relevant. Citizen's Income is one of the most powerful of the policy proposals popularized by the Greens in the 1980s, and has now been taken up by many others, on both the Left and the Right. Citizen's Income has been around as an idea (under other names, most recently Basic Income) since the 1920s, long before the current wave of Green thinking. Briefly, it is an income which will be paid to all citizens, irrespective of their age. For children it would replace child benefit, and for older people it would replace the retirement pension. The attractions of Citizen's Income are that it will get rid of many social security benefits, and most particularly means-tested benefits. The income would be paid to all, irrespective of whether they were in work or not. Their savings, other income, or marital status would not affect the payment (Fitzpatrick 1999).

Citizen's Income is intended to give everyone the opportunity to work in the economy in the way in which they want. It recognizes the value of unpaid work—domestic labour and caring work—by giving those who perform this work a wage. It acknowledges the value of low-paid work, often carried out for community purposes, by providing a supplement that will enable people to be able to afford to do it. Additionally, Citizen's Income is an increasingly useful tool in the employment market of the late twentieth century, where part-time work has multiplied at the expense of full-time jobs. The problems regarding its implementation lie in the area of cost, how it will be possible to afford the income, and the level at which the income should be set. Clearly it is an extremely contentious proposal, for it goes against the grain of the emerging bipartisan consensus on social security and employment summarized in the phrase 'welfare to work'. Yet the government has introduced a working families tax credit scheme for those with children on low incomes, ensuring that they receive a 'minimum income' by paying benefit to them for the amount by which their income falls below a threshold. It has been suggested that this scheme could be extended in the direction of a minimum income by redesigning it as an active citizen's credit which would be paid to all those who were working in paid or unpaid work, with children or without children (Williams and

Windebank 2001: 168–79). Among the main objections to a universal Citizen's Income without qualification is that it would offend notions of fairness, the very same principle which makes some kinds of social security fraud so unpopular. The Commission on Social Justice called for a 'Participation Income', a variation on Citizen's Income which tackles the problem of 'getting something for nothing' by requiring some evidence of participation, either by having caring responsibilities or being 'available for work' (Commission on Social Justice 1994). Another fundamental objection is that the Citizen's Income is predicated upon a redistribution of resources from one citizen to another which will require a state with tax-raising and tax-spending powers, something that the anarchist wing of the Greens want to rule out.

Other proposals espoused by Greens are of much more recent provenance. Local Exchange Trading Schemes (LETS) have proliferated, particularly in the USA, Canada, and the UK. These are token economies which enable services and work to be performed for tokens or credits which can then be used to obtain other services. Members of the schemes themselves decide who they are going to exchange their tokens with and for which services. The coverage of these schemes is haphazard in the UK and they have not made major inroads into local economies. One study of five LETS in the UK found that about 40 per cent of the activities were domestic work and all could have been paid for in cash (Seyfang, cited in O'Riordan 1997: 18).

The problem of such schemes is that they have not managed to escape their 'green' alternative image, so that in areas where they would be of most help enabling people to get jobs done which they cannot afford to pay for in the formal economy, they are not around. In part this is because of the lack of time available to people at certain stages of their life—for example, single mothers—and in part it is because of the restrictive social security laws which are designed to combat fraud and which mean that any money earned over the income disregard will be deducted from one's benefit. Hudson has highlighted the barriers to LETS being successful in low-income areas: too few community activists who could champion the scheme, insufficient attention to marketing the scheme in clear language, a lack of confidence among local people as to their skills and abilities, a limited supply of services on offer in the scheme, and the fear that local people might go into debt, i.e. using up all their tokens and not earning any by providing services (Hudson et al. 1999: 3) (see Box 19.3). LETS schemes do, however, constitute an acknowledgement of the amount of work which goes on outside the formal economy. The government tends to view the schemes as a springboard to employment in the formal economy, but there would appear to be little evidence that is occurring (Williams and Windebank 2001: 162).

Time banks are another way in which people can volunteer to give up some of their time to help others. Members 'deposit' their time in a bank and then can claim it back when they need something done themselves. The idea originated in the USA, where there are now over 250 time banks, but it is still in its infancy in the UK (Boyle 1999).

Community enterprise schemes aim to provide work in areas which are run down and have suffered greatly from the restructuring of the British economy over the past two decades. These areas are characterized by high unemployment, poor housing, underperforming schools, and poor public transport. They are often in inner-city areas or

Box 19.3 Potential of LETS to re-engage individuals in the local economy

Social exclusion can mean	*LETS offers*
Lack of money/income to buy materials needed to exchange in formal of informal production	Reduced need for money for buying goods or services which individuals may otherwise not be able to afford
Social isolation resulting in fewer chances to hear of work or other opportunities	A social network within which exchanges can take place
Lack of requisite skills or reduced chance to use existing or develop new skills	Skills development through exchange
Low self-esteem and self-confidence	Improved confidence for those not in paid work and greater sense of self-worth
High cost or difficulty accessing credit	Zero-interest credit
Low money circulation	High local currency circulation and trading

(Hudson et al. 1999: 9)

outer 'sink' estates. Credit unions are a key form of community enterprise. Financial exclusion is linked to social exclusion: it is estimated that 26 per cent of people have no current account with a bank or a building society. 'The groups without bank accounts tend to be women, the young, the old, the unemployed, those both in low-paid jobs and more likely to live in rented accommodation' (Conaty and Mayo 1997). Credit unions offer saving facilities for those who are outside the traditional banking system, providing loans at low interest to their members. The rules of credit unions generally require members to live and work locally (Pearce 1993).

ECOLOGICAL TAX REFORM

Taxation is at the heart of social policy. It allows the state resources to redistribute between citizens if it so chooses and permits it sufficient income to provide services for those citizens. Taxes are raised in a variety of ways: on incomes, in the form of social insurance contributions, on sales of goods in shops, and on imports of goods into the country. Fifty per cent of taxes in the European Union are taxes on employment (Tindale 1997). Greens argue that if governments want to move towards more sustainable policies then they have to consider changing the nature of taxation (Robertson 2002). Given the fact that all governments wish to encourage the level of employment, taxes on a 'good' such as a job should be reduced, while taxes on 'bads' such as pollution should be increased. There is an additional benefit claimed for pollution and environmental taxes, namely that they could enable the reduction of taxes on employment, such as National Insurance in the UK. Thus there would be a 'double dividend' of more employment, and the cost to employers of an extra worker would fall.

Clearly, poor people might need protection from such changes. Pollution taxes can be socially regressive—that is to say, they may fall most heavily on those who are least able to bear the cost. This can be illustrated by one of the most debated examples of an ecological tax proposal: a continuing and substantial increase in the tax on petrol. Such a tax would penalize those who live in rural and semi-rural areas where there is no alternative for many people to using the car if they wish to reach their work and other amenities. Proponents of ecological taxation admit the force of this argument, and propose that payments should be made to such motorists to compensate them for the extra costs which they would have to bear. However, this is not the only tax that could be levied in support of an environmentally friendly transport policy. It is widely acknowledged that the existence of free parking at work has been one of the major reasons why the use of the car has greatly increased for commuter journeys over the last twenty years. Taxing employers for this parking space would, if it was passed onto the employee, discourage the use of the car for these journeys. Those on low incomes are clearly hit the hardest when domestic fuel taxation is increased, and the state would need to protect them with rebates and by subsidizing better standards of insulation in the home.

The Green perspective on health policy is a preventive one, with an emphasis on clean environments, alternative medicine, and reducing pollution levels (Draper 1991). The new emphasis on public health by the Labour government reinforces the links between health and other policy areas, particularly housing. Housing represents a major area where the impact of environmental 'goods' and 'bads' can be seen. Houses and the households that live in them use a great deal of energy and generate considerable waste: energy and materials are used to construct the houses in the first place; they use a range of fuels for lighting, heating, cooking, and the running of the household appliances; and the occupants produce waste that has to be disposed of. These are all areas where environmental gains and losses are considerable, and where social policies can seek a better balance (Bhatti et al. 1994). The growth in household formation has highlighted the conflict between protection of the Green Belt and the desire of many house buyers to live in country locations. The Department of the Environment has estimated that housing for another 4.4 million extra households will be required by 2016 but, as McLaren et al. (1998: 129) note, 'While car travel is cheap, demand for detached and semi-detached country homes remains high.'

A major area for environmental taxation is water consumption. Water is a precious asset, vital for human beings and all life forms on the planet, yet in the Western industrialized countries it is used profligately. There are now well-worked-out policies to cut back on water use: a combination of water metering and different tariffs for different household sizes. Here again, low-income consumers need protection. Water tariffs need to be designed so that where there is extra demand in a household, it can be compensated for; for example, those receiving child benefit could claim an additional allowance (Herrington in O'Riordan 1997).

CONCLUSION: HOW NEW IS GREEN SOCIAL POLICY?

Green perspectives are usually concerned with welfare in the widest sense: green writing has been hostile to the notion of the welfare state, drawing on a tradition of anarchism with its critiques of large-scale, bureaucratic state structures. From this perspective the idea of the welfare state is a contradiction in terms. Welfare and community care should come from the activities of families, friends, and the local community. Professionals can all too easily become disempowering, removing the capacity of men and women to help themselves. Greens believe that individuals and communities need to define their needs for themselves. Much of this thinking is not new or different from mainstream social policy ideas on community development, although some versions of community enterprise are 'greener' than others. Recently it has been suggested that Paul Hirst's vision of an 'associative democracy', where self-governing community organizations become the primary forms for political life and public services and the state becomes secondary, are a possible 'greenprint' for community development (Achterburg 1996; Hirst 1994).

In most areas of social policy the green perspective offers nothing new in the sense of policy ideas. Any novelty comes from the priority which it accords an environmental perspective. To some extent this is because the practice of those who work in and those who direct the welfare state is still conducted within a framework of everyday institutions—hospitals, social services departments, and social security offices—which are predicated upon profligate use of energy. This is especially the case with the car, a technology which has transformed the practice of welfare state professionals but on the other hand made some vital facilities expensive and time-consuming to visit for the carless. Among these we can number not only the poorest and many disabled people but also all children and many adults. Hillman et al. (1990) have shown how the right of children to walk the streets safely to school has been largely removed in this country, but the rights and welfare of the carless in general have been severely curtailed by the hegemony of the motor vehicle, thus contributing to a decline in their welfare.

The green perspective will not change whole areas of policy. However, the commitment to sustainable development at both local and central government level means that the debate is now beginning to concern itself with the 'how' rather than the 'why' of sustainability. The discourse around 'quality of life' does have the potential to link environmental issues and social policy. For example, community care services are going to be needed in a society informed by environmental considerations just as much as the present capitalist society, though their nature and form will change. Sustainability implies a commitment to local services on grounds of energy-saving and access. As we have seen in the example quoted earlier of Lancashire County Council, how far people have to travel to services—the mobility cost of access—is important. For social service departments to take this seriously would mean returning to the ideas of local patch organization recommended by Roger Hadley twenty years ago (Brown et al. 1982). The importance of the locality is revealed as shop closures, small business failures, and the decline of public transport and public spaces exacerbate its decline. This bears most heavily upon the poor—those without the resources to enjoy private transport—who are far less able to escape a poor environment.

Case Study 19.1 9 Lives

How do you make sustainable development meaningful to people?
Brighton and Hove City Council, like numerous other local authorities, had engaged in various Local Agenda 21 activities throughout the 1990s. But they knew that sustainable development still remained a piece of jargon to most of the people of the city. In order to get the message across to the wider public they came up with a project in 2001 which would have wider appeal. Taking their cue from reality television and makeover shows they advertised for nine people who would be willing to spend nine weeks changing their lives in a more sustainable direction.

The nine people chosen were helped in their quest for a more sustainable lifestyle by a team of experts assembled and paid for by the Council, including an energy consultant, a transport consultant, a personal fitness trainer, and environmental consultants. The nine agreed to video their experiences and extracts were shown on the project web site: www.ninelives.tv which attracted 80,000 hits during the nine weeks. Coverage was given in the Council's own newspaper and in the Brighton *Evening Argus* together with local television and radio. Out of the 100 or so people who applied, the nine selected were:

Name	*Occupation*	*Aim*
Nicole	Personal assistant	To stop thinking about work so much
		To save £20 a week on shopping bills
		To recycle waste at work and at home
Thamsanga	Student psychiatric nurse	To save £30 a week towards reducing my overdraft, partly by cutting my mobile phone bill costs
		To cook an Indian meal for four using an organic vegetable box and a budget of £12
Vicky	Young mother	To make my garden more child and wildlife friendly
		To stop smoking and stay calm
		To complete an IT course
Dawn	Registered blind	To learn new artistic skills and create a piece of tactile art
		To cook and serve a meal at a vegetarian restaurant
Eric	Writer and comedian	To find ways of becoming greener
		To make some money out of organizing an event
		To find time out every week and to do something for myself that has a positive effect on the environment

Name	*Occupation*	*Aim*
Chris	Healthy Schools Coordinator	To get a better work–life balance and form a band to sing with To avoid becoming a two-car household To create a new outfit from recycled clothing to wear while performing in my band
Ruth	Writer on mind, body, and spirit issues	To work out a household budget and save £10 a week To plan a weekly food shop and eat healthily without meat for nine weeks To clear the clutter from my house and recycle it
Jan	Writer	To spend a week in a freelance TV company and get feedback on my screen play To exercise three times a week including a bike ride To use my car only for essential trips and heat my flat with minimal impact on the environment
Dudley	Retired	To join a twice-weekly yoga class and stick at for nine weeks To cook a healthy meal for friends using ingredients with minimum packaging To reduce the contents of my dustbin by half

Clearly this attempt to make sustainable lives more popular and high-profile owed some of its appeal to the holistic nature of the project, and it is noticeable how much emphasis the participants placed on changing the routine activities of their lives—travelling, cooking, working—which do nonetheless contribute to unsustainable practices. The 9 Lives project would appear to indicate that many people are interested in moving towards more sustainable lifestyles but need advice, assistance, and encouragement.

Ecological citizenship is promoted by some Greens as a way for populations in the advanced industrial societies to remember their obligations to the poor world and hence to restrain their consumption: 'to live more simply so that others may simply live.' The twenty-first century could mean that 'First world communities . . . will need to accept declining material living standards, the elimination of employment in certain industry sectors and geographic regions . . . and significant transfers of resources back to the Third World' (Christoff, in Doherty and de Geus 1996). In any version of sustainable development, even in its weakest interpretation, behavioural change is required. But this is politically unpopular, and governments in Western democracies are dependent upon responding to the mood of electorates. These are not necessarily selfish in their attitudes—the public opinion polls show that there is a widespread support for environmental and green views—but change can be much harder to achieve. A good test of this will come in the next few years as the Labour government grapples with weaning the British public away from its over-reliance on the car. Car dependency is now firmly entrenched in the UK and other advanced industrial societies, yet the use of the car has to be cut back drastically if the carbon emissions which lead to global warming are to be reduced. The 9 Lives project in Brighton was an imaginative attempt to work out the implications of sustainability in everyday life (see Case Study 19.1).

The social policies discussed will improve the 'quality of life' for some people. But far too many people, it must be said, are also registering their dissatisfaction with the way that some other people behave which affects their local environment: allowing their dogs to foul the pavement, vomiting in a doorway after a heavy session at the pub, thieving from cars, playing loud music at all hours of the day and night, and drug dealers plying their trade on the street. This behaviour degrades not only the local environment but also the 'quality of life' for their neighbours. Some of the worst of this behaviour is to be found in the poorest areas of our cities and on 'sink' estates—the unacceptable face of a society which is committed to freedom, choice, and privatized lifestyles. Communitarianism offers one response which stresses that communities need to be supported in enforcing their collective majority view about what passes for acceptable behaviour (Etzioni 1995; 1997; Tam 1998). Green citizenship is related to this in the sense that, like communitarians, its exponents believe that individuals gain much of their identity from the local community and presumably communitarians would not want to damage the local environment as well. Indeed, they are active in fostering a social ecology of sound local relationships. The costs of environmental pollution are most often experienced by those on the lowest incomes whilst they suffer from poor public transport and low-quality environment.

A sustainable social policy will have to be one which protects the poorest and vulnerable while at the same time delivering environmental benefits. The environmental agenda of the twenty-first century will need to address the traditional concerns of social policy—need, welfare, social justice equity—but in the context of sustainable development.

REFERENCES

Achterburg, W., 'Sustainability, community and democracy'. In Doherty and de Geuss (1996).

Bahro, R. (1982), *Socialism and Survival*. London: Heretic Books.

—— (1986), *Building the Green Movement*. London: GMP.

Barclay, P. (ed.) (1982), *Social Workers: Their Roles and Tasks*. London: National Institute for Social Work Bedford Square Press.

Beck, U. (1992), *Risk Society: Towards a New Modernity*. London: Sage.

Benn, M. (1998), *Madonna and Child: The Politics of Modern Motherhood*. London: Cape.

Bhatti, M., Brooke, J., and Gibson, M. (eds.) (1994), *Housing and the Environment: A New Agenda*. London: Chartered Institute of Housing.

Boyle, D. (1999), *Funny Money: In Search of Alternative Cash* London: HarperCollins.

Brown, P., Hadley, R., and White, K. J. (1982), 'A case for neighbourhood-based social work and social services'. In Barclay (1992).

Buckingham-Hatfield, S. P. (1998), *Constructing Local Environmental Agendas*. London: Routledge.

Cahill, M. (2002), *The Environment and Social Policy*. London: Routledge.

—— and Fitzpatrick, T (eds.) (2002), *Environmental Issues and Social Welfare*. Oxford: Blackwell.

Carter, N. (2001), *The Politics of the Environment*. Cambridge: Cambridge University Press.

Commission on Social Justice (1994), *Social Justice: Strategies for National Renewal*. London: Vintage.

Conaty, P., and Mayo, E. (1997), *A Commitment to People and Place: The Case for Community Development Credit Unions*. York: Joseph Rowntree Foundation.

Daly, H. E., and Cobb, J. B. (1990), *For the Common Good: Redirecting the Economy towards Community, the Environment and a Sustainable Future*. London: Green Print.

DEFRA (Department for Environment, Food and Rural Affairs) (2002), *Achieving a Better Quality of Life: Review of Progress towards Sustainable Development*. London: DEFRA.

Dobson, A. (ed) (2000), *Fairness and Futurity*. Oxford: Oxford University Press.

—— (2000), *Green Political Thought*, 3rd edn. London: Unwin Hyman.

Doherty, B., and de Geus, M. (eds.) (1996), *Democracy and Green Political Thought: Sustainability, Rights and Citizenship*. London: Routledge.

Draper, P. (1991), *Health through Public Policy: The Greening of Public Health*. London: Green Print.

Ehrlich, P. (1968), *The Population Bomb*. New York: Ballantine.

Etzioni, A. (1995), *The Spirit of Community: Rights, Responsibilities and the Communitarian Agenda*. London: Fontana.

—— (1997), *The New Golden Rule: Community and Morality in a Democratic Society*. London: Profile.

Fitzpatrick, T. (1999), *Freedom and Security: An Introduction to the Citizen's Income Debate*. London: Routledge

—— and Cahill, M. (eds.) (2002), *Environment and Welfare: Towards a Green Social Policy*. Basingstoke: Palgrave Macmillan.

Friends of the Earth/New Economics Foundation (1997), *Quality of Life Briefing Paper No. 3*. London: New Economics Foundation.

Garner, R. (2000), *Environmental Politics*, 2nd edn. Basingstoke: Macmillan.

Giddens, A. (1991), *Modernity and Self Identity: Self and Society in the Late Modern Age*. Cambridge: Polity, press.

Gray, J. (1993), *Beyond the New Right: Markets, Governments and the Natural Environment*. London: Routledge.

Hardin, G. (1968), 'The tragedy of the commons', *Science* 162: 1243–8.

Hillman, M., Adams, J., and Whitelegg, J. (1990), *One False Move . . . A Study of Children's Independent Mobility*. London: Policy Studies Institute.

Hirst, P. (1994), *Associative Democracy: New Forms of Economic and Social Governance*. Cambridge: Polity Press.

Hudson, H., Newby, L., Hutchinson, N., with Harding, L. (1999), *Making 'LETS' Work in Low Income Areas*. London: Forum for the Future.

Hulsberg, W. (1987), *The West German Greens: A Social and Political Profile*. London: Verso.

Humphrey, M. (ed.) (2001), *Political Theory and the Environment*. London: Cass.

Jackson, T. (1995), *Material Concerns: Pollution, Profit and Quality of Life*. London: Routledge.

—— Marks, N., Ralls, J., and Stymme, S. (1998), *Sustainable Economic Welfare in the UK 1950–1996*. London: New Economics Foundation.

Jacobs, M. (ed.) (1997), *Greening the Millennium: The New Politics of the Environment*. Oxford: Blackwell.

—— (1999), *Environmental Modernisation*. London: Fabian Society.

Lamb, R. (1996), *Promising the Earth*. London: Routledge.

Lancashire County Council (1997), *Lancashire's Green Audit 2: A Sustainability Report*. Preston: Lancashire County Council.

Leach, P. (1994), *Children First: What Our Society Must Do and Is Not Doing for Children Today*. London: Penguin.

McLaren, D., Bullock, S., and Yousuf, N. (1998), *Tomorrow's World: Britain's Share in a Sustainable Future*. London: Earthscan.

Macnaghten, P. (1995), *Public Perceptions and Sustainability in Lancashire*. Preston: Lancashire County Planning Department.

Maslow, A. H. (1954), *Motivation and Personality*. New York: Harper.

Max-Neef, M. (1992), 'Development and human needs'. In P. Ekins and M. Max-Neef (eds.), *Real-Life Economics: Understanding Wealth Creation*. London: Routledge.

Mellor, M. (1997), *Feminism and Ecology*. Cambridge: Polity.

Naess, A. (1988), 'The basics of deep ecology', *Resurgence* 126: 4–7.

Offer, A. (ed.) (1996), *In Pursuit of the Quality of Life*. Oxford: Oxford University Press.

O'Riordan, T. (ed.) (1997), *Ecotaxation*. London: Earthscan.

Pearce, J. (1993), *At the Heart of the Community Economy: Community Enterprise in a Changing World*. London: Calouste Gulbenkian Foundation.

Pepper, D. (1993), *Eco-Socialism: From Deep Ecology to Social Justice*. London: Routledge.

—— (1996), *Modern Environmentalism: An Introduction*. London: Routledge.

Porritt, J. (1984), *Seeing Green: The Politics of Ecology Explained*. Oxford: Blackwell.

Robertson, J. (1989), *Future Wealth: A New Economics for the 21st Century*. London: Cassell.

—— (2002), 'Eco-taxation in a green society'. In Fitzpatrick and Cahill (2002).'

Ryle, M. (1988), *Ecology and Socialism*. London: Radius.

Sargisson, L. (2001), 'What's wrong with ecofeminism?' In Humphrey (2001).

Saunders, P. (1995), *Capitalism: A Social Audit*. Buckingham: Open University Press.

Schor, J. (1992), *The Overworked American: The Unexpected Decline of Leisure*. New York: Basic Books.

Seed, P., and Lloyd, G. (1997), *Quality of Life*. London: Jessica Kingsley.

Selman, P. (1996), *Local Sustainability: Managing and Planning Ecologically Sound Places*. London: Paul Chapman.

Tam, H. (1998). *Communitarianism: A New Agenda for Politics and Citizenship*. London: Macmillan.

Tindale, S. (1996), *Jobs and the Environment*. London: Institute for Public Policy Research.

—— (1997), 'The political economy of environmental tax reform'. In Jacobs (1997).

Weale, A. (1992), *The New Politics of Pollution*. Manchester: Manchester University Press.

Whitelegg, J. (1997), *Critical Mass: Transport, Environment and Society in the Twenty-First Century*. London: Pluto Press.

Williams, C., and Windebank, J. (2001), *Revitalising Urban Neighbourhoods: An Assisted Self Help Approach*. Aldershot: Ashgate.

World Commission on Environment and Development (Chairman Gro Brundtland) (1987), *Our Common Future*. Oxford: Oxford University Press.

FURTHER READING

M. Cahill, *The Environment and Social Policy* (London: Routledge, 2002). Explores the themes in this chapter.

M. Cahill and T. Fitzpatrick (eds.), *Environmental Issues and Social Welfare* (Oxford: Blackwell, 2002) A series of chapters which cover both the political philosophy and the policy implications of green thought for social policy.

N. Carter, *The Politics of the Environment* (Cambridge: Cambridge University Press, 2001). Green political thought, parties and movements and environmental policy making are all covered.

A. Dobson, *Green Political Thought*, 3rd edn. (London: Routledge, 2000). A lucid guide to green thought, with an emphasis on the challenges for contemporary society from dark greens.

T. Fitzpatrick and M. Cahill (eds.) *Environment and Welfare* (Basingstoke: Palgrave Macmillan, 2002). A review of the implications for social policy of the environmental crisis.

M. Huby, *Social Policy and the Environment* (Buckingham: Open University Press, 1998). Demonstrates the interrelationship of environmental and social issues through a discussion of key policy areas.

L. Martell *Ecology and Society* (Cambridge: Polity Press, 1994). A clear and readable sociological account.

D. McLaren, S. Bullock, and N. Yousuf, *Tomorrow's World: Britain's Share in a Sustainable Future* (London: Earthscan, 1998). Makes the case for reducing consumption and improving our quality of life using the concept of 'environmental space'.

D. Pepper, *Modern Environmentalism: An Introduction* (London: Routledge, 1996). An extremely thorough and authoritative guide to the varieties of green thought and environmental movements, situating them in the context of the history of ideas.

J. Whitelegg, *Critical Mass: Transport, Environment and Society in the Twenty-First Century* (London: Pluto Press, 1997). Demonstrates how our car dependency has produced enormous problems of congestion, ill health, and inequality.

USEFUL WEBSITES

Agenda 21 United Nations 1992: www.un.org/esa/sustdev/agenda21text.htm

Sustainable Development Commission: www.sdcommission.gov.uk/index.htm

Department for Environment, Food and Rural Affairs (DEFRA): www.defra.gov.uk/

Department for Transport (DfT): www.dtlr.gov.uk/about/dtlr/02.htm

House of Commons Environmental Audit Committee: www.parliament.uk/commons/selcom/eahome.htm

Sustainable Scotland: www.scotland.gov.uk/

Sustainable Wales: www.wales.gov.uk/themesustainabledev/index.htm

Sustainable Development in Northern Ireland: www.nics.gov.uk/env.htm

Friends of the Earth: www.foe.org/

Green Peace: greenpeace.org.uk

GLOSSARY

dark green Broad term describing the ideology of those who take a tough view of the changes needed to preserve the natural environment and to return it to ecological balance. Generally dark greens believe that very substantial, possibly revolutionary, changes to the economy and other social institutions are necessary. Contrasted with **light green**.

deep ecology The welfare of human and non-human forms of life on the planet have value in themselves. Change will come about for humans at the individual level, and there is value in all viewpoints, so that change has to come through non-violent persuasion.

ecocentric view Sees humans as one part of the natural ecosystem and argues for a sense of respect for nature. Usually allied to a deep suspicion of bureaucracy and technology.

ecological modernization The belief that economic growth need not lead to greater environmental damage. Its proponents argue for environmental policy controls because they believe that these will lead the economy towards innovation, which will not only reduce the environmental impact but promote resource-intensive industries.

environmental justice The recognition that environmental hazards are closely linked to race and poverty, and that poor people live in the most environmentally hazardous environments.

Index of Sustainable Economic Welfare Conventional economic indicators such as GDP (Gross Domestic Product) do not necessarily measure welfare. The Index of Sustainable Economic Welfare takes into account personal consumer expenditure, but then adjusts this to take account of such factors as income inequality, unpaid domestic labour, environmental degradation, depletion of natural resources, and long-term environmental damage. It was pioneered by Daly and Cobb (1990) in the USA, and has been adapted for the UK (Jackson et al. 1998).

light green Broad term describing the ideology of those who believe in the possibility of policies that will sustain and improve the quality of the natural environment and which are at the same time largely compatible with existing economic and social arrangements. Contrasted with **dark green**.

Malthusian Pertaining to the views of Thomas Malthus (1766–1834), who in his book *Essay on the Principle of Population* argued that there were natural limits to growth in human population and to the capacity of the economy to provide for that population.

quality of life Used in green debates to refer to a view that individual and collective welfare is not solely provided by consumption but must also include such environmental 'goods' as clean air, clean water, and lack of noise pollution, as well as social goods such as low crime rates, public parks, and health and social services.

risk society A society with uncertainties and hazards created by the limited ability of humankind to dominate nature and the environment. Also used to describe the uncertainties faced by individuals in their personal lives as the result of the demise of tradition.

sustainability/sustainable development Classically defined by the Brundtland Commission (World Commission on Environment and Development 1987) as 'development that meets the needs of the present without compromising the ability of future generations to meet their own needs'. Embodies the notion of inter-generational equity, meaning that the stock of resources bequeathed to our children, both natural and manmade, should be the same as that inherited by us. Similarly includes the concept of intra-generational equity or social justice between the rich and poor worlds. Equally, there is a commitment to participation for all people who will be affected by decisions which will impinge upon their quality of lives.

technocentric The belief that the application of science and technology can deal with environmental problems without any fundamental alteration to the economic system.

20

Comparative Social Policy and the European Union

Jochen Clasen

CONTENTS

INTRODUCTION

It is often said that social policy can no longer be studied without a comparative perspective. Mature welfare states are undergoing similar socioeconomic trends, facing common challenges, and tend to respond to social problems such as unemployment or poverty in fairly similar ways. Demographic ageing and low birth rates, for example, are problems which cause financial problems for sustaining national pension systems in most Western countries, albeit to differing extents (Castles 2002). Smaller households and less extensive family networks put pressure on policy-makers to provide more public social care services for older citizens—yet low growth rates and increasing economic internationalization put limits on the financial scope for expansion. In short, studying national social policy in isolation seems increasingly questionable due to the growing impact of external influences on national social policy formation and the increasing interdependence between countries.

Yet what do we gain from investigating social policy across countries, and what kinds of comparison can be made? This question is addressed in the first section of the chapter. The subsequent sections revolve around three further questions. Which patterns of social policy differences and similarities can be identified across modern European welfare states and, apart from describing the latter, what does 'comparative' in studying and researching social policy across countries mean? Finally, confining the perspective to member states of the European Union, are countries still the appropriate unit for comparative study of social policy? In other words, to which extent has the growing influence of the EU rendered comparisons of national social policy systems meaningless?

COMPARATIVE PERSPECTIVES AND THEIR RELEVANCE FOR THE STUDY OF SOCIAL POLICY

Social policy might broadly be understood as encompassing programmes which are aimed at securing or enhancing the wellbeing and the life chances of individuals. Conventionally, the study of these policies tended to be confined to Western countries and the ways in which they publicly provide, or regulate, core programmes such as cash benefits, housing, health, and social services. Yet beyond these generally accepted central areas of social welfare, there is a range of other policies which might legitimately be included. Tax allowances, tax credits or exemptions, for example, are in many ways simply alternatives to providing social security (cash) transfers in the sense that they raise the income of certain individuals or households. Education, active labour market policies, occupational health and health and safety issues impinge on an individual's state of welfare by providing opportunities for, or by directly improving the level of, social and material protection. Non-public forms of welfare production on the part of voluntary organizations, families, or individuals are also important sources for the wellbeing of large parts of the population. Shifting the focus to more than one country is a powerful reminder of the relevance of such a wider perspective applied to the study of social policy. In comparative social policy it is an inherent perspective.

One term, several meanings

Most types of social policy analysis could be regarded as comparative in the sense that observed phenomena or types of social problem (such as poverty, homelessness, or unemployment) are compared against a certain point of reference. Often the latter might merely be implicitly assumed rather than openly stated. However, some sort of benchmark is required for assessing, interpreting, or evaluating differences and similarities. Does this mean that there is nothing distinctive about comparative social policy as opposed to other forms of research designs? This question has been extensively deliberated in texts on methods of comparative social research generally (Kohn 1989; Øyen 1990; Ragin 1987; 1991; Hantrais and Mangen 1996) as well as comparative social policy in particular (Clasen 1999; Kennett 2003). Without rehearsing the arguments here, what seems commonly accepted is the fact that a cross-national perspective adds to methodological problems such as generating comparable data, identifying appropriate concepts which can be applied across countries, and achieving a sufficient sensitivity towards the different historical and cultural contexts in which national social policies are embedded.

Treating comparative as synonymous with cross-national is a common shorthand understanding in most contemporary writing on social policy. However, 'nation' is sometimes not the appropriate terminology to be applied in spatial comparisons. Countries belonging to the same nation might be compared, as was the case for studies of divergent forms of social policy delivery in East and West Germany before unification. Nations rather than countries would be the chosen units of comparisons for studying policy differences across Scotland, England, and Wales. Rather than cross-national, the term cross-cultural, or cross-societal, might be preferred for studies with a specific focus or research interest, such as norms and values in respect of redistribution or solidarity, even where the boundaries of different countries are the same as cultures or societies.

A second objection to treating 'comparative' as synonymous with 'cross-national' rests on the fact that the nation (or country) might not be the most useful unit of comparison. The prevalence of a social problem in particular localities within countries (such as forms of social exclusion) might make cross-regional comparisons the more appropriate strategy, covering one or more areas from several countries or within the same country. In other words, countries as units for comparisons might be too large—or too small. In the first case, given its cultural diversity, a study of patterns of informal support systems aimed at covering an entire country such as India would generate a wealth of material for intra-country comparisons. In the latter case, a comparison of social policy norms embedded within religious belief systems, for example, might draw on countries for illustrative purposes, but would go beyond nation-states as units of comparison.

In short, depending on the particular aim of a comparative study, sub-national entities (local authorities, regions, federal states) or supra-national organizations (such as the EU) might be the more appropriate unit of analysis. Indeed, much research which has been labelled cross-national or cross-country is in fact a comparison of particular (and not necessarily representative) regions or towns within different countries. There are often good methodological reasons for such a strategy (e.g. Bradshaw et al. 1993a), which should be made explicit.

Finally, comparisons might be inter-temporal rather than (or as well as) cross-national in character. Comparing policy processes during '**critical junctures**' in the historical development of particular programmes within a single country (e.g. periods when major legislative changes were made) might be an appropriate research strategy for improving our understanding of the forces which have shaped modern forms of social policy.

Box 20.1 Historical and cross-national comparison on nationalized health care

Nearly all western European governments have considered proposals for introducing national health care systems at one time or another. In a historical and comparative investigation, Ellen Immergut (1992b) asked why some governments (e.g. Sweden) succeeded while others (e.g. France or Switzerland) failed. She examined these three countries in detail and rejected potential explanatory factors such as different ideologies within national medical associations (all initially objecting to the nationalization of health care) or their respective organizational strength. Neither did other factors, such as political demands for national health care from unions and leftist political parties in particular, and differences in the relative strength of the latter, explain differences in political outcomes. Instead, Immergut emphasizes political institutions and the ways in which they 'establish the rules of the game' and strongly influence how 'policy conflicts will be played out' (p. 63). In a careful historical analysis of major decision-making processes during the postwar decades she analysed the impact which different political arenas (executive, legislative, or electoral) exerted on national policy-making. It was not the power or influence of particular actors per se that was important, she argued, but how the latter were influenced by arenas which provide different 'veto points': constitutional rules in France, the possibilities of popular referenda in Switzerland, and the strong position of the political executive vis-à-vis the parliament in Sweden. These veto points heavily impinge on political outcomes, in this case facilitating or hindering the establishment of national healthcare systems.

Combining comparisons over a long time span with those across countries has proved to be a very effective strategy. Ellen Immergut (1992a) applied such an approach to a seminal study in which she illustrates that differences in formal political institutions (such as electoral, legislative, and executive systems) explain much cross-national variation in contemporary health care provision (see Box 20.1).

What is gained from studying social policy across countries?

Potentially there are a number of academic as well as non-academic benefits arising from studying social policy within a comparative perspective (for convenience, from now on understood as synonymous with cross-national). To begin with the latter, investigating welfare programmes in other countries in order to learn lessons has a long tradition. For example, in 1908 Lloyd George famously visited Germany and studied its pension system (Ritter 1986). More recently, the international cross-fertilization of ideas in the process of reforming welfare systems seems to have spread. The influence of US American thinking on British reforms in the area of social security is a good case in point (Deacon 2002).

To some extent the growing interest in comparative social policy can be regarded as a response to political events and processes, as well as to common economic challenges and social processes. The collapse of the **command economies** in central and eastern European countries after 1989 set in motion a search for social policy models which would accompany the transition towards market economies. The influence of external agencies in this process, such as the **World Bank** or the **IMF**, has been considerable, as social policy analysts have shown (Deacon 1997). Within the EU, the European Commission has gained in influence not only in economic but also in social policy formation, pushing reforms which would allow a stronger level policy coordination across member states (see below). This has spurned comparative social policy research across member states as well as between the so-called **European social model** and patterns of welfare provision in the USA and Japan, for example.

But there are also good academic reasons why a comparative perspective is becoming an increasingly attractive strategy—even to social policy students who are primarily interested in domestic welfare programmes. At one level, and provided methodological problems of comparisons can be overcome, a comparison of domestic policies with similar arrangements elsewhere can be used as a form of evaluation or test. One way of assessing the effectiveness or efficiency of a particular labour market scheme—a health-screening programme or model of home help services, for example—would be to compare it with analogous policies in one or several other countries. The answer to the question 'what works where and why?' is important for both social policy analysts and, potentially at least, policy-makers, since learning from other countries might be a step towards improving domestic policy.

On a more abstract level, some central inquiries in social policy have always been formulated within cross-national frameworks. For example, the question why Western countries have developed into welfare states during the twentieth century (measured by, for example, the increase in the rate of **GDP** spent on social expenditure or the introduction and spread of social rights) has been a major topic of academic debate for many decades (see Pierson 1998 for an excellent overview). Of course, in principle such an investigation can be restricted to the emergence and evolution of social policy within a single country. The impact of the influence of enlightened thinkers and their ideas, the role of increased economic prosperity, growing public demands for welfare, government ideologies, the power of organized labour, and other factors could all be carefully studied in a historically sensitive project on domestic policy trajectory. However, it would seem rather limiting if developments in other countries with similar trends in social policy were to be ignored. Widening the research by including more countries enlarges the empirical basis for testing hypotheses, and thus renders potential findings much more robust. In other words, a cross-national rather than single-country research design might be the more theoretically promising strategy.

There is another basic but major justification for looking across borders, associated with what C.W. Mills (1976) called '**the sociological imagination**'. While Mills more directly referred to the ability of the possessor of this imagination to grasp history and biography and to place his or her daily experience into a wider structural and historical framework, a similar type of understanding and reflection can be reached by studying and comparing countries or societies. Even a fairly preliminary observation of, in this case, the ways in which other countries respond to similar social problems, organize welfare services, underwrite social rights, or interprete values such as solidarity or equality tends to lead to reflections about domestic social policy arrangements—and the realization of how much is often taken for granted. Indeed, it might often be some form of 'sociological imagination' which inspires new questions. For example: how do we explain the different emphasis which otherwise similar countries place on family policies? Why do unemployed people, pensioners, or lone parents fare considerably better in some countries than in others? Why are some countries able to sustain expensive welfare programmes which require high levels of tax revenue while a similar approach seems inconceivable elsewhere? Why do countries with similar average living standards have very different levels of homelessness? These and other questions would be typical points of departure in comparative social policy research. Before discussing some examples of the latter, the following section will illustrate some more broad cross-national similarities and differences in social policy.

CROSS-NATIONAL VARIATIONS OF SOCIAL POLICY IN EUROPE

A global perspective?

Most early systematic academic analyses of social policy reflected different national preoccupations. The empirical study of the problem of poverty, for example, has a long tradition in British social policy and continues to be a major concern in academic research. By contrast, the **Arbeiterfrage** (the 'workers question', that is, how to socially integrate the growing mass of industrial workers in the existing social structure during the second half of the nineteenth century) has been a more central concern for social policy debates and analysis in Germany. As a consequence, not so much poverty but forms of income maintenance during periods out of work due to illness, unemployment, or retirement have been at the centre of academic (and political) concern for some time.

To some extent these national social policy concerns have been superseded by debates which are more international and comparative in nature, to the extent that criticisms have been made against analyses which remain not only single country-based but confined to western Europe or to economically advanced countries, such as those belonging to the OECD (see Jones Finer 1999). Social policy research since the 1980s widened the scope to developing countries, with some studies having adopted an explicitly comparative focus (e.g. MacPherson and Midgley 1987). In many cases it is interesting, or sometimes essential, to broaden the scope of cross-national analysis beyond Europe, particularly if social policy variation is a prime interest. In order to capture different value systems underpinning welfare provision or the different roles of families and informal networks in the provision of welfare services, a broad comparative perspective seems appropriate. However, even a more narrow European perspective can serve the purpose of illustrating some of the similarities and differences in social policy arrangements which have inspired cross-national studies of social policy.

Social policy in eight member states of the European Union: some aggregate figures

A conventional starting point for observing cross-national differences in social policy is based on data on social expenditure. Fig. 20.1 provides an overview of social protection

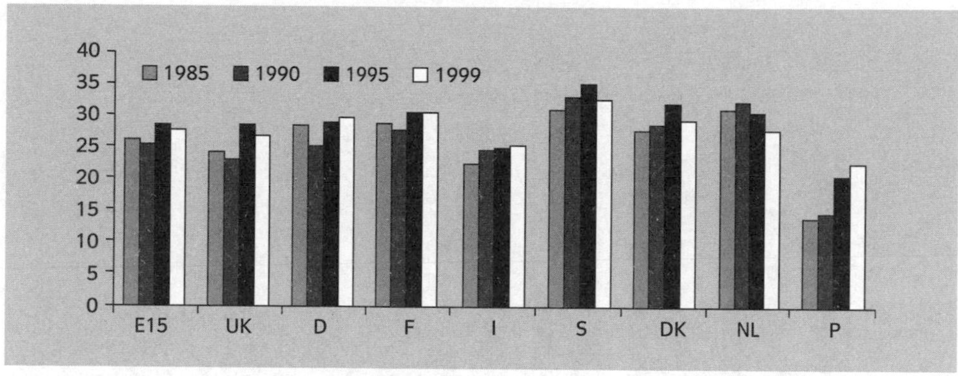

Figure 20.1 Social protection expenditure (as % of GDP)

Source: Eurostat (1994; 2001). © European Communities 1994–2002.

spending in eight member states of the European Union, plus the average across all fifteen states. The countries are geographically spread, include the three large economies of Germany, France, and the UK, and cover long-standing as well as recent EU member states. In order to adjust for different population size, social spending is measured as a share of national Gross Domestic Product (GDP). Of course, as always in comparative social policy, there are problems of comparability. Some areas (such as education) are excluded, while indirect spending (such as tax subsidies) are difficult to identify consistently across countries in compatible ways, and thus left out. Also, while taking the economic output of a country into account, measuring social expenditure as a share of GDP is always liable to differences in national business cycles at certain points in time. Nevertheless, the figure gives an indication of the different efforts which countries make in social policy, and of the magnitude of social expenditure in some countries (such as Sweden). However, it also shows that countries have moved closer together since the mid-1980s, i.e. that the differences in social policy spending have become smaller, with southern European countries such as Portugal apparently catching up with the more mature European welfare states.

Some degree of convergence is also observable in respect to the ways in which EU countries finance social policy. In principle, there are four forms of revenue: taxation, contributions from protected persons (social insurance contributions), contributions from their employers, and other forms of receipts from a variety of sources such as interest and dividends, co-payments for prescriptions, and so on. The relative share of the latter has not altered significantly during the 1990s, remaining below 10 per cent of all social protection revenue in 1999 across the EU (see Fig. 20.2) but closer to 20 per cent in Portugal and the Netherlands. By contrast, tax funding (referred to as general government revenue) has lost in relevance in countries which traditionally put a strong emphasis on taxation, such as Denmark and the Netherlands, but has become more important in countries such as France, Italy, and Germany (see Fig. 20.3). The background for this trend is a concomitant reduction of the share of employers' contributions in those countries as an attempt to reduce non-wage labour costs which, although contracting, generally remain higher in continental countries than in the UK, Ireland, or Scandinavia.

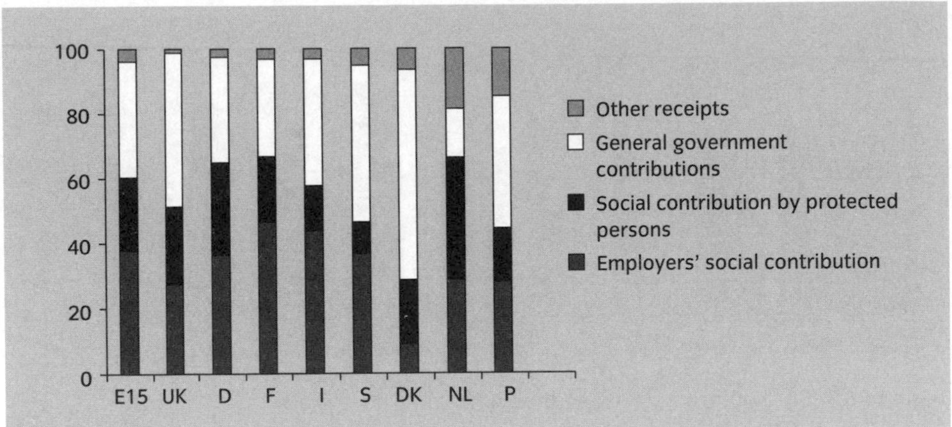

Figure 20.2 Social protection receipts by type in 1999 (as % of total receipts)

Source: Eurostat (1994; 2002). © European Communities 1994–2002.

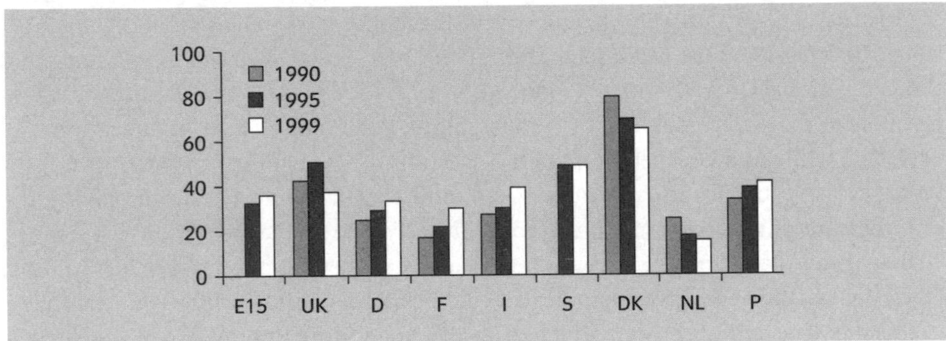

Figure 20.3 General government contributions (as % of total receipts)

Source: Eurostat (1994; 2002). © European Communities 1994–2002.

As to the type of social policy, there are two basic forms in which programmes can be delivered: as **cash transfers** (pensions, parental allowances, sickness benefits, etc.) or as **benefits in kind** (goods and services such as health care, housing, child care, and home help). Fig. 20.4(a) reveals that some EU states make a relatively strong effort to provide benefits in kind, such as Sweden and Denmark, while others such as Italy, the Netherlands, and Germany put a relatively strong emphasis on cash transfers. If the same perspective is applied not to the aggregate but to specific areas of social policy where both forms of support are commonly made, cross-national differences are even more apparent. Support for families with children, for example, can either be in kind (e.g. child care services) or cash (child benefits). While all eight countries reviewed here provide both types of assistance, Sweden and Denmark stand out as 'service' states. As Fig. 20.4(b) indicates, the provision of benefits in kind for children (i.e. childcare arrangements) in the two Scandinavian countries seems to have a much greater importance than in the other EU states.

Typical problems and risks which social policy spending aims to ameliorate include unemployment, poverty, homelessness, and social exclusion. All of these problems can be defined, and thus measured, in different ways within and across countries (see the discussion

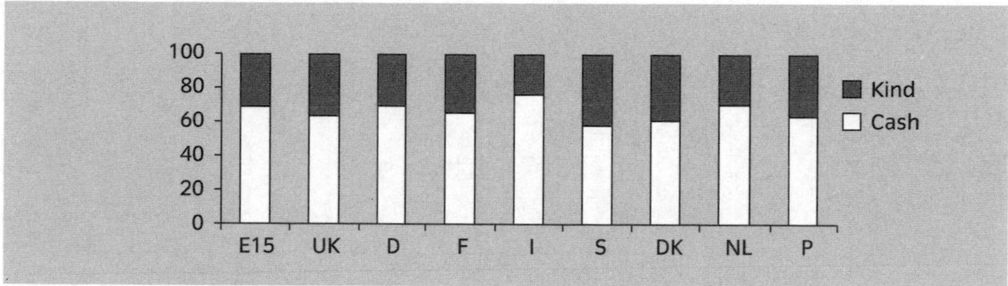

Figure 20.4(a) Distribution of total social protection by type in 1999 (%)

Source: Eurostat (2002). © European Communities 1994–2002.

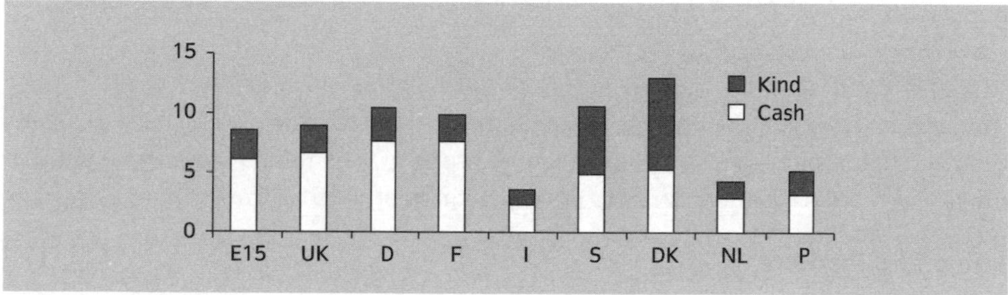

Figure 20.4(b) Distribution of social protection for family/children by type in 1999 (% of total social benefits)

Source: Eurostat (2002). © European Communities 1994–2002.

on inequality and poverty in Chapter 5 of this volume). Without rehearsing the methodological and theoretical problems involved, for the purpose of illustrating cross-national variation Fig. 20.5 displays the relative risk of poverty in the eight countries, defined as the share of the population with income below 60 per cent of median national income—before and after the receipt of benefits. The chart is derived from the EU's first joint report on social inclusion, agreed by EU leaders at the summit in December 2001 (EU 2001) with data derived from the **European Community Household Panel**. It shows that poverty rates—before the effect of transfers, except for pensions, is taken into account—are fairly close to the EU average in six countries but not in the UK and perhaps surprisingly, Sweden. The difference between the first and the second column indicates the effect which social transfers have on reducing poverty, which is considerable in all countries except Italy. However, the second column shows that differences in the extent of poverty remain substantial across EU member states. Denmark, closely followed by Sweden and the Netherlands, all have poverty rates which are well below the EU average and close to half of those in the UK, which is the country at the other end of the spectrum, followed by Portugal and Italy.

For particular groups of benefit claimants a similar picture emerges. The risk of poverty amongst unemployed people in the UK, for example, is particularly acute. Applying the same poverty indicator as above and using data from the European Community Household Panel, Duncan Gallie and colleagues (2001) showed that almost half of British unemployed were poor in the mid-1990s, which was a rate far higher than in any other of the eleven EU countries covered in their study. The same study suggests that moving from employment into unemployment carries a higher risk of poverty in

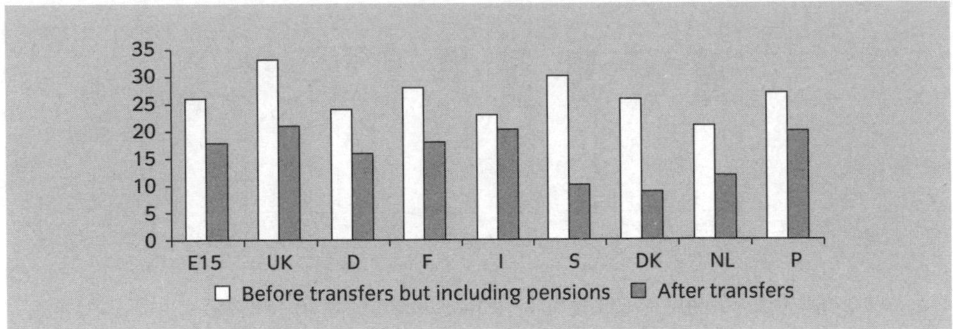

Figure 20.5 People at risk of poverty, before and after social transfers, 1998 (% of total population)

Source: EC (2001). © European Communities 1994–2002.

Britain than in any of the other countries of the sample. In other words, it is not simply the case that poor people in Britain are more prone to becoming unemployed, but that unemployment leads more easily to poverty than in other countries.

Some implications

Aggregate data on the relative scale of problems such as poverty or long-term unemployment, or the extent and type of funding can provide clues about differences in the delivery of social protection, about the groups of actors which are likely to be involved in policy making, and even about differing ideas as to notions of solidarity, redistribution, and need. For example, in countries with a relatively high proportion of contributory rather than tax-funding, benefits tend to be proportional to previous earnings rather than flat-rate. As principal contributors, employers and employees are often involved in the administration of benefits which are sometimes regarded as 'deferred wages' and thus represent an important element in the processes of collective bargaining between **social partners.** Trade unions and employer organizations cooperate in matters of social insurance in Germany, for example, and the administration of unemployment insurance is entirely the responsibility of trade unions in Sweden or Denmark. By contrast, the absence of similar institutional arrangements, and the preference of flat-rate rather than earnings-related transfers, gives governments more power over social policy and also creates a different set of interests, such as between taxpayers on the one hand and benefit claimants on the other. In the UK, for example, social (national) insurance benefits are not regarded as an element of worker's remuneration, and the contributory principle is much less prominent than elsewhere in the EU, except perhaps for Ireland (Clasen 2001). Indeed, national insurance contributions in the UK have become all but another form of taxation, unlike in many other European countries, where they are an earmarked form of collective resources which is separate from general government expenditure. In comparison with the UK, this makes it more difficult for many European governments to simply cut back contributory-based benefits.

Thus, even where national levels of spending might not be too dissimilar, cross-national differences can be significant as far as the role of actors and institutional structures are concerned. Two examples have demonstrated this well. Giuliano Bonoli (2000) compared pension policies in three western European countries, France, Switzerland, and the UK. He showed that, despite similar challenges such as demographic ageing, patterns of policy reform differed substantially across countries, with actors and interests strongly influenced by the type of pension financing, institutional arrangements, and differences in wider national policy-making frameworks. Richard Freeman (2000) investigated the ways in which healthcare systems have evolved and are currently organized in five European countries. He identifies a country group in which national healthcare services have been established (Italy, Sweden, and the UK) and others in which healthcare is based on principles of social insurance (Germany and France). Using such a perspective he is able to point to similarities within the groups, and clear differences across them, with respect to the ways in which organizational patterns influence the composition and strength of vested interests in healthcare policy, and also impinge on the role and perceptions of doctors, patients, and the wider public.

Finally, different eligibility rules reveal cross-national variation regarding prevailing notions of who is and who is not deemed to deserve access to social policy. The latter can be based on need or on previous contributions, or can arise from membership of a social group. A certain period or number of contributions is usually required in social insurance programmes before eligibility to a pension or sickness allowance is established. Citizenship, reaching retirement age, or being a parent of a dependent child are typical criteria for benefits which are 'universal' in the sense that neither need nor contributions are deemed relevant in establishing eligibility. State pensions in Denmark or universal child benefits in most European countries are examples of the latter. The extent of means-testing in European welfare systems indicate the relative strength of the principle of need, i.e. the notion that resources should (primarily) be targeted at poor people. Within a European context, this idea has always been somewhat more prominent in the UK and Ireland. Elsewhere other objectives seem more important, such as the involvement of the middle classes as beneficiaries of social policy in order to create welfare states which act as an integral and integrating institution in society. Despite an increased relevance of means-testing also in other countries, the needs orientation in the UK and Ireland has remained more prominent than anywhere else in the EU. In 1996, for example, about one fifth of total welfare spending in the UK, and one third in Ireland, was based on means-testing, compared with well below 5 per cent in Denmark, Austria, Belgium, and Sweden (EC 2000: 80).

COMPARATIVE SOCIAL POLICY IN THE ANALYSIS OF NATIONAL WELFARE STATES AND PROGRAMMES

There are many books which discuss social policy instruments, outcomes, and policy developments, with individual chapters devoted to particular countries, providing a flavour of national policy developments. But often these texts lack criteria which would make them explicitly comparative in any analytical sense. For example, disparate country chapters often come without a common analytical framework, systematic structure, or even set of common topics. At times there is little attempt to introduce central concepts, or no discussion of how these have been operationalized; as a consequence, drawing comparative conclusions is difficult.

And yet early systematic comparisons go back to the 1960s and 1970s, concentrating on social administration (Rodgers et al. 1968) and later social policy (e.g. Kaim-Caudle 1973; Rodgers et al. 1979). Driven by the idea that there is considerable knowledge and insight to be gained from looking across countries, these pioneering studies briefly designed an analytical framework and then proceeded with 'constructive descriptions' (Stebbing in Rodgers et al. 1979: xii) and intensive country-by-country discussions of social policy programmes, aims, and forms of delivery. This empirical engagement with social policy in a range of countries was extremely valuable at the time, but many aspects were quickly outdated. Also, very few in-depth comparative studies made any claims to theoretical advancement. Heclo's seminal book (1974) on differences and similarities in the development of unemployment insurance and pension programmes in the UK and Sweden was one of the rare exceptions.

Accessing information about national social policy systems has become much easier since then, not least due to the publication of specialized texts on particular countries (e.g. Jones 1990; Olsson 1990; Clasen and Freeman 1994), the establishment of new journals which regularly feature articles on comparative social policy (e.g. the *Journal of European Social Policy*), and efforts made by supra-national agencies such as the EU or the OECD to harmonize data and thus facilitate cross-national analyses. As a consequence, the value of publications of largely descriptive accounts of national social policy programmes has become rather limited when no attempt is made to connect individual country analyses to a wider conceptual framework which would allow inferences about, for example, causes for cross-national convergence or divergence.

Comparative welfare state studies: from welfare effort to welfare regimes

Often as the result of collaborative research frameworks, intensive comparative accounts of social policy developments within developed welfare states were conducted in the 1980s, such as the one developed by Peter Flora and colleagues which produced landmark publications (Flora and Heidenheimer 1981; Flora 1986). The core explanatory variables in these studies were variations in national welfare effort, i.e. the relative share of the national product which is devoted to social policy programmes. Other indicators of welfare state growth were the timing of social policy legislation and the growth in programme coverage. The interest in these dependent variables links them to earlier studies conducted in the 1960s and 1970s which, on the basis of statistical observations, argued that the emergence and development of welfare states has to be regarded as a response to socioeconomic pressures developed within industrialized societies and growing capacities to meet demands (Cutright 1965; Wilensky 1975). In the 1970s and 1980s these explanations were questioned in studies which pointed to political factors, and in particular the strength of organized labour, as a crucial variable of welfare state expansion (see Shalev 1983).

The current version of this ongoing debate about causes of welfare state development emphasises the diversity and the coexistence of several paths towards post-industrialism in accordance with the notion of the existence of different types or **welfare regimes** around which countries cluster (Esping-Andersen 1990). Gøsta Esping-Andersen's seminal book has impinged on much comparative social policy in the 1990s and beyond. Building on earlier categorizations of welfare states (Titmuss 1974), his typology was original in the sense that it was derived from a systematic empirical investigation of similarities and differences across developed industrialized countries at the time.

One of Esping-Andersen's starting points was the argument that the level of social spending is a rather poor 'proxy' variable for social policy (Esping-Andersen 1993). Indeed, a high level of expenditure provides little information as to the degree of redistribution achieved in a particular country or the ways in which welfare programmes ameliorate, perpetuate, or reduce social divisions or income inequality. Instead, an understanding of the impact of welfare states on the social structure of a given country requires a study of the ways in which national welfare programmes are structured and delivered. Applying such a perspective to eighteen OECD countries allowed the identification of three distinct 'welfare regimes':

> institutional arrangements, rules and understandings that guide and shape concurrent social-policy decisions, expenditure developments, problem definitions, and even the response-and-demand structure of citizens and welfare consumers. (Esping-Andersen 1990: 80)

Esping-Andersen argues that the provision of social policy and the interaction between markets, states, and families follows a certain logic which differs across the three clusters of welfare states. For example, social policy in 'liberal' welfare states is predominantly aimed at providing support mainly for low-income groups. Consequently, there is an emphasis on means-tested social assistance benefits and only modest universal transfers, and an active encouragement of the use of non-state alternatives such as private forms of social protection. Esping-Andersen regards countries such as the USA, Australia, Canada, and, to a lesser extent, the UK as belonging to this group. A second regime type, the 'corporatist' or 'conservative' welfare state, aims to preserve status differentials by providing transfers which are closely linked to previous earnings. Since social rights are attached to class and status (e.g. with separate programmes for white- and blue-collar workers, and benefits covering family dependants), private forms of welfare provisions are much less prevalent than in liberal welfare states. Continental European countries such as Germany, France, and Italy belong to this cluster. The third, 'social democratic' type aims to foster cross-class solidarity and equality. Generous benefits, also for the less well-off, and universal forms of support predominate, with the state acting not only as compensator for lost earnings but also as principal provider of care services for children and older people. Social policy in Scandinavian countries such as Sweden, Norway, and Denmark is arguably embedded within such a framework.

Empirically, Esping-Andersen distinguished the three clusters by their respective degrees of **'de-commodification'** and **'stratification'**. The latter indicator refers to the type of social structure which welfare programmes promote and is composed of a measurement, consisting of the degree of corporatism (number of distinct public pension schemes), etatism (pension expenditure on government employees), average levels of benefit universalism and benefit equality, and proportions of spending on means-tested social expenditure, private pensions and private healthcare (see Esping-Andersen 1990: 70–1). 'De-commodification' is understood as the degree to which. . . . 'individuals, or families, can uphold a socially acceptable standard of living independently of market participation' (Esping-Andersen 1990: 37). In other words, welfare states differ in the extent to which they allow benefit recipients to remain outside of the labour market (see Box 20.2).

Esping-Andersen's welfare state typology stimulated major debates in comparative social policy. Some commentators questioned the academic value of constructing clusters of welfare states (e.g. Baldwin 1996), but many others emphasized the need to identify

Box 20.2 De-commodification as a central concept in Esping-Andersen's welfare regimes

One of the two central indicators which Gøsta Esping-Andersen (1990) employs to distinguish between welfare states is the level of 'de-commodification'. With developing capitalism, for the majority of the population the survival outside the labour market became increasingly difficult, work became waged work, and labour therefore commodified. Only the gradual establishment of social rights lowered workers' reliance on the labour market somewhat during times of sickness, unemployment, or retirement. The historical expansion of the welfare state can therefore be regarded as a process of de-commodification, and countries can be compared in accordance with the degree of de-commodification.

Using data from the early and mid 1980s, Esping-Andersen calculated the degree of de-commodification for pension, sickness, and unemployment programmes in eighteen OECD countries. He took account not only of the generosity of transfers but also of benefit duration, access to benefits (eligibility rules), and the ways in which benefits are funded, weighted by the percentage of the relevant population covered. For example, the index for pensions has been constructed as consisting of the levels of both the minimum pension and the standard pension, the number of years to qualify, the proportion of pensions funded by contributors rather than taxation, and the share of people above retirement age who are actually in receipt of a pension. He then scored individual programmes for each country and produced rank orders. These showed the lowest (combined) de-commodification scores for Australia, the USA, Ireland, and the UK. For average workers in these 'liberal' welfare states the degree of market independence achieved by social policy is therefore low and the pressure to return to paid work high. By contrast, the highest scores were registered for Scandinavia which means that the same welfare state programmes enable Swedish or Danish workers more easily and for longer periods to survive without participation in the labour market.

The concept of de-commodification is a crucial indicator in Esping-Andersen's three-way classification of welfare states and has become an important reference point in comparative social policy. However, it is not free from theoretical and conceptual problems, and questions have been raised about the ways in which Esping-Andersen has applied the concept. Francis G. Castles and Deborah Mitchell (1993), for example, criticized the somewhat arbitrary low weighting which was ascribed to some programmes simply because they are means-tested.

more than three distinct welfare regimes. Stephan Leibfried (1993), for example, argued that southern European ('Latin Rim') countries could not simply be regarded as evolving versions of one of the three types but display characteristics which made them different. This has also been claimed by Maurizio Ferrera (1996), who pointed to characteristics such as a fragmented nature of social security, the mix between public and non-public forms of welfare provision, and the role of clientelism and patronage which combined form a distinct southern European welfare state (but critically, see Kastrougalos 1996). Beyond Europe, Castles and Mitchell (1993) pointed to methodological and conceptual problems in Esping-Andersen's typology (such as the treatment of means-testing; see Box 20.2). Esping-Andersen's 'liberal' welfare states arguably consist of two groups, with the UK, Australia, and New Zealand pursuing similar welfare goals as in Scandinavia (poverty reduction, income equalization) but by means of redistributive instruments rather than high social expenditure.

Other criticisms of Esping-Andersen's approach (for reviews see Abrahamson 1999; Arts and Gelissen 2002) revolved around the notion of welfare regimes (are they **ideal types** or actual systems?), the problem of assigning particular countries to particular clusters, the dynamic nature of welfare states, and the question of regime shifts. The exclusive focus on income transfers has been regarded as another major problem. Placing welfare services such as health and social care at the centre of the analysis would have produced a different clustering of countries (Kautto 2002). The two 'conservative' welfare states of France and Germany, for example, with similar patterns in the provision of social security, differ considerably in the means and the extent to which they provide care for children and support parents (Rostgaard and Fridberg 1998). The inclusion of the role of unpaid care provided by families and networks would help to attain a more adequate understanding of women's relationship with the welfare state, which cannot be reduced to that of a paid worker (Lewis 1992). Recently Esping-Andersen (1999) has acknowledged the relevance which households play in different countries within the overall production of welfare.

Despite, or perhaps because of, these various forms of criticism, Esping-Andersen's welfare regime approach has remained a major reference point and contribution to the study of comparative social policy to date. Also, his classification has proved to be fairly solid, even though a case can be made for extending the categories to four or even five (with the 'conservative' type as the most heterogeneous) and for repositioning some countries if the focus of analysis is a certain programme or policy field rather than welfare state per se. What is more, the reference to welfare regimes (implying a certain logic of social policy provision) helps to locate the study of comparative social policy within a wider framework, highlighting national configurations and interdependencies between welfare and other policy areas such as industrial relations, labour market policy, or national production systems (Ebbinghaus and Manow 2001). Indeed, it is difficult to find any macro-level comparisons of European welfare states which does not refer to the 'three worlds of welfare capitalism', critically or otherwise. This is the case even for cross-national comparisons of social policy which concentrate on particular aspects of social policy rather than welfare states, and which are more interested in welfare outcomes rather than configurations of welfare production.

Evaluative comparisons in social policy

Rather than concentrating on welfare states and on the causes of their development, another strand of cross-national social policy analysis focuses on particular types of social policy intervention (e.g. Bradshaw and Piachaud 1980) or on particular problems such as poverty (Walker et al. 1983). Since the 1980s the developments of new and improved data sets, such as the Luxembourg Income Study or the European Community Household Panel, has helped to provide a more robust empirical basis for comparative research of this type which is more interested in evaluating the effectiveness of welfare programmes, such as the impact of national income transfer programmes on poverty (Mitchell 1991) or the effect of unemployment on individuals and families (Gallie and Paugam 2000).

Much of this type of analysis produces rank orders of countries, sometimes with the idea of 'learning' from those countries which seem to be better than others at dealing with social problems or providing social policy in a more effective way. Another more academic value of these types of systematic comparative analyses is to demonstrate how multi-faceted and complex social policy interventions can be, and thus how superficial and at times misleading tables in the media can be which arguably show differences in the extent to which countries support particular social groups.

Simple comparisons of child benefit rates, for example, would misrepresent the overall effort which countries make to help families with the cost of children. For example, while some countries place an emphasis on universal or means-tested child benefits, others choose tax allowances, or a combination of the two. This has been shown by a project coordinated by Jonathan Bradshaw and colleagues at York University in 1992 (Bradshaw et al. 1993a; 1993b). The study brought together a large team of researchers in order to provide information and data with the aim of identifying the structure of national 'child support packages' in fifteen countries. Apart from benefits and tax allowances, other forms of support included in the study were help with the cost of childcare, schooling, and healthcare for children, but also housing allowances, which can be dependent on the size of a family. Once the structure of these components was identified for each country, the value of child support packages was calculated. Here it is important to recognize that the level of support which countries provide often discriminates between different family types (see Box 20.3). Thus, rather than one child support package, the value of a multitude of packages had to be computed for each country, producing tables with countries ranked in accordance with support levels by income, number and age of children, family type and employment status. The summary ranking showed some similarity with Esping-Andersen's welfare regimes, with Scandinavian countries among the most and Anglo-Saxon countries among the least generous countries, but there were also considerable deviations. The UK, for example ended up with a middle position while France, from this perspective, seems to be much closer to Norway and Denmark than to other 'conservative' welfare states such as Germany or Italy. However, findings of more recent investigation of the same type, covering twenty-two countries, bear little relationship to the ranking which would have been predicted using Esping-Andersen's regime approach (Bradshaw and Finch 2002).

Box 20.3 Evaluating the level of child support across fifteen countries

In the early 1990s, Jonathan Bradshaw and colleagues (1993a; 1993b) investigated different ways in which thirteen European countries, plus Australia and the USA, help families with the cost of bringing up children, and also compared the relative generosity of national support packages. Rather than interviewing families, the research was based on legislation and regulations concerning tax treatment and the entitlement to and level of cash transfers and other forms of support, e.g. with pre-school care or healthcare consumption for eight different model families with between one and four children of different ages. National currencies were made comparable by using 'purchasing power parities' which, unlike exchange rates, take account of differences in the cost of living across countries.

The findings show that it is difficult to provide an answer to the question which country is the most generous in supporting families because of cross-national variations in outcomes. Comparing countries before or after the cost of housing makes a difference, for example, and there are some significant variations in the level of child support which applies to different families within countries. Some, for example, target their efforts on families with low income (Germany, USA, UK), others favour large families irrespective of earning levels (France, Belgium, Luxembourg), and some (including Norway, France, and Luxembourg) are particularly generous to lone parents. An average rank order across these and other variations however shows that Norway, France, Luxembourg, Denmark, and Belgium are, generally, the most supportive welfare states for families with children. The least generous countries are Spain, Greece, Ireland, Portugal, and the USA. In 2001, Bradshaw and Finch (2002) repeated the study and extended it to twenty-two countries. It showed a substantial improvement of the UK's position compared with the early 1990s, but indicates that Austria provides a child support package which is considerably more generous than anywhere else, followed by Luxembourg and Finland.

COUNTRIES AS UNITS OF COMPARISON? THE ROLE OF THE EUROPEAN UNION

The discussion so far has shown that European countries retain distinctive characteristics in the patterns in which markets, states, and families interact in the provision of social protection. On the other hand, as outlined in the last but one section, at a broad level indicators such as social expenditure and types of revenue for social policy suggest that some degree of convergence is taking place. This process is being reinforced by actions at the level of the European Union.

European social integration: only a question of market-building?

The development of European integration across member states of the European Union is predominantly based on economic rationales. The ambition to create a single European market with free movement of goods, investment, services, and labour has been a central driving force since the 1950s, and was cemented by the adoption of a single currency in 1999 which now applies in twelve of the fifteen EU countries. But as a corollary of economic integration some social policy intervention is all but inevitable. For example, free movement of labour would be difficult to reconcile with a lack of recognition of pension rights and entitlement, to benefits for citizens who work in member countries other than their own. Equally, minimum social standards help to put a brake on countries who otherwise might be tempted to gain a competitive advantage over others by lowering the social (non-wage) costs for companies and thus undercut prices (a process which has been referred to as '**social dumping**'). As a consequence, there has been some form of social policy legislation at EU level, but one which was characteristically confined to employment-related aspects such as health and safety at work, working conditions, minimum standards, or regulating the length of the working week.

However, unlike national welfare states, the form of EU intervention is largely regulatory, and does not guarantee rights to social benefits which, paid out of a European social budget, individual citizens could claim. Even at the beginning of the twenty-first century, a European welfare state which, taking over from national governments, would provide programmes such as pensions, healthcare, or social services seems inconceivable because of a number of barriers. Most importantly, the EU lacks legislative power and financial resources, such as a designated form of tax revenue which would fund these core social policy areas. What is more, because of their popularity and electoral significance, there is little political will among member states to transfer sovereignty from the national to the EU level to such an extent.

Most commentators therefore regard the EU influence over national social policy-making as rather limited—and also remain sceptical about the prospects of a harmonization of national social policy regimes. In fact, the EU's reliance on only broadly defined guidelines and flexible forms of implementation might leave sufficient space for further divergence rather than convergence of national social policy provision, as Geyer (2000b) argues. But this is not to say that the EU has not had any influence on social policy across its member states. In fact, it can be shown that the degree of social policy activities and intervention has steadily grown since the 1950s (for extensive discussions, see Falkner 1998; Hantrais 2000; Geyer 2000a; Kleinman 2002).

Essentially a process of creating a common economic sphere, the six founding members of the then EEC (European Economic Community) assumed that a higher level of social welfare would follow from increased economic activity which was to be achieved via regulations concerning the free movement of workers between member states or the freedom to provide services. Yet even the Rome Treaty, signed in 1957, included some more explicit areas of social policy intervention, such as improved working conditions, equal pay between men and women, and holiday pay. The latter policies were insisted upon by France in order to prevent a potential competitive disadvantage, and can thus be seen not so much as driven by concerns over social welfare but as accompanying elements of economic integration and fostering the mobility of labour.

However, while early social policy activities were rather rudimentary and geared towards mobile workers and creating gender equality in pay and social rights, over the past twenty years or so the EU has become an increasingly influential force in the shaping of social policy regulation within member states. The Social Action Programme (1974–6) was aimed at improving employment, living, and working conditions and encouraging cooperation between employees and employers. However, the worsening economic climate in the mid-1970s contributed to a rather mixed and more modest output than had been anticipated, even though important directives were passed in the areas of equal treatment for men and women and health and safety, as well as the establishment of several European networks and observatories aimed at monitoring social policy developments in the member states.

The 1980s were dominated by the preparations for the completion of the single market. Although social policy was not a major element of the Single European Act of 1986 (the first major revision of the Rome Treaty), the then president of the Commission, Jacques Delors, with the support of the pro-European French President Mitterrand and the German Chancellor Kohl, was keen to expand the so-called European 'social dimension' in order to increase public support for further economic and political integration. This became explicit in the growing emphasis on involving social partners in matters of social policy (the so-called **'social dialogue'**) and the increased use of Structural Funds in order to reduce regional disparities. Another example was the stronger decision-making power of the EU facilitated by the adoption of qualified (rather than unanimous) majority voting in some areas, such as health and safety at work.

Disagreement over the growing European social policy competence in the run-up to the Maastricht European Council in 1991, which formally created the European Union, led to the famous British 'opt-out' from the so-called **'Protocol on Social Policy'** which was signed by the other eleven member countries and annexed to the Treaty. It extended the principle of qualified majority voting to further areas, such as working conditions, information for and consultation of workers, and equality between men and women. The British opt-out was later rescinded by the incoming Labour government in 1997 and formally incorporated in the Amsterdam Treaty of the same year, paving the way for European directives on areas such as parental leave, atypical forms of employment, working time, and sex discrimination which now apply across all EU member states. The Amsterdam Treaty also for the first time explicitly mentioned the fight against social exclusion as one of the areas in which the EU was to adopt a more active role.

In short, while the EU influence over social policy matters has remained limited in the sense that it continues to be restricted to areas which are fairly close to the labour market, an increasing EU influence in these areas can be observed. At the same time, while attempts at directly harmonizing national policies stalled in the early 1990s, other less legalistic forms of influencing policy making have been pursued since then, particularly in areas such as the fight against social exclusion (see Ferrera et al. 2002) or the coordination of national employment policies (Goetschy 2001)—see Box 20.4. Fixing common objectives, encouraging cooperation between member states, benchmarking, promoting best practice, conducting evaluations, requesting regular progress reports, and issuing recommendations have now become principal forms of policy intervention as part of the so-called **'open method of coordination'** (de la Porte et al. 2001) which is paramount in these two areas.

Box 20.4 The European Employment Strategy

Since the mid-1990s a growing EU involvement in employment policy can he observed, later formalized as the European Employment Strategy (EES). The origins of this strategy go back to the European Council in Essen in 1994 and the Amsterdam Treaty in 1997, which stressed that employment was a 'matter of common concern', and also stressed the need for coordination of employment policies across member states (see Goetschy 2001). At the Luxembourg Job Summit, which was held in 1997, it was decided that the European Council was to draft annual Employment Guidelines to be translated into National Action Plans for Employment (NAPs) to be submitted by member states. The plans are then analysed jointly by the Council and the Commission and the results presented in a Joint Employment Report. The findings of this report provide the basis for the reshaping of future guidelines and country-specific recommendations for member states' employment policies (see www.eu-employment-observatory.net/introframeset_en.htm).

One of the cornerstones of the EES is the shift from 'welfare to work'. For example, the Council asks the member states to quantify targets for people to be transferred from what are called 'passive' income support systems to 'active' employment-related measures, and to increase the overall number of unemployed who are being offered training or jobs by a certain margin. What kind of direct and lasting effect the EES will have in practice is probably difficult to assess at this stage. However, the requirement of annual reporting is likely to increase cross-national transparency and, potentially at least, will improve levels of comparability of national policy performances and thus facilitate cross-national evaluations. This can be assumed to exert some influence over and above symbolic policy-making at member state level.

Limited but growing: other forms of EU influence on social policy in Europe

As shown, applying new methods of governance, employment policy and tackling social exclusion are two fields in which the EU is gaining political profile, in addition to areas such as occupational health, working conditions, and labour mobility. By comparison, as long as EU activities in the more classic social policy fields such as healthcare, social services, family policy, or housing remain as limited as they are, the creation of a welfare state in the conventional sense at the European supra-national level seems a long way off. And yet national sovereignty over social policy formation has eroded over the decades while EU influence has grown. Not that long ago, benefits were largely restricted to citizens of a particular country and their consumption was restricted to the home country. As Leibfried and Pierson (1995a) show, neither stipulation holds any longer for many transfers. Even though the extent of loss of national sovereignty differs between types of social benefit, as the result of an ever-increasing number of legal rulings by the European Court of Justice, national governments can no longer exclude non-national EU citizens from social rights or stop the exportability of benefit entitlement to other EU countries. This applies particularly to benefits which can be regarded as providing a minimum level of social protection (such as a minimum pension) but also for family allowances and other long-term (particularly in-kind) benefits. By contrast, national governments have managed to hold onto sovereignty over transfers which are tightly linked to individual contributions (social insurance), and unemployment insurance transfers especially.

This outcome is not so much the result of a deliberate political move towards a European welfare state but of a conflict between maintaining national autonomy over welfare state matters versus the completion of a single open market with full European labour mobility and the freedom to provide services in other member states. Public monopolies, such as in healthcare delivery or pension provision, might be interpreted as contravening freedom of enterprise, for example. The arena for this ongoing struggle has been the European Court of Justice in a series of complex legal processes in which, as Leibfried and Pierson (2000: 279) put it, 'supranational efforts to broaden access and national efforts to maintain control go hand in hand, and are calibrated from conflict to conflict and court case by court case'.

In other words, as a form of spillover and brought about by legal rather than by direct political action, the process of economic or market integration has been accompanied by an incremental process of social policy 'homogneization' (Leibfried and Pierson 2000) across the EU. Its driving parameters (exportability of benefits; non-exclusivity; freedom to provide services) have increasingly influenced national welfare state reform processes and outcomes and can be expected to do so even more in the future.

This has consequences for the study of comparative social policy within the EU. On the one hand, abandoning nations as units of comparison seems rather premature because most social policy-making (funding, spending, delivering) is still decided at national rather than at EU level. What is more, apart from some specific areas (health and safety at work) or social groups (migrant workers) the EU has not replaced national institutions as principal legislator, and certainly not as revenue base or provider of social policy. However, it would equally be misleading to disregard the increasing impact of EU legislation on the content and process of national social policy reforms, or to dismiss the extent to which sovereignty over some social policy fields has been transferred from national governments to supra-national EU governance. Indirect EU action (legal rulings as an outcome of market-building) and direct action both in fields relevant to social policy (convergence criteria for the European Monetary Union or attempts at tax harmonization) and in social policy proper (e.g. the European Employment Strategy) exert pressure on national welfare state reforms. In sum, the lesson for comparative analyses of social policy at European level is to acknowledge that governments of member states can still 'choose' social policy options but, as Leibfried and Pierson (2000: 288) put it, 'they do so from an increasingly restricted menu'. The impact of the EU will vary depending on the particular policy field, but the interaction between the EU and national social policy formation will continue to be a major area of study within comparative social policy for some time to come.

CONCLUSION

While not all comparative studies of social policy are cross-national in character, the study of social policy has become increasingly comparative in nature, and the comparative analysis of social policy has become firmly embedded within most university courses on the subject. The chapter has discussed a number of reasons for such a growth of the comparative perspective, some of which are of an academic nature and others to do with the growing sense of cross-country interdependence and similarities in the challenges which mature, as well as many developing, welfare states face today. The chapter has also illustrated that otherwise similar countries, such as those within the European Union, continue to display considerable differences both in the extent of social problems, such as poverty, in the ways in which social policy is financed, and in the magnitude of national resources devoted to social policy. However, the latter particularly indicates a process of policy convergence in Europe.

While there might be many reasons for the scale of national resources devoted to social policy, the influence of the EU as a determining factor for social policy development in its member states is becoming ever more apparent. This does not means that national boundaries are no longer relevant for comparative social policy analysis. The prospect of a European welfare state replacing core social policy programmes at national level is perhaps as remote as ever. While this might be good news for those who like to study cross-national social policy, the nature of comparisons is increasingly likely to be influenced by direct and indirect supra-national developments, and not only within Europe.

KEY LEGISLATION

1957 Treaty establishing the European Economic Community (EEC) in Rome.

1992 Treaty on European Union (EU) signed in Maastricht in February 1992. Agreement and protocol on Social Policy which was concluded by all member states with the exception of the UK.

1993 Green Paper on European Social Policy. Options for the Union (COM(93) 333).

1994 White Paper on European Social Policy—a way forward for the Union (COM(94) 333); an important document setting out the EU's role in social policy.

1997 Signing of Amsterdam Treaty; the UK giving up its opt-out position and signs the Social Chapter.

REFERENCES

Abrahamson, Peter (1999), 'The welfare modelling business', *Social Policy and Administration* 33(4): 394–415.

Arts, W., and Gelissen, J. (2002), 'Three worlds of welfare capitalism or more? A state-of-the-art report', *Journal of European Social Policy* 12(2): 137–58.

Baldwin, P. (1996), 'Can we define a European welfare state model?' In B. Greve (ed.), *Comparative Welfare Systems*. London: Macmillan.

Bonoli, G. (2000), *The Politics of Pension Reform: Institutions and Policy Change in Western Europe*. Cambridge: Cambridge University Press.

Bradshaw, J., Ditch, J., Holmes, H., and Whiteford, P. (1993a), *Support for Children: A Comparison of Arrangements in Fifteen Countries*. DSS Research Report No. 21 London: HMSO.

—— —— —— —— (1993b), 'A comparative study of child support in fifteen countries', *Journal of European Social Policy* 3(4): 255–72.

—— and Finch, N. (2002), *A Comparison of Child Benefit Packages in 22 Countries*. DWP Research Report No. 174. Leeds: Corporate Document Services.

—— and Piachaud, D. (1980), *Child Support in the European Community*. London: Bedford Square Press.

Castles, F. (2002), 'Public expenditure and population ageing: why families of nations are different'. In Clasen (2002: 141–55).

—— and Mitchell, D. (1993), 'The worlds of welfare and families of nations'. In F. Castles (ed.), *Families of Nations: Patterns of Public Policy in Western Democracies*. Aldershot: Dartmouth.

Clasen, J. (ed.) (1999), *Comparative Social Policy: Concepts, Theories and Methods*. Oxford: Blackwell.

—— (2001), 'Social insurance and the contributory principle: a paradox in contemporary British social policy', *Social Policy and Administration* 35(6): 641–57.

—— (ed.) (2002), *What Future for Social Security? Debates and Reforms in National and Cross-National Perspective*. Bristol: Policy Press.

—— and Freeman, R. (eds.) (1994), *Social Policy in Germany*. London: Harvester Wheatsheaf.

Cutright, P. (1965), 'Political structure, economic development, and national social security programs', *American Journal of Sociology* 70: 537–50.

de la Porte, C., Pochet, P., and Room, G. (2001), 'Social benchmarking, policy, policy making and new governance in the EU', *Journal of European Social Policy* 11(4): 291–307.

Deacon, A. (2002), *Perspectives on Welfare*. London: Palgrave.

Deacon, B. (1997), *Global Social Policy*. London: Sage.

Ebbinghaus, B., and Manow, P. (eds.) (2001), *Comparing Welfare Capitalism*. London: Routledge.

EC (European Community) (2000), *Social Protection in Europe*. Luxembourg: Office for Official Publications of the European Communities.

—— (2001), *Joint Report on Social Inclusion, Part I: The European Union*. Luxembourg: Office for Official Publications of the European Communities.

Esping-Andersen, G. (1990), *The Three Worlds of Welfare Capitalism*. Cambridge: Polity Press.

—— (1993), 'The comparative macro-sociology of welfare states'. In L. Moreno (ed.), *Social Exchange and Welfare Development*. Madrid: Consejo superior de investigaciones cientificas.

—— (1999), *Social Foundations of postindustrial economies*. Oxford: Oxford University Press.

Eurostat (1994), *Detailed Tables European Social Statistics: Expenditure and Receipts, 1980–1992*. Luxembourg: Office for Official Publications of the European Communities.

—— (2001), *Detailed Tables European Social Statistics: Expenditure and receipts, 1980–1999*. Luxembourg: Office for Official Publications of the European Communities.

—— (2002), *Statistics in Focus*. Luxembourg: Office for Official Publications of the European Communities.

Falkner, G. (1998), *EU Social Policy in the 1990s: Towards a Corporatist Policy Community*. London: Routledge.

Ferrera, M. (1996), 'The southern model of welfare in Europe', *Journal of European Social Policy*, 6(1): 17–37.

—— Matsaganis, M., and Sacchi, S. (2002), 'Open coordination against poverty: the new EU "social inclusion process" ', *Journal of European Social Policy* 12(2): 227–39.

Flora, P. (ed.) (1986), *Growth to Limits*. Berlin: De Gruyter.

—— and Heidenheimer, A. J. (eds.) (1981), *The development of welfare states in Europe and America* (New Brunswick, NJ: Transaction Books).

Freeman, R. (2000), *The Politics of Health in Europe*. Manchester: Manchester University Press.

Gallie, D., and Paugam, S. (eds.) (2000), *Welfare Regimes and the Experience of Unemployment in Europe*. Oxford: Oxford University Press.

—— —— and Jacobs, S. (2001), 'Unemployment, poverty and social isolation: is there a vicious circle of social exclusion?' Paper presented at Euresco conference on 'Labour Market Change, Unemployment and Citizenship in Europe', Helsinki.

Geyer, R. (2000a), *Exploring European Social Policy*. Oxford: Oxford University Press.

—— (2000b), 'The state of European Union social policy', *Policy Studies* 21(3): 245–61.

Goetschy, J. (2001), 'The European employment strategy from Amsterdam to Stockholm: has it reached its cruising speed?', *Industrial Relations Journal* 32(5): 401–18.

Hantrais, L. (2000), *Social Policy in the European Union*, 2nd edn. London: Palgrave.

—— and Mangen, S. (eds.) (1996), *Cross-National Research Methods in the Social Sciences*. London: Pinter.

Heclo, H. (1974), *Modern Social Politics in Britain and Sweden: From Relief to Income Maintenance*. New Haven, Conn.: Yale University Press.

Immergut, E. (1992a), *Health Politics. Interests and Institutions in Western Europe*. Cambridge: Cambridge University Press.

—— (1992b), 'The rules of the game: the logic of health policy-making in France, Switzerland and Sweden'. In Steinmo et al. (1992: 57–89).

Jones, M. A. (1990), *The Australian Welfare State*. London: Allen & Unwin.

Jones Finer, C. (1999), 'Trends and developments in welfare states'. In Clasen (1999: 15–33).

Kaim-Caudle, P. R. (1973), *Comparative Social Policy and Social Security: A Ten-Country Study*. London: Robertson.

Kastrougalos, G. (1996), 'The Greek welfare state: in search of an identity', *Journal of European Social Policy* 6(1): 39–60.

Kautto, M. (2002), 'Investing in services in West European welfare states', *Journal of European Social Policy* 12(1): 53–65.

Kennett, P. (ed.) (2003), *Handbook of Comparative Social Policy*. Cheltenham: Elgar.

Kleinman, M. (2002), *A European Welfare State? European Union Social Policy in Context*. Basingstoke: Palgrave.

Kohn, M. L. (ed.) (1989), *Cross-National Research in Sociology*. Newbury Park, Calif.: Sage.

Leibfried, S. (1993), 'Towards a European welfare state?' In C. Jones (ed.), *New Perspectives on the Welfare State in Europe*. London: Routledge, 133–56.

—— and Pierson, P. (1995a), 'Semisovereign welfare states: social policy in a multitiered Europe'. In Leibfried and Pierson (1995b: 43–77).

—— —— (eds.) (1995b), *European Social Policy: Between Fragmentation and Integration*. Washington, DC: Brookings Institution.

—— —— (2000), 'Social policy'. In Wallace and Wallace (2000: 267–92).

Lewis, J. (1992) 'Gender and the development of welfare regimes', *Journal of European Social Policy* 2(3): 159–73.

MacPherson, S., and Midgley, J. (1987), *Comparative Social Policy and the Third World*. Brighton: Wheatsheaf.

Mills, C. W. (1976), *The Sociological Imagination*. Oxford: Oxford University Press.

Mitchell, D. (1991), *Income Transfers in Ten Welfare States*. Aldershot: Avebury.

Olsson, S. E. (1990), *Social Policy and the Welfare State in Sweden*. Stockholm: Arkiv.

Øyen, E. (ed.) (1990), *Comparative Methodology: Theory and Practice in International Social Research*. London: Sage.

Pierson, C. (1998), *Beyond the Welfare State? The New Political Economy of Welfare*, 2nd edn. Oxford: Polity Press.

Ragin, C. (1987), *The Comparative Method*. Berkeley: University of California Press.

—— (1991), *Issues and Alternatives in Comparative Social Research*. Leiden: Brill.

Ritter, G. A. (1986), *Social Welfare in Germany and Britain: Origins and Development*. Leamington Spa: Berg.

Rodgers, B., with Doron, A., and Jones, M. (1979), *The Study of Social Policy: A Comparative Approach*. London: Allen & Unwin.

—— Greve, J., and Morgan, J. S. (1968), *Comparative Social Administration*. London: Allen & Unwin.

Rostgaard, T., and Fridberg, T. (1998), *Caring for Children and Older People in Europe: A Comparison of European Policies and Practices*. Copenhagen: Danish National Institute of Social Research.

Shalev, M. (1983) 'The social democratic model and beyond', *Comparative Social Research* 6: 315–51.

Steinmo, S., Thelen, K., and Longstreth, F. (eds.) (1992), *Structuring Politics: Historical Institutionalism in Comparative Analysis*. Cambridge: Cambridge University Press.

Titmuss, R. M. (1974), *Social Policy*. London: Allen & Unwin.

Walker, R., Lawson, R., and Townsend, P. (1983), *Responses to Poverty in Europe*. London: Heineman.

Wallace, H., and Wallace, W. (eds.) (2000), *Policy-Making in the European Union*, 4th edn. Oxford: Oxford University Press.

Wilensky, H. L. (1975), *The Welfare State and Equality: Structural and Ideological Roots of Public Expenditure*. Berkeley: University of California Press.

FURTHER READING

For discussions about applying various methods and approaches in comparative social research generally two good sources are L. Hantrais and S. Mangen (eds.), *Cross-National Research Methods in the Social Sciences* (London: Pinter, 1996) and C. Ragin, *The Comparative Method* (Berkeley: University of California Press, 1987). More focused on comparative analysis of social policy are J. Clasen (ed.), *Comparative Social Policy: Concepts, Theories and Methods* (Oxford: Blackwell, 1999), and P. Kennett (ed.), *Handbook of Comparative Social Policy* (Cheltenham: Elgar, 2003).

Esping-Andersen's *Three Worlds of Welfare Capitalism* (Oxford: Polity Press, 1990) remains the definitive starting point for the discussion of welfare regimes and regime theory. For his response to the debate in the 1990s and a reflection on extending the analysis, see G. Esping-Andersen, *Social Foundations of Postindustrial Economies* (Oxford: Oxford University Press, 1999). For overviews of the regime theory and welfare typologies, see P. Abrahamson, 'The welfare modelling business', (*Social Policy and Administration* 33(4) (1999): 394–415) and also W. Arts and J. Gelissen, 'Three worlds of welfare capitalism or more? A state-of-the-art report', (*Journal of European Social Policy* 12(2) (2002): 137–58).

For an attempt of evaluating the relevance of the EU as influencing social policy in Europe, the collection edited by S. Leibfried and P. Pierson, *European Social Policy. Between Fragmentation and Integration* (Washington, DC: Brookings Institution, 1995) remains a classic source. For more recent reviews and debates about the development of EU social policy and the degree and the ways in which the EU influences social policy formation in member states, see L. Hantrais, *Social Policy in the European Union*, 2nd edn. (London: Palgrave, 2000); R. Geyer, *Exploring European Social Policy* (Oxford: Oxford University Press, 2000), and M. Kleinman, *A European Welfare State? European Union Social Policy in Context* (Basingstoke: Palgrave, 2002).

Comparative social policy books and monographs have found their way into the catalogues of most academic publishers of social science texts, and most national and particularly international journals more frequently carry cross-national social policy articles. The *Journal of European Social Policy* should perhaps be singled out for the space it devotes to comparative articles and the regular monitoring of social policy initiatives at EU level.

GLOSSARY

Arbeiterfrage is German and literally translates as 'the workers question'. It refers to the debate about how to socially integrate the growing mass of industrial workers in the existing social structure during the second half of the nineteenth century.

benefits in kind are social policy provisions which are administered as services (rather than cash transfers), e.g. health care, education, home helps, foster care etc.

cash transfers is an expression for all types of social policy provision which, in contrast to benefits in kind, are made as monetary support to individuals or families. In Britain (but not the US) cash transfers have become synonymous with social security.

command economies is one of many terms which describes the former communist central and east European countries, highlighting the fact that their economies did not function on a free-market basis but were to a large extent politically planned.

critical junctures are brief historical periods of intense policy debates during which changes in policy direction are likely.

de-commodification is a central concept in Esping-Andersen (1990). Welfare states (or particular social policy programmes) differ in the degree of de-commodification, i.e. the extent to which they allow benefit recipients to withstand the pressure to return to the labour market.

European Community Household Panel A large-scale comparative survey involving interviews with the same representative households and individuals over a number of years. Covering initially twelve European countries in 1994, the ECHP is under the responsibility of Eurostat, the Statistical Office of the European Communities.

European Social Model This term is defined somewhat vaguely. It has been used by the EU as an expression of common values in member states, including democracy, individual rights, free collective bargaining, equality of opportunity, and market economy as well as social welfare and social solidarity. Essentially it emphasizes that economic competitiveness and social progress are not in conflict but go hand in hand.

GDP stands for Gross Domestic Product and is an expression of the total value of goods and services produced within a given period (normally a year) within a given country. The increase (or decrease) of GDP is a conventional indicator of the growth (or decline) of the domestic economy.

ideal types are central to the sociology of Max Weber. For Weber, ideal types do not exist in empirical reality but as conceptual thought figures which highlight characteristics of phenomena to be analysed. In comparative welfare state research, Esping-Andersen's three worlds of welfare capitalism (1990) can be regarded as ideal types in the sense that the Swedish welfare state, for example, is an empirical reality which can be measured against Esping-Andersen's ideal type of a social democratic welfare state.

IMF stands for International Monetary Fund. The Fund promotes international monetary cooperation, exchange stability, and orderly exchange arrangements. It provides temporary financial assistance to countries to help ease balance of payments adjustment—and can therefore play an important role in the of social policy decision-making processes.

Luxembourg Income Study An international collaboration that collects household data from participating countries and makes it comparable and electronically available to interested researchers. It has greatly facilitated comparative analyses on poverty and income inequality.

open method of coordination (OMC) A form of policy coordination at the EU level. Agreed upon at the Lisbon Summit of March 2000, the OMC has become a means of spreading best practice within the EU and thereby achieving greater convergence. Its mechanisms include fixing guidelines at the EU level and translating them into national and regional policies by setting specific targets, adopting quantitative and qualitative indicators and benchmarks, and monitoring and evaluating policy development. The OMC has become a central tool for the European Employment Strategy and the EU 'social inclusion' process.

The Protocol on Social Policy allowed eleven EU member states to proceed in implementing their 'agreement on social policy' in 1991. As it proved impossible to reach agreement among the then twelve EU members, a solution was found in the form of an 'opt-out' for the UK from the social policy provisions of the Maastricht Treaty to which the Protocol was annexed in December 1991.

Social Dialogue A central institution in EU social policy-making after the Social Agreement of the Maastricht Treaty in 1992. It seeks to involve the **social partners** in matters of EU social policy, and requires the Commission to consult social partners before initiating policy in the area related to employment. Within the remit of the Social Dialogue, the Commission's role is to provide relevant information for policy-making and to facilitate negotiations between the social partners. Social partners can initiate and formulate policy and determine which form of legislative instrument should be chosen for policy implementation, including collective agreements rather than formal adoption by the European Council Structural Funds.

social dimension Areas of social policy competence where minimal standards are set at the EU rather than national level, e.g. in matters concerning workers residing in a member state other than their own, or moving between member states, and in labour market-related areas such as equal treatment, health and safety measures, and working conditions.

social dumping A term which has been used to denote one possible outcome of economic and political integration between the member states of the EU. It refers to companies which might decide to move to countries where wages and wage-related social contributions are low.

social partners A term is used in some European countries, and also by the EU, as a description of employer and employee (e.g. trade union) organizations. Within the EU, social partners have adopted an increasingly important role as policy initiators in the area of social policy. They are free to initiate and formulate policy and determine which form of legislative instrument should be chosen for policy implementation, including collective agreements rather than formal adoption by the European Council.

sociological imagination A term coined by C.W. Mills (1976). Mills referred to the ability of the possessor of this imagination to grasp history and biography and to place his or her daily experience into a wider structural and historical framework. A similar type of understanding and reflection can be reached by studying and comparing countries or societies.

stratification is another central concept in Esping-Andersen (1990), who refers to it as the type of social structure which welfare programmes help to promote, and employs it as a composite measurement consisting of the degree of corporatism (e.g. number of distinct public pension schemes), etatism (pension expenditure on government employees), average levels of benefit universalism and benefit equality, plus spending on means-tested social expenditure, private pensions, and private healthcare.

welfare regime Implies the existence of a certain logic of social policy provision, and specific configurations in which markets, states, and family (or households) interact in the provision of welfare in a given country.

World Bank, or International Bank for Reconstruction and Development, one of the world's largest sources of development assistance. It works with government agencies, non-governmental organizations, and the private sector to formulate assistance strategies mainly to developing countries. As a consequence, it can have a considerable impact on social policy debates.

PART FIVE

CONSEQUENCES AND OUTCOMES OF SOCIAL POLICY

21

The Impact of Social Policy

Chris Pickvance

CONTENTS

INTRODUCTION

Social policy is inextricably linked with the idea of need. In the earlier chapters in the book, and particularly in Part 4, the way in which government action has addressed need in the different fields of social policy has been detailed. In this chapter we examine some of the problems in assessing the effects of these policies.

We start by discussing what is meant by social policy, and how to measure it, and in subsequent sections we go on to examine the impact of social policy on individuals and on society as a whole.

MEASURING SOCIAL POLICY

In this chapter we are concerned only with social policy in the form of government policy. This still leaves the question of which policies belong to this category. The first issue is whether social policy should be defined narrowly as policy which seeks to ensure a minimum level of welfare for all, or to reduce inequalities in welfare, or whether broader definitions should be used. For example, is higher-education provision part of social policy, and should all policy which seeks to achieve social, as opposed to economic, goals be included? The second issue is whether we should restrict ourselves to what is conventionally labelled as social policy. A number of policies indirectly aimed at helping the poor are are not labelled social policy, such as urban and regional policies in support of activities in deprived areas. On the other hand, labels are not an accurate guide to the purposes of a policy. Social policies may have a mix of objectives and their 'social' content is less than figures of spending on social policy would suggest. While social policies can generally be defined as those policies which seek to meet welfare need irrespective of their label, we will not go into a detailed discussion of the limits of this definition. We will adopt an illustrative approach, and give some examples of the problems of assessing the impact of social policy.

Whatever choice is made about the definition of social policy, we must be able to measure the volume of social policy in order to establish its impact. To explore this deceptively simple question we examine in turn what is meant by meeting need, since this is the usual description of the purpose of social policy, and how to measure the volume of social policy.

Social policy comes in three forms:

- Regulation, i.e. the establishment of constraints on the actions of individuals and firms so as to increase social welfare. These extend from food standards to building standards.
- Taxation, i.e. the differential levying of taxes so as to protect the poorest groups or groups with a particular need. Two examples are income tax, which exempts those with the lowest income, and is set at increasing rates at higher income levels, and the lower rate of VAT on electricity and gas, which recognizes that energy represents a larger proportion of household budgets for poor households.
- Provision, where government spending is used in pursuit of social welfare aims. This takes two main forms:
    1. benefits in kind, or services, such as education or personal social services;
    2. cash benefits, such as pensions, and housing benefit.

For reasons of space this chapter will mainly be concerned with provision in the form of services. Cash benefits are considered in Chapter 12. In considering what is meant by meeting welfare needs we first examine how welfare needs can be measured.

Measuring welfare needs

The most debated issue concerns how to measure need quantitatively. There are three approaches to measuring need (see also Chapter 5). One can:

- rely on subjective judgements (e.g. by asking service users). This is often referred to as 'felt' or 'expressed' need;
- rely on expert judgements (e.g. by asking the professionals or managers involved in providing a service). This is usually referred to as 'normative need';
- assume that existing provision meets needs (e.g. by taking the current cost per capita of meeting a particular need for each person in a need category as a measure of need).

Each approach has certain drawbacks. The first is open to the possibility that people will express 'unrealistic' needs, and the second is open to the objection that professionals and managers will define needs 'generously' so as to defend the status quo or expand employment opportunities in their organizations. The third approach is optimistic since it does not allow for any shortfall in meeting need, and is also crude since it is based on numbers of people in categories rather than individuals and their needs. In practice the second and third approaches overlap, since existing provision is partly based on expert opinion: but it is also based on cost constraints. Most often, calculations of need for a category are based on the third method, by multiplying the cost of existing provision per person and demographic estimates of the number of people in the need category. For example, the need for primary education is based on the number of children of primary-school age in an area and the average education spending per child. The fact that need is often calculated in respect of those living in an area, and that there are inter-area variations in need, is central to the idea of territorial justice, discussed below.

A further useful distinction is between the **horizontal** and **vertical dimensions of need**. These are closely related to the concepts of 'breadth' and 'depth' (or 'intensity') of need. The proportion of the population in need is referred to as the 'horizontal' dimension, while the average level of need per person (and hence the level of service (or benefit) provided to each) is referred to as the 'vertical' dimension. A given sum of money could be used to provide a limited service to many or a more adequate service to a minority. The horizontal dimension thus reflects the level of **take-up**, i.e. the proportion of those eligible who actually receive the service or benefit. This is a misleading term, since it implies that the cause is ignorance, lack of effort or interest, or pride among the potential recipients, rather than any poor management or lack of effort by the providers.

The debate about measuring need tends to leave aside the more fundamental question of whether the forms in which education, healthcare, housing, or personal social services are provided do meet people's needs. Policy debates often take for granted that existing forms of provision are largely on the right lines, and that if the right groups are gaining access to a service their needs are being met. But critics would argue that existing forms of provision often represent the interests of providers rather than those of consumers, and that people's expressed needs are highly conditioned by what is available in society. The debate about whether services meet needs is therefore often about who is receiving the service, which is a different question. It starts from the expert's view rather than the recipient's view and does not ask what benefit recipients derive from the service or benefit. However, innovation in service provision does take place, both instigated by professionals ('community care' for elderly people) and by users, e.g. some forms of 'community care' demanded by disabled people.

Meeting welfare needs

It is easier to ask what is meant by 'meeting need' than to give an answer. A primary school-age child has a need for education. This is a societal value embodied in the state requirement, in the UK, that compulsory education extends from 5 to 16. If state schools were the only way of meeting this need, then we could say that the need for primary level state education in an area depended on the number of primary-age children. This leads to the **principle of uniform service provision**, which implies that uniform provision enables uniform meeting of needs. It could, for example, lead to an identical per pupil allocation of funds for primary education in all areas. But this is only one possibility.

An alternative is that in some areas, e.g. in inner cities or deprived outer council estates, a greater input of resources is needed in primary schools to compensate for the disadvantaged situation from which the children come. In other words, to provide equality of opportunity, unequal provision of a particular kind is required to meet needs equally. This is the **principle of proportional service provision**. It implies that where needs among a population group are unequal, provision should be proportional to need. (The parallel principles in the case of cash benefits are universalism and selectivity—see Chapter 12.)

The two principles may be used together. In education, for example, resources are allocated partly on a per pupil basis and partly in recognition of special situations.

Finally it is worth mentioning a closely related idea: the principle of **territorial justice**. This concept was introduced by Davies (1968; see also Boyne and Powell 1991) in recognition of the fact that most services are provided on an area basis, and need varies from one area to another. Territorial justice refers to a situation where the provision of services (health, personal social services, etc.) in different areas varies in proportion to inter-area differences in need. It should be noted that territorial justice is a relative concept since it does not concern the absolute level of provision. It could mean that need is met equally badly in different areas or that it is met equally well.

Measuring the volume of social policy

Finally, in order to assess the impact of social policy we need to be able to tell whether more or less of it is being provided. In other words we need to be able to measure the volume of social policy.

Two types of measure of social policy will be considered here: input measures and output measures. A third type of measure, an outcome measure, is discussed in the next section since it refers to the impact of social policy.

An **input measure** of a social policy is a measure of the various inputs used to provide a service. The simplest input measure is spending. This covers the wages and salaries of all the staff employed, the goods and services used, and capital spending. But what improves the overall state of welfare in a service area is how well services are directed to those in need. This depends on how much of the service is produced and how appropriately it is allocated, which in turn depends partly on the amount of spending on the items listed above and partly on the efficiency with which they are combined and managed. Another input measure is based on the number of direct providers of social services, for example, the number of GPs or teachers employed, or more commonly the number of GPs per 100,000 population or the average class size. This has the advantage that it is 'closer' to service provision than a money measure, but has the weakness that social policy outcomes depend on all inputs and how they are combined (and not only the number of direct providers).

A second type of measure is known as an **output measure** because it measures the volume of the service itself, e.g. healthcare or personal social services, and hence gets closer to the idea of a measure of the welfare produced by the service. 'Service-based measures' include the number of 'patient treatment episodes' in hospitals (since one patient may need a series of treatments) or the number of children living in local authority-run children's homes. 'Access-based measures' include the proportion of people waiting more than one year for hospital treatment. These need to be used in conjunction with service-based measures since they do not refer directly to the services received.

Obviously there is some connection between input measures and output measures, since without resources no services could be provided; but output measures have the advantage that they take account of how spending translates into the provision of services. The problem with service-based output measures is that they do not distinguish between more and less appropriate or successful service provision. For example, repeated attempts to treat the same illness would show up as increased healthcare provision even if the treatment was misdirected. The problem with access-based measures such as waiting-list length, which is popular with politicians, is that they assume that people's need for the service is equal. In fact the need for hospital treatment varies in urgency, and overall welfare may be better served by the proportional than by the uniform principle of provision, i.e. by giving priority in treatment to those with the most urgent need even if they have not waited very long.

Since it would make little sense to spend more on or provide more of a service irrespective of the need for it, both input and output measures are usually calculated *for a region or district* and are considered in conjunction with the need for treatment *in that area*. In other words, territorial justice is sought.

It should be noted that all of the measures (sometimes called 'performance measures' because they are a way of judging welfare providers comparatively) have unintended consequences. In particular, their introduction is likely to have an effect on how the service is organized, how services are provided, and how statistics are collected. In particular, service-providing organizations are likely to take steps to boost their performance on the measures on which they are assessed, possibly by worsening their performance on activities that are not assessed. For example, if hospitals are judged by the length of waiting lists for in-patient treatment but not by waits for outpatient treatment, they may be tempted to shift resources into the measured activity. Whether there is a net benefit to patients is debatable.

In general the problem with these measures is that they are generated by provider organizations and do not necessarily measure what service recipients consider important. For example, if the 'waiting time' for an operation is calculated from the time when the decision is made that a patient needs the operation, this ignores the time elapsing between the patient making initial contact and receiving the decision. Also, if a patient has to be seen by a second consultant the measure of 'time on the waiting list' starts again.

Thus it can be seen that the assumption that more spending on a social policy means more welfare turns out to be questionable. Everything depends on how the spending is used, how it is allocated between areas, how it is targeted on groups in need, and how far measures of performance distort the way organizations work.

In the case of social policies which take the form of cash benefits, input measures (spending) are usually used. The main limitation of *total* spending measures of cash benefits is that they are a product of the numbers receiving the benefit (which depends on the number eligible and the level of take-up) and the level of the benefit. A rising trend in spending on a cash benefit may be because of an increase in claimants rather than because of an increase in generosity of benefit levels. Ideally, therefore, both take-up and benefit level need to be known. In contrast, output measures are not generally used. One reason is that cash benefits are used directly by those receiving them to obtain increased welfare. There is no professional involvement. In theory one could examine whether inputs in the form of cash benefits are converted into a welfare 'output' by the recipient, or whether they are 'diverted' to some other purpose. The possibility that cash benefits are not translated by their recipients into welfare outputs leads to the provision of benefits in a non-transferable form (as in the US system of food stamps) or the payment of cash directly to the provider of welfare (as in the UK, when housing benefit is paid direct to landlords).

In sum, both input and output measures of social policies are either conceptually debatable or difficult to apply in practice, and hence need to be treated with caution.

MEASURING THE IMPACT OF SOCIAL POLICY

The question of how to establish the impact of social policy is a particular case of the general issue of how to identify cause–effect relations. This is a thorny problem in all social scientific work. There are two main reasons for this. First, society is complex and many possible causes operate simultaneously, which makes it difficult to identify the effect of a single cause (or, rather, set of causes) such as a social policy. For example the number of people experiencing poverty depends on the effectiveness of social policy, but also on demographic and labour market processes (such as birth rates, household formation and dissolution rates, migration rates, job availability, and wage levels). Second, social science has to find a path through the thicket of claims made by politicians, officials, and others about the effect of social policy. These claims may be more intended to take credit and avoid blame than to make a careful assessment.

To claim that social policy has had an impact of some type, three conditions must be met:

- The social policy must occur before the effect claimed for it. This is perhaps too obvious to need stating. But it is not uncommon for success to be claimed for a new policy on the basis of trends which had been in existence before it was introduced.
- Variations in the policy must be associated with variations in the claimed effect. This is the familiar point that if two things are causally related they will vary together. However, the reverse is not true. Events or processes which occur together or rise and fall over time together are not necessarily linked by cause–effect relations. Causation is more than correlation. This is not an easy condition to meet, since the presence of multiple causes means that cause–effect relations may be hard to disentangle.
- The nature of the causal process(es) linking the policy with its claimed effect must be identified or hypothesized. This requirement is also difficult to meet. First, causal connections are not directly observable but are matters of inference. Writers belonging to different theoretical schools disagree both about what causal connections are likely to exist and about what evidence would establish that they do. Debates about causal connections cannot be settled by an 'appeal to the facts' because of the disagreement about which 'facts' are relevant. Second, as mentioned above, many causes are in operation and they may be hard to identify and separate. Comparison with other countries, or with the same country in the past, may be helpful, but only if it is assumed that there are common processes operating and no significant differences—a matter which again may be debated between theoretical schools. Third, we are only aware of some of the causes which operate. Scientific progress involves identifying new causal links and improving our understanding of policy impact.

These complexities can be illustrated when we examine what are known as **outcome measures** of social policy because they are believed to measures the result of the policy. Examples are the level of morbidity (ill health) in an area, school examination results, or the life expectation of elderly people receiving 'community care'. The attraction of this type of measure is that it comes closest to being an indicator of impact in the sense of additional welfare due to social policy. The drawback of such measures is that that they measure the outcome of a large number of processes of which the social policy of interest is only one. (The term 'outcome measure' is thus a misnomer.) For example, school exam results reflect the ability of children admitted to a school and the extent of parental support, as well as the efforts of the school; and morbidity reflects nutrition, living and working conditions, and environmental effects as well as healthcare. Unless the causal influence of these processes can be taken into account the impact of a social policy cannot be identified. A further issue concerns the timing of outcome measures. While in some cases an immediate measure is appropriate, in others, e.g. preventive healthcare, outcomes need to be measured over a longer period. Social policy can also have wider impacts on society, as shown later in the chapter.

Two more general points about assessing the impact of social policy must be made. First, it is important to distinguish between the aims and the effects of a social policy.

The aims of a policy refer to the intentions of policy-makers or of those involved in implementing the policy. These may themselves conflict and/or change over time. In some cases they are even modified retrospectively in the light of changing government priorities. Hence, although every policy has aims there is a degree of flexibility about them which makes them an unstable yardstick by which to judge the success of a policy. In our case this does not matter, since we are concerned with the effects of social policy, and aims are distinct from effects.[1] However in practice it is difficult to avoid some reference to aims. Secondly, there is no necessary connection between pressure groups or lobbies who are influential in bringing a policy into existence and the effects of the policy. One cannot say that because a pressure group was influential that the population category the group is fighting on behalf of is the main beneficiary. Policies rarely have single aims: they may be the result of pressure from multiple sources outside government and as they pass through the government machine they may be shaped by further pressures. Moreover, they can have unintended consequences. The effects of a policy can only be assessed in the way indicated above.

In sum, there are very considerable problems in establishing the effects of social policy, and we need to pay attention to the methods used by those who claim to have identified their effects. Hence any claims made about the impact of social policy need to be regarded with caution.

THE IMPACT OF SOCIAL POLICY ON INDIVIDUAL HOUSEHOLDS

In this section we present analyses of the impact of one social policy, healthcare, on individual households, and of the combined impact of several services on individuals using the '**social wage**' approach.

First, it is useful to have a general picture of the pattern of spending on social policy. The shares of social policy spending going on services and on cash benefits are roughly equal. In 2000/1 public spending on health accounted for 5.5 per cent of GDP, on education 5.1 per cent, on personal social services 1.4 per cent, and on housing 0.3 per cent (excluding housing benefits which account for 1.3 per cent). Spending on cash benefits including housing benefits amounted to 11.0 per cent of GDP (HM Treasury 2002: tables 3.5 and 3.6).

Second, it is helpful to list the different elements which may account for the current level of social policy spending:

- the extent of horizontal need, i.e. to provide the service or benefit to more or less people;

[1] There are various reasons why policy aims may not be achieved: the level of funding may be inadequate; people may respond to the policy in unexpected ways (e.g. people may fail to take up a benefit because it is felt to be stigmatizing; elderly people may divest themselves of assets in order to be eligible for state support for their housing); or countervailing processes are present (e.g. low-income households who need home improvement grants most are less likely to take them up if they cover only part of the cost of the work needed).

- the extent of vertical need, i.e. to provide lower or higher levels of service or cash benefit according to the needs of the recipient;
- cost: this reflects salary levels, and other costs which vary between parts of the country;
- efficiency: the more efficient the provision the more that can be provided for a given level of spending.

The main difficulty of assessing the impact of social policy from spending figures is to assess the roles of these four elements.

- Horizontal need is easy to estimate in some cases (e.g. the number of school-age children) but difficult in others (e.g. the number entitled to mobility allowance, which depends on a doctor's assessment).
- Vertical need is more difficult to estimate because it implies that different people within a need category have different needs (e.g. different children have different intensities of need).
- If salary costs rise, any increase in spending may not translate into increased service provision, so this is a crucial element. Inflation can be taken into account in either of two ways. Actual spending each year is recorded in 'money terms' or 'current prices' and therefore will rise simply because of inflation. If allowance is made for the rise in the general price level (i.e. for the increase in prices for *all* goods and services) the result is a figure referred to as **real spending**. Alternatively, if allowance is made for the rise in prices of those goods and services in the sector concerned (e.g. health or education) the result is referred to as 'volume terms spending' or **volume spending**. If the prices of the goods and services bought with social policy spending rose at the same rate as prices generally, real spending and volume spending would be identical. In practice the price of goods and services purchased with most types of social policy spending goes up relatively faster than the general rate of inflation.[2] Spending in 'real terms' or 'real spending' thus underestimates the rate of inflation in the field of social policy and overestimates the value of social policy inputs. 'Volume spending' allows for inflation experienced in the social services but understates the value of social policy inputs, since it assumes that if the number of, say, teachers remains the same their productivity remains the same. In practice, through the use of computers or improved management, these teachers may become more productive. Neither real nor volume spending is a perfect measure of inputs, and Sefton (1997) suggests that the truth lies somewhere between them.

[2] This is known as the 'relative price effect', and occurs because employees are a crucial part of the service being provided in the social policy sphere and hence the chance of saving money by substituting employees by machines is very limited. In contrast in manufacturing industry this option is normal. The consumer does not mind if higher wages lead employers to replace workers by machines. Indeed, the involvement of robots becomes a selling point in the marketing of cars. There is no sign of this happening in the social policy field: the caring quality of nurses or the ability to inspire of teachers cannot be replaced by machines. It is true that computers are heavily used in education and in administration in all areas of social policy, but they only partly save money, since they require new staff to be employed and may raise the quality of the service.

- Lastly, efficiency is the most difficult element to measure. It relates to the conversion of inputs into outputs and is therefore affected by the uncertainties surrounding both of these measures.

The impact of healthcare on individual households

We now examine the impact of social policy on individual households by using the example of healthcare.

Health is the largest service in terms of public spending. Although 10 per cent of the population is covered by private health insurance, this is used mainly for elective surgery, and private expenditure on healthcare accounts for less than 3 per cent of public health care costs (Le Grand and Vizard 1998: 98). Public spending on healthcare is therefore the dominant form of healthcare. The overall aim of health policy is to improve the nation's health. Secondary aims are to achieve greater equity between groups and places, to use resources efficiently, and to be responsive to changes in need and in medical knowledge. The majority of spending is on hospital care.

What is the volume of healthcare being provided and what is its impact? The simplest input measure of healthcare is health spending. In general, increased spending can only be taken to mean that need is being better met (either horizontally or vertically) if we can be sure:

- that the need for the service has not increased;
- that costs have not gone up so that the same spending buys less of the service. Hence the need to look at real and volume spending;
- that efficiency, i.e. the conversion of inputs into outputs, has not fallen.

If need has increased, costs have risen, or efficiency has fallen, higher spending will be needed to meet need at the same level.

Between 1981 and 1995 real spending on the National Health Service rose 55 per cent, but volume spending rose only 28 per cent (Le Grand and Vizard 1998: table 4.1).[3] But how did this increase in inputs match the change in needs? A demographically based estimate of needs suggests that over the 1981–95 period a 10 per cent increase was needed simply to meet the greater demands on healthcare due to people living longer (Le Grand and Vizard 1998: table 4.4) Hence volume spending on health inputs increased by about 1.8 per cent per year faster than needs in this period.

How did these inputs vary by region and by social group? The regional distribution of real health spending per capita on all items (e.g. including both hospitals and primary care provided by GPs) between 1985 and 1994 shows an increase in the spread between regions: the 'coefficient of variation', a statistical measure of spread between regions, increased from 0.103 to 0.143 (Le Grand and Vizard 1998: table 4.8). No data are available to compare this with the changing regional distribution of need for healthcare. But Le Grand and Vizard conclude that 'unless there was also a growing and matching inequality in need, this suggests that regional inequalities may be increasing' (1998: 104).

[3] In places my classification of services as inputs or outputs or my interpretation of the data diverges from that in Glennerster and Hills (1998).

In other words, territorial injustice in this respect is increasing. This trend is despite an explicit policy introduced in 1976, following the Resource Allocation Working Party, aimed at reducing regional inequalities.

Another measure of variation of inputs by region, the number of GPs per 100,000 population, shows that here too regional variation increased between 1975 and 1995. Thus while the average number of GPs per 100,000 in the UK rose from 48 to 61, it ranged from 43 (Trent) to 58 (Scotland) in 1975, and from 53 (North Western) to 76 (in Scotland) in 1995 (Le Grand and Vizard 1998: table 4.9).

The variation in input measures of health services used by different social groups has been studied but while research in the 1970s showed that professionals and managers received 40 per cent higher spending per ill person than the semi- and unskilled, later studies found no such bias (quoted in Le Grand and Vizard 1998: 107).

Thus while, overall, inputs may have increased faster than needs, the distribution of these inputs between regions implies considerable and possibly widening territorial injustice. As a result the impact of health service provision on health is likely to have been less than it could have been.

Turning to output measures of healthcare, two types are available: measures of the services received by different social groups, and access-based measures. In the case of the former, studies of the use of services suggest that poorer groups visit GP surgeries more than better-off groups (assuming their need is reflected in their age distribution) and are more often hospital inpatients, whereas better-off groups phone their GPs more and make more use of outpatient treatment (Evandrou, referred to in Le Grand and Vizard 1998: 107). On the other hand, South Asians and Caribbeans make less use of both inpatient and outpatient services than their needs would suggest.

As far as access-based measures are concerned, waiting lists for inpatient treatment grew from 628,000 in 1981 to 729,000 in 1991, and for all treatment from 948,000 in 1991 to 1,164,000 in 1997 (Le Grand and Vizard 1998: 99). However, the proportion waiting over one year fell from 24 per cent in 1988 to 1 per cent in 1996 (Le Grand and Vizard 1998: table 4.6). The latter reflects the targeting of policy to reduce waiting times. In 2001, in the face of continuing difficulties in reducing waiting lists, the Secretary of State for Health announced that waiting list lengths would no longer be used as targets. Instead, by 2005 the government aimed to reduce the maximum time spent on waiting lists to six months.

What was the impact of these healthcare inputs and outputs on health? The most commonly used outcome measures are mortality and morbidity rates. There is conflicting evidence about mortality rates. The life expectation for men and women, allowing for differences in the size of each age cohort, increased from 70.4 to 71.5 between 1974 and 1994, and the male–female gap narrowed slightly. On the other hand, class differences for males dying between 20 and 64 have increased: unskilled workers in this age range were 1.8 times more likely to die than professionals in 1970/2 but 2.9 times more likely to do so by 1991/3 (Le Grand and Vizard 1998: table 4.10).

Evidence on morbidity shows an increase in self-reported chronic and acute illness between 1974 and 1994, even when the effect of the ageing population is taken into account. This may be linked with the increase in waiting lists mentioned earlier. But class differences in chronic and acute illness have not increased over time (Le Grand and Vizard 1998: fig. 4.2 and table 4.12).

As mentioned earlier, these outcomes reflect many other processes besides the public spending on health. However, if inputs have indeed risen faster than needs in total, then it is likely that it is the maldistribution of inputs and outputs (such as access to hospital and GP care) between need categories (social or spatial) which explains why the effect on morbidity has not been greater. On the other hand, non-health service factors such as lifestyles, and domestic, work, and environmental situations, may have counteracted the positive effects of healthcare provision.

The impact of all services: the 'social wage' approach

We now turn to an attempt to make a wider assessment of the impact of social policy by looking at three services.

Debates about the overall impact of social policy have centred around two propositions. The first is that social policy helps the poor, and this is because it was set up to do so and because it achieves its aims. The second is that social policy benefits the middle class disproportionately because the middle class is well informed, well organized, and well connected, and (a) ensures the services it benefits from are provided and well funded and (b) is efficient in taking advantage of the best services that are available. This claim was advanced by Le Grand (1982), who argued that there had been a middle-class 'capture' of the welfare state, preventing it from realizing its aims.

One way to examine this type of broad argument is to assume that the value of the services provided is equal to the cost of providing them and then to measure how these costs are distributed among different social groups. This involves:

- establishing the total cost of a particular service;
- subtracting that part which cannot be allocated to households;
- establishing what use is made of this service by different social groups or categories;
- breaking down the cost of the service among groups in proportion to their usage of it.

This approach is known as the 'social wage' approach since it sees services (along with payments in kind) as increasing people's welfare in the same way as the spending power afforded by a wage. The approach allows us to translate services into quantitative terms and see who receives most and who least. However, it does have disadvantages. It is based on data on expenditure and therefore suffers from the defects of input measures mentioned earlier. Also, since different households have different levels of need, a calculation of who benefits is only an approximate answer to the more interesting question 'who benefits and was it in proportion to need?' Ideally we need to take into account different levels of need related to age, gender, ethnicity, etc. The approach thus ignores questions of inefficiency and poor targeting (by need group and spatially), inappropriate service provision, needs which are unmet, etc.[4]

[4] A further question of method concerns the unit of measurement. If the household is chosen it means that large and small households are equated, and the fact that the value of benefits and services is split between all the members of the household is not allowed for. In 1993 the average household size was highest in the

Table 21.1 Distribution of value (£ per person) of health, education, and housing services by income quintile, 1979, in 2000/2001 prices

	Health	Education	Housing	Total
Bottom	632	430	203	1,265
2nd	501	573	167	1,241
3rd	418	585	155	1,158
4th	406	501	119	1,026
Top	406	394	84	883
All	473	496	146	1,115

Source for Tables 21.1–21.5: data supplied by Tom Sefton—see footnote 5.

A recent publication by Sefton (2002) allows us to address the question of who gained more and less from spending on three social services over the whole 1979–2000/1 period. Tables 21.1–21.5 show the levels of spending per person on the three services, healthcare, education, and housing[5] for individuals in the five **income quintiles** in successive years. The figures in the tables have all been adjusted to 2000/1 prices and are therefore comparable. Table 21.6 summarizes the distribution between quintiles, based on the ratio of service spending received by the lowest quintile divided by the spending received by the highest quintile. This ratio would be 1 if the richest quintile received the same amount as the poorest, and above 1 if the poorest quintile received more than the richest.

The tables can be read in several ways. First, the figure for all services and all income groups shows that over the period there has been a 47.4 per cent real increase in spending per individual, from £1,115 to £1,644, on all these services. This is a little less than the real growth of GDP. Secondly we can see that the total spending on health per person has risen fastest (£473 to £790, 67 per cent) followed by education (£496 to £668, 34.7 per cent) and housing (£146 to £186, 27.4 per cent).

Thirdly, Table 21.6 shows that for all three services the ratio of spending received by the poorest quintile to the share received by the richest quintile moves up from 1.43 in

lowest-income quintile and lowest in the highest-income quintile, and the second income quintile had the largest share of elderly people. Hence if the household is the unit the two lowest-income quintiles need more than 20 per cent each of the value of services and benefits. If the individual is chosen as the unit of measurement, this problem is avoided, but the savings made when people live with others is also ignored.

[5] Housing excludes housing benefit and mortgage interest tax relief. It is mainly made up of the discounts received by tenants buying their council housing and subsidies to social housing rents (economic rent 'less gross rent'. Higher-education spending is allocated to parents of students. I would like to acknowledge the kindness of Tom Sefton, Centre for Analysis of Social Exclusion, London School of Economics, in making these tables available to me. They are the tables on which the bar charts in fig. 6 in his report (Sefton 2002) are based, but are not included in the report.

Table 21.2 Distribution of value (£ per person) of health, education, and housing services by income quintile, 1987, in 2000/2001 prices

Income quintile	Health	Education	Housing	Total
Bottom	656	597	310	1,563
2nd	632	525	179	1,337
3rd	525	597	143	1,265
4th	477	525	95	1,098
Top	406	442	60	907
All	539	537	158	1,234

Table 21.3 Distribution of value (£ per person) of health, education, and housing services by income quintile, 1993, in 2000/2001 prices

Income quintile	Health	Education	Housing	Total
Bottom	692	740	239	1,671
2nd	788	609	239	1,635
3rd	668	656	131	1,456
4th	561	561	84	1,205
Top	513	489	24	1,026
All	644	611	143	1,399

Table 21.4 Distribution of value (£ per person) of health, education, and housing services by income quintile, 1996/7, in 2000/2001 prices

Income quintile	Health	Education	Housing	Total
Bottom	747	748	267	1,762
2nd	860	609	277	1,746
3rd	708	667	145	1,420
4th	574	566	101	1,241
Top	479	507	40	1,026
All	674	619	166	1,459

Table 21.5 Distribution of value (£ per person) of health, education, and housing services by income quintile, 2000/2001, in 2000/2001 prices

Income quintile	Health	Education	Housing	Total
Bottom	919	819	292	2,030
2nd	1,051	719	262	2,032
3rd	807	671	194	1,672
4th	628	637	134	1,399
Top	545	493	50	1,088
All	790	668	186	1,644

Table 21.6 Ratio of share of spending on services received by bottom quintile divided by share received by top quintile

Income quintile	Health	Education	Housing	Total
1979	1.56	1.09	2.42	1.43
1987	1.62	1.35	5.17	1.72
1993	1.35	1.51	9.96	1.63
1996/7	1.56	1.48	6.68	1.72
2000/1	1.69	1.66	5.84	1.86

Source: calculated from Tables 21.1–21.5.

1979 from to 1.86 in 2000/1. This table also allows the effects of changes of government to be seen. It shows that the 1979–87 Conservative governments achieved a considerable change in pro-poor direction, but in the next decade there was no further improvement. The Labour government, however, added to the pro-poor direction of policy. Interestingly in health the change on the pro-poor direction is least marked (1.56 in 1979 to 1.69 in 2000/1) with no net change over the whole Conservative period of office. In education the change is much greater and occurs in every single period shown. Finally, in housing the general level of pro-poor policy is strong throughout the period, and peaks in 1993.

To make sense of these patterns and changes it is necessary to look at their components. This is done at length in Sefton (2002). The shares received by particular income groups reflect their need for the service and their use of it. The large size of the pro-poor effect of housing spending is because it refers to subsidies to social housing only. By contrast, education and healthcare are used by all income groups. Widening participation in higher education has the effect of making education spending more pro-poor, as does reliance by higher income groups on private healthcare. There is also evidence that the next to lowest income group uses health care more than the lowest quintile, which may explain why this quintile receives the most health care spending in tables 21.3–21.5.

The relation between age and income plays a key part since 'lower income groups contain a high proportion of children and pensioners, who are the most intensive users of welfare services' (Sefton 2002: 9). The fact that children benefit most from education and older people receive most healthcare therefore also means that lower income groups receive more of these two services. However, Sefton shows that if the age effect is allowed for there is still a net pro-poor effect in the distribution of the social wage in 1996/7 and 2000/1.

At the end of this discussion of the impact of social policy on households and individuals we can see that the easier data to present are on real and volume spending. Information on efficiency has rarely been referred to and is a source of potential error. However, the major difficulty in estimating the impact of social policy lies in measuring the scope and intensity of need. The eagle-eyed reader will have noticed that statements about need have usually been either statements attributed to unidentified experts or assumptions based on demographic trends which assume that provision at some time in the past was meeting need adequately. This is frustrating given the scale of spending on social policy and the importance of need to measures of the outcome of this spending.

THE IMPACT OF SOCIAL POLICY ON SOCIETY

We now consider the wider social impacts of social policy. This is a very large field and we shall be selective.[6] We examine the following arguments:

- that social policy increases social stability; and
- that social policy undermines the market mechanism for allocating resources.

One preliminary point needs to be made. This is that the discussion of wider effects encounters even more problems of identifying cause–effect relations than our discussion of the impact of social policy on different social groups. One reason for this is that the causal links in question relate to broader and more nebulous concepts like 'social stability'. The other reason is that in saying that social policy has a wider impact of a particular type, a comparison has to be made with a hypothetical situation in which that social policy was absent, or took a different form—what is known as the 'counterfactual' because it is something that did not happen! This can be done by comparing the UK today either with the UK previously, when the social policy was absent or different in form, or with other advanced capitalist societies. The problem in the first case is to allow for the other changes which will have occurred since the policy was introduced or

[6] For a more extensive discussion of the societal impacts of social policy see George and Wilding (1984: ch. 4–7). The effects of social policy on the labour force and particularly on women's employment are also very significant.

changed, and in the second to allow for the other relevant differences between the UK and the other societies chosen. These two difficulties mean that there is inevitably greater reliance on the plausibility of the causal inference, and this means that writers of different theoretical persuasions will tend to advance their own interpretations of the wider impact of social policy. Thus the reader needs to be particularly cautious about accepting claims made about the wider impacts of social policy.

Social policy and social stability

One of the most widely held views about social policy is that it contributes to the stability of society. This belief has often been used by politicians and reformers in advocating social policy measures. They have asserted that by introducing reforms social disorder or even revolution would be avoided. The clear message is that social policy has a stabilizing effect. But advocates of reform have a vested interest and are likely to adopt whatever arguments they think will help win support for their case. The fact that claims are made that social policy has a stabilizing effect does not mean that such effects actually exist. To establish whether they do or not, we need to look beyond the statements of interested parties. We examine the three elements of the claim that social policy has a stabilizing effect: that it reduces the number of deprivations, that it individualizes social problems, and that it reduces conflict.

1. Social policy reduces the number of deprivations

Social policy undoubtedly averts or ameliorates some of the situations which arose before it existed. Cash benefits and services are available to a wide variety of groups in need. Even allowing for a certain degree of mis-targeting, incomplete take-up, stigmatization, inappropriate services, and cash benefits which are too low in value, it is undeniable that social policy has the effect of reducing the level of deprivation. However, social policy also has a second effect: to increase the number of deprivations and increase the demands made for policy measures. This is because the number of deprivations is not fixed, but is subject to a 'demonstration effect' by which the success of social policy measures in one sphere creates pressure for further intervention in the same or other spheres. For example, the precedent of state intervention in the form of council housing led to subsequent pressure on government to widen the responsibilities of councils to include provision for homeless people. Paradoxically, therefore, social policy can *increase* the number of deprivations which are labelled as social problems, as well as averting or lessening the impact of such problems through remedial action.

2. Social policy individualizes social problems

Typically the individualized mode of dealing with problems in the social policy sphere leads people to experience deprivations as individuals. For example, if a particular job or work place is hazardous the individual workers may be treated by health services as individuals and no attempt made to discover the common cause of their symptoms. Likewise, if there is a recession, the consequent job losses lead individuals into unemployment and poverty, and they are treated as individuals by the agencies they contact in order to obtain social security benefits and services. The common source of their situation is eclipsed from view. In the case of benefits to which not all are entitled there is a stronger sense of fragmentation. Clearly the various social services are set up in a way which emphasizes individual need and the provision of services and benefits to meet it, rather than the common sources which give rise to these needs. This has an isolating or fragmenting effect, and reduces the probability of group action among those involved. However this does not rule it out altogether. The effectiveness of the movement of disabled people is a case in point (Campbell and Oliver 1996).

3. Less deprivation means less conflict and greater social stability.

The third argument is that social policy, by reducing the number of deprivations and individualizing social problems, makes it less likely that groups will demand change and this strengthens social stability.

The connection between deprivation and social instability is a complex one. Every society generates a wide variety of situations ranging from ill-health to unemployment and poverty. There are three factors which determine whether they lead to conflict. First, people's expectations must be high enough to regard them as deprivations. Second, people must feel they are deprivations that can be changed, rather than that they are unalterable. Third, people must believe that the government or other agency is capable of responding to group action.

But is it correct to assume that, in the absence of social policy, deprived groups would engage in social conflict? In fact this is debatable. Research on social movements suggests that the most deprived groups typically lack confidence in themselves and are much less likely to engage in collective action than middle-class groups which are not deprived but have high expectations and are effective in mobilizing themselves (Neidhardt and Rucht 1991).

The further question of whether, if conflict occurs, it is a source of instability is a large one. There are various views about how stable advanced capitalist societies are and what are the main sources of division within them. Marxist writers argue that capitalist–worker conflicts have the greatest potential to destabilize society, and that conflicts around consumption issues such as social services are of secondary importance. Others would argue that the consumption sphere is as least as, if not more, important as a source of conflict, and that consumption-based conflicts can be just as destabilizing for society. For example, for owner-occupiers housing is a large investment and the largest monthly expenditure, and hence could generate strong conflicts. Taking the two views together one might suggest that if the lines of division in consumption conflicts coincide with those in work-based conflicts there is a greater potential for instability, but where consumption divisions cross-cut production divisions the effect is to mitigate the strength of conflict.

To explore these ideas Dunleavy and Husbands interviewed a sample of people about their voting in the 1983 general election. This revealed that within each social class, council tenants were more likely vote Labour and home-owners to vote Conservative, with those in other tenures having an intermediate position (Dunleavy and Husbands 1985: table 6.13). This made it clear that housing tenure had an association with voting over and above the relation between class and voting. They went on to reason that dependence on public transport or access to a private car might also affect voting. They found that those without a car were least likely to vote Conservative, those with one car more likely, and those with two or more cars most likely, and that this was true within each class category (table 6.14). These two findings are consistent with the idea that housing and transport consumption do generate different interests (as measured by voting), though this may not lead to conflict. Other writers argue that prior values condition both voting and consumption choices (Heath et al. 1985: 44–57).

Hence the consumption sphere is a source of different interests as well as of common interests. Whether consumption-based interests give rise to conflict depends on how far consumption divisions coincide with work-based divisions. Conflict also depends on the types of demand made by those with common interests. One argument is that demands which challenge the way society is organized have a greater destabilizing potential than those which do not. However, in practice this potential is not realized, since only small minorities make radical demands. This leads to a second view that it is demands which do not challenge society but which have considerable support which give rise to the most conflict, and that these can be destabilizing although they are not demands for radical change. This could be seen in trade union demands in the UK in the late 1970s. Lastly the existence of conflict and whether it has destabilizing effects also depends on the institutions available for reaching compromise. Compared to France, where direct and often violent action is quite usual, in the UK government is relatively open and this encourages negotiation and the channelling of protest into peaceful and less destabilizing forms.

In sum, it has been argued that the likelihood (a) that deprived individuals will engage in collective action and conflict and (b) that any action will be destabilizing is much less than often suggested. In the absence of social policy most deprivations would lead to resignation rather than collective action, and any conflict would not necessarily be destabilizing. It follows that insofar as it reduces deprivation, social policy increases social stability only to a limited extent, contrary to what is often claimed.

We have thus suggested that social policy (a) both expands and reduces deprivations, (b) encourages a view of social problems as something experienced individually, and (c) to a limited extent reduces the amount of collective action that would be taken by deprived groups. It can thus be concluded that social policy on balance helps social stability, but that it encourages forces in both directions.

Social policy and the market mechanism

A second argument about the wider impact of social policy is that it introduces a system of allocating resources which is in contradiction with the market mechanism, and that this is threatening in a capitalist type of society.

The starting point is the idea that markets are the central means of allocating resources in capitalist societies. They allow people to obtain resources according to their ability to pay the current price. This is held to be an efficient mechanism because the price people are willing to pay is taken to be a measure of the value they give to that resource: if they value it more highly they will be willing to pay more for it. Hence the market is an efficient way for society to allocate resources between individuals, and an efficient way to enable individuals to choose between different items of spending. This leads to the idea that the market mechanism provides people with an incentive to earn more so that they can obtain more resources. In all these respects, therefore, the market mechanism is held to be socially beneficial.

By contrast, the allocation of services and cash benefits according to need has no place for ability to pay as a principle. Allocation by need is held to be more socially efficient because need is not necessarily indicated by ability to pay, and groups with low incomes would consume less than they need if the market mechanism were the only one operating. Instead, need-based allocation relies on expert judgements about what levels of need people have, and this is claimed to lead to a more efficient allocation of resources. Critics, however, would say that allocation according to need is unsatisfactory because:

- Expert opinion is not reliable due to experts' self-interest arising from their role in the process of provision.
- It leads to both overconsumption and overproduction because price does not act as a rationing device to indicate people's preferences.
- It weakens the motivation to work, since services and cash benefits are not allocated according to effort.

In appearance, therefore, social policy introduces a principle of allocation which threatens the market principle which is central to the operation of capitalism. Let us examine the arguments for and against.

The arguments for the idea that social policy is incompatible with the market principle are as follows:

- Services and cash benefits in social policy are allocated according to need, not ability to pay. In practice these services and benefits do not meet need adequately, but that does not alter the fact that the principle is one of needs-based allocation. In the case of housing, on the other hand, policy is concerned with political goals as much as with meeting need (see Chapter 17). The implication is that people whose need is less than their ability to pay receive more than they would receive if social policy did not exist and they had to rely on their wages to purchase education and healthcare. The market principle would lead to the callous view that these groups deserve less and are over-consuming. But such a view is so extreme that it would be difficult to find a serious advocate for it. This suggests that the market principle of allocation is combined in capitalism with values which limit its application.
- A second argument is that social policy weakens the incentive to work, and is thus threatening to market allocation. This argument is applied particularly to cash benefits paid to those without work and looking for work. This argument would be most convincing if all allocation was according to need, rather than only social policy measures. In fact, as long as most people are reliant on wages for their income the incentive to work is considerable. In the case of benefits paid to unemployed people, it is claimed that if benefits are a high percentage of the wages people receive when in work they will be discouraged from finding employment. But the failure of benefit levels to keep pace with wages means that the proportion of unemployed people who would be discouraged from taking employment by the level of benefits is declining continuously.

The arguments that need-based allocation does not undermine market allocation are as follows:

- The most challenging argument is that market allocation is not as efficient in resource allocation or as crucial to motivation as is claimed. One example would be to ask whether in the USA, where total spending on healthcare is much higher as a share of GNP than in the UK and mostly takes place through market allocation (e.g. private health insurance), this is a more efficient allocation of resources. Critics would argue that the 'market' in healthcare in the USA leads to over-treatment, as hospitals and doctors are paid by insurance companies rather than patients directly. In contrast, advocates of need-based allocation in the UK would say that it discourages over-consumption of health services because of the public spending constraints applying to it.
- The second argument complements the preceding one. It is that need-based allocation is actually indispensable in advanced capitalist societies. Social policy spending helps to create a productive (i.e. healthy, educated, and disciplined) labour force, and to shield the private sector from direct responsibility for workers who are made redundant. It also embodies values about minimum welfare levels and preferences for greater equality, which are social values which exist within advanced capitalist societies but which cannot be achieved by the market principle.

This is part of a broader view about the role of the public sector in capitalist societies. The dominant idea is that public spending is unproductive and parasitic on the private sector because it is a burden on taxes which could either be cut or used to benefit the private sector directly. But this is a very one-sided view. Public sector employment is 23 per cent of the total and generates income tax itself, and the private sector is highly dependent on public spending, e.g. on infrastructure, industrial support, public sector orders, loan guarantees for exports, and bail-outs in case of emergency. This suggests that the private and public sectors are interdependent. The productivity of one depends on the other. Hence the indispensability of need-based allocation in capitalist societies.

We would therefore suggest that social policy introduces a principle of allocation which is complementary rather than contradictory with market allocation, as long as values favouring the achievement of minimum levels of welfare for all and some steps towards equality are prevalent in society. If need-based allocation were to become dominant rather than subordinate as a principle, that would undermine the functioning of capitalism. But this is not the case.

CONCLUSION

The two wider impacts of social policy we have discussed show that it contributes to social stability, and that it is not threatening to capitalism despite being based on a principle which contradicts the market principle. Earlier, when looking at the impact on individuals and households, we concluded that on balance social policy distribution is pro-poor, but we found it difficult to be clear about the degree to which social policy raises social welfare, for some people absolutely, or reduces inequality because initial definitions of needs are so varied and so open to question and judgement.

REFERENCES

Boyne, G., and Powell, M. (1991), 'Territorial justice: a review of theory and evidence', *Political Geography* 10: 263–281.

Campbell, J., and Oliver, M. (1996), *Disability Politics*. London: Routledge.

Davies, B. P. (1968), *Social Needs and Resources in Social Services*. London: Michael Joseph.

Dunleavy, P., and Husbands, C. T. (1985), *British Democracy at the Crossroads*. London: Allen & Unwin.

George, V., and Wilding, P. (1984), *The Impact of Social Policy*. London: Routledge.

Glennerster, H., and Hills, J. (eds.) (1998), *The State of Welfare*, 2nd edn. Oxford: Oxford University Press.

Heath, A., Jowell, R., and Curtice, J. (1985), *How Britain Votes*. Oxford: Pergamon.

HM Treasury (2002), *Public Expenditure Statistical Analyses 2002–3*. London: HMSO.

Le Grand, J. (1982), *The Strategy of Equality*. London: Allen & Unwin.

—— and Vizard, P. (1998), 'The National Health Service: crisis, change or continuity?' In Glennerster and Hills (1998).

Neidhardt, F., and Rucht, D. (1991), 'The analysis of social movements: the state of the art and some perspectives for further research'. In D. Rucht (ed.), *Research on Social Movements*. Frankfurt: Campus/Boulder, Colo.: Westview Press.

Sefton, T. (1997), *The Changing Distribution of the Social Wage*. STICERD Occasional Paper No. 21. London: London School of Economics.

—— (2002), *Recent Changes in the Distribution of the Social Wage*. London: Centre for Analysis of Social Exclusion, London School of Economics.

FURTHER READING

The Glennerster and Hills collection *The State of Welfare* (2nd edn., Oxford: Oxford University Press, 1998) is an indispensable source of data and interpretation on the impact of social policy. The earlier book by George and Wilding, *The Impact of Social Policy* (London: Routledge, 1984) is particularly useful for its discussion of societal impacts of social policy. Books which explore the role of taxation as a social policy measure are J. Hills, *New Inequalities: The Changing Distribution of Income and Wealth in the UK* (Cambridge: Cambridge University Press, 1996) and J. Hills, *The Future of Welfare* (2nd edn., York: Joseph Rowntree Foundation, 1997). Richard Wilkinson's *Unhealthy Societies: The Afflictions of Inequality* (London: Routledge, 1997) is a stimulating account of the degree to which industrial societies, and particularly the UK, remain affected by differences in most measures of welfare.

GLOSSARY

horizontal dimension of need Number of people with a given level of need.

input measure Measure of resources used in providing a service or benefit, e.g. spending, number of staff employed.

income quintiles The division of a population, such as individuals or households, into a hierarchy of five parts each containing equal numbers. The bottom quintile would contain the fifth with the lowest incomes, and so on to the top fifth, containing those with the highest incomes. The income of each quintile is usually given in the form of the average income of all the units in it.

outcome measure Type of measure (of social policy) which looks at final impact, e.g. level of illness, examination results.

output measure Measure of volume of service produced, e.g. number of patients treated, number of council houses built, number of people receiving home help. An intermediate measure between input measures and outcome measures.

principle of proportional service provision Principle according to which provision varies in proportion to need.

principle of uniform service provision Principle according to which provision is equal per member of group in need.

real spending Spending which has been adjusted for the effect of the general level of inflation in the economy.

social wage If public spending is treated as a source of benefits to individuals, then the value of the services and cash payments received per household can be termed a 'social wage' since it is like a form of income.

take-up The extent to which all those entitled to a service or benefit receive it.

territorial justice A situation where the provision of services in different areas varies in proportion to inter-area differences in need.

vertical dimension of need Need defined in terms of its hierarchical distribution amongst similar units, such as individuals or households, such that some are said to have higher needs than others.

volume spending spending which has been adjusted for the effect of the level of inflation experienced in a particular sector, e.g. education.

22

New Thinking in Social Welfare

Tony Fitzpatrick

CONTENTS

INTRODUCTION

Social policy has a reputation for being a laggard when it comes to new theoretical developments and innovations. As a field of study that is quite interdisciplinary it often seems to be catching up with what is happening in other subject areas, joining the party just as everyone else is leaving. But the element of truth in this characterization easily disguises another truth, which is that the subject's very nature gives it a degree of flexibility and agility that other disciplines may lack. For while other disciplines are exploring new ideas, spending time testing them against established concepts and frameworks, and frequently leading themselves down blind alleys, social policy is able to borrow what it needs and apply it rapidly (if sometimes belatedly) to its traditional concerns. In turn, social policy offers other subjects a real-world reference point that can act as a needed corrective to the overly abstract flights into which they sometimes launch themselves. So if it is sometimes late for the party this is because it feels no need to join for the sake of joining. It is therefore far more than the application of sociological, political, economic, cultural, and philosophical ideas to welfare institutions. When it comes to theoretical innovation social policy is neither a professional nor a layman but, rather, something of a gifted amateur.

The most obvious aim of this closing chapter is to introduce you to a variety of the new debates with which social policy scholars and researchers are beginning to wrestle. Some of these are already fairly well established and some are still in their early, tentative stages. In writing it I have had to work from within various constraints. First, I have excluded those areas that are covered substantially in other chapters. Second, there are many (many!) debates about which I know relatively little. For instance, the issue of how welfare states are affected by religious context and conflict is one that has surfaced from time to time but I cannot claim to know very much about it. Third, a certain amount of subjective judgement is involved. In other words, the following discussions reflect those areas that I consider to be important, but this certainly does not mean that I am any kind of fortune teller. Finally, there are constraints of space and so I have excluded recent innovations in concepts and methodology. Basically, I have opted for depth rather than breadth, though this is still something of a whistle-stop tour. These points made, I suspect that much of what follows will be of even greater central importance to future editions of this book.

GLOBALIZATION

The advent of globalization

Globalization is a concept that manages to frighten almost everyone at some point yet, at its simplest, it refers to the contemporary process through which different parts of the world become increasingly interconnected and interdependent. Think of an obvious example. When the attack on the USA occurred on 11 September 2001 the pictures were instantly beamed around the globe to a worldwide audience. The event occurred *as people were watching it.* Contrast this with other historical events, e.g. the American Revolution or the *Titanic* disaster, where the audience was only formed hours, days, and sometimes weeks after the event itself (depending upon how far back in time you go). Information and Communication Technologies (ICTs) have connected the world together. Another example. Many now insist that the twenty-first century will experience a deteriorating natural environment with all sorts of repercussions for human and non-human life (see Chapter 19). This means we are all in it together. There is no part of the world which is immune from pollution, for instance, and so what happens in one region is intimately dependent upon what happens in all the others.

Now, sceptical readers will already be shaking their heads. Hang on, they say, this process of interconnection and interdependency is as old as society itself. What is so special about the contemporary world? This is a perfectly reasonable question and, in fact, it points to the central dispute with some people believing that globalization is real and others believing that it is not, some believing that globalization is new and others believing that it is very old indeed. We will explore these issues in a moment. For now, it is worth explaining that those who insist that globalization is recent and very real do so by identifying a paradigm shift. Take the **nation-state**. Nation-states have existed for centuries and relationships between them of one sort or another have always existed, but what some insist is that it is the relations which are becoming more important: rather than 'nodes' determining the relations that join them together it is the relations that shape the nodes. Castells (1996 1997 1998) talks repeatedly of **networks** in a constant state of flux having replaced the stable hierarchies and top-down structures of traditional modernity. Therefore, if you want to understand nation-states (and firms and social movements and any other kind of node) you have to analyse the networks out of which they are formed. Therefore, some believe that globalization involves the reshaping of social space and time (Giddens 1991; Harvey 1989): the way in which the world gets both bigger and smaller. We can access more of it and do so more quickly than ever before. Robertson (1992) says that globalization is in fact the interpenetration of the local and the global as local events often have global effects and global events usually have local consequences.

This is where the controversies really begin to bite (Fitzpatrick 2001: 163–75). At the risk of simplification we can identify the following four positions (Held et al. 1999). The first is maintained by those who not only insist that globalization is real but who welcome it for one reason or another. Call these people the 'sponsors' (see Box 22.1). Ohmae (1995), for instance, believes that because there is now a single global economy in the process of formation the nation-state is gradually dying away: there are no longer any national boundaries for the state to police and defend. This means that we should shape our social institutions and practices to meet the demands of a global free market. Such also seems to be the position of the International Monetary Fund, the World Bank, and the World Trade Organization.

The second position is held by those who also believe that ours is an age of globalization but who regarded it with less optimism: these are the 'sceptics' (see Box 22.2).

Box 22.1 From the end of the Nation State

'Put simply, in terms of real flows of economic activity, nation states have already lost their role as meaningful units of participation in the global economy of today's borderless world.'

(Kenichi Ohmae, The End of The Nation State)

Box 22.2 From Globalization

'. . . the pressure to pull down the last remaining barriers to the free movement of money and money-making commodities and information goes hand in hand with the pressure to dig new moats and erect new walls . . .'

(Zygmunt Bauman, *Globalization*)

Box 22.3 From Globalization in Question

'. . . we remain sceptical about the more extreme claims for economic globalization, whilst at the same time acknowledging that the international economy has changed radically in structure and forms of governance from those that prevailed in the long boom from the early 1950s to the 1973 oil crisis.'

(Paul Hirst and Grahame Thompson, *Globalization in Question*)

Bauman (1998), for instance, thinks that globalization is essentially a process whereby the affluent detach themselves physically and symbolically from the poor, producing new forms of social and spatial inequalities. And environmentalists are often sceptics, welcoming some aspects of globalization (the worldwide consciousness of ecological problems) but not necessarily others (the drive towards a deregulated, consumerist capitalism, for instance).

Thirdly, there are those who deny that 'globalization' is an appropriate description of what is happening in the world today: the 'doubters'. Doubters introduce an historical perspective into the discussion, pointing out that any analysis of contemporary changes must involve a comparison between the present and the past. Hirst and Thompson (1999), for instance, identify more continuities with the past than discontinuities (see Box 22.3). There is nothing unique about our time, they maintain, we have been here before: between the 1870s and the First World War we also experienced a series of economic, political, and technological leaps. We may be experiencing considerable changes but these are not describable as globalization.

The final position is taken by those who insist that globalization is a complete myth promoted by those who have most to gain from the worldwide adoption of unrestrained capitalism (Bourdieu 1999): the 'hecklers' (see Box 22.4). For the hecklers, what others call globalization is nothing more than the latest stage in the capitalist backlash against the post-war settlement, when the interests of capital and labour balanced each other out in the context of a mixed economy and a welfare state. Therefore, the debate is a conjurer's trick which we should recognize as a diversionary sleight-of-hand. Instead, we should focus upon the underlying forces whereby the powerful and the disempowered struggle against one another.

Box 22.4 From Acts of Resistance

'It is a myth in the strong sense of the word, a powerful discourse, an *idée force*, an idea which has social force, which obtains belief. It is the main weapon in the battles against the gains of the welfare state. European workers, we are told, must compete with the least favoured workers of the rest of the world. The workers of Europe are therefore offered as a model countries which have no minimum wage, where factory workers work twelve hours a day for a wage which is between a quarter, and fifth of European wages, where there are no trade unions, where there is child labour, and so on.'

(Pierre Bourdieu, *Acts of Resistance*)

Social policy and globalization

Where does social policy fit into all of this? Basically, the debate concerning globalization and social policy follows the same contours as those sketched above. The initial running was made by sponsors bringing a range of arguments to bear (World Bank 1994). They began by insisting that the economic conditions of post-Second world War social policy are no longer in place. A country could no longer reflate its economy in order to reduce unemployment because the closer integration of economies means that international investors can quickly disinvest and search for another country in which interest rates are higher and so the returns to capital are greater. For similar reasons, social expenditure has to be reduced because investors are more able to avoid the punitive rates of taxation upon which such expenditure depends. Affluence is therefore generated not through the management of demand but through a deregulation of the economy's supply side, meaning that workers have to become much more flexible in their habits and expectations.

Because the welfare state represents an expensive source of rigidity, it has to be reformed accordingly. The sponsors have consequently advocated either its complete dismantling or its replacement by a series of safety nets that the state can provide for the very poor, with everyone else having to purchase private forms of insurance and welfare in the free market. Those countries that refuse to go down this road will be less attractive to investors and so invite the kind of economic collapse that will destroy the welfare state anyway. At their most extreme, sponsors have anticipated a 'race to the bottom' whereby nations try to underbid each other by offering ever-lower wages, ever-lower rates of taxation, and ever-more residual forms of state welfare.

This is an alarming and (for many) a persuasive account, but does it stand up to scrutiny? For the sponsors to be correct, it must be the case that those countries with low taxation, low wage levels (at the bottom end of the market), and few state welfare services are flourishing more than ever in the global economy. However, by the mid-to late 1990s there was enough evidence to suggest that this was not the case and that no great race to the bottom was occurring. Gough (1996), for example, shows that there is no simple correlation between the welfare state and economic prosperity. Some countries with generous welfare states were flourishing and some were not; some countries which *lacked* generous welfare states were flourishing and some were not. So the idea that you deregulate and, hey presto, you experience higher productivity and affluence was just too simplistic. Therefore, the 'cynic' might point out that globalization is invoked by sponsors who want to promote that which they claim is unavoidable: an unequal, low-taxation society.

Those who wish to defend the welfare state therefore took heart from these kinds of research findings and the idea that globalization is not a *fait accompli*, nor just a simplistic form of economic integration, but is shaped by and through local contexts (Sykes et al. 2001). This is the notion of 'path dependency'. Globalization cannot 'hollow out' national economies because an economy is moored in a diverse series of social and cultural institutions, practices, and assumptions. For instance, the Scandinavian social democracies are not going to accept passively the dismantling of their welfare states, because the welfare state is rooted in their sense of collective self, historical inheritance, and national identity. In fact, welfare state generosity might well be *attractive* to international investors because of the social cohesion and security they engender, in contrast to free-market nations where inequalities and insecurities might undermine the productivity of the workforce. The thesis of path dependency therefore states that 'context matters', and so even if economies are integrating at the global level this will manifest itself in different ways in different nations. The local appropriates the global.

Yet having reached this point there are many researchers who nevertheless reserve a certain pessimism regarding globalization and its implications for social policy (Bonoli et al. 2000). Even if globalization does not imply the contraction of welfare states (though some contraction was visible throughout the 1990s, even in the Scandinavian social democracies), it has brought to an end the era of expansion. For in the decades after the Second World War welfare states grew as a means of stabilizing the economy and creating jobs. However, because of a range of factors (not all of them due to globalization) this upward trajectory has now halted. Electorates will no longer tolerate high levels of taxation, the private sector will no longer tolerate over-regulation, consumers will no longer tolerate being dictated to by public-sector producers. The welfare state has therefore reached its limits, and the best we can do is to defend it in terms of new imperatives: competition rather than solidarity, inclusion rather than equality. We have entered the era of what Pierson (2001) calls 'permanent austerity', where we can no longer 'have it all' but have to make trade-offs between conflicting aims. This, then, is the position of the sceptics: those who identify globalization as real but who are more pessimistic about its implications than the sponsors.

Finally, we might reject all of the above arguments on the grounds that they each represent a capitulation to the conservative, neo-liberal agenda that has been attacking the post-Second World War settlement since the 1970s. For hecklers, the debate concerning globalization is a diversion from some deeper conflicts, though one which might carry echoes of those conflicts within it. For instance, it might well be that the struggle between capital and labour is now emerging at an international level, but that we are being sidetracked from recognizing the full importance of this struggle by concentrating upon national social policies. Even for those who question it, globalization can still appear as a irresistible force that overwhelms our collective ability to shape our personal and social destinies. Lurking always within the discourse of globalization is a preference for market forces and an assumption that the market cannot be resisted. Therefore, we should not be distracted by the myths of globalisation but recognize that the terrain of social policy consists, as always, of a conflict between those who do and those who do not possess power.

POSTMODERNISM AND POST-STRUCTURALISM

Postmodernism

Postmodernism came to prominence in the 1980s, and its longevity has perhaps surprised both its supporters and its critics. The former expected it to revolutionize the humanities and social sciences to the point where they would no longer be recognizable; its critics anticipated that postmodernism would be a transitory fashion. Both sides were wrong, because both neglected the extent to which postmodernism throws new light on some old ideas without thereby making those ideas redundant.

Postmodernism was born of a disillusionment with the radical politics of the 1960s and 1970s. Because the 'New Left' had failed to offer an alternative both to welfare capitalism and to Communism some felt that radical politics had missed its final opportunity to dominate the historical stage. Postmodernism therefore represents the introversion of those who felt that the Left had, temporarily at least, nowhere else to go. For some postmodernists it represented the death of the modern project, i.e. the belief that society was on an upward trajectory of progress and emancipation; for others, postmodernism was the opportunity to rethink fundamental assumptions and categories in order that radicalism could be reconstructed.

Postmodernism has become easy to caricature since it is often taken to refer to anything that is ironic, relativist, superficial, playful, or obsessed with identity. But a quick review of one of its most influential thinkers reveals that it has to be taken more seriously than this.

Lyotard's (1984) basic idea is that 'metanarratives' are no longer available to us. A metanarrative is a system of thought that attempts to understand the social world within a single, all-encompassing critique. Marxism is one such 'grand narrative' in that it ultimately seeks to explain society in terms of material production and class struggle. But Lyotard insisted that such explanations are based upon 'essences' that can only explain the world by reducing it to narrow categorical boundaries. Therefore, a broader understanding comes not by reducing the world to some kind of inner essence or core but by understanding the particular localities from which we start. The job of philosophy and science should not consist of trying to map the world in its entirety, to provide a universal account that is true for all people at all times, but of clarifying and elucidating the local narratives of the philosopher and the scientist. Inquiry is not the search for truth but a necessary reminder that what we think of as the truth is always dependent upon a particular context. Postmodernism for Lyotard is therefore a kind of attitude, or an intellectual orientation that displays 'incredulity towards metanarratives'.

Such ideas came under considerable attack from other social theorists. Jurgen Habermas (1987) alleges that postmodernism is nothing more than a philosophical justification for conservatism. The implication of Lyotard's ideas is that the local must predominate over the universal and that modern conceptions of progress and emancipation have been based upon delusionary premises. But what else is this but a restatement of the kind of philosophical and political conservatism that dates back at least to Edmund Burke in the eighteenth century? For Habermas, the idea that the modern project has failed is objectionable. What has failed is not **modernity** per se but particular forms of modernity. Rather than collapsing into postmodernist pessimism, then, we must attempt to reinvigorate the modern project on new grounds.

This debate has now been circulating back and forth since the early 1980s, and although the original sound and fury has long since died down (or at least evolved into other forms) it succeeded in placing at the centre of contemporary thought the question regarding modernity and the prospects for social improvement. Do we still live in an age describable as modern (theorists often make reference to 'advanced modernity' and 'late modernity') or have we passed into a postmodern one? Is it still realistic and desirable to strive for progress and emancipation?

Social policy and postmodernism

The relevance of these questions to social policy consists in the simple fact that because state welfare is undoubtedly an important part of the modern project, a proper understanding of social policy changes depending upon which interpretation of the condition of modernity we prefer. As a simple definition, social policies attempt to raise levels of individual and social wellbeing through collective forms of organization. But if, as postmodernists insist, such an endeavour is based upon naive universal narratives then our notion of social policy has to alter radically (Leonard 1997; Carter 1998; Rodgers 2000).

Think of the following example. The discipline of social policy is arguably based upon the view that there is such a thing as human nature, that this consists of certain basic needs, and that the job of welfare systems is to enable those needs to be fulfilled. But if human nature is a fiction, a mirage that we wasted several centuries pursuing through the wastelands of modernity, and if needs are constructed through language rather than being prior to language, then the very rationale of state welfare is undermined. This is one of the reasons why some social policy commentators are very suspicious of postmodernism, accusing it of providing an intellectual justification of anti-welfare state politics.

However, others believe that we should not be so quick to abandon postmodern ideas. At its extreme postmodernism certainly seems to embrace a kind of pessimistic nihilism that is antithetical to the subject of social policy. Yet this does not mean that every aspect of postmodern theory should be abandoned. The following two influences seem most relevant.

First, postmodernism draws attention to the way in which our identities are complex and plural, consisting not of a few simple elements (occupation, sex, age, etc.) but of a multiple variety of representations, divisions, and relations (see Box 22.5). This is why some worry that postmodernism diverts us from the bread-and-butter issues of class and justice, but it might also be that a postmodern perspective allows us to combine those

Box 22.5 Identity

Your identity is not stable but is in a constant state of flux and you do not carry it around like an internal set of baggage but constantly reconstruct it through and with an engagement with the identities of others. Identity is 'differential' rather than 'essential'. Postmodernism is therefore suited to a society in which the expressive self and consumerist lifestyles have come to dominate.

issues with questions of how to recognize and respect others. Nancy Fraser (1997) insists that the future of radical politics lies in the attempt to reconcile material redistribution with cultural recognition. If so, then welfare institutions have to be based not just upon distributive criteria but also upon forms of cultural empowerment.

Secondly, although some postmodernists want us to abandon universal frames of reference and meaning, others have demanded that **universalism** become more sensitive to local variations. We can, for instance, still identify universal needs which acknowledging that in order for needs to be fulfilled that have to be translated into a local context. We may all need autonomy (Doyal and Gough 1991), but the specific meaning of autonomy may vary from place to place and from time to time. And if this is the case it follows that the means of guaranteeing autonomy have to vary also. The wellbeing that is delivered to one person may not be suitable for another. So, rather than a one-size-fits-all kind of universalism, social policies have to derive from universal principles that are sensitive to the particular environments upon which policies impact. This could imply that, rather than leaving it to experts to deliver welfare 'from the top down', welfare reform should aim to empower citizens 'from the bottom up' and ensure that welfare services are rooted more firmly in civil society.

Post-structuralism

Post-structuralism is related to postmodernism, but the two should not be confused, as the former tends to be more focused and methodological. Post-structuralists agree with postmodernists that we cannot transcend the contexts in which we are embedded, but they insist that those contexts have to be understood as consisting first and foremost of 'signs'. A sign is the basic unit of meaning, the atom of language. Traditionally, we have thought of language as a transparent medium, a means for revealing the world as it really is and of communicating with that external reality. But for post-structuralists signs do not relate to anything which is 'external'; instead, a sign only ever relates to other signs, and meaning derives not from a correspondence with a world that is outside of language because there *is* nothing outside of language. In order for something to be real it has to be named. Therefore, reality is not prior *to* language but is only ever an effect *of* language. So meaning is not a correspondence of signs to reality but the endless supersession of signs in a 'stream of signification'. The central post-structuralist claim is that 'the world is a text' and a text only ever means something in its differences from other texts. Inquiry is therefore not about the discovery of truth (because truth is another text) but the interpretation and endless reinterpretation of textual signs.

Post-structuralists therefore make constant reference to the idea of 'discourse', by which is meant this self-reference of language to itself.

Perhaps the most influential post-structuralist is Foucault (1984). Foucault investigates the conditions (the **discourses**) through which knowledge and ideas are generated. He sets out to understand discursive practices through a 'genealogical' approach which closely traces the history and operation of power within a number of institutional settings, e.g. prisons, asylums, clinics. These settings are not based upon true ideas about the world; instead, they are the means by which the truth-claims of some dominate the truth-claims of others through the production of knowledge and power. Power not only consists of repression but is also the means by which subjects and subjectivities are formed. We can make claims about the world only through the discursive web of practices; we speak only insofar as we are spoken through institutional knowledge and signification.

For what we do as institutional participants is to separate out the normal from the deviant and to disperse ourselves across the spectrum of normality. We are disciplined, and discipline ourselves through the discursive norms of institutions. The key metaphor for Foucault is the 'panopticon'. The panopticon was a design for a prison that would use the least number of prison officers to survey as many prisoners as possible. The prisoners would not know when they were being observed and so would need to act as if they were under constant surveillance. Foucault treats this as a metaphor for the institutions of modernity: the mutual surveillance of all under the gaze of normalization. What he is invoking is not an Orwellian dsytopia (although these have certainly haunted the modern period) because there is no final distinction between the panopticon's guards and its prisoners. Each one of us is both.

Social policy and post-structuralism

As with postmodernism, many within social policy have condemned these ideas as dangerous or simply irrelevant. If truth really is nothing more than a demeanour of power, then this renders the business of social critique redundant. Unless we have firm grounds for knowing what is and is not essentially real, unless we can get outside of language and discourse, then we cannot discern what is wrong with the world nor develop any idea how to put it right. However, some argue that far from rendering political struggle redundant post-structuralism simply draws attention to the inevitability of struggle, to the impossibility of utopia, and to the endlessness of conflict (Laclau and Mouffe 1985). We are more likely to improve the condition of the weak and disadvantaged if we abandon the pretence that creating the perfect society is just a matter of devising a complete 'social theory of everything'. It was this illusion that drugged Marxism into the nightmares of state communism. Therefore, the relevance of post-structuralism to social policy is not easy to dismiss, and the following two areas seem to be most relevant.

First, the notion of **surveillance** has been influenced ideas about governance and freedom (Rose 1999). Traditionally, governance and power have been separated out: the Right has demanded (market) freedom instead of (state) governance; the Left has demanded governance as a means of creating higher forms of freedom than those permitted by the capitalist market. But for post-structuralists the ineluctability of power

Box 22.6 Bodies and society

Foucault draws attention to the extent to which bodies are medicalized and managed within modern societies. The contemporary obsessions with fitness, dieting, youth, beauty, cosmetic surgery and health reflect the ways in which bodies may be disciplined, with so much social interaction hinging upon judgements concerning bodily appearance: how we appear to others and how others appear to us relates to assumed deviations from, or approximations to, some cultural norm.

and discourse means that freedom is a technology of governance and governance is the medium of freedom. We govern ourselves through our freedoms.

Take the welfare state. Proponents of state welfare defend it for many reasons, but almost always do so on the basis that it increases the sum of freedom: redistribution and social cohesion improve the freedom not only of the poorest but of the affluent also. Yet because the welfare state depends upon the intimate cataloguing, classification, sorting, and regulation of each of us from cradle to grave, its presence saturates those aspects of our lives that we still, somehow, insist upon defining as private. Yet this does not mean (as the Right imagines) that dismantling the welfare state would reclaim the spaces of privacy, since there simply is no space that is immune from the disciplinary gaze. The irony is that we continue to work with eighteenth-century notions of public and private that have long since been made redundant by the social technologies of modernity. If we read the welfare state as one such technology, then we have redefined our understanding of social policy.

Second, the body has become more important to social policy critiques (see Box 22.6). Indeed, disability theorists have long drawn attention to the means by which 'disabled' bodies are represented as less than, rather than different, from 'abled' bodies. In short, when we look at bodies we are looking not just at the corporeality of the physical body but at the way in which it is commodified, fetishized, and managed by a complexity of expert discourses. The body is therefore a site of social struggle, and we gain a clearer understanding of social policies if we analyse their effects upon bodies and the spatial and temporal environments which are formed through bodily movement and interaction.

RISK SOCIETY

The debate concerning risks and risk society touches upon some of themes already explored in the preceding two sections. A risk society is in many respects a global society given that risks (whether environmental, technological, economic, medical, etc.) do not respect national borders, and the fact that we may experience the very same risks as those who are spatially distant from us is arguably one indication that we live in a globalizing era. The debate also relates to those concerning postmodernism. Those who describe ours as a risk society tend not to argue that we have passed from modernity to postmodernity, but they seem to believe that we now live in an age of advanced or 'reflexive' modernity. One of the key figures in this respect is Ulrich Beck (1992).

Beck's basic argument is fairly simple. It is not the end of modernity and the beginning of postmodernity that we have reached, but the end of *first* modernity and the beginning of *second* modernity. The first modernity was an age of industrial progress and all political and social institutions were designed to generate 'goods' (welfare, growth, resources) in a world that was taken to be stable, knowable, and scientifically calculable. By contrast, the second modernity that emerged in the latter part of the twentieth century is a risk society characterized by the attempt to limit, manage, and negotiate a way through a series of 'bads' and hazards. Beck had been struck by the worldwide consequences of the Chernobyl and Bhopal disasters, and the way in which invisible but deadly contagion had crossed spatial borders (national boundaries) and temporal borders (since the effects will be felt for generations) without any respect for the tidy assumptions of industrial modernity. For instance, nuclear and industrial pollution undermines the simple class hierarchies of the industrial order, affecting the ghettos of the rich as well as those of the poor. Generalizing, he proposed that these were simply the most extreme examples of the riskiness of second modernity. It is not that the world has become a more dangerous place: it is that hazards are the unintended consequences of our centuries-old attempt to pacify and control the world. The second modernity is therefore the first modernity turned in on itself in a process of reflexive modernization, and coping with riskiness necessitates the democratization of science and policy-making: decisions can no longer be left to technocratic elites but must involve all of us.

Of what relevance is all of this to social policy (Taylor-Gooby 2000)? The welfare state was a direct descendant of industrialism, of urbanization and collectivism that has been concerned both with the production of goods through economic wealth generation and with the just distribution of those goods through social institutions. If this type of industrial society has been superseded, then the welfare state's traditional roles of economic intervention and social management can be identified as one of the main sources of risks. Through the principle and systems of social insurance and universal provision the welfare state has always been concerned with the calculation and amelioration of collective risks. Today, not only are those 'safety systems' less effective but they are, themselves, the origins of risk and insecurity: insurance against old age, unemployment, and sickness is aimed at the predictable and collective events of the life course and not at the individualized contingencies of risk society.

The UK social policy literature is now replete with discussions of risk, anxiety, insecurity, and a host of similar concepts (Culpitt 1999; Manning and Shaw 2000). Kemshall (2002), for example, discusses the extent to which 'needs' are being reconstituted as 'fears' so that the state no longer sees its job simply as providing certain levels of income, shelter, healthcare, etc. but also as addressing the anxieties and insecurities that people experience. Therefore, criminal policy is now more of a central governmental concern than ever and, what is more, the state often legitimates extensions of its surveillance powers by arguing that they will fight crime and terrorism and so make the world safer and more secure, i.e. ease people's fears. A risk society may therefore inspire social policies that embody either collectivism or individualism, and which are either progressive or punitive, depending upon how they are interpreted politically.

The risk society thesis has not gone unchallenged. Many complain that it oversimplifies recent social developments and overestimates the extent to which the social world really has changed. Beck has come in for particular criticism by arguing that we no longer live in a class society but in a society where inequalities are 'biographical' and so difficult to generalize into social strata. Such criticisms aside, the concept of risks have undoubtedly captured the imagination of many social scientists and theorists since it was first popularized in the 1980s.

NEW TECHNOLOGIES

Information and communication technologies

Some social policy theorists have recently been taking an increasing interest in the debate concerning information society and ICTs (Loader 1998; Fitzpatrick 2003a; see Box 22.7). ICTs include all forms of computer-based information systems (informatics), Internet-related technologies, and cyborg (machine–body interface) technologies. In - developed societies it is now virtually impossible to live and work without encountering one or all of these, and as we experience the convergence of televisions, personal computers, and mobile/video phones over the next few years the new technologies will become even harder to avoid.

To a large extent, the debate concerning the information society assumes that we now live in a post-industrial network society, though one whose basic characteristics have

Box 22.7 Social policy and information and communication technologies

ICTs are relevant to social policy in a variety of ways:

- Computer availability and literacy: the extent to which schools and universities are online, the quality of the skills being taught, the implications of home computers for the learning process, and the implications for distance learning.
- Government publications can be increasingly accessed with relative ease: the web pages of government departments can now provide at least some information for researchers, welfare rights advisers, and campaigners
- There are those who allege that ICTs make it easier for those with the will and the resources to evade national tax authorities, placing a question mark over the future funding of generous welfare services.
- These technologies bear consequences for employment levels, research and development, and supply-side interventions in the labour market.
- Cyberspace is the realm of financial globalization, which supposedly flows over and around the immobilities of welfare states.

been carried over from the industrial hierarchies of the post-Enlightenment. This means that although the debate is highly contemporary it is built around some familiar themes. First, to what extent do ICTs empower or disempower individuals and under what circumstances should the state have the power to monitor ICT-related messages or determine what is posted on the web? Second, do ICTs bring people together in new 'cyber-communities' or help to fragment society? Third, can ICTs enhance democracy, civic association, the public sphere, citizenship, and the political process, or might they perpetuate a widespread alienation and estrangement from public affairs? Finally, are ICTs the means by which a surveillance society of social control is enhanced or the means by which the holders of power can be made visible and brought to account? Running throughout these debates is a contest between the technophiles for whom ICTs can do no wrong and the technophobes who concentrate upon the negative effects of ICTs.

The implications of ICTs for welfare reform may be either positive or negative (see Case Study 22.1). On the optimistic side, ICTs may empower people and help to reduce social disadvantage. For example, if the use of computers and 'remote technology'

Case Study 22.1 Digital divisions

'The internet revolution has created a new underclass of people in rural and remote areas who are being excluded from the brave new world of teleworking, virtual shopping, and online public services by lack of access to technology. That is the conclusion of research, to be published this week, which warns the much-hyped potential for new technologies to "render distance obsolete" is not being realized. Despite confident predictions that the expansion of information and communications technologies (ICT) would bridge social divides—between urban and rural and rich and poor—the UK's knowledge economy currently threatens to bypass large areas of the country, leaving them "trapped in a cycle of low skills/low value work".

The research calls on the government to treat access to technology as just as important as access to transport and health care.

"Those unable to travel easily to work, to access ICT, shop or socialise are in danger of becoming excluded from our increasingly mobile society, missing out on the opportunities available, and penalised for their lack of mobility," the authors conclude.

Rural communities stand, in theory, to gain most from technologies which allow them to work, shop or access services electronically. But the researchers found that home-based teleworking remains an urban phenomenon, rising fastest in London where congestion and the costs of commuting provide good reasons for people to want to work from home.

Part of the problem, according to the authors, has been failure to identify demand and social requirements. The failure of teleworking in the countryside, for example, may be because working life still requires regular face-to-face contact with employers, colleagues and clients.

The report concludes that mobile technologies offer the best platform for breaking this cycle, with services from customised weather reports and skills training to remote health care and e-democracy all delivered through wireless networks to mobile phones, notebook computers and handheld devices.

The researchers criticise the government for "missing a trick" by failing to find innovative ways of using mobile technologies to bridge the digital divide between urban and rural. They point out that while it is possible to get bus timetables via a mobile in London, this service is unheard of in the vast majority of rural areas.

Zapping the problems

In Sweden, an initiative called MobiLearn tackles the problem of teleworkers—"nomads"—not being able to attend corporate training events. It uses 3G cellular networks and high-speed internet access to provide learning sessions which workers can access where and when they choose.

The Llwybr Pathway initiative, led by Powys county council, has spent £10.3 m on projects to improve access to information and communications technology, e-commerce and infrastructure development in rural Wales.

Researchers in New York found that, even in a densely-packed city, there was less access to high-speed internet connections in low-income areas such as Harlem. NYC wireless was set up to provide bandwidth to poorer people through partnerships with housing associations, park authorities and recreation centres.'

(Stuart Millar, 'Rural area have-nots lose out on the net' The *Guardian*, 4 March 2002)

in healthcare can ensure that more people are treated than in conventional medical settings, then such 'telemedicine' provides an obvious bonus. Similarly, ICTs may enable new forms of community and social participation to emerge, assisting the objectives of social inclusion. Then again, the implications could also be malign. There is evidence that the dissemination of ICTs is leading to a 'digital divide' where social inequalities based upon income and wealth are being replicated and even strengthened. Furthermore, we may experience the emergence of a 'self-service' welfare system where individuals are given the basic tools to access the information network and so, supposedly, have no excuses for failure. This might represent a digitally updated version of Victorian self-help with penalties for 'the undeserving'. However, we are not helpless in the face of these new developments, and, as with the risk society debate, much depends upon our political response to them.

New genetics

One of the most contentious areas of the new technologies concerns that of genetics. The term 'new genetics' is usually meant to distinguish recent technological developments from the earlier history of the science when eugenic assumptions were sometimes prominent—**eugenics** being applied in its most disturbing and virulent form in Nazi Germany in the 1930s and 1940s.

The 'new genetics', however, emphasizes humanitarian goals that were anathema to many eugenicists. For instance, through somatic cell therapy we can address debilitating conditions such as Alzheimer's and Parkinson's diseases; with genetically modified (GM) foods, it is alleged, we can cure world hunger; and through the creation of

Cartoon 22.1 'That's strange. This new microchip sewn under my skin is supposed to open the door and put the kettle on.'

(Stan McMurtry, *Daily Mail*, 27 August 1998)

transgenic species we can solve medical conditions like haemophilia. However, critics allege that despite these potential advantages the new genetics also has worrying implications: if people are able to breed designer babies then this might create a 'genetic underclass'; GM foods are capable of undermining biodiversity and so are possibly dangerous; genetic engineering might discriminate against disabled people—for a review of the recent literature see Fitzpatrick (2001).

There are five main areas where genetics and social policy interact most clearly. First, there are implications for healthcare and health costs. Will genetic innovations make us less dependent upon medical biotechnology or more dependent? Will they lower healthcare costs in the long term or raise them? Second, there are implications for insurance systems. The genetically disadvantaged may have to pay higher premiums than others and may even be refused any coverage. Also, people may be more reluctant to be genetically screened for life-threatening conditions if the resulting information is to be released to insurance companies. Third, there are implications for workplace discrimination. Workers and job applicants may be judged not on proven ability but on their genetic endowments. Fourth, the patenting of genes and of gene-related techniques may hand excessive amounts of power over to biotechnology companies. Finally, the combination of genetics and ICTs, known as 'bioinformatics,' has implications for individual privacy. Does this combination assist in the creation of a surveillance society?

SOCIAL MOVEMENTS

The debate concerning social movements is another one of those that is now well established and has been wielding an influence upon the discipline of social policy since the 1980s at least. Nevertheless, the debate can still appear novel given the continuing arguments regarding the salience, or otherwise, of class as a useful analytical concept. Class analysis has dominated the traditions of social science. The problem is that such analysis can often ossify into an interpretation of society that allots primacy to grand, socio-structural hierarchies and interprets individuals as little more than the bearers of their class, as class actors first and foremost. By contrast, an analysis that treats individuals as the basic units of society can seem more dynamic and relevant, though many have certainly tried to balance individualistic factors out with 'structural' ones (e.g. Bourdieu 1977; Elster 1985).

The debate concerning social movements could be thought of as one such balancing act since the attempt is here being made to capture the dynamism of individual interaction without losing sight of deeper social processes and structures (Della Porta and Diani 1999). Therefore, individuals are located less in terms of class and more in terms of groups, associations, crowds, protests, blocs, factions, and all forms of social, cultural and political movement. The emphasis here is therefore upon diversity and plurality: a 'movement' is not only a collection of actors who share common goals but a process of collective action within a given social conjuncture. A social movement is a mobilization in opposition to that which the movement's members believe threatens their identity, values, or interests. It is a network whose lifespan may be either short or long and which may either be formal and highly organized (something akin to a political party or pressure group) or informal and loosely organized (something which is leaderless and more spontaneous). As such, social movement theories really date from the 1960s, when a host of non-class-specific movements arose both to challenge old forms of injustice and to promote new forms of politics. The civil rights/liberties movement, the women's movement, the student movement, the gay and lesbian movement, the Green movement, the peace/anti-war movement, and the anti-nuclear movement all signalled an evolution in political consciousness and organization that did not fit neatly into the sociological categories of the time.

Social movements are often taken to be concerned with:

- particular issues that are often conceptually broadened out into universalistic values and concerns;
- civil society rather than state institutions and political power;
- openness and flexibility rather than with rule-governed hierarchies.

So whereas the 'party' and the 'union' were the archetypes of the early twentieth century, by the end of the century these were considered by many to be too bureaucratic and resistant to change.

Perhaps the most contentious issue is whether 'social movement' should replace 'class' as an analytical tool (Eder 1993; Maheu 1995). It might be claimed that we no longer live in a class society, that income and occupation no longer define who we are or what we might achieve in life. Therefore, an analysis based upon social movements more fully captures the texture of contemporary social changes. On the other hand, we seem to live in societies in which inequalities are more prevalent than ever, and so, although there is some mobility up and down the social ladder the categories of class are those still best suited to understanding the distribution of power. Another perspective says not that 'class' and 'class society' are redundant but that the meaning of these terms has to adapt to capture the contemporary emphasis upon self, culture, identity, and lifestyle. And while political radicals have traditionally looked to the working class as the engine of historical progress, some insist that the lever of progress can no longer be located within any single social group but emerges *sui generis* through the contingent interaction of class (both working and middle class) and non-class-specific actors. Therefore, 'class' and 'social movement' are not necessarily opposed to one another at all.

There are perhaps two key ways of relating social movements to social policy (cf. Martin 2001). First, we need to appreciate the extent to which welfare systems are themselves responsible for the rise of the so-called 'new' social movements which emerged in the 1960s and 1970s (see above). According to Offe (1987) these can be explained as a consequence of rising prosperity, educational opportunities, and the growth of the public sector. The great distributional conflicts appeared to have been solved, but particular injustices persisted. New social movements therefore emerged due both to the successes and the continuing failures of postwar welfare capitalism. Second, social movements have also wielded an influence upon social policies themselves. This has certainly been the case with the women's movement, for instance, which has altered our understanding of the public and private, of citizenship rights and duties, and of the importance for social wealth of domestic labour and unpaid work.

What of the future? Inglehart (1990) believes that the welfare state is a victim of its own success and has made itself redundant by satisfying the basic needs of income, shelter, and so forth. State welfare is therefore the source of a post-materialist society within which state welfare itself struggles to flourish. For Inglehart, then, social movements must be analysed according to post-materialist categories and objectives, implying that our conceptions of social needs and social problems have to alter accordingly. To some extent this accords with the approach of Fraser (1997) which I mentioned briefly when discussing postmodernism. Fraser does not imagine that material conflicts have become redundant (certainly not after the ascendancy of conservatism in the 1980s and 1990s) but that such conflicts are inseparable from struggles over status and recognition. Therefore, if state welfare services are to have a progressive future we have to find theoretical and practical ways of reconciling the aims of redistribution and recognition (Fitzpatrick 2003b)—or rather, of understanding how the material and the cultural and inevitably intertwined.

SOCIAL INCLUSION

We conclude this chapter with a brief look at social inclusion. Traditionally, social policy has been concerned with concepts such as **inequality** and **poverty**, but three political developments have shifted the focus somewhat. First, the conservatism espoused by the likes of Thatcher and Reagan insisted that, far from being unjust, inequality was desirable both as a source of individuals' incentives and as a sign of economic dynamism and growth. Therefore, there was no such thing as poverty other than the self-imposed poverty of those (the work-shy, the feckless, and the criminally minded) who had brought it on themselves. So conservatives shifted attention towards those they held to have excluded themselves from mainstream society. Second, this concern with social exclusion was shared by many European commentators whose influence grew with the growth of the European Union (EU) in the 1980s. But whereas conservatives attributed social exclusion to individuals' deficiencies, the EU drew upon a continental philosophical tradition, one that highlighted the social fabric of solidarity and interdependence. Social exclusion was therefore explained as a decline in the systems of solidarity, in the institutions that bind people together. Finally, the Third Way's reinvention of social democracy for a post-conservative society, one which came to dominate the mid-to late 1990s, placed an emphasis on social *inclusion*. In fact, the Third Way could be defined as a search for new means of including all within the social body without relying upon strong redistributive measures that many feared would alienate affluent and aspirational voters (see Case Study 22.2).

Case Study 22.2 Tony Blair and welfare reform

'In welfare, for too long, the right had let social division and chronic unemployment grow; the left argued for rights but were weak on responsibilities. We believe passionately in giving people the chance to get off benefit and into work. We have done it for one and a quarter million. But there are hundreds of thousands more who could work, given the chance. It's right for them, for the country, for society. But with the chance, comes a responsibility on the individual—to take the chance, to make something of their lives and use their ability and potential to the full.

In my speech on welfare reform at Toynbee Hall three years ago I set out the challenge. We must give the unemployed youth the skills to find a job; give the single mother the childcare she needs to go out and work; give the middle-aged man on a disability benefit the support and confidence to go back into the office. And we must not only lift people out of poverty. We must transform their horizons, aspirations and hopes as well—through helping people get the skills they need for better jobs, and through giving them chance to save and build up a nest egg.

Only in this way will we drive up social mobility, the great force for equality in dynamic market economies. To do all that, ours has to be an enabling welfare state—one which helps people to help themselves.'

(Extract from a speech by Tony Blair on welfare reform, 10 June 2002)

Box 22.8 Linking poverty and social exclusion

- Some believe that what we used to call poverty should now be referred to as social exclusion in order to capture the different ways in which social stratification now occurs. So whereas class and social background used to be the key determinants, it is now the case that a lack of skills and opportunities (whether due to policy failures or individuals' failings or both) is the determining factor.
- Others suggest that poverty and social exclusion describe the same phenomenon, but whereas the former relates to Anglo-American conditions the latter refers to that of the traditions and cultures of continental European.
- Or it may be that poverty refers to a situation (a lack of income or employment) whereas social exclusion denotes the processes of social marginalization which many experience. Poverty is therefore 'static' whereas social exclusion is more of a dynamic concept. This implies that some of those who are poor are not necessarily socially excluded (e.g. students) and some who are socially excluded are not necessarily poor (e.g. affluent pensioners in rural areas).

Therefore, social policy research has come to regard social inclusion as a key point of reference (Byrne 1999). The question is, how should this concept be related to that of poverty? There are three basic answers to this question (see Box 22.8).

The main controversy centres upon the extent to which a low income, relative to the average, is the principal source of social exclusion. If it is, then this may imply that government should redistribute in order to reduce levels of both poverty and social exclusion (Hills et al. 2002). If what is lacking is paid employment (rather than income per se) then the government should aim to create jobs (or at least nurture the economic conditions that lead to job growth) and to improve the economy's supply side, i.e. the employability of its workforce. But if what is lacking is a willingness on the part of the excluded to find employment, then government ought to prod people into the labour market through a series of sticks (coercive measures) and carrots (incentives).

These are the main elements of the debate concerning exclusion and inclusion. Although there is no space here to review each and every recent development in the debate, two areas certainly deserve a mention: time and social capital.

Time

Although we are not reviewing it here, much has been made in recent years of the importance to social science of space, i.e. of the way in which individuals trace geographical patterns through their social environment. Yet the concept of time is still crucial and, in fact, has influenced a school of 'life course research' that brings together the dynamic and the structural features of inclusion and exclusion. Two recent examples illustrate this.

Leisering and Leibfried (1999) observe that most life histories periodically demonstrate some degree of poverty: poverty is not a fixed characteristic of certain disadvantaged groups but is a life event, reaching well into the middle class, that we negotiate our way through using state welfare institutions. Socioeconomic structures exist, but within those hierarchies can be found a diversity of biographical trajectories. Poverty transcends class boundaries as a temporal dynamic of all income groups. Therefore, the objective duration of poverty has to be understood in terms of the subjective orientations of poor individuals, i.e. how they contextualize that experience in terms of their life histories, using public institutions as coping strategies. What this implies is that we, including the poorest, are all competent actors who determine the course of their lives within certain constraints. Insofar as it is confined to transitional periods in individuals' lives, the trick is to devise life-course policies that use poverty strategically by constructing institutional supports that offer bridges through those periods (Esping-Andersen 1999). Some vertical redistribution is justifiable but, ultimately, these transitional bridges must be built upon updated forms of social insurance.

Gershuny's (2000) research agrees with much of this. He finds that since the 1960s most countries have experienced an increase in the time available for leisure, that men now perform more unpaid work and women more paid work, and, finally, that those on higher incomes work more and those on lower incomes now possess more leisure. Accordingly, there has been a general shift in the service economies of developed nations from 'low-value' to 'high-value' services. High-value economies are usually to be found in social democratic countries, where the satisfaction of basic needs has facilitated the emergence of more sophisticated tastes that drive a virtuous circle of high-value production and consumption. One implication of this is that whereas high-value economies are inconsistent with large degrees of income inequality, such inequalities are ultimately only reduced by raising the productivity of human capital (skills, experiences, qualifications, networks) rather than through tax-and-spend redistribution. In our new information societies, public regulation must be geared towards further reductions in working hours and to other 'time-use policies'.

So according to the research of Leisering, Leibfried, and Gershuny the traditional measures for producing social justice (such as tax-and-spend redistribution, higher welfare spending, and an expanding public sphere) are now less important than policies which look at the life-course as a whole and which enable individuals to survive the periods of low income that most of us experience at one time or another. This is an analysis that dovetails nicely with that of the Third Way (Giddens 1998).

Social capital

The Third Way also draws from recent debates concerning social capital. Traditionally, social science has been concerned with physical capital, i.e. with the means of production from which social wealth is generated. The term 'social capital' also refers to a source of wealth and wellbeing, but signifies not the physical aspects but the social ones: the extent to which people are connected to each other through types of formal and informal association and the quality of those networks, i.e. whether they integrate people together in participative relations that are conducive to civic and economic health. Social capital is therefore the glue that allows society to cohere. Although the term did not originate with him, the key figure in recent years is Robert Putnam (2000).

Putnam argues that social capital has been on the decline in developed countries (though his research has concentrated upon Italy and America) for many years now.

This means that as individualistic habits and attitudes have taken root so the less visible, but no less important, practices that weave us together below the social surface have begun to unravel. Such processes manifest themselves as a reduction in levels of trust and reciprocity. People are more wary of each other than they used to be, more fearful of dangers (both real and imagined), and adopt a contractualist approach to others whereby actions are performed only when there is a demonstrable gain to be made. Putnam's influential illustration of this is the figure of the isolated bowler. Whereas Americans were once very sociable, associating together in a variety of clubs and societies, today they are more likely to engage in activities on a solitary basis. The number of bowling clubs has declined, for instance, and Americans are now more likely to go bowling alone. Therefore, the solitary bowler is, for Putnam, the symbol of the decline of neighbourliness and civic engagement.

Putnam's research has been criticized on a number of grounds: that he underestimate the extent to which old forms of association have been replaced by new ones (e.g. through the medium of ICTs) and that he has no clear explanation for social capital's decline. However, his thesis has been popular with social democrats who, having reconciled themselves to the inevitability of capitalism, wish to emphasize the inability of free markets (and perhaps many aspects of state welfare) to nurture the social capital upon which social integration depends. Therefore, 'social capital' has worked its way into the political vocabulary and is used to explain any number of things: the decline in electoral turnout, rises in levels of crime and incivility, reductions in charitable effort and voluntary work, reluctance to contribute to the community, and so forth. The thesis is therefore handy for those who wish to create a social capitalism.

The implications for the welfare state are therefore ambivalent. On the one hand, state welfare might be taken as an example of the kind of social capital that once prevailed, as a sign that people once recognized their common fate and interdenendency. Then again, it might also be possible to blame state welfare for that decline. By emphasizing rights rather than responsibilities, by soaking up public resources, and by giving power to politicians and public-sector workers, the welfare state has produced the hollowing out of civil society, of the spaces where people relate to each other on a familial and communal basis. Therefore, although those in the political centre have latched onto the debate, the concept of social capital does not replace the more familiar ideological arguments of politics. Whether social capital has declined, why it has done so, and what the possible solutions might be are all issues upon which people fundamentally disagree. This implies that the nature of, explanations for, and solutions to the problem of social exclusion are similarly political. The debate concerning social capital contributes to that concerning the future of social policies but does not replace it.

CONCLUSION

At the beginning of this chapter I stated that its most obvious aim was to introduce a variety of the new debates. Yet its ultimate purpose has been to underline the point that the future of the discipline shows every sign of being as diverse and as interesting as its past. The subjects covered here are not likely to replace most of social policy's traditional concerns, and nor should they, but they will contribute to the discipline's 'outer margins', the places where it overlaps with some recent developments across the social sciences. Those interdisciplinary channels are two-way: they are means by which social policy can learn from others but also how others can learn from social policy. As such, the 'core' and the margins of social policy also have much to learn from one another. The subject always has been and always will be concerned with the means by which the state intervenes in order to address social problems and fulfil social needs. Recent theories in no way alter that focus. However, they can enable us to refine our focus and develop our understanding of what 'state', 'intervention', 'social problem', and 'social needs' actually imply for the twenty-first century. We therefore return to where this book began by remembering that we should not be afraid to carry the past with us, even as we rush into the future.

REFERENCES

Bauman, Z. (1998), *Globalization*. Cambridge: Polity Press.

Beck, U. (1992). *Risk Society*. London: Sage.

Bonoli, G., George, V., and Taylor-Gooby, P. (2000), *European Welfare Futures*. Cambridge: Polity Press.

Bourdieu, P. (1977), *An Outline of a Theory of Practice*. Cambridge: Cambridge University Press.

—— (1999), *Acts of Resistance*. Cambridge: Polity Press.

Byrne, D., (1999). *Social Exclusion*. Milton Keynes: Open University Press.

Carter, J. (ed.) (1998), *Postmodernity and the Fragmentation of Welfare*. London: Routledge.

Castells, M. (1996), *The Rise of the Network Society*. Oxford: Blackwell.

—— (1997), *The Power of Identity*. Oxford: Blackwell.

—— (1998), *The End of Millennium*. Oxford: Blackwell.

Culpitt, I. (1999), *Social Policy and Risk*. London: Sage.

Della Porta, D., and Diani, M. (1999), *Social Movements*. Oxford: Blackwell.

Doyal, L., and Gough, I. (1991), *A Theory of Human Needs*. London: Macmillan.

Eder, K. (1993), *The New Politics of Class*. London: Sage.

Elster, J. (1985), *Making Sense of Marx*. Cambridge: Cambridge University Press.

Esping-Andersen, G. (1999), *Social Foundations of Post-Industrial Economies*. Cambridge: Cambridge University Press.

Fitzpatrick, T. (2001), *Welfare Theory: An Introduction*. London: Palgrave.

—— (ed.) (2003a), *New Technologies and Social Policy*, special edition of *Critical Social Policy*.

—— (2003b), *After the New Social Democracy*. Manchester: Manchester University Press.

Foucault, M. (1984), *The Foucault Reader*, ed. P. Rabinow. Harmondsworth: Penguin.

Fraser, N. (1997), *Justice Interruptus*. London: Routledge.

Gershuny, J. (2000), *Changing Times*. Oxford: Oxford University Press.

Giddens, T. (1991), *Modernity and Self-Identity*. Cambridge: Polity Press.

—— (1998), *The Third Way*. Cambridge: Polity Press.

Gough, I. (1996), 'Social welfare and competitiveness', *New Political Economy* 1(2): 210–32.

Habermas, J. (1987), *The Philosophical Discourse of Modernity*. Cambridge: Polity Press.

Harvey, D. (1989), *The Condition of Postmodernity*. Oxford: Blackwell.

Held, D., McGrew, A., Goldblatt, D., and Perraton, J. (1999). *Global Transformations*. Cambridge: Polity Press.

Hills, J., Le Grand, J., and Piachaud, D. (eds.) (2002), *Understanding Social Exclusion*. Oxford: Oxford University Press.

Hirst, P., and Thompson, G. (1996), *Globalisation in Question*. Cambridge: Polity Press.

Inglehart, R. (1990), *Culture Shift in Advanced Society*. Princeton, NJ: Princeton University Press.

Kemshall, H. (2002), *Risk, Social Policy and Welfare*. Milton Keynes: Open University Press.

Laclau, E., and Mouffe, C. (1985), *Hegemony and Socialist Strategy*. London: Verso.

Leisering, L., and Leibfried, S. (1999), *Time and Poverty in Western Welfare States*. Cambridge: Cambridge University Press.

Leonard, P. (1997), *Postmodern Welfare*. London: Sage.

Loader, B. (ed.) (1998), *Cyberspace Divide*. London: Routledge.

Lyotard, J.-F. (1984), *The Postmodern Condition*. Manchester: Manchester University Press.

Maheu, L. (ed.) (1995). *Social Movements and Social Classes*. London: Sage.

Manning, N., and Shaw, I. (eds.) (2000), *New Risks, New Welfare*. Oxford: Blackwell.

Martin, G. (2001), 'Social movements, welfare and social policy: a critical analysis', *Critical Social Policy* 21(3): 361–83.

Offe, C. (1987), 'Challenging the boundaries of institutional politics: social movements since the 1960s'. In C. S. Maier (ed.), *Changing Boundaries of the Political*. Cambridge: Cambridge University Press.

Ohmae, K. (1995), *The End of the Nation State*. London: HarperCollins.

Pierson, P. (2001), 'Post-industrial pressures on the mature welfare states'. In P. Pierson (ed.), *The New Politics of the Welfare State*. Cambridge: Cambridge University Press.

Putnam, R. (2000), *Bowling Alone*. New York: Simon & Schuster.

Robertson, R. (1992), *Globalisation*. London: Sage.

Rodgers, J. (2000), *From a Welfare State to a Welfare Society*. London: Macmillan.

Rose, N. (1999), *Powers of Freedom*. Cambridge: Cambridge University Press.

Sykes, R., Palier, B., and Prior, P. (eds.) (2001). *Globalisation and European Welfare States*. London: Palgrave.

Taylor-Gooby, P. (ed.) (2000), *Risk, Trust and Welfare*. London: Macmillan.

World Bank (1994), *Averting the Old Age Crisis*. London: Oxford University Press.

FURTHER READING

T. Fitzpatrick, *Welfare Theory: An Introduction* (London: Palgrave, 2001). A recent textbook covering most of the major issues and debates in theories of social policy and the welfare state.

G. Lewis, S. Gewirtz, and J. Clarke, *Rethinking Social Policy* (Milton Keynes: Open University Press, 2000). A wide-ranging introduction to a variety of policy-related issues.

C. Pierson, *Beyond the Welfare State?* (Cambridge: Polity Press, 1998). 'An influential overview of key theoretical influences and ideas on contemporary welfare systems.

GLOSSARY

discourses Refer to the ways in which language is inscribed within the world to the extent that we can never get 'beyond' language and perceive or understand the world without reference to naming, signification, and description. The concept expresses the idea that as well as being something we speak, linguistic signs and representations are that out of which our subjectivities and identities are formed.

eugenics The genetic assumptions and practices (sterilization and selective breeding) that prevailed in the early decades of the twentieth century, based upon conceptions of biological determinism and, frequently, upon racist notions of biological inferiority and superiority. Though associated with Nazi Germany, forms of eugenics were also practiced in countries like Australia and Sweden until the 1970s.

inequality Implies that the distribution of social resources is concentrated more upon some than upon others and may be either justified (if this distribution is based upon efforts, choice, and merit) or unjustified (if based upon relations of oppression, discrimination, and class).

modernity A period of social development whose chronology is disputed. However, many associate modernity with the post-seventeenth century Age of Enlightenment in which the emphasis was upon progress, rationality, and secularization. Some believe that this age of modernity is now finished or at least coming to an end.

nation-state The conjunction of political and national boundaries, so that the authority of the state is contained within determinate geographical borders. Nation-states emerged from the seventeenth to the nineteenth centuries and represent the most common forms of modern citizenship and social association. However, some insist that the sovereignty of the nation-state has never been absolute.

networks Flexible, web-like forms of interaction and interrelationship. More 'horizontal' than the hierarchies and structures with which social science has traditionally been concerned, some insist that networks are becoming the organizational archetypes of human societies.

poverty Poverty denotes a lack of material resources (especially income) and thus basic social needs that remain unmet.

surveillance The practice of scrutinizing a given population. Surveillance may be overt or covert, and refers not only to a perceptual apparatus but also to systems of classification and cataloguing. Surveillance may possess social effects that are beneficial or harmful, and sometimes both simultaneously.

universalism In this context, universalism is a philosophical tenet which insists that knowledge, truth, and moral values are the same for all people at all times. Universalism therefore presupposes the existence of a world that has objective existence, i.e. is independent of mind and social context, and is usually contrasted with philosophies of relativism.

Index

D

E

I

N

Q

R

S

T

W

Y

List of Boxes

List of Figures

List of Tables